HERALDS OF THE GOOD NEWS

HERALDS OF THE GOOD NEWS

*Isaiah and Paul "In Concert" in the Letter
to the Romans*

BY

J. ROSS WAGNER

BRILL
LEIDEN · BOSTON · KÖLN
2002

This book is printed on acid-free paper.

Die Deutsche Bibliothek – CIP-Einheitsaufnahme

Wagner, J.Ross:
Heralds of the good news : Isaiah and Paul "In Concert" in the letter to
the Romans / by J. Ross Wagner: – Leiden ; Boston; Köln : Brill, 2002
(Supplements to Novum testamentum ; Vol. 101)
ISBN 90–04–11691–5

Library of Congress Cataloging-in-Publication Data

Library of Congress Cataloging-in-Publication Data is also available

ISSN   0167-9732
ISBN   90 04 11691 5

PRINTED IN THE NETHERLANDS

For Ronda

οὐ μὲν γὰρ τοῦ γε κρεῖσσον καὶ ἄρειον
ἢ ὅθ᾽ ὁμοφρονέοντε νοήμασιν οἶκον ἔχητον
ἀνὴρ ἠδὲ γυνή.

Homer, *Odyssey* 6:182–184

CONTENTS

ACKNOWLEDGEMENTS

The writing of this book has spanned several major transitions in my family's life: relocating from Durham, NC, to Princeton, NJ; moving from graduate studies in the university to full-time teaching on a theological faculty; and growing from a family of three to a family of six. Numerous people have offered us their support, guidance, and friendship during these years. It would be impossible simply to name them all in this brief space, let alone to acknowledge them properly. Nevertheless, it is a privilege to record here something of the immense debt of gratitude I owe to family, friends, and colleagues.

This study began as a doctoral dissertation defended at Duke University in April, 1999. Generous financial support for my graduate work was provided by the Pew Charitable Trusts, who awarded me a Pew Younger Scholars Fellowship, by A Foundation for Theological Education, who named me a John Wesley Fellow, and by the Graduate Department of Religion of Duke University, who granted me a departmental fellowship. While at Duke, I had the privilege of thinking through my reading of Romans in conversation with colleagues in seminars and at several professional meetings. Among those who interacted with early versions of my thesis and offered helpful—and often challenging—critiques, particular thanks are due Bruce Fisk, Jack Levison, Diana Swancutt, Chris Stanley, W. D. Davies (ל"ז), and Tom Wright. I also had the good fortune to study with a number of outstanding professors at Duke, including James L. Crenshaw, Orval S. Wintermute, and Melvin K. H. Peters, who hooked me on Septuagint studies with his contagious enthusiasm for the subject and his kind encouragement of my first efforts in that field.

My sincere thanks go to the members of my dissertation committee, generous and patient mentors all: Eric M. Meyers, D. Moody Smith, and James C. VanderKam (Notre Dame). Professor E. P. Sanders gave unstintingly of his time both as an advisor and as a teacher. Going well beyond what is normally expected of a second reader, he offered detailed and incisive comments on two drafts of the dissertation that forced me to refine and sharpen my arguments.

If I have at points been too stubborn to heed his remonstrances, the fact remains that his influence on my thinking about Paul, as well as about early Judaism and early Christianity in general, is profound—and I am deeply grateful. To Richard Hays, I can only offer what seems to me to be a very inadequate expression of appreciation for many hours spent reading and discussing this study in its various drafts (including taking time out during the Final Four of the 1999 NCAA Men's Basketball Tournament to read the last two chapters!). My investigation clearly builds on his own ground-breaking research into Paul's reading of scripture, yet he has encouraged me to think my own thoughts, and he has treated me more as a colleague than as a student. I am grateful for his generous spirit and wise counsel and, above all, for the gift of his friendship.

I completed the dissertation during my first year of teaching at Princeton Theological Seminary. President Thomas Gillespie and Dean James Armstrong generously supported my writing with a course reduction and ample research assistance. A warm and collegial faculty and a bright and earnest student body have made this a truly wonderful environment in which to write and teach. Several present and former PTS students contributed significantly to the revision of this study. The keen eye of my friend Shane Berg, now a doctoral candidate in New Testament at Yale, has saved me from a number of embarrassing errors; moreover, his sound editorial judgment has greatly improved the flow of the argument. Thanks go as well to Robert Jacobs for checking citations to modern works and for revising the bibliography, and to Bill Pinches for carefully proofreading the manuscript and helping prepare the indexes.

Portions of Chapter Five have already appeared in print as "The Christ, Servant of Jew and Gentile: A Fresh Approach to Romans 15:8–9," *Journal of Biblical Literature* 116 (1997): 473–85 and "The Heralds of Isaiah and the Mission of Paul: An Investigation of Paul's Use of Isaiah 51–55 in Romans," in *Jesus and the Suffering Servant: Isaiah 53 and Christian Origins* (ed. W. H. Bellinger, Jr. and W. R. Farmer; Harrisburg, PA: TPI, 1998), 193–222. Professor Gail O'Day, editor of the *Journal of Biblical Literature*, and Mr. Henry Carrigan, Editorial Director at Trinity Press International, have kindly granted permission to reprint this material here in revised form.

The preparation of this volume was delayed a year by the premature birth and chronic illness of our twin girls, Naomi and Claire. I am grateful for the patience and kindness of Pim Rietbroek, Louise

Schouten, and the rest of the editorial team at Brill, who have graciously allowed me to extend my deadline more than once. There is simply no way to express the depth of my gratitude for the multitude of friends around the world who have prayed for us, encouraged us, and served us during this difficult time. Colleagues and students at the seminary, members of our local church, and friends from the community provided hot meals, often two or three times a week, for nearly twelve months. Our families, who have been a constant source of strength through the ups and downs of graduate study, made great personal sacrifices to help us through the past year. Time would fail me to tell of all those who cared for our older children, helped to feed the babies, dropped by unannounced to lend a hand with household chores, sent a card or gift to encourage us, or offered a warm embrace and a listening ear. We have seen the church be the church, and it is a beautiful thing.

As I write these words, Claire and Naomi are beginning to take their first halting steps and to say their first words. Their health has greatly improved over the past few months. Together with their older brothers, Nathaniel and Caleb, they make life a constant blur of noisy, joyful activity that prevents me from taking myself or my work too seriously. That is a precious gift indeed.

To Ronda, my dearest friend and my partner in life for twelve years, I dedicate this book as one of the fruits of our mutual labors. Together we have walked some dark valleys, and, by God's grace, we have come through them together. What flows between us is too deep for words.

Ross Wagner
Princeton, New Jersey
Feast of St Clare of Assisi, 2001

LIST OF FIGURES

LIST OF ABBREVIATIONS

AB	Anchor Bible
ABD	D.N. Freedman, (ed.), *Anchor Bible Dictionary*
AGJU	Arbeiten zur Geschichte des antiken Judentums und des Urchristentums
ALUOS	*Annual of Leeds University Oriental Society*
AnBib	Analecta biblica
ANRW	*Aufstieg und Niedergang der römischen Welt*
ASNU	Acta seminarii neotestamentici upsaliensis
ASTI	*Annual of the Swedish Theological Institute*
ATAbh	Alttestamentliche Abhandlungen
ATDan	Acta theologica danica
AusBR	*Australian Biblical Review*
AUSS	*Andrews University Seminary Studies*
BA	*Biblical Archaeologist*
BASOR	*Bulletin of the American Schools of Oriental Research*
BDAG	W. Bauer, F. W. Danker, W. F. Arndt, and F. W. Gingrich, *Greek-English Lexicon of the New Testament and Other Early Christian Literature* (3d ed.)
BDB	F. Brown, S. R. Driver, and C. A. Briggs, *A Hebrew and English Lexicon of the Old Testament*
BDF	F. Blass, A. Debrunner, and R. W. Funk, *A Greek Grammar of the New Testament*
BDR	F. Blass, A. Debrunner, and F. Rehkopf, *Grammatik des neutestamentlichen Griechisch*
BETL	Bibliotheca ephemeridum theologicarum lovaniensium
BFCT	Beiträge zur Förderung christlicher Theologie
BHT	Beiträge zur historischen Theologie
Bib	*Biblica*
BibOr	Biblica et orientalia
BJRL	*Bulletin of the John Rylands University Library of Manchester*
BJS	Brown Judaic Studies
BNTC	Black's New Testament Commentaries
BT	*The Bible Translator*
BTB	*Biblical Theology Bulletin*
BZ	*Biblische Zeitschrift*
BZAW	Beihefte zur ZAW
CBQ	*Catholic Biblical Quarterly*
CBQMS	Catholic Biblical Quarterly Monograph Series
ClQ	*Classical Quarterly*
ConBOT	Coniectanea biblica: Old Testament Series
ConNT	Coniectanea neotestamentica
CRINT	Compendia Rerum Iudaicarum ad Novum Testamentum

CSCO	Corpus scriptorum christianorum orientalium
DBSup	*Dictionnaire de la Bible: Supplément*
DJD	Discoveries in the Judaean Desert (see Bibliography for individual volumes, s.v. "DJD")
DSD	*Dead Sea Discoveries*
Ebib	Etudes bibliques
EKKNT	Evangelisch-katholischer Kommentar zum Neuen Testament
ErIsr	*Eretz-Israel*
ETL	*Ephemerides theologicae lovanienses*
ETR	*Etudes théologiques et religieuses*
EvQ	*Evangelical Quarterly*
EvT	*Evangelische Theologie*
FB	Forschung zur Bibel
FBBS	Facet Books, Biblical Series
FRLANT	Forschungen zur Religion und Literatur des Alten und Neuen Testaments
Hatch-Redpath	E. Hatch and H. A. Redpath, *A Concordance to the Septuagint*
HeyJ	*Heythrop Journal*
HNT	Handbuch zum Neuen Testament
HNTC	Harper's New Testament Commentaries
HSM	Harvard Semitic Monographs
HSS	Harvard Semitic Studies
HTR	*Harvard Theological Review*
HTS	Harvard Theological Studies
HUCA	*Hebrew Union College Annual*
IBC	Interpretation: A Bible Commentary for Teaching and Preaching
ICC	International Critical Commentary
IDB	G. A. Buttrick (ed.), *The Interpreter's Dictionary of the Bible*
IDBSup	K. Crim (ed.), *IDB: Supplementary Volume*
Int	*Interpretation*
JAAR	*Journal of the American Academy of Religion*
JANESCU	*Journal of the Ancient Near Eastern Society of Columbia University*
JAOS	*Journal of the American Oriental Society*
JBL	*Journal of Biblical Literature*
JECS	*Journal of Early Christian Studies*
JETS	*Journal of the Evangelical Theological Society*
JJS	*Journal of Jewish Studies*
JNES	*Journal of Near Eastern Studies*
JQR	*Jewish Quarterly Review*
JSJ	*Journal for the Study of Judaism in the Persian, Hellenistic and Roman Periods*
JSNT	*Journal for the Study of the New Testament*
JSNTSup	Journal for the Study of the New Testament—Supplement Series

JSOT	*Journal for the Study of the Old Testament*
JSOTSup	Journal for the Study of the Old Testament—Supplement Series
JSP	*Journal for the Study of the Pseudepigrapha*
JSPSup	Journal for the Study of the Pseudepigrapha—Supplement Series
JSS	*Journal of Semitic Studies*
JTS	*Journal of Theological Studies*
KD	*Kerygma und Dogma*
LD	Lectio divina
LEH	J. Lust, E. Eynikel, and K. Hauspie, *A Greek-English Lexicon of the Septuagint*
LSJ	Liddell-Scott-Jones-McKenzie, *Greek-English Lexicon* (9th ed. with Revised Supplement)
MeyerK	H. A. W. Meyer, Kritisch-exegetischer Kommentar über das Neue Testament
MHT	J. H. Moulton, W. F. Howard, N. Turner, *A Grammar of New Testament Greek* (4 vols.)
MM	J. H. Moulton and G. Milligan, *The Vocabulary of the Greek Testament*
MNTC	Moffatt New Testament Commentary
MSU	Mitteilungen des Septuaginta-Unternehmens
Neot	*Neotestamentica*
NICNT	New International Commentary on the New Testament
NICOT	New International Commentary on the Old Testament
NovT	*Novum Testamentum*
NovTSup	Novum Testamentum Supplements
NTAbh	Neutestamentliche Abhandlungen
NTS	*New Testament Studies*
NTTS	New Testament Tools and Studies
OBO	Orbis biblicus et orientalis
OBT	Overtures to Biblical Theology
OTL	Old Testament Library
OTP	J. H. Charlesworth (ed.), *The Old Testament Pseudepigrapha*
OtSt	*Oudtestamentische Studiën*
PTMS	Pittsburgh Theological Monograph Series
PTSDSSP	The Princeton Theological Seminary Dead Sea Scrolls Project
RAC	*Reallexikon für Antike und Christentum*
RB	*Revue biblique*
REJ	*Revue des études juives*
RevExp	*Review and Expositor*
RevQ	*Revue de Qumran*
RHPR	*Revue d'histoire et de philosophie religieuses*
RivB	*Rivista biblica italiana*
RSR	*Recherches de science religieuse*
SBB	Stuttgarter biblische Beiträge
SBG	Studies in Biblical Greek
SBLAS	SBL Aramaic Studies

SBLDS   SBL Dissertation Series
SBLMS   SBL Monograph Series
SBLSCS   SBL Septuagint and Cognate Studies
SBLSP   *SBL Seminar Papers*
SBT   Studies in Biblical Theology
SD   Studies and Documents
SE   *Studia Evangelica I, II, III* (= TU 73 [1959], 87 [1964], 88 [1964], etc.)
SJLA   Studies in Judaism in Late Antiquity
SJT   *Scottish Journal of Theology*
SNTSMS   Society for New Testament Studies Monograph Series
SPB   Studia post-biblica
SSEJC   Studies in Scripture in Early Judaism and Christianity
SR   *Studies in Religion/Sciences religieuses*
ST   *Studia theologica*
STDJ   Studies on the Texts of the Desert of Judah
SWJT   *Southwestern Journal of Theology*
TDNT   G. Kittel and G. Friedrich (eds.), *Theological Dictionary of the New Testament*
TLZ   *Theologische Literaturzeitung*
TRu   *Theologische Rundschau*
TS   *Theological Studies*
TU   Texte und Untersuchungen
TynBul   *Tyndale Bulletin*
USQR   *Union Seminary Quarterly Review*
UUÅ   Uppsala Universitetsårsskrift
VT   *Vetus Testamentum*
VTSup   Vetus Testamentum Supplements
WBC   Word Biblical Commentary
WMANT   Wissenschaftliche Monographien zum Alten und Neuen Testament
WTJ   *Westminster Theological Journal*
WUNT   Wissenschaftliche Untersuchungen zum Neuen Testament
ZAW   *Zeitschrift für die alttestamentliche Wissenschaft*
ZNW   *Zeitschrift für die neutestamentliche Wissenschaft und die Kunde der älteren Kirche*
ZTK   *Zeitschrift für Theologie und Kirche*

CHAPTER ONE

SCRIPTURE, THEOLOGY, AND MISSION IN THE LETTER TO THE ROMANS

> Paul, a slave of Christ Jesus, called to
> be an apostle, set apart for the gospel
> of God, which God announced before-
> hand through his prophets in holy writ-
> ings concerning his son . . .
>
> *Romans 1:1–3*

From the opening words of his letter to the Roman churches, Paul reveals himself to be both a "missionary theologian"[1] and a "hermeneutic theologian."[2] That is, Paul presents his apostolic mission as one that proclaims and interprets the gospel and Israel's scriptural traditions in the service of creating and sustaining communities called into existence by God's grace and love in Jesus Christ. The epistle to the Romans reflects the dynamic interplay of a number of influences and constraints on Paul's thought. Foundational convictions, experiences and practices of mission, scriptural interpretation, cultural and historical contexts—all shape and reshape one another in Paul's ongoing struggle to make sense of God's design for Israel and to faithfully fulfill his own divinely-ordained role in the outworking of that plan.[3]

Nowhere is this complex and dynamic interrelationship of scripture, theology, and mission more apparent than in Paul's consistent representation of Isaiah as a fellow preacher of the good news. A striking feature of the letter to the Romans is the apostle's frequent invocation of the oracles of Isaiah, not only through direct quotations,

---

[1] On this topic, see the penetrating insights of Dahl 1977b.

[2] So Beker 1986:10.

[3] As Dahl observes, "a systematic outline of [Paul's] theological doctrines becomes at best an accurate and useful map, a two dimensional projection without depth or movement (Dahl 1977b:71). Several of the proposals for doing "Pauline theology" arising out of the Pauline Theology Group of the Society of Biblical Literature urge that Paul's theology may be more adequately conceptualized as a dynamic *activity* rather than as a relatively static set of convictions (see, for example, Bassler 1993 and Kraftchick 1993).

but also through more indirect modes of allusion and intertextual echo. Citations from Isaiah account for nearly half of Paul's explicit appeals to scripture in Romans.[4] Moreover, at a number of points in the letter the prophet Isaiah virtually takes on a life of his own and becomes a second voice, speaking in concert with the apostle concerning God's plan to redeem Israel and the nations. Isaiah "cries out on behalf of Israel," affirming God's unremitting faithfulness even in the midst of judgment.[5] Isaiah boldly "dares to speak" of God's astonishing embrace of Gentiles, while God's own people stand off at a distance, estranged and unresponsive.[6] Isaiah sings of the root of Jesse who comes to unite Jew and Gentile into a single community of worship and praise.[7] Even where he is not named, the ancient prophet's words are a weighty and palpable presence, whether Paul is wrestling with Israel's resistance to God's righteousness or interpreting the crucial role his own mission plays in the redemptive plan of God.[8]

Three interlocking questions motivate the study that follows. First, how did Paul, as an ancient reader, approach the book of Isaiah?[9] In what form (or forms) did he encounter the book? What were the

---

[4] Compare the slightly different lists of citations (due to the use of different criteria for identifying quotations) in Koch 1986:21–24, Smith 1988:270–72, and Hübner 1997:1–219. The term "scripture" presupposes the existence of a particular community with a particular set of beliefs and practices (see Lindbeck 1988). In this work, when I speak of Paul's reading of "scripture," I refer to what *Paul*— and presumably his first hearers—would have taken as holy writ. This is not necessarily coextensive with the "canon" of scripture (another term that is meaningful only in relation to a particular interpretive community) later recognized by rabbinic Judaism or, in various forms, by Christian churches (see Collins 1995a; Sundberg 1964). I avoid the term "Old Testament" as anachronistic for Paul. "Hebrew Bible" is similarly an inappropriate term for this study, both because it presupposes canonical decisions not made until a later period in a particular Jewish community, and also because, as will become evident, Paul's use of Israel's scriptures in his letters suggests that he read them primarily (if not solely) in one or more *Greek* versions.

[5] Rom 9:27–29. Unless otherwise noted, all translations of ancient texts are my own.

[6] Rom 10:20–21.

[7] Rom 15:12.

[8] For a list of citations of and allusions to Isaiah in Romans identified in this study, see p. 342 below (Figure 6.1).

[9] With reference to Paul, I will avoid terms such as First, Second, and Third Isaiah, since there is no evidence that readers in the Second Temple period recognized these particular divisions of the book or that they considered the book as a whole to be anything other than the collected oracles of Isaiah of Jerusalem. I will, however, occasionally use the terms as a convenient shorthand for referring to the major blocks of the book, 1–39, 40–55, 56–66. Interestingly, more recent crit-

interpretive assumptions and techniques with which he read and appropriated the prophet's words? Second, how did Paul's understanding of the gospel and of his own particular calling as an apostle shape his reading of Isaiah,[10] and, conversely, how did Isaiah's oracles help to form Paul's conception of his own message and mission? Finally, how does this interplay of scripture, theology, and mission come to expression in the particular argument of the letter to the Romans,[11] and to what extent can attention to these questions enrich a reading of the letter?

Two factors justify this concentration on Paul's letter to Rome. First, because of the unique circumstances in which it was written, Romans represents Paul's most explicit reflection on his own mission and its relation to God's promises to Israel. Although by almost any reckoning Paul's genuine letters were all written within the brief span of a decade or so, Romans represents a stage in Paul's thinking about his mission and about the fate of Israel that is not reflected in his earliest correspondence.[12] As he writes this letter, he is nearing the completion of his mission in the eastern Mediterranean and

icism of Isaiah has tended to blur the clear divisions once found between First, Second, and Third Isaiah. For surveys of approaches to Isaiah ancient and modern, see Carr 1992; Sheppard 1992, 1996; Sommer 1996b.

[10] The importance of Paul's vocation as apostle to the Gentiles for the development and shape of his theology has long been recognized. Writing forty years ago on the topic of Paul's "missionary theology," Nils Dahl insisted that Paul's "theology and his missionary activity were inseparable from one another" (Dahl 1977b [1956]:70). Similarly, Johannes Munck recognized that "Paul's apostolic consciousness in its eschatological form stands in the centre of his personality and theology" (1959:42). Ferdinand Hahn concurs, noting that Paul's "view of the mission is inseparable from his entire theological thought" (1965:97). More recently, Arland J. Hultgren has argued that Paul's mission is "integrally related to his identity and thought" (1985:125). Significantly, E. P. Sanders begins his biographical study of Paul with the chapter, "Paul's Mission," explaining, "[Paul's] theology was bound up with a view of himself and his role in God's plan; it was not, perhaps, determined entirely by his self-perception, but certainly not separable from it. . . . His job description was this: Apostle to the Gentiles in the Messianic Era" (1991:2–3; see also Barrett 1995; O'Brien 1995).

[11] If "Paul's theology" is best conceptualized as an *activity* rather than as a relatively static set of convictions, then Paul's interpretation of scripture should be understood along similar lines, as something best observed "in the wild"—that is, in the context of the dynamic, unfolding arguments of his letters. To simply capture, dissect, and catalogue his interpretations of scripture is inevitably to render them dull and lifeless specimens of ancient exegesis.

[12] Romans is clearly not an exercise in systematic theology, but a contingent response to particular churches in specific historical circumstances; at the same time, the letter does represent the fruit of many years of deliberate and intense theological reflection in the service of mission (cf. Bornkamm 1991).

is attempting to lay the groundwork for a new thrust westward to Spain.[13] At the same time, as he prepares to accompany the "offering of the Gentiles" to Jerusalem (Rom 15:16),[14] Paul is painfully aware of the growing paradox of the early Christian mission: While Gentiles joyfully receive the gospel in ever growing numbers, it is becoming increasingly apparent that the majority of Paul's fellow Jews are not finding his message to be "good news."[15]

This leads to my second reason for focusing on Romans. Faced with new opportunities for the Gentile mission and wrestling with the apparent inertia of the mission to Israel, Paul turns to scripture—notably Isaiah—in an attempt to make sense of this paradoxical situation.[16] Among Paul's letters, Romans contains by far the greatest number of quotations of and allusions to Isaiah.[17] Moreover,

---

[13] The continuing debate over the purposes of Romans cannot be pursued here. However, Romans 15:14–33 suggests that Paul's desire to lay the groundwork for extending his mission to the western Mediterranean (with Rome as his base of operations) is one important reason for the letter. See N. T. Wright's suggestive hypothesis (1995:34–36). See also Dunn 1988b:856; Beker 1980:71–74; Jewett 1982; Wedderburn 1991; Jervis 1991.

[14] It may well be that Paul has been rehearsing such arguments as are found in Romans 9–11 in preparation for his impending visit to Jerusalem (see p. 36 and n. 128 below). At the same time, there is no reason to deny that these chapters also address real issues in the Roman churches.

[15] Stark 1996:49–71 provides a much-needed corrective to the view that Christianity ceased to spread among Jews after the wars with Rome. Employing the tools of sociological analysis alongside what historical data is available, Stark argues that the phenomenal numerical growth of the early church is explicable only if the community continued to attract a steady stream of Diaspora Jews. Stark's findings are not incompatible with the view that Paul and others were deeply troubled by the fear that the mission to their kinspeople was failing, however. The early followers of Jesus seem to have expected a massive turning of Jews to their messiah (cf. Acts 3:19–21). But by 50 CE, this new Jewish sect would have numbered perhaps 1,400 people, including Gentiles—a far cry from a national movement (Stark 1996:7). And with the continuing influx of Gentiles, the ever-decreasing ratio of Jews to Gentiles might well have led someone such as Paul to believe that the mission to Israel had stalled out.

[16] The observation of D.-A. Koch (1986:101) is suggestive:
Je stärker Paulus sich veranlaßt sieht, seine eigene Position theologisch zu klären, desto intensiver wird zugleich auch die Beschäftigung mit der Schrift und ihre Verwendung in seinen Briefen.

[17] Among the undisputed letters of Paul, the following contain explicit quotations of Isaiah (those with a citation formula of some sort): Romans (15); 1 Corinthians (3); 2 Corinthians (2); Galatians (1). Although the criteria for determining allusions are more imprecise (see below, pp. 11–13), the recent study by Florian Wilk (1998) finds allusions to Isaiah in these letters: Romans (12); 1 Corinthians (6); 2 Corinthians (5); Galatians (2); Philippians (2); 1 Thessalonians (3). Cf. Figures 6.1 and 6.2 below, pp. 342–43.

Romans 9–11, with its dense concentration of scriptural citations and allusions, comprises the longest sustained interpretive argument in Paul's writings. As such, the letter to the Romans provides a unique opportunity to study the interconnections between Paul's interpretation of scripture, his theological convictions, and his own sense of calling and mission. A close reading of Romans 9–11 and Romans 15 will reveal just how significantly the convictions Paul expresses in these chapters—particularly his stubborn insistence on God's enduring faithfulness to his covenant people Israel—have been molded and shaped by his wrestling with Israel's scriptures. At the same time, this investigation will show how radically Paul rereads scripture in light of his belief that, in Christ, God has decisively revealed his righteousness for Israel and for the world and that God is working out his redemptive plan in the present time through Paul's own ministry.

PAUL'S USE OF SCRIPTURE IN RECENT STUDY

The last several decades have witnessed a steady blossoming of interest in the question of how early Jewish and Christian communities interpreted their sacred texts.[18] In the context of this larger movement in the study of ancient Judaism and Christianity, a great deal of attention has been devoted to the use of Israel's scriptures by Paul and other New Testament authors. Much of the discussion has focused on identifying the hermeneutical assumptions and interpretive techniques in play as Jesus' earliest followers struggled to understand the significance of Jesus' life, death, and resurrection in the light of Israel's scriptures.[19] There appears to be a growing consensus that the use

---

[18] The literature on this topic is vast and rapidly expanding. Helpful surveys are found in Sæbø 1996; Mulder 1988; Carson and Williamson 1988; Ackroyd and Evans 1970; Smith 1972. The volumes in the Studies in Scripture in Early Judaism and Christianity Series offer wide exposure to the problems and issues currently under discussion. See Evans 2000; Evans and Sanders 1993, 1997, 1998; Evans and Stegner 1994; Charlesworth and Evans 1993.

[19] Barnabas Lindars (1961) and C. H. Dodd (1952a, 1952b) believe that scriptural interpretation arose in service of the *kerygma*. Don Juel (1988) traces early Christian exegetical activity specifically to the need to understand and defend the confession that the crucified and risen Jesus is Israel's *messiah*. While Lindars and Juel see these readers engaged primarily in atomistic exegesis of isolated bits of text, Dodd argues that certain larger passages of scripture are foundational to early Christian theology.

of scripture by the early Christians must be examined not only, or even principally, in light of later rabbinic taxonomies of interpretive strategies and techniques,[20] but as part of the larger phenomenon of biblical interpretation in the Second Temple period in all its bewildering variety.[21]

On the narrower question of Paul's appropriation of Israel's scriptures, a number of recent studies have significantly advanced the discussion both of Paul's citation practices and of the interpretive strategies that shape his use of scripture.[22] The careful investigations of Paul's citation technique by Dietrich-Alex Koch and Christopher D. Stanley have argued convincingly that Paul's biblical quotations point to his reliance on Greek *Vorlagen*[23] and that Paul himself has often modified the text of his citations to fit them into the context

---

[20] The lists of *middot* attributed to Hillel and to R. Ishmael are attempts to describe and discipline methods of interpretation that have a long history prior to the codification of such "rules" and that have a much wider cultural currency than simply "rabbinic" tradition. Lists of rabbinic *middot*, with brief explanations, may conveniently be found in Stemberger 1996:15–30 and Mielziner 1968:117–87. See also Bloch 1955, 1957; Gertner 1962; Loewe 1990; Porton 1979; Seeligmann 1953. Instone Brewer 1992 offers the most careful recent treatment of early proto-rabbinic exegesis. The similarities between the *middot* and interpretive conventions common in the wider Greco-Roman context are analyzed by David Daube (1949, 1977). See also Lieberman 1950; Alexander 1990. Daniel Boyarin and Michael Fishbane, among others, have revealed a hermeneutical sophistication and artistry in rabbinic exegesis hardly imaginable on the basis of attention to the *middot* alone. See Boyarin 1990; Fishbane 1989, 1998. The most thorough attempt to relate Paul's interpretation of scripture to that of the rabbis remains Bonsirven 1939; see also Cohn-Sherbok 1982.

[21] Such an approach begins by recognizing the interpretive activity inscribed within the canonical texts themselves. The landmark study of such "inner-biblical" exegesis is Fishbane 1985 (see also Fishbane 1977a, 1977b, 1980, 1982). In addition to works cited previously, important investigations of "post-biblical" exegesis include Barton 1986; Blenkinsopp 1981; Charlesworth 1987; Davies 1983; Ellis 1978; Kugel and Greer 1986; R. N. Longenecker 1975; M. P. Miller 1971; Patte 1975; Schmitt 1979; Vermes 1973, 1975; Zink 1963. See most recently J. Kugel's massive compendium of early Jewish interpretations of biblical narratives (1998).

[22] Surveys of the history of research on Paul's use of scripture are readily available. One of the most comprehensive reviews of older literature is found in C. D. Stanley 1992b:3–28. See also Hays (1989:5–14) for a critique of previous attempts to conceptualize Paul's hermeneutic. Litwak 1998 considers a number of developments since Hays's study.

[23] Koch 1986; Stanley 1992b. A particular strength of these two studies is that they take into account the growing body of research on the Septuagint, including the critical work on the text of the LXX undertaken by the Göttingen *Septuaginta-Unternehmen*. As a result, Koch's and Stanley's studies completely supersede E. E. Ellis's earlier investigation of Paul's citations (1957), which relies on too narrow a base of evidence for the text of the LXX in Paul's time (cf. Barr 1994). De Lagarde's

of his argument and to enable them to communicate more clearly the point he desires to make.[24]

In a 1997 monograph, however, Timothy H. Lim calls into question the confidence with which scholars have identified Pauline adaptations of scriptural citations. He argues that the degree of textual plurality and fluidity in the first century is far greater than either Koch or Stanley allows,[25] and he insists that any attempt to reconstruct Paul's *Vorlage* must consider the full range of available witnesses to the scriptural text, not simply those now extant in Greek.[26] Although Lim does think that Paul occasionally modified the wording of his biblical text,[27] he rightly seeks to take full account of the possibility that Paul encountered in Greek a textual variant for which the only evidence now survives in a text written in another language. Moreover, Lim notes that Paul may have drawn upon textual variants for which no evidence of any kind remains apart from Paul's citation.[28] Finally, Lim believes that Paul could read Hebrew and Aramaic, and on this basis he assumes that Paul would regularly have consulted scriptural texts written in these languages, perhaps occasionally even making his own translations into Greek.[29]

---

basic theory of Septuagint origins (an *Urtext* which later branched into different text-forms) has come to dominate the field of Septuagint studies (see the brief histories of research in Tov 1997:10–15; Peters 1992:1096–97). The Göttingen LXX (in distinction from Rahlfs's 1935 *Handausgabe*) seeks both to reconstruct the *Urtext* for each book and to present as fully as possible the extant witnesses to the text.

[24] A major difference between the two studies is that Stanley limits his investigation to citations explicitly marked for the reader by means of a citation formula, an interpretive gloss (e.g., 1 Cor 15:27), or a disruption of the syntax of the sentence (e.g., Rom 10:18; Stanley 1992b:56–57). Koch, on the other hand, employs a looser set of criteria for identifying an appeal to scripture and thus considers many unmarked appropriations of the biblical text. Stanley's narrow focus suits the limited purpose of his study, but it cannot offer a comprehensive account of Paul's use of scripture (cf. Porter 1997:81–82).

[25] Lim 1997a:12–18. Lim basically adopts the position laid out by Tov 1982. For recent discussion of the impact of the Qumran finds on theories of the development of the biblical text, see Ulrich 1998, 1999; Greenspoon 1998.

[26] This includes the important evidence supplied by both biblical and non-biblical scrolls discovered in and around Qumran.

[27] The bulk of Lim's work (1997a) seeks to compare Paul's approach to scripture with the handling of the biblical texts in the Qumran *pesharim*. However, his extremely conservative methodology leads him to identify only a handful of clear adaptations of the text of scripture in the *pesharim* and in Paul's writings. For critiques of Lim's approach, see Stanley 1998; Wagner 2001.

[28] See further Wilcox 1988.

[29] Lim takes it for granted that Paul could read Hebrew and Aramaic, primarily on the basis of Paul's putative education in a pharisaical school in Jerusalem (in

However, even if, for the sake of argument, one accepts Lim's account of Paul's linguistic competence,[30] his further claims that Paul engaged in comparison of textual variants across two or more languages, that he was reluctant to rely on a Greek translation, and that his quotations reflect the use of non-Greek texts must be demonstrated *from the citations themselves*. This Lim does not do. Having called into question the consensus opinion (articulated most forcefully by Koch and Stanley) that Paul consistently utilized a Greek text much like the LXX, and having argued for the necessity of an investigation of Paul's biblical text that attends closely to Hebrew evidence as well as Greek, Lim concludes his study without actually undertaking such an investigation on a comprehensive scale.[31] One of the goals of the present study, then, is to take up Lim's challenge to examine the full range of available witnesses to the text of Isaiah in order to see whether the hypothesis that Paul's citations sometimes depend on a Hebrew text rather than on a form of the LXX is actually borne out by the evidence.[32]

---

addition to the testimony of Acts, Lim appeals to Galatians 1:4 and Philippians 3:5 as evidence for Paul's competence in Hebrew; see Lim 1997a:161–68). He further believes that Paul would have "been uneasy with an over-reliance upon the words of his Greek biblical quotations" (164) and so would have sought to compare textual variants across several languages in order to find the text that best expressed the meaning of the passage as Paul understood it; only as a last resort, so one infers, would Paul alter the text himself (cf. the similar theory employed by Stendahl 1954 to explain the nature of the non-Markan biblical quotations in Matthew's gospel; but see the critique of Stendahl's work in Gundry 1967:155–59).

[30] W. D. Davies, though holding a view of the apostle's background similar to Lim's in important respects, is far more cognizant of the significant problems posed for such historical reconstructions by the paucity of our sources (1999). See also the careful sifting of evidence concerning Paul's linguistic competence by Du Toit 2000:392–401.

[31] Lim offers more extensive analyses of Pauline texts in his dissertation (1991) than he does in the published version (1997a), but even in the earlier work his investigation of Paul's citations along the lines he proposes is far from complete. Lim recognizes this fact, observing that "a comprehensive study of all the Pauline quotations from the perspective of textual plurality is a desideratum. A thorough study will have to be done once all the Qumran biblical scrolls have been properly edited and published" (1997a:149). Now that publication of all of the biblical texts of Isaiah from Qumran is complete (see the Appendix, pp. 361–62), the present study of Paul's use of Isaiah in Romans will be able to offer a substantial contribution toward such a comprehensive investigation.

[32] This will require an examination of the evidence not only of the Dead Sea scrolls, but also of the Isaiah Targum, the Peshitta, and the Vulgate. I will also evaluate afresh the Greek evidence for Paul's citations of and allusions to Isaiah. In this way, where my investigation agrees with Koch and/or Stanley, it will stand as additional testimony rather than a mere restatement of their conclusions.

While Koch, Stanley, and Lim focus primarily on reconstructing Paul's *Vorlage* and describing Paul's citation technique, other recent interpreters have concentrated their efforts on the task of exploring the hermeneutical assumptions and interpretive strategies that drive Paul's appropriation of Israel's scriptures. By far the most influential recent work on this front has been done by Richard B. Hays. In his seminal volume, *Echoes of Scripture in the Letters of Paul*,[33] Hays argues that Paul's letters reflect the apostle's deep engagement with Israel's scriptures:

> Paul's great struggle is not a struggle to assert his own authority over Scripture; it is, rather, a dialectical struggle to maintain the integrity of his proclamation in relation to Scripture and the integrity of Scripture in relation to that proclamation, to justify his startling claims about what the God of Israel had elected to do in Jesus Christ.[34]

Particularly important to Hays's investigation is a concept borrowed from modern literary criticism, that of "intertextual echo."[35] By means of this literary device, an author poetically alludes to a prior text in a way that "generates new figuration."[36] Echo often involves a trope known as "metalepsis" or "transumption," through which an author evokes another text in such a way that significant points of contact between the new text and its precursor remain unexpressed,

---

[33] Hays 1989. Responses to *Echoes*, with a further rejoinder by Hays, may be found in Evans and Sanders 1993:42–96. See also the insightful review by Hans Hübner (1991). Hübner himself has done important work on Paul's use of scripture (1984, 1993, 1997).

[34] Hays 1989:158–59.

[35] Hays acknowledges his indebtedness to the work of John Hollander (1981). Note that in Hays's usage, "intertextuality" refers to the *diachronic* influence of specific precursor texts on an author's work, not, as in the work of R. Barthes, J. Kristeva, and their followers, to the *synchronic* semiotic matrix within which a text "converses" with all of the other "texts," written and unwritten, available in a culture. On the important distinctions between these conceptions of "intertextuality," see Clayton and Rothstein 1991. Hays's approach to intertextuality shares much methodological common ground with the massive study of "inner biblical exegesis" by Michael Fishbane (1985). Benjamin D. Sommer (1998) has fruitfully adopted a similar notion of intertextuality to investigate the use of earlier traditions in Deutero-Isaiah.

[36] Hollander 1981:ix; quoted in Hays 1989:19. Echo is thus a subspecies of allusion. Hollander distinguishes the two more by *effect* than by anything else: echo is "a way of alluding that is inherently poetic rather than expository, and that makes new metaphor rather than learned gestures." I will follow Hays in making no systematic attempt to distinguish "echo" from "allusion", although generally "echo" will refer to more oblique methods of alluding to a prior text. For further reflection on how allusion "works," see the perceptive analysis of Ben-Porat 1976; cf. Morawski 1970.

inviting readers to complete the trope themselves by supplying the transumed connections. In the case of Paul, intertextual echo nearly always functions in tandem with more obvious references to scripture, including citations marked by introductory formulas and more explicit modes of allusion. In fact, the most impressive examples of intertextual echo Hays adduces are almost without exception the reverberations of the wider context of a scriptural text that Paul cites explicitly.[37] The "complex intertextual matrix" of Paul's letters

> proves hospitable to the proliferation of metalepsis. . . . In this literary setting even overt quotation can become a mode of troping: citations allude to their original contexts, and the most significant elements of intertextual correspondence between old context and new can be implicit rather than voiced, perceptible only within the silent space framed by the juncture of two texts.[38]

Hays's close readings of key passages in Paul's letters emphasize just how radical and even scandalous are the apostle's reinterpretations of Israel's scriptures; at the same time, he shows convincingly that these scriptural texts exercise a pervasive influence on Paul's conception of the gospel. Particularly where Paul employs the device of intertextual echo, scripture maintains its own voice over against Paul's, continually forcing the apostle to articulate his gospel in terms that are faithful to the scriptural story of God's election of Israel:

> Paul's allusive manner of using Scripture leaves enough silence for the voice of Scripture to answer back. Rather than filling the intertextual space with explanations, Paul encourages the reader to listen to more of Scripture's message than he himself voices. The word that Scripture speaks where Paul falls silent is a word that still has the power to contend against him.[39]

Paul's use of the figure of echo reveals the extent to which his thought is permeated and shaped by Israel's scriptures. He is convinced that,

---

[37] While attention has naturally focused on the figure of echo in Hays's work and on his criteria for discerning echoes, the extent to which his study relies on indisputable instances of citation and allusion often goes unnoticed. Hays allows his ear to be tuned by disciplined attention to Paul's explicit appropriations of scripture.

[38] Hays 1989:155. Similar intertextual effects involving quotation and allusion are explored in the context of biblical as well as rabbinic texts by Fishbane and Boyarin (see n. 20 above). *Contra* Wilcox, who asserts that citation, as opposed to allusion, does not assume the reader's familiarity with the original context (1979:237), Hays shows that such a sharp distinction between citation and allusion does not apply in many cases where Paul quotes scripture (cf. van Dodewaard 1955).

[39] Hays 1989:177.

despite its radical newness, the gospel he preaches stands in deep continuity with the witness of the biblical texts to God's continuing faithfulness to the covenant with Israel:

> Paul finds the continuity between Torah and gospel through a hermeneutic that reads Scripture primarily as a *narrative* of divine election and promise. . . . Within this narrative framework for interpretation, Paul's fragmentary references to and echoes of Scripture derive coherence from their common relation to the scriptural story of God's righteousness. Though the quotations appear eclectic and scattered, they usually must be understood as allusive recollections of the wider narrative setting from which they are taken.[40]

Hays cautions that discerning intertextual echoes is "less a matter of method than of sensibility."[41] Nevertheless, he does offer seven criteria for evaluating alleged instances of intertextual echo.[42] Far from constituting a set of rules that can be mechanically applied to texts, these seven criteria function as "modestly useful rules of thumb"[43] whose application is "an art practiced by skilled interpreters within a reading community," resulting in "an *aesthetic* judgment pronounced upon the fittingness of a proposed reading."[44] Hays concedes that, especially in the case of echoes, the criteria may lead only to a judgment about the relative probability of a particular echo. Consequently, careful readers can and do disagree about whether or not particular Pauline texts should be regarded as allusions to or echoes of scripture.

Of these seven criteria, five are particularly important for my purposes here: "Volume," "Recurrence," "Historical Plausibility,"

---

[40] Hays 1989:157–58. Other studies that draw attention to the coherence of Paul's citations and allusions with larger narrative and structural patterns found in their scriptural contexts include: Via 1974; J. A. Sanders 1975b; Smith 1988:279–88; Wright 1991:263–65; Stockhausen 1989, 1993; O'Day 1990; Scott 1992; Keesmaat 1994a, 1994b; Wagner 1998a. Of course, the view that Paul normally paid no regard to the larger context of his citations continues to live on happily in many quarters.

[41] Hays 1989:21.

[42] Hays 1989:29–32. They are: (1) Availability; (2) Volume; (3) Recurrence; (4) Thematic Coherence; (5) Historical Plausibility; (6) History of Interpretation; (7) Satisfaction.

[43] Hays 1998:212.

[44] Hays 1998:209; emphasis original. Porter (1997:83–84) misses the mark when he criticizes Hays for failing to offer a rigorous set of criteria, as if interpretation were simply a matter of hitting on the right methodology. While methodological rigor is crucial for certain purposes, it fails miserably as a strategy for reading literature, particularly for such metaphorically-charged literature as Paul's letters.

"Thematic coherence," and "Satisfaction."[45] *Volume* refers primarily to the degree of verbal correspondence between the alleged echo and the source text.[46] Verbal connections that are distinctive to a particular text can be particularly important for identifying the source of an echo.[47] The volume of a given echo also depends on the prominence it is given in Paul's argument. An echo that occurs at a crucial point in the discussion or in close connection with an explicit citation will tend to have a higher volume.

The criterion of *Recurrence* recognizes that an argument for the influence of a particular source text on an author is normally cumulative. In other words, the case for an alleged echo becomes stronger if the author has a pattern of drawing on that text or its larger context elsewhere.[48] In this way, for example, explicit citation of a passage can render further echoes of that same passage much more plausible than they would appear if considered only by themselves.

Historical Plausibility takes seriously the author's cultural environment and inherited traditions of interpretation. It is imperative to set Paul's reading of scripture in its larger historical and cultural context. Donald Juel remarks, "History can provide constraints on imaginative readings of the text: Given knowledge of the first century, some readings are implausible."[49] It is just as true, however,

---

Countless dull and lifeless readings of Paul's letters, and particularly of his scriptural citations and allusions, can be chalked up to methodological *rigor mortis*. By way of illustration one might recall two contrasting scenes in the movie, *The Dead Poets Society* (Touchstone Pictures, 1989). In the first, the students are directed by the author of their literature textbook to analyze poetry "scientifically" by plotting its elements on a graph. In the second scene, a group has gathered outdoors at night to *experience* poetry as they take turns reading it aloud to one another in the firelight. The film leaves no doubt as to which reading strategy allows the "dead poets" to return to life and to speak in powerful—and unexpected—ways to a new generation.

[45] As Hays notes (1989:29–30), "Availability" is not really an issue when it comes to Paul's use of scripture (though it is much less clear what his original audience knows of scripture; see below, pp. 33–39). "History of Interpretation" is best used not as a negative criterion to exclude possible echoes from consideration, but as a positive stimulus to hear Paul's appeals to scripture in new and perhaps unfamiliar ways.

[46] I exclude from consideration cases where there is an alleged "conceptual connection" but no clear verbal link.

[47] Fishbane stresses the importance of verbal links for identifying cases of "aggadic exegesis"; particularly significant are clusters of terms from the source text that appear to have been reorganized exegetically by the tradent (1985:285).

[48] This point is emphasized by B. D. Sommer in his study of Deutero-Isaiah's employment of earlier traditions (1998:35). Cf. the similar claim by B. S. Rosner (1994:19–20).

[49] Juel 1994:27.

that knowledge of exegetical techniques and traditions available in Paul's cultural context can open our eyes to new interpretive possibilities.[50] The final two criteria are closely related, if more elusive. *Thematic Coherence* refers to the "fit" of the proposed echo both with the argument that the author is developing and with the way the author appropriates other precursor texts. As will become apparent, my identification and analysis of fainter echoes of Isaiah in Romans is guided by the patterns I have discerned through examining Paul's explicit citations. *Satisfaction* is another way of saying that "the proof of the pudding is in the eating." Ultimately, the test of a proposed reading is its ability to make sense of Paul's larger argument. The criterion of "satisfaction" reminds us that reading is a communal activity. Our interpretations are shaped by and ultimately responsible to the judgments and sensibilities of larger communities of readers.[51]

THE APPROACH OF THE PRESENT INVESTIGATION

My own investigation of Paul's reading of Isaiah in Romans stands on the shoulders of the four studies just discussed, even as it attempts to extend their insights to address a new set of questions. Though differing (sometimes significantly) with respect to the details, Koch,

---

[50] On the related question of the extent to which the first readers of Romans could have understood Paul's more allusive references to Isaiah, see pp. 33–39 below.

[51] In the present instance, I read Paul both as a member of the academic community of biblical scholars and as a member of a two thousand-year-old faith community that claims both Romans and Isaiah as scripture. One's context is like a window—it both permits and restricts vision (cf. Wilken 1989; Melugin 1996, 1998). The questions I ask of Paul's letters and the interpretive methods I employ are inevitably shaped by these two communities, as well as by my wider historical and cultural contexts. For example, the Holocaust has given a particular sense of urgency to the task of rereading Paul's letters in the service of critical reflection on the relationship between the Church and Israel in the present day. As C. H. Cosgrove reminds us, as interpreters we become "co-accountable" with the text for its meaning (1996:87; see further Cosgrove 1997). Recognizing that readers and reading communities contribute an essential element to the interpretive process—that texts do not simply have "meaning" in and of themselves—does not imply, however, that the text and its author are thereby completely subsumed under the interpreter's will to power. Awareness of our own situatedness and of the "otherness" of the text under consideration opens the way for a "hermeneutic of love," in which we approach the task of interpretation much as we would a conversation with someone we respect and esteem. That is, from within our own context we may

Stanley, and Lim all agree that Paul adapted the wording of his scriptural text to conform more closely to his own understanding of its meaning as well as to serve his immediate rhetorical purposes. Ironically, though each of them devotes a great deal of effort to analyzing "external evidence" for Paul's *Vorlage* (i.e., the various ancient witnesses to the scriptural text), it is apparent from their discussions that in many cases the decision to attribute a particular variant to Paul rather than to his text finally turns on "*internal* evidence"—that is, on their own understanding of what Paul is driving at in the larger context of his argument.[52] Yet it is precisely here that these previous studies are least convincing, for they do not consistently pursue the kind of close reading of Paul's letters that penetrates to the underlying hermeneutical logic driving Paul's appropriations of scripture. The privilege of building on the insights of these previous studies, as well as the more limited focus of the present investigation on one single letter and on a smaller set of citations and allusions, will allow greater attention to be devoted to the *logic and function* of Paul's appropriations of Isaiah. My interest in determining as nearly as possible Paul's *Vorlage* and identifying his adaptations of the scriptural text will serve the larger purpose of understanding how Paul actually reads and employs Isaiah in the context of his unfolding argument in Romans.

In many respects, the work of Richard Hays on Paul's use of Israel's scriptures is foundational to this larger aim of the present study.[53] Like Hays, I seek to uncover the hermeneutical logic that guides Paul's reinterpretations of scripture by undertaking a close reading of Paul's argument and by paying special attention to Paul's use of intertextual allusion in its subtler as well as in its more overt forms. My methodology differs from Hays's, however, in its system-

---

make a genuine attempt to understand and articulate another's perspective in terms they would approve (on the rationale for such a dialogical approach to interpretation, see further Patte 1999:52–54; Wright 1992:50–64). A similar hermeneutic has been advocated by Nancy Jay, who argues for and models a dialogical method of ethnographic research that she terms "interpretive sociology" (1992:xxv–xxvi, 13–14).

[52] This is true even for Stanley (1992b), who hopes to minimize this "subjective" element by assigning a probability rating to each alleged Pauline alteration of the scriptural *Vorlage*. He then constructs his profile of Paul's citation techniques using only what he considers to be the most obvious cases of authorial adaptation.

[53] Hays, along with many others, has noted the particular importance that Isaiah seems to have for Paul: it is "statistically and substantively the most important scriptural source for Paul" (1989:162).

atic employment of a text-critical investigation of Paul's *Vorlage* as a tool for exposing Paul's interpretive strategies and aims[54] and in its greater attention to the relevance of other Second Temple literature for understanding Paul's reading of Isaiah in the apostle's cultural and historical context.[55]

My procedure in what follows will be to examine Paul's citations of and allusions to Isaiah in the context of Paul's argument as it unfolds in Romans. This will necessitate a close reading of relevant portions of the letter, including attention to Paul's appeal to other passages of scripture, for it is often the case, particularly in Romans 9–11,

---

[54] By combining the text-critical focus of Koch, Stanley, and Lim with the attentiveness to the poetic effects of Paul's citations and allusions modeled by Hays, the present study adopts a method that is analogous to "reasoned eclecticism" in the field of textual criticism, where both "external" and "internal" evidence are given careful consideration when evaluating textual variants (see Holmes 1995).

[55] The detailed investigation of Paul's use of Isaiah by Florian Wilk (1998) became available to me only after the present study was well on its way to completion. In this doctoral dissertation, written at the University of Jena under the direction of Berndt Schaller, Wilk undertakes a thorough examination of the text and function of Paul's citations of and allusions to Isaiah throughout the undisputed letters. He organizes Paul's interpretations of Isaiah under four headings: "Christusbotschaft," "Selbstverständnis," "Israelfrage," and "Parusieerwartung." By comparing the manner in which Isaiah is used in each letter, Wilk then attempts to trace the development of Paul's interpretation of the prophet throughout his apostolic career. He argues, as do I, that Paul's self-understanding and theology are shaped by his reading of large sections of Isaiah from the standpoint of his calling as apostle to the Gentiles (see especially 340–80, 401–408; see also Wilk 1999). Despite areas of overlap, however, the basic approach of the present study is significantly different from that of Wilk. While Wilk's focus is more wide-ranging, encompasing all of Paul's letters, it is also less able to explore the function of Paul's citations and allusions in their particular epistolary contexts. The present inquiry attempts to delve more deeply into the function of Isaianic texts in the context of Paul's argument in Romans. Whereas Wilk aims to trace the development of Paul's reading of Isaiah over time, I seek to provide a "thick description" of the ways in which Paul's reading of Isaiah shapes and is shaped by a particular set of circumstances and problems. Furthermore, while Wilk for the most part restricts his study to Paul's citations of and allusions to Isaiah, I devote a significant amount of attention to the relationship between Paul's reading of Isaiah and his interpretation of other scriptural texts in Romans. Finally, by attending closely to other interpretations of Isaiah roughly contemporaneous with Paul's, the present study is able to situate Paul's reading of scripture in its larger cultural context in a way that has not been done before. My interaction with Wilk's thesis—as with most other secondary literature—will largely be limited to the footnotes. It appears to me that our approaches to the question of Paul's reading of Isaiah are to a large extent complementary, and it may well be that the points at which we agree will carry greater weight by virtue of having been arrived at independently.

that Paul cites Isaiah as part of a larger scriptural argument involving a number of different texts.[56]

For each citation of or allusion to Isaiah,[57] I will compare Paul's wording[58] with:

1) the critically reconstructed text of LXX Isaiah[59] as well as variant readings in the manuscript tradition of the LXX;[60]

---

[56] It will thus be necessary to ask to what extent Paul's reading of Isaiah differs from his interpretation of other scriptural voices: Is Isaiah in any way unique for Paul, or is it in his eyes merely, as Barton puts it, part of "the seamless fabric of the oracles of God" (1986:150)?

[57] For the purposes of this study, "citations" are those appropriations of scripture marked for the reader either by a citation formula or by some other explicit textual feature (e.g., the sudden shift in pronouns in Rom 9:7; cf. Stanley 1992b:56–57; Fox 1980). "Allusion" and "echo" will be used somewhat interchangeably for unmarked appropriations of scripture, although "echo" normally denotes a more oblique reference than "allusion."

[58] The New Testament manuscript tradition of Paul's citations must be evaluated carefully, since it appears that scribes tended to harmonize NT citations of scripture with their LXX form (Metzger 1992:197–98). A fresh examination of the evidence leads me to part company with the editors of NA^{27}/UBS^4 at a very significant point (see below pp. 84–85).

[59] Ziegler 1939a.

[60] In this study I use the term "LXX" to refer to the *initial* Greek translation of a biblical book (cf. Peters 1992:1093–94). In most cases there exists a critically-reconstructed text (in the Göttingen LXX), which is employed here with constant attention to the apparatus. Where the Göttingen series is incomplete, I use the Cambridge LXX (which normally reproduces B, but which includes an extensive critical apparatus); where necessary, I also consult the edition of Holmes and Parsons (1798–1827). Rahlfs's edition (1935) is used only where the precise reading of the LXX text is not at issue. Of course, I do not assume that Paul's *Vorlage* exactly matched the reconstructed *Urtext* of the Göttingen edition. As J. W. Wevers remarks, "The countless readers of the LXX throughout the centuries only had copies, in fact, copies of copies. . . . These manuscripts are all eclectic in nature, i.e. they are based on a complicated and often untraceable textual genealogy" (1998:xxxvii). In referring to variants from the "LXX" that reflect later developments of the *Urtext*, I follow Wevers in speaking of the "LXX tradition." It is crucial to recognize that in the first century, the text of the Greek translation of Israel's scriptures was in a state of flux. The initial translations into Greek of biblical books originally written in Hebrew and Aramaic did not simply suffer the normal vagaries of textual transmission: there is also strong evidence for intentional, if unsystematic, revision of the LXX in the first century. Some changes appear to have been intended as "improvements" of the Greek style. More significant for my purposes, however, are a class of textual alterations that represent attempts to bring the LXX closer to one of a variety of Hebrew text-forms (see Barthélemy 1963; Hanhart 1984; Wevers 1968, 1982; Brock 1992; the extended discussion of the issue in Stanley 1992b:37–51 is quite helpful). The clear implication for the present study is that where Paul's citations or allusions differ from the "LXX" (as critically reconstructed) and appear to reflect a text closer to that now preserved in MT, *this does not prove that Paul was drawing directly on a Hebrew text*. Rather, he may well have been using a text of the LXX that had previously been revised toward a Hebrew exemplar. In fact, in some

2) the evidence of the later Greek versions, the church fathers, and quotations in other NT writings;[61]

3) the available evidence for Hebrew forms of the text, including MT, the Dead Sea Scrolls,[62] the Isaiah Targum, and the Peshitta.[63]

My aim will be, where possible, to distinguish Paul's *Vorlage* from modifications Paul himself has made to his text. I am particularly interested in the interpretive and rhetorical ends Paul's modifications appear to serve. Where evidence is available, I will compare Paul's reading of Isaiah with interpretations of the same passage in other Second Temple Literature.[64] This will entail a close examination of the LXX, 1QIsaᵃ, Targum, and Peshitta for evidence of exegetical activity on the part of their tradents.[65] The goal, however, is not to establish Paul's *dependence* on particular exegetical traditions, but to set

---

cases where Paul seems to be utilizing a revised text of Isaiah LXX (e.g., Isa 8:14 in Rom 9:33; Isa 52:7 in Rom 10:15), there is additional evidence apart from Paul's citation for the existence of just such a revision (see pp. 126–36 and 170–74). On the form of Paul's Greek text of Isaiah in particular, see n. 86 below.

[61] As P. Katz notes, the later Greek versions—all *post-Christian*—are potentially of great value for New Testament studies. For example, they may be able to shed important light on developments in the meaning and usage of Greek words in the centuries after the original translation of the LXX (Katz and Ziegler 1958:270–71).

[62] Citations of the Dead Sea Scrolls follow the format: scroll name/number, fragment number(s), column number, and line number(s). So, for example, 4Q161 frgs. 8–10 3.6–13 refers to lines 6–13 of column three of the joined fragments 8 through 10 of 4Q161. I normally follow the numbering of the *editio princeps*; for the *pesharim*, however, I follow the revised text of Charlesworth 2001. For the *Hodayot*, I adopt the numbering of García Martínez and Tigchelaar 1997–98 (following the reconstruction of Stegemann/Puech) and provide Sukenik's numbers (1955) in brackets.

[63] See the Appendix for an annotated list of the editions and specialized studies consulted for each of these ancient witnesses.

[64] I make no pretense of offering a true comparative study of the use of Isaiah in Paul and in writings contemporaneous with his letters. Such a project would require treating each individual document on its own terms before attempting a comparison among them. In the present investigation, it is Paul's citations and allusions that set the agenda and raise the questions I pose to these other Jewish texts. I will occasionally refer to other NT appropriations of Isaiah in the present study, but, again, only in the service of my investigation of Paul's interpretive activity. Here too, comparative work must await fuller studies of each NT author or writing on its own terms. A broad survey of interpretations of Isaiah in the Second Temple Period, in both Jewish and emerging Christian communities, is provided by the essays in Broyles and Evans 1997; see also Anderson 1988a; Knibb 1996. For the interpretation of Isaiah in Christian tradition, see Sawyer 1996; Manley 1995. Due to the difficulty of dating rabbinic traditions reliably, only rarely will I consider the evidence of rabbinic exegesis as a means of illuminating Paul's interpretations of Isaiah. See the cautions and guidelines offered in Alexander 1983; Vermes 1980; Evans 1995; Rendtorff 1993a.

[65] It has long been appreciated that "the ancient versions of the Bible are

Paul's reading of Isaiah in its wider cultural and historical context.[66]

At the same time, drawing on Hays's concept of "intertextual echo," I will listen for the resonances in Romans of the wider Isaianic settings of the texts that Paul appropriates through citation or allusion.[67] Here, my focus will primarily be on *Paul's* reading of Isaiah—to the extent that it can be discerned from the text of Romans itself[68]—

---

themselves also part of exegetical literature" (Vermes 1970:203). The literature on this topic is voluminous. See Brock 1974, 1988 for concise overviews of the issues. James Barr's study of ancient approaches to translation (1979) remains a standard work; see also Muraoka 1994; Seeligmann 1961. The extent to which the ancient translators were also exegetes continues to be debated. R. Hanhart argues with regard to all of the books of the LXX that "deviations from the MT must be noticed but should only in the rarest cases be taken as the peculiar expression of the translator by means of which he wants to interpret—let alone reinterpret—his *Vorlage*" (1992:342; cf. Hanhart 1983). In contrast, M. Goshen-Gottstein has contended that a significant number of variant readings in the LXX are *exegetical* in nature and do not necessarily reflect use of a Hebrew *Vorlage* different from MT. See his programmatic essay (1963) as well as Tov 1999 (note, however, the cautions of Tov 1984; Elwolde 1997). Similarly, M. P. Weitzman concludes with regard to the Peshitta: "It is safest to attribute the maximum to the translators' activity. This implies keeping to a minimum the assumption of variant readings and hence of scribal change in the copying either of the Hebrew or of the Syriac text" (1999:69). Goshen-Gottstein's edition of Isaiah for the Hebrew University Bible Project (1995) offers numerous astute observations on readings in the versions as well as in the Dead Sea Scrolls. For further literature on interpretation in the ancient versions, see the Appendix.

[66] E. P. Sanders notes, "Parallels *are* often illuminating, as long as one does not jump from 'parallel' to 'influence' to 'identity of thought'" (1977:11; emphasis original). See S. Sandmel's now famous essay (1962); cf. Donaldson 1983. I will be looking not primarily for identical interpretations of scripture in Paul and his contemporaries but for analogous ways of appropriating and interpreting a text. Note the similar approach of Paul Dinter (1980): Rather than seeking to find a "coherent trajectory of interpretation . . . that somehow predetermined Paul's use" of the motifs of "remnant" and "stone," Dinter seeks, "through a synoptic comparison, to understand the possibilities over against which Paul contemporized the traditions that are at the heart of his exposition in Romans 9–11" (163; emphasis removed).

[67] It is important to note that attention to intertextuality plays a subsidiary role in my investigation of Paul's *Vorlage* and of his possible adaptations of the text of his citations. The concept of intertextual echo comes into play at this stage of the investigation only to the extent that, by shedding light on possible motivations for an alleged Pauline adaptation, it may serve as a source of "internal evidence" for a particular text-critical judgment.

[68] That is, as an interpreter, my concern is not with the *writer* of Romans—the particular historical figure who produced the letter and who exists *outside* the text—but with the *author* "Paul" who emerges through the process of interpreting Romans (and the undisputed Pauline corpus as a whole). For this distinction, and on the relation between writer and author, see Nehamas 1981, 1986, 1987. According to Nehamas, "the author is postulated as the agent whose actions account for the text's features; he is a character, a hypothesis which is accepted provisionally, guides interpretation, and is in turn modified in its light" (1981:145; cf. Booth's "implied author"

not, in most cases, on what the first hearers of Paul's letter might have picked up from his use of Isaiah in Romans.[69]

In the chapters that follow, I will attempt to maintain three foci of attention: (1) the Isaianic texts and their wider settings in the book of Isaiah; (2) Paul's interpretive strategies in relation to those particular texts (and possibly to their wider contexts); (3) Paul's ongoing argument in Romans, including his appropriation of other scriptural texts. Though it may be heuristically useful to attempt to separate the strands of scriptural text, scriptural interpretation, and epistolary context for the purpose of analysis, such a procedure is also fraught with danger: the whole thing may simply unravel in our hands. Ultimately, then, the sort of analysis undertaken here must constantly attend to a close reading of Paul's letter itself; to do otherwise would be to destroy the beauty, strength, and coherence of the intricate interpretive tapestry that Paul weaves in the service of his apostolic ministry to the Roman believers (Rom 15:14–15).

READING ISAIAH IN THE FIRST CENTURY

A few introductory remarks will help set Paul's reading of Isaiah in its wider cultural and historical context. Although many of the problems and issues touched on here easily warrant a book-length treatment in their own right, my goal for the present is simply to sketch the picture of Paul as an ancient reader that informs this investigation.

[1961]). Nehamas argues that the author, while not identical with the writer, must however be "a plausible historical variant of the writer" (1986:689; cf. 1981:145). Thus, my interest in "Paul" as author of Romans and interpreter of Isaiah will require me to attend as fully as possible to the cultural and historical context within which Paul's letters emerged. For a perceptive account of the crucial role one's portrait of "Paul" plays in the interpretation of his letters—no less for the modern than for the ancient reader—see Mitchell 2000:409–439. She contends: "Chrysostom's interpretation of Paul in its vigorously author-centered way illustrates that, at least for epistolary texts, a separation of the author from his writings is simply impossible" (436).

[69] These questions are not entirely separable, however. See the discussion of the problem in Hays 1989:25–33. For a more audience-centered approach to Paul's scriptural quotations, see Stanley 1997, 1999. On the question of Paul's actual audience in Rome, see pp. 33–39 below.

How Did Paul Encounter the Book of Isaiah?

Attention to the realia of books and readers in the ancient world is necessary if one's conception of Paul's reading of Isaiah is not to be hopelessly anachronistic.[70] It is difficult to imagine the apostle travelling thousands of miles on foot carrying the full scroll of Isaiah along with him.[71] Even with access to the text of Isaiah, the physical characteristics of the scroll form,[72] combined with the almost complete absence of aids to the reader, may well have rendered it time consuming and tedious to look up and compare passages, particularly in a text of this size.[73]

In light of the practical difficulties involved in handling the full scroll of Isaiah, it is reasonable to postulate that Paul—to the extent that he utilized written texts of scripture—employed, in addition to biblical scrolls, personal notebooks of excerpts culled from the scriptures by himself or by others. This suggestion is similar to the "testimony book" hypothesis proposed by J. Rendel Harris, except that it does not limit the purpose of excerpting to apologetic or polemical ends. Moreover, it does not require one to suppose there ever existed a single *Urbuch* of excerpts passed from hand to hand.[74] The

---

[70] H. Y. Gamble has assembled an impressive amount of material on this topic and has provided a keen analysis of its significance for a wide range of issues in the study of early Christianity (1995). See also Millard 2000 and the older, but still valuable work by F. G. Kenyon (1951).

[71] Stanley suggests that the cost of books would have made private ownership of scriptural texts prohibitive for all but the wealthy (1999:127). However, in his exhaustive study of books and readers in the early church, Gamble notes that the cost of books does not appear to have been a factor limiting Christian access to the scriptures (1995:55, 231, 233, 237). Moreover, Stanley himself recognizes the distinct possibility that wealthy Christians may have purchased scriptural texts for their congregation's use (1992b:73 n. 27).

[72] It is just possible that Paul had access to Isaiah in codex form. In a fascinating essay, Michael McCormick (1985) suggests that the necessity for early Christian missionaries such as Paul to carry scriptural texts on their travels may have led to the early adoption of the codex form in Christian circles. He argues that two of the principal advantages of the codex over the roll are its ease of transport and its capacity to hold large texts (Gamble notes that the third-century Chester Beatty Codex VII, which originally contained 224 pages, held the entire book of Isaiah [1995:67]). McCormick further observes that twelve of the seventeen surviving non-Christian codices assigned by Roberts and Skeat to the second century probably belonged to doctors and teachers, who frequently had occasion to travel with their books and manuals.

[73] The Great Isaiah Scroll from Qumran (1QIsaᵃ) now measures just over 24 feet in length; its original length may have been more than 24 ½ feet (Trever 1950:xiv).

[74] For the testimony-book hypothesis, see especially J. R. Harris 1916–20. A

practice of extracting passages from larger texts and collecting them in personal notebooks is well attested for the first century.[75] In fact, several striking examples of such collections of scriptural excerpts have been discovered among the Dead Sea Scrolls,[76] including one collection of Isaianic texts promising the "consolation" of Israel.[77]

The qualification introduced in the previous paragraph, "to the extent that Paul utilized written texts of scripture," is an important one. *Ancient interpreters relied heavily on memory even in conjunction with the use of written texts.* Paul in particular was raised in a culture that deeply valued an intimate acquaintance with Israel's scriptures. In such an environment, the memorization of large portions of scripture was probably the norm.[78] This observation holds whether Paul is thought to have been raised in Tarsus or educated from an early age in Jerusalem.[79] Though we know little about what it would have meant to be a *diaspora* Pharisee, there is every reason to suppose that it would have entailed a high regard for and close acquaintance with Israel's sacred texts, at least in their Greek form.[80]

---

concise discussion of Harris's hypothesis and critical responses to it is found in Paget 1994:90–100. The earlier proposal of Edwin Hatch (1889b:203; cf. 1889a) appears far more plausible than Harris's version of the hypothesis. Rather than positing a single, fairly fixed set of texts used by Christian polemicists, as did Harris, Hatch suggested that early Jewish and Christian interpreters made use of multiple anthologies that varied in content. Paul may well have created his own anthologies of *excerpta* and also borrowed from anthologies collected by others. Over time, it would not be surprising if there began to be a significant degree of overlap in the texts found in such manuals. See further Kraft 1960, 1961.

[75] A survey of the evidence for the use of anthologies in the ancient world is provided by Hodgson 1979. For fuller discussion and development of the hypothesis of biblical *excerpta*, with suggestive parallels from the Greco-Roman world and from Qumran, see Gamble 1995:24–28; Albl 1999; Chadwick 1969; C. H. Roberts 1970; Koch 1986:247–55, 99–101; Stanley 1992b:69–79, 255–56; Lim 1997a:150–58; Tov 1995; Duncan 1997; White 1990.

[76] The discovery of catena texts at Qumran such as 4QMidrEschat[a,b] (= 4Q174 + 4Q177), 4QTest (4Q175), and 4QTanḥ (4Q176) has revived interest in the testimony-book hypothesis by providing for the first time a roughly contemporaneous parallel to these putative early Christian anthologies. See Fitzmyer 1957; Lim 1997a:152–54; White 1990.

[77] See Stanley 1992a.

[78] On memorization as a fundamental component of education in antiquity, see Marrou 1956; Safrai 1976. On the interrelationship between writing and memorization in the transmission of Christian tradition, see Gerhardsson 1961, 1964. For important correctives to Gerhardsson, note the series of studies by M. S. Jaffee (1992, 1994, 1995).

[79] See the judicious discussions of this question by Davies 1999 and Du Toit 2000.

[80] Josephus (*J.W.* 2.162; *Life* 191; cf. Acts 22:3; 26:5) notes the Pharisees'

Most studies of Paul's use of scripture have taken it for granted that memorization played a significant role in Paul's appropriation and interpretation of Israel's sacred texts. However, this idea has recently been disputed by both Koch and Stanley.[81] They are most convincing when they argue against those who explain Paul's inexact citations of scripture by positing memory lapses on the part of the apostle. Stanley points out the contradiction inherent in appealing to Paul's faulty memory to account for variants in his citations and allusions while simultaneously attributing verbatim agreements with a known *Vorlage* to the excellence of Paul's memory rather than to his use of written texts. In fact, Stanley and Koch have demonstrated convincingly that Paul often *purposefully* adapts his scriptural citations to fit his own argument. In addition, they have plausibly argued that in some cases the evidence points to Paul's use of *written* texts.[82] But while Koch and Stanley have made it impossible any

---

reputation for exactness (ἀκριβεία) in interpretation of and obedience to the Law; cf. A. I. Baumgarten 1983; Mason 1991:89–96.

[81] The principal arguments are found in Stanley 1992b:16–17; 69–71; cf. Koch 1986:93–99. I will focus my critique on the arguments adduced by Stanley (many of which he adopts from Koch), since he offers the more compelling statement of the case.

[82] See Stanley 1992b:69–71. The strongest evidence for Paul's use of a written text involves citations that appear to reflect an early revision of the LXX (see n. 60 above and the discussions below of Isaiah 28:16/8:14 [pp. 126–36] and Isaiah 52:7 [pp. 170–74]). Stanley considers the possibility that Paul had originally memorized these "non-standard" renderings, but deems it

> unlikely that [Paul] would have continued to adhere to such idiosyncratic traditions in view of his constant exposure to the standard language of the Septuagint. The fact that he quotes other passages from the same books in full agreement with the Septuagint makes such an explanation all the more unlikely (1992b:70–71 n. 21).

This argument assumes that Paul's memorization of a text would have rendered him unable to tolerate or to remember variant versions of a particular verse or passage. Yet it is far from obvious that such would have been the case. Many modern Christians know at least two versions of the Lord's prayer, for instance, and they do not seem to have too much difficulty substituting "debts" for "trespasses" as the occasion requires—though embarrassing mistakes are known to occur! It is not hard to imagine that had Paul known the book of Isaiah by heart, he might still have stumbled upon a rendering of a particular passage that was more useful for his purposes and either remembered it or jotted it down in his notebook for future reference. Frederick W. Norris notes that the Patristic writers "compared manuscripts and translations" as they interpreted scripture (1994:457). The argument for Paul's knowledge of a diversity of text-types, while it may strongly suggest his use of written notes, is no proof that he did not also memorize scripture. For a reevaluation of the actual extent of textual diversity in Paul's citations of Isaiah, however, see n. 86 below.

longer to invoke a "memory lapse" to explain away what might otherwise appear to be an intentional modification of the text, *they have
not shown thereby that Paul's authorial adaptations preclude his knowing scriptural texts by heart.* Deliberate modifications may be made to memorized texts as well as to written ones.[83] Stanley will allow memorization
as a possibility in the case of "such well-known passages as the Ten
Commandments."[84] In Paul's case, however, there is every reason
to think that what was "well known" would have included large portions of Israel's scriptures.[85]

---

[83] For example, like many people of my generation who went through confirmation
in a mainline Protestant church, I can quote the King James Version of Psalm 23
perfectly. But when I recite the psalm for my four-year-old, I purposefully mod-
ernize the language in order to communicate the meaning of the psalm in terms
he can understand.

[84] Stanley 1992b:79 n. 49.

[85] So also Hengel 1991:34–37. Stanley seems somehow to know which portions
of scripture Paul (not to mention his contemporaries) would have known well, and
which portions would have been less familiar. He argues that in Paul's letters "even
well-known biblical passages are often quoted 'inaccurately' while more obscure
texts are cited nearly verbatim" (1992b:17). Stanley includes the following among
these allegedly "obscure texts" cited accurately by Paul: "Ps 68.10 (Rom 15.3), Deut
32.43 (Rom 15.10), Ps 5.10 (Rom 3.13), Ps 18.5 (Rom 10.18), etc." (1992b:17
n. 49). This list is quite surprising, considering that, next to Isaiah, the book most
frequently quoted by Paul is the Psalms. Not only does Paul quote Psalm 68:23–24
LXX in Romans 11:9–10 (see below, pp. 257–65), this psalm was apparently appropriated very early on by Christians to interpret Jesus' Passion. Barnabas Lindars
writes:
> The largest contribution to the Passion apologetic comes from Psalm 69 [68
> LXX], which is undoubtedly the most important of these psalms.... It is clear
> that it was found useful *as a whole* by the early Christians (1961:99; emphasis
> original; see the whole section, 99–108).

Even more amazing is Stanley's claim that Deuteronomy 32 was a relatively "obscure"
text. Leaving aside the question of the use of Moses' Song in other Jewish literature (see below, pp. 191–92), Paul himself directly quotes from Deuteronomy 32 in
Romans 10:19 (Deut 32:21b), Romans 12:19 (Deut 32:35), and Romans 15:10 (Deut
32:43). There are also a number of fairly strong allusions to Moses' Song in Paul's
letters: Romans 11:11–14 (Deut 32:21b); 1 Corinthians 10:20a (Deut 32:17); 1
Corinthians 10:22 (Deut 32:21a); Philippians 2:15 (Deut 32:5). On the crucial role
Deuteronomy 32 plays for Paul in Romans, see below Chapters 3, 4, 5, and 6.
See further Bell 1994. Hays's comment is quite pertinent here (1989:164):
> The Song of Moses, read as a prophetic prefiguration of God's dealings with
> Israel through the gospel, becomes in Paul's hands a hermeneutical key of equal
> importance with the prophecies of Deutero-Isaiah.... Deuteronomy 32 contains
> Romans *in nuce.*

Interestingly, the Book of Hebrews, which may reflect some "Pauline" influence
(Hurst 1990:107–24, 131–33), quotes two of the passages from Moses' Song cited
by Paul in Romans: 32:35–36 (Heb 10:30) and 32:43 (Heb 1:6). In each case, the
citation in Hebrews includes a different portion of the verse than that quoted by

Let me be clear: I do not wish to deny that Paul may have had frequent recourse to written texts of scripture; neither do I dispute that the apostle may have compiled notebooks of scriptural excerpts, carried them along on his travels, and consulted them when composing his letters. However, the conclusion Stanley wishes to draw from all of this, that Paul knew Israel's scriptures *primarily* through the medium of written texts, simply does not follow.[86] Stanley believes, along with Koch,[87] that Paul's quotations are the product of intense study and reflection prior to their incorporation in his letters, but Stanley's hypothesis that Paul developed his interpretations of scrip-

---

Paul, showing that the author clearly knows the Song apart from the bits quoted in Paul's letter to the Romans. The fact is, we have no way of knowing which portions of scripture would have been "obscure texts" for Paul. There is thus no *a priori* justification for treating a verbatim citation of a particular passage as evidence that Paul quoted from a written text rather than from memory.

[86] Stanley argues that the diversity of text-types represented by Paul's citations from Isaiah strongly suggests that he did not use a single Isaiah scroll (and, presumably, that he did not have a single version of Isaiah memorized; Stanley 1992b:68 n. 15; 73 n. 27; 255 n. 12). However, in a largely positive review of Stanley's monograph, James Barr has questioned whether Stanley rightly grasps the importance of recognizing the *relative value* of the textual witnesses to Isaiah for reconstructing Paul's *Vorlage* [Barr 1994:597–600]. An examination of the examples adduced by Stanley to show the "diffuse textual situation" for Paul's quotations of Isaiah in Romans reveals that Paul's text normally agrees with one of the major "Alexandrian" uncials (A Q), the chief representatives of the text-family that Ziegler (1939a:21–36) considers to be the most reliable witnesses to Isaiah LXX (see Stanley 1992b:255 n. 12; for "11:14," read 14:11; *contra* Stanley, 1:17 is not a quotation from Isaiah). Only in Romans 9:33 (Isa 8:14) and Romans 10:15 (Isa 52:7) is there strong evidence for Paul's use of a revised text of LXX Isaiah. (The order of verbs and clauses in Romans 10:20 is, as Stanley admits, a "wholly uncertain" case [1992b:255 n. 12]; in Romans 9:28 Paul agrees with the "Hexaplaric" uncials B V against A Q in reading κύριος rather than θεός, but this type of alteration by itself does not carry much weight, particularly with κύριος σαβαώθ appearing in Romans 9:29.) Koch shows that the same pattern of agreement with Alexandrian witnesses holds outside of Romans as well (the only exceptions are the citations of Isaiah in 1 Corinthians 14:21 and 15:54, which he believes reflect a revised text of LXX Isaiah; Koch 1986:48–51; cf. Wilk 1998:17–42). Far from demonstrating that most of Paul's quotations from Isaiah could not have come from a single manuscript, *the textual evidence strongly suggests that Paul knew Isaiah in a form very close to the "Alexandrian text" of LXX Isaiah.* It is not possible to determine on this basis whether Paul had a personal copy of Isaiah that he toted around (cf. the possibly historical reminiscence in 2 Timothy 4:13), whether he had the book memorized, or whether he had access at various times to copies of the book that all had a similar textual character (which, it should be noted, is close to the putative *Urtext* of LXX Isaiah), but the evidence is certainly compatible with my hypothesis that Paul knew Isaiah by heart in Greek (cf. n. 82 above; see further the discussions of Romans 9:33 and 10:15 below, pp. 126–36 and 170–74 respectively).

[87] Koch 1986:257–85.

ture "through continued meditation on the verses contained in his anthology"[88] sounds more like a description of a modern-day "Bible verse memory program" than an account of how ancient Jews, such as Paul, learned and interpreted scripture. Still more incredible is Stanley's assumption that once Paul expended the labor to find and excerpt a passage, he promptly forgot all about its original setting:

> The fact that a number of Paul's citations are used in a sense quite foreign to their original context is easily understood if Paul is pictured as copying his citations not directly from the pages of Scripture, but rather from a diverse collection of biblical texts in which the only link with the original context is the one that is preserved in the compiler's mind.[89]
>
> At least some of Paul's more fanciful interpretations of the biblical text could have arisen from the fact that the original context was no longer available to him at the time of composition.[90]

It is far easier to attribute the kind of intricate linking of texts and contexts one finds in Paul's use of Isaiah in Romans[91] to Paul's memorization of the book of Isaiah than to imagine him repeatedly (at many times and in various places!) rolling and rerolling the scroll, combing the text for passages to excerpt and then making interpretive connections on the basis of those excerpts and his (limited) recollection of their contexts. The "foreignness" of Paul's interpretations to the original scriptural contexts of the citations is best explained, not by assuming that at the moment of writing he did not recall the wider setting of a verse he had previously copied into his notebook, but by recognizing that Paul's gospel and mission have driven him to a radical rereading of scripture. In other words, Paul's "misreading" of scripture derives from his convictions as a missionary theologian, not from his lack of familiarity with Israel's sacred texts.

Rather than posing the question in terms of mutually exclusive alternatives—*either* memorization *or* use of written texts and anthologies of excerpts—we should imagine Paul interacting with scripture in a *variety* of modes, including meditation on memorized passages,

---

[88] Stanley 1992b:78.

[89] Stanley 1992b:78. That Stanley thinks Paul is "the compiler" is clear from his prior suggestion that "Paul copied his excerpts from a variety of manuscripts housed at sites all around the eastern Mediterranean world, where he was a constant traveler" (78).

[90] Stanley 1999:137.

[91] I hope to demonstrate in the four chapters that follow the appropriateness of such a characterization of Paul's use of Isaiah in Romans.

hearing of spoken texts, personal reading of written texts, and collection of and reflection on excerpts from larger texts. Such a multi-
faceted approach, though it may require a less "rigorous" methodology
in the study of Paul's appropriations of scripture, is absolutely
neccessary to capture the complex reality of books and readers in
the first century.

While a detailed survey of the evidence is impossible here, two
examples will sufficiently illustrate this latter point for the purposes
of this study.[92] The introduction to 2 Maccabees alludes to the various ways first-century readers could be expected to interact with
texts. Describing their purpose in condensing the five-volume history
of the Maccabees by Jason of Cyrene into a single book, the authors
state:

> We have aimed to please those who wish to read, to make it easy for
> those who are inclined to memorize, and to profit all readers (2 Macc
> 2:25, NRSV).
>
> ἐφροντίσαμεν τοῖς μὲν βουλομένοις ἀναγινώσκειν ψυχαγωγίαν, τοῖς δὲ
> φιλοφρονοῦσιν εἰς τὸ διὰ μνήμης ἀναλαβεῖν εὐκοπίαν, πᾶσι δὲ τοῖς ἐντυγχά-
> νουσιν ὠφέλειαν.

Even though they make no pretension to be writing scripture, the
authors clearly assume that some of their readers will want to *memorize* the work for their own enjoyment and edification.

Although it comes from several centuries later, Augustine's advice
to readers of scripture reflects the sizable challenge Paul and his
Jewish contemporaries faced as they approached the task of interpreting a vast scriptural corpus collected in numerous scrolls:

> The first rule in this laborious task is, as I have said, to know these
> books; not necessarily to understand them but to read them so as to
> commit them to memory or at least make them not totally unfamiliar.[93]

In order to understand obscure or ambiguous passages, Augustine
says, one must compare them with perspicuous and indisputable ones.

---

[92] A fascinating collection of essays surveying the multiplicity of ways people in
Greco-Roman society—including the illiterate majority—encountered and interacted
with written texts is found in *Literacy in the Roman World* (ed. J. H. Humprey; Journal
of Roman Archaeology Supplement Series 3, 1991). See especially Beard 1991.
These studies offer an important supplement and corrective to William V. Harris's
masterful account of the place of the written word in ancient society (1989). See
further Botha 1992a; Bowman and Woolf 1994; Goodman 1994b; Lane Fox 1994.
[93] Cuius operis et laboris prima observatio est, ut diximus, nosse istos libros, etsi

But how does one locate the proper texts for such a comparison? The bishop advises,

> Here memory is extremely valuable; and it cannot be supplied by these instructions if it is lacking.[94]

Since memory was considered a necessary aid to the use of written texts, there is no reason to think that Paul's use of biblical scrolls or anthologies of quotations implies that he did not have the passage memorized by heart as well.[95] I assume, then, that one cannot exclude either memory or written texts as possible sources for Paul's citations and allusions in Romans. Instead, the *variety* of ways in which Paul encountered scripture must constantly be kept in mind.[96]

Finally, it is important to note that when I speak of Paul "reading" scripture, I am employing the term in its broadest sense of "interpreting," which entails both comprehending a text (whether spoken, written, or memorized)[97] and performing an interpretation of that text in a particular context (such as the letter to the Romans).

---

nondum ad intellectum, legendo tamen vel mandare memoriae vel omnino incognitos non habere (*De Doctrina Christiana*, 2.30; Green 1995:70–71).

[94] In qua re memoria valet plurimum; quae si defuerit non potest his praeceptis dari (*De Doctrina Christiana*, 2.31; Green 1995:70–71). Although we should not imagine a situation of widespread literacy among Christian laypeople, neither should we think that Augustine was addressing an elite guild of scholars. He offers his work to all "those with the will and the wit to learn" (Haec tradere institui volentibus et valentibus discere [Preface, 1; Green 1995:2–3).

[95] Martin S. Jaffee speaks of the "interpenetration of the oral and written registers" evident both in Paul and in the Rabbis (1995:71). His comments (70–71) are worth quoting at some length, for they provide an important perspective on Paul from outside the field of New Testament studies:

Over the past fifteen years or so a number of scholars . . . have presented models of rabbinic literary culture as one in which written and oral texts were in constant mutual penetration. . . . The rabbinic deployment of scriptural verses for a variety of rhetorical purposes reveals a total oral mastery of the written text. . . .

. . . .Paul seems no less capable of deploying an apt scriptural quotation than any Sage, nor of making his own points through adept scriptural citations and allusions. And Sages' scriptural quotations are, no less than Paul's, quotations from memory in service of more ambitious rhetorical constructions. I fail to see what significant difference one can find between Pauline and rabbinic oral mastery of Scripture. Paul knew his Greek text as thoroughly as Sages knew their Hebrew version. I assume he learned it by both hearing it and reading it, just as they did theirs. But, having mastered it, the written text was useful as a mnemonic aid, not a crutch.

[96] See further Graham 1987.

[97] Paul Achtemeier (1990) emphasises the "oral/aural" nature of reading and writing in the first century.

The act of reading is intimately and inextricably bound up with the
act of interpretation, and this was no less true in the ancient world
than it is today. Although the invention of the printing press and
the rise of enlightenment philosophy have conspired to obscure for
us moderns the irrefrangible nature of this connection,[98] for ancient
readers, the realization that reading entails interpretation would have
been inescapable. Fred Norris explains:[99]

> Reading a text in antiquity ordinarily meant reading aloud a manu-
> script usually without word divisions or punctuation marks and cor-
> recting the errors as one went along. Sometimes readers compared
> manuscripts; sometimes they had only one exemplar. But each reader
> always expected errors. The printing press was what impressed us with
> uniformity of spelling and grammar in copies of texts. No early Christian
> theologian ever had that cancerous luxury. The texts we now study
> were then in flux at the level of the black marks because those black
> marks were created by scribes who themselves belonged to worship-
> ping communities and by readers who knew that the words or letters
> were not always correct. Why call their changes "corruptions" even in
> an ironic way, when the scribes themselves did not think that they
> had in their hands "incorrupt" texts? Perhaps they are among the most
> "honest" readers of antiquity because they wrote down what they
> "knew" the text said.[100]

In adapting the wording of his scriptural texts to serve his interpretive ends, then, Paul reveals himself to be not some iconoclastic
religious reformer or cunningly deceptive orator, but a person of his
own time.[101]

---

[98] Though even we cannot escape the problem completely. With what tone of
voice is one to read Jesus' answers to the high priest (Matt 26:64) and to Pilate
(Matt 27:11)? Are the centurion's words upon the death of Jesus (Mark 15:39) to
be heard as confession or taunt? (For the latter reading, see Juel 1994:74 n. 7).

[99] Norris 1994:456. Norris is speaking with reference primarily to the Patristic
period, but his observations—both concerning reading practices and concerning the
state of the scriptural texts—are equally applicable to Paul and his contemporaries.

[100] Norris is here responding to Bart Ehrman's provocative phraseology (Ehrman
1993). While appreciative of much in the book, Norris chides Ehrman for failing
to press his knowledge of literary theory to its logical conclusion in the realm of
textual criticism by repudiating the notion that an "original text" ever circulated
apart from living communities of readers who interpreted and shaped the text.
Commenting on the prodigous text-critical labors of Origen, Norris says, "He never
saw the correction of black marks as a task separate from reading the texts in and
for the community" (Norris 1994:457).

[101] Stanley has convincingly shown that with respect to citation technique, "for
the most part Paul adhered to the normal literary practices of his day," practices
that are in evidence among Jewish as well as non-Jewish writers (1992b:350). Pursuing

Isaiah and the Story of Israel's Restoration

A further matter to address at the outset of this study is what can be known about the ways in which Isaiah was being interpreted by Paul's contemporaries. A full answer to this query would require a series of studies of the use of Isaiah in other writings at least as extensive as the present investigation of Paul's letter to Rome. Nevertheless, it is fairly clear that in the Second Temple period, Isaiah was not read within a context narrowly circumscribed by the literary boundaries of the book itself. Rather, interpreters freely culled oracles from Isaiah and from throughout the prophetic writings and assembled them in accordance with the larger stories they told about God and Israel.[102]

One of the foundational narratives shared by a wide range of Jewish groups was the story of Israel's sin, punishment, and (future) restoration by God. This complex of ideas, termed by E. P. Sanders "Jewish Restoration Eschatology," was founded on the conviction that God had established an eternal covenant with Israel.[103] Because of their unfaithfulness to that covenant, Israel had suffered the penalty of exile from the land. But God refused to annul the promises he had made to his people. The prophets announced that God would surely deliver his people from exile and plant them once again securely in the land. Although at first blush the return from exile in Babylon

---

a more narrow basis of comparison, Lim (1997a) has also found important similarities in the approaches of Paul and the Qumran *pesharists* to their sacred texs.

[102] See Barton 1986:150. By "story"and "narrative" I refer not to a literary genre, but to the way people articulate the larger conceptions they hold concerning the cosmos and their place in it. A full discussion of this usage may be found in Wright 1992:38–44, 65–80, 122–37. According to Wright, these foundational stories attempt to answer the questions: "Who are we?" "Where are we?" "What is wrong?" and "What is the solution?" (123). For the concept of "story" applied to Pauline theology in particular, see Hays 1983, 1991; Petersen 1985; Witherington 1994; Wright 1991:258–67.

[103] Extensive discussion of biblical and post-biblical texts may be found in E. P. Sanders 1985:77–119, 1992:289–98; Wright 1992:215–23; see also Jeremias 1958; E. P. Sanders 1987. Second Temple writings that evince a continued hope for restoration include Bar 2:30–35 (cf. 1:15–3:8); 4:21–5:9; *Pss. Sol.* 11; 17:28–31; 11QPs^a (11Q5) 22.1–15 (Hymn to Zion); Tob 13–14. On the latter text, see S. Weitzman 1996. Sanders cautions that "eschatological expectation is not generally clear and consistent, and there certainly is not any one combination of various hopes that constitues a set theology" (1985:87). In referring to the "story" of Jewish Restoration Eschatology, then, I am speaking of a narrative whose basic outline is clear—God will restore his covenant people as promised—but whose detailed plotline is developed in diverse ways in the surviving literature.

30 CHAPTER ONE

appeared to be the fulfillment of these grand visions of redemption
and restoration, the brutal realities of continued subjection to foreign nations and unremitting internal strife belied these hopes. As a
result, the faithful looked to the future for the full realization of these
prophecies.[104] For some, Israel's restoration lay in the far distant future.[105] For others, fulfillment of the prophetic word was near at hand.[106]

---

[104] Cf. *4QFlorilegium* (4Q174) frgs. 1–2 1.15, ". . . as it is written in the book of
Isaiah the prophet for the last days" (אשר כתוב בספר ישעיה הנביא לאחרית ה[ימים]).
Fishbane appeals to Julius Wellhausen's happy turn of phrase, "the elasticity of
hope," to explain this reinterpretation of prophecy against an eschatological hori-
zon (Fishbane 1985:485; quoting Wellhausen 1899). See further Carroll 1978, 1980.

[105] N. T. Wright has argued that there was in first-century Judaism a widespread
belief that Israel was still in exile. His discussion and further references may be
found in Wright 1992:268–72. See more recently the collection of articles edited
by J. M. Scott (1997); see also Scott 1993a, 1993b, 1994. While the language of
"exile" was one way Second Temple Jewish groups narrated their present plight,
this conceptualization was by no means a universal feature of restoration eschatology. One could speak of hope for future restoration without employing the language of exile or focusing one's hopes entirely on a renewed residence in the Land.
A. T. Kraabel (1987:57–58) notes that during this period, many Jews *chose to leave*
Palestine:

> Over the centuries many Jews left the Homeland voluntarily, as did other peo-
> ple from peripheral areas of the Mediterranean who sought their fortunes in the
> centers of power of the Hellenistic and Roman world. These individuals did not
> understand themselves to be in exile, but rather welcomed and desired immi-
> gration as part of a new situation that was also under the control of Providence.
> Just as the rabbis spiritualized the Temple and its cult, so the Diaspora Jews
> spiritualized the Homeland. . . . The Diaspora was not Exile; in some sense it
> became a holy land too.

Paul is an intriguing figure in that he seems to have spiritualized the concept of
"land" (see Davies 1974:219–20) while continuing to employ the metaphorical language and thought patterns of restoration eschatology, including the general story-
line of exile and redemption. In the following chapters, I will often speak of Paul's
appropriation of Isaiah's story of exile and restoration as one of his ways of con-
ceptualizing metaphorically the present plight of Israel. I am not claiming, however, that "exile" was Paul's sole—or even primary—way of understanding Israel's
plight; nor am I defending the view that most of Paul's contemporaries considered
the exile to be ongoing.

[106] The Qumran covenanters, for example, apparently viewed themselves as the
proleptic realization of Israel's promised restoration. Note their appropriation of
Isaiah 40:3 as a depiction of the community's existence and purpose (1QS 8.13–14;
9.19–20). Those who join the community are preparing the way for the Lord's
return to Zion. See McCasland 1958; Talmon 1993:245–54; Brooke 1994;
Charlesworth 1997b. Note also the employment of the "shoot" (נצר) of Isaiah 11:1
in the Hodayot, apparently as a reference to the community (1QHa 14[6].15;
15[7].19; 16[8].6, 10). At the same time, it is clear that the covenanters did not
believe that Israel's restoration had yet been fully realized. Note the clear statement
of confidence in the *future* fulfillment of Isaiah's prophecies of restoration (cf. Isa
53:4–5; 26:19; 61:1) in 4Q521 frg. 2 2.11–12:

ונכ²דות שלוא היו יעשה אדני כאשר ד[בר] 11
12 [כי] ירפא חללים ומתים יחיה ענוים יבשר

It is this larger cultural "story" that lies behind Paul's appropriation of Isaiah in Romans to speak both of his own mission to the
Gentiles and of Israel's present and future relationship with their
God.[107] At the same time, Paul tells a particular version of this story,
one that cannot be explained solely by reference to other contemporary interpretations.[108] When I speak of the "story" of God's relationship with Israel that Paul finds in Isaiah, Deuteronomy, or
elsewhere in Israel's scriptures, I am referring to a construct of Paul's
that forms the context for his reflections, in the light of Israel's sacred
texts, on what God is doing in the world. Paul did not, so far as
we know, write anything like a commentary on Isaiah.[109] Romans,
like Paul's other letters, is a contingent response to a particular group
of churches in particular historical circumstances.[110] Thus, any coherence in Paul's interpretation of Isaiah is necessarily an extrapolation

---

[11] The glorious deeds that have not (yet) taken place, the Lord will do, just as
he sa[id], [12] [for] he will heal the wounded and give life to the dead; he will
proclaim good news to the poor . . .
A strikingly similar list of God's eschatological deeds of salvation appears in Matthew
11:5 // Luke 7:22.

[107] A number of recent studies suggest that this story, in one form or another,
significantly shapes many of the New Testament writings. See, for example, Wright
1992; Swartley 1994; R. Watts 1997; Marcus 1992, 1995; Allison 1993; Moessner
1989, 1999; Pao 2000. This is not to suggest that there is a general consensus
regarding the influence of larger scriptural narratives on the writings of the New
Testament. Many scholars continue to believe that the use of Israel's scriptures by
Paul and other New Testament authors depends to a great extent on rather narrow connections between texts, often amounting to little more than shared terminology. The hypothesis that Paul read scripture in light of larger narrative patterns
is thus still very much in need of demonstration through careful analysis of each
of his citations and allusions.

[108] Barton cautions, "There cannot be any *a priori* way of establishing what the
'prophetic' books meant to those who read them in our period: one can discover
the meaning they were thought to have only by seeing what kinds of information
people in fact turned to them to discover . . ." (1986:151).

[109] Lim's attempt to compare Paul's citation technique to that of the Qumran
pesharists (1997a) fails to take sufficient account of the fact that they are working
within the constraints of completely different genres.

[110] To anticipate a possible objection to my thesis—that Paul fails to quote particular texts that would appear to be ideal for his reinterpretation of Isaiah as a
story about the restoration of Israel and the mission to the Gentiles—it must be
insisted that in no sense is Paul interpreting Isaiah for its own sake, but rather for
the sake of an argument determined in large part by the exigencies that called forth
his letter in the first place. We do not have a Pauline exposition of Isaiah, but only
indirect reflections of his interpretation of the prophetic text. It should not be surprising, then, that some texts that appear (to us) to be potentially useful were not
actually used by Paul. In any case, the argument from silence ("Why didn't Paul

from the evidence of the letters themselves.[111] To the extent that dis-
covering "Isaiah's story," or rather, the particular "story" manifested
in Paul's interpretation of Isaiah, is an imaginative act of interpretation, this "story" is also a construct of my own making.[112] Ultimately,
the value of my reconstruction of the "story" Paul finds in Isaiah
and in other scriptural texts will have to be measured by its ability
to make sense of what Paul actually does with these texts in his letters.[113] My hypothesis that Paul read large sections of Isaiah as a

---

quote *x*?") is a tenuous one given our small sampling of Paul's actual teaching and
correspondence.

[111] Compare James Kugel's description of his study of ancient midrash as an
exercise in "reverse engineering" (Kugel 1990:251–53). Richard Hays draws on the
work of N. Frye, P. Ricoeur and R. Funk to describe the organic relationship
between story and non-narrative discourse (1983:20–28). Stories consist of both a
sequential plot (*mythos*) and an overall pattern or theme (*dianoia*) that, while not separable from the narrative, captures the sense or point of the story as a whole. Just
as one can retell a story by recapitulating its sequence of events, one can also recall
the *dianoia* of the story in non-narrative modes of discourse. Hays explains (28):
   (1) There can be an organic relationship between stories and reflective discourse because stories have an inherent configurational dimension (*dianoia*) which
   not only permits but also demands restatement and interpretation in non-narrative
   language.
   (2) The reflective restatement does not simply repeat the plot (*mythos*) of the
   story; nonetheless, the story shapes and constrains the reflective process because
   the *dianoia* can never be entirely abstracted from the story in which it is manifested and apprehended.
   (3) Hence, when we encounter this type of reflective discourse, it is legitimate
   and possible to inquire about the story in which it is rooted.
As Paul looks ahead in Romans to new opportunities for mission and wrestles with
the challenge posed to his gospel by Israel's unbelief, he engages in just this type
of reflective discourse, seeking understanding of his present situation by returning
to the scriptural narratives that tell the story of God's plan to redeem Israel and
the cosmos.

[112] The following account Hays offers of his hermeneutic captures succinctly the
general approach of the present study as well (1989:27–28):
   My design is to produce late twentieth-century readings of Paul informed by intel-
   ligent historical understanding: to undertake a fresh imaginative encounter with
   the text, disciplined and stimulated by historical exegesis. The legitimacy of such
   a project rests on a single key hermeneutical axiom: that there is an authentic
   analogy—though not a simple identity—between what the text meant and what
   it means. One might call this a proposal for "common sense" hermeneutics: common sense not only because it is the way that sympathetic critics and faith communities have ordinarily read Scripture but also because it rests upon an assumption
   that readers ancient and modern can share a common sense of the text's meaning.
For further discussion (pro and con) of the usefulness of the concept of "story" for
understanding Paul's theology, see the various methodological proposals in Hay
1993; Johnson and Hay 1997.

[113] There is, finally, no "scientific" method of interpretation that can guarantee
that the coherence—or incoherence—we find is not at least partially constructed

prophetic word concerning his own role in the eschatological restoration of Israel and the extension of that salvation to the Gentiles will have to be tested repeatedly through close attention to each of his citations of and allusions to Isaiah.[114]

READING ROMANS IN THE FIRST CENTURY

The First Recipients of the Letter

Because my interests center on *Paul's* reading of Isaiah as it may be recovered from the text of Romans,[115] I will, for the most part, refrain from speculating about the variety of responses Paul may have evoked from his first hearers. Nevertheless, I do think that Paul intended to communicate with real communities of believers in Rome. It is necessary, therefore, to consider briefly the extent to which the first recipients of Romans might have been able to understand Paul's frequent scriptural allusions and echoes.

Chris Stanley has recently argued that most members of Paul's churches (which, Stanley thinks, were largely composed of illiterate Gentiles)[116] would have lacked the necessary "hearer competence" to appreciate Paul's more allusive evocations of scripture.[117] In the case of Romans, Stanley's view would appear to be supported by the widely-held reconstruction of the history of the Roman churches that sees the supposed expulsion of all Jews under Claudius (usually dated to 49 CE; cf. Acts 18:2) as the decisive event in the life of the communities to which Paul wrote. These suddenly Gentile-only churches,

---

by the interpreter. The only safeguard against solipsism is to continually test our interpretations against the text and to submit our readings to the judgment of other interpreters.

[114] It is not necessary to my hypothesis that every single appeal of Paul to Isaiah be consistent with the larger reading I am proposing. Just as the claim that Paul at times adopts scriptural language and employs it for his own purposes unrelated to the original meaning or context does not necessarily suggest that he always, or even customarily, worked this way, so also the hypothesis that Paul saw a larger "story" in Isaiah does not require that he always had this story in mind when drawing on Isaiah's langugage. The force of my argument will ultimately depend on the cumulative weight of the evidence rather than on my exegesis of one particular quotation or allusion considered in isolation from the others.

[115] See n. 68 above.

[116] On the extent of literacy in the ancient world, see the works cited in n. 92 above.

[117] Stanley 1999:139; note the similar concerns of Tuckett 2000:407–411.

deprived of the influence of Jewish believers for a number of years, would allegedly have had little access to or interest in the scriptures of Israel. By the time Paul wrote Romans, so the theory goes, the Jewish believers had begun to return to Rome; but what had once been a mixed church was now dominated by Gentiles who would have been unable to follow Paul's scriptural arguments and who, in any case, were none too receptive to the heritage and traditions of their returning Jewish brothers and sisters.[118]

This historical reconstruction has serious problems, however. There are compelling reasons to doubt that an explusion of Jews on such a grand scale ever took place under Claudius.[119] Apart from this "vacuum" theory, however, there is no strong reason to assume that Gentiles greatly outnumbered Jews in the Roman churches.[120] Moreover, it becomes far more difficult to believe that these Gentiles—who shared a common life with Jewish believers who presumably *were* concerned to understand their confession of Jesus as the Christ in relation to Israel's scriptures and traditions—would have been completely unfamiliar with or uninterested in these sacred texts.

Ultimately, the historical evidence available to us does not allow a firm judgment to be reached on the composition of the Roman churches or on the "hearer-competence" of Paul's empirical audience (who in any case probably represented *varying degrees* of familiarity with Israel's scriptures and with Jewish interpretive traditions).[121] As a result, a reader-focused approach to Paul's use of scripture in Romans that depends heavily on a reconstructed *historical* audience is clearly inadequate by itself for interpreting the letter on historical, let alone literary or theological, grounds.

---

[118] Wiefel 1991; similarly Dunn 1988a:xliv–liv; Fitzmyer 1993:76–78.

[119] See Leon 1960:23–27; Abel 1968; Smallwood 1981:207–208, 210–16; Barclay 1996:303–306; Mason 1994. J. Murphy-O'Connor hardly exaggerates when he concludes, "The Jewish vacuum . . . is a myth" (1996:333).

[120] See Stark 1996:49–71. That Paul chooses to address his letter principally to Gentiles is another matter. More on this below.

[121] Stanley rightly emphasizes the importance of recognizing "the diverse literary capabilities and backgrounds of the members of Paul's congregations" (1999:144). As he notes, "Such an analysis will produce not one but many possible 'meanings' for Paul's biblical quotations, reflecting the diverse literary capabilities and experiences of the many people in his churches" (142). But Stanley himself curiously gives pride of place to the least competent hearers imaginable. He does not appear to recognize the contradiction involved in advising interpreters both "to assume no more audience knowledge of Scripture than would be required to make minimal sense of Paul's explicit biblical quotations" and at the same time "to allow room

A more fruitful reader-oriented approach to Romans, though remaining attentive to historical data, has focused on the audience encoded in the letter itself, the so-called "ideal reader."[122] Observing that Paul claims authority to speak to the Romans on the basis of his calling as "apostle to the Gentiles" and that he addresses his remarks specifically to Gentiles in Romans 1:5, 13; 11:13; 15:15–16, one can argue that the ideal readers (or, better, hearers) of the letter are Gentiles. Moreover, from the demands Paul's argument places on the hearers, one can infer that these are Gentiles who have more than a passing acquaintance with Jewish practices and beliefs and who have a fairly good grasp of Israel's scriptures.[123]

Yet it must be admitted that the theoretical construct of the ideal reader has its limitations as a tool of historical inquiry. There is no way to be certain that the theoretical construct of the ideal hearer actually represents any of the first real empirical hearers of the letter. It is always possible that Paul seriously misjudged the hearer-competence of his audience in Rome.[124] Alternatively, Paul may not have aimed simply to reach the lowest common denominator among his audience or worried whether his arguments were immediately understandable to all. I suggest as an analogy here the letter to the Galatians, where Paul addresses complex scriptural arguments to his formerly pagan converts (cf. Gal 4:8). E. P. Sanders comments:

> [Paul's] argumentation reveals partly his own education—he argues the way he was taught—and partly the education of his third party opponents ("they," "some," Gal. 1:7; 5:12, etc.), not the education of his Galatian Gentile converts.[125]

If Paul aimed the intricate scriptural arguments in Galatians in large part at his opponents, perhaps he similarly crafted his rhetoric in

---

for significant variation in the level of knowledge of various individuals within the church" (136). If "Paul seems to have crafted his quotations in such a way that readers with very little biblical knowledge could grasp his essential point" (138), is this a reason to limit an investigation of the rhetorical effects of Paul's quotations to their impact on those in his audience least familiar with Israel's scriptures?

[122] See Stowers 1994:21–33 and, more generally, Iser 1974; Suleiman and Crosman 1980.

[123] See Wedderburn 1991:50–59; Hays 1989:29. For the argument that the encoded readers include "a significant number of Jewish Christians," see Guerra 1995:22–42 (quotation from p. 32).

[124] Murphy-O'Connor (1996:334) argues that the diatribe style of Romans 1–11 betrays Paul's lack of familiarity with the actual situation of the Roman churches.

[125] Sanders 1983:182. Similarly, Stanley 1999:135, 139–41.

Romans with an eye toward people not explicitly encoded in the
letter. Though his rhetorical strategy addresses Gentiles explicitly,[126]
Paul may well have intended his arguments to be *overheard* by Jewish
Christians in the Roman congregations.[127] In light of the concerns
Paul expresses in Romans 15:25–32, it is also worth considering the
extent to which his upcoming visit with the church in Jerusalem may
have shaped the development of his argument in Romans, particularly Romans 9–11.[128]

Unfortunately, as Denis Feeney observes, "The search for the ideal
contemporary reader's response makes it practically impossible to
entertain the notion of *a diverse, contentious initial audience.*"[129] The challenge of imagining such an audience leads us to consider just how
Paul's letter would have been received by the Roman believers.

The Reception of Paul's Letter in
the Roman Churches

Hypotheses about the hearer-competence of Paul's first audience normally envision only a first encounter with Romans by a fairly homo-
geneous group of listeners. The resulting reconstructions of the
recipients of Paul's letter are thus rather flat and static. Yet it is no
more adequate for interpretation to imagine only one hearing of the
letter than it is to suppose that these first listeners all heard Paul
the same way. It strains credulity to believe that Romans, having
once been read out in the assembly, would never have been reread,
discussed, or debated again by these diverse congregants. And if
Romans continued to have a place in the common life of these communities, might not Paul's rich dialogue with scripture through citation, allusion, and echo have sparked a desire in his listeners to
become interpreters capable of hearing the multitude of scripture voices

---

[126] Though note the address in Romans 7:1 to "those who know the Law."

[127] So also Watson 1986:171. Jewish believers are among those greeted by Paul
in Romans 16. E. P. Sanders observes that "Romans is unique in the Pauline correspondence in containing so many clues to the presence of Jewish Christians among
the readership" (1983:184). Although it does not seem to shape his reading of the
letter significantly, Stowers leaves room for such considerations to influence one's
approach to the rhetoric of Romans: "I am not denying that either the encoded
readers or any likely empirical readers associated with Jews and had Jewish followers of Christ among them" (1994:33).

[128] So, for example, Bornkamm 1991, 1971:88–96; Jervell 1991; Beker 1980:72;
Williams 1980:247–48; E. P. Sanders 1983:184.

[129] Feeney 1995:311 n. 45 (emphasis mine).

testifying to Paul's gospel? Indeed, Paul appears to have intended his interpretive arguments to model for his churches a way of reading Israel's scriptures in the new light of the gospel. Where the apostle reflects explicitly on his eschatological and ecclesiocentric hermeneutic, he does so in order to commend this way of reading to his listeners (e.g., Rom 15:4; 4:23–24; cf. 1 Cor 10:11). Perhaps, then, Paul's frequent references to Israel's scriptures in Romans provoked some among his first hearers to *acquire* the familiarity with these sources necessary to grasp his argument fully.

This suggestion becomes more plausible when it is recognized that Paul's letter was most likely copied, discussed, and even studied by the Roman churches to whom it was sent. We know that the Corinthian assembly discussed Paul's "prior letter" at some length; when they could not agree on the meaning of Paul's instructions or desired further clarification of some things he had said, they sent him a letter of their own (1 Cor 7:1; cf. 5:9–11). In the case of Romans, the circulation of these letters among a number of house churches (cf. Col 4:15–16) almost certainly involved making multiple copies of the letters for future reference:

> The first recipients of a Pauline letter were probably no better able than we to digest it at one reading and would have wished to retain it for subsequent consideration. *Paul himself may well have hoped or expected that his letters would not only be heard but also studied.*[130]

Moreover, it is difficult to imagine a "teaching office" in these early Pauline communities, however informal (1 Cor 12:28–29; cf. Eph 4:11; 1 Tim 3:2; 2 Tim 2:2, 24), that did not involve the interpretation of apostolic teaching—including Paul's letters—to some degree.[131] This would certainly have entailed multiple public readings of the letters, for this was the way most people in Greco-Roman society encountered written texts.[132] For this reason, the fact that perhaps most members of the Pauline communities would not have been able to read for themselves would not have been a significant barrier to their close acquaintance with Paul's letters (or, for that matter, with Israel's scriptures).[133]

---

[130] Gamble 1995:97 (emphasis mine).
[131] On the correlation of literacy and leadership in the early churches, see Gamble 1995:9–10.
[132] See Achtemeier 1990.
[133] Cf. Gamble 1995:1–10, 212–213.

In addition, it is quite likely that the bearers of Paul's letters were
charged by the apostle with the further responsibility of helping to
interpret them.[134] R. F. Ward considers the reading of Paul's letters
in Corinth from the standpoint of social conventions in antiquity as
well as from the modern perspective of performance studies. As Ward
notes, "the rendering of Paul's letter by a trusted emissary" was a
means by which Paul could re-establish a powerful presence in the
Corinthian church:

> When Paul's emissary stood before the Corinthians to speak the let-
> ter, he [in the case of Romans, "she"; cf. Rom 16:1–2] would have
> internalized the contents of the letter and would be prepared to inter-
> pret the whole of Paul's logos to the Corinthians. . . . In any case, Paul
> must have carefully considered the ability of his reciter to render his
> text in accordance with the standards of excellence of the time. Titus
> or some other emissary, through the skillful rendering of Paul's letter,
> intended to guide the audience through an *experience* of the situation
> from Paul's perspective. . . .
>   . . . Given the conventions of performing letters in antiquity, we can
> imagine the reciter giving Paul's letter fullness, not simply by render-
> ing the written word but by adding oral commentary in the spirit and
> attitude of Paul himself.[135]

The interpretive authority with which Paul's letter-carriers were thus
invested may explain why Paul's personal commendation of his emis-
saries was necessary (e.g., 1 Cor 16:15–18; Rom 16:1–2; Phil 2:25–30).
Similarly, Paul frequently commends his coworkers, conferring on
them authority to interpret his teaching and carry out his directives
(1 Cor 4:16–17; 16:10–11; 2 Cor 8:16–24; Phil 2:19–24).

Gamble further argues that "the Pauline mission, both before and
after Paul's death, was substantially invested in texts carrying the
apostle's teaching";[136] these texts allowed Paul's words to be heard
and reheard by the congregations that copied and preserved them.
Evidence for the early circulation of Paul's letters beyond the original communities to which they were addressed is found in the textual tradition of Romans (1:7, 15) and 1 Corinthians (1:2; cf. Ephesians

---

[134] The bearer of a personal letter often conveyed information about the sender
beyond that contained in the letter itself (note, within the Pauline corpus, Col 4:7–9
and Eph 6:21–22). For examples from ancient letters, see further Botha 1992b; Cox
1998:81–82; Doty 1973:45–46; Jewett 1988; Mitchell 1992:649–51.

[135] Ward 1995:104–105 (emphasis original).

[136] Gamble 1995:99.

1:1), where in some manuscripts the original addresses have been replaced with more generic formulas.[137] Fairly wide distribution of authentic Pauline letters is also a necessary condition for the production and circulation of pseudonymous letters of Paul, a process that appears to have begun shortly after his death.[138] Moreover, quotations from Paul in Clement of Rome, Ignatius of Antioch, and Polycarp of Smyrna in the late first and early second centuries attest to the early spread of Paul's letters over a fairly extensive geographical area.[139] The enduring value ascribed to Paul's letters is further suggested by the relatively early process of gathering them into a collection[140] and developing a theological rationale for their continued reading in the church.[141]

The foregoing discussion suggests that to confine one's interpretive interests to what listeners might have picked up on the first hearing of Romans is to seriously underestimate the actual impact of this letter on a community that took its message seriously. The implications of all of this for the present investigation are profound. For example, it will be necessary to attend to the totality of Paul's argument in Romans 9–11 and to cultivate a sensitivity to the ways in which Romans 11 is already adumbrated in chapter 9. The listener who becomes familiar with the whole of Romans will, on subsequent readings, hear Paul's discussion of the remnant in Romans 9 in conversation (and perhaps in deep tension) with the ultimate conclusion Paul reaches in Romans 11 that "all Israel will be saved."[142] Consequently, although my investigation largely follows Paul's argument as it develops through Romans 9–11 and reaches its climax in Romans 15, I will also step back from time to time in order to consider the significance of the shape of Paul's argument in the letter as a whole for the interpretation of a particular passage.

---

[137] Gamble 1995:98. Note also the evidence for the omission of the greetings in chapter 16 in some MSS of Romans (see further Gamble 1977).

[138] Gamble 1995:99.

[139] On the "prompt transfer of letters throughout the Greco-Roman world," see Epp 1991 (quoted words are from p. 55).

[140] Gamble finds here the origin of the codex as the dominant form of the book among Christians (1995:58–65, 99–101; see also Gamble 1990).

[141] Dahl 1962; Gamble 1995:59–62; Mitton 1955; Trobisch 1994.

[142] Cf. Hays 1989:67; Meeks 1990:112–18; Cosgrove 1996:274–76. The full force of this point came home to me recently as I watched the film *Jesus of Montreal* (written and directed by Denys Arcand; Orion Pictures, 1989). This brilliant and creative retelling of the Jesus narrative through the story of a troupe of actors who put on an unconventional Passion Play (a genuine "two-level drama") has a densely

❋

With this methodological ground-clearing now complete, the way is open to turn to Paul's letter itself in order to examine Paul's citations of and allusions to Isaiah in the context of the larger argument he develops in Romans. I begin with Romans 9–11 since most of these citations and allusions cluster in this section of the letter.[143] My investigation of Paul's use of Isaiah in Romans 9–11 falls into three chapters, corresponding to the three principal issues or questions that organize Paul's argument:[144]

Chapter 2: Romans 9:1–29:   It is not as though God's word (cf. 9:4–5) has failed (9:6).

Chapter 3: Romans 9:30–10:21:   But then why have Gentiles attained righteousness while Israel has not (9:30–32)?

Chapter 4: Romans 11:1–36:   God has not rejected his inheritance, has he (11:1)?

In Chapter Five, I examine the citations in Romans 15 in light of the patterns and strategies of interpretation discerned in Romans 9–11.[145]

The final chapter draws together the results of the investigation and suggests some of the implications of my findings for the study of Paul's interpretive practices and for broader questions of Pauline theology. In brief, I argue that Paul's citations of and allusions to Isaiah

---

allusive texture that requires multiple viewings to appreciate fully. For example, in the opening scene of the film, an advertising executive remarks concerning a young actor, "I want his head." Only as the film progresses does it become apparent that this actor is the "John the Baptist" figure, and only in light of one of the final scenes of the film is it clear in what John's "beheading" consists. Although many of this film's significant allusions to the gospel narratives will be obvious to viewers educated in the West, most people—even those with a solid Christian education—will miss numerous more subtle allusions and ironies. To recognize them requires subsequent viewings of the film in light of its ending. In a very real sense, then, the film becomes more complex—and more enjoyable—the more one watches it.

[143] Figure 6.1 (p. 342 below) lists the citations of and allusions to Isaiah treated in this study according to their location in Romans.

[144] For a different, though in many ways complementary, analysis see Aageson 1986.

[145] The citations of Isaiah in Romans 2 and Romans 14 are discussed in excurses to Chapters 3 and 5, respectively.

reflect the apostle's sustained and careful attention to the rhythms and cadences of individual passages as well as to larger stories and motifs that run throughout the book. Moreover, Paul's frequent conflation and juxtaposition of Isaianic oracles with other texts from Israel's scriptures—notably Deuteronomy 29–32—reveals a deliberate interpretive strategy, in which Isaiah's distinctive message is shaped by the testimony of other scriptural witnesses. Throughout Romans, Isaiah is heard in concert not only with Paul, but also with a wider chorus of scriptural voices who lend the cumulative weight of their authority to Paul's argument.

Through his revisionary rereading of Isaiah, Paul finds in the prophet's words both a prefiguration of his own apostolic mission to the Gentiles and a prophecy of Israel's resistance to the gospel. At the same time, Paul joins Isaiah in insisting that the existence of a remnant of Israel in the present time vouchsafes the future redemption of "all Israel." By adopting as his own the stories Isaiah and his fellow scriptural witnesses tell about God's unquenchable love for his people, Paul is able to maintain confidently that the God who is now embracing Gentiles as his own will be faithful to redeem and restore his covenant people Israel as well, so that Jew and Gentile can with one voice laud the incomparable mercy of their God.

CHAPTER TWO

"IF THE LORD OF HOSTS HAD NOT LEFT US SEED . . ."
ISAIAH IN ROMANS 9:1–29

> It is not as though the word of
> God has fallen.
>
> *Romans 9:6*

In Romans 9–11, scriptural testimonies entwine with Paul's own interpretive comments to create a majestic tapestry displaying the righteousness of the God of Israel.[1] My purpose in this and the following two chapters is to illuminate the artistry with which Paul interweaves explicit and allusive references to Isaiah into this thick web of scripture and interpretation. This will require a close reading of Romans 9–11 as a whole, with careful attention not only to Paul's invocations of Isaiah, but also to the apostle's appeals to other scriptural witnesses, for Paul frequently employs Isaiah as part of a larger exegetical argument comprising a number of different texts. Indeed, I will argue that Paul's reading of Isaiah cannot be fully understood apart from his interpretation of key texts from the Torah, Psalms, and other prophetic books.

The dense and multi-layered texture of the argument in Romans 9–11 suggests that, long before dictating this particular letter, the apostle has reflected deeply on the issues he treats here.[2] Although it is occasionally proposed that Paul himself is surprised by the turn he takes in chapter 11,[3] I hope to show convincingly that in Romans

---

[1] In addition to the major commentaries on Romans, recent studies of Romans 9–11 include: Aageson 1983, 1987; Dinter 1980; Hays 1989:63–83; Hübner 1984; E. E. Johnson 1989; J. D. Kim 2000; De Lorenzi 1977; B. W. Longenecker 1989; Maillot 1982; Munck 1967; Piper 1993; Räisänen 1987, 1995; Siegert 1985; Stowers 1994; Watson 1986:160–74; Westerholm 1996; Wright 1991:231–57; Zeller 1973. This list could easily be made many times longer, of course. See the useful survey of scholarship by Räisänen (1988).

[2] Cf. Dodd 1932:148–50; Aune 1991:294.

[3] The extreme view is represented by B. Noack, who argues: "The paragraphs from ix.1 to xi.10 do not contain the slightest hint at the final solution, simply because that solution does not yet exist" (1965:166). Rather, "the solution is granted Paul during his wrestling with the problem, the mystery is revealed to him at the

9–10, Paul is already preparing the way for the eloquent encomium on God's mercy that brings his argument to a close in Romans 11. Thus, while my discussion follows the thread of Paul's argument through Romans 9–11, I will often pause to step back and consider the larger design of the tapestry Paul is in the process of weaving.

The problems Paul addresses in Romans 9–11 are adumbrated much earlier in the letter.[4] In the thematic statement of Romans, Paul asserts that his gospel is

> the power of God for the salvation of everyone who believes—for the Jew first, and equally for the Greek—for in it the righteousness of God is revealed from faith to faith... (Rom 1:16–17).

In this compact sentence, Paul asserts that the "righteousness of God"—that is, God's faithfulness to rescue his covenant people Israel and to vindicate them before their oppressors[5]—is revealed in what God has now accomplished in the death and resurrection of Jesus. The promises of redemption and restoration for Israel are at long last being realized. Moreover, the benefits of Israel's redemption are available to Jew and Gentile alike on precisely the same basis.[6] Paul unpacks the significance of these claims in the chapters that follow.

---

very moment of his dictating the second part of ch. xi, vv. 13–36" (165). Cautiously supportive of Noack's notion of Spirit-inspired "spontaneous composition" is Aune 1983:252–53. For a somewhat different account of the relationship between prophecy and scriptural interpretation, see Gillespie 1994.

[4] For Romans 9–11 as central to (though not necessarily *the* center of) the theological argument of the letter, see among recent commentators, Wright 1991:234; Beker 1986; W. S. Campbell 1982; Hooker 1990:3; Dunn 1988b:519. The tendency to see Romans 9–11 as integral to the letter is a welcome corrective to the long-dominant interpretation that marginalized these chapters (for a concise history of interpretation, see Beker 1980:63–64; a more extensive survey is found in E. E. Johnson, 1989:110–23). At the same time, there is no reason to lurch to the opposite extreme and conclude that chapters 1–8 are merely a "preface" to 9–11 (as does Stendahl 1976:29; see the critique of Stendahl by E. P. Sanders 1978).

[5] This definition of "God's righteousness" in Paul (and in Isaiah) will be supported by the detailed exegetical arguments of the present study. It is by no means, however, a novel definition of the phrase. For a similar understanding of "the righteousness of God" in Paul, see Williams 1980; Beker 1986:14–15; Dunn 1998:334–46; Hays 1992; E. P. Sanders 1977:491–92; Kuyper 1977; Dahl 1977c; Käsemann 1969, 1971; Stuhlmacher 1965; Kertelge 1971; Dodd 1932:9–13. The most thorough investigation of "righteousness" language in Isaiah LXX is that of J. W. Olley (1979); see also Fiedler 1970. For a critique of Olley's study, see pp. 103–104 n. 192.

[6] E. P. Sanders forcefully draws attention to the crucial role the inclusion of Gentiles *qua* Gentiles plays in the construction of Paul's thought. He argues that

Two of his primary concerns are to establish that it is πίστις, rather than observance of the covenant markers established by the Law, that designates one as belonging to the people of God and, further, to demonstrate that this is what God has always intended and thus what Israel's scriptures have always proclaimed.

It is not until Romans 9, however, that Paul squarely faces the problem of reconciling his claim that God's righteousness has now been revealed in the gospel with the hard fact that, by and large, Israel has rejected the apostolic message.[7] When, in Romans 8, Paul appropriates the terminology of *Israel's* election for his *Gentile* churches,[8] the issue of God's faithfulness to his own people, which has simmered on the back burner since 3:1–8, finally boils over and demands the apostle's sustained attention.

ABRAHAM AND THE DRAMA OF ELECTION: ROMANS 9:1–13

Romans 9:1 marks a sharp turn in the argument of the letter. The mood of triumphant confidence (in the midst of suffering!) in God's unfailing, immutable love to "us" through Christ, so stirringly hymned by Paul in Romans 8:38–39, is shattered by a sudden outpouring of anguish over Israel's continuing resistance to the salvation that is theirs by inheritance (9:1–5). Invoking the example of Moses interceding for Israel, Paul expresses his passionate love for his kin κατὰ σάρκα. For their sake, he could wish himself cut off from Christ, even as Moses had prayed that God might blot him out of his book rather than refuse to forgive Israel's worship of the golden calf (Exod 32:32). At this point in the argument, Paul does not explain in detail what has gone wrong with Israel. However, this faint echo of Israel's idolatrous rebellion against God will prove to be the first note of a much more extensive leitmotif of Romans 9–11.

---

the main thrust of Romans is the equal standing of Jew and Gentile before God (1977:488–91).

[7] See above, p. 4 n. 15.

[8] Note υἱοί (8:14, 19); υἱοθεσία (8:15, 23; cf. 9:4); τέκνα θεοῦ (8:16, 21); ἀγαπάω (8:28, 37; cf. ἀγαπητοὶ θεοῦ, 1:7); πρόθεσις (8:28); προγινώσκω (8:29); προορίζω (8:29); καλέω (8:30); κλητός (8:28, 30); ἐκλεκτοὶ θεοῦ (8:33); ἀγάπη (8:35, 39). On the connections between Romans 8 and 9, see further N. Elliott 1990:253–63.

The catalogue of Israel's privileges in vv. 4–5 serves to intensify the sense of irony and tragedy that God's people should fail to realize their inheritance at this climactic moment in God's redemptive plan. And yet it is just these gifts of God's grace that undergird Paul's confidence in God's unbroken commitment to his people (Rom 11:1–2) and in God's ultimate triumph over their present rebellion (11:29).[9]

The apostle turns to scripture to explain how it is that, despite Israel's stubborn resistance to the gospel, the word of God promis-

---

[9] For "promises" to the patriarchs, see also Romans 9:8–9; 15:8. For "covenant," see also Romans 11:27. The term "covenant" is rather rare in Paul (8 times in the undisputed letters). In Romans, διαθήκη appears only at 9:4 (in the plural) and at 11:27. Consider, however, E. P. Sanders's observation concerning the relative infrequency of the term "covenant" in rabbinic literature:

> It has frequently been urged as evidence against the primacy of the covenantal conception in 'late Judaism' that the word 'covenant' does not often appear. . . . I would venture to say that it is the *fundamental nature of the covenant conception which largely accounts for the relative scarcity of appearances of the term 'covenant' in Rabbinic literature.* The covenant was presupposed, and the Rabbinic discussions were largely directed toward the question of *how* to fulfil the covenantal obligations (1977:420–21; emphasis original).

Sanders notes that "similar observations could be made about most of the rest of the literature" from the period 200 BCE–200 CE (421). Although Sanders rightly emphasizes that Paul's christology—particularly his concept of "participation in Christ"—distinguishes his "pattern of religion" from the "covenantal nomism" of Palestinian Judaism in crucial ways, others have found Paul's thought to be more deeply indebted to the covenant conception so widespread in Second Temple Judaism than Sanders allows. See M. D. Hooker's incisive critique (Hooker 1982); note also Wright 1991, 1995; Hays 1995. Sanders's inattention to Paul's use of scripture may help to account for his conclusion that "covenant" no longer functions as a central category of Paul's thought. In a review of *Paul and Palestinian Judaism*, N. A. Dahl, while judging the "chief results of Sanders's argument" to have been firmly established, observes,

> Sanders would have sharpened, rather than weakened, his argument if he had more fully realized that the identity of the risen Lord with the crucified Messiah, Jesus, is at the center of Paul's theology; *that we cannot fully understand Paul without paying serious attention to his interpretation of Scripture;* and that Paul really meant what he said about righteousness by faith and about the sanctity of the law and *the remaining validity of God's promises to Israel* (1978:157; emphasis mine).

In the present study, I seek to demonstrate that, although the actual *term* διαθήκη plays little role in Paul's discussion, the concept of God's covenant faithfulness to Israel functions as an indispensible presupposition of Paul's thought in Romans 9–11. As Hays has recognized, a crucial part of such a demonstration will involve showing in detail "that Paul actually draws consistently on covenant language *and exposits scripture in a way that highlights covenant themes*" (1995:86; emphasis mine).

ing Israel's restoration has not fallen to the ground.[10] Although Paul's first significant appropriation of Isaianic language does not appear until verse 20, the tightly woven texture of his argument makes it imperative to follow his line of reasoning from the beginning. In fact, Paul's use of Isaiah in Romans 9:20 can be properly understood only in the context he has established through the numerous scriptural quotations and allusions in the preceding verses. By concentrating on two of Israel's foundational narratives—the Abraham saga and the exodus—Paul frames his discussion of Israel's present plight in terms of God's covenant faithfulness to Israel in the past.[11] It is against this complex backdrop, layered with allusions to covenant and redemption, that Paul performs his own particular interpretation of Isaiah.

Beginning in Romans 9:6, Paul contends that enjoyment of the blessings graciously bestowed on Abraham has always come through promise and election rather than solely through physical descent. Paul's argument here consists of a highly selective and abbreviated retelling of Israel's history, beginning with the promise of descendants to Abraham and reaching to Israel's rebellion, exile, and beyond.[12] This retelling consists primarily of the evocation of key moments in Israel's history through citations of and allusions to scripture, interpreted by Paul's rhetorical questions and comments.[13]

---

[10] A faint echo of Isa 40:7–8 in Romans 9:6 subtly enhances Paul's point: οὐχ οἷον δὲ ὅτι ἐκπέπτωκεν ὁ λόγος τοῦ θεοῦ (Rom 9:6).
ἐξηράνθη ὁ χόρτος, καὶ τὸ ἄνθος ἐξέπεσε, τὸ δὲ ῥῆμα τοῦ θεοῦ ἡμῶν μένει εἰς τὸν αἰῶνα (Isa 40:7–8 LXX; cf. σ΄, which has λόγος for ῥῆμα).

[11] See R. Watts 1997:34–45 for a discussion of the importance of a community's "founding moment" in shaping a group's ideology.

[12] Readings of Romans 9–11 in terms of an abstract "doctrine of election" thus fail to recognize that Paul's understanding of election is driven by the very particular story of God's relationship with Israel and of the eschatological inclusion of the Gentiles in the people of God (a story in which Paul himself plays a major role).

[13] See Eisenbaum (1997:89–133) for an analysis of the relationship of retelling to direct quotation (see further Savran 1988). Though Eisenbaum claims that the author of Hebrews pits the two modes of scriptural presentation against one another (the author uses "scriptural prooftexts to argue against the continuation of traditional religious practices contained in scripture" [131–32]), we will see that Paul employs both retelling and quotation as *complementary* witnesses to the larger story of Israel he is telling in Romans 9–11. See also Stegner 1984. On the phenomenon of "rewritten Bible" more generally, see Nickelsburg 1984.

An elaborate network of verbal links binds together Paul's argument in Romans 9:6–29. Especially significant is the clustering of terms around two related themes: sonship and election (Fig. 2.1). Nearly all of the scriptures cited by Paul in these verses carry one or more of these key terms,[14] lending a certain unity and focus to what on any reckoning is a complex and difficult argument.[15]

Figure 2.1: Two Key Themes in Romans 9:6–29

Sonship	"Children" (τέκνα), vv. 7, 8 (3x) "Seed" (σπέρμα), vv. 7 (2x), 8, 29 "Son(s)" (υἱός), vv. 9, 26, 27
Election	"Call" (καλέω) vv. 7, 12, 24, 25, 26 "Promise" (ἐπαγγελία), vv. 8, 9 "Election" (ἐκλογή), v. 11 "Purpose" (πρόθεσις), v. 11 [cf. 8:28] "Love" (ἀγαπάω), vv. 13, 25 (2x) [cf. 11:28; 1:7] "Mercy" (ἐλεέω/-άω), vv. 15 (2x), 16 and (ἔλεος), v. 23. "Will" (θέλω), vv. 18 (2x), 22 "Plan" (βούλημα), v. 19

[14] On occasion the terminological link does not appear in the portion actually cited by Paul, as in Romans 9:12 (Gen 25:23, but see 25:25 and context) and possibly in 9:20 (Isaiah 45:9; but see 45:11 and discussion below). Note the reappearance of many of these terms in chapter 11: "Call" (κλῆσις) 11:29; "Election" (ἐκλογή), 11:5, 7, 28; "Beloved" (ἀγαπητός), 11:28; "Mercy" (ἐλεέω/-άω), 11:30, 31, 32 and (ἔλεος), 11:31.

[15] Carol Stockhausen (1989) highlights Paul's interest in larger narrative sections of scripture and shows how important both verbal and narrative/thematic links are to Paul's concatenation of citations from various parts of the scriptures. She argues that Paul's comparison of the ministries of the old and new covenants in 2 Corinthians 3 is founded on his reading of the Pentateuchal narrative about Moses veiling his face (Exod 34:29–35). Paul interprets this narrative with the help of a set of scriptural texts that are linked both with the Exodus text and with one another through a network of key terms. Stockhausen has found a further example of this method, which she suggests is basic to Paul's exegesis of scripture, in Galatians 3–4, where the Abraham narrative serves as Paul's primary text (1993). A similar exegetical pattern may underlie Romans 9:6–29; here, however, it is not a single Pentateuchal narrative that forms the basis for Paul's reflections, but rather Paul's larger retelling of Israel's story from Abraham through the exodus to rebellion and ultimately to exile. The narrative that Paul is interpreting is not a discrete passage of scripture, but rather his own construction of Israel's past based on his selective appropriation of key episodes in Israel's history.

The burden of Paul's case is that the status of sonship, which qualifies one to inherit the blessings promised to Abraham and his descendants, has always depended on God's gracious election rather than merely on physical descent from the patriarchs.

Paul attempts what amounts to a redefinition of "Israel"[16] by creating in vv. 6–7 a distinction between "children" of Abraham (τέκνα = οἱ ἐξ Ἰσραήλ) and "seed" of Abraham (σπέρμα = Ἰσραήλ). Appealing to Gen 21:12,[17] he then links "seed" with two important terms, "call" and "promise," setting the "children of promise" over against "children of the flesh." Only the children of promise are reckoned (λογίζομαι) as "seed" by God[18] and thus only they are "children of God." Consequently, the privilege of "adoption as sons" (υἱοθεσία), that is, of being τέκνα τοῦ θεοῦ—said in 9:3–4 to belong to Paul's kinspeople κατὰ σάρκα, the "Israelites"—actually belongs not to the "children of the flesh," but only to those descendants of Abraham

---

[16] The tension created by this redefinition, combined with Paul's continued use of the term "Israel" for ethnic Israel as a whole (9:31; 11:2, 7), creates an exegetical crux in 11:26: the meaning of "all Israel will be saved." (I discuss this latter text in Chapter 4; cf. the problems surrounding Gal 6:16, "the Israel of God.") Significantly, a similar question regarding the referent of "seed" drives much of the dramatic tension of the Abraham saga in Genesis. God's promises to Abraham specifically are directed to his "seed" (see e.g., Gen 12:7; 13:15–16; 15:5, 18; 16:10; 17:1–14, 19; cf. Rom 4:13, 16). As the story develops, it becomes clear that "seed" does not refer to all of Abraham's descendants, but first to Isaac, and then to Jacob and his children. Paul is exploiting this feature of the earlier narrative to serve his polemical redefinition of Abraham's true family.

[17] ἐν Ἰσαὰκ κληθήσεταί σοι σπέρμα. Here, a quotation is signalled not by a citation formula, but by a syntactical dislocation, the switch to the second person pronoun, σοι. For this technique of marking a citation, see M. Fox 1986; cf. Stanley 1992b:56–57. Paul's interpretive comment is introduced by τοῦτ' ἔστιν (v. 8; also in Rom 10:6, 7, 8). This phrase is not limited to exegetical comments, but is also used to clarify Paul's own statements (Rom 1:12; 7:18; Phm 12).

[18] Paul's argument in Romans 4 also centers on the definition of "seed." There, Paul's main point is that among Abraham's "seed" are included both Jews and Gentiles (4:16). In Romans 9, Paul attempts to show that belonging to Israel "after the flesh" is not sufficient to be considered "seed" of Abraham. In both arguments, however, Paul is engaged in the same project of redefining the concept of descent from Abraham in terms of faith in God's gracious promise (note the conjunction of these terms in 4:13–14, 16) rather than physical descent. Jews who are Abraham's "seed" are those who not only follow Abraham in circumcision, but who also follow his example of faith (4:12, 16). In Romans 9:6–29, the language of faith has been completely eclipsed by Paul's focus on God's election, apart from—and even despite—human response, as the sole basis on which one is reckoned to be Abraham's "seed." Beginning with 9:30, however, the language of faith will return to the argument as the corollary to election.

who are "children of promise."[19] The identification of "promise" with
the scriptural announcement that Sarah will give birth to a son
(v. 9)[20] completes this stage of the argument, establishing Paul's contention that the "children of promise" are descendants of one particular child of Abraham, Sarah's son Isaac, through whom God has
promised to call "seed" for Abraham (v. 7). Paul's choice of terms
("call," "promise," "reckon") emphasizes that the election of Isaac
and his descendants depends solely on God's gracious purpose.

This crucial claim that membership in "Israel" is due to God's
election and not simply to physical descent is elaborated further as
Paul continues to follow the outline of the patriarchal narratives and
trace the theme of the inheritance of Abraham's blessing. Not only
in the case of Abraham, but also in the stories of Isaac and his children, only some of the physical descendants inherit the promises.
Although Esau and Jacob are conceived at the same time, by the
same father, only the younger is chosen as heir.[21] The election of
Jacob rather than Esau, Paul emphasizes, rests on no human action,
good or bad (vv. 11–12),[22] but derives solely from "God's purpose,
in accordance with [his] choice" (ἡ κατ' ἐκλογὴν πρόθεσις τοῦ θεοῦ)—
the same gracious purpose in effect when God (ὁ καλούντων) deter-

---

[19] Who these "children of promise" are remains unspecified at this point in the
discussion. A full answer awaits Romans 9:24–29, and indeed, the conclusion of
Romans 11.

[20] The citation, marked both by an introductory formula, "This word is [a word]
of promise," and by a shift in speakers (see n. 17 above), is a conflation of Gen
18:10 and 14.

[21] *T. Job* 1:5–6 offers an intriguing Second Temple reflex of the story of the
election of Jacob rather than Esau. Job's (second set of) children are "a chosen
and honored race," not because they are *his* children—for Job is a descendant of
Esau—but because they are children of his second wife, Dinah, the daughter of
Jacob (ὑμεῖς δὲ γένος ἐκλεκτὸν ἔντιμον ἐκ σπέρματος Ἰακωβ τοῦ πατρὸς τῆς μητρὸς
ὑμῶν).

[22] "Works" here approaches the sense of "human activity in general." The phrase,
"works of the law," used throughout Galatians (2:16 [3x]; 3:2, 5, 10), is found in
Romans 2:15; 3:20, 28. Subsequent references to "works" in Rom 4:2, 6 are probably to be understood in light of this fuller phrase, since Paul is discussing the relationship between Abraham's faith and circumcision. "Works" in 9:32 is also associated
with observance of the law. In light of Paul's usage in the rest of the letter, the
remaining occurrences of "works" in 9:12 and 11:6 probably also carry the connotation, "works of the law." The immediate context of 9:12, however, specifies
"works" as τι ἀγαθὸν ἢ φαῦλον (v. 11; cf. 2 Cor 5:10) and contrasts them with
God's gracious calling (cf. 9:16). This may suggest a generalization of "works" to
include human effort of any kind, while not excluding "works of the law" as the
particular type of human effort with which Paul is most immediately concerned in
Romans. Cf. I. H. Marshall 1996:345 and n. 21, 356; Moo 1983a.

mined to "call" σπέρμα for Abraham through Isaac.[23] God, who spoke "the word of promise" to Sarah regarding Isaac (v. 7), speaks a shocking word to Rebekah that reverses the normal customs of inheritance: "The older shall serve the younger."[24]

Paul interprets this oracle by means of a later prophet's reflection on the story: "Jacob I loved, but Esau I hated."[25] While Paul's quotation of Malachi appears to be motivated primarily by the terminological link,[26] the wider context of this citation in Malachi suggests that the logic of Paul's argument is deeply rooted in the native soil of Israel's scriptures. For Malachi too, not all "from Jacob" constitute the "Jacob" whom God has loved. Throughout the book, the prophet indicts the people for their continuing rebellion against God. Only a portion of Israel, "those who fear the Lord" (οἱ φοβούμενοι τὸν κύριον, 3:16–21 LXX), will experience God's promised redemption. In arguing that in the present time "not all from Israel are Israel," then, Paul is simply extending the logic of a narrative pattern established in the stories of Israel's national origins, a pattern which continued to shape the prophetic understanding of the nature of God's election of Israel.[27]

Moses and the Drama of Redemption: Romans 9:14–18

Paul now anticipates the obvious objection to the case he has been assembling: If election rests with God and has no connection with human desert, is God then unjust in choosing some and rejecting others?[28] The apostle shrewdly frames this objection as a leading

---

[23] And, significantly, the same divine plan on which Paul tells his hearers to set their hope as those who have been called by God (8:28, οἴδαμεν δὲ ὅτι τοῖς ἀγαπῶσιν τὸν θεὸν πάντα συνεργεῖ εἰς ἀγαθόν, τοῖς κατὰ πρόθεσιν κλητοῖς οὖσιν).

[24] Here, a quotation formula, ἐρρέθη αὐτῇ ὅτι, introduces a citation of scripture.

[25] The quotation from Malachi 1:2–3 is marked with an explicit citation formula, καθὼς γέγραπται. Paul advances the name "Jacob," destroying the chiasm of the original, but emphasizing the identity of the heir of the promise. Note the relationship of "love" and "call" in Paul's quotation of Hos 2:25 in 9:25. Cf. also the similar conjunction of terms for election (including "seed of Abraham") in Isa 41:8: σὺ δέ, Ισραηλ, παῖς μου Ιακωβ, ὃν ἐξελεξάμην, σπέρμα Αβρααμ, ὃν ἠγάπησα.

[26] Jacob and Esau are mentioned together in scripture outside Genesis only in Joshua 24:4; 1 Chronicles 1:34 LXX; Obadiah 18; Malachi 1:2–3.

[27] See further Evans 1984a.

[28] This query actually reprises a concern voiced as early as Romans 3:5 but allowed to lie dormant until now.

question whose very form suggests the correct answer: τί οὖν ἐροῦμεν; μὴ ἀδικία παρὰ τῷ θεῷ;[29] Paul defends his emphatic μὴ γένοιτο by quoting God's own words to Moses (Exod 33:19): "I will have mercy on whom I have mercy, and I will have compassion on whom I have compassion."[30] This quotation is linked to the preceding argument by the idea of God's freedom to choose the objects of his mercy and love; moreover, the recurrence of "mercy" in Romans 9:23, σκεύη ἐλέους, serves as a catchword indicating that in v. 15 Paul is beginning a line of argumentation that stretches to v. 23 and beyond. The verb "have mercy" (ἐλεέω) thus joins the group of terms Paul liberally employs in these chapters to speak of God's gracious choice: "call," "promise," "election," purpose," "love" (see Fig. 2.1).

The importance of "mercy" for the ensuing discussion in chapters 9–11 is adumbrated by Paul's interpretive comment on the quotation in Romans 9:16, as he characterizes God as "the one who shows mercy."[31] This thematic connection with the preceding verses does not exhaust the significance of Exodus 33:19 for Paul's argument, however. For one who knows the source of the quotation, the apostle's point is far more telling. These words are spoken in response to Moses' intercession on behalf of Israel after the rebellion of the golden calf, an episode Paul has already evoked in 9:3 with his wish to be cut off from Christ for his people's sake. Despite Israel's grave sin of idolatry, Moses asks for and receives confirmation of God's continued favor for Moses and for Israel (33:12–17). In response, he requests a vision of the Lord's glory (33:18). God promises to make his glory pass before Moses and to proclaim his name, "the Lord," a name that he further characterizes or defines by the phrase quoted by Paul, "I will have mercy on whom I have mercy, and I will have compassion on whom I have compassion" (33:19). At the point in the exodus narrative where Israel has failed utterly, God remains faithful—not because of human willing or striving, not because of Israel's merit, but because of God's own mercy (cf. Rom 9:16). God

---

[29] Paul's question faintly echoes Deuteronomy 32:4 (θεὸς πιστός, καὶ οὐκ ἔστιν ἀδικία). On Paul's use of Deuteronomy 32 in general, see Bell 1994.

[30] The quotation follows LXX exactly but for the omission of the initial καί.

[31] ἄρα οὖν οὐ τοῦ θέλοντος οὐδὲ τοῦ τρέχοντος ἀλλὰ τοῦ ἐλεῶντος θεοῦ. For the introduction of an interpretive conclusion with ἄρα οὖν, see also v. 18 (cf. Rom 7:3). Paul's remarks parallel his earlier assertion that God's choice is based not on the human being who "works" but on God alone, "the one who calls" (ἐκ τοῦ καλοῦντος, v. 12).

is not unjust, according to this line of reasoning, because God remains faithful to his promises despite Israel's failure.

God's revelation of his merciful character finds further explication in the account of the Lord's actual appearance to Moses, proclaiming:

> The Lord, the *compassionate* and *merciful* God, patient, and *full of mercy*, and true; maintaining justice and showing *mercy* to thousands. . . .

> Κύριος ὁ θεὸς οἰκτίρμων καὶ ἐλεήμων, μακρόθυμος καὶ πολυέλεος καὶ ἀληθινὸς καὶ δικαιοσύνην διατηρῶν καὶ ποιῶν ἔλεος εἰς χιλιάδας . . . (Exodus 34:6–7 LXX).

These words are invoked repeatedly throughout Israel's sacred writings as a way of characterizing the intimate connection between God's very nature and his commitment to his people.[32] They are not a speculative theological proposition about the divine nature, but a profound summary of the very particular story in which God shows his faithfulness by keeping his promises *to Israel*, even when his people are unfaithful to their God. By drawing on Exodus 33:19 and the larger narrative characterization of Israel's God of which it is a part, Paul argues not simply that God is free to be merciful to whom he will, but more specifically that God has freely chosen to be merciful to Israel and to keep his covenant with his people even in the face of their unfaithfulness and idolatry.[33] Lingering in the background of Romans 9, these echoes of Exodus 32–34 foreshadow the conclusion to which Paul's argument is driving, that despite the present unbelief of many within Israel, God has not forsaken his people (Rom 11:1–2), but has determined to show mercy to "all Israel" (11:25–32).

But God's freedom to be merciful has, for Paul, another side: namely, God's freedom *not* to show mercy, but to turn human rebellion to his own purposes, as in the case of Pharaoh (Rom 9:17).[34]

---

[32] See, for example, Num 14:18; Neh 9:17; Ps 85:15 LXX; 102:8 LXX; 144:8 LXX; Joel 2:13; Hos 2:19–20 LXX; Jonah 4:2; Nah 1:3; Wis 15:1; Sir 5:4; 18:11; Pr Man 7.

[33] This is not to suggest that Paul (or the biblical writers, for that matter) thought God's mercy was limited to Israel. Indeed, Paul is faced with the necessity of composing Romans 9–11 precisely because he has insisted that God saves Jews *and Gentiles* on exactly the same basis. It is rather to insist that for Paul, God is known not in the abstract, but through the story of God's election of Abraham and his descendants, through whom God has determined to bless all nations. Käsemann thus misses the mark when he suggests that Paul appeals to Israel's story in Romans 9 only in order to find timeless theological "types" (1980:264).

[34] Paul introduces his quotation of Exodus 9:16 with the phrase, λέγει γὰρ ἡ

The primary connection of thought here seems to be the antithesis between "show mercy" and "harden," as Paul's interpretive gloss in v. 18, phrased in a manner reminiscent of the quotation from Exodus 33:19 (Rom 9:15), indicates: "Therefore, he shows mercy to whom he will, and he hardens whom he will." The example of Pharaoh provides a striking contrast to the previous illustration of God's mercy toward Israel. The verb σκληρύνω does not actually appear in the verse cited by Paul (Exod 9:16), but a notable feature of the exodus narrative (including, in the immediate context, Exod 9:7, 12, 34, 35) is the repeated statement that God hardened Pharaoh's heart.[35] Here we have a clear case of Paul's awareness of the larger context of a quotation and his exegetical interest in elements of the narrative not explicitly cited. Significantly, Paul's highly abbreviated and allusive retelling of the story presupposes his audience's familiarity with the story of the exodus.

The purpose of God's hardening of Pharaoh is important for Paul's use of this episode in Romans 9, and indeed it is the focus of the passage from Exodus that he actually quotes (Exod 9:16):

γραφὴ τῷ Φαραὼ ὅτι. This personification of scripture (note the parallel in v. 15, λέγει [ὁ θεός]) not only enlivens and strengthens Paul's rhetoric with multiple authoritative voices; at a deeper level, it also reveals Paul's fundamental theological conviction that scripture is a living voice. Scripture speaks to Pharaoh (Rom 9:17) and preaches the gospel to Abraham (Gal 4:30). Through scripture, Paul's "co-workers"—Isaiah and "Righteousness from Faith"—boldly proclaim to Israel the message of the gospel (Romans 10:6–8, 16). Similar attitudes toward scripture are evidenced by the prominence of verbs of "saying" in the citation formulas in Philo, the Dead Sea Scrolls, and rabbinic literature. See Ryle 1895:xlv; Elledge 2001; Bernstein 1994; Fitzmyer 1960–61; Horton 1971; Metzger 1951; Bonsirven 1939:29–31.

[35] The verb σκληρύνω appears 14x in Exodus LXX (out of 17x in the Pentateuch and 37x in the LXX as a whole). The statement that God hardened Pharaoh's heart introduces the 10 plagues and serves as a refrain after each plague. God is said to harden Pharaoh's heart (σκληρύνω) in Exod 4:21; 7:3; 9:12; 10:1, 20, 27; 11:10; 14:4, 8, 17 (the passive voice, used to indicate divine action, appears in 7:22; 8:19; 9:35). The verb βαρύνω is also used to speak of the divine hardening of Pharaoh's heart (Exod 8:15, 9:7 [both passive]), as is κατισχύω (7:13). Exod 9:12 LXX makes it clear that God ordained (συντάσσω) that Pharaoh's heart be hardened (so also the repeated phrase, "as the Lord said" in 7:13, 22; 8:15, 19; 9:35). Three times Pharaoh is said to have hardened himself so as not to let the people go (βαρύνω, Exod 8:32 and 9:34; cf. 1 Sam 6:6; σκληρύνω, Exod 13:15). The author of the biblical narrative (and, also, apparently, Paul) saw no conflict between attributing the same action both to God and to humans, although the emphasis in Exodus rests on God's action. In only two other instances is God said to have "hardened" someone: Sihon, king of Heshbon (Deut 2:30), and Israel (Isa 63:17). For God as cause of the Egyptians' hatred of Israel, see Ps 104:25 LXX.

For this very reason I raised you up[36]—so that I might show my power through you and so that my name might be proclaimed in all the earth.

εἰς αὐτὸ τοῦτο ἐξήγειρά σε ὅπως ἐνδείξωμαι ἐν σοὶ τὴν δύναμίν μου καὶ ὅπως διαγγελῇ τὸ ὄνομά μου ἐν πάσῃ τῇ γῇ.

As his comment in Romans 9:18 and his subsequent discussion in vv. 22–24 make clear, Paul reads the two ὅπως clauses separately, as dual aspects of God's overall purpose. On the one hand, God raises Pharaoh up in order to show his power (v. 18, "he hardens whom he will"); on the other hand, God delivers Israel from captivity in order that his name might be proclaimed throughout the world ("and he shows mercy to whom he will").

This latter purpose suggests perhaps another connection in Paul's thought between Exodus 9:16 and Exodus 33:19 (and its wider context), where the proclamation of the Lord's *name* consists in the declaration of his mercy, freely shown to those he chooses.[37] For Paul, God's hardening of Pharaoh must be understood in relation to his determination to show mercy to Israel and so to proclaim his glory throughout the earth.[38] In like manner, Paul will aver that God's ultimate aim in the present time is to show his glory through redeeming "vessels of mercy," both Jew and Gentile (Rom 9:23; cf. 11:32–36).

But this is to run ahead of Paul's argument. The bitter irony at

---

[36] Paul's quotation has the verb ἐξεγείρω where LXX reads διατηρέω. Ἐξεγείρω is an appropriate, if uncommon, rendering of Hebrew עמד (hiphil); the simple ἐγείρω occurs for this Hebrew form in Daniel LXX 8:18; Sirach 10:4; 1 Esdras 5:43 (= Ezra 2:68); 8:78 (= Ezra 9:9). It is unclear whether Paul himself is the source of the reading ἐξεγείρω or whether he has drawn on a Greek text revised toward a Hebrew exemplar (cf. Stanley 1992b:107–108). Paul's citation, along with the Hebrew text, focuses on God's purpose in Israel's captivity/exodus considered as a whole. That Pharaoh has been allowed any power over Israel at all is only because of God's design. In contrast, the LXX, with διατηρέω, emphasizes that although God could have destroyed Pharaoah long ago, he prolonged Pharaoh's disobedience in order to show his power and glory. In Romans 9:22, there is a change of perspective that brings Paul closer to the interpretation of Exodus 9:16 LXX, as Paul underscores the great patience with which God bore with "the vessels of wrath." Paul's focus on God's patience with Pharaoh in Romans 9:22 could derive from his own exegetical reflection on the exodus story as easily as from a knowledge of the variant διατηρέω attested by LXX.

[37] See above, pp. 52–53; for further terminological links between Exodus 33:19 and Exodus 9:16, see below, pp. 73–74.

[38] For an exploration of the theme in Romans 9 that God's ultimate purpose is to display his glory in showing mercy, see Piper 1993. Even God's act of "hardening" some serves his merciful purpose of redeeming his people.

this stage in Paul's discussion is that Israel appears to have taken on the role of Pharaoh, refusing to recognize the redemption offered them in Christ. Even more scandalous is the idea implied by Paul's emphasis on God's sovereign choice to have mercy or to harden—that it is God himself who has hardened Israel.[39] And, indeed, Paul recognizes the scandal and hastens to address it.[40]

THE POTTER AND THE CLAY: ROMANS 9:19–21

The imaginary interlocutor who objects to Paul's theodicy does so in language laden with overtones of Job's heart-rending protests against the apparent injustice of God.[41] By framing his interlocutor's objection in terms reminiscent of Job's complaints,[42] Paul stacks the deck in his favor, subtly portraying such questions as outrageous, both on the grounds that, for Paul at least, no one can claim to be blameless before God[43] and because the questions themselves are improper for a mere creature to ask of the creator. It is the latter point that Paul's rebuke emphasizes: "O human,[44] who are *you* who

---

[39] Note Paul's use in Romans 11:7 and 25 of πωρόω/πώρωσις (p. 240 n. 68 and pp. 276–78). The idea that God has hardened Israel's heart is not original to Paul, but is rooted in the tradition of penitential prayer attested, for example, by Isaiah 63:17 LXX: "Why have you caused us to stray from your path, Lord? Why have you hardened our hearts so that we do not fear you? (τί ἐπλάνησας ἡμᾶς, κύριε, ἀπὸ τῆς ὁδοῦ σου, ἐσκλήρυνας ἡμῶν τὰς καρδίας τοῦ μὴ φοβεῖσθαί σε;). Interestingly, the speaker appeals in the preceding verse to God's mercy (ἔλεος) and compassion (οἰκτιρμοί) and to the fact that Israel bears God's name (ἀπ' ἀρχῆς τὸ ὄνομά σου ἐφ' ἡμᾶς ἐστι). While it is impossible to know if Paul had this passage in mind while composing Romans 9, it is clear that he has tapped into language and thought patterns thoroughly at home in scripture.

[40] The objection Paul addresses here actually breaks the flow of his argument, for v. 22 continues the exposition of Exod 9:16 begun in v. 17 (see pp. 71–74).

[41] Ironically, in the episode immediately following Exodus 9:16, Pharaoh for the first time admits that God's judgment against him is just: "I have sinned this time. The Lord is just, but I and my people are ungodly" (ἡμάρτηκα τὸ νῦν· ὁ κύριος δίκαιος, ἐγὼ δὲ καὶ ὁ λαός μου ἀσεβεῖς, Exod 9:27). In contrast, Paul's interlocutor insinuates that God's choice to harden some and to have mercy on some is *unjust* (9:19; cf. v. 14, μὴ ἀδικία παρὰ τῷ θεῷ;).

[42] Compare Romans 9:19a with LXX Job 33:9–10 and Romans 9:19b with LXX Job 9:19; 41:2b-3; see also Wis 11:21; 12:12. Though not marked as a citation, Paul's wording in Romans 11:35 is very close to Job 41:3 (see p. 302). There is a marked citation of Job 5:12–13 in 1 Corinthians 3:19. In addition, Philippians 1:19 may allude to Job 13:16.

[43] Paul has argued that the fact of universal sinfulness shuts every mouth that would presume to complain against God (Romans 3:19; cf. 3:23).

[44] For use of the vocative, ὦ ἄνθρωπε, as a means of addressing a hypothetical

answers back to God?" (ὦ ἄνθρωπε, μενοῦνγε σὺ τίς εἶ ὁ ἀνταπο-κρινόμενος τῷ θεῷ; Rom 9:20a).[45]

To drive home the point that such questions are inappropriate for a creature to ask the Creator, Paul takes up a metaphor—found in both prophetic and wisdom literature—that likens human beings before God to clay in the hands of a potter: "Will the thing formed say to the one who formed it, 'Why have you made me thus?'" (Rom 9:20b).[46] The basic meaning of the figure is illuminated by the rhetorical question in the following verse—the potter has authority over the clay to make from it whatever he chooses. The metaphor thus supports Paul's contention that God is free to show mercy or to harden as he wills (9:18).[47] To anyone familiar with Israel's scriptures, however, it would also be evident that Paul is drawing on a traditional metaphor for God's relationship to creation, and, more

---

interlocutor, see Rom 2:1, 3. Paul's use of the particle μενοῦνγε, though perhaps not used in "the sort of straightforward negation which is normally the context of adversative μὲν οὖν in classical literature" (Thrall 1962:35; cf. Rom 10:18), heightens the sharpness of Paul's rebuttal as he pointedly questions the questioner ("you interrogate God—but the real question is, 'Who are *you* to arrogate such a right to yourself?'").

[45] Here again, the faintest echo of Job may be discerned, for when Job finally is confronted by God and challenged to answer (σὺ δέ μοι ἀποκρίθητι, 38:3; cf. 40:2), he refuses: "But for my part, what answer shall I give to these things? I will put my hand over my mouth; once I have spoken, but I will not add to it a second time" (ἐγὼ δὲ τίνα ἀπόκρισιν δῶ πρὸς ταῦτα; χεῖρα θήσω ἐπὶ στόματί μου· ἅπαξ λελάληκα, ἐπὶ δὲ τῷ δευτέρῳ οὐ προσθήσω. Job 40:4b–5 LXX). Paul similarly challenges his interlocutor to show humility before God.

[46] This metaphor is found in various forms in Isa 29:16; 45:9; 64:8; Jer 18:1–12; Sir 33:7–13; Wis 15:7–17; 1QS 11.22; *LAB* 53:13; *T. Naph.* 2:2–5. The description of human beings as fashioned from clay (cf. Gen 2:7) appears frequently in the *Hodayot* to emphasize the lowly position of human creatures before their God: 1QH[a] 9[1].21–23; 11[3].23–25; 12[4].29; 18[10].3–7; 19[11].3; 20[12].24–32; 23[18].12. See further Aageson 1983:249–54.

[47] In light of recurrent echoes of Job in Romans 9:19–20a, we should note Job's self-description in response to his vision of God (42:6 LXX): "Therefore I despised myself and melted away, I consider myself dirt and ashes" (διὸ ἐφαύλισα ἐμαυτὸν καὶ ἐτάκην, ἥγημαι δὲ ἐμαυτὸν γῆν καὶ σποδόν). See also the description of human beings, and Job in particular, as fashioned from clay (πηλός): Job 10:9; 30:19; 33:6; cf. Gen 2:7. Interestingly, *LAB* 53:13 combines the potter/clay topos with language reminiscent of Job 1:21, "The Lord has given and the Lord has taken away. Blessed be the name of the Lord." In Pseudo-Philo's expansive retelling of the calling of Samuel, Eli reacts to the news that he and his family will be wiped out by saying: Will the object formed answer back him who formed it? (Si respondebit plasma ei qui eum plasmavit?) So I cannot answer back when he, the faithful giver, wishes to take away what he has given. Holy is he who has prophesied; I am under his power (Jacobson 1996:181, 1129).

specifically, to his people Israel. It is worth asking, then, what rhetorical and theological weight echoes of this tradition might lend to Paul's larger argument. Particularly important for my purposes are the strong connections between Paul's appeal to the metaphor of potter and clay and the use of this figure in Isaiah's oracles.

Isaiah 29:16/45:9 in Romans 9:20: The Text

Although there is in Romans 9:20 no explicit marker of a quotation, Paul's phraseology recalls Isaiah 29:16 LXX and, more distantly, Isaiah 45:9 LXX (Fig. 2.2).

Figure 2.2: Isaiah 29:16 LXX and Isaiah 45:9 LXX in Romans 9:20

Key: single underline agreement between Rom 9:20 and Isa 29:16
 double underline agreement between Rom 9:20 and Isa 45:9
 italic agreement among all three column

Isaiah 29:16 LXX	Romans 9:20	Isaiah 45:9 LXX
οὐχ ὡς ὁ πηλὸς τοῦ κεραμέως λογισθήσεσθε;		ποῖον βέλτιον κατεσκεύασα ὡς πηλὸν κεραμέως; μὴ ὁ ἀροτριῶν ἀροτριάσει τὴν γῆν;
μὴ ἐρεῖ τὸ πλάσμα τῷ πλάσαντι· οὐ σύ με ἔπλασας; ἢ τὸ ποίημα τῷ ποιήσαντι· οὐ συνετῶς με ἐποίησας;	μὴ ἐρεῖ τὸ πλάσμα τῷ πλάσαντι· τί με ἐποίησας οὕτως;	μὴ ἐρεῖ ὁ πηλὸς τῷ κεραμεῖ· τί ποιεῖς, ὅτι οὐκ ἐργάζῃ οὐδὲ ἔχεις χεῖρας;

Paul's question, τί με ἐποίησας[48] οὕτως, paraphrases the statement in Isaiah 29:16c LXX, οὐ συνετῶς με ἐποίησας. Both formulations challenge the wisdom of the creator.[49] Paul has changed the statement

---

[48] The variant ἔπλασας in Romans 9:20 (D, Peshitta) probably represents an assimilation to Isaiah 29:16b (but see n. 49).

[49] Paul's citation agrees with LXX against MT in that neither Paul nor LXX

in Isaiah to a question by omitting οὐ συνετῶς, adding τί (possibly under the influence of 45:9c),[50] and supplying οὕτως in order to make it clear that what is being challenged is not the mere *fact* of being created but the *form* that creation has taken.[51] This wording provides a better parallel to the presumptuous questions in v. 19, which Paul now likens to the complaint of the clay against the potter.[52] Further verbal connections with Isaiah 29:16 (and with Isaiah 45:9) are established through the use of the terms πηλός and κεραμεύς in Romans 9:21.

Linking Isaiah 29:16 and 45:9: lxx and Targum

Although Paul's wording closely resembles Isaiah 29:16, the possibility of an allusion to 45:9 as well should not be excluded from consideration. The common theme and shared terminology (πηλός, κεραμεύς, ποιέω, μὴ ἐρεῖ) may have suggested to Paul a connection between the two passages.[53] Moreover, a study of the rendering of

---

has an equivalent for the objective pronominal suffix on לעשׂהו (the addition of αὐτό(ν) in B, V, and many Hexaplaric and Lucianic mss is clearly a secondary assimilation to MT). In several mss (88 301 Syrohexapla), 29:16 ends with ἔπλασας. Their omission of the rest of the verse (29:16c) is perhaps the result of haplography due to homoioteleuton. The Lucianic ms 93 likewise omits 29:16c, but reads a final ἐποίησας rather than ἔπλασας. Although Paul's *Vorlage* may have similarly suffered haplography, it is quite possible, in light of his other alterations to the end of the citation, that the omission in Romans 9:20 of the words intervening between πλάσαντι and με ἐποίησας is to be traced to Paul himself.

[50] In so doing, Paul would have altered the sense of τί from "what" to "why." Koch (1986:144 n. 13) thinks it unlikely that Isaiah 45:9 has shaped Paul's wording here because he can detect no other influence of this passage on the apostle's argument. As I will argue below, however, not only are there formal parallels in the Targum to what I suggest is Paul's conflation of Isaiah 29:16 and 45:9, there are also plausible echoes of 45:9 in the context of Paul's argument.

[51] *Contra* Koch (1986:144 and n. 13), who comments, "hier die Geschöpflichkeit als solche—illegitimerweise—Gott gegenüber als Argument gebraucht wird." As Romans 9:21 makes clear, it is not being a creature, but rather being a vessel intended for destruction, that calls forth the protest against God's justice.

[52] For a similar statement of the futility of questioning God, see Job 9:12 (cf. Wis 12:12): τίς ἐρεῖ αὐτῷ· τί ἐποίησας; The resemblance of Romans 9:20b to the language of Job may be not insignificant in light of the Job-like diction noted above in Romans 9:19–20a (L. T. Johnson [1997:151] considers Romans 9:20 "a mixed citation/allusion to Isa 29:16 and Job 9:12").

[53] In Hebrew, the texts are linked by the words חמר, יצר, עשׂה, אמר. See Figure 2.3 below for the Hebrew texts. In his study of Deutero-Isaiah's use of earlier biblical texts, B. D. Sommer argues that Isaiah 45:9–10 echoes 29:16 (1998:104, 258–59 nn. 95–96; cf. Sommer 1996a:177 nn. 43–44). H. G. M. Williamson states the matter even more forcefully: "Isa. 29:16 and 45:9 may be regarded as a firm example of the literary influence of the earlier part of Isaiah on the latter" (1994:63).

these two verses in the LXX and Targum shows that other ancient readers noted a relationship between these Isaianic potter texts.

The textual history of the LXX suggests that some of its tradents were influenced by an exegetical tradition linking these two passages. A number of manuscripts add a phrase to the end of 45:9 reflecting the language of 29:16b: μὴ ἀποκριθήσεται τὸ πλάσμα πρὸς τὸν πλάσαντα αὐτό;[54] Furthermore, it is just possible that the verb ἐποίησας in 29:16c, which lacks a Hebrew equivalent, was supplied by the translators under the influence of 45:9c.[55]

The rendering of the Isaiah Targum provides more unambiguous evidence of an interpretive linking of Isaiah 29:16 and 45:9. The identical phrase, "Is it possible that the clay will say to its maker, 'You did not make me'?" (הֶאְפְשַׁר דְּיֵימַר טִינָא לְעָבְדֵיהּ לָא עֲבַדְתַּנִי), appears in both verses, though the Targum translates the remainder of each verse differently, in keeping with the sense of their respective Hebrew originals. Significantly, the phrase shared by Targum Isaiah 29:16 and 45:9 includes a number of features found in one or the other of the Hebrew passages but not in both. The composite nature of the targumic phrase may be seen in Figure 2.3.

---

[54] B, most Lucianic MSS, numerous other witnesses (S* has τῷ προσπλάσαντι). This variant cannot be explained as an assimilation to MT, and so it almost certainly has its roots in an inner-septuagintal attempt at harmonization of the two oracles. Though this phrase is clearly a secondary addition to LXX Isaiah (there are no grounds for supposing that the variant was known to Paul), it may well reflect a much earlier exegetical tradition. M. Goshen-Gottstein finds a further connection between the original form of Isaiah 45:9 LXX and the larger context of 29:16. He suggests that the Septuagint rendering of חֶרֶשׂ אֶת־חַרְשֵׂי אֲדָמָה in Isaiah 45:9 as μὴ ὁ ἀροτριῶν ἀροτριάσει τὴν γῆν derives from Isaiah 28:24, where יַחֲרֹשׁ הֶחָרֹשׁ is translated μέλλει ὁ ἀροτριῶν ἀροτριᾶν (1963:153–55). The manuscript tradition lends indirect support to his argument, for a large number of MSS add to 45:9 yet a further phrase from 28:24 (ὅλην τὴν ἡμέραν = כָּל הַיּוֹם) either before or after ὁ ἀροτριῶν or after τὴν γῆν. All of this strongly suggests that later tradents recognized and sought to enhance the connections between Isaiah 45:9 and 28:24.

[55] It has long been recognized that the LXX translator of Isaiah frequently solves exegetical difficulties by reference to similar passages within the book: "La traduction de la LXX d'Is compare constamment les passages susceptibles de s'éclairer mutuellement" (Laberge 1978:120; he offers examples of this phenomenon on pp. 118–120). Kutscher comments, "One sometimes finds that the [LXX] translator has been influenced by a different passage either from the same or from another book of the Bible. This is so largely in places where there are exegetical or other difficulties" (1974:76). The same procedure was followed by the scribe of 1QIsaᵃ (76; cf. 73–77, 306–308, 312–13). Kutscher observes, "This of course implies that the scribe knew the book quite well, perhaps even by heart" (312). See also Ziegler 1934:13, 25–30, 135–75; Zillesin 1902:249–52. More generally, see Muraoka 1973. In the present instance, however, the use of ποίημα/ποιέω in the immediate context may provide a sufficient explanation of the final ἐποίησας.

Figure 2.3: Isaiah 29:16 and 45:9 in MT and Targum

Key:	single underline	Words drawn from Isaiah 29:16 (Heb) only
	double underline	Words drawn from Isaiah 45:9 (Heb) only
	italic	Words common to both Hebrew texts

Isaiah 29:16 MT	Tg. Isaiah 29:16	Tg. Isaiah 45:9	Isaiah 45:9 MT
הפככם	הלמהפך עובדיכון אתון בען	יי דמדמי למקם לקביל פתגמי ברוהי	הוי רב את יצרו
אם כחמר היצר יחשב	הא כמא דטינא ביד פחרא כין אתון חשיבין קדמי	ורחיץ דייטבון ליה צלמי פחרא דעבידין מעפר אדמתא	חרש את־חרשי אדמה
כי יאמר מעשה לעשהו לא עשני	הַאֶפשר דיימר טינא לעבדיה לא עבד חני	הַאֶפשר דיימר טינא לעבדיה לא עבד חני	ה יאמר חמר ליצרו מה תעשה
ויצר אמר ליוצרו לא הבין	ובריתא דתימר לברהא לא חכימת לי	ועובדך לית ידין ליה	ופעלך אין ידים לו

The verbs יֹמר and עבד are common to the two texts (Heb. עשׂה, אמר). From 45:9 MT come the word טינא, "clay" (Heb. חמר; 29:16 MT reads מעשה, "the thing made") and the second person verb עבדתני (Heb. תעשה; 29:16 MT has third person, עשׂני). From 29:16 MT, the Targum draws the negative particle, the tense of the verb, and the direct object of the verb. In addition, it appears likely that the rendering לעבדיה reflects לעשׂהו of 29:16b MT rather than ליצרו of 45:9 MT.[56]

The Targum's composite phrase is of considerable significance for our study for two reasons. First, the fact that its translators made an exegetical connection between Isaiah 29:16 and 45:9 suggests that

---

[56] In the overwhelming majority of cases, the Isaiah Targum employs √עבד as an equivalent for Hebrew √עשׂה, as it does at the end of the shared phrase (לא עבדתני). In contrast, Hebrew √יצר is most often represented in Tg. Isaiah by √תקן or by √ברא, as in 45:9a (Tg. ברוהי = Heb. יצרו) and in 29:16c (Tg. ובריתא, לברהא = Heb. ויצר, ליצרו). Compare the Peshitta of these verses, where √ܥܒܕ = √עשׂה and √ܓܒܠ = √יצר. An alternative explanation is possible, however, when it is noted that in the two clear cases in which Tg. Isaiah translates the Hebrew √יצר with √עבד, the reference is to making idols (44:9; 44:10). The Targum's interpretive rendering of 45:9b as a polemic against those who hope in "the potter's idols (צלמי פחרא) made (עבידין) from the dust of the ground," could explain the choice of √עבד as a lexical equivalent for the Hebrew √יצר in 45:9c, without requiring the targumists' recourse to 29:16b.

Paul, as an ancient reader of Isaiah, could plausibly have made this connection as well, whether or not he knew the same exegetical tradition attested by the Targum.[57] Second, the composite nature of the phrase shared by Targum Isaiah 29:16 and 45:9 provides a formal analogue to Paul's conflated allusion in Romans 9:20. As suggested above in Figure 2.2, Paul follows Isaiah 29:16 closely, but by including an important word (τί) found only in 45:9, he gives the question a sense more appropriate to its context in Romans. On the level of technique, then, Paul's method of conflating two similar texts finds a parallel in the Targum. It remains to be seen whether Paul's interweaving of Isaiah 29:16 and 45:9 on the formal level reveals an exegetical connection between the two texts that illuminates his appropriation of them in Romans 9.

Isaiah 29:16/45:9 in Context

If Paul's language is drawn from Isaiah 29:16/45:9, what might be the connection of thought between his argument in Romans 9 and these Isaianic oracles? In its context,[58] the question in Isaiah 29:16 reflects a challenge to the divine wisdom and power by those who have put their hope for deliverance from Assyria in their own plans and devices.[59] Isaiah 28–29, part of the larger section 28–33, consist of a series of woes interspersed with promises of salvation.[60] In

---

[57] The variants in the LXX noted above show that readers of Isaiah in Greek were also capable of making a connection between the two passages. Thus, whether or not Paul knew Isaiah in a non-Greek form is irrelevant to the present discussion. In the absence of firm dates either for the addition to Isaiah 45:9 LXX of the phrase from Isaiah 29:16 LXX or for the present form of the Targum, it is not possible to be certain that the interpretive traditions underlying these translations pre-date Romans. Although it is not unlikely that Paul was aware of a tradition linking the two passages, he himself may have connected them on the basis of their shared terminology and ideas alone.

[58] Paul appears to have been familiar with the passage as a whole; he quotes from Isaiah 29:10 in Romans 11:8 (see pp. 240–54) and from 29:14 in 1 Corinthians 1:19; cf. his use of Isaiah 28:11–12 in 1 Corinthians 14:21, Isaiah 28:16 in Romans 9:33, 10:11, and possibly Isaiah 28:22 in Romans 9:28 (see pp. 97–99).

[59] The issue of divine versus human wisdom is clearly brought out in 29:14–16, but it is implicit in the whole passage. Note the comparison of God to a wise farmer in 28:23–28.

[60] Note the use of οὐαί to mark divisions of thought within the larger section 28–33 (28:1; 29:1; 29:15; 30:1; 31:1; 33:1). Because Paul does not quote from 30–33, I limit my focus here to the first three units in 28–29. See further G. Stansell 1996:70–71.

this prophetic chiaroscuro, the woes are aimed primarily at the lead-ers of Ephraim (28:1–4) and Judah (28:7–22; esp. v. 14), who reject the word of the Lord and dismiss the prophet's message as nonsense fit only for children (28:9–13).[61] Refusing to trust in their God (28:12, 15), they devise their own plans for warding off the Assyrian threat, plans that presumably involve an alliance with Egypt (cf. 30:1–5). Isaiah excoriates their scheme as a covenant with death, a search for security in a lie (28:15). The Lord vows to expose the folly of their trust in other gods by bringing their plans to nought. At the same time, he himself establishes a "stone" in Zion, promising that "the one who trusts in it will not be ashamed" (28:16).[62] The prophet's message is clear: Only those who trust in the Lord will be spared, for like a mighty flood, the coming calamity will sweep away the rebellious schemes of Judah's leaders (28:17–22).

Yet God does not intend the complete destruction of Israel; rather, his purpose is to purify and save a remnant of the people (cf. 28:5–6). As a wise farmer knows when to stop plowing and when to plant, as those who thresh different types of grain know what tools to employ and how to preserve the valuable part of the crop undam-aged, so God's "strange work" of judgment will ultimately result in salvation for Israel (28:23–29; cf. vv. 5–6). The point is made unmis-takably clear in the LXX, which offers words of comfort to Israel in v. 26, "And you shall be instructed by the judgment of your God, and you shall rejoice,"[63] and in v. 28, "For I will not be angry with you forever, neither shall the voice of my bitter wrath (cf. v. 21) trample you down."[64]

---

[61] Paul quotes Isaiah 28:11–12 in 1 Cor 14:21. See Lanier 1991; Hays 1997:238–40; Stanley 1992b:197–205; Koch 1986:111–12, 122–23, 151, 268–69; Wilk 1998:27–30, 49–50, 105–112, 179–82, 226–30.

[62] Paul quotes this verse, in combination with Isa 8:14, in Rom 9:33; 10:11 (see pp. 126–57 and 168–70).

[63] καὶ παιδευθήσῃ κρίματι θεοῦ σου καὶ εὐφρανθήσῃ. In contrast, MT speaks of the farmer being well-instructed by God: ויסרו למשפט אלהיו יורנו.

[64] οὐ γὰρ εἰς τὸν αἰῶνα ἐγὼ ὑμῖν ὀργισθήσομαι, οὐδὲ φωνὴ τῆς πικρίας μου καταπατήσει ὑμᾶς. In MT, v. 28 is a continuation of the parable, and not a direct promise of hope to Israel: כי לא לנצח אדוש ידושנו והמם גלגל עגלתו ופרשיו לא ידקנו. The LXX appears to have abandoned the parable form in order to make its mean-ing plain. This technique is characteristic of the LXX translators (Swete 1914:325–29) as well as of the targumists (Stenning 1949:xiii–xiv) and reflects the translator's deci-sion to transmit the meaning of the source text at the expense of its form.

Isaiah 29 continues with an oracle of woe against Jerusalem
(29:1–4)[65] followed by a promise of salvation through God's judgment on the nations that war against Zion (29:5–8). But Judah's
leaders perceive nothing of God's purposes. Isaiah's explanation is
that God himself has made his people drunk with a spirit of stupor
and has blinded their eyes, rendering prophets and leaders insensible so that they do not comprehend God's work of judgment and
salvation (29:9–12 LXX; cf. 6:9–10).[66] The prophet characterizes the
nation's adherence to God as mere pretense, an empty devotion to
human commandments and teachings, while their hearts are far from
God. As a result, God has vowed to confound their wisdom and
understanding (29:13–14).[67] The deep irony expressed in 29:15–16
centers on the fact that the people act as though their wisdom is
greater than God's: "Who has seen us and who knows us or what
we are doing?" (29:15).[68] Their foolishness is exposed by Isaiah with
a series of rhetorical questions:

> Will you not be considered as the clay of the potter? The thing formed
> doesn't say to the one who formed it, "You did not make me," does
> it? The thing made doesn't say to its maker, "You did not make me
> wisely," does it?
>
> οὐχ ὡς ὁ πηλὸς τοῦ κεραμέως λογισθήσεσθε; μὴ ἐρεῖ τὸ πλάσμα τῷ
> πλάσαντι· οὐ σύ με ἔπλασας; ἢ τὸ ποίημα τῷ ποιήσαντι· οὐ συνετῶς με
> ἐποίησας; (Isaiah 29:16).

"Μὴ γένοιτο," Isaiah might have answered, had he spoken Greek.
The wisdom of the creator is far greater than that of the creature.
God himself will save his people in a way they do not expect;[69] he

---

[65] Although 29:1 appears to address Ariel as a city in Moab (cf. 2 Kdgms 23:20;
1 Chr 11:22), the "double translation" in v. 7 of צביה וכל אריאל על הצבאים clearly
identifies Ariel with Jerusalem: ὅσοι ἐπεστράτευσαν ἐπὶ Αριηλ, καὶ πάντες οἱ στρα-
τευσάμενοι ἐπὶ Ιερουσαλημ.

[66] Paul quotes in Romans 11:8 what appears to be a conflation of Isaiah 29:10
with Isaiah 6:9–10 and Deuteronomy 29:4 LXX (see pp. 240–57).

[67] Paul quotes Isaiah 29:14 in 1 Corinthians 1:19 (discussions in Koch 1986:152–53,
273–75; Stanley 1992b:185–86; Wilk 1998:18–19, 44–45, 101–105, 160–62, 246–48,
393). Interestingly, the LXX apparently takes this verse as a prediction of the exile:
διὰ τοῦτο ἰδοὺ προσθήσω τοῦ μεταθεῖναι τὸν λαὸν τοῦτον καὶ μεταθήσω αὐτοὺς καὶ
ἀπολῶ τὴν σοφίαν τῶν σοφῶν καὶ τὴν σύνεσιν τῶν συνετῶν κρύψω.

[68] τίς ἡμᾶς ἑώρακεν καὶ τίς ἡμᾶς γνώσεται ἢ ἃ ἡμεῖς ποιοῦμεν;

[69] The reference in Isaiah 29:17 to the imminent destruction of "Lebanon" may
well have been understood by many in Paul's time as a prophecy of the downfall
of Rome. Note the interpretation in 4QpIsaᵃ (4Q161) frgs. 8–10 3.6–13 of "Lebanon"
(Isaiah 10:34) as נדולי ביד יתנ[נו] אשר כתיאים[ה] (line 12 [cf. line 7]; similarly, 4QSM

himself will remove their deafness and blindness (29:17–24).[70] Even those who, out of misguided trust in their own wisdom, oppose God's wisdom will be transformed: "Those who go astray in spirit will learn understanding, and those who grumble will learn to obey" (29:24 LXX).[71] The challenge of the clay to the potter, then, is part of a larger narrative in Isaiah 28–29 in which Israel doubts God's wisdom and power to save them, trusting instead in their own schemes for deliverance.

Isaiah 45:9 likewise involves a disputation between God and his people; once again the issue revolves around Israel's persistent questioning of God's wisdom and power to save them. Having received lavish promises of return from exile and restoration to the land, Israel balks at God's announcement that his chosen instrument to effect this deliverance is Cyrus, his "anointed one" (44:21–45:8).[72] The absurdity of Israel's challenge to God's wisdom is likened to the clay questioning the potter's skill or to a child objecting to its own conception and birth:

μὴ ἐρεῖ ὁ πηλὸς τῷ κεραμεῖ· τί ποιεῖς, ὅτι οὐκ ἐργάζῃ οὐδὲ ἔχεις χεῖρας; ὁ λέγων τῷ πατρί· τί γεννήσεις; καὶ τῇ μητρί· τί ὠδινήσεις; (Isa 45:9–10).

These outrageous images are matched only by the spectacle of Israel audaciously questioning God's plan for his own children or commanding him concerning how he ought to deal with the work of his hands:

ἐρωτήσατέ με περὶ τῶν υἱῶν μου καὶ περὶ τῶν θυγατέρων μου καὶ περὶ τῶν ἔργων τῶν χειρῶν μου ἐντείλασθέ μοι (v. 11).[73]

Indeed, Isaiah frames Israel's challenge to God with strident affirmations of God's incomparable wisdom and power as the creator of the universe:

[4Q285], frg. 5). Discussion of these texts may be found in Vermes 1992:88–89; Rosenthal 1969–70:29; Brooke 1991; cf. Lichtenberger 1996. R. P. Gordon (1990:93) notes that the identification of "Lebanon" as the nations and/or their kings is found several times in Targum Jonathan (1 Kgs 7:2; 10:17, 21; Isa 2:13; Ezek 31:15 and Zech 11:1; cf. 4QpNah [4Q169] frgs. 1–2 2.3–9). On midrashic interpretations of "Lebanon," see further Vermes 1973:26–39.

[70] Isaiah 29:18 thus reverses the judgment imposed by God in 29:9–12.

[71] καὶ γνώσονται οἱ τῷ πνεύματι πλανώμενοι σύνεσιν, οἱ δὲ γογγύζοντες μαθήσονται ὑπακούειν.

[72] See further R. Watts 1990.

[73] In context, these words should be taken as ironic commands.

> I, the Lord, am God, and there is none besides: I am the one who formed light and made darkness, the one who makes peace and creates evil: I, the Lord, am God, the one who does all these things (Isaiah 45:6b–7).

> I made the earth and human beings upon it; by my hand I established the heavens, I commanded all the stars (Isaiah 45:12).[74]

Acknowledgment of God's wisdom and power as creator should suffice to quell Israel's suspicions that God is somehow not acting wisely or justly in delivering them in his chosen way.[75] But Isaiah's designation of God specifically as *Israel's* maker further deepens the irony that his people should object to his redemptive plan. The repeated designation of God as the "maker" (ὁ πλάσας/ὁ πλάσσων) of Israel in 44:21–45:8 (and often in Isaiah 40–55)[76] reveals an important connotation of the metaphor of God as potter in Isaiah. Rather than representing a childish attempt by God to assert his sovereignty over his people through brute force ("It's *my* pot and I can smash it if I want to"), the affirmation that God is Israel's maker implies a far more intimate relationship. This is the language of election.[77] Indeed, Isaiah 45:10 offers a metaphor parallel to that of potter and clay in which God is likened to Israel's father and mother. Similarly, 45:11 God calls Israel not only "the works of my hands," but also "my sons and my daughters." For God to call himself Israel's maker is to reaffirm that they belong specially to him, and he to them.

In Isaiah 40–55, the reminder that God has formed Israel consistently leads to the promise that he will redeem them from their present distress, that judgment will not be God's final word.[78] This

---

[74] On the relationship of creation and redemption in Deutero Isaiah, see Fishbane 1979a, 1985:354–57; Harner 1967; Ludwig 1973; von Rad 1965, 1966; Rendtorff 1954, 1993b; Stuhlmueller 1959, 1967, 1970.

[75] Note the promises in 45:8, 13 that God's raising up Cyrus will result in δικαιοσύνη (justice/salvation).

[76] ὁ πλάσας, Isaiah 27:11; 43:1; 44:2 (all parallel to ὁ ποιήσας); 49:5; ὁ πλάσσων, 44:24; cf. ἔπλασα: 43:7; 44:21. Also note the related designations of God as creator or maker of Israel: ὁ κτίσας σε, 45:8; ἐγὼ κτίζω σε [= Ἰσραηλ], 54.16—where the sense is quite different from MT; ὁ ποιήσας, 27:11; 43:1; 44:2; 51:13; ὁ ποιῶν, 54:5; ἐποίησα, 43:7; 46:4. These terms are concentrated almost exclusively in Isaiah 40–55, with 27:11 representing the only occurrence of this image outside 40–55.

[77] In 44:2, the reminder to Israel that God is the one who "made you" and "formed you from the womb" is sandwiched between two designations of Israel as "the one whom I have chosen," ὅν ἐξελεξάμην, 44:1, 3.

[78] The statement that God is Israel's maker occurs as part of an announcement of redemption in 43:1, 7; 44:2, 212, 24; 45:8; 46:4; 54:5, 16. In 51:13, Israel's fear

promise of redemption clearly informs the image of God as potter in 45:9. Leading up to the potter/clay metaphor in 45:9 are three separate occurrences of the motif of God as Israel's maker. The announcement of deliverance through Cyrus is introduced by the affirmation that because God has made Israel his servant, he will take away their sins. Israel is called to remember these things and turn to God so that he may redeem them (44:21–23). In 44:24, God as "maker" stands parallel to God as "redeemer" (ὁ λυτρούμενος) of Israel;[79] these titles become the basis for the announcement that Jerusalem will be rebuilt and Judah inhabited through the agency of Cyrus. Finally, 44:24–45:8 emphasizes God's status as sole creator of the universe, celebrates his intent to bring mercy and righteousness on the earth, and powerfully reiterates God's special relationship to Israel: "I am the Lord, the one who created you."[80]

It is this affirmation, "I created you," that immediately precedes the potter/clay analogy. In likening Israel's questioning of God to a lump of clay challenging the potter who is forming it, Isaiah 45:9 trades on this wider theme of God as maker and redeemer of his people. God, as Israel's creator, has graciously and freely chosen them to be his own, thereby committing himself to redeem them; it is all the more shocking, then, that Israel responds by questioning God's wisdom and justice in employing Cyrus as their deliverer. Israel has not only stepped out of their proper place as creature in relation to the Creator, they have forgotten the special care that God has promised to show for the people he himself has formed.[81]

Paul's use of the potter/clay metaphor in the unfolding argument of Romans 9–11 is remarkably congruent with the way this figure

---

of other gods is especially tragic since it means that they have forgotten "the God who made" them. Quite striking is 27:11, where it is said that judgment will come on Israel *despite* the fact that God has made them; the people's sin is thus portrayed as especially heinous. By chapter 40, the tone of the book has clearly changed, and God reaffirms his creation of Israel in order to reassure them that he will not fail to save them.

[79] Note also 54:5, where ὁ ποιῶν σε is parallel to ὁ ῥυσάμενός σε. Cf. 43:1, where the characterization of God as the one who "made" Israel is followed by the call not to fear ὅτι ἐλυτρωσάμην σε.

[80] ἐγώ εἰμι κύριος ὁ κτίσας σε (45:8).

[81] In contrast, note the use of the potter/clay metaphor in the penitential prayer in Isaiah 64:8–9, where it functions (in parallel with father/child terminology) to remind *God* of his special relationship to Israel and his concomitant responsibility to care for and redeem them: "And now, Lord, you are our father, and we are clay, all of us the work of your hands. Do not be exceedingly angry with us. . . ."

functions in Isaiah 29:26/45:9. Both of these Isaianic passages set
the clay's challenge to the potter in the context of Israel's confrontation with God over his chosen means of redemption. Israel is
portrayed as blind and deaf, doubting God's wisdom and resisting
his appointed means of redemption, either by relying on their own
schemes for salvation or by questioning God's plan of deliverance.
Paul's contention in Romans 9–11 is that contemporary Israel is
similarly engaged in a struggle with God's redemptive plan, questioning God's wisdom and justice (Rom 9:19–20) and preferring
"their own righteousness" (Rom 10:3) to the righteousness from God
that has come through Christ. Even if they would have been lost
on most hearers of Romans, these deep thematic correspondences
suggest how Paul himself may have found these passages from Isaiah
useful in his reflection on Israel's current plight.

Disputing God's Wisdom: Isaiah 29:16/45:9 in 1qs

Evidence from a contemporaneous interpreter of Isaiah lends weight
to my hypothesis. The allusion to Isaiah 29:16/45:9 in 1QS 11.22
provides an intriguing parallel to the way I have suggested Paul reads
the potter/clay passages as disputes concerning the wisdom of God's
plan for delivering his people. In the hymn of praise that concludes
1QS (10.9–11.22), the psalmist, acutely aware of his own sinfulness,
proclaims that his hope for salvation rests in God's mercy and faithfulness alone. The poet repeatedly grounds his hope in "the righteousness (צדקה, צדק) of God."[82] "God's righteousness" in this hymn
signifies not only that God, unlike humans, unfailingly does what is
right, but, more specifically, that God remains faithful to redeem
those who trust in him and choose his ways.[83] For the psalmist,
"righteousness" belongs not only with "judgment" (משפט) and "truth"
(אמת), but also with "mercy" (חסדים), "compassion" (רחמים), "goodness" (טוב), "glory" (תפארת), and "salvation" (ישועה; 1QS 11.11–15).

---

[82] צדקות אל (10.23); צדקת אל (10.25; 11.12); צדקותו (11.3); מקור צדקתו (11.5; cf.
11.6, צדקה); מקור צדקת אמתו (11.14); צדקתו (11.14); צדק (11.15). Cf. 10.11, ולאל
אומר צדקי. The English translation of 1QS quoted here is that of Charlesworth
1994:49, with minor modifications. The Hebrew text (edited by E. Qimron) is taken
from the same volume.
[83] On the range of meanings of צדק, צדקה, and related words in the Dead Sea
Scrolls, see E. P. Sanders 1977:305–12 (cf. Przybylski 1980:13–38). Ziesler (1972:85–103)
also emphasizes the covenantal associations of this word group.

Because God is righteous, he can be trusted to do what is right.[84] More specifically, because God is righteous, he mercifully delivers those who have no other hope than him. At this point at least, the poet of the Community Rule and Isaiah (and Paul!) dwell in the same world of thought.

Most significant for my purposes, however, is the link the poet forges between God's righteousness and God's wisdom[85] and the manner in which this connection illuminates his use of Isaiah 29:16/45:9. Twin affirmations of God's power and wisdom in contrast to human frailty and corruption (11.9–11, 17–22) frame both the psalmist's confession that the righteousness and mercy of God are his only hope for salvation and his consequent prayer to God for deliverance (11.11–17). This literary device sets the question of God's faithfulness to deliver those who trust in him firmly within the larger problem of God's sovereignty over creation. Indeed, the psalmist's plea for deliverance is founded on his conviction that, because God is the one who directs all things by his wisdom and might, he can be counted on to save his people (11.17–18). God alone is the source of the psalmist's hope, for there is no human being who can even begin to grasp God's ways, let alone dispute his plans (11.18–20).

This insight is driven home in the poem's last line by means of a rhetorical question crafted from Isaiah 29:16/45:9:

> What can clay [חמר] and that which is shaped (by) hand [ויצר יד] dispute; and what does it understand in order to give counsel? (11.22).[86]

As taken up in 1QS 11.22b, the potter/clay imagery of Isaiah not only suggests the humble and transient nature of human beings (cf. 11.20–22) but also the utter futility of such a creature daring to question God's plans. It is this latter point that receives the greatest emphasis. The final question of the poem,"What does [clay]

---

[84] Note the contrast in 1QS 10.23 between God's "righteousness" (צדקות) and human "unfaithfulness" (מעל).

[85] Though he never uses the word חכמה, the poet extols God's "knowledge" (דעת, 11.11), "design" (מחשבת, 11.11, 19), "will" (רצון, 11.17, 18), "counsel" (עצה, 11.18; cf. לעצת, 11.22), "mysteries" (רזין, 11.19), "wonders" (נפלאות, 11.19), and "wondrous mysteries" (רזי פלא, 11.5). In addition, he acknowledges God as the source of "knowledge" (דעת, 10.12; 11.3, 6, 15, 17–18).

[86] מה ישיב חמר ויוצר יד ולעצת מה יבין. I have altered the last line of Charlesworth's translation to bring out more clearly the force of the infinitive + ל, לעצת. As I understand it, the point is not the clay's inability to *understand* God's counsel but rather its lack of wisdom to *give* counsel to God.

understand in order to give counsel?" (ולעצת מה יבין) recalls the concluding stich of Isaiah 29:16, לא הבין, but with a crucial twist. Rather
than reading these words as a quotation of the clay's challenge to
the potter, the psalmist interprets them as a statement of the obtuseness of the vessel. The absurdity of the clay questioning the potter's
wisdom or presuming to advise him[87] is further highlighted by the
fact that the language of the allusion—"dispute" (ישיב), "counsel"
(לעצת)—recalls the previous declaration in 1QS 11.18: "There is no
one besides you to dispute your counsel" (להשיב על עצתכה). Tied
together by this *inclusio*, the entire section in which the poet sets
his allusion to Isaiah 29:16/45:9 (1QS 11.17–22) grounds the hope
of divine deliverance in the incomprehensible wisdom and power
of God.

The allusion to Isaiah 29:16/45:9 in 1QS 11.22 functions in its
new setting in a manner remarkably similar to the role the potter/
clay metaphor plays within its wider context in Isaiah. Both texts
understand the question of the clay to be a brazen challenge to
God's wisdom, power, and faithfulness to deliver his people. The
significance of this observation for my study of Paul's reading of
Isaiah 29:16/45:9 must be stated carefully. I am not claiming that
Paul's interpretation of the Isaianic potter/clay passages depends on
1QS or even on a shared exegetical tradition. Rather, 1QS 11.22,
written by someone who was a near contemporary of Paul both
chronologically and culturally, provides an important touchstone for
testing the plausibility of my contention that Paul reads Isaiah
29:16/45:9 in a manner sensitive to the wider literary and theological contexts of these passages.

In drawing on the imagery of potter and clay, Paul has clearly
tapped into a widely-used metaphor with a broad range of possible
resonances. While his language betrays a close connection with the
text of Isaiah, it is likely that Paul knew of further reflexes of the
metaphor as witnessed in other prophetic and wisdom texts.[88] Numerous
echoes evoked by Paul's use of the potter and clay metaphor whis-

---

[87] There may be a faint echo here of Isaiah 40:13 as well: ואיש עצתו יודיענו, "and
who, as his counselor, has instructed him (= יהוה)?" 1QIsaᵃ, as corrected by a second hand, reads: ואיש עצתו יודיענה, "and who, as his counselor, has made her
(= רוח יהוה) known?" (cf. Brownlee 1964:220–21).

[88] For a discussion of the function of this imagery in Jeremiah 18:1–12, Sirach
13:33, Wisdom 15:7, and *T. Naphtali* 2:2–5, see Wagner 1999b:81–87. It is also
probable that the metaphor had currency outside written texts, as part of Paul's
larger cultural heritage. Interestingly, the targumists connect Jeremiah's oracle concerning the potter and clay with Isaiah 29:16 by employing in Jeremiah 18:6b and

per suggestively around the edges of his argument. God's wisdom as creator; his sovereign freedom to form vessels for honor and vessels for dishonor alike; his unique commitment to Israel, which yet does not preclude his judging the nation or redeeming it as he sees fit— all of these themes come together in Romans 9:20–21 in the service of Paul's larger apology for God's justice and mercy in the present time. Paul is not engaged in speculation about God's power over creation in the abstract; rather, he is wrestling here, as throughout Romans, with God's particular relationship to Israel as their creator and with the paradox of Israel's continued resistance to God's purposes for them.

VESSELS OF WRATH/VESSELS OF MERCY:
ROMANS 9:22–24

Having established (to his own satisfaction, at least) God's right to have mercy on whom he will and to harden whom he will (v. 18), to form "vessels for dishonor" as well as "vessels for honor" (v. 21), Paul returns to the question of God's purpose in doing so. Not surprisingly, in what follows, Paul will turn once again to Isaiah in order to interpret God's dealings with Israel. Paul's appeal to Isaiah in Romans 9:27–29 is incomprehensible, however, apart from the verses that lead up to it. As a result, following the flow of Paul's argument will prove crucial to my reading of the Isaianic material in Romans 9:27–29.

Paul's understanding of the apparent hardening of Israel in the present is shaped by his reading of the exodus narrative as a paradigm for God's redemptive activity. In Romans 9:22–23, Paul weaves

---

Isaiah 29:16a an identical phrase that is itself composed of elements drawn from the Hebrew texts of both verses: "Behold, as the clay in the hand of the potter, so are you regarded before me":

Isa 29:16a	יחשׁב	היצר	כחמר אם
Tg. Isa 29:16a/ Tg. Jer 18:6b	קדמי חשׁיבין כין_אתון	ביד פהרא	כמא דטינא הא
Jer 18:6:b	בידי בית ישׂראל	כן-אתם היוצר	ביד הנה כחמר

We saw earlier that a similar type of pastiche translation binds together Tg. Isaiah 29:16 and 45:9 (pp. 60–62). Through the use of these composite phrases, the targumists establish a three-way relationship among these potter-clay texts, with 29:16 as the middle term, suggesting that Isaiah 29:16, Isaiah 45:9, and Jeremiah 18:6 have been read in light of one another.

together key terminology and concepts from both Exodus 33:19 (cited in Romans 9:15) and Exodus 9:16 (cited in Romans 9:17). In fact, the two ὅπως clauses of Exodus 9:16/Romans 9:17 decisively shape Paul's argument in vv. 22–23.[89]

Paul draws on the first ὅπως clause of Exodus 9:16 to explain God's purpose in creating "vessels for dishonor": "Wanting to show his wrath and to make his power known," he says, "God with great patience bore with vessels of wrath, prepared for destruction" (v. 22). These words can be heard as a loose commentary on the exodus narratives, in which God bears patiently with Pharaoh's obduracy and duplicity. God's deferral of wrath provides the occasion for a series of ten plagues that vividly demonstrate his power over the Egyptians and their gods. The LXX version of Exodus 9:16 emphasizes this point, reading "for this reason *you have been preserved*, that I might show my power through you . . ." (ἕνεκεν τούτου διετηρήθης).[90] Indeed, in the book of Exodus and throughout Israel's scriptures, the exodus from Egypt, including the plagues and the victory over Pharaoh's army at the Sea, is regarded as a unique display of God's power.[91]

The idea that God patiently defers his wrath against foreign oppressors of Israel also provides a way for later generations to understand God's apparent failure to deliver Israel from foreign powers. The prophets announce that Assyria and Babylon, instruments used by God to discipline Israel, will themselves be destroyed once they have done their work.[92] Until then, God bears with these sinful nations

---

[89] See Figure 2.4 below. Cf. the similar analysis of Dahl (1977d:145).

[90] Even if Paul did not know this variant (see n. 36 above), he could have drawn the same conclusion from his reading of the narrative as a whole.

[91] For the exodus as the work of God's strength, see Exod 7:4 (δύναμις); 15:6, 13; 32:11 (ἰσχύς). Note also χείρ (3:20; 7:4; 9:3, 15; 15:6, 9); χεὶρ κραταιά (3:19; 6:1; 13:3, 9, 14, 16); ἡ δεξιά (15:6, 12); βραχίων ὑψηλός (6:1, 6; 32:11; cf. τὸ μέγεθος βραχίονός σου, 15:16). Echoes of this tradition are found in Isaiah (e.g., Isa 50:2; 51:9–11). See further Fishbane 1979b; 1985:358–68.

[92] The phrase σκεύη ὀργῆς is used in Jeremiah 27:25 LXX [MT 50:25] and in Symmachus' version of Isaiah 13:5 to describe the nations that serve as "instruments for the working of God's wrath" against Babylon (710 attributes the reading in Isaiah 13:5 to Aquila as well, perhaps erroneously: nowhere else does Aquila translate זעם with ὀργή; cf. Reider 1966:175, 275). Dahl (1977d:145 n. 28) suggests that ἤνεγκεν in Romans 9:22 alludes to Jer 27:25 (ἐξήνεγκεν τὰ σκεύη ὀργῆς αὐτοῦ). Also relevant is Isaiah 10:5–19: In the hand of the Assyrians is ἡ ῥάβδος τοῦ θυμοῦ μου καὶ ὀργῆς (10:5). Later these foreign oppressors are figuratively described as God's axe, saw, staff, and stick (10:15). Similar ideas about the nations as tools of God's wrath are found in Deuteronomy 32, 1 Samuel 4–6, and Habakkuk 1–2.

in order to use them for the purpose of refining and redeeming his own people. In this respect, Paul's argument in Romans 9:22–23 is thoroughly grounded in a traditional Jewish conception of how God works in history to make even ungodly nations serve his purposes.

In line with this tradition, Paul's emphasis falls on the fact that God's ultimate design is the redemption of his elect people. In Romans 9:23, he reads the second ὅπως clause of Exodus 9:16 as a statement of God's intent for the "vessels for honor" that he has formed: ". . . and in order to make known the riches of his glory for vessels of mercy, which he prepared beforehand for glory."

Figure 2.4: Exodus 9:16 (Rom 9:17) and Romans 9:22–23

Exodus 9:16 (Rom 9:17)	Romans 9:22–23
εἰς αὐτὸ τοῦτο ἐξήγειρά σε ὅπως ἐνδείξωμαι ἐν σοὶ τὴν δύναμίν μου	²²εἰ δὲ θέλων ὁ θεὸς ἐνδείξασσαι τὴν ὀργὴν καὶ γνωρίσαι τὸ δυνατὸν αὐτοῦ . . .
καὶ ὅπως διαγγελῇ τὸ ὄνομά μου ἐν πάσῃ τῇ γῇ	²³καὶ ἵνα γνωρίσῃ τὸν πλοῦτον τῆς δόξης αὐτοῦ ἐπὶ σκεύη ἐλέους ἃ προητοίμασεν εἰς δόξαν

As Figure 2.4 shows, there are no exact verbal correspondences between Exodus 9:16 and Paul's formulation in Romans 9:23, but there is an important connection of thought that arises both from Paul's understanding of the larger context of Exodus 9:16 and from his use of Exodus 33:19 and context to interpret Exodus 9:16.[93] An important theme of the early chapters of Exodus is the revelation of God's name. Twice Exodus narrates the self-disclosure of God's name to Moses (3:1–22; 6:2–8); in both cases God's name is bound up with his promise to rescue Israel from Egypt and to establish them as his very own people. Thus, it is through the act of redemption

---

The parallel phrase, "vessels of mercy" (Rom 9:23), may suggest that "vessels of wrath" in Romans 9:22 should be understood to mean "vessels that are themselves the objects of God's wrath" rather than "vessels that work God's wrath." However, in light of the prophetic view that God will punish the nations he uses to discipline Israel, one does not need to choose between the two meanings for "vessels of wrath" (so, rightly, Hanson 1981).

[93] See above, pp. 52–55.

74 CHAPTER TWO

that the meaning of God's name is truly known.[94] Significantly,
Pharaoh's first response to Moses' message from the Lord is, "Who
is he that I should obey his voice . . .? I don't know the Lord" (Exod
5:2). The plagues that follow are repeatedly described as revelations
of God's name both to the Egyptians[95] and to Israel.[96] In context,
then, the statement in Exodus 9:16 that God intends for his name
to be proclaimed in all the earth means that God determines to be
known as the one who has powerfully redeemed his people from
Egypt.

These observations help to explain how Paul could understand
the proclamation of God's name in Exodus 9:16 to consist in the
revelation of "the riches of his glory toward vessels of mercy whom
he prepared for glory." Paul's interpretive logic becomes even clearer,
however, once it is realized that he has read Exodus 9:16 through
the lens of Exodus 33:19 (cited earlier in Romans 9:15 in connection with Exodus 9:16). In Exodus 33:18, Moses requests a vison of
God's glory. God promises to reveal his glory to Moses and says
that in doing so he will call out his name before Moses. This name,
"the Lord," is immediately specified further by the phrase, "I will
have mercy on whom I have mercy, and I will have compassion on
whom I have compassion" (33:19).[97] This connection between God's
name, God's glory,[98] and God's character as one who shows mercy
by redeeming his people is reprised a few verses later in the actual
narration of God's self-revelation to Moses (Exodus 34:6–7). With
the help of Exodus 33:19 and context, then, Paul reads God's
announcement to Pharaoh in Exodus 9:16 as a paradigmatic statement of God's design both in hardening and in showing mercy to
those he has created, a design whose ultimate goal is the revelation
of God's glory through his redemption of his people.

But who are these "vessels of wrath" and "vessels of mercy" about
whom Paul is speaking? Paul moves quickly to identify the "vessels

---

[94] See further Seitz 1999.
[95] Exod 7:5, 17; 8:10; 9:14. Similarly, the defeat of Pharaoh's army at the Sea
is regarded as a revelation of God's name: Exod 14:4, 17–18.
[96] Exod 6:7–8; 10:1–2.
[97] In Hebrew, this self-description resembles that offered in Exodus 3:14. The
similarity is lost in Greek due to the translation of אהיה אשר אהיה by ὁ ὤν in Exodus
3:14 LXX.
[98] For "glory" in parallel with God's "name," see also Ps 101:16 LXX; Isa 24:15;
66:19.

of mercy" with "us"—both Jews and Gentiles—and to support this identification with citations from scripture. More problematic, however, is the identification of "vessels of wrath." It might be supposed in light of the argument of Romans 9 to this point that the category "vessels of wrath" includes the majority of Israel, who have not obeyed the gospel. Insofar as Paul has made a distinction between "those from Israel" and "Israel" and between "children" of Abraham and Abraham's "seed," equating the former at least implicitly with Ishmael, Esau, and Pharaoh, such an identification is not unthinkable. Working against it, however, is Paul's stubborn insistence that Israel as a whole has *not* been rejected, despite their present obduracy. If Paul totters on the brink of identifying disobedient Israel with "vessels of wrath prepared for destruction," he never actually plunges over this precipice. In fact, Paul argues passionately in chapter 11 that God remains committed to his covenant people and that God will soon redeem "all Israel." Already in Romans 9 there have been strong undercurrents tugging Paul's logic in this direction, as echoes of the wider scriptural settings of the texts Paul has cited linger around the edges of his argument, whispering insistently of God's promises to save his people.[99]

All this suggests that Paul's comments in Romans 9:22–23 might be read in light of the direction his argument ultimately takes in Romans 11.[100] But is such a reading possible? The sentence that begins in 9:22 with the particle εἰ, lacking an apodosis,[101] is commonly translated as a hypothetical question ("What if . . ."). Paul's syntax is taken as a case of aposiopesis, and the apodosis is understood to be something along the lines of, "God has every right to

---

[99] The quotations in Romans 9:25–29 continue to function this way as well. See Hays 1989:66, 158; so also Dahl 1977d:146–47.

[100] Framing the issue this way presumes, of course, that Paul's argument in Romans 9–11 was thought through to a great extent before he started dictating it (see pp. 43–44).

[101] The atttempt of A. Nygren (1949:372) to find the apodosis in v. 23 (with the main verb of the clause carried over from the protasis) has not received widespread support, but it may deserve further consideration. Nygren's reading clearly brings out Paul's emphasis on God's mercy:

> If God, to show his wrath and make known his power, in his longsuffering, had patience with the vessels of wrath which were ready for destruction, so [he also had it] in order to make known the riches of his glory for the vessels of mercy, which he has prepared beforehand for glory (1949:372).

Although he analyzes 9:23 as an instance of anacoluthon, Fitzmyer's interpretation of the sentence is much the same as Nygren's (1993:570).

do so," or—more laconically—"so what?"[102] This way of reading the
sentence coheres with Paul's emphasis on God's authority in 9:21
(as well as with the tone of his rather curt dismissal of the imaginary
interlocutor's objection in 9:19–20). However, I have already noted
the influence of the structure and phraseology of Exodus 9:16 and
33:19 on Romans 9:22–23. If Paul is indeed interpreting these texts
in the protasis of the condition, then the first half of the protasis,
"If . . . God endured with great patience vessels of wrath prepared
for destruction . . .," refers first of all to God's longsuffering endurance
of Pharaoh's rebelliousness. And rather than making a timeless theological statement in 9:22–23, Paul is drawing a *comparison* between
how God acted at the exodus and how he is presently at work calling out a people for himself. In his haste to identify the "vessels of
mercy" (9:24), Paul simply fails to complete the comparison.[103]

Since the second term of the comparison is left unexpressed, it is
unclear just how Paul would have finished it. One possibility is that
he intended to draw a simple analogy between Pharaoh and unbelieving Israel: just as God bore with Pharaoh for a time and then
annihilated him, so God is presently bearing with Israel's disobedience, but will soon bring judgment on the obdurate and destroy
them. Against this interpretation is the fact that in Romans 11 Paul
explicitly denies that God has forsaken his people (11:1–2) or that
Israel has stumbled so as to "fall" (11:11). Rather, the present "insensibility" that has come on a portion of Israel is only temporary; at
the right time, God himself will come to deliver "all Israel" (11:25–27).
Although Paul does call unbelieving Israelites "enemies with respect
to the gospel," he is quick to add that this is "for the sake of you
[Gentiles]" and to avow that "with respect to election, Israel is
beloved on account of the fathers" (Rom 11:28). It is thus difficult
to read the strongly predestinarian language of Romans 9:22 as a
reference to Israel in its present, but temporary, state of unbelief.

A second possibility for finishing the comparison comports more
closely with Paul's argument in Romans 9–11 as a whole. This is

---

[102] As in John 6:62; Acts 23:9 (cf. BDF §482; Robertson 1934:1203). This type
of aposiopesis is found in classical texts: "When the conclusion is *it is well* (καλῶς
ἔχει) or the like, it is often omitted" (Smyth 1956, §2352a; italics original). However,
Cranfield notes that in every case of such an ellipsis, "the sense has to be understood from the context" (1979:493).

[103] Romans 9:22–24 would then be an instance of anacoluthon rather than of
aposiopesis, at least as BDF defines the latter term (cf. BDF §467).

to read vv. 22–23 as the first term of an (uncompleted) *qal-vaḥomer* argument, "If . . . God endured with great patience vessels of wrath prepared for destruction . . .," and to supply the apodosis: "*how much more will he bear patiently with Israel, the people whom he has chosen as his own inheritance [cf. 11:1], until their time of hardening is over?*" Understood in this way, the thought would be similar to that stated in 11:11–16, 25–32: Israel's loss has resulted in the Gentiles' gain (in order to show the riches of God's glory for vessels of mercy . . ., 9:23); Israel's full inclusion will be more glorious still (the unstated apodosis of 9:22–23). On this reading, unbelieving Israel is not finally identified with the "vessels of wrath," but rather contrasted with them; since God's calling of Israel is irrevocable (11:29), Israel too will become a "vessel of mercy" (11:31).

Admittedly, this is to import into Romans 9:22–24 convictions that Paul does not state clearly until chapter 11,[104] or, in other words, to read these verses in light of what follows rather than in light of what Paul has already said.[105] In favor of this reading is that it finds in the total argument of Romans 9–11 a certain measure of coherence, in that Paul's insistence in Romans 11 on the continuing election of Israel is adumbrated already in Romans 9.[106] This reading is also consistent with my contention that the echoes of the scriptural texts Paul cites in chapters 9–11—texts that speak of God's commitment to save his people Israel—combine to form a counter-

---

[104] Though note that Romans 2:4 has spoken of God's μακροθυμία as having the purpose of leading its objects to repentance, so that perhaps the predestinarian tone of 9:22, "prepared for destruction" need not be heard as an irrevocable decree of reprobation.

[105] Cf. Cranfield's comment on 9:22–23a (1979:497):
The relations between God's patient enduring of vessels of wrath, the showing of His wrath, and the manifestation of the wealth of His glory upon vessels of mercy, will be illuminated by 9.30–11.36. We shall see there that the ultimate purpose of that patience of God toward rebellious Israel which is depicted in 10.21 includes the salvation of rebellious Israel itself (chapter 11).

[106] P. Ellingworth notes the important transitional function of these verses in Romans 9–11:
In the wider setting of Paul's argument, 9,22 may perhaps be compared to a creaking hinge. It is a hinge, in that it forms the transition between the previous argument about God's freedom and the following argument about his mercy. . . . The hinge of 9,22 creaks, quite apart from the grammatical incoherences of the passage, because the relation between God's freedom and his mercy has not yet reached mature expression: the two are held together provisionally by the concept of μακροθυμία (cf. 2,4). Later, especially in 11,25–32, the relation is (not, indeed, logically defined, but) theologically more fully expressed (1978:401).

melody that gradually swells in volume until it becomes the dominant strain of chapter 11.

Whether this reading of Romans 9:22–24 be deemed persuasive
or not, it is clear that Paul, having drawn both on the analogy of
God as potter and on the exodus narrative to explain the outworking of God's redemptive purposes in the present time, fails to identify explicitly the current analogue to Pharaoh and other "vessels of
wrath" from the past. The reader is left hanging, and the present
status of unbelieving Israel remains for the time being an open question.[107] Instead, Paul quickly turns his attention to the recipients of
God's free mercy—those who have been called from among both
Jews and Gentiles.

CALLED FROM AMONG JEWS AND GENTILES:
HOSEA AND ISAIAH IN ROMANS 9:24–29

In returning to the language of "calling" in Romans 9:24, Paul creates a neat *inclusio* with the preliminary stages of his argument (Rom
9:7, 12), driving home once again the point that God's free mercy
is the sole ground for inheriting the blessing promised to Abraham
and his descendants.[108] A string of intertwined quotations from Hosea
and Isaiah supports Paul's claim that, in Christ, God has called Jews
and Gentiles together to be his people (Rom 9:25–29).[109] The apostle names both prophets, thus distinguishing between the two different
sources of his quotations.[110] However, the fact that Paul actually
conflates the words of Hosea and Isaiah in Romans 9:27 suggests

---

[107] For a perceptive analysis of Paul's use of suspense in Romans and its implications for reading the letter, see Cosgrove 1996.

[108] καλέω: 9:24, 25, 26; see 9:7, 12. This *inclusio* is strengthened by the reappearance in the quotations in Romans 9:25–29 of two other key terms seen earlier in the chapter, "sons" and "seed" (υἱοί: 9:26, 27; see 9:9; σπέρμα: 9:29; see
9:7 [2x], 8).

[109] Hos 2:23 LXX (2:25 MT) in Rom 9:25; Hos 1:10 LXX (2:1 MT) in Rom
9:26; Isa 10:22–23 in Rom 9:27–28; Isa 1:9 in Rom 9:29.

[110] Romans 9:25: ὡς καὶ ἐν τῷ Ὡσηὲ λέγει; Romans 9:27: Ἡσαΐας δὲ κράζει
ὑπὲρ τοῦ Ἰσραήλ; Romans 9:29: καὶ καθὼς προείρηκεν Ἡσαΐας. Note that, of the
two, only Isaiah appears as an actual person who is speaking: "Isaiah cries out."
Romans 9:25 introduces the following citation with the phrase, "as indeed he (it)
says in Hosea," thereby distinguishing Hosea as a book from the speaker (either
Scripture [cf. Rom 9:17] or God). In contrast, Isaiah will remain an important
"character" in the subsequent discussion (Rom 9:29; 10:16, 20; 15:12).

that he read these prophetic texts in light of one another.[111] The significance of this observation for understanding Paul's interpretive strategy will become apparent as we proceed.[112]

Romans 9:24 explicitly states the claim in support of which Paul adduces the following testimony from Hosea and Isaiah. Consequently, v. 24 sets the parameters within which these citations are to be interpreted. Paul's formulation in v. 24 betrays his Israel-centered worldview: "[God] called us—*not only* from among the Jews. . . ." Here Paul simply assumes Israel's continuing election; he feels no need to argue the point that Jews are among those called by God. The accent of v. 24 falls on the surprising inclusion of Gentiles along with Jews as "vessels of mercy": "[God] called us—not only from among the Jews *but also from among the Gentiles.*"[113]

It is common to analyze Paul's argument in Romans 9:25–29 as taking up the terminology of 9:24 in chiastic fashion, with Hosea's words addressed to the Gentiles and Isaiah's to the Jews. But Paul's appropriation of these scriptural testimonies is far more complex and multilayered than this neat analysis might suggest. To appreciate the full force of this point, it will be necessary to attend both to the interpretive logic by means of which Paul intertwines these prophetic oracles and also to the significant ways in which the larger scriptural contexts of these citations shape Paul's own argument in Romans 9.

A Surprising Reversal: Hosea 2:23/1:10 in Romans 9:25–26

Getting the Gentiles "In": Hosea in Romans

Paul's first quotation combines elements from Hosea 2:23 LXX (2:25 MT) and Hosea 1:10b LXX (2:1b MT). By making several crucial alterations to these verses, Paul weaves his citation firmly into the argumentative fabric of Romans 9. At the same time, these modifications accentuate his interpretation of Hosea's words as God's promise to call a people not only from among the Jews, but also from among the Gentiles.

---

[111] Recall the Targum's similar strategy with regard to Isaiah 29:16/45:9, as well as my argument that Paul similarly conflated Isaiah 29:16/45:9 in his appropriation of the potter/clay metaphor (see pp. 59–62).

[112] See especially pp. 89–92 below.

[113] In light of Paul's re-use of the two purpose clauses of Exodus 9:16 in Romans 9:22–23, v. 24 may be heard as a reinterpretation of the phrase, "in all the earth" (Exod 9:16c).

Figure 2.5: Hosea 2:23 LXX and Hosea 1:10b LXX in Romans 9:25–26

Hosea 2:23 LXX	Romans 9:25–26	Hosea 1:10b LXX
καί ἐλεήσω τὴν Οὐκ ἠλεημένην καὶ ἐρῶ τῷ Οὐ λαῷ μου· λαός μου εἶ σύ [καὶ ἐλεήσω τὴν Οὐκ ἠλεημένην]	²⁵ὡς καὶ ἐν τῷ Ὡσηὲ λέγει· καλέσω τὸν οὐ λαόν μου λαόν μου καὶ τὴν οὐκ ἠγαπημένην ἠγαπημένην· ²⁶καὶ ἔσται ἐν τῷ τόπῳ οὗ ἐὰν κληθήσονται· οὐ λαός μου, ἐκεῖ κληθήσονται υἱοὶ θεοῦ ζῶντος	καὶ ἔσται ἐν τῷ τόπῳ οὗ ἐρρέθη αὐτοῖς· οὐ λαός μου ὑμεῖς, κληθήσονται καὶ αὐτοὶ υἱοὶ θεοῦ ζῶντος

Hos 2:25 MT: וְזֵרַעְתִּיהָ לִּי בָּאָרֶץ וְרִחַמְתִּי אֶת־לֹא רֻחָמָה וְאָמַרְתִּי לְלֹא־עַמִּי עַמִּי־אַתָּה וְהוּא יֹאמַר אֱלֹהָי

Hos 2:1b MT: וְהָיָה בִּמְקוֹם אֲשֶׁר־יֵאָמֵר לָהֶם לֹא־עַמִּי אַתֶּם יֵאָמֵר לָהֶם בְּנֵי אֵל־חָי

In citing Hosea 2:23 Paul omits the initial καί and changes the verb ἐρῶ to καλέσω (Figure 2.5).[114] In so doing, he forges a strong link with the second half of his composite quotation (κληθήσονται [2x], Hos 1:10b/Rom 9:26). The verb καλέω also recalls both the immediate context of his argument (οὓς καὶ ἐκάλεσεν, v. 24) and the earlier occurrences of this verb as a term for divine election in Romans 9:7, 12. Additional prominence is given καλέω by Paul's omission of ἐλεέω in the next clause.[115] The result is that the single verb καλέω

---

[114] Paul's reading καλέω in Hosea 2:23 (Rom 9:25) has no support in the Greek textual tradition, although it is an appropriate translation for the underlying Hebrew אמר (cf. the LXX at Hosea 1:10, where אמר is rendered by both ἐρῶ and καλέω). In view of the close correspondence of Paul's citation elsewhere to the wording of the LXX, however, it is not necessary to suppose that Paul used anything but a Greek text of Hosea. His lexical choice in citing Hosea 2:23 may have been influenced not only by the wording of Hosea 1:10, but also by the use of καλέω in Hosea 1:4, 6, 9, where the prophet's children are first named.

[115] This is almost certainly a Pauline omission: not only does it lack support in

now governs both halves of the sentence in Romans 9:25. Paul further modifies the syntax to suit his choice of καλέω, turning direct speech into indirect speech in the first clause[116] and creating a parallel construction in the second clause by the addition of the objective complement ἠγαπημένην, signifying the change of name.[117]

More strikingly, Paul reverses the order of clauses in the original, placing the reference to οὐ λαός μου first.[118] This alteration of the text is particularly significant, for it is by means of the appellation "not my people" that Paul gains hermeneutical leverage over the text, wresting from it the astounding conclusion that the promise of return from exile and national restoration for Israel in Hosea is really an announcement of God's embrace of *Gentiles* as his own people. Paul hyper-extends the logic of reversal inherent in Hosea's salvation oracles, with the result that the scope of "not my people" now embraces not only covenant-breaking Israel, but also the Gentiles, who once were excluded from God's covenant altogether.

It is more difficult to be sure that Paul himself is responsible for using ἀγαπάω rather than ἐλεέω in Romans 9:25b. Although the participle of ἐλεέω might actually have served Paul better by providing a further verbal link to the theme of God's mercy, which runs as a leitmotif throughout Romans 9–11,[119] the external evidence suggests that the reading ἠγαπημένην should be traced to Paul, rather than to his *Vorlage*.[120]

---

the manuscript traditions of either LXX or MT, it also coheres with the other alterations Paul has made to the syntax of his *Vorlage*.

[116] As a result of this, "not my people" shifts from dative (indirect object) to accusative (direct object), "my people" changes from nominative (predicate complement in direct speech) to accusative (objective complement in indirect speech), and the subject and verb ("you are") used in direct speech drop out.

[117] These changes in syntax, including the addition of the second ἠγαπημένην, have no support in the manuscript traditions of LXX or MT.

[118] This order of clauses is found also in the quotation of Hosea 1:6, 9 in 1 Peter 2:10. The switch makes sense in both instances because of each author's focus on the new status of Gentile Christians as the people of God. Textual evidence for common use of a written "testimony" collection seems slight in this case—1 Peter has ἠλεημένοι, while Paul has the distinctive reading ἠγαπημένη. The transposition of elements, even entire lines, in quotations or allusions is a phenomenon attested in a number of biblical and Second Temple texts. See further the study of P. C. Beentjes (1982), who suggests that many such inversions are rhetorically motivated.

[119] E.g., 9:15 (2x), 16, 23; 11:30, 31, 32. Note especially 11:30, "Just as you [Gentiles] were once disobedient to God, but now you have been shown mercy. . . ."

[120] *Contra* Stanley 1992b:112. A number of witnesses substitute ἠγαπημένη for ἠλεημένη in several of the following occurrences of the name: 1:6, 8; 2:1; 2:23 (2x), but only V 407 and the Coptic versions do so in every occurrence (though at 1:6

If this hypothesis is correct, and the variant originated with Paul, what might be the interpretive payoff of Paul's lexical choice? In Romans 9:24–26, those whom God has "called," who formerly were "not loved", are given a new name, "beloved." This transformation of "not loved" to "beloved" recalls Paul's earlier discussion of Jacob and Esau (τὸν Ἰακὼβ ἠγάπησα, τὸν δὲ Ἠσαῦ ἐμίσησα),[121] where ἀγαπάω belongs to a cluster of terms (including καλέω) within the semantic field of election (Rom 9:11–12; cf. 11:28). By echoing the earlier allusion to the Jacob/Esau story in this way, Hosea's words intimate a reversal of the divine exclusion of Esau (= the Gentiles) from God's mercy.[122]

The shocking nature of this interpretive move should not be minimized. Notwithstanding Paul's earlier use of the Jacob/Esau narrative to argue for God's freedom to exclude some from "Israel," the intertextual relationship established here between this story of Israel's ancestor (as Paul has retold it) and Hosea's oracle suggests that God's mercy is powerful enough to reverse even the logic of exclusion that

---

the Achmimic is the only Coptic version to support ἠγαπημένη). The verb רחם, however, is normally translated by these same witnesses with ἐλεέω elsewhere in Hosea (1:6, 7; 2:4; 14:4). The only exceptions are the variants at 1:6 (Coptic reads ἀγαπάω [Μϵ]) and 2:23 (B, V, 407, Coptic, and a few other witnesses read ἀγαπήσω τὴν οὐκ ἠγαπημένην, where the choice of verb is most likely influenced by the choice of ἠγαπημένη for the following participle). Significantly, in the entire LXX, ἀγαπάω translates רחם only in Zech 10:6, Isa 60:10, and Ps 17:1. Consequently, the instances of the variant reading ἠγαπημένη in the textual tradition of Hosea LXX are probably best understood as the result of assimilation to Paul's version of the name of Hosea's daughter rather than as the source of his wording.

[121] Malachi 1:2–3 in Romans 9:13.

[122] In light of the venerable Jewish interpretive tradition that regards Esau/Edom as a cipher for the nations, "Esau I have hated" could well have been heard by Paul and his contemporaries as a statement of the exclusion of the Gentiles in general. H. W. Wolff observes, "In the exilic and postexilic period Edom is elsewhere too the very personification of Israel's enemies in the world of the nations: Isa 34:2, 5ff.; Ezek 36:5; Joel 3:2, 12, 19; Amos 9:12" (Wolff 1986:63). Wolff argues that in the final arrangement of the Book of the Twelve in the Hebrew canon, "Edom" serves to link together thematically the books of Joel, Amos, and Obadiah. As a bridge between Joel and Obadiah, Amos 9:(11–)12 picks up the reference to Edom in Joel 3:19 and connects Edom with Jerusalem and with the nations in general, a connection then elaborated further in Obadiah 16–21 (1986:17). Interestingly, Tg. Isaiah 34:5–9 appears to identify Edom with Rome (רומי). "Edom" frequently serves as a code name for Rome in the Talmud and in Aphrahat (M. P. Weitzman 1999:64–65). This metonymic use of Edom to stand for the nations appears to be behind the exegetical transformation of Amos 9:12 in the LXX (cf. Acts 15:17), where אדם is revocalized אָדָם and דרש is read in place of ירש (cf. the use of דרש in Isa 11:10) to produce the rendering: ὅπως ἂν ἐκζητήσωσιν οἱ κατάλοιποι τῶν ἀνθρώπων τὸν κύριον (see further de Waard 1965:25 and Braun 1977).

is often the corollary of belief in divine election. In this way, Paul subverts any conception of Israel's election that would deny the blessing of Abraham to Gentiles *qua* Gentiles.[123]

Paul's strong "misreading" of this prophetic oracle coheres with his interpretive practices elsewhere in Romans, for he consistently seizes on such negative appellations as "not my people ... not loved" as hermeneutical warrants for finding references to Gentiles in scripture. The Gentiles are those "not pursuing righteousness" (9:30; cf. Isa 51:1), "no nation at all ... a nation without understanding" (10:19; Deut 32:21), "those not seeking me ... those not asking for me" (10:20; Isaiah 65:1), "those to whom it was not announced concerning him ... those who have not heard" (15:21; Isaiah 52:15).[124] This bold move reveals one of Paul's fundamental interpretive strategies: Israel's scriptures are read as testimony to the surprising reversal wrought by God's grace, in which those apparently outside the scope of God's mercy are included among the people God has redeemed for himself.[125] Paul's hermeneutic of reversal is far-ranging and profound in its effects, necessitating a radical rereading of texts foundational to Israel's understanding of election. Projected through this interpretive lens, Hosea's moving depiction of God's passionate commitment to his people Israel is refracted and refocused into a prophecy of the "riches of God's glory" now showered upon *Gentile* "vessels of mercy."

---

[123] This is not to suggest that first-century Jews thought all Gentiles were excluded from God's love and concern; such was clearly not the case (see Donaldson 1997:51–78 for an extensive analysis of the complexity and variety of early Jewish views on the present and future fate of Gentiles). Nevertheless, Israel's sense of being chosen by God clearly marked Gentiles out as being "other," and various means of conversion were in place for those Gentiles who wanted to cross over the boundary and join God's people. Paul is not challenging the idea of election or erasing all boundaries between the people of God and those outside; rather, he is redefining the basis on which Jew and Gentile come to be part of God's people. His problem arises in relating this new basis to the election of Israel, which Paul insists has not been superseded.

[124] Paul's statement in Romans 4:17 that Abraham believed God's promise that he would be the father of many nations because he had faith in God ". . . who calls into being the things that are not" (καλοῦντος τὰ μὴ ὄντα ὡς ὄντα) may similarly allude to the inclusion of Gentiles among Abraham's descendants ἐκ πίστεως. Compare the characterization of the Corinthian (Gentile) Christians as τὰ μὴ ὄντα in 1 Cor 1:28.

[125] For a clear statement of this conviction outside a context specifically dealing with division between Jew and Gentile, see 1 Cor 1:26–31 and the discussion in Wagner 1998b.

Paul's modifications to the second half of this combined citation (Hos 1:10b LXX) provide further evidence that he understands Hosea's oracles to envision not only the redemption of Israel, but also the calling of "some from among the Gentiles." His quotation reads (with 𝔓⁴⁶ F G a b d* Peshitta): καὶ ἔσται ἐν τῷ τόπῳ οὗ ἐὰν κληθήσονται οὐ λαός μου ἐκεῖ κληθήσονται υἱοὶ θεοῦ ζῶντος.[126] It is highly probable that Paul himself is the source of these variations from Hosea 1:10b LXX.[127] The use of κληθήσονται in place of ἐρρέθη

---

[126] F G (but not 𝔓⁴⁶ and the Old Latin MSS) have ὑμεῖς after μου. 𝔓⁴⁶ reads ἐάν, although some witnesses read ἄν (𝔓⁴⁶ reads ἐάν where other witnesses have ἄν also in 1 Cor 11:34). The use of ἐάν for ἄν after relative pronouns is a common feature not only in the LXX and NT, but also in the papyri (particularly in the first two centuries CE). See further Deissmann 1903:201–205; Mayser 1906:152; BDF §107; MHT 1:42–43. On the character of 𝔓⁴⁶, see Royse 1981. The reading of Hosea in 𝔓⁴⁶ et al. finds no support in the manuscript tradition of the Septuagint; neither does it clearly represent an adaptation toward the MT. Given the probability that a later scribe would be more likely to harmonize a quotation to the LXX than to introduce a variant (J. K. Elliott 1995:326; Metzger 1992:197–98), it would appear that the majority reading is clearly secondary and that 𝔓⁴⁶ and its Western allies preserve the original text of Romans 9:26a (so also Zuntz 1953:174; cf. Kilpatrick 1980:66).

[127] Although recognizing the evidence in favor of the text of 𝔓⁴⁶ et al., Stanley rejects it for two reasons: he argues that οὗ (ἐ)άν is rare in Hellenistic Greek, and he appeals to the "awkwardness of the Future Indicative that accompanies it" (1992b:113 n. 86). Neither of these considerations is persuasive, however. First, the adverbial construction οὗ (ἐ)άν is *not* uncommon in Hellenistic Greek. In addition to appearing elsewhere in Paul (1 Cor 16:6), it is found just over fifty times in the Septuagint; about one third of these occurrences are variations on the expression (πᾶς) τόπος οὗ (ἐ)άν . . . (ἐκεῖ). Two examples stand out as particularly close structural parallels to Paul's adapted citation of Hosea: (1) Numbers 9:17: καὶ ἐν τῷ τόπῳ οὗ ἂν ἔστη ἡ νεφέλη ἐκεῖ παρενέβαλον οἱ υἱοὶ Ισραηλ; (2) Nehemiah 4:14: ἐν τόπῳ οὗ ἐὰν ἀκούσητε τὴν φωνὴν τῆς κερατίνης ἐκεῖ συναχθήσεσθε πρὸς ἡμᾶς. The construction is further attested in Clement of Rome (1 Cl 54.2), in inscriptions, and above all in papyri (for abbreviations, see Oates et al. 1992). In addition to references cited in BDAG (s.v. οὗ 1.b) and MM (464), note P. Lond., Vol. 2, 220.2.23–24: ἡ δὲ χεὶρ ἤδε κυρία ἔστω πανταχοῦ οὗ ἐὰν ἐπιφέρηται. Variations on this formula, all using οὗ (ἐ)άν, occur dozens of times in the papyri (e.g., BGU, Vol. 3, 988.2.13; BGU, Vol. 6, 1264.30; 1265.21–22; 1274.14–15; 1275.20). Another common clause also employs οὗ (ἐ)άν: ἀποδότοσαν . . . ἐν τῇ κώμῃ οὗ ἐάν συντάσσωσι (PSI, Corr. I, 1150.35; cf. BGU, Vol. 6, 1275.15; 1277.19; BGU, Vol. 10, 1943.11; 1944.10; PSI, Vol. 10, 1098.23–24; P. Yale, Vol. 1, 51, FrB, 11). Note also P. Hib, Vol. 2, 197: κ]αι τὸν χῶρον οὗ ἂν ἦι. Second, while it is true that the future indicative rarely follows (ἐ)άν, this construction is attested for both classical and hellenistic Greek (in the NT, see Mark 8:35; Acts 7:7). One of the characteristics of hellenistic Greek vis-à-vis classical dialects is the increasing "intermixture of the future indicative and the aorist subjunctive" (BDF §363), with the result that "the connection between the mood and the conjunction (e.g. subj. after ἄν) is becoming less determined" (MHT 3:107 n. 1). See further Goodwin 1892, §197; LSJ [s.v.

is explicable entirely on internal grounds. Paul has already substituted a form of καλέω for ἐρῶ in 9:25b; the identical move here produces a three-fold repetition of this key *Stichwort* in 9:24–25, binding the two excerpts from Hosea to one another and to the affirmation that they are adduced to support. In keeping with the change of verb, Paul also changes direct discourse into indirect (as above in Rom 9:25/Hos 2:23), thus obviating the need for αὐτοῖς and ὑμεῖς.

Particularly important for Paul's use of this quotation is the shift from ἐν τῷ τόπῳ οὗ to ἐν τῷ τόπῳ οὗ ἐάν . . . ἐκεῖ. While the first phrase might be taken to refer to a specific place and time (as in Hosea's reference to God's punishment of Israel),[128] Paul's οὗ ἐάν transforms Hosea's oracle into a more expansive prophecy embracing the Gentiles as well as Israel. *Wherever* people are estranged from God, there God is now actively calling out a people for himself.[129] Paul's rereading of this text locates the realization of Hosea's prophecy within the context of his own mission, which he understands as a call to preach the gospel wherever Christ is not named (Rom 15:18–24). Indeed, his choice of the future form κληθήσονται lends a heightened sense of expectation to the oracle: Hosea's vision will certainly come to pass.[130] In fact, Paul claims, it is *already* a reality in the community—composed of both Jews and Gentiles—that God has now called into being through the apostolic mission (Rom 9:24).

ἄν, A.I.2b]; Radermacher 1925:173–74; Mayser 1926:285; Robertson 1934:958–59, 1421; BDF §380 [3]; §371 [2]; MHT 3:116. See also Moorhouse 1946, 1959; Macleod 1956; Hulton 1957. That ὅς (ἐ)άν followed by the future is relatively rare would actually appear to *favor* the hypothesis that 𝔓⁴⁶ preserves the original reading; rather than creating a new reading by introducing a fairly uncommon construction, scribes would be more likely to smooth out the syntax here by assimilating the quotation to the LXX.

[128] Cf. W. D. Davies 1974:196.

[129] Although the reading ἐκεῖ in Hosea 1:10b LXX is attested by a wide variety of MSS, including the important Alexandrian uncial A, it probably represents assimilation to Paul's quotation (though Koch's explanation [1986:54, 174] that this variant is the result of an inner-Greek development cannot be ruled out). If original to LXX, ἐκεῖ may reflect the translator's attempt at a clear rendering of the Hebrew idiom (cf. the parallel move made in the Peshitta, ܬܡܢ) rather than use of a *Vorlage* that varied here from the text preserved in MT.

[130] Porter observes, "Where a choice is offered between the Subjunctive and the Future, the Future is the more heavily marked semantically" (1989:414). "In relative clauses, the Future has a sense of expectation missing from the Subjunctive" (415).

Is Israel "Out"? Hosea 2:23/1:10 in Context

It would be ironic, to say the least, if Paul's hermeneutic of reversal were taken to imply that Israel is now excluded from God's
mercy, as if in Paul's "misreading" of Hosea Gentiles have now
entirely replaced Jews as the recipients of the prophetic word of consolation. Such an explanation of Paul's scriptural argument in Romans
9:25–26 is precluded, not only by his vehement denial in Romans
11 that God has forsaken his people Israel, but also by the immediate context in which this quotation from Hosea is set. For in his
interpretive introduction to the citation, Paul *takes it for granted* that
"some from among the Jews" are called by God (Rom 9:24).[131] Thus,
in the context of Paul's argument in Romans 9:24–25, the appellations "my people" and "beloved" must also embrace those Jews who
have, as a result of God's call, experienced the restoration promised
in Hosea.[132] The following quotations from Isaiah (Rom 9:27–29)
confirm this interpretation, for they aver that a remnant of Israel
will be saved, a remnant whom Isaiah calls by a name that functions as a technical term in Romans 9 for those who inherit the
blessings of Abraham: "seed" (Rom 9:29; cf. 9:7, 8).

Moreover, the original setting in Hosea of the oracles Paul quotes
here exerts a strong pull on the logic of Paul's argument in Romans
9. The book of Hosea testifies to God's fierce determination to overcome his people's unfaithfulness and to restore them to himself. An
examination of the context of Hosea 1–2 will show how deeply Paul's
appropriation of Hosea 2:23 and 1:10 is rooted in the larger story
Hosea tells about Israel and their God.

The book of Hosea opens with the account of Hosea's marriage
and the offspring it produces. These children are given ominous-
sounding names whose meanings portend imminent doom for Israel.
The name "Jezreel" announces judgment on the bloodstained rul-
ing dynasty of Israel, while "Not Pitied" and "Not My People" signify God's renunciation of the covenant and his determination to
judge Israel's unfaithfulness. The name of Hosea's third child is par-

---

[131] Note E. P. Sanders's appeal to what is *assumed* in rabbinic debates as evidence of the Rabbis' foundational convictions (e.g., 1977:81–84, 182, 235–37, 420–21;
1990:171–72, 250–52, 320–22).
[132] Dahl comes to a similar conclusion (1977d:146): "The relative clause inserted
in Rom 9:24 is probably to be understood as a parenthesis. The quotations from
Hosea do not refer to the Gentiles alone, but to all the vessels of mercy."

ticularly striking, for it signifies the reversal of the ancient covenant formula epitomizing God's special relationship with Israel. The promise, "I will be your God and you will be my people,"[133] now is repudiated by the author of the covenant himself: "You are not my people and I am not your [God]."[134]

Following hard on the heels of this oracle proclaiming inexorable doom, however, comes an announcement of apparently unconditional redemption (Hosea 1:10–2:1 LXX [2:1–3 MT]):

> And it will happen that in the place where it was said to them, "You are not my people," even they will be called sons of the living God.
>
> καὶ ἔσται ἐν τῷ τόπῳ, οὗ ἐρρέθη αὐτοῖς οὐ λαός μου ὑμεῖς, κληθήσονται καὶ αὐτοὶ υἱοὶ θεοῦ ζῶντος (Hos 1:10b LXX).

This stark juxtaposition of oracles of doom and salvation, which has troubled interpreters both ancient and modern,[135] reveals a tension inherent in the prophet's message. Because of the covenant, God has determined to judge his people's sins.[136] Nevertheless, God remains faithful to his promises and will mercifully redeem and restore Israel to himself. Judah and Israel will be gathered together under one ruler, and "they will go up from the land" (1:11 LXX; 2:2 MT)[137] a phrase that may refer to the multiplication of the people[138] but that can also be understood as a reference to the return from exile. Targum Jonathan explicitly reads the text this way, glossing "the place" (2:1 MT [1:10 LXX]) as, "in the place to which they were exiled among the sons of the peoples,"[139] and translating the following verse, "and they shall go up out of the land of their exile."[140]

---

[133] ἔσομαι ὑμῶν θεὸς καὶ ὑμεῖς ἔσεσθέ μου λαός (Lev 26:12). Cf. Exod 6:7; 19:5–6; 23:22; Psa 49:7 LXX; Jer 7:23; 11:4; Ezek 36:28.

[134] ὑμεῖς οὐ λαός μου καὶ ἐγὼ οὔκ εἰμι ὑμῶν (Hos 1:9). Ziegler (1939a) capitalizes εἰμί suggesting that it be read as a name: "I am not your 'I am.'" This echo of Exod 3:14 would highlight the rupture of the covenant bond even more dramatically. For a similar suggestion, see Schildenberger 1959:191.

[135] Particularly since the message of judgment resumes immediately in 2:2 LXX (2:4 MT). See the brief history of interpretation in Macintosh 1997:33–35.

[136] Cf. Amos' startling words to Israel: "You only have I known of all the families of the earth—therefore I will punish you for all your iniquities" (Amos 3:2 NRSV).

[137] ἀναβήσονται ἐκ τῆς γῆς; וְעָלוּ מִן־הָאָרֶץ.

[138] Cf. Isa 11:1 LXX, where ἀναβαίνω = "shoot up" (of a plant). In this case, "the day of Jezreel" would be a play on the meaning of זרע, "to sow" (cf. Hosea 2:22–23 LXX [24–25 MT]). So also Harper 1905:247; Wolff 1974:28.

[139] בְּאַתְרָא דְאִיתְגְלִיאוּ לְבֵינֵי עַמְמַיָא.

[140] וְיִסְקוּן מֵאֲרַע גָלוּתְהוֹן.

Although in its present form Targum Jonathan dates from well after
the Second Temple Period, it is possible that the Targum preserves
a reading of Hosea in terms of national restoration after exile that
was current in Paul's day.[141]

The following oracles proclaiming certain judgment on Israel for
their idolatry (2:2–13 LXX [2:4–15 MT]) finally give way to the
depiction of Israel's restoration after judgment in terms of a new
exodus (2:14–23 LXX [16–25 MT]).[142] Once again God will lead
his people into the wilderness, there to renew his covenant with
them.[143] Portraying the Lord as the faithful husband of adulterous
Israel, Hosea announces that God will woo Israel back to himself
(2:14 LXX [2:16 MT]). God's faithfulness and mercy will overcome
his people's unfaithfulness. The thrice-repeated covenant formula
(2:19–20 LXX [21–22 MT]) resounds with terminology quite at
home in Paul's discussion of God's character in Romans:

> I will betrothe you to myself forever, and I will betrothe you to myself
> in *righteousness* and in *justice* and in *mercy* and in *compassion*, and I will
> betrothe you to myself in *faithfulness*, and you shall know the Lord.

> καὶ μνηστεύσομαί σε ἐμαυτῷ εἰς τὸν αἰῶνα καὶ μνηστεύσομαί σε ἐμαυτῷ
> ἐν <u>δικαιοσύνῃ</u> καὶ ἐν <u>κρίματι</u> καὶ ἐν <u>ἐλέει</u> καὶ ἐν <u>οἰκτιρμοῖς</u> καὶ
> μνηστεύσομαί σε ἐμαυτῷ ἐν <u>πίστει</u>, καὶ ἐπιγνώσῃ τὸν κύριον.[144]

The renaming of Hosea's children, signifying the restoration of God's
covenant with Israel, brings the announcement of redemption to
completion and closes the unit 1:2–2:23 LXX (1:2–2:25 MT). The
name "Jezreel" (v. 22 LXX [24 MT]) is taken up in Hebrew by a
play on words (lost in Greek) in the following verse (וזרעתיה/יזרעאל)
promising the multiplication of the nation in its own land. The reversal of the names "Not Pitied" and "Not My People" seals the renewal
of the covenant as Israel responds, "You are the Lord, my God"
(2:23 LXX). This recurrence of the three names in 2:22–23 LXX
(24–25 MT) forges a tight link with the earlier announcement of
salvation in 1:10–2:1 LXX (2:1–3 MT).

---

[141] Cf. *b. Pesaḥ* 88a for a similar reading of Hos 2:2 MT from a later time period.

[142] κατὰ τὰς ἡμέρας ἀναβάσεως αὐτῆς ἐκ γῆς Αἰγύπτου, 2:15.

[143] "Hosea has a doctrine of redemption by recapitulation. God will take Israel
back into the desert, and begin all over again" (Anderson and Freedman 1980:203).

[144] Note the echo of Exodus 34:6–7 (see the earlier discussion of the importance
of this passage for Paul, pp. 52–53).

In combining Hosea 2:23 and 1:10 LXX in his citation, Paul demonstrates a clear awareness of their function in the larger context of Hosea 1–2 as promises of the future redemption of Israel from judgment and exile.[145] If in his interpretation of Hosea Paul expands the category of the people of God to embrace (some) Gentiles, he does not thereby exclude (all) Jews. Rather, in light of the gospel, Paul radically reconceives the basis on which anyone, Jew or Gentile, experiences the redemption promised to Israel in their sacred writings. There is thus a fundamental *asymmetry* in the principle of "reversal" so foundational to Paul's conception of what God has done in Christ, an asymmetry rooted in Paul's vision of the ultimate purpose of God to shower mercy on all, Jew and Gentile alike. Although the climactic statement of this grand Pauline theme awaits the thundering finale of Romans 11:32–36, this foundational conviction serves as a crucial presupposition of Paul's reading of scripture throughout Romans 9–11.

Reading Hosea through Isaiah-Colored Glasses
Paul's appropriation of Hosea's oracles promising national restoration to Israel in the context of his argument in Romans 9 does give rise to a serious objection, however: How is Paul able to misread Hosea's lavish promise of restoration for *all* of Israel as a more restricted announcement of salvation for a portion of Israel—"us . . . *from among* the Jews" (Rom 9:24)? The obvious answer is that Paul's reinterpretation is motivated by the hard reality of the early mission to Israel, which has attracted a relatively small percentage of Jews to the Jesus movement. What is of principal interest here, however, is the way in which Paul finds support in Israel's scriptures for his belief that God has intended this outcome all along. From a hermeneutical point of view, the key to understanding Paul's radical rereading of LXX Hosea 1:10b; 2:23 is found in Romans 9:27b—ostensibly part of the first quotation from Isaiah—where Paul conflates Isaiah 10:22 and Hosea 1:10a LXX.[146]

---

[145] The reference in Hosea 3:5 LXX to "the end of days" would have further confirmed to a first century reader such as Paul that Hosea's words envisioned a time well beyond the prophet's own day. For Paul, that time has now arrived (1 Cor 10:11).

[146] The substantial verbal agreement between the two passages no doubt first suggested to Paul the connection between the texts. The similar contexts in which they

Figure 2.6: Isaiah 10:22a LXX and Hosea 1:10a LXX in Romans 9:27

Key: single underline   agreement between Rom 9:27 and Isa 10:22a
        double underline   agreement between Rom 9:27 and Hos 1:10b
        italic   agreement among all three columns

Isaiah 10:22a LXX	Romans 9:27	Hosea 1:10a LXX
καὶ ἐὰν γένηται ὁ λαὸς *Ισραηλ ὡς ἡ ἄμμος τῆς θαλάσσης* τὸ κατάλειμμα αὐτῶν σωθήσεται	Ἡσαίας δὲ κράζει ὑπὲρ τοῦ Ἰσραήλ· ἐὰν ᾖ ὁ ἀριθμὸς τῶν υἱῶν *Ισραηλ ὡς ἡ ἄμμος τῆς θαλάσσης* τὸ ὑπόλειμμα σωθήσεται	καὶ ἦν ὁ ἀριθμὸς τῶν υἱῶν *Ισραηλ ὡς ἡ ἄμμος τῆς θαλάσσης*

Isa 10:22a MT: כִּי אִם־יִהְיֶה עַמְּךָ יִשְׂרָאֵל כְּחוֹל הַיָּם

Hos 2:1a MT: וְהָיָה מִסְפַּר בְּנֵי־יִשְׂרָאֵל כְּחוֹל הַיָּם

In Romans 9:27, Paul reproduces verbatim all of the wording shared by Hosea 1:10a LXX and Isaiah 10:22a LXX apart from the initial καί (Figure 2.6). He follows Isaiah in retaining the conditional form of the oracle, but he adopts Hosea's fuller wording, ὁ ἀριθμὸς τῶν υἱῶν Ισραηλ.[147] This phrase evokes the words Paul cited from

---

are found—God's judgment on his rebellious people and his promise to redeem them despite their unfaithfulness—would have further strengthened the connection. While Stanley leaves open the possibility that Paul's conflation of Hosea 1:10b and Isaiah 10:22a may be due to a memory lapse, he inclines toward the view that Paul has a definite reason for the conflation (1992b:114–15). He cites as "an attractive explanation" Koch's hypothesis that Paul wants to avoid calling the whole of Israel λαός (as he has so named Gentiles in 9:25–26), reserving this term for the "remnant" (Koch 1986:167–68). This explanation falters on the fact that Paul elsewhere refers to *disobedient* Israel as λαός (10:21; 11:2). A more plausible explanation for Paul's choice of ἀριθμὸς τῶν υἱῶν over λαός would be his desire to forge a link with the words of the preceding quotation, υἱοὶ θεοῦ ζῶντος (Hos 1:10b/Rom 9:26). I suggest below a still deeper logic for Paul's conflation, however.

[147] *Contra* Lim 1991 (who is perhaps too eager to trace Paul's variants back to a Hebrew *Vorlage*), Paul's use of ᾖ rather than γένηται (Isa 10:22a) tells us nothing about the text(s) from which he drew his quotation. There is no reason to suppose that Paul's ἐὰν ᾖ "may be a direct translation of Isa 10.22[1QpIsa] [*sic*; read 4QpIsaᵃ (4Q161) frgs. 2–6 2.6] הי[ה] אם" (Lim 1991:156). As far as the LXX is concerned, wherever ἐὰν ᾖ occurs, it translates יהיה אם, never היה אם. The translation ἐὰν γένηται is even more common for יהיה אם than is ἐὰν ᾖ. However, the same translator can use both equivalents (Gen 28:20/34:15; Isa 1:18 [ἐὰν ὦσιν]/10:22). Interestingly, the one occurrence of היה אם in the LXX is translated ἐὰν γένηται (Deut 22:20).

Hosea 1:10b just previously—υἱοὶ θεοῦ ζῶντος (Rom 9:26)—but in an ironic fashion. As Isaiah laments, it is tragically *not* the case that all "the sons of Israel" are among the "sons of the living God" who are now experiencing the restoration promised to the remnant.[148]

The interpretation of Hosea 1:10a found in LXX would have facilitated Paul's restriction of Hosea's promises to a portion of Israel. In contrast to MT, which understands the comparison of "the number of the sons of Israel" to "the sand of the sea" as a promise of blessing and growth for the future, the LXX translator reads it as a description of Israel in the *past*, before God's judgment on the nation. Although MT has וְהָיָה (a common marker for the future in prophetic texts) twice in Hosea 2:1, the Greek text (LXX 1:10) translates only the second with its normal equivalent: καὶ ἔσται,[149] rendering the first with the imperfect, καὶ ἦν, instead.[150] This alternation of tenses does not appear to be due to a Hebrew *Vorlage* reading וַיְהִי;[151] it is more likely a deliberate interpretive move designed to connect 1:10a with the announcement of judgment in 1:9 and to drive a wedge between 1:10a and the announcement of restoration in 1:10b.[152] As a result, the "sand of the sea" (1:10a LXX [2:1a MT]) describes the blessing enjoyed by Israel *before* their rebellion and God's judgment on the nation. By implication, it is a much smaller group that remains after judgment to receive the promise of restoration (1:10b LXX [2:1b MT]; 2:23 LXX [2:25 MT]).[153]

Paul's move to limit the scope of Hosea 1:10 LXX to a portion of Israel would have been facilitated by his reading of Hosea's words in light of the similar oracle in Isaiah 10:22, where Isaiah draws a striking contrast between the present multitude of Israelites, "like the sand of the sea," and the far smaller remnant that will be saved

---

[148] Recall Paul's earlier distinction between "all from Israel/children of the flesh" and "Israel/children of promise/children of God" (Rom 9:6–9).

[149] Cf. Hosea LXX 1:5; 2:1b, 18, 23; 4:9. This translation is standard throughout the Book of the Twelve and in Isaiah.

[150] Elsewhere in Hosea LXX, καὶ ἦν renders וַיְהִי (7:11); cf. καὶ ἐγένοντο for וַיִּהְיוּ in Hos 9:10.

[151] 4QXII^g [4Q82] supports the reading of MT, וְהָיָה, in Hos 2:1. The possibility of a variant *Vorlage* cannot be completely ruled out, however. Cf. a similar variant in the text of Isaiah 10:22, where 4QpIsa^a (4Q161) frgs. 2–6 2.6 alone reads [ה]יֹהְ against יִהְיֶה found in 1QIsa^a; 4QpIsa^c (4Q163) frgs. 5, 6–7 2.14; MT.

[152] So Wolff 1974:24, note a. In line with MT, α′ and σ′ read ἔσται rather than ἦν.

[153] Though note the promise of *future growth* for restored Israel in Hosea 2:23 LXX (καὶ σπερῶ αὐτὴν ἐμαυτῷ ἐπὶ τῆς γῆς) and the similar implication of the play on "Jezreel" in Hebrew (Hosea 2:3, 24–25 MT).

through the judgment that is coming. Paul's conflation of these texts
in Romans 9:27b suggests that he has indeed interpreted Hosea 1:10;
2:23 and Isaiah 10:22–23 in tandem. Isaiah's oracle concerning the
remnant provides the lens through which Paul refracts the words of
Hosea as he projects them onto the screen of his contemporary situation and sees that Hosea's promise of restoration and blessing is
vouchsafed not to "all from Israel" (9:6), but rather to "us, whom
God has called, not only *from among* the Jews, but also from among
the Gentiles" (9:24).[154]

Judgment and Hope, Remnant and Seed:
Isaiah in Romans 9:27–29

In Romans 9:27, Paul calls a second witness to confirm the truth of
this remarkable claim: Ἡσαΐας δὲ κράζει ὑπὲρ τοῦ Ἰσραήλ. Through
Paul's rhetorical invocation, Isaiah himself stands before the Roman
congregations, testifying in his own voice together with Paul concerning God's plan for Israel. The weight of the prophet's "presence" enhances both the authority and the immediacy of his oracles
(Isa 10:22–23 and 1:9).[155]

The precise force of Isaiah's words in the context of Romans 9
has been the subject of much debate, however. Paul's brief introductory phrase in 9:27 presents the interpreter with two interrelated
problems. First, does the particle δέ signal a strong disjunction ("but,
in contrast") or does it function as a weaker adversative merely signalling a change of focus ("now, as for Israel")?[156] Second, does Isaiah

---

[154] Such a reading would likely have been the product of careful exegetical and
theological reflection prior to Paul's adaptation of these quotations to his argument
in Romans. The Peshitta (Gelston 1980) betrays an analogous understanding of
Hosea 1:10a that may also have been influenced by the parallel text in Isaiah 10:22.
It begins Hosea 1:10a with a plus relative to MT and LXX: "and if" (ܘܐܢ), a
reading found in its translation of Isaiah 10:22 (Heb, כִּי־אִם). This plus in Hosea
1:10a may be an attempt to connect 1:10 closely with 1:9 and so to read 1:10 as
a further oracle of doom (cf. Macintosh 1997:33 n. 12).

[155] See also Romans 9:29; 10:16; 10:20; 15:12. Note Paul's similar use of "Moses"
as a character who speaks the words of scripture (e.g., Rom 10:5, 19; so also
"David" in Rom 4:6; 11:9). Paul's emphasis on Isaiah as a person is not unparalleled. For "Isaiah" as a person who spoke the words of scripture, see also Matt
3:3; 4:14; 8:17; 12:17; 13:14; 15:7; John 1:23; 12:38, 39, 41; Acts 28:25; CD-A
4.13; 6.8; 11QMelch (11Q13) 2.15. For "Isaiah" as a name for the book, see Mark
1:2; 7:6; Luke 3:4; Acts 8:28, 30; 4QFlor (4Q174) frgs. 1–2 1.15; 4QTanh
(4Q176) frgs. 1–2 1.4; CD-A 7:10.

[156] Romans 10:19–21 illustrates well the importance of context in determining
the precise nuance to be given this conjunction. Δέ in 10:20 signals a change of

cry out with prophetic urgency *"concerning* Israel" or *"for the sake of/ on behalf of* Israel"?[157] Although in Hellenistic Greek the semantic range of ὑπέρ partially overlaps with that of περί, "concerning,"[158] ὑπέρ commonly has the sense, "on behalf of" or "for the sake of."[159] A common interpretation of Romans 9:27 takes κράζω ὑπέρ in the sense, "cry out concerning," and reads δέ as a strong adversative. As a result, Isaiah's words appear primarily as a message of judgment or condemnation for Israel. If, however, κράζω ὑπέρ is heard as, "cry out on behalf of," and δέ is understood to signal a shift in topic rather than a strong antithesis,[160] Paul's introduction raises the expectation in hearers that Isaiah's message will proclaim good news for Israel, just as Hosea's words have celebrated the inclusion of Gentiles in God's people.

Because Paul's words are so ambiguous,[161] the introductory formula is of little help by itself in determining the import of Isaiah's words. It must be admitted that both *"concerning* Israel" and *"for the sake of/on behalf of* Israel" are defensible translations of ὑπὲρ Ἰσραήλ.[162] The precise nuance ascribed to ὑπέρ in Romans 9:27a ultimately depends on one's sense of the function of the quotations themselves in the larger context of Romans 9. Interpretive debate must consequently focus on the quotations, with attention devoted both to their

---

speakers without suggesting that one stands in opposition to the other, while in 10:21, δέ marks what is clearly a more decisive contrast. In each case, it is the structure of the larger discourse, and not the meaning of the particle by itself, that determines how strong an adversative sense ought to be ascribed to δέ. Cf. Robertson, 1934:1184: "there is in the word no essential notion of antithesis or contrast." J. D. Denniston, commenting on the function of δέ in classical Greek, notes: "As a connective, δέ denotes either pure connexion, 'and', or contrast, 'but', with all that lies between" (1950:162).

[157] For κράζω introducing prophetic discourse, see John 1:15; 7:28, 37; 12:44. In Josephus *Ant.* 10.117, κράζω is parallel to κηρύσσω in a description of Jeremiah's prophetic activity during the siege of Jerusaelm. *Contra* Aageson (1983:216 n. 21; 256), κράζω itself does not connote a threat.

[158] Zerwick 1963:31. Later scribes often interchanged ὑπέρ and περί in NT mss (BDAG, s.v. ὑπέρ, 3). Zerwick notes that the use of ὑπέρ for περί "is in the NT practically restricted to Paul: Rom 9,27; 1 Cor 4,6; 2 Cor 5,12; 7,14; 8,23; 9,2; 12,5 etc." (1963:31; cf. BDF §231). I argue below that Romans 9:27 does not belong in this list, however.

[159] E.g., Rom 10:1 (contrast 11:2); 1 Cor 15:3; 2 Cor 5:14, 15, 20, 21.

[160] For which ἀλλά would be better suited.

[161] Contrast the judgments concerning ὑπέρ in this passage by BDAG (1031 s.v. ὑπέρ, 3: "oft. at the same time in the sense 'in the interest of' or 'in behalf of'") and by Riesenfeld 1972:224 ("with reference to").

[162] By no means, however, does κράζω ὑπέρ mean "cry out *against.*" Compare the very different senses of ἐντυγχάνω ὑπέρ τινος (intercede for, Rom 8:27, 34; Heb 7:25) and ἐντυγχάνω κατά τινος (Rom 11:2; 1 Macc 8:32; 10:61, 63; 11:25).

context in Paul's larger argument and to the reminiscences these citations evoke of their wider settings in Isaiah.

Isaiah's words are normally understood to function in Romans 9:27–29 as an announcement of judgment on Israel/the Jews, of whom "[only] a remnant will be saved."[163] Indeed, such a construal of Isaiah's testimony is unavoidable.[164] Paul's argument throughout Romans 9 has *presupposed* that because of the failure of many in Israel to embrace the gospel, they are now cut off from the blessings that God promised them (Rom 9:1–5). Paul has further claimed that not all "from Israel" actually constitute the "Israel" whom God has chosen, and he has identified the "vessels of mercy" called by God as "us . . . *from among* the Jews . . ." (9:24) rather than as the nation of Israel as a whole. In this context, Isaiah's dark words concerning the remnant left to Israel after a judgment of Sodom-like proportions stand in stark contrast to the apostle's appropriation of Hosea's oracle as a glowing announcement of God's embrace of Gentiles.

At the same time, to hear in Isaiah's words *only* the language of judgment is to remain insensible to the numerous echoes in these prophecies of the larger scriptural story that tells of God's stubborn fidelity to Israel. Within the book of Isaiah itself—particularly when read in a cultural context shaped by Second Temple Jewish stories of Israel's election by God—the language of "remnant" and "seed" resonates with promises of a future and a hope for Israel on the other side of judgment. There is thus a real tension in Paul's use of these two quotations from Isaiah, a tension that derives ultimately from their larger setting in Isaiah's story of a God who determines not only to judge, but also to redeem, his people. Paul does not resolve this tension until the end of Romans 11. It is crucial to recognize, however, that the solution at which Paul finally arrives is already present germinally in his quotations from Isaiah in Romans 9:27–29. To see how this is so, it will be necessary to attend first to the form in which Paul has cited these oracles and to the broader

---

[163] Cf. the ironic allusion in the curse of Deuteronomy 28:62 LXX to God's promise to Abraham that he will have innumerable descendants:
You will be left few in number, though you were numerous as the stars of heaven, for you did not listen to the voice of the Lord your God.
καὶ καταλειφθήσεσθε ἐν ἀριθμῷ βραχεῖ, ἀνθ᾽ ὧν ὅτι ἦτε ὡσεὶ τὰ ἄστρα τοῦ οὐρανοῦ εἰς πλῆθος, ὅτι οὐκ εἰσηκούσατε τῆς φωνῆς κυρίου τοῦ θεοῦ ὑμῶν.
[164] See the strong statement of this view by Käsemann, *Romans*, 274–76.

contexts in Isaiah from which they are drawn. Only then will it be possible to step back and appreciate the extent to which these texts shape Paul's argument in Romans 9–11 as a whole.

Isaiah 10:22–23: The Text of the Citation

As noted above, in Romans 9:27 Paul conflates the opening words of Isaiah 10:22 with the similar passage from Hosea 1:10a, producing a catch-word link "υἱοί" with the end of the preceding quotation (Rom 9:26/Hos 1:10b). Other features of Paul's quotation appear to be less significant for his particular interpretation of Isaiah 10:22–23 (see Fig. 2.7 below). For the LXX reading κατάλειμμα, Paul has the related term ὑπόλειμμα. While this variant may well derive from Paul

Figure 2.7: Isaiah 10:22–23, Hosea 1:10a, and Isaiah 28:22b in Romans 9:27b–28

Key: single underline   agreement between Rom 9:27b–28 and Isa 10:22–23
        double underline   agreement between Rom 9:27 and Hos 1:10b
                            or between Rom 9:28 and Isa 28:22b
        italic   agreement among all three columns

Isaiah 10:22–23 LXX	Romans 9:27–28	Hosea 1:10a LXX
²²καὶ <u>ἐὰν</u> γένηται ὁ λαὸς *Ισραηλ* *ὡς ἡ ἄμμος* *τῆς θαλάσσης* <u>τὸ</u> κατάλειμμα αὐτῶν σωθήσεται	²⁷Ἠσαΐας δὲ κράζει ὑπὲρ τοῦ Ἰσραήλ· <u>ἐὰν</u> ᾖ <u>ὁ ἀριθμὸς τῶν υἱῶν</u> *Ἰσραὴλ* *ὡς ἡ ἄμμος* *τῆς θαλάσσης,* <u>τὸ</u> ὑπόλειμμα σωθήσεται·	καὶ ἦν <u>ὁ ἀριθμὸς τῶν υἱῶν</u> *Ισραηλ* *ὡς ἡ ἄμμος* *τῆς θαλάσσης*
		Isaiah 28:22b LXX
<u>λόγον γὰρ συντελῶν</u> <u>καὶ συντέμνων</u> ἐν δικαιοσύνῃ ²³ὅτι λόγον συντετμημένον *ποιήσει* ὁ θεὸς ἐν τῇ οἰκουμένῃ ὅλῃ	²⁸<u>λόγον γὰρ συντελῶν</u> <u>καὶ συντέμνων</u> *ποιήσει* <u>κύριος</u> <u>ἐπὶ τῆς γῆς.</u>	διότι συντετελεσμένα καὶ συντετμημένα πράγματα ἤκουσα παρὰ <u>κυρίου</u> σαβαωθ ἃ *ποιήσει* <u>ἐπὶ</u> πᾶσαν τὴν <u>γῆν</u>

himself,[165] Paul's use of Isaiah 10:22–23 does not depend on the change in wording.[166]

Hos 2:1a MT: וְהָיָה מִסְפַּר בְּנֵי־יִשְׂרָאֵל כְּחוֹל הַיָּם

Isa 10:22–23 MT: ²²כִּי אִם־יִהְיֶה עַמְּךָ יִשְׂרָאֵל כְּחוֹל הַיָּם שְׁאָר יָשׁוּב בּוֹ
כִּלָּיוֹן חָרוּץ שׁוֹטֵף צְדָקָה
²³כִּי כָלָה וְנֶחֱרָצָה אֲדֹנָי יְהוִה צְבָאוֹת עֹשֶׂה בְּקֶרֶב כָּל־הָאָרֶץ

Isa 28:22b MT: כִּי־כָלָה וְנֶחֱרָצָה שָׁמַעְתִּי מֵאֵת אֲדֹנָי יְהוִה צְבָאוֹת
עַל־כָּל־הָאָרֶץ

Ziegler notes that variation in the initial preposition of a compound word is a fairly common occurence in the transmission-history of LXX Isaiah and often entails no significant change in meaning.[167] Paul's choice of ὑπόλειμμα is best explained by analogy with this type of lexical transformation. The omission of five words of Isaiah 10:22c–23a from Paul's quotation likewise appears to be fairly insignificant for his exegesis of the passage, although it does smooth out the rather choppy syntax of the LXX.[168] If unintentional, this gap may have arisen as a result of simple parablepsis due to homoioarcton (συντέμνων/συντετμημένον).[169]

---

[165] Although κατάλειμμα is found in 𝔓⁴⁶ ℵ¹ D F G Ψ 33. 1739*. 1881, it clearly represents a revision toward the univocal reading of the LXX textual tradition. NA²⁷ rightly follows ℵ* A B 81 1739ᶜ in adopting ὑπόλειμμα. Cf. Zuntz 1953:174; Koch 1986:142; Stanley 1992b:116.

[166] Paul rings the changes on the λείπω word-group in Romans 9–11: ὑπόλειμμα (9:27); ἐγκαταλείπω (9:29); ὑπολείπω (11:3); καταλείπω (11:4); λεῖμμα (11:5).

[167] Ziegler 1939a:68–69, 87, with examples. The noun κατάλειμμα occurs four times in Isaiah LXX (10:22; 14:22, 30; 37:30: ὑπόλειμμα is never a variant reading) and the adjective κατάλοιπος three (15:9; 21:17; 46:3), while forms of the related verb καταλείπω are fairly frequent (47x). In contrast, the noun ὑπόλειμμα never occurs in Isaiah LXX, while ὑπόλοιπος (11:11) and ὑπολείπω (4:3) are found only once each. The later versions α′ σ′ θ′ have τὸ ὑπόλειμμα for LXX τὸ καταλειφθὲν ὑπόλοιπον in Isaiah 11:11 (MT has שְׁאָר, as in Isa 10:22), and α′ has ὑπολείπω in 11:11 and 24:6, where LXX reads καταλείπω.

[168] In what are clearly secondary harmonizations, a number of NT manuscripts fill in some or all of the missing words (see Metzger 1994:462). No extant manuscript of LXX Isaiah lacks the words omitted by Paul.

[169] See Koch 1986:82–83; more cautiously, Stanley 1992b:116–17. The haplography hypothesis might be supported by the argument that because δικαιοσύνη fits well with Paul's use of the term in Romans to describe God's covenant faithfulness/saving power, Paul would have been unlikely to omit the word if he had read it in his *Vorlage*. However, speculation concerning what Paul "would have found useful" is an extremely tenuous basis on which to reconstruct his *Vorlage*.

Two other variants may more confidently be ascribed to Paul. The first, the use of κύριος for ὁ θεός in Romans 9:28/Isaiah 10:23, has little support in LXX manuscripts.[170] At the same time, κύριος helps to bind 10:23 to Paul's next quotation from Isaiah 1:9 (κύριος σαβαώθ, Rom 9:29), making it quite possible that the apostle himself is responsible for this lexical variant.[171] The second variant, the reading ἐπὶ τῆς γῆς for ἐν τῇ οἰκουμένῃ ὅλῃ, may also represent a Pauline modification of the text, for the latter phrase appears in all but one witness to LXX Isaiah.[172]

Taken together, these minor variants suggest that Paul has conflated Isaiah 10:22–23 with the strikingly similar oracle in Isaiah 28:22b (see Fig. 2.7 above). Although Paul's choice of κύριος could be explained solely as a technique for establishing a link with his next quotation (Isaiah 1:9/Romans 9:29), it is suggestive that 28:22b reads κύριος σαβαώθ, the exact appellation for the deity used in Isaiah 1:9.[173] Similarly, Paul's substitution of γῆ for οἰκουμένη might be seen merely as another example of lexical variation lacking exegetical significance,[174]

---

[170] The reading (ὁ) κύριος is found mainly in Hexaplaric manuscripts and is probably secondary.

[171] According to Stanley, Paul "normally" reproduces the divine names in his *Vorlage* faithfully (1992b:68 n. 15, 70). However, the fact that Paul normally agrees with the Alexandrian witnesses to Isaiah (see p. 24 n. 86) makes his agreement with the Hexaplaric uncials B V at this point somewhat suspect. As mentioned above, the occurrence of κύριος σαβαώθ in the very next verse suggests a motivation for Paul to have made the change. Certainty on this point is, of course, impossible.

[172] Tertullian, the sole witness for ἐπὶ τῆς γῆς in LXX Isaiah, appears to have been influenced by the wording of Paul's quotation. He also reads κύριος for ὁ θεός in this verse in agreement with Paul.

[173] Isaiah 28:22b thus would have served as a bridge of sorts between Isa 10:23 and Isa 1:9 for Paul. This explanation is obviously speculative, and it does not account for the fact that Paul wrote κύριος in Rom 9:28 rather than the complete phrase κύριος σαβαώθ (which would have further enhanced the verbal connection with Rom 9:29). It must be conceded as well that κύριος σαβαώθ appears 52 times in LXX Isaiah; as a result, the value of this title by itself as evidence for the influence of Isaiah 28:22 in Paul's quotation of 10:23 is correspondingly diminished. Were there other good reasons for supposing that Paul used a Hebrew text of Isaiah, it would be important to note that MT reads אֲדֹנָי יְהוִה צְבָאוֹת at 10:23. This might account for Paul's use of κύριος (but why not σαβαώθ?) as well as explain the verbal link between 10:23 and 1:9, rendering unnecessary the appeal to 28:22b as a middle term.

[174] Neither word is clearly more "Pauline" than the other. While οἰκουμένη appears in Paul only in a quotation of the OT (Ps 18:5 LXX/Rom 10:18, in parallel with γῆ), γῆ shows up only five times in the undisputed letters, and of these occurrences, three are in OT quotations (1 Cor 8:5; 15:47; Rom 9:17/Exod 9:16; Rom 10:18/Ps 18:5; 1 Cor 10:26/Ps 23:1 LXX).

but again, Isaiah 28:22b LXX contains the word chosen by Paul.[175]

Moreover, a close look at the LXX suggests that the translator of Isaiah also was aware of the relationship between these two passages (Figure 2.8).

Figure 2.8: Isaiah 10:22c–23 and Isaiah 28:22b in LXX and MT

Isa 10:22c–23 LXX	Isa 10:22c–23 MT	Isa 28:22b MT	Isa 28:22b LXX
λόγον γὰρ συντελῶν καὶ συντέμνων	כָּלְיוֹן חָרוּץ שׁוֹטֵף		
ἐν δικαιοσύνῃ ὅτι λόγον συντετμημένον	צְדָקָה כִּי כָלָה וְנֶחֱרָצָה	כִּי־כָלָה וְנֶחֱרָצָה	διότι συντετελεσμένα καὶ συντετμημένα πράγματα
		שָׁמַעְתִּי	ἤκουσα
[ὁ θεὸς] ποιήσει ὁ θεὸς ἐν τῇ οἰκουμένῃ ὅλῃ	אֲדֹנָי יְהוִה צְבָאוֹת עֹשֶׂה בְּקֶרֶב כָּל־הָאָרֶץ	מֵאֵת אֲדֹנָי יְהוִה צְבָאוֹת עַל־כָּל־הָאָרֶץ	παρὰ κυρίου σαβαωθ ἃ ποιήσει ἐπὶ πᾶσαν τὴν γῆν

In MT, Isaiah 10:23c and 28:22b share the phrases כִּי כָלָה וְנֶחֱרָצָה, אֲדֹנָי יְהוִה צְבָאוֹת, and כָּל־הָאָרֶץ. Although the LXX renders these phrases somewhat differently lexically and syntactically,[176] it retains a significant amount of semantic parallelism. There are also important verbal connections between the two passages. The verbs συντελέω and συντέμνω occur together in LXX Isaiah only in Isaiah

---

[175] The Hebrew text may indicate that the focus of Isaiah 10:23 is not the whole world, but the Land of Israel (אֶרֶץ carries both senses). Dinter is right in noting that the LXX excludes this interpretation (Dinter 1980:207–209). The choice of οἰκουμένη emphasizes the world-wide scope of Isaiah's oracle, though LXX Isaiah also uses γῆ to denote the entire earth (e.g., Isa 6:3). However, Paul's choice of γῆ rather than οἰκουμένη and his omission of the adjective with γῆ (ὅλος, Isa 10:23; cf. πᾶς, Isa 28:22) certainly should not be seen as a restriction of the scope of Isaiah's oracle (*contra* Koch 1986:149); there is no evidence that γῆ for Paul refers to anything other than the whole earth. Paul's shift from accusative to genitive with ἐπί likewise does not appear to be exegetically significant (ἐπὶ γῆς is found in 1 Cor 8:5 [also 4x in Col and 3x in Eph]; ἐπὶ γήν never occurs in the Pauline literature. The sample is too small to generalize further about Paul's usage).

[176] The translation of both verses is characterized by a certain amount of free-

10:22 and 28:22b. More revealingly, the relative clause, ἃ ποιήσει, added to smooth out the syntax in 28:22b, reflects the diction of 10:23.[177]

As in the case of Romans 9:20, where Paul's conflation of Isaiah 29:16 with Isaiah 45:9 finds parallels in the interpretive activity of early Jewish translators of Isaiah (LXX and Targum), so here the LXX rendering of Isaiah 10:22–23 and 28:22b suggests either that Paul is following an exegetical tradition that linked these verses or that he made a similar connection himself based on his close knowledge of the two passages.[178] It may be the case that Paul's quotation of Isaiah 10:22–23 has been influenced by Isaiah 28:22b (perhaps even unconsciously) at the level of diction only. Yet the fact that in just a few verses (Rom 9:33; 10:11) Paul will quote from a neighboring passage, Isaiah 28:16, at least raises the possibility that Isaiah 28 has played a more significant role in shaping Paul's thought in Romans 9:27–28.[179] Before examining this further, however, it is necessary to

---

dom. While the equivalencies συντελέω = √כלה and συντέμνω = √חרץ are consistent, LXX does not render כלה in 10:23 with a separate word, but rather translates כלה ונחרצה as λόγον συντετμημένον (λόγος is more likely a carry-over from 10:22 than an indication of a *Vorlage* reading מלה [so Goshen-Gottstein 1995:42; Ziegler 1934:140]). Whereas LXX supplies λόγος in 10:22–23, it adds πράγματα in 28:22. Similarly, כל־הארץ becomes ἡ οἰκουμένη ὅλη in 10:23 and πᾶσα ἡ γῆ in 28:22.

[177] There is no equivalent for these words in MT (and no reason to suppose that the *Vorlage* of the LXX contained an equivalent phrase).

[178] Fishbane (1985:490) notes that in the Hebrew text "the language of [Isa 10:22–23] is echoed in Isa. 28:15–22, which also deals with the Assyrian advance." Not only does Daniel 9:26–27 borrow the terminology of Isaiah 10:22–23, Daniel 11 appears to be heavily indebted to both Isaiah 10:22–23 and 28:15–22 (490). Like Paul, the author of Daniel 11 reinterprets Isaiah's prophecies typologically, finding them fulfilled in the events of his own day (489–91). More indirectly, the manuscript tradition of the Peshitta at Isaiah 28:22 betrays interference from the parallel passage, Isaiah 10:23, at some point in the process of textual transmission. At Isaiah 28:22, ms B.21 Inferiore (Brock's 7a1) and a Jacobite lectionary (Brock's 916) read ܥܒܕ from 10:23 in place of ܡܢ ܫܡܥܬ (= MT, שמעתי מאת), attested by the majority of witnesses and adopted by Brock as the more original reading. The Peshitta's rendering of 10:22–23 and 28:22 agree quite closely with MT, making Septuagintal influence less likely as an explanation for the variant; rather, we have in these mss an independent example of the conflation of 10:22–23 with 28:22. On the question of the relationship between LXX and Peshitta in Isaiah, see Delekat (1957), who argues that agreements between the Peshitta and the LXX are to be traced to use of a common tradition (cf. Delekat 1958, which argues that LXX Isaiah has been influenced by an Aramaic targum). See further M. P. Weitzman 1999:68–86.

[179] On Isaiah 28:16 in Romans 9:33; 10:11, see pp. 126–57 and 168–70. A further reason to think that Isaiah 28:22 may have influenced Paul's quotation of

look more closely at the passage from which Paul clearly does draw his quotation.

Isaiah 10:22–23 in Context

The function of Isaiah 10:22–23 LXX in its context provides an important clue to the sense of Paul's quotation in Romans 9:27–28. The opening chapters of Isaiah (1–12) present God's indictment of Israel and announce God's imminent judgment on his wayward people in the form of an Assyrian invasion that will all but wipe out the nation.[180] Although brief rays of hope occasionally pierce the dark clouds of impending doom (most notably the Davidic oracle in 9:1–7), Isaiah's message is grim. In 9:8–10:4, a series of oracles rebuke Israel's pride and injustice. The prophet's relentless predictions of destruction are punctuated only by the frightening refrain: "For all this, [his] wrath is not turned back (ἀναστρέφω), but [his] hand is still upraised" (9:12, 17, 21; 10:4).[181] Further judgment appears certain, for despite their suffering, Israel has refused to turn back (ἀναστρέφω) and seek the Lord (9:13).

At 10:5, however, a crucial shift of topic and of tone is signalled by the cry, "Woe to the Assyrians!" From this point on in Isaiah 10–12, the prophet's message becomes one of comfort to Israel as God's wrath is redirected toward their enemies. Although the Assyrians have been God's appointed instrument for punishing Israel's sins,

10:22–23 is his clear interest in Isaiah 28–29, both in Romans and in 1 Corinthians (see his citation of 28:11–12 in 1 Cor 14:21 and his various appeals to chapter 29 [29:16/ Rom 9:20; 29:10/Rom 11:8; 29:14/1 Cor 1:19]).

[180] The arrangement of the opening chapters of Isaiah has been the subject of a great deal of discussion. See Sweeney 1988; Bartlett 1996; Seitz 1993:19–113; Ackroyd 1978; Anderson 1988b. I can do no more here than provide a thumbnail sketch of these chapters in order to set the stage for the oracles under consideration. Recent research has made it clear that these early chapters have undergone redaction in light of the shape of the book of Isaiah as a whole (Sweeney 1988; Seitz 1991; Williamson 1994, 1997; Jones 1955; Rendtorff 1993c; Carr 1993). One result of this final redaction is that the Assyrian threat now serves as a prefiguration of the Babylonian exile (Seitz 1991:201; Clements 1980a:424–33). If an ancient reader such as Paul shows no sign of distinguishing between texts that are addressed to the Assyrian crisis and those that speak to the later trauma of exile in Babylon, it may point as much to a sense for the overall shape of the message of the book of Isaiah as to a lack of modern historical-critical sensibilities.

[181] This refrain is first found in 5:25, suggesting that 6:1–9:7 has been inserted into an earlier cycle of oracles. For the importance of this observation for understanding the shape of Isaiah, see Ackroyd 1978:43–44; Anderson 1988b:239; Seitz 1993:46, 88.

they themselves have acted arrogantly, crediting their victories to their own might rather than acknowledging the Lord's sovereignty. In a fascinating interpretive addition, the LXX likens their boasting to the hubris displayed by the builders of the tower of Babel (10:5–11).[182] As a result, "in that day" when God finishes (συντελέω) disciplining his people, he will turn his white-hot anger on Assyria and consume their pride like wildfire (10:12–18). The magnitude of the devastation will be such that those remaining will be few enough that a child will be able to list them by name (10:19).

The following oracle (10:20–23) explicitly contrasts the fate of the remant of Israel (τὸ καταλειφθὲν Ισραηλ) "in that day" with the remnant of Assyria (οἱ καταλειφθέντες) mentioned in the previous verse.[183] No longer will Israel put their hope in Assyria for deliverance (οὐκέτι μὴ πεποιθότες ὦσιν ἐπὶ τοὺς ἀδικήσαντας αὐτούς); now the survivors "will trust in God (ἔσονται πεποιθότες ἐπὶ τὸν θεὸν), the holy one of Israel, in truth, and the remnant of Jacob will [trust] in God, the mighty one (10:20–21)." The double occurrence of the idiom εἶναι πεποιθὼς ἐπί τινα in Isaiah 10:20 recalls Isaiah's previous use of this phrase to describe those who remain faithful to the Lord in contrast to those who encounter him as a stumbling stone (Isaiah 8:14, 17).[184] Now the entire remnant of Israel receives this characterization as faithful ones who fear the Lord and treat him as holy.[185]

Verses 22–23 affirm that Israel's deliverance by God is certain. Though far less numerous than the descendants once promised to Abraham,[186] the remnant *will* be saved (10:22).[187] The allusion to the

---

[182] Καὶ ἐὰν εἴπωσιν αὐτῷ Σὺ μόνος εἶ ἄρχων, καὶ ἐρεῖ Οὐκ ἔλαβον τὴν χώραν τὴν ἐπάνω Βαβυλῶνος καὶ Χαλαννη, οὗ ὁ πύργος ᾠκοδομήθη; (Isaiah 10:8–9 LXX). The identification of Χαλαννη as the location where the Tower of Babel was built is probably an exegetical deduction from Genesis 10:10–11; 11:2 (so also Seeligman 1948:47, 78).

[183] Note the structural parallelism established through the use of καὶ ἔσται + temporal phrase at the beginning of the announcement of Assyria's punishment (10:12) and at the outset of this oracle of salvation for Israel (10:20; cf. 10:27).

[184] Paul draws on Isaiah 8:14 LXX in Romans 9:33 to emphasize the necessity of faith/trust (see pp. 136–42 and 151–55).

[185] Note the repeated use of the phrase εἶναι πεποιθὼς ἐπί τινα in LXX Isaiah to describe those who trust in the Lord rather than in idols, human beings, or foreign nations (17:7–8; 31:1; 33:2; 36:7; 37:10; 50:10; 58:14).

[186] See Gen 13:16; 15:5; 16:10; 22:17.

[187] Note that MT plays here on the name of the prophet's son (שוב ישוב שאר; cf. 10:21; 7:3). The LXX translator sacrifices this wordplay in order to introduce a more explicit statement of salvation (cf. Brockington 1984:81).

Abrahamic covenant in v. 22a works simultaneously at two levels. Comparison with the sand of the sea cannot but highlight the magnitude of the devastation the population has experienced at the hands of the Assyrians. At the same time, however, by recalling God's unconditional promise to Abraham, these words remind Israel of God's faithfulness to the covenant he has graciously initiated. The preservation of a remnant of Israel thus holds out hope for a realization of this promise of innumerable descendants on the other side of judgment.

This line of thought is developed more explicitly in two further allusions to the Abraham saga in the book of Isaiah. The first, found in Isaiah 48:18–19, also employs the metaphor of descendants as numerous as grains of sand in order to highlight the disparity between the bright promise given to Abraham and the harsh reality of Israel's decimation by Babylon.[188] The prophet laments what could have been, had Israel remained faithful to God: "If you had hearkened to my commandments . . . your seed would have been like the sand (ἐγένετο ἂν ὡς ἡ ἄμμος τὸ σπέρμα σου) and the offspring of your womb like the dust of the earth" (Isa 48:18–19a).[189] Yet the recollection of God's promise to Abraham immediately calls forth a renewed affirmation of God's commitment to preserve his people: "But now you surely shall not be eradicated, neither shall your name be destroyed from before me!" (48:19b).[190] This declaration finds its realization in the return from Babylon, portrayed as a new exodus (48:20–21).

---

[188] Although these examples come from Deutero-Isaiah (generally recognized to have its distinct theological viewpoint, sometimes in tension with that of First Isaiah), an ancient reader such as Paul would not have made such a distinction. More likely, Paul, like many other ancient Jewish interpreters (see Barton 1986:276 n. 16), would have tended to read all of Isaiah in light of the theology of Deutero-Isaiah. Cf. *b. B. Bat.* 14b, which describes the book of Isaiah (including chapters 1–39!) as "full of consolation," in contrast to Ezekiel, which prophesies "destruction" at the beginning of the book and "consolation" only at the end: ויחזקאל רישיה חורבנא וסיפיה נחמתא וישעיה כוליה נחמתא.

[189] The phrase, "the offspring of your womb" (τὰ ἔκγονα τῆς κοιλίας σου, 48:19), echoes the terminology found in the deuteronomic blessing/curse formulas (Deut 28:4, 11, 18, 35; cf. 7:13). According to Isaiah, Israel has forfeited this covenant blessing. Nevertheless, God remains faithful and will preserve Israel's name (= descendants) by rescuing them from Babylon (48:20–21). Compare the similar thought in Deut 30:9, where the blessing on "the offspring of your womb" is bestowed again on Israel after their deliverance from exile.

[190] The LXX begins a new thought after 48:19a (cf. the placement of *'atnaḥ* in MT), reading 48:19b as a promise of *hope* for the future: οὐδὲ νῦν οὐ μὴ ἐξολεθρευθῇς,

The call to remember Abraham and Sarah in Isaiah 51:2–3 links together even more clearly the return from exile with the renewed promise of numerous descendants: "He was [only] one, and I called him and blessed him and loved him and multiplied him" (51:2). Just as once God chose and multiplied the descendants of Abraham, so he will again comfort Zion and make her prosper (51:3).

In both Isaiah 48:18–19 and 51:2–3, the promise of descendants to Abraham serves as a reminder of God's faithfulness to Israel and grounds Israel's hope for future blessing from God. It is likely, then, that the allusion to "the sand of the sea" in Isaiah 10:22 would similarly be heard with overtones not only of judgment but also of restoration.

My hypothesis that Isaiah 10:22–23 LXX functions in its context primarily as an oracle of salvation is further confirmed by the observation that the LXX translator has rendered 10:22c–23—and its parallel in 28:22b—in such a way as to remove the explicit language of destruction found in the Hebrew (כליון, כלה; see Fig. 2.8 above). Rather than announcing an imminent *devastation* of the entire land out of which "only" a remnant of Israel will survive, Isaiah 10:22c–23 LXX functions as a coda to the prophet's oracle of salvation (10:20–23), proclaiming the *swift accomplishment of redemption* for the remnant of Israel throughout the inhabited world.[191] Isaiah 10:22c–23 assures Israel that in righteousness[192] God is already completing and

---

οὐδὲ ἀπολεῖται τὸ ὄνομά σου ἐνώπιόν μου. Contrast the rendering of 48:19b by the NRSV (with most English translations) as a further statement of what *would have been*: "their name would never be cut off or destroyed from before me."

[191] So rightly Dinter 1980:204–207. P. R. Ackroyd (1978:44) argues for a positive meaning for these verses in the MT as well.

[192] The question of the meaning of δικαιοσύνη in Isaiah LXX is a complex one. Olley (1979) rightly argues that in LXX Isaiah, as in "secular" Greek generally, the word lies within the semantic field of "justice" (note the parallel κρίμα in 5:16; 9:6). However, Olley's study, which attempts to distance the δικ– word group in Isaiah LXX semantically from its Hebrew counterpart (√צדק), fails to take sufficient account of the fact that, due to frequent collocation with terms related to ἐλεέω and σῴζω, the δικ– word-group in LXX Isaiah also carries the unmistakable connotation of God's *faithfulness to deliver* his people: God acts justly precisely in that he saves the people with whom he has made covenant (cf. Ziesler 1972:52–69). The adequacy of Olley's lexicographical approach, which focuses primarily on the putative meaning of the word group to native Greek speakers, is called into question by E. Tov's observation that such an approach "alone cannot be satisfactory due to the comprisal within the language of the LXX of many un-Greek elements derived from the source languages" (1976:529). Moreover, Olley underestimates the degree to which exposure to Isaiah LXX might reshape a native Greek speaker's

even cutting short their punishment in order to speed their deliverance.[193] For Paul, as a reader of LXX Isaiah, then, 10:22–23 would not sound a single, somber note of judgment and ruin. On the contrary, these verses strike a complex chord rich with scriptural overtones heralding the imminent end of this period of severe chastisement and underscoring the certainty of redemption for the remnant of Israel.[194]

The similar phrase in Isaiah 28:22b, with which Paul appears to have conflated his citation of 10:22–23, functions in an analogous manner in its Isaianic context. The collocation of συντελέω and συντέμνω in Isaiah 28:22b emphasizes both the swiftness of God's justice and also his mercy in shortening the time of chastisement in order to hasten Israel's deliverance. Isaiah 28:22 comes at the end of an oracle castigating those who have "made a covenant with death" and put their hope in false gods. The prophet exhorts them not to rejoice (εὐφραίνω, 22a),[195]—perhaps referring to their (unwar-

---

understanding of the semantic range of "righteousness" terminology. C. Rabin observes that readers of translations are not "seriously perturbed" when encountering words "used in ways that would not normally occur in original texts of the receptor language" (1968:9). This is because

> the force of context is such that even some degree of deviation from the meanings with which the reader or listener is familiar will not spoil the sense. . . . We may call this ability of the context to absorb semantic deviation "semantic tolerance". . . . The degree of tolerance is considerable; it varies, naturally, with the purpose of the text. We may assume it to be . . . particularly large in the translation of a religious text (9–10).

Rabin further notes that peculiar usages of words in a translation can eventually have an effect on the usage of those words in the receptor language itself (10–11; cf. Muraoka 1984). Again, one would suppose that this process would be especially noticeable in the case of words used in religious contexts, such as δικαιοσύνη and its cognates.

[193] Compare Isaiah 10:12, which promises that God will take vengeance on Assyria and deliver his people ὅταν <u>συντελέσῃ</u> κύριος πάντα ποιῶν ἐν τῷ ὄρει Σιων καὶ ἐν Ιερουσαλημ. See also Isaiah 55:11: οὕτως ἔσται τὸ ῥῆμά μου, ὃ ἐὰν ἐξέλθῃ ἐκ τοῦ στόματός μου, οὐ μὴ ἀποστραφῇ, ἕως ἂν <u>συντελεσθῇ</u> ὅσα ἠθέλησα καὶ εὐοδώσω τὰς ὁδούς σου καὶ τὰ ἐντάλματά μου. Note the use of these two verbs together in the interpretation of the oracle in Daniel 5:26–28 LXX as an announcement of the imminent end of the Babylonian kingdom: συντέτμηται καὶ συντετέλεσται ἡ βασιλεία σου. Compare the similar idea in Mark 13:20//Matthew 24:22, where God has determined to cut short (κολοβόω) the time of tribulation so that the elect will survive.

[194] Dinter 1980:22 notes that λόγον συντελῶν καὶ συντέμνων ποιήσει κύριος supports Paul's opening affirmation, οὐχ οἷον ἐκπέπτωκεν ὁ λόγος τοῦ θεοῦ (Rom 9:6).

[195] The sense of the LXX is not entirely clear here (if the translator is not paraphrasing, it appears that he took תתהללו to be from √עלז, "rejoice," instead of √ליץ "be proud, scornful").

ranted) confidence that the prophesied judgment will not touch them (28:15, 17b–18a)—lest their punishment be made even more severe. Isaiah assures them that God will speedily execute his sentence. At the same time, 28:22b urges them to submit because their chastisement will be short-lived. The following parable of the farmer (28:23–29a) has as its main point the wisdom of God, who knows the right measure of discipline to employ and who will not be angry forever so as to destroy his people (28:28). If they will only submit to God's discipline, God will instruct them and give them a true reason for rejoicing (εὐφραίνω, 28:26).[196]

In terms of "volume," the echoes of Isaiah 28:22b in Romans 9:28 are admittedly quite faint. It may be Paul has unconsciously conflated the two passages. On the other hand, since Paul draws frequently on Isaiah 28–29, it is quite possible that he recognized the connections of thought and language between the two passages in Isaiah. Whether intentional or not on Paul's end, for those who have ears to hear the reverberations of Isaiah 28:22b in Romans 9:28 enrich and amplify the note of imminent deliverance for a people suffering under divine wrath sounded by Isaiah 10:22–23.

As a result of the firm pledge of salvation offered in Isaiah 10:20–23, the following oracle (διὰ τοῦτο, 10:24) addresses Israel using the covenant formula, "my people." The prophet exhorts them not to be fearful, for God's wrath will soon turn against their oppressors (10:25), and God will deliver them. The terminology of the following verses evokes the Davidic oracle of 9:1–7,[197] preparing the way for the prophecy in chapter 11 of the Spirit-filled scion of David who will arise to rule the Gentiles.[198] The entire section closes with a resounding hymn of thanksgiving, celebrating the fact that the Lord has now turned away his wrath[199] and has shown mercy to his

---

[196] See pp. 62–65 and 142–51 for further discussion of the LXX translator's rendering of Isaiah 28–29.

[197] Note Μαδιαμ (9:4; 10:26); compare ἀφαιρεθήσεται ὁ ζυγὸς ὁ ἐπ᾽ αὐτῶν κείμενος (9:4) with ἀφαιρεθήσεται ... ὁ ζυγὸς αὐτοῦ ἀπὸ τοῦ ὤμου σου, καὶ καταφθαρήσεται ὁ ζυγὸς ἀπὸ τῶν ὤμων ὑμῶν (10:27) and καλεῖται τὸ ὄνομα αὐτοῦ· μεγάλης βουλῆς ἄγγελος (9:6) with ἀναπαύσεται ἐπ᾽ αὐτὸν ... πνεῦμα βουλῆς (11:2). The foregoing connections are found in MT as well. LXX Isaiah alone has at 10:26 τῇ ὁδῷ τῇ κατὰ θάλασσαν, an echo of 9:1, ὁδὸν θαλάσσης (Isaiah 10:26 MT speaks of God lifting his rod over the sea, an allusion to the exodus).

[198] I treat Paul's use of Isaiah 11:10 below, pp. 317–28.

[199] ἀπέστρεψας τὸν θυμόν σου, 12:1. Contrast the insistent refrain of the judgment oracles: οὐκ ἀπεστράφη ὁ θυμός (5:25; 9:12, 17, 21; 10:4).

people, and reaffirming Israel's trust in God,[200] who has become their salvation.

Within the overall flow of Isaiah 1:1–12:6, then, the oracle Paul quotes (10:22–23) comes *after* the major turning point of 10:5 and functions as part of a proclamation of *comfort* to Israel in light of the impending judgment on their enemy, Assyria. Though set against the backdrop of Israel's unfaithfulness and their consequent chastisement by God, the dominant note of 10:22–23 LXX is one of confidence and trust that God will soon turn and deliver his people.

"A Remnant Will Be Saved": Hearing Isaiah 10:22–23 in Romans 9
When we turn to the place of Isaiah 10:22–23 in Paul's larger argument in Romans 9, it is important, in light of the interpretive debate that rages over the force of this citation, to note both what Paul assumes with regard to Israel's present situation as he quotes this text and what positive point he is attempting to establish by means of Isaiah's testimony. Paul's appropriation of this oracle maintains much of the tension of its original context in Isaiah 1–12, where it sits at the transition point between the message of condemnation and the celebration of God's gracious deliverance of his people. The Israel addressed in Isaiah 10:20–23 is in dire straits, suffering under Assyrian oppression as a result of its unfaithfulness to God. Similarly, Paul has labored in Romans 1–3 to establish the view that Israel— like the rest of humanity—is held captive by sin and so presently stands under God's judgment.[201] In Romans 9–11, the apostle's expressions of deep anguish at Israel's present plight (9:1–5; 10:1; cf. 11:13–14) indicate clearly that in Paul's view, his kinspeople stand in desperate need of deliverance. Paul's wish to be cut off from Christ for the sake of his people, which evokes images of Moses' intercession for idolatrous Israel, makes absolutely no sense unless Paul believes that a substantial part of Israel (cf. 9:24) currently stands under God's wrath.

---

[200] πεποιθὼς ἔσομαι ἐπ᾽ αὐτῷ (Isa 12:2) echoes the salvation oracle of 10:20–21 (cf. 8:14, 17).

[201] E. P. Sanders's contention that Paul began with the "solution" (Christ as universal savior) and worked backwards to his analysis of the "plight" of Israel and of all humanity (universal subjection to the power of sin) rightly emphasizes the revolutionary effect on Paul's thought of the apostle's encounter with the risen Christ (1977:474–511). However, this insight should not be taken to imply that Paul himself was not firmly persuaded of the validity of his analysis of Israel's plight.

When Paul calls Isaiah forth to speak in Romans 9:27–29, then, he imaginatively places Israel in a situation analogous to that originally addressed by the prophet, a situation in which Israel is already experiencing God's judgment. As in Isaiah 10:22–23, so also in Romans 9 the echo of the promise to Abraham of descendants like the sand of the sea dramatically heightens the numerical disparity between the "sons of Israel" and the remnant that is saved.[202] It is on this aspect of the correspondence between Isaiah 10:22–23 and Paul's own situation that many interpreters have focused when they argue that Paul appeals to Isaiah in Romans 9:27–28 in order to pronounce condemnation on Israel.

Where this interpretation of Paul's rhetoric goes astray, however, is in its failure to recognize that, as a result of Paul's trope, the prophet's words in Romans function as they do in their context in Isaiah—as a message of *hope* in the midst of disaster, as a *promise* that Israel yet has a future. The rhetorical function of Romans 9:24 is crucial: Paul tells his hearers in advance what Hosea and Isaiah will say: namely, that God has graciously called "us" as vessels of mercy. If Hosea has provided Paul exegetical leverage to include Gentiles in this group, it is evident that Isaiah testifies to the salvation of some "from among the Jews." Only a reading that ignores Paul's plain interpretive statement in 9:24 can maintain that Isaiah 10:22–23 functions in Romans 9 as an announcement of condemnation on Israel and a grim declaration that "only" a remnant will be saved. Paul invokes Isaiah, not in order to establish the fact that Israel is suffering under God's wrath, but to claim that by calling "us . . . from among the Jews," God is faithfully preserving a remnant of Israel and bringing his people's chastisement to an end.[203]

---

[202] Although "sons of Israel" in Romans 9:27 (Isa 10:22/Hos 1:10a) would seem to parallel the immediately preceding "sons of the living God" in Romans 9:26 (Hos 1:10b), it is clear that for Paul, the "sons of Israel" stand *over against* the "sons of the living God" and "the remnant," for it is these latter two groups alone who are now experiencing God's deliverance. This move is in line with Paul's earlier attempt to distinguish between "all from Israel" and "Israel" in Romans 9:6–13.

[203] Compare the interpretation of this passage in in 4QpIsa[a] (4Q161) frgs. 2–6 2.1–9. Although the text is fragmentary, the pesharist seems to understand 10:22–23 as a reference to the impending eschatological war with the Kittim (i.e., Rome) from which Israel will emerge victorious over their oppressors (cf. 4QpIsa[c] [4Q163] frgs. 5, 6–7 2.11–20). 4QpIsa[a] frgs. 2–6 2.6–9 identifies the saved with those who are "planted" in the land (see Isa 60:21; 61:3), an image used elsewhere in the scrolls to portray the community as the restored people of God (cf. 1QS 11.8; CD-A 1.7; 1QH[a] 14[6].15; 16[8].4–26).

Moreover, the preservation of this remnant does not imply for Paul the end of Israel as a whole; on the contrary, it insures Israel's continued survival. In Isaiah 10, the allusion to God's promise to Abraham of innumerable descendants does not function merely as a bittersweet recollection of past blessings now forfeited. At a deeper level, it serves as a reminder of God's faithfulness to his covenant with Abraham and thus as a word of hope for the future. This hope is presently embodied in the remnant that is preserved through judgment.[204]

That hope for the restoration of Israel becomes the dominant connotation of "remnant" language in the Second Temple Period has been well documented. E. P. Sanders captures the essence of this development:

> In the post-biblical literature the theme of a threatened punishment which will leave only a remnant recedes. Remnant terminology, especially various terms designating the suvivors as 'poor' and 'lowly', is often retained; but the emphasis is on reassembly, freedom from oppression and foreign dominion, punishment of the Gentiles and the like, not on the further winnowing of Israel.[205]

A few examples of the way remnant language functions in this period will suffice to illustrate Sanders's point:

> From the days of our fathers to this day we have been in great guilt; and for our iniquities we, our kings, and our priests have been given into the hand of the kings of the lands, to the sword, to captivity, to plundering, and to utter shame, as at this day. But now for a brief moment favor has been shown by the LORD our God, to leave us a remnant [פליטה], and to give us a secure hold within his holy place, that our God may brighten our eyes and grant us a little reviving in our bondage (Ezra 9:7–8 RSV).[206]

---

[204] Commenting on the remnant motif in the Hebrew Bible, L. V. Meyer makes the general observation, "Because the catastrophe is understood to be an act of divine judgment, the survival of a viable remnant is, correspondingly, an act of divine mercy" (1992:670).

[205] E. P. Sanders 1985:95. Similarly, R. E. Clements states that while one would overreach the evidence in speaking of a "fixed concept" of the remnant in the postexilic period, "the return of the remnant became an image and model of Jewish hope, and thereby the concept of a remnant entered into a central position in Jewish eschatological hope" (1980b:118). See further the massive study by G. F. Hasel (1974) and, for the Second Temple Period, the unpublished dissertations by R. W. Huebsch (1981) and P. E. Dinter (1980, esp. 191–231). James W. Watts (1988) discusses the literature from the New Testament side. For a quite different reading of the evidence, see M. A. Elliott 2000.

[206] In contrast, Ezra 9:13–14 contemplates the dreadful possibility that Israel's

But the Lord will never abandon his mercy or nullify any of his words; he will never wipe out the descendants of his chosen one, or take away the seed of him who loved him. So he gave a remnant to Jacob, and to David a root from his own family (Sir 47:22 NRSV [modified]).[207]

But because he remembered the covenant with the first ones [the patriarchs], he left a remnant for Israel and did not give them over to destruction (CD-A 1.4–5).[208]

I take comfort in spite of the tumult of the people and the uproar of the kingdoms when they gather together, [for] I [kn]ow that you will soon raise up a reviving of life among your people and a remnant among your inheritance, and you will purify them to cleanse them of guilt (1QH[a] 14[6].7–8).[209]

Clearly, in wrestling with the question of God's faithfulness to Israel in Romans 9–11, Paul has drunk deeply of the logic of Israel's scriptures as they were interpreted in the Second Temple Period. For Paul, the salvation of the remnant upholds God's covenant faithfulness and pledges the eventual salvation of "all Israel" (11:26).[210] The hopeful conclusion with which Paul's argument ends in Romans 11 is thus already foreshadowed in his appropriation of Isaiah's promise of a remnant in Romans 9.[211] In order to appreciate the full force of

---

persistence in sinning might provoke God to destroy the nation utterly, leaving no remnant and, thus, no future:

> After all that has come upon us for our evil deeds and for our great guilt, seeing that you, our God, have punished us less than our iniquities deserved and have given us such a remnant [פליטה] as this, shall we break your commandments again and intermarry with the peoples who practice these abominations? Would you not be angry with us until you destroy us without remnant or survivor [שארית ופליטה]? (Ezra 9:13–14 NRSV).

For "without remnant" as a phrase denoting complete annihilation, see also 1QS 4.13–14; 5.13; 1QM 1.5–7; 4.1–2; 14.5; 1QH[a] 14[6].32; CD-A 2.6–7.

[207] ὁ δὲ κύριος οὐ μὴ καταλίπῃ τὸ ἔλεος αὐτοῦ καὶ οὐ μὴ διαφθείρῃ ἀπὸ τῶν λόγων αὐτοῦ οὐδὲ μὴ ἐξαλείψῃ ἐκλεκτοῦ αὐτοῦ ἔκγονα καὶ σπέρμα τοῦ ἀγαπήσαντος αὐτὸν οὐ μὴ ἐξάρῃ· καὶ τῷ Ιακωβ ἔδωκεν κατάλειμμα καὶ τῷ Δαυιδ ἐξ αὐτοῦ ῥίζαν.

[208] ‏ובזכרו ברית ראשנים השאיר שארית לישראל ולא נתנם לכלה.

[209] ‏7 ואנחמה על המון עם ועל שאון מ[מ]לכות בהאספם [כי יד]עתי אשר 8 תרים למצער‏ ‏מחיה בעמכה ושארית בנחלתכה ותזקקם להטהר מאשמה‏

Note the echoes of Isaiah 13:4 (‏שאון מ[מ]לכות בהאספם‏ ... ‏המון עם‏) and Ezra 9:8 (‏מחיה‏).

[210] Clements remarks that in the post-exilic period, the remnant are viewed as "the instruments through whom salvation could be brought to all Israel, and even to the Gentiles" (1974:108). Similarly, Hasel speaks of "the inherent potentiality of renewal of the remnant, no matter what its size" (1962:735).

[211] Interestingly, "remnant" appears only once in Isaiah 40–66 LXX (46:3, κατάλοιπον). In the latter half of the book, the idea of a remnant gives way to the

this claim, however, it is necessary to turn to Paul's next citation of Isaiah and to the description there of the remnant of Israel as "seed."

Isaiah 1:9: God Has Left Us Seed

Paul prefaces his second quotation from Isaiah with the phrase, "And just as Isaiah has foretold" (καὶ καθὼς προείρηκεν Ἡσαΐας, Rom 9:29). In contrast to his previous citation formula (Rom 9:27), where the rhetorical trope of Isaiah offering his testimony *viva voce* accentuated the immediacy of the prophetic word, Paul here highlights the predictive/oracular dimension of Isaiah's words. His introduction implies that what has happened to Israel is not a surprising development but the fulfillment of God's plan, of which Israel has long been apprised.[212]

The adverb "just as" (καθώς) makes it clear that Paul intends the second quotation from Isaiah to support the first. Consequently, "seed" must refer to the same group as "the remnant" in the previous quotation. Two verbal links further connect the citations. The verb ἐγκαταλείπω, "leave [a remnant]," in Romans 9:29 (Isa 1:9) recalls the "remnant," ὑπόλειμμα, in Romans 9:27 (Isa 10:22), while κύριος σαβαώθ (Rom 9:29) echoes κύριος in the previous verse. Since the quotations are obviously intended to make the same point, this verse shares the same basic interpretive problems as Isaiah 10:22–23. As I will show, however, the citation of Isaiah 1:9 provides decisive evidence that Paul's appeal to Isaiah in Romans 9:27–29 is intended as a word of *hope* for the remnant—and ultimately for Israel as a whole.

Aside from the omission of the initial καί, Paul's quotation follows LXX exactly (Fig. 2.9). This appears to be a clear case where Paul's argument is furthered by an interpretation of Isaiah 1:9 distinctive to LXX. Although the Hebrew word שָׂרִיד ("survivor[s]; remnant") is normally translated in LXX by a term with a similar semantic range, the LXX translator renders it here as σπέρμα.[213]

---

promise of the return of the nation as a whole (though God still vows the destruction of the wicked within Israel: see esp. Isaiah 65–66).

[212] Paul argues this point explicitly in Romans 10:18–21 (see pp. 180–217).

[213] Although it was not recognized by Hatch-Redpath, T. Muraoka is certainly correct in his identification of this equivalency (1998:144). Deuteronomy 3:3 provides the only other instance of this lexical equivalency in LXX. Elsewhere, שָׂרִיד is rendered by καταλείπειν (Lam 2:22); κατάλειμμα (Judg 5:13; 4 Kgdms 10:11); κατάλοιπος (Jer 29 [47]:4); ὑπόλειμμα (Job 20:21); σῴζειν (Josh 8:22; 10:33, 40; Job 18:19; Jer 49 [42]:17; 51 [44]:14); διασῴζειν (Josh 10:20, 28, 30, 37, 39, 40;

This term not only provides a link to "sons" in Romans 9:27 (Isaiah 10:22a/Hos 1:10a) and 9:26 (Hosea 1:10b), but it also recalls the initial stage of Paul's argument, where "seed" functions as a technical term for the true descendants of Abraham (Rom 9:7–8).

Figure 2.9: Isaiah 1:9 LXX and Romans 9:29

Isaiah 1:9 LXX	Romans 9:29
καὶ εἰ μὴ κύριος σαβαωθ ἐγκατέλιπεν ἡμῖν σπέρμα, ὡς Σοδομα ἂν ἐγενήθημεν καὶ ὡς Γομορρα ἂν ὡμοιώθημεν	καὶ καθὼς προείρηκεν Ἡσαΐας· εἰ μὴ κύριος σαβαὼθ ἐγκατέλιπεν ἡμῖν σπέρμα, ὡς Σόδομα ἂν ἐγενήθημεν καὶ ὡς Γόμορρα ἂν ὡμοιώθημεν

Isa 1:9 MT:　　　לוּלֵי יְהוָה צְבָאוֹת הוֹתִיר לָנוּ שָׂרִיד כִּמְעָט כִּסְדֹם הָיִינוּ לַעֲמֹרָה דָּמִינוּ

The concept of "seed" is crucial both for grasping the significance of Isaiah 1:9 in its context in LXX Isaiah and for comprehending Paul's appropriation of this verse in his argument in Romans. In its present form, Isaiah 1 introduces the main problems of the book of Isaiah: Israel's unfaithfulness to God (1:2–4, 10–15, 21–23), their unresponsiveness even to severe chastisement (1:5–9), and the certainty of yet further judgment (1:24–25, 28–31). At the same time, it extends God's invitation (and warning) to repent and be forgiven (1:16–20), promising the ultimate removal of Israel's sins by a gracious God who will not utterly destroy his people, but who will instead remove the wicked from Israel's midst and reestablish his people in righteousness (1:24–27). Isaiah 1:7–8 speaks of the devastation of Judah at the hands of invading armies, who have razed its cities and devoured the produce of the land. Beleaguered Zion stands alone in the midst of a scene so bleak it evokes images of the cataclysmic ruin of Sodom and Gomorrah (1:9b).[214] Significantly, however, Isaiah

---

11:8); φεύγειν (Obad 14); διαφεύγειν (Josh 10:28, 30, 33); ἐκφεύγειν (Sir 40:6); ἐπήλυτος (Job 20:26); ζωγρεία (Num 21:35; Deut 2:34); ὁ περιών (Job 27:15). Compare Isaiah 1:9 in the Peshitta (ܟ݁ܘܒܐ) and Targum (שיזבא). Vulgate, *semen*, follows LXX.

[214] For Sodom and Gomorrah as bywords for total annihilation, see Amos 4:11; Zeph 2:9; Isa 13:19; Jer 27:40 (50:40 MT), 30:12 (49:18 MT); cf. 2 Pet 2:6; Jude 7. See also the curse for breaking the covenant threatened in Deuteronomy 29:22–23:

refuses to make a direct comparison of Zion's fate with that of Sodom and Gomorrah: "We *would have become* as Sodom, and we *would have been* like Gomorrah." He stops short of this because of one crucial difference: "The Lord of hosts has left us σπέρμα."

As we saw above with regard to the concept of the "remnant," so also here God's preservation of Israel's "seed" vouchsafes the ultimate restoration of the nation.[215] That this is the clear connotation of "seed" language in Isaiah 1:9 may be seen from two types of passages found in Isaiah. The first cluster of texts affirm God's election of Israel and on this basis promise redemption and restoration to their "seed."[216]

> But you, Israel, Jacob my servant, whom I chose, seed of Abraham, whom I loved. . . . I chose you and did not abandon you. Don't be afraid, for I am with you (41:8–10d).[217]

> Don't be afraid, for I am with you. I will bring your seed from the east, and I will gather you from the west (43:5).[218]

The next generation . . . will see the devastation of that land and the afflictions with which the LORD has afflicted it—all its soil burned out by sulfur and salt, nothing planted, nothing sprouting, unable to support any vegetation, like the destruction of Sodom and Gomorrah, Admah and Zeboiim, which the LORD destroyed in his fierce anger (NRSV).

[215] "The purpose of [Isa 1:9] is clearly to offer some element of alleviation of the preceding threat (vv. 5–8) and to suggest the idea of a remnant through whom the future would be secured" (Clements 1980a:425). Cf. Dinter (1980:347–56), who reaches conclusions similar to those of the present study regarding the meaning of "seed" language in LXX Isaiah.

[216] The idea of God's commitment to bless the "seed" of Abraham derives ultimately from the patriarchal narratives (Gen 12:7; 13:15–16; 15:5, 18; 16:10; 17:1–14, 19; 21:12; 22:17; 24:7, 60; 26:3–4, 24; 28:4, 13–14; 32:12; 35:12; 48:4). The blessing on Abraham and his seed is recalled numerous times elsewhere in Israel's scriptures (Exod 32:13; 33:1; Num 23:10; 24:7; Deut 1:8; 4:37; 10:15; 11:9; 34:4; Josh 24:3; 2 Chr 20:7; Neh 9:8). In addition, it is widely evoked in the Second Temple Period as the ground for Israel's confidence in God's enduring fidelity to his covenant (e.g., Sir 44:21; Pr Azar 36; *Pss. Sol.* 9:9; 18:3; *Jub.* 13:20–21; 16:17–18, 26, 28; 17:3; 18:15; 19:9, 21–24; 22:9–10; 24:22; 27:1, 22–23; 32:9; *LAB* 4:11; 8:3; 10:2; 12:4; 14:2; 18:5; 21:9; 23:5, 12–13; 49:6; 4 *Ezra* 3:15; *T. Mos.* 3:9; *T. Ab.* [A] 8:7; *T. Levi* [B] 3:16; 7:1; *Gk. Apoc. Ezra* 3:10; *T. Job* 1:5; *1 En* 10:3; 1QM 13.7; 4Q504 frg. 5 2.1–2; Luke 1:55; Acts 7:5). God's promise to bless Abraham's seed also functions as a foundational assumption of Paul's arguments in Galatians 3–4 and Romans 4.

[217] σὺ δέ, Ισραηλ, παῖς μου Ιακωβ, ὃν ἐξελεξάμην, σπέρμα Αβρααμ, ὃν ἠγάπησα . . . . ἐξελεξάμην σε καὶ οὐκ ἐγκατέλιπόν σε, μὴ φοβοῦ, μετὰ σοῦ γάρ εἰμι (41:8–10a LXX).

[218] μὴ φοβοῦ, ὅτι μετὰ σοῦ εἰμι· ἀπὸ ἀνατολῶν ἄξω τὸ σπέρμα σου καὶ ἀπὸ δυσμῶν συνάξω σε.

Thus says the Lord God who made you and who formed you from the womb: "You will still be rescued—do not fear, my servant Jacob, and my beloved Israel, whom I chose. For when they thirst, I will give water to those who travel in a waterless land; I will place my spirit on your seed and my blessings on your children . . ." (44:2–3).[219]

By the Lord they will be vindicated, and in God they will be glorified—all the seed of the sons of Israel (45:25).[220]

And I will lead seed from Jacob and seed from Judah out [of exile], and they will inherit my holy mountain. My elect and my servants will inherit [it] and they will dwell there (65:9).[221]

Just as the new heaven and new earth which I am making remain before me, says the Lord, so will your seed and your name endure (66:22).[222]

In contrast, the second group of texts prophesy the annihilation of other nations or of the wicked by promising the destruction of their "seed."[223]

And I will rise up against them [the Babylonians], says the Lord of Hosts, and I will destroy their name and their remnant and their seed (14:22).[224]

And [the flying serpent] will consume your seed with famine and your remnant it will consume (14:30).[225]

And I will destroy the seed of Moab and Ariel and the remnant of Adama (15:9).[226]

---

[219] οὕτως λέγει κύριος ὁ θεὸς ὁ ποιήσας σε καὶ ὁ πλάσας σε ἐκ κοιλίας Ἔτι βοηθηθήσῃ, μὴ φοβοῦ, παῖς μου Ιακωβ καὶ ὁ ἠγαπημένος Ισραηλ, ὃν ἐξελεξάμην· ὅτι ἐγὼ δώσω ὕδωρ ἐν δίψει τοῖς πορευομένοις ἐν ἀνύδρῳ, ἐπιθήσω τὸ πνεῦμά μου ἐπὶ τὸ σπέρμα σου καὶ τὰς εὐλογίας μου ἐπὶ τὰ τέκνα σου. . . .

[220] ἀπὸ κυρίου δικαιωθήσονται καὶ ἐν τῷ θεῷ ἐνδοξασθήσονται πᾶν τὸ σπέρμα τῶν υἱῶν Ισραηλ.

[221] Note the use of ἐκλεκτοί in parallel with σπέρμα: καὶ ἐξάξω τὸ ἐξ Ιακωβ σπέρμα καὶ τὸ ἐξ Ιουδα, καὶ κληρονομήσει τὸ ὄρος τὸ ἅγιόν μου, καὶ κληρονομήσουσιν οἱ ἐκλεκτοί μου καὶ οἱ δοῦλοί μου καὶ κατοικήσουσιν ἐκεῖ.

[222] ὃν τρόπον γὰρ ὁ οὐρανὸς καινὸς καὶ ἡ γῆ καινή, ἃ ἐγὼ ποιῶ, μένει ἐνώπιόν μου, λέγει κύριος, οὕτως στήσεται τὸ σπέρμα ὑμῶν καὶ τὸ ὄνομα ὑμῶν.

[223] This motif is present elsewhere in Israel's scriptures: e.g., Num 24:20; Deut 3:3; 1 Kgdms 2:31; 24:22; 3 Kgdms 11:1; 17:20; Ps 20:11 LXX; 36:28 LXX.

[224] καὶ ἐπαναστήσομαι αὐτοῖς, λέγει κύριος σαβαωθ, καὶ ἀπολῶ αὐτῶν ὄνομα καὶ κατάλειμμα καὶ σπέρμα.

[225] ἀνελεῖ δὲ λιμῷ τὸ σπέρμα σου καὶ τὸ κατάλειμμά σου ἀνελεῖ.

[226] καὶ ἀρῶ τὸ σπέρμα Μωαβ καὶ Αριηλ καὶ τὸ κατάλοιπον Αδαμα. Dinter takes αἴρω σπέρμα here and in 48:14 to signify "raise up seed," but this meaning is highly improbable in these contexts. Nowhere in Isaiah LXX is the phrase used for the preservation of Israel's "seed" (1980:347–48). Note that σπέρμα is parallel

Because I loved you I accomplished your will against Babylon to destroy the seed of the Chaldeans (48:14).[227]

The seed of those who rebelled has perished (33:2).[228]

The idea that the preservation of "seed" guarantees a nation's continued survival *and future growth* continues to have widespread currency in the Second Temple Period. Once again, representative examples will suffice to make the point:

For even in the beginning, when arrogant giants were perishing, the hope of the world took refuge on a raft, and guided by your hand left to the world the seed of a new generation (Wis 14:6 NRSV).[229]

But in all of them [i.e., previous epochs] he raised up for himself those called by name in order to leave survivors for the land and to fill the face of the world with their seed (CD-A 2.11–12).[230]

God's mercy in preserving Israel's seed even in the midst of judgment attests to his unswerving commitment to the covenant he made with his people. In 1 Esdras 8, Ezra acknowledges that God would have been fully justified in blotting out Israel completely. Because of God's faithfulness to his promises, however, God has disciplined Israel, not by uprooting the plant altogether, but by drastically pruning it down to the root. The fact that a "root" and "seed" and "name" have been left to Israel is a sign of grace that keeps alive the hope of their survival and future multiplication in the land:

"Were you not angry enough with us to destroy us without leaving a root or seed or name? O Lord of Israel, you are faithful; for we are left as a root to this day" (1 Esdras 8:88–89 NRSV [8:85–86 LXX]).[231]

---

to "remnant" in this (κατάλοιπον) and the preceding two examples (κατάλειμμα). Like "seed," a "remnant" is a guarantee of a nation's future (cf. Isaiah 6:12 LXX, "those left will multiply in the land": οἱ καταλειφθέντες πληθυνθήσονται ἐπὶ τῆς γῆς).

[227] ἀγαπῶν σε ἐποίησα τὸ θέλημά σου ἐπὶ Βαβυλῶνα τοῦ ἆραι σπέρμα Χαλδαίων.

[228] ἐγενήθη τὸ σπέρμα τῶν ἀπειθούντων εἰς ἀπώλειαν.

[229] καὶ ἀρχῆς γὰρ ἀπολλυμένων ὑπερηφάνων γιγάντων ἡ ἐλπὶς τοῦ κόσμου ἐπὶ σχεδίας καταφυγοῦσα ἀπέλιπεν αἰῶνι σπέρμα γενέσεως τῇ σῇ κυβερνηθεῖσα χειρί (Wis 14:6).

[230] ¹¹וּבְכוּלָם הֵקִים לו קְרִיאֵי שם לְמַעַן הָתִיר פְּלִיטָה לָאָרֶץ וּלְמַלֵא ¹²פְּנֵי חֵבֵל מִזֵּרְעָם

[231] οὐχὶ ὠργίσθης ἡμῖν ἀπολέσαι ἡμᾶς ἕως τοῦ μὴ καταλιπεῖν ῥίζαν καὶ σπέρμα καὶ ὄνομα ἡμῶν; κύριε τοῦ Ισραηλ, ἀληθινὸς εἶ· κατελείφθημεν γὰρ ῥίζα ἐν τῇ σήμερον. That preservation of "seed" ensures the future growth of a nation is, as we have seen, attested also by the fact that the destruction of "seed" signifies the ultimate act of divine judgment, the complete annihilation of a people. This use of the seed metaphor is found in Second Temple writings as well. See, for example, *Pss. Sol.* 17:7, 9; *Jub.* 16:9; 21:22 (cf. 4QJub^d [4Q219] 2.26–27; 4QJub^f [4Q221] frg. 1, lines 3–4); *Jub.* 24:30–32; 35:14; 36:9; *1 En.* 22:7; *T. Sim.* 6:3.

Similarly, the prayer in *4QWords of the Luminaries*[a] (4Q504) frgs. 1–2 5.6–14 attributes the preservation of Jacob's seed to God's covenant faithfulness:[232]

> [6]. . . In spite of all this [Israel's sin and exile] you did not despise [7]the seed of Jacob and you did not abhor Israel [8]so as to destroy them and break your covenant with them. [9]For you alone are the living God and there is none beside you. You remembered your covenant [10]by bringing us out [of captivity] in the sight of the nations and not abandoning us [11]among the nations. You showed favor to your people Israel in all [12]the lands to which you had scattered them so that they would return [13]to their senses and turn back to you and heed your voice, [14]just as you had commanded by the hand of Moses, your servant.[233]

When Paul appropriates Isaiah's oracle, then, it is with full knowledge of this widely used metaphor of "seed" as the pledge of a *future* for Israel.[234] What is potentially scandalous in Paul's appeal to Isaiah 1:9 is his claim that it is none other than he and his fellow Jewish believers ("us, whom God has called . . . from among the Jews," 9:24) who are the seed of Israel preserved by God. It must be insisted, however, that Paul does not thereby exclude the rest of Israel from God's mercy.[235] Rather, in light of the connotations of "seed" so

---

[232] This text is a portion of the Friday prayer, whose theme is the Lord's covenant faithfulness to Israel and his consequent commitment to deliver them (cf. the reference to the Lord in the benediction [frgs. 1–2 7.2], "who delivers us from every distress" [אשר הצילנו מכול צרה]). The most extensive work on this text has been done by Esther G. Chazon (1992, 1997, and Forthcoming). See also Falk 1997:59-94, esp. p. 67.

[233] [6]. . . בכול זואת לוא מאסתה [7] בזרע יעקוב ולו נעלתה את ישראל [8] לכלותם להפר בריתכה אתם כי אתה [9] אל חי לבדכה ואין זולתכה ותזכור בריתכ[ה] [10] אשר הוצאתנו לעיני הגוים ולוא עזבתנו [11] בגוים ותחון את עמכה ישראל בכול [12] [ה]ארצות אשר הדחתם שמה להשיב [13] אל לבבם לשוב עודך ולשמוע בקולכה [14] [כ]כול אשר ציותה ביד מושה עבדכה

Note that lines 6–11 allude to the curse of exile and subsequent deliverance promised in Leviticus 26:44–45, while lines 11–14 appropriate the language of Deuteronomy 30:1–2 with its assurance that God will gather repentant Israel from the ends of the earth. God's past faithfulness to deliver his people from exile becomes the foundation for the present community's hope for forgiveness and restoration. God has poured his holy spirit on them (15) so that they too will seek God in their distress (16–17).

[234] In this light, the (metaleptically suppressed) connection between σπέρμα in Romans 9:29 (Isa 1:9) and σπερῶ in Hosea 2:23a LXX ("I will sow her for myself in the land"; cf. Hos 2:23b in Rom 9:25) becomes highly suggestive, for it places God's preservation of Israel's seed in the context of covenant renewal.

[235] Compare Paul's carefully nuanced discussion of Abraham's "seed" in Romans 4. While claiming that the promise of "seed" envisions the inclusion of "many nations" in Abraham's family—not only Jacob's descendants (4:16, 18)—Paul is at

evident in Isaiah and so widely diffused in Second Temple literature, it is clear that Paul's reference to the "seed" in Romans 9:29
carries with it the germ of his conclusion in 11:26 that God will
certainly redeem "all Israel." On the way to this conclusion, Paul
will point to himself—ἐκ σπέρματος Ἀβραάμ (Rom 11:1)—as proof
that God has not abandoned Israel *and that more will be saved.*

These two Isaianic prophecies of remnant (Isa 10:22–23) and seed
(Isa 1:9) function *together* in Romans 9:27–29 not only to evoke the
severe judgment of God on wayward Israel, but also to foreshadow
God's ultimate restoration of his people.[236] Israel's present tragedy
by no means fades from view (see Rom 9:30ff.!), but through these
quotations Paul insists that because God has in the present time preserved a remnant and seed, Israel's hope of restoration remains very
much alive. The "remnant" spoken of by Isaiah does not refer to
barren survivors destined to die off one by one (like Fenimore Cooper's
Chingachgook and Uncas), but to seed that will germinate, sprout,
and blossom into a renewed Israel.[237] Because God remains faithful
to his covenant with Israel, a remnant—and, ultimately, "all Israel"—
will be saved.[238]

---

pains not to exclude Israel from the referent of "seed." Significantly, Abraham is
the "father of the circumcision," even as Paul insists that circumcision alone is not
enough; "seed" refers to "those who are not only of the circumcision but who also
follow in the footsteps of the faith of our father Abraham, which he had while still
uncircumcised" (4:12).

[236] So Meeks rightly observes:

In light of this further development [i.e., Paul's quotation of Isa 1:9], then, we
see that we would have been wrong to read "only a remnant" in v. 27—not
because the negative judgment implied by the "only" is absent from the Isaiah
passages as Paul reads them, but because the "only" would foreclose the other
side of the prophet's word, the promise that Paul also hears there (1990:113).

[237] Note the confluence of the language of "remnant" and of "seed" in Isaiah
37:31–32 (parallel to 4 Kgdms 19:30–31):

Those who remain in Judea will take root below and produce seed above, for
those who remain will go forth from Jerusalem, and those who are delivered
[will go forth] from Mount Zion—the zeal of the Lord Sabaoth will do this.
καὶ ἔσονται οἱ καταλελειμμένοι ἐν τῇ Ιουδαίᾳ φυήσουσι ῥίζαν κάτω καὶ
ποιήσουσι σπέρμα ἄνω. ὅτι ἐξ Ιερουσαλημ ἐξελεύσονται οἱ καταλελειμμένοι
καὶ οἱ σῳζόμενοι ἐξ ὄρους Σιων· ὁ ζῆλος κυρίου σαβαωθ ποιήσει ταῦτα.

[238] On this reading, it is clear that although there is a clear progression of ideas
in Paul's argument, there is no strong disjunction of thought between Romans 9
and Romans 11. Paul does not, as is often alleged, suddenly reject his remnant
theory in Romans 11 (despite all the arguments he has advanced up to this point)
in order to allow for the salvation of all of Israel. Although ample room must be
left for Paul to be unsystematic and even self-contradictory (that is, to be human),

✳

In Romans 9:25–29, Paul has marshalled an impressive pair of witnesses for his claim that God has called Gentiles as well as Jews as vessels in which to pour out his mercy and display his glory throughout the world (9:24). The texts he selects from Hosea and Isaiah share important terminological connections. Just as significant, however, are the wider conceptual correspondences among these oracles. All three of the quotations Paul adduces speak of the restoration of Israel after a period of apostasy and consequent divine judgment. While Paul hyper-extends promises of redemption and restoration for Israel so that they now encompass Gentiles, he does not thereby exclude Israel from the scope of these oracles. On the contrary, through appropriating these prophetic promises of restoration after judgment for his own situation, Paul locates contemporary Israel in the same position as Isaiah's audience, between desolation and hope. In the present time, Israel suffers under the wrath of God and desperately needs to hear the message of reconciliation and release proclaimed by Isaiah—and now by Paul himself.

Before Paul can develop further how his gospel is good news for Israel (cf. Rom 1:16–17), however, he must explain where Israel has gone wrong. Significantly, Isaiah will play a pivotal role in the development of this stage of his argument as well.

---

there is no particular virtue to be found in readings that overemphasize the unsystematic character of his thought at the expense of attending as closely as possible to the logic (foreign though it may seem to us) of his actual argument in these chapters. Käsemann's hermeneutic of charity (1980:viii) is instructive:

> Until I have proof to the contrary, I proceed on the assumption that the text has a central concern and a remarkable inner logic that may no longer be entirely comprehensible to us.

CHAPTER THREE

"A DISOBEDIENT AND CONTRARY PEOPLE"
ISAIAH IN ROMANS 9:30–10:21

> Not all have believed the gospel, just
> as Isaiah says: "Lord, who has believed
> our message?"
>
> *Romans 10:16*

THE CONTINUING INFLUENCE OF ISAIAH 1:9

In Romans 9:30–10:21, Paul traces the etiology of Israel's failure to embrace the gospel.[1] The apostle's segue from Isaiah's proclamation of hope for the remnant/seed of Israel (Rom 9:27–29, citing Isa 10:22–23; Isa 1:9) to an analysis of Israel's present disobedience (Rom 9:30) replicates the rhetorical move found in Isaiah 1:9–10. Despite the glimmer of hope offered in Isaiah 1:9, in the very next verse the prophet abruptly renews his fierce indictment of God's unfaithful people. Although Isaiah has stopped short of equating Zion's fate with that of Sodom and Gomorrah (1:9), he immediately reemploys the analogy in a shocking address to his audience: "Hear the word of the Lord, you rulers of Sodom ... you people of Gomorrah" (1:10). His call to "give heed to the law of God" (νόμος θεοῦ) implies that they have missed the point of the Law. Their sacrifices, their holy days—even their prayers—are in vain, because of their wicked and unjust practices (1:11–17).

Like Isaiah, Paul claims that Israel has wrongly understood the purpose or τέλος of the Law.[2] Despite Israel's strenuous pursuit of the Law, their efforts have been in vain, for they have failed to recognize

---

[1] As elsewhere in Romans, a rhetorical question ("What then shall we say?") signals a turn in the argument (3:1, 3b, 5c, 9, 27a, 31; 4:1, 9; 6:1, 15; 7:7, 13; 8:31; 9:14, 19, 30; 10:18–19; 11:1, 7, 11, 19; cf. Boers 1981).

[2] Many of Paul's quotations and allusions invoke the important Isaianic themes of hearing, seeing, and understanding, either explicitly or implicitly through the device of intertextual echo. The key text, of course, is Isaiah 6:9–10, from which numerous passages throughout Isaiah take their bearings. See Clements 1985:101–104; Williamson 1994:30–56, esp. 46–51; Rendtorff 1989.

that the τέλος of the Law—God's righteousness—is Christ, and that
this righteousness is available to all solely on the basis of πίστις (10:4).
Central to Paul's account of how Israel has missed the τέλος of the
Law (while Gentile outsiders have attained it) is a scriptural cita-
tion (Rom 9:33) woven out of strands culled from Isaiah 28:16 and
Isaiah 8:14.

Stumbling in Mid-Race: Romans 9:30–10:4

Before examining this citation more closely, however, it is necessary
to consider briefly the larger argument Paul is constructing in Romans
9:30–10:4. Although this section of Romans is fraught with exegetical
stumbling-stones, as it were, I will forge ahead and offer a reading
of these verses that will provide a context sufficient for understanding Paul's quotations of Isaiah, without allowing the many other
problems crying out for attention in this passage to impede our
progress unduly. The test of my interpretation will be its ability to
provide a coherent reading of Paul's argument in this section as a
whole.

The key to understanding Paul's intricate and compact argument
is found in the complex interplay among several important terms—
δικαιοσύνη, νόμος, πίστις—within the overarching context of his
extended metaphor of a footrace.[3] All three terms finish the contest
together in Romans 10:4, and (perhaps surprisingly for those who
cannot ignore Luther's vociferous cheering on the sidelines) they all
end up on the winning team, thanks to the crucial addition of the
star athlete and MVP, Χριστός. To understand how Paul pulls off
this theological (not to say metaphorical) *tour de force* requires that
we track closely the numerous twists and turns in his reasoning, paying particular attention to the role played by the citation from Isaiah
that anchors his entire argument.

The language of "righteousness" (δικαιοσύνη) appears for the first
time in Romans 9 in 9:30, but the concept has not been far from
the surface in Paul's previous discussion of how God has called out
a people for himself from among both Jews and Gentiles. The term

---

[3] Athletic imagery is a favorite item in Paul's rhetorical repertoire (see the similar collection of terms in Phil 3:12–16). See further Pfitzner 1967. On the race
metaphor in Romans 9–11, see the insightful discussion in Stowers 1994:303–306;
312–16.

"righteousness" is best understood within the larger story Paul tells about Israel's God, who has committed himself not only to save Israel from their enemies, but also to incorporate Gentiles into his people.[4] For Paul, the δικ– word group belongs to the same broad semantic field as other terms for deliverance/salvation that have been prominent in 9:1–29: ἀγαπάω (9:13, 25 [2x]); ἐλεέω (9:15 [2x], 16; cf. v. 23); καλέω (9:7, 12, 24, 25, 26); σῴζω (9:27). God's "right-eousness" refers to God's power and faithfulness to deliver and vin-dicate his people.[5] With reference to human beings, "righteousness" becomes one of several terms used by Paul to describe the rela-tionship with God that results from being redeemed and incorpo-rated into God's people ("being righteoused," δικαιοῦμαι).[6]

Paul's compact phrase, "Gentiles . . . have obtained righteousness" (9:30), encapsulates the point made more poetically by Hosea: Some Gentiles have been called by God, welcomed as his beloved people, adopted as "sons" (Romans 9:24–26). The shocking—even scan-dalous—nature of what God has done for these Gentiles is exposed by Paul's admission that they were "not pursuing righteousness." In Paul's bizarre version of "The Tortoise and the Hare," the Gentiles who have beaten Israel across the finish line were not even running in the race to begin with![7]

---

[4] See p. 44 n. 5.

[5] Cf. Romans 1:16–17. Although Käsemann was wrong about "the righteousness of God" being a technical term of "apocalyptic" (see Matlock 1996), it is an extremely important concept found frequently in the Psalms and Isaiah, as well as in Jewish literature outside the NT. While Käsemann's notion of God's righteousness as *heilset-zende Macht* captures a crucial dimension of the concept, his explication of it pri-marily in cosmic terms does not take sufficient account of the particularity of God's covenant with Israel in Paul's thought.

[6] For the term, "to righteous," and the significance of the passive voice for Paul's usage of the word as a "transfer term," see Sanders 1977:544–45. The position adopted here attempts to set Sanders's insight concerning Paul's use of the δικ– word group as "transfer" terminology more explicitly within a covenantal context, so as to highlight the continuity for Paul between what God has done for Jew and Gentile in Christ and God's promises to Israel (yet without underplaying Paul's sense of the radical newness of what God has done in Christ). It may be that my account of "righteousness" in Paul's thought owes more to Romans, while Sanders's is more indebted to Galatians. Although it would be interesting to see to what degree my understanding of "righteousness" might illuminate Paul's argument in Galatians, such an investigation would require another monograph in itself.

[7] For διώκω in the context of a footrace, see Phil 3:12, 14. For καταλαμβάνω used of attaining the thing one is pursuing, see Phil 3:12, 13; Sir 11:10; in a mil-itary context, see Gen 31:23; Exod 15:9; Deut 19:6; 4 Kgdms 25:5. Sirach 27:8 voices one of the foundational axioms of wisdom literature, that the one who pur-sues what is right will attain it: ἐὰν διώκῃς τὸ δίκαιον καταλήμψῃ καὶ ἐνδύσῃ αὐτὸ

In describing the Gentiles as "those not pursuing righteousness," Paul takes up a description of Israel employed by Isaiah, οἱ διώκοντες τὸ δίκαιον (Isa 51:1), and turns it on its head. In keeping with his hermeneutic of finding Gentiles in negative descriptions of those outside God's people,[8] Paul here creates a negative description of his own and finds this one, like the others, reversed by God's act of deliverance in Christ. Significantly, Paul immediately clarifies the nature of the righteousness Gentiles have obtained: it is righteousness ἐκ πίστεως. This qualification will prove vital to Paul's explanation of why Israel has failed so far to finish the race.[9]

While Paul thus coopts and reverses an Isaianic characterization of God's people to speak of Gentiles, he also employs the same phrase in its positive form to talk about Israel. Here too, however, he has made a crucial alteration to Isaiah's words. As a result, Israel is now depicted as zealously pursuing, not δικαιοσύνη, but νόμος δικαιοσύνης (9:31). The translation of this phrase is difficult, but in context it should probably be understood as "the Law that leads to righteousness."[10] That is, νόμος refers here not to a general princi-

---

ὡς ποδήρη δόξης. Paul's formulation here completely reverses such expectations. Wilk's suggestion (1998:316–17) that in Romans 9:30 Paul alludes to Isaiah 59:9 (διὰ τοῦτο ἀπέστη ἡ κρίσις ἀπ᾽ αὐτῶν καὶ οὐ μὴ καταλάβῃ αὐτοὺς δικαιοσύνη) appears unlikely, especially since in Isaiah 59:9 it is δικαιοσύνη who is pictured pursuing wayward Israel (59:7–8). An allusion to Isaiah 51:1 (see below) and the metaphor of a footrace would be sufficient to explain Paul's choice of words in Romans 9:30–31 without recourse to Isaiah 59:9.

[8] See p. 83.

[9] Although Paul constructs a binary opposition of Jews versus Gentiles, he has just argued from Isaiah 10:22–23 and Isaiah 1:9 that even now God has called some "from among the Jews" as "vessels of mercy" (Rom 9:24–29). Note Paul's parallel formulation in Romans 11:7, where his statement that Israel has failed to obtain righteousness receives the important qualification that "the remnant according to the election of grace" *has* experienced the deliverance promised by God. Heaviest on Paul's mind in Romans 9–11 are the questions *unbelieving Israel* raises for his gospel; hence, he often falls back into language that suggests a Jew/Gentile dichotomy, even though elsewhere he clearly states that some within Israel have already attained righteousness in Christ. E. P. Sanders suggests to me that this is an example of Paul's "general tendency to use bi-polar language in a situation that requires three terms" (private correspondence).

[10] Cf. Romans 7:10: ἡ ἐντολὴ ἡ εἰς ζωήν. So Cranfield 1979:507–508 (see also Cranfield 1975a); Käsemann 1980:277; Rhyne 1981:98–102, 1985. My reading of the syntax is basically the same as Cranfield's (1979:507–510), though we disagree about the meaning of Paul's critique. Where Cranfield finds an attack on the *legalistic* observance of the Law (cf. Cranfield 1964), E. P. Sanders and others have more plausibly located Paul's concern with "works" in the *exclusiveness* of Jewish covenant markers such as Sabbath, dietary laws, and circumcision (1983:38). I will argue that Romans 9:31 must be viewed from the perspective of Romans 10:4.

ple, but to the Jewish Law, and it is this Law that Paul claims leads to righteousness.[11]

Although it initially appears as though Paul is setting up a contrast between two kinds of righteousness, δικαιοσύνη ἐκ πίστεως and νόμος δικαιοσύνης,[12] in order to drive a wedge between Law and "righteousness from faith," his argument takes a surprising turn in the second half of v. 31. Paul claims that in running after the νόμος δικαιοσύνης, Israel failed to "catch up with"—not righteousness, as one might expect—but the Law (νόμος) itself.[13] As it stands, not only has Israel not attained the goal of righteousness, they have not yet

---

Paul maintains that pursuing the Law "as if from works" has led Israel astray because he is convinced that the righteousness to which the Law leads is the righteousness that is available through Christ for *all* who believe. Though Sanders rightly dismisses the idea that Paul is concerned with "legalism," he is only partially correct in saying, "Israel's failure is not that they do not obey the law in the correct way, but that they do not have faith in Christ" (1983:37). Paul's point is precisely that the correct way to obey the law *is* to have faith in Christ! As far as I can ascertain, the particular collocation, νόμος δικαιοσύνης, occurs elsewhere in Second Temple Jewish literature only in 4QpIsaᵉ [4Q165] frgs. 1–2 line 3 (probably a comment on Isa 40:11 [so Horgan 1979:134]) and in Wisdom 2:11. The former text (נלה אֵת תורת הצ]דק[) is too fragmentary to be of use, particularly since it is not possible to tell from the context whether תורה means "teaching" or, more specifically, "the [Mosaic] Law." In Wisdom 2:11, the sense of the sentence seems to be that "might makes right" (ἔστω δὲ ἡμῶν ἡ ἰσχὺς νόμος τῆς δικαιοσύνης, τὸ γὰρ ἀσθενὲς ἄχρηστον ἐλέγχεται), and νόμος has here the broader meaning, "principle, rule." While Paul's phraseology is close to that of Wisdom, the context of his argument suggests that the terms νόμος and δικαιοσύνη in Romans 9:30–10:4 carry significantly different connotations than they do in Wisdom 2. Consequently, I will not pursue any further the question of an allusion to Wisdom 2:11 here.

[11] This reading of Romans 9:30–10:4 stands in obvious tension with statements Paul makes elsewhere about the Law, most notably in Galatians 2:21 (οὐκ ἀθετῶ τὴν χάριν τοῦ θεοῦ· εἰ γὰρ διὰ νόμου δικαιοσύνη, ἄρα Χριστὸς δωρεὰν ἀπέθανεν). It is, however, closer in thought to Romans 7:10–13. Much confusion has resulted from attempting to harmonize too quickly Paul's argument in Romans 9:30–10:4 with these other passages. It is not necessary to view Paul's statements about the Law as completely inconsistent and self-contradictory to appreciate the influence of the particular situation he is addressing on the manner in which he frames the issue of the relationship of Law to faith and righteousness. I will confine my attention to the present passage rather than attempting to pursue here the general problem of Paul's relationship to the Law.

[12] This is clearly Paul's intent in Philippians 3:5–11, where he sets ἡ δικαιοσύνη ἡ ἐν νόμῳ/ἡ ἐμὴ δικαιοσύνη ἡ ἐκ νόμου over against ἡ διὰ πίστεως Χριστοῦ [δικαιοσύνη]/ἡ ἐκ θεοῦ δικαιοσύνη ἐπὶ τῇ πίστει (on the relationship of this passage to Rom. 10:5–6, see pp. 158–59 n. 122).

[13] The variant, νόμον δικαιοσύνης [ℵ² F Ψ 1881 𝔐 lat sy], removes the difficult turn taken by Paul, but also effectively destroys his argument (as does P. Schmiedel's conjectural emendation, δικαιοσύνην). The reading νόμον is clearly the better-attested—and more difficult—reading.

caught up with the very Law that would lead them to the goal. It is crucial to note that Paul does not criticize Israel for pursuing the Law (it is, as he has just said, the "Law that leads to righteousness"). Neither does he indicate that the "righteousness" to which the Law leads is any different from the righteousness already obtained by the Gentiles, although he does not quite say yet that the Law leads to "righteousness from faith."[14] What *is* clear at this point in Paul's argument is that if Israel had been able to overtake the Law that they were pursuing, they would have gone on to obtain righteousness as well. In contrast to the Gentiles, who were not in the game at all, Israel has been running the right race.[15]

Why then has Israel, though pursuing the "Law that leads to righteousness," been unable to overtake the Law? Paul answers, "because not from faith, but as if from works (ὅτι οὐκ ἐκ πίστεως ἀλλ᾽ ὡς ἐξ ἔργων). They stumbled over the stumbling stone . . ." (9:32). Unfortunately, Paul's elliptical style in 9:32 poses quite an obstacle of its own to interpreters. The context requires us to supply to the ὅτι clause something along the lines of, Ἰσραὴλ ἐδίωκε νόμον δικαιοσύνης οὐκ ἐκ πίστεως. . . . As a result, "not from faith . . ." describes their manner of pursuing the Law rather than characterizing the nature of the Law itself.[16] The Law, according to Paul, is rightly pursued ἐκ πίστεως. Israel, however, has been running as if it could be obtained ἐξ ἔργων.[17] As a result, right in the middle of the race they have run smack into "the stone of stumbling" placed on the track by God himself—a stone that can only be avoided by ὁ πιστεύων ἐπ᾽ αὐτῷ (Romans 9:32–33).

Just what Paul means by pursuing the Law "from faith" rather than "as if from works" is, not surprisingly, the subject of heated debate. While a full answer to this question is bound up with numerous other decisions that have to be made about "faith" and "works" in Romans and in Paul's thought generally, the immediate context

---

[14] See my discussion of Romans 10:4–13 below, pp. 157–70.

[15] Paul's race metaphor stays alive well into chapter 11 (see Rom 11:11–12).

[16] Rightly, Cranfield (1979:509). Paul's statement in Galatians 3:12, "the Law is not ἐκ πίστεως," is set in the context of a quite different argument (*contra* T. D. Gordon 1992).

[17] The importance of the particle ὡς (*as if*) should not be overlooked. By means of ὡς, Paul differentiates between what Israel (mistakenly) thinks and the way Paul claims things actually are (so Barrett 1957:193, Cranfield 1979:510, Sanday and Headlam 1902:280). Again, the problem is not pursuing the Law, but pursuing it in the wrong manner.

deserves the closest scrutiny in any attempt to understand these phrases as Paul employs them in *this* argument. In particular, Paul's second diagnosis of Israel's plight in 10:1–3 should be understood as filling out the abbreviated narrative of 9:31–33.[18]

In Romans 10:1, Paul reiterates his intense desire and prayer that Israel experience salvation. "Salvation" (σωτηρία) here reprises the theme of "righteousness" from 9:30–31. In addition, the phrase εἰς σωτηρίαν anticipates its counterpart in 10:4, εἰς δικαιοσύνην. This further confirms the interpretation that "righteousness" language in Paul refers to God's power and faithfulness to save his people and to the consequences of that act of deliverance.[19] Romans 10:4 makes it clear that this righteousness is available "to all who *believe* (πιστεύω)," echoing Paul's earlier phrase, "righteousness from *faith* (ἐκ πίστεως)" (9:30).

Although Israel's "zeal for God" is real, it is "not according to knowlege" (οὐ κατ᾽ ἐπίγνωσιν).[20] They "do not understand (ἀγνοοῦντες)[21] the righteousness of God" and seek instead to establish "their own righteousness." As a result, Israel "has not submitted (οὐχ ὑπετάγησαν) to God's righteousness."[22] The juxtaposition of Romans 9:30–33 with 10:1–4 makes it clear that Israel has been attempting to establish "their own righteousness" precisely by pursuing the Law as if it were ἐξ ἔργων. In contrast, "God's righteousness," the "righteousness ἐκ πίστεως," has been revealed to be none other than Christ, the τέλος to which the Law, pursued ἐκ πίστεως, has been leading all the time (10:4).

---

[18] I find the arguments of Lambrecht (1999) for a major break between Romans 9:33 and 10:1 to be unconvincing.

[19] See p. 44 n. 5. On the parallel use of "salvation" and "righteousness" in Romans 9–10, see further pp. 161, 168.

[20] Aageson (1983:239–40) notes the verbal link with Romans 1:28, where the Gentiles are portrayed as refusing to acknowledge God (οὐκ ἐδοκίμασαν τὸν θεὸν ἔχειν ἐν ἐπιγνώσει). On ἐπίγνωσις in Paul as entailing obedience, see Bultmann 1964:707–708; cf. Sullivan 1963.

[21] Ἀγνοέω has a range of meanings from "not know" to "not understand" to "disregard." The second seems preferable here in light of the preceding "not according to knowledge," although something closer to the third sense is suggested by Paul's later denial that Israel has not "heard" or "known" and by his subsequent appeal to Isaiah, who calls Israel λαὸς ἀπειθῶν καὶ ἀντιλέγων (Rom 10:19–21).

[22] Note the striking parallel to this statement in Romans 8:7 that "the mind of the flesh" does not submit to "the Law of God" (incidentally, the only other time submission to God is mentioned in Romans): διότι τὸ φρόνημα τῆς σαρκὸς ἔχθρα εἰς θεόν, τῷ γὰρ νόμῳ τοῦ θεοῦ οὐχ ὑποτάσσεται, οὐδὲ γὰρ δύναται. This parallel suggests that Paul identifies ἡ τοῦ θεοῦ δικαιοσύνης with the νόμος δικαιοσύνης

My focus on Paul's reading of Isaiah will help to expose the logic underlying Paul's contention that Israel has pursued the Law ἐξ ἔργων because of their ignorance of, and indeed outright resistance to, "the righteousness of God." Paul explicitly anchors his play-by-play analysis of Israel's misstep to a citation of scripture drawn from Isaiah 28:16/8:14. The most obvious connection between the passage Paul cites and Romans 9:30ff. is the catchword πιστεύω.[23] Yet given the evidence adduced thus far for Paul's sensitivity to the wider settings of many of his scriptural citations, it is reasonable to hope that a closer look at Isaiah 26:18/8:14 and their contexts may elucidate more precisely Paul's critique of Israel, including what he means by ἐκ πίστεως, ἐξ ἔργων, and "the righteousness of God."

Isaiah 28:16/8:14 in Romans 9:33: The Text

Paul's introduction (9:32b-33a) modifies a phrase borrowed from the quotation, προσέκοψαν τῷ λίθῳ τοῦ προσκόμματος. By anticipating the wording of his citation, Paul guides the reader toward its proper interpretation.[24] From the outset, Israel is linked with those who stumble over the stone and, correspondingly, set in opposition to those who "believe/trust in it" (ὁ πιστεύων ἐπ᾽ αὐτῷ). Curiously, Paul does not go on to identify the "stone" explicitly. In the absence of a clear christological interpretation of the citation at this point in Paul's argument (as is found, for example in 1 Peter 2:4–8), it is all

---

(the law rightly pursued ἐκ πίστεως) and sets *both* over against Israel's "own righteousness."

[23] The notion of stumbling also fits well with the larger "race" metaphor Paul constructs. One wonders whether the metaphor suggested the quotation to Paul, or vice versa.

[24] Paul does not name Isaiah as the source of this quotation, employing instead one of his usual introductory formulas, καθὼς γέγραπται (Rom 1.17; 2.24; 3.4, 10; 4.17; 8.36; 9.13, 33; 10.15; 11.8, 26; 15.3, 9, 21; 1 Cor 1.31; 2.9; 2 Cor 8.15; 9.9; cf. γέγραπται: Rom 12.19; 14.11; 1 Cor 1.19; 3.19; 9.9; 10.7; 14.21; 15.45; Gal 3.10, 13; 4.22, 27). This formula effectively substitutes for Isaiah's, "Thus says the Lord." Fitzmyer (1960–61:8–9) notes that this formula is found in the LXX (e.g., 4 Kgdms 14:6; Dan 9:13 θ′) and that it corresponds to the formula כאשר כתוב found in the Dead Sea Scrolls (8–9). On quotation formulas in the Qumran *pesharim*, see further Elledge 2001; see also Bernstein 1994; Metzger 1951. One cannot argue from silence that Paul did not know (or care that his readers knew) the source of this quotation, for Paul rarely provides a reference more specific than "it is written." However, we should pay all the more attention to the rhetorical effect created by the instances in which Paul does name Isaiah or another figure as the speaker of the words he quotes. See p. 78 n. 110.

the more important to inquire how the identity and role of the "stone" within the book of Isaiah may have influenced Paul's choice of texts here.

My first task is to address the question of the source of Paul's citation and to suggest why he conflated these particular texts in this manner. Paul's composite citation takes an A–B–A form, with a portion of 8:14 spliced into the middle of 28:16. The most obvious cause for this conflation appears to be the word λίθος shared by the two texts. In effect, Paul's juxtaposition of the two passages allows 8:14 to define the nature of the stone spoken of in 28:16. This identification of the stone in 28:16 with that in 8:14 appears elsewhere in early Christian exegesis. In fact, there is good evidence to suggest that this interpretive move had already been made by the author or editor of Isaiah 28 and then further developed by the translator of the LXX.[25] Before considering the possibility of Paul's indebtedness to previous interpreters, however, I will focus on the formal aspects of the citation itself.

The form of text that Paul cites in Romans 9:33 and the extent of his own authorial adaptations are complex and highly controverted questions, particularly when one entertains the possibility of a pre-Pauline origin for this composite citation (whether in Hebrew or in a Greek version other than LXX). Careful attention to the details of the quotation itself reveals clearly the numerous difficulties and uncertainties involved in reconstructing Paul's *Vorlage*.[26] By pursuing a close analysis of these questions, however, I will be able to offer a far more nuanced account of Paul's multi-layered relationship to the text of Isaiah.

---

[25] The critical consensus that Isaiah 28–33 derives from the same general time period as Isaiah 1–12 is based in part on the numerous connections between the two sections of the book in vocabulary, in thought, and even in structure (see Seitz 1993:204–207). These connections—though not the critical hypotheses they have engendered in the modern period—would have been obvious to ancient readers/memorizers of Isaiah as well.

[26] See the extended discussions in Lindars 1961:169–86; Snodgrass 1977–78; Black 1971–72:11–14.

Figure 3.1: Isaiah 28:16 LXX and Isaiah 8:14a LXX in Romans 9:33

Key: single underline agreement between Rom 9:33 and Isa 28:16
      double underline agreement between Rom 9:33 and Isa 8:14a
      italic   agreement among all three columns

Isaiah 28:16 LXX	Romans 9:33	Isaiah 8:14a LXX
διὰ τοῦτο οὕτως λέγει κύριος Ἰδοὺ ἐγὼ ἐμβαλῶ εἰς τὰ θεμέλια Σιων λίθον πολυτελῆ ἐκλεκτὸν ἀκρογωνιαῖον ἔντιμον εἰς τὰ θεμέλια αὐτῆς, καὶ ὁ πιστεύων ἐπ᾽ αὐτῷ οὐ μὴ καταισχυνθῇ	ἰδοὺ τίθημι ἐν Σιὼν λίθον προσκόμματος καὶ πέτραν σκανδάλου, καὶ ὁ πιστεύων ἐπ᾽ αὐτῷ οὐ καταισχυνθήσεται	καὶ ἐὰν ἐπ᾽ αὐτῷ πεποιθὼς ἧς, ἔσται σοι εἰς ἁγίασμα, καὶ οὐχ ὡς λίθου προσκόμματι συναντήσεσθε αὐτῷ οὐδὲ ὡς πέτρας πτώματι [καὶ ἐὰν πεποιθὼς ἧς ἐπ᾽ αὐτῷ... οὐχ ὡς... οὐδὲ ὡς... συναντήσεσθε αὐτῷ]

Isa 28:16 MT: לָכֵן כֹּה אָמַר אֲדֹנָי יְהוִה הִנְנִי יִסַּד בְּצִיּוֹן אָבֶן אֶבֶן בֹּחַן פִּנַּת
               יִקְרַת מוּסָד מוּסָּד הַמַּאֲמִין לֹא יָחִישׁ

Isa 8:14 MT: וְהָיָה לְמִקְדָּשׁ וּלְאֶבֶן נֶגֶף וּלְצוּר מִכְשׁוֹל לִשְׁנֵי בָתֵּי יִשְׂרָאֵל לְפַח
               וּלְמוֹקֵשׁ לְיוֹשֵׁב יְרוּשָׁלִָם

The text of Isaiah 28:16a cited in Romans 9:33 agrees once with MT against LXX in reading ἐν Σιων (MT: בצּיון; LXX, εἰς τὰ θεμέλια Σιων). The initial verb τίθημι differs from LXX (ἐγὼ ἐμβαλῶ) with regard to use/non-use of the independent pronoun,[27] lexical choice,[28] and verb tense.[29] An additional minor variation between Romans

---

[27] Hebrew texts read הנני. At this point, the LXX is closer to the Hebrew from the standpoint of literal representation of each feature of the original.

[28] In the LXX, τίθημι never translates the Hebrew root יסד.

[29] The present tense might reflect either the use of a variant Hebrew text or a different vocalization of the consonants found in MT (cf. Lim 1997a:148–49). 1QIsa[a] (מיסד) and 1QIsa[b] (יוסד) have participles, while MT's perfect (יִסַּד) could also be vocalized as a participle (יֹסֵד). Such a *Vorlage* (or variant pointing of יסד) is suggested by α′ σ′ θ′, ἰδοὺ ἐγὼ θεμελίων Σιων. Interestingly, the author of the Epistle of Barnabas employs τίθημι in the introduction to his quotation of Isaiah 28:16 (where, with LXX, he has ἐμβαλῶ), suggesting that he knew both text forms (*Barn.*

9:33 (οὐ καταισχυνθήσεται) and Isaiah 28:16 LXX (οὐ μὴ καταισχυνθῇ) locates the former slightly closer to the Hebrew,[30] although this may be explained as merely an inner-Greek variant rather than an attempt at a more woodenly literal representation of the Hebrew.[31] On the other hand, in the final clause of 28:16, Paul's version shares with LXX two elements lacking in MT: namely, the conjunction καί before ὁ πιστεύων and the prepositional phrase, ἐπ αὐτῷ.[32] In addition, the common use of a form of καταισχύνω represents a significant agreement between Paul and LXX, particularly in light of the difficulty of the Hebrew idiom and the quite divergent translations found in the versions.[33] Of course, the composite citation in Romans stands apart from both MT and LXX in substituting the description of the stone found in Isaiah 8:14 for that belonging to Isaiah 28:16.

Paul's citation of Isaiah 8:14 in Romans 9:33 shares three important words with the LXX version: λίθον (LXX, λίθου; cf. the form λίθον found in Isa 28:16 LXX); προσκόμματος (LXX, προσκόμματι); πέτραν (LXX, πέτρας). However, Paul's version also differs significantly from LXX. For LXX πτώματι, the text found in Romans reads σκανδάλου.[34] Moreover, Paul's citation lacks several words uniformly

---

6:2–3; see Harris 1916–20, 1:31; Bauckham 1988:311). There is no clear evidence that Pseudo-Barnabas knew Paul's letters (Paget 1994:207–14; Hvalvik 1996:34).

[30] Romans 9:33 renders the single Hebrew negative with a single Greek negative. Οὐ alone is employed by α′ σ′ θ′.

[31] Both expressions are acceptable Greek. While the construction found in LXX is perhaps more emphatic, the sense of expectation attached to the future tense may have better suited Paul's eschatological framework. The reading of Western witnesses (D F G) at Romans 9:33 (οὐ μὴ καταισχυνθῇ) probably represents a secondary harmonization with LXX.

[32] The prepositional phrase has the obelus in 88 and is omitted by several, principally Hexaplaric, witnesses. In all likelihood, this omission represents a secondary harmonization with MT. The variant πᾶς in Romans 9:33 clearly arose by assimilation to Paul's citation of the verse in Romans 10:11 (cf. Metzger 1994:463).

[33] Isaiah LXX elsewhere translates חוש (hif.) by ἐγγίζω (5:19) and by συνάγω (60:22). The translator may have solved the problem of the meaning of לֹא יָחִישׁ by drawing on the idiom לֹא יֵבוֹשׁ found at 29:22, 45:17, 49:23, 50:7 (בוש = αἰσχύνω), and at 54:4 (בוש = καταισχύνω). At Isa 28:16, α′ σ′ θ′ translate οὐ σπεύσει. In contrast, the Peshitta reads, "he will not *be afraid*" (ܢܕܚܠ ܠܐ), while Tg. has, more expansively, "when trouble comes, they will not *be shaken*" (בְּמֵיתֵי עָקָא לָא יִזְדַּעְזְעוּן). The antiquity of the Targum's rendering is supported indirectly by echoes of this portion of Isaiah 28:16 in 1QHa and in 1QS: לוֹא תחזיע (1QHa 14[6].27); לוֹא תזדעזע (1QHa 15[7].9); בל יזדעזעו, parallel to בל יחישו (1QS 8.7–8).

[34] Elsewhere in Isaiah LXX, מכשול is translated by σκῶλον (57:14). An examination of the Reider/Turner index reveals that Aquila regularly translates √כשל with a form of σκανδαλ– (Reider 1966:286). Apparent exceptions to this rule probably result from misattribution of these readings to Aquila (p. 34, s.v. ἀσθενεῖσθαι;

attested by the LXX textual tradition (but not by any Hebrew text).[35] Where the quotation in Romans 9:33 diverges *grammatically* from LXX, it agrees with MT and with the later Greek translations of Aquila, Symmachus and Theodotion. Romans 9:33 has καί where LXX reads οὐδέ, and Paul's phrases λίθον προσκόμματος . . . πέτραν σκανδάλου render more exactly the Hebrew construct chains, ולאבן נגף . . . ולצור מכשול.[36]

The overall impression one derives from this mass of data is that Paul's citation depends on a Septuagint text that has been reworked at points to bring it closer to a Hebrew exemplar. Significantly, where Paul's quotation diverges from LXX Isaiah in 28:16b and in 8:14, in all but one instance it does so in agreement with a Hebrew text[37] and/or with one of the later Greek translators.[38] At the same time, it is not possible to make a strong case that any of the differences between Paul's citation and the LXX originated with Paul himself.[39] This evidence strongly suggests that Paul used a manuscript of the Septuagint that had already been revised toward a Hebrew form of the text. Curiously, however, the "distance" of this text from LXX varies within Paul's citation. Paul's text is furthest from LXX in its rendering of Isaiah 28:16a and Isaiah 8:14. Its proximity to LXX is greatest in Isaiah 28:16c, where Romans 9:33 shares with LXX—against all other witnesses—both the additional phrase, ἐπ᾽ αὐτῷ, and

---

p. 230, s.v. συντρίβεσθαι). In the LXX, σκάνδαλον is found for מכשול in 1 Kgdms 25:31; Ps 118:165.

[35] LXX οὐχ ὡς . . . οὐδε ὡς may be explained as loose equivalents for Hebrew ו and ל, called forth by the overall interpretation of the text pursued by the translator (Ziegler 1934:95, following Fischer 1930:23, suggests that a reading ולא לאבן, perhaps arising from dittography, could account for the interpretation of the LXX. Goshen-Gottstein 1995:31 doubts this account, apparently attributing the LXX reading to the translator's interpretive freedom with the *Vorlage*). The words συναντήσεσθε αὐτῷ lack any Hebrew counterparts and find no support in other Greek versions; their presence is clearly due to the LXX translator's interpretive activity.

[36] Cf. Aquila: καὶ εἰς λίθον προσκόμματος καὶ εἰς στερεὸν σκανδάλου. The versions σ΄ and θ΄ have the same grammatical structure: καὶ εἰς λίθον προσκόμματος καὶ εἰς πέτραν πτώματος (though a fragment of Eusebius cites σ΄ as reading εἰς πέτραν σκανδάλου).

[37] It does not seem possible to specify this as a revision toward a "proto-masoretic" text, since at no point in these verses does the Greek point to a reading that is distinctively characteristic of MT.

[38] See above regarding the tense of τίθημι; the phrase ἐν Σιων; the construction λίθον προσκόμματος . . .; καί; the use of σκάνδαλον. The omission of ἐγώ in Paul's citation has no parallel in other witnesses.

[39] As is possible, for example, in the case of πᾶς in Paul's re-citation of Isaiah 28:16c in Romans 10:11, discussed below (cf. Stanley 1992b:123–25).

the use of καταισχύνω as a lexical equivalent for Hebrew חוש.[40] It is difficult to explain the sole difference from LXX in the citation of 28:16 (the form of the verb οὐ καταισχυνθήσεται) as an intentional revision toward a more literal rendering of the Hebrew. We are thus presented with the curious phenomenon of a single verse, Isaiah 28:16, whose latter half stands in close agreement with LXX while its former half—along with the bit of 8:14 joined to it—appears to have undergone a hebraizing revision. It may be that the revision of LXX hypothesized here took place in a fairly haphazard manner,[41] or that it proceeded according to some other principle than a desire for the closest possible conformity at every point with a Hebrew exemplar.[42]

A Pre-Pauline Testimony? The Evidence of 1 Peter

Significant agreements between the text cited in Romans 9:33 and the (un-conflated) quotation of these Isaianic passages in 1 Peter have led a number of scholars to the hypothesis that Paul draws his quotation from a pre-existing testimony-book or anthology of quotations.[43] Figure 3.2 lays out the texts of Romans 9:33 and 1 Peter 2:6, 8 so that an exact comparison may be made between them.

In place of the prophetic introduction found in Isaiah 28:16 LXX, "thus says the Lord," both Paul and the author of 1 Peter employ formulas signalling a quotation from scripture, although neither names the source as Isaiah.[44] At Isaiah 28:16a, Romans 9:33 and 1 Peter 2:6 agree with one another exactly up to the word λίθον; they thus share in common the divergences from and agreements with LXX noted previously. At this point, however, where Paul's citation inserts phrases from Isaiah 8:14, 1 Peter continues to quote 28:16b.

---

[40] Note also the absence in MT of an equivalent for καί before ὁ πιστεύων.

[41] See below, p. 134 n. 53; cf. pp. 16–17 n. 60; Tov 1997:11.

[42] Such a principle should have entailed at least the omission of ἐπ᾽ αὐτῷ (see n. 32 above).

[43] Cf. pp. 20–21 above. See further Lindars 1961:169–81; Aageson 1983:116–120; Albl 1999:265–85, esp. 271–75.

[44] There is no further citation formula in 1 Peter 2:6–8 after v. 6, although quotations from Psalm 117:22 LXX and Isaiah 8:14 are woven into the interpretive comments in vv. 7–8. Note that the author prepares for this scriptural catena and its interpretation as early as v. 4 through employing the key terms λίθον . . . ἀποδεδοκιμασμένον . . . ἐκλεκτὸν ἔντιμον. On the use of scripture in 1 Peter, see Bauckham's insightful discussion (1988:309–13).

Figure 3.2: Romans 9:33 and 1 Peter 2:6, 8

Key: single underline   agreement of both Rom and 1 Peter with LXX
       double underline   agreement of Rom and 1 Peter *against* LXX
       italic   unique agreement of 1 Peter with LXX
       roman   reading unique to Rom or 1 Peter

1 Peter 2:6	Romans 9:33	1 Peter 2:8
διότι περιέχει ἐν γραφῇ· ἰδοὺ τίθημι ἐν Σιὼν λίθον	καθὼς γέγραπται· ἰδοὺ τίθημι ἐν Σιὼν λίθον προσκόμματος καὶ πέτραν σκανδάλου	καὶ λίθος προσκόμματος καὶ πέτρα σκανδάλου
†ἀκρογωνιαῖον ἐκλεκτὸν ἔντιμον † καὶ ὁ πιστεύων ἐπ᾽ αὐτῷ οὐ μὴ καταισχυνθῇ	καὶ ὁ πιστεύων ἐπ᾽ αὐτῷ οὐ καταισχυνθήσεται	
†LXX, πολυτελῆ ἐκλεκτὸν ἀκρογωνιαῖον ἔντιμον εἰς τὰ θεμέλια αὐτῆς†		

The text in 1 Peter 2:6 varies at two points from the LXX, omitting several words (πολυτελῆ . . . εἰς τὰ θεμέλια αὐτῆς) and inverting the order of two of the descriptions of the stone.[45] Paul's quotation picks up again at Isaiah 28:16c. Here, 1 Peter 2:6 agrees with LXX verbatim, as does Romans 9:33 (apart from the variant οὐ καταισχυνθήσεται discussed above).

From Isaiah 8:14, both Paul and the author of 1 Peter quote only the two phrases describing the stone.[46] Significantly, 1 Peter 2:8 reads with Romans 9:33—and against LXX—the word σκάνδαλον (found in α′ and also, according to Eusebius, in σ′). In addition, 1 Peter agrees with Romans (cf. α′ σ′ θ′ MT) in the grammatical form of

---

[45] The apparatus of NA[27] indicates the variety of readings in the mss at 1 Peter 2:6; the version attested in B C et al. (adopted by NA[25]) is almost certainly an assimilation to LXX. The remaining variations can best be explained as instances of haplography due to homoioteleuton.

[46] Both NT authors quote the text with καί rather than οὐδέ as in LXX. See p. 130 n. 35.

the phrases λίθος προσκόμματος . . . πέτρα σκανδάλου, over against
LXX Isaiah's λίθου προσκόμματι . . . πέτρας πτώματι.

The striking correspondences between Romans 9:33 and 1 Peter
2:6, 8, particularly where both differ from LXX, point in the direction of a common source,[47] perhaps a revised LXX text or an anthology of scriptural quotations.[48] What is of particular significance for
the present study is the high probability that the actual *conflation* of
texts—and the consequent omission of at least the words, ἀκρογω-
νιαῖον ἐκλεκτὸν ἔντιμον—is to be attributed to Paul.[49] The quite
different ways in which these texts are presented in Romans and
1 Peter provides an important clue to the form in which Paul will
have encountered these texts in his *Vorlage*. Romans 9:33 conflates
Isaiah 28:16 and 8:14, while 1 Peter 2:6–8 separates Isaiah 28:16
and Isaiah 8:14 by means of a third "stone" text, Psalm 117:22 LXX.[50]
It appears, then, that these texts were *not* conflated in the source
shared by Romans and 1 Peter, but that Paul himself wove them together as they now appear in Romans 9:33. Such a reconstruction is
far simpler than supposing that the author of 1 Peter, Penelope-like,

---

[47] That 1 Peter depends directly on Romans for these quotations is unlikely (see
further p. 134 n. 51 below).

[48] The combination of Isaiah 28:16 and 8:14 appears occasionally in early Christian
literature, but clear evidence for a single written testimony source is lacking. The
conflation of Paul's distinctive form of Isaiah 28:16 with Isaiah 8:14 is found twice
in Tertullian (*Adv. Marc.* 5.5; *Adv. Jud.* 14) and once in the fourth-century *Dialogue
of Athanasias and Zacchaeus*, §111 (Kraft 1960:345). These two authors may well depend
on Romans for the connection of these Isaianic texts rather than on a separate collection of excerpts. While I consider it likely that *Barn.* 6:2–4 depends on reading
Isaiah 28:16 and 8:14 together (so Prigent 1961:171), I agree with Kraft's assess-
ment that the evidence for Barnabas' use of Isaiah 8:14 in the introduction to his
quotation of 28:16 is "inconclusive" (1960:345 n. 77). The only explicit trace of
Isaiah 8:14 is the noun συντριβή (cf. Isa 8:15, συντριβήσονται; but note also 28:12,
σύντριμμα; 28:13, συντριβήσονται). E. G. Selwyn's hypothesis that Paul and the
author of 1 Peter make common use of an early Christian hymn or rhythmical
prayer is interesting, but undemonstrable (1947:268–77).

[49] It may well prove impossible to identify additional Pauline adaptations with
any degree of certainty.

[50] The interpretation of these "stone" texts in 1 Peter explicitly focuses on the
christological significance of these passages to a much greater degree than does
Paul, yet, like Paul, the author discusses these texts in an *ecclesiological* context. I am
skeptical whether one can trace within the NT lines of development in the interpretive tradition surrounding these verses (or even be certain in which direction
"development" proceeded); such a project assumes a much larger (and even more
tenuous) hypothesis about the shape of early Christian interpretation of the scriptures. For an attempt to show development, however, see Lindars 1961:169–86.
For the use of "stone" texts by patristic authors, see Kraft 1960:344–45; J. R. Harris
1916–20, 1:18–19, 26–32; 2:19–20, 59–61, 137–39; Albl 1999:279–83.

first meticulously unravelled the conflated texts before proceeding to
reweave them—along with additional strands from Isaiah 28:16—
into a different pattern altogether.[51]

The nature of the source from which both Paul and the author
of 1 Peter drew these Isaiah passages remains unclear. The existence
of various scriptural anthologies with fairly wide circulation among
early Christian preachers has been shown to be a thoroughly plausible hypothesis, but the use of such an anthology in any particular
instance remains a matter of conjecture.[52] In the case of Isaiah 28:16
and 8:14 in Romans and 1 Peter, a plausible explanation for the
non-septuagintal characteristics of these quotations would be their
common use of a version of LXX Isaiah revised (unevenly) toward
a Hebrew exemplar.[53]

Even if Paul has created his conflated quotation in Romans 9:33
by drawing texts from a pre-existing collection of excerpts, it does
not follow that the larger Isaianic contexts of these passages are
unimportant for understanding Paul's use of these texts. We should

---

[51] It is conceivable that the author of 1 Peter drew his citations from Paul's letter to the Romans, but again, he would not only have had to pull apart Paul's
combined quotation, he also would have had to supply the words missing from
Isaiah 28:16. Consequently, it seems unlikely that the author of 1 Peter depended
on Romans, rather than on a common source, for his quotation of Isaiah 28:16
and 8:14. See the similar line of reasoning in Kraft 1960:345; Dodd 1952a:42–43.
Only one other passage of scripture is shared by Romans and 1 Peter, Hosea 2:23
LXX (Rom 9:25; 1 Peter 2:10); however, 1 Peter does not share Paul's distinctive
reading, οὐκ ἠγαπημένη.

[52] Selwyn's astounding claim that ἐν γραφῇ (1 Pet 2:6) "proves ... that St. Peter
was here quoting from a documentary source other than the text of scripture itself"
(1947:163) is convincingly refuted by J. R. Michaels (1988:102–103).

[53] Cf. Michaels 1988:103. Stanley objects that tracing the identical text-form of
Isaiah 8:14 in Romans and 1 Peter to their common use of a "corrected" manuscript of Isaiah requires one to suppose that they also both just happened to choose
an *unrevised* manuscript of Isaiah LXX for their citations of 28:16 (1992b:120–21
n. 109). However, this argument ignores the "hebraizing" character of Paul's citation of Isaiah 28:16a. Moreover, in claiming that Paul's citations of Isaiah 8:14 and
28:16 could not have come from the same manuscript, Stanley assumes that the
hypothetical revision of LXX Isaiah toward a Hebrew exemplar would have resulted
in a text of uniform character, despite the fact that the available evidence for early
revisions of the LXX suggests that such modifications were made on a much more
haphazard basis. Stanley himself (1992b:46 n. 41) quotes F. M. Cross's description
of the proto-Lucianic recension as "a light sprinkling of readings derived from the
Palestinian textual family . . . to which the Old Greek was sporadically corrected"
(Cross 1972:116). Cross concludes, "At most the proto-Lucianic text is a light revision of the Old Greek, consisting of occasional corrections to the closely allied
Palestinian text" (1972:125 n. 26 [Stanley mistakenly gives the reference as p. 120
n. 30]). See further Stanley 1992b:45 n. 39.

not assume that Paul's occasional use of a pre-existing collection of scriptural texts precludes his knowledge of the fuller contexts of these passages in their source texts.[54] Paul would have encountered scripture in multiple modes. A more adequate model would view Paul's relationship with scripture as multi-dimensional, potentially including in any given instance familiarity with the use of scriptural traditions in early Jewish and Christian teaching, an acquaintance with collections of excerpts (his own or others'), and his own careful reading of particular passages in their wider literary contexts, including his memorization of large portions of scripture.[55] This is not to baldly assert that Paul never quotes or alludes to Israel's scriptures without regard for the wider context of a passage. Rather, each case of citation or allusion must be argued individually, through a full exploration of the evidence, with the burden of proof resting on the shoulders of the one advancing a hypothesis about the source of Paul's wording and his knowledge (or lack thereof) of its wider context. At the same time, a convincing demonstration of my claim that the great majority of Paul's quotations and allusions to Isaiah in Romans must be understood in terms of his construal of the sense of a larger portions of the book requires not only a consideration of each passage by itself, but also a critical evaluation of the cumulative evidence provided by the study as a whole.[56]

In the present instance, the hypothesis that Paul is aware of the original settings of Isaiah 8:14 and 28:16 in the book of Isaiah certainly warrants further investigation, particularly in light of the fact that Paul, both elsewhere in Romans 9–11 and in 1 Corinthians, clearly shows interest in Isaiah 28–29, drawing on texts as close to our present passage as 28:11–12 (1 Cor 14:21) and 28:22 (Rom 9:27).[57] Moreover, as I will demonstrate below, the text of Isaiah 28–29 resounds with numerous echoes of Isaiah 8. It is quite

---

[54] This is an important assumption that underlies much of Stanley's work on Paul's use of scripture, but one whose validity he never convincingly demonstrates (see pp. 22–25).

[55] See above pp. 20–27.

[56] For which see Chapter 6 below. In his detailed and careful study of Deutero-Isaiah's use of other texts, Sommer similarly notes that when investigating an author's allusive use of sources, it is necessary to rely on cumulative argumentation. For instance, finding a clear allusion to a particular source increases the likelihood that the author is alluding to that same source in a case where the alleged allusion is less transparent (1998:35; cf. Hays 1989:30).

[57] Note also Isa 29:10/Rom 11:8; Isa 29:14/1 Cor 1:19; Isa 29:16/Rom 9:20.

conceivable that Paul's own close reading of Isaiah 28–29 could have suggested to him the connection with Isaiah 8, whether or not he first became aware of such a link through a pre-existing anthology of quotations. Thus, it is necessary to explore the extent to which Paul's use of Isaiah 8:14 and 28:16 may be illuminated by attending to the function and interrelation of chapters 8 and 28–29 within the book of Isaiah.

Isaiah 28:16/8:14 in Romans 9:33: The Context

How much Paul's appropriation of Isaiah 8:14 and 28:16 in Romans 9:33 owes to the wider contexts of these verses in the book of Isaiah can only be revealed through a careful reading of both the Isaianic texts and Romans. I will first sketch briefly the function of Isaiah 8:14 and 28:16 in their immediate literary settings and also note the significant interconnections between the two passages established within the book of Isaiah itself. This investigation will set the stage, as we return to Romans 9:33, for a greater appreciation of the extent to which Paul draws on the text of Isaiah as he creatively reinterprets scripture in light of the larger argument he is developing in Romans 9–11.

The Stone of Stumbling

The exegetical quandaries facing modern readers of Isaiah 8 were no less acute for ancient interpreters, as the bold divergence of the LXX and Targum from the Hebrew text (and from one another) attests.[58] In the preceding discussion, I noted the importance of a partially-revised form of the LXX text for explaining Paul's composite quotation in Romans 9:33. Consequently, I will pay close attention here to the sense of Isaiah 8 as it stands in the LXX, offering along the way further evidence that Paul's interpretation of these verses presupposes his use of a Septuagintal version of Isaiah.

Isaiah 8 LXX continues to address the threat to Ahaz and to the Davidic dynasty introduced in Isaiah 7. The kings of Damascus (Aram) and Samaria (Israel) have formed a coalition in order to contain Assyrian aggression in the region. In an attempt to compel Judah to join them, they have plotted to overthrow Ahaz and to install an

---

[58] On Isaiah 8 LXX see van der Kooij 1997a:519–29; Seeligmann 1948:105–107; Ziegler 1934:95–96. For the Targum, see the notes in Chilton 1987:18–20.

otherwise unknown puppet ruler in his place (7:1–6). Their anti-Assyrian policy evidently has won strong support even within Ahaz's own kingdom (8:6). Isaiah, however, assures Ahaz that his enemies' plot will not succeed; God, though he disciplines his people by means of such foreign threats, will not forsake Israel: "For whenever my fierce anger comes, again I will heal [you]."[59]

In response to this promise of deliverance, Ahaz is called to believe (πιστεύω) the word the Lord has spoken (7:7–9). Ahaz's failure to trust, represented by his pious-sounding refusal to ask for a divine sign (7:10–13), nevertheless calls forth from the prophet a sign of hope for God's people: the promise of a coming ruler who will exemplify genuine trust in God (7:14–16).[60] For Ahaz and the people of Judah as a whole, however, there is a more immediate promise of punishment (7:17). God is about to raise up Assyria as his instrument of judgment to chastise not only the northern nations threatening Judah, but also the southern kingdom itself (7:18–25).

A two-part episode involving writing in a scroll and naming Isaiah's child opens Isaiah 8 (8:1–4). These enacted prophecies signal the imminent plundering of Damascus and Samaria at the hands of the Assyrian invaders. There is little room for Judah to take comfort at this message, however, for the Lord immediately condemns the people of Jerusalem for their willing complicity in the rebellious plots of the northern kings and announces that Assyria will overrun and devastate the land of Judah as well (8:5–8b). Yet as before, God does not intend the utter destruction of his people. Though Aram, Israel, and Assyria plot against them, God will ultimately bring the schemes of Judah's enemies to nought (cf. 7:7; 10:25). The repeated affirmation, "God is with us" (8:8c, 10c), frames a defiant proclamation to the nations that it is the God of Israel who controls world events; though he disciplines his people, God will not forsake them.

---

[59] ὅταν γὰρ ὀργὴ τοῦ θυμοῦ μου γένηται, πάλιν ἰάσομαι, 7:4b LXX. MT reads quite differently here: בְּחֳרִי־אַף רְצִין וַאֲרָם וּבֶן־רְמַלְיָהוּ. The LXX translator makes the interesting move of drawing on the Lord's previous words of commission to Isaiah in 6:10 (μήποτε ἴδωσιν τοῖς ὀφθαλμοῖς καὶ τοῖς ὠσὶν ἀκούσωσι καὶ τῇ καρδίᾳ συνῶσι καὶ ἐπιστρέψωσι καὶ ἰάσομαι αὐτούς) in a way that highlights God's gracious commitment ultimately to redeem Israel despite their present obduracy.

[60] It is intriguing to note that the LXX translator has rendered vv. 15–16 in such a way as to present this child-to-be-born as one who (unlike Ahaz) instinctively chooses good and rejects evil:

πρὶν ἢ γνῶναι αὐτὸν ἢ προελέσθαι πονηρά, ἐκλέξεται τὸ ἀγαθόν· διότι πρὶν ἢ γνῶναι τὸ παιδίον ἀγαθὸν ἢ κακόν, ἀπειθεῖ πονηρίᾳ τοῦ ἐκλέξασθαι τὸ ἀγαθόν ...

The following oracle, from which Paul's quotation is drawn, describes a response to the present crisis that contrasts starkly with the reaction of the majority of the people. It is a response of faith and trust in God (8:11–16).[61] Because the LXX differs so significantly from MT in these verses, it will be helpful to provide the entire passage:

[11]οὕτως λέγει κύριος· τῇ ἰσχυρᾷ χειρὶ ἀπειθοῦσι τῇ πορείᾳ τῆς ὁδοῦ τοῦ λαοῦ τούτου λέγοντες· [12]μήποτε εἴπητε σκληρόν· πᾶν γάρ, ὃ ἐὰν εἴπῃ ὁ λαὸς οὗτος, σκληρόν ἐστι· τὸν δὲ φόβον αὐτοῦ οὐ μὴ φοβηθῆτε οὐδὲ μὴ ταραχθῆτε· [13]κύριον αὐτὸν ἁγιάσατε, καὶ αὐτὸς ἔσται σου φόβος. [14]καὶ ἐὰν ἐπ᾽ αὐτῷ πεποιθὼς ᾖς, ἔσται σοι εἰς ἁγίασμα, καὶ οὐχ ὡς λίθου προσκόμματι συναντήσεσθε αὐτῷ οὐδὲ ὡς πέτρας πτώματι· ὁ δὲ οἶκος Ιακωβ ἐν παγίδι, καὶ ἐν κοιλάσματι ἐγκαθήμενοι ἐν Ιερουσαλημ. [15]διὰ τοῦτο ἀδυνατήσουσιν ἐν αὐτοῖς πολλοὶ καὶ πεσοῦνται καὶ συντριβήσονται, καὶ ἐγγιοῦσι καὶ ἁλώσονται ἄνθρωποι ἐν ἀσφαλείᾳ ὄντες. [16]τότε φανεροὶ ἔσονται οἱ σφραγιζόμενοι τὸν νόμον τοῦ μὴ μαθεῖν.

[11]Thus says the Lord, "With a strong arm they rebel against following in the way of this people, saying, [12]'No longer say a hard [i.e., stubborn, rebellious] thing; for everything this people says is hard. Do not fear what they fear and do not be troubled. [13]The Lord—*him* shall you sanctify, and *he* will be your fear. [14]And if you trust in him, he will be for you a sanctuary, and you will not encounter him as the obstruction of a stone or as the obstacle of a rock.' But the house of Jacob is in a snare, and they are lying in a trap in Jerusalem. [15]For this reason many will become weak through them, and they will fall and be broken, they will draw near and be captured—people dwelling in safety. [16]Then those who seal up the Law in order not to learn [it] will be exposed."

This interpretive move—along with the reading παρθένος in v. 14, of course—may have later facilitated Christian appropriation of this oracle as a christological prophecy. Also important for such a christological interpretation were the numerous interconnections between the Immanuel oracle in chapter 7 and the oracle in chapter 9 heralding the birth of a royal son (Seitz 1993:74–75, 84–87). Seitz argues that the larger shape of Isaiah points to Hezekiah as the focus of these oracles, leading to a clear contrast between Ahaz' lack of faith in the present episode and the faithful behavior of Hezekiah under a similar threat from Assyria in Isaiah 36–39 (1993:60–87; cf. Seitz 1991:195–96; Ackroyd 1982; Clements 1991).

[61] The opening boundary of this section of chapter 8 is clearly delineated by the use of the introductory formula, "thus says the Lord." Identifying its conclusion is more problematic. Despite the paragraph divisions in Ziegler 1939a, v. 16 evidently continues the topic of the preceding verses (so Seeligmann 1948:105; van der Kooij 1997a:523). The speech formula, καὶ ἐρεῖ, in v. 17 may mark a division of thought, although repetition of the phrase, πεποιθὼς εἶναι, forges a strong link with v. 14. Similarly, the shift in speaker at v. 19 may indicate a new section; it connects closely, however, with the theme of refusal to give heed to νόμος introduced in v. 16. In any event, it is clear that the oracles in vv. 17–22 continue to develop themes introduced in vv. 11–16.

The oracle speaks of two groups of people whose reactions to the Assyrian threat fall at opposite ends of the spectrum. The first group is referred to as "this people" (ὁ λαὸς οὗτος, 8:11, 12). Standing as it does in sharp contrast to the covenant formula, "my people," frequently found in Isaiah's messages of consolation, this appellation represents a jarring distantiation of God from his people. "This people" have already been characterized in Isaiah 6:9–10 as blind and deaf and without understanding. The phrase continues to carry a negative valence in chapter 8, and indeed, throughout the rest of the book.[62] In Isaiah 8:6, it is "this people" who have rejected the smoothly-flowing waters of Siloam in favor of submitting to rule by the coalition of northern kings. This group—further identified in 8:14–15 as "the house of Jacob," those "in Jerusalem," "many," "people dwelling in security"—will encounter God as a snare and stumbling stone.[63] In context, "this people" must also encompass "those who seal up the Law in order not to learn [it]" (8:16)[64] and those who take counsel with spiritists and mediums (8:19) rather than relying on the aid provided by the νόμος (8:20).

The second group remains unnamed, but it is characterized both by implacable opposition to "this people" and by unwavering trust in God. These are the ones who vigorously rebel (τῇ ἰσχυρᾷ χειρὶ ἀπειθοῦσι)[65] against "following the way of this people" (8:11).[66] They

---

[62] "This people" appears again in chapters 28–29, which I will argue are closely related verbally and thematically to Isaiah 8 (cf. 28:11, 14; 29:13, 14). Elsewhere, the phrase is found in Isaiah 3:17; 9:16; 65:3. Given Paul's use of Hosea 2:23; 1:10 earlier in Romans, it is unlikely that the covenantal implications of the name "this people" escaped his notice. Seeligmann 1948 (and van der Kooij 1997a after him) misses the negative valence of "this people"; as a result, while he also finds in Isaiah 8 LXX two groups—the faithful and those who forsake God's Law—he misidentifies "this people" as the faithful.

[63] *Jub.* 1:9–10 (cf. 4QJub[a] [4Q216] 2.6–7) employs terminology from Isaiah 8:14–15 to describe the consequences of Israel's idolatry (see J. C. VanderKam in DJD XIII, 10, note to line 7).

[64] In contrast, in Isaiah 8:16 MT it is Isaiah's disciples who are to seal up the testimony and the teaching (תורה) among themselves.

[65] For χεὶρ ἰσχυρά in a description of armed resistance, see its two other occurences in LXX: Num 20:20; 1 Macc 11:15. Note also the description in the Immanuel oracle of the child to come as one who resists (ἀπειθέω) evil in order to choose good (Isa 7:16). The verb ἀπειθέω appears in LXX Isaiah 1:23 and 65:2 where MT reads √סרר (cf. its use in 59:13 where MT has the noun סרה); perhaps here the translator understood the Hebrew verb in his *Vorlage* to be a form of √סרר. Alternatively (Goshen-Gottstein 1995:31 n. 11[2]), the translator may have read the verb as a form of √סור (so α′σ′ θ′ 1QIsa[a] Peshitta; contrast MT, pointed וְיִסְּרֵנִי [from √יסר]).

[66] *4QFlorilegium* (4Q174) frgs. 1–2 1.14, commenting on Ps 1:1, employs a modified

set themselves over against "this people/the house of Jacob" by
eschewing rebellious speech (v. 12).[67] Instead of fearing what "this
people" fear, they determine to regard the Lord alone as holy and
to fear only him (v. 13).

The LXX rendering of 8:14 further drives home the point that
trusting in God is the proper response to the present crisis. The
translator solves the major exegetical problem in v. 14[68] by supplying a key phrase from v. 17 (πεποιθὼς ἔσομαι ἐπ' αὐτῷ) and by turn-

---

phrase from Isaiah 8:11 to speak of the righteous as "those who turn from the path
[of the wicked]": [הרשעים] פשר הדב[ר.•••]סרי מדרך (in doing so, it further attests the
root √סור read by the scribe of 1QIsaᵃ and possibly by the translator of LXX
Isaiah; see previous note). A quotation of Isaiah 8:11a follows in line 15 with the
citation formula: "As it is written in the book of Isaiah the prophet for the last
days" (אשר כתוב בספר ישעיה הנביא לאחרית [ה]ימים). 1QSa [1Q28a] 1.1–3 identifies
"the sons of Zadok—the priests—and the men of their covenant" as "those who
turned from walking in the way of the people" (אשר סר[ו מל]כת ב[דרך העם). Similarly,
11QMelchizedek [11Q13] 2.24 interprets "Zion" (Isa 52:7) as those who "establish
the covenant, who turn from walking in the way of the people" (הסרים מלכת [בד]רך
העם). In CD, the rebels are those who "did not depart from the way of traitors"
(לא סרו מדרך בונדים; CD-A 8.4–5 = CD-B 19.17), while the "penitents of Israel"
(שבי ישראל) "turned from the way of the people" (סרו מדרך העם; CD-A 8.16 =
CD-B 19.29; cf. the pejorative comment about "those who returned to the way of
the people," ושבו עוד אל דרך העם, CD-B 20.23–24). In contrast, CD-A 1.13 uses
the appellation, "those who turn from the way" (סרי דרך), to describe the apos-
tates in Israel (note the catchword link סרר/סור with Hosea 4:16, cited in CD-A
1.13–14; cf. CD-A 2.6; 1QS 10.21: ס(ו)ררי דרך). G. J. Brooke has suggested that
the use of this phrase in CD-A 1.13 is rooted in an interpretation of "Isaiah 8:11
and its context (8:11–16)," perhaps under the influence of the use of part of Isaiah
8:11–16 in 4QJubᵃ 2.7–9 [*Jub.* 1:9–10, echoing Isa 8:14–15] (1997c:114–15). Against
Brooke's hypothesis is the telling absence of the qualifier העם, "[way of] the people," which would tie the phrase in CD-A 1.13 clearly to Isaiah 8:11. The "way"
is known elsewhere as a description of the community's life and may ultimately
derive from an interpretation of Isaiah 40:3 (see McCasland 1958). If Brooke is
right in hearing an echo of Isaiah 8:11 here, however, it would reveal a surprising
tolerance in the same document for quite different interpretations/appropriations of
the same text (i.e., CD-A 1.13 vs. CD-A 8.16 = CD-B 19.29).

[67] The adjective σκληρός and related words are part of a frequently-employed
scriptural *topos* describing Israel's rebelliousness (e.g., Isa 48:4; Deut 31:27; Judg
2:19; Bar 2:33; σκληρότης: Deut 9:27; σκληροκαρδία/σκληροκάρδιος: Deut 10:16;
Jer 4:4; Ezek 3:7; Sir 16:10; σκληροτράχηλος: Exod 33:3, 5; 34:9; Deut 9:6, 13;
Sir 16:11; Bar 2:30; σκληρύνω [τ. καρδίαν; τ. τράχηλον; τ. νῶτον]: Deut 10:16;
4 Kgdms 17:14; 2 Chr 30:8; 36:13; Neh 9:16, 17, 29; 1 Esd 1:46; Ps 94:8; Jer
7:26; 17:23; 19:15; *Pss. Sol.* 8:29).

[68] I.e., the apparent need for a clear break between למקדש and ולאבן despite the
waw on the latter. MT solves the problem by supplying an *'atnaḥ* at למקדש, producing two distinct thought units. For a modern solution that creates a single unit
of thought by emending למקדש to למקשר, "conspiracy" (cf. 8:12), see J. D. W.
Watts 1985:119 note 14.a (cf. BHS, note a on v. 14). An alternative to emendation is offered by Evans 1985.

ing the first half of the verse into a conditional sentence: ἐὰν ἐπ᾽ αὐτῷ πεποιθὼς ἧς. . . . According to Isaiah 8:14 LXX, those who trust in God[69] will *not* encounter him as the obstruction of a stone or as the obstacle of a rock, but as a sanctuary.[70] Instead, they will wait on God, even though God has turned his face away from the "house of Jacob." Isaiah 8:17 underscores their resolve: "I will trust in him." The LXX creates a tight verbal link between 8:14 and 8:17 through the insertion of "If you trust in him" into v. 14.[71] It thereby not only makes trust in God the thematic center of gravity of the passage but also brings Isaiah and his followers within the orbit of this unnamed group of the faithful (vv. 17–18).

In light of Paul's appropriation of this text in Romans 9:30ff. to explain Israel's misstep, it is significant to note that, in the Isaianic context, trust in God entails *adherence to* the νόμος.[72] Verses 16–18 set the faithful one who trusts in God over against those who refuse to learn the Law, clearly implying that willingness to learn and obey the Law characterizes those who wait for and trust in God. Similarly, according to verses 19–20, God gave the Law as a help, freely available to his people,[73] so that they would not seek out mediums and spiritists. Instead, through the aid provided by the Law, they ought to rely on their God alone (8:19: οὐκ ἔθνος πρὸς θεὸν αὐτοῦ;). For Isaiah, then, adherence to the Law sets those who trust in God apart from the unfaithful ones who stumble and fall. I will return to this

---

[69] I noted above the use of πεποιθὼς εἶναι in Isaiah 10:20 to characterize Israel's attitude when they turn back to God (p. 101).

[70] The Targum similarly creates a conditional sentence out of 14a, but it interprets למקדש negatively, in line with the following prediction of stumbling: ואם לא תקבלון ויהי מימריה בכון לפורען ולאבן מחי "And if you do not listen, his Memra will become in your midst an avenger and a stone of striking. . . ." Ziegler argues that a common *Schultradition* lies behind LXX and Targum here (1934:96). The *formal* similarity of their interpretations must not mask the significant divergence of *content*, however. It may be that the coincidence of the two translations at this point is due to a common stock of techniques for dealing with translational difficulties rather than to a shared exegetical tradition.

[71] The translator's rendering, "the house of Jacob" (cf. MT, "the two houses of Israel"), further links v. 14 with v. 17.

[72] It is probable that תורה in Isaiah 8:16 originally carried the more general sense "teaching," since it seems to refer to the prophet's own instruction (note the mention of disciples, למדי). However, the LXX rendering of the verse (compare 8:20) apparently takes νόμος in its later, more restricted sense, of the Mosaic Law (see Seeligmann 1948:104–105; Dodd 1935:25–41). Paul would most likely have understood νόμος in Isaiah 8 in this narrower technical sense.

[73] This appears to be the sense of περὶ οὗ [τοῦ νόμου] οὐκ ἔστι δῶρα δοῦναι περὶ αὐτοῦ; in contrast, the services of a medium (8:19) come at a price.

point shortly when examining the role of the Law in Israel's mis-step according to Paul.

"The One Who Trusts in Him Will Not Be Ashamed"

A similar situation of deep internal division forms the background for Isaiah 28:16 and its wider context, chapters 28–29.[74] As before, the rift results from two quite different responses to Israel's God, who is working through foreign nations to bring both judgment and deliverance to his people.[75]

As in chapter 8, Isaiah employs the language of "faith/trust" (πεποίθα/πιστεύω) to differentiate between those who have remained faithful to God and those who have apostatized. The appellation "this people," employed in 8:11–12, appears frequently in 28–29 as a pejorative term for God's rebellious people (28:11, 14; 29:13, 14). Prominent among the rebels are the "leaders of this people in Jerusalem," (28:14)[76] whom the prophet characterizes as "the ones who vainly place their trust in a lie" (οἱ πεποιθότες μάτην ψεύδει, 28:17). The "lie" refers to the belief that they will escape the judg-ment with which God is about to visit his people at the hands of the Assyrians (28:15). They have placed their confidence in a deliv-erer other than God, probably, in light of 30:1–7 and 31:1–3, to be identified as Egypt.[77] The prophet vividly denounces their idolatrous pact as a "covenant with death . . . an agreement with Hades" (28:15, 18) and vows that it shall not stand (28:17–19).[78] He describes their

---

[74] I confine my investigation to 28–29 based on two considerations: the occur-rence of a clear break at 30:1 (note the use of οὐαί to mark topical shifts at 28:1; 29:1, 15 (2x); 30:1; 31:1; 33:1) and the fact that Paul does not quote from 30–33. Seitz notes that, among critical scholars, there is as yet no real consensus regard-ing the structure of Isaiah 28–33 (1993:203).

[75] Recall the earlier discussion of the general flow of thought in Isaiah 28–29 LXX (pp. 62–65).

[76] Note "priest" and "prophet," 28:7; cf. 29:10, "their prophets and their lead-ers, the ones who see hidden things." *Contra* Dinter (1980:279), there is no reason to believe that the LXX translator has only *foreign* oppressors in view.

[77] Compare Isaiah 28:17 (οἱ πεποιθότες μάτην ψεύδει) with 30:3 (τοῖς πεποιθόσιν ἐπ' Αἴγυπτον) and 31:1 (οἱ ἐφ' ἵπποις πεποιθότες καὶ ἐφ' ἅρμασιν . . . καὶ οὐκ ἦσαν πεποιθότες ἐπὶ τὸν ἅγιον τοῦ Ισραηλ). Additional terminological links with Isaiah 30 include συνθήκη (28:15; 30:3), σκεπάζω (28:15; 30:2; cf. 30:3, σκέπη); αἰσχύνη/ ὄνειδος (28:16; 30:3, 5). The irony of this pact with Egypt should not be missed: to return to Egypt (30.2; 31:1) would be to repudiate the Lord's greatest act of deliverance in favor of the very gods so soundly and publicly defeated in the exo-dus. This "plan" or "covenant" represents the polar opposite of the "new exodus" heralded by Isaiah.

[78] Perhaps a sarcastic allusion to Egypt's cult of Osiris (so also J. D. W. Watts

fate in words eerily reminiscent of Isaiah 8:15: they will fall, be broken, and be taken captive in the coming disaster (28:13).

In contrast, the Lord announces that he himself is setting in Zion's
foundation "a precious stone, a chosen and honored cornerstone."
In Hebrew, the image seems to be that of a foundation stone inscribed
with the motto, "the one who trusts [in YHWH] will not be
ashamed."[79] In this figure, the stone merely bears the maxim; it is
not a symbol for YHWH.

Some later tradents, however, did seek to identify the stone more
precisely. The Targumist, in a fairly interpretive rendering of the
whole passage, read this as a prophecy of the Roman emperor.[80]
Among the Dead Sea Scrolls, the Rule of the Community and several of the *Hodayot* apparently understood Isaiah 28:16 as a reference to the founding of their community. Although none of these
compositions quotes Isaiah 28:16 explicitly, the "chosen stone"[81] and
"precious cornerstone"[82] that "will not be shaken"[83] are prominent
among the numerous building images fashioned into elaborate
metaphorical monuments to the solidity of the new community that

---

1985:369). Note the transformation of this text in Wisdom 1:16–3:12, where the
"covenant with death" is made by adherents of a philosophy of *carpe diem* who per-
secute the righteous ones who trust in God (οἱ πεποιθότες ἐπ' αὐτῷ, 3:9). By identifying the unfaithful with Gentile idolators in opposition to righteous Jews, Wisdom
takes Isaiah 28 in the opposite direction from Paul, who makes room for Gentiles
among those Jews who trust in the "stone" of 28:16 (Rom 10:11) while explicitly
identifying those who stumble with the majority of Israel. For Wisdom's use of
Isaiah, see Skehan 1940; Suggs 1957; Beentjes 1997; Nickelsburg 1972:58–82;
Winston 1979:17, 20–21.

[79] So also Kaiser 1974:254 (see 253 for other interpretations).

[80] בכין כדנן אמר יי אלהים האנא ממני בציון מלך תקוף ניבר ואימתן
אחקפיניה ואחסניניה אמר נביא וצדיקיא דהימינו באלין במיתי עקא לא יזדעזעון
"Therefore thus says the Lord God, 'See, I am appointing in Zion a king—a
severe, mighty, and fearsome king.' 'I will harden him and strengthen him,' says
the prophet. 'And the righteous ones who believe these things—when trouble
comes, they will not be shaken.'"
A messianic reference is quite unlikely here (*contra* Evans 1984a:565) in light of
28:17–20, which portrays the king as the one who sends Israel into exile (so Chilton
1987:55–57).

[81] אבני בחן (1QHᵃ 14[6].26); cf. חומת בחן (1QHᵃ 15[7].9); חומת הבחן (1QS 8.7).

[82] פנת יקר (1QS 8.7). This text apparently refers to "the council of the community" rather than to the community as a whole. Note, however, the echo of Isaiah
28:16 in 1QS 5.5 in reference to the calling of all who enter the community: ליסד
מוסד אמת לישראל.

[83] לוא תתחזעזע (1QHᵃ 14[6].27; לוא תזדעזע (1QHᵃ 15[7].9; בל יזדעזעו, parallel to
בל יחיש (1QS 8.7–8).

God has founded.[84] The use of Isaiah 28:16 to speak of the *Yaḥad*—
beleaguered and isolated amidst the widespread unfaithfulness of
Israel, yet unmoved—appears particularly fitting in light of the wider
setting of Isaiah 28:16, with its sharp distinction between those who
trust in YHWH and the majority who have apostatized.

In the LXX, however, there is a crucial addition to Isaiah 28:16:
"the one who trusts *in him* will certainly not be ashamed" (ὁ πιστεύων
ἐπ' αὐτῷ οὐ μὴ καταισχυνθῇ). Faith or trust *in the "stone"* characterizes
those who will be delivered by God from the coming crisis. The
precise identity of this stone remains curiously ambiguous. The
antecedent of "him" may well be God, despite the abrupt shift from
first to third person. Isaiah's warning to Ahaz and his followers in
Isaiah 7:9 (ἐὰν μὴ πιστεύσητε οὐδὲ μὴ συνῆτε) provides the closest parallel and, interestingly, the only previous use of πιστεύω in Isaiah. In
Isaiah 7:9, it is clear that the object of trust is God. However, the
potential for a determined interpreter to find textual warrant in the
LXX for identifying the "stone" with someone other than God
remains.[85] I will examine below how Paul exploits this feature of the
text in the course of his argument in Romans 9:30–10:13.

In addition to speaking of "faith/trust," Isaiah 28 makes rather
elaborate use of the language of "hope" (ἐλπίς).[86] What divides the
two groups addressed by Isaiah is the *object* of their hope. The prophet
excoriates those who place their hope and trust not in Israel's God,
but in a "lie" (28:15), in "Hades" (28:18). Their hope will prove ill-
founded; when disaster comes, it will strike at break of day, and "in
the night, there will be evil hope" for them (28:19). In contrast to

---

[84] Among these images we should also take special note of one drawn from Isaiah
28:17, [מה]א משקלה ומשקלת קו משפט (1QHᵃ 14[6].26); cf. משקלת השמש . . . נכון קו (1QHᵃ
16[8].21–22). For detailed discussion of the use of building imagery in the Dead
Sea Scrolls, see Betz 1957.

[85] Early Christian interpreters such as the author of 1 Peter understood this to
be a prophecy of Christ (1 Peter 2:4–10). Interestingly, on this foundational christological interpretation of the stone passages the author of 1 Peter erects an image
of the community not unlike that known from 1QS and 1QHᵃ: his addressees are
living stones, fitted together by God to form a spiritual temple.

[86] The frequent reference to "hope" in chapter 28 (10 of 16 occurrences of ἐλπίς
in Isaiah) lends a tight thematic unity to this chapter in its LXX version. In fact,
the translator introduces this notion even where it lacks a plausible basis in the
Hebrew text before him (28:4, 5, for צבי; 28:19, for זועה). Note also the more
understandable—but still interpretive—use of ἐλπίς for קו in 28:10 [2x], 13 [2x],
17 and the possible exchange by the translator of √חסה for √חזה in 28:18 (cf. 28:15,
where ἐλπίς = מחסה; see notes in Goshen-Gottstein 1995:108–110).

the disaster that awaits "this people" (apparently the vast majority of Jerusalemites and their leaders, 28:14), the Lord promises, "In that day, the Lord of Hosts will be the crown of hope, the diadem of glory, for the *remnant of my people* (τῷ καταλειφθέντι μου λαῷ, 28:5). For those who trust (28:16), the Lord promises to make his merciful judgment their hope (28:17); his judgment and strength will protect them from destruction (28:6).

In Isaiah 28, then, as in chapter 8, Israel as a whole has sought deliverance apart from God. Only the remnant who remain faithful to the Lord, who are characterized by hope and trust in him alone, receive the promise of deliverance.

Isaiah in Stereo: Recollections of Isaiah 8 in Isaiah 28–29
There is solid precedent in the book of Isaiah itself—and particularly in its LXX version—for the interpretive relationship between Isaiah 8:14 and 28:16 that Paul draws by conflating these passages in Romans 9:33. Numerous verbal and thematic connections between chapter 8 and chapters 28–29 suggest that at the compositional level, Isaiah 28–29 is intended to be read in light of Isaiah 8.[87] Close analysis of the LXX version of these chapters will bear this hypothesis out.

The most obvious link between Isaiah 8:14 and 28:16 is, of course, the prominent image of God as "stone" and the promise that the one who trusts in him will be vindicated. The particular wording of Isaiah 28:16 LXX (ὁ πιστεύων ἐπ᾽ αὐτῷ) suggests that the translator rendered this passage with Isaiah 8:14, 17 in mind. The phrase ἐπ᾽ αὐτῷ in Isaiah 28:16 LXX has no parallel in the Hebrew text, but it does appear in Isaiah 8:17 (πεποιθὼς ἔσομαι ἐπ᾽ αὐτῷ, where ἐπ᾽ αὐτῷ corresponds to MT, לו) and in the similar phrase added to 8:14 by the LXX translator (ἐὰν ἐπ᾽ αὐτῷ πεποιθὼς ᾖς).[88] The diction of 8:14, 17 may also have influenced the translator's rather interpretive rendering in 28:17, where he characterizes those who do not

---

[87] In speaking of the influence of Isaiah 8 on 28–29, I am consciously adopting the perspective of a reader who encounters these texts sequentially, rather than making a claim about the relative priority of either text. The dating of the materials in Isaiah 28–29 is still disputed, although a good portion of the material within these chapters is commonly attributed to Deutero-Isaiah.

[88] On the addition to Isaiah 8:14 LXX, see pp. 140–41 (cf. Ziegler 1934:95). Curiously, in his detailed analysis of Isaiah 28–33 LXX, Laberge (1968, 1978) does not discuss the reading ἐπ᾽ αὐτῷ in Isaiah 28:16.

trust in God as "those who vainly trust in a lie" (οἱ πεποιθότες μάτην ψεύδει).[89]

The network of relationships extends well beyond these few verses, however. A number of additional passages spread througout Isaiah 28–29 betray the influence of terminology and concepts found in Isaiah 8. In Hebrew, Isaiah 8:15 and 28:13 share a string of four verbs describing the fall of those who refuse to rely on God: "they will stumble . . . and be broken, they will be snared and be captured" (see Fig. 3.3).[90] Nowhere else in Isaiah do even two of these Hebrew verbs appear together.[91]

Figure 3.3: Isaiah 8:15 and 28:13 in LXX and MT

Key: <u>single underline</u>   agreement between Isa 8:15 MT and 28:13 MT
<u>double underline</u>   agreement between Isa 8:15 LXX and 28:13 LXX

Isaiah 8:15 LXX	Isaiah 8:15 MT	Isaiah 28:13 MT	Isaiah 28:13 LXX
		ילכו	ἵνα πορευθῶσι
ἀδυνατήσουσιν	וכשלו	וכשלו	καὶ πέσωσιν
ἐν αὐτοῖς πολλοὶ	בם רבים	אחור	εἰς τὰ ὀπίσω
καὶ πεσοῦνται	ונפלו		
καὶ συντριβήσονται	ונשברו	ונשברו	καὶ κινδυνεύσουσι
καὶ ἐγγιοῦσι	ונוקשו	ונוקשו	καὶ συντριβήσονται
καὶ ἁλώσονται	ונלכדו	ונלכדו	καὶ ἁλώσονται

The echo of Isaiah 8:15 in 28:13 is discernable in the LXX also. In the LXX, the parallelism is not as neat—in part because in 8:15 the translator evidently mistook ונוקשו (κινδυνεύσουσι in 28:13) for ונגשו (ἐγγιοῦσι)[92]—but nevertheless, the correspondence is quite strik-

---

[89] MT, "and hail will sweep away the shelter of a lie" (ויעה ברד מחסה כזב). On the problems in relating the LXX translation of this verse to a Hebrew *Vorlage*, see Laberge 1978:11–12.

[90] Noted also by Stansell 1996:86–87. Irwin 1977 fails to note most of the verbal connections that exist between chapters 28–29 and 8, however.

[91] The verb יקש occurs in Isaiah only in these two verses, while לכד is found in only two other verses (only one other time in the *niphal*).

[92] Goshen-Gottstein (1995:32) thinks this resulted from an error in hearing (cf. Fischer 1930:23). In addition, the order of terms differs between the two verses (a number of Hexaplaric and Lucianic witnesses transpose κινδυνεύσουσι and συντριβήσονται in order to match 28:13 MT).

ing. In both cases, those who will fall, be broken, and be captured are just those Israelites who refuse to put their trust in God and his word (8:14; 28:16).[93]

In retracing the steps of the LXX translator, we see once again the capacity of an ancient interpreter to compare related passages, phrases, and even single words that are widely dispersed throughout a sizable text. Although the translator of Isaiah may represent a special case due to the particular exigencies of his task of translation as well as interpretation, it is unlikely that his work was isolated from the wider traditions and practices of exegesis in Jewish communities. Indeed, rabbinic exegesis is well known for its juxtaposition of widely separated passages, largely on the basis of shared vocabulary or theme. The textual tradition of the scriptures also bears witness to the powerful influence of parallel passages on the transmission of the text, both in its original languages and in the versions.[94] We should

---

[93] The occurrence in Isaiah 29:4 and 8:19 of a rare phrase used to describe the spirits of the dead consulted in divination—οἱ φωνοῦντες ἐκ/ἀπὸ τῆς γῆς—provides an additional point of contact between chapters 8 and 28–29. In the entire LXX, this phrase appears elsewhere only in Isaiah 19:3, in the context of a declaration of judgment on the false gods of Egypt (The Hebrew equivalent, אוֹב, likewise occurs only in Isaiah in 8:19; 19:3; 29:4. It is found elsewhere [16x] in the Hebrew Bible only in the Pentateuch, the Deuteronomic History and Chronicles. In addition, the verb צפף, "chirp," unique to Isaiah, is used in connection with the dead only in 8:19 and 29:4 [it appears in 10:14; 38:14 of birds]. This latter correspondence between chapters 8 and 28–29 is lost in the LXX.). Although the Greek phrase resembles terminology employed in the well-known narrative of 1 Kingdoms 28:3–25 (cf. Sir 46:20), where Saul consults the ghost of Samuel through a medium (ἐγγαστρίμυθος, 1 Kgdms 28:3, 7 [2x], 8, 9; οἱ γνώστας ἀπὸ τῆς γῆς, 1 Kgdms 28:3, 9), the LXX translator does not appear to have employed 1 Kingdoms as a guide for the translation of the underlying Hebrew terms. While 1 Kingdoms renders ידענים by γνώσται (as does σ′ at Isa 8:19), LXX Isaiah uses ἐγγαστρίμυθοι; for אוֹב, 1 Kingdoms employs ἐγγαστρίμυθος, but LXX Isaiah translates האובות and אוֹב as οἱ φωνοῦντες ἀπὸ τῆς γῆς. More probably, the translator derived the meaning of אוֹב through his own comparison/ conflation of the three passages in which this word appears in Isaiah. From the context of 29:4 (והיה כאוב מארץ קולך), he hit upon the translation φωνέω ἐκ τῆς γῆς for אוֹב, drawing inspiration from the following word, φωνή (= קוֹל). He then used this equivalent for the other occurrences of אוֹב in 8:19 and 19:3, where there is in Hebrew no mention of the ground (ארץ). In turn, the plural אובות from 8:19 and 19:3 was carried over into 29:4 (so Laberge 1978:24, 119. Cf. α′: μάγος, Isa 8:19; 29:4; σ′: γνώστης, Isa 8:19; but ἐγγαστρίμυθος, Isa 29:4). For the listener who perceives this echo of Isaiah 8:19 in 29:4, the effect is to highlight the certain doom of those who will not trust in the Lord. The very ones who sought safety in false gods (8:19) will become like the spirits of the dead to whom they have looked for guidance (29:4).

[94] See the numerous examples for both testaments discussed in Schildenberger 1959.

not underestimate the close knowledge of the book of Isaiah possible for ancient readers—particularly those with "scholastic" interests—who regarded it as a sacred text. To what degree Paul's use of Isaiah betrays such intimacy with the text is, of course, the point at issue in the present work; the preceding discussion, however, offers an important reference point for evaluating what evidence we do have concerning Paul's reader-competence and interpretive strategies in their historical and cultural contexts.

Yet another node in the network of relationships connecting Isaiah 28–29 with Isaiah 8 is formed by the conjunction of Isaiah 29:11 and 8:16. Both of these verses speak of the sealing of a book, employing vocabulary that appears nowhere in Isaiah outside these two passages (Greek, σφραγίζω; Hebrew, חתם). In 8:16 LXX, the prophet predicts the exposure to God's judgment of those who "seal up the νόμος so as not to learn it" (οἱ σφραγιζόμενοι τὸν νόμον τοῦ μὴ μαθεῖν). In contrast to the Hebrew text, in which it is Isaiah's "testimony" (תעודה) and "teaching" (תורה) that are being sealed up among his disciples, in the LXX this νόμος is none other than God's Law, and those who seal it up do so out of rebellion against God. When Isaiah later cries out that, because of Israel's divinely-inflicted blindness and stupor (29:10; cf. Romans 11:8), all of God's deeds of judgment and salvation (πάντα τὰ ῥήματα ταῦτα) will be for them like "the words of *this* sealed book" (ὡς οἱ λόγοι τοῦ βιβλίου τοῦ ἐσφραγισμένου τούτου, 29:11), it is tempting to understand here a reference by the LXX translator[95] to the book of the Law that the disobedient have sealed up in order to disregard it (8:16). Because they have refused to hearken to God's Law, they are unable to discern God's ways in the present crisis.

Further evidence of the relationship between Isaiah 8 and Isaiah 28–29 at the compositional level may be found in the closing verses of the latter section, Isaiah 29:17–24. This passage, a promise of imminent redemption, draws together a number of terms and ideas from chapters 8 and 28–29. Verse 18, "In that day, the deaf will hear the words of a book" (λόγους βιβλίου), recalls "the words of this sealed book" (οἱ λόγοι τοῦ βιβλίου τοῦ ἐσφραγισμένου τούτου) mentioned in 29:11. If, as I have suggested, 29:11 is linked verbally to

---

[95] Note that an equivalent for τούτου is lacking in MT (not surprisingly, it is omitted in Hexaplaric and Lucianic witnesses to LXX), 1QIsaᵃ, Targum, Peshitta, Vulgate.

8:16, the implication is that "the deaf" will now hear God's Law aright.[96] The second half of 29:18 promises that the eyes of the blind—eyes that are in darkness and gloom (οἱ ἐν τῷ σκότει καὶ οἱ ἐν τῇ ὁμίχλῃ ὀφθαλμοὶ τυφλῶν)—will be able to see. This oracle thus reverses the curse of 8:22, where those who rebel against God encounter σκότος ὥστε μὴ βλέπειν.[97] In connection with the reference to deafness in 29:18a, the language of blindness here recalls the important Isaianic theme of the blinding of Israel by God (6:9–10), last mentioned in 29:10.

At the heart of this densely allusive passage (29:22–23) lies the clearest indication that the LXX translator has not only recognized the presence of threads tying chapters 8 and 28–29 together within the book of Isaiah but has also pulled the knot joining the two "stone" texts tighter still. The Hebrew text of Isaiah 29:23 recalls 8:12–13 by its use of the verbs עָרַץ and קָדַשׁ, which occur in the *hiphil* only in these two passages in Isaiah. Absent is any overt connection with 28:16. The verbal link with chapter 8 found in Hebrew is maintained in the LXX, through the use of the verbs ἁγιάζω and φοβέω in both 8:12–13 and 29:23.

What is of greater interest, however, is the fact that in the LXX, this recollection of the "stone" passage of chapter 8 is tightly bound up with another allusion, this time to the "stone" saying in 28:16.

> For this reason, thus says the Lord to the house of Jacob, whom he set apart from [among the descendants of] Abraham: "Now you shall *not be ashamed*, O Jacob, and now Israel shall not turn his face. But when their children see my works, on my account they shall *sanctify* my name. They shall *sanctify* the holy one of Jacob and they shall *fear* the God of Israel."

> διὰ τοῦτο τάδε λέγει κύριος ἐπὶ τὸν οἶκον Ιακωβ, ὃν ἀφώρισεν ἐξ Αβρααμ· οὐ νῦν αἰσχυνθήσεται Ιακωβ, οὐδὲ νῦν τὸ πρόσωπον μεταβαλεῖ Ισραηλ· ἀλλ᾽ ὅταν ἴδωσι τὰ τέκνα αὐτῶν τὰ ἔργα μου, δι᾽ ἐμὲ ἁγιάσουσι τὸ ὄνομά μου καὶ ἁγιάσουσι τὸν ἅγιον Ιακωβ καὶ τὸν θεὸν τοῦ Ισραηλ φοβηθήσονται (Isaiah 29:22–23).

In 29:22, the word of the Lord comes to "the house of Jacob" vowing, "Now Jacob will not be ashamed" (οὐ νῦν αἰσχυνθήσεται). This

---

[96] Cf. the call, μάθετε ἀκούειν, in 28:19 and the further use of hearing as a metaphor for obedience in 28:12, 23. Note also the prophecy in 29:24 that "the grumblers will *learn* to obey" (μαθήσονται ὑπακούειν).

[97] So also Clements 1985:104.

oracle echoes the promise made in 28:16 that the one who trusts in the "stone" will certainly not be ashamed (οὐ μὴ καταισχυνθῇ).[98] The following verse borrows the religious language of 8:12–13 in order to depict the positive counterpart to "not being ashamed": "But when their children see my works,[99] through me they will sanctify (ἁγιάζω) my name. They will sanctify (ἁγιάζω) the holy one of Jacob, and they will fear (φοβέω) the God of Israel" (29:23). As already noted, this statement recalls Isaiah 8:12–13, where those who sanctify and fear the Lord (κύριον αὐτὸν ἁγιάσατε καὶ αὐτὸς ἔσται σου φόβος) do not encounter him as a stone of stumbling.[100]

The conjunction of key phrases from *both* Isaianic "stone" passages strongly suggests that the translator has read these texts in light of one another. Hearing the two stone passages together enriches them both: The notion of trusting in God (28:16) receives fuller explication through the ideas of sanctifying and fearing the Lord (8:12–13). Likewise, to those who experience God as a sanctuary (8:14) is extended the explicit promise of ultimate vindication (28:16). As a result of God's eschatological intervention, Israel's renewed loyalty to God, described in the language of 8:12–13, results in Israel's vindication, expressed in terms of the positive promise of 28:16.

Considered all together, there is a substantial body of evidence suggesting that Paul's interpretive decision to read Isaiah 8:14 and 28:16 together in Romans 9:33 is rooted in the much larger interrelationship of chapters 8 and 28–29 within the book of Isaiah. Moreover, there are strong reasons to believe that this interrelationship was noted by pre-Pauline tradents such as the LXX translator, who through his distinctive rendering of Isaiah 8:14, 28:16,

---

[98] This correspondence is not found in the MT, which reads לֹא יְחִישׁ at 28:16, but לֹא יֵבוֹשׁ at 29:22. The echo arises from a decision made previously by the translator in his rendering of 28:16. This does not necessarily mean that the echo was unintended, for as we saw above (n. 93) with regard to LXX Isaiah 29:4/19:3/8:19, the Isaiah translator is quite capable of comparing a number of widely separated verses and rendering them in similar ways. It is even conceivable, then, that 29:22–23 has influenced the translator's departure from MT in 28:16.

[99] Or, conceivably, "But when they see their children, my works" (ἀλλ᾽ ὅταν ἴδωσι τὰ τέκνα αὐτῶν τὰ ἔργα μου).

[100] There is an additional connection between Isaiah 29 and Isaiah 8 in the LXX due to the translator's distinctive rendering of 8:14, where it is not "the two houses of Israel" (Hebrew) that encounter God as a stone of stumbling, but "the house of Jacob" (cf. 8:17). In 29:22 LXX (addressed to "the house of Jacob"), we see a reversal of this situation, but expressed in terms of 28:16 ("not ashamed") rather than via the language of stumbling found in 8:14.

and 29:22–23 has drawn the verbal connections between chapters 8 and 28–29 tighter still.[101]

Ripples Created by the Isaianic "Stone" Passages in Romans 9:30–10:4

Viewing Romans 9:30–10:4 through the lens shaped by my reading of the larger contexts of Isaiah 8:14 and 28:16 allows several significant features of Paul's larger argument to come into sharper focus. First, over both Isaianic "stone" passages hovers the specter of bitter division within Israel. In the face of serious threats to Israel's national security by foreign powers, the majority of "this people" and their leaders have forsaken YHWH, placing their hope for deliverance not in their God, but in the gods and rulers of foreign nations. Only a small remnant remains faithful to Israel's God. Similarly, Paul writes out of a context of deep division within Israel, this time brought about through the preaching of the gospel. Just as Isaiah viewed himself as one of a small remnant of the faithful, Paul too employs remnant terminology to speak of "us . . . from among the Jews" whom God has now saved (Romans 9:24, 27–29; cf. 11:5).

Futhermore, in both Isaiah 8 and Isaiah 28–29, what divides the two groups of Israelites is their trust (or lack of trust) in God's power and faithfulness to deliver them from the present crisis. Trust in God plays a prominent role in these passages (πέποιθα, 8:14, 17; cf. 28:17; πιστεύω, 28:16; cf. 7:9). To those who trust in him, God promises vindication and deliverance. In the coming crisis, they will not be ashamed (28:16), nor will they encounter God as a stone of stumbling (8:14). In contrast, those who do not trust in YHWH but put their faith in "a lie" (28:17) will fall and be broken (8:15; 28:13).

This motif of faith/trust is central to Paul's criticism of Israel in Romans 9:30–10:4 and, indeed, throughout Romans 10. Absent from Paul's argument since Romans 6:8, the πίστις/πιστεύω word group suddenly becomes prominent in Paul's discussion once again, occurring thirteen times in 9:30–10:21. The Gentiles have believed and thereby obtained "the righteousness ἐκ πίστεως." But because Israel did not pursue the "Law that leads to righteousness" ἐκ πίστεως, they have been unable to overtake the Law (Romans 9:33). Instead, they

---

[101] It lies beyond the scope of this study to trace the relationship between Isaiah 8 and 28–29 in the other versions or in the history of exegesis. A significant collection of material for such an investigation has been assembled in the text-critical study of Léo Laberge (1968; published in part as Laberge 1978).

have become like those in Isaiah 8 and 28–29 who stumbled because
of their lack of faith.[102]

Isaiah 8 and 28–29 LXX offer Paul an important precedent for
his insistence that Israel's lack of faith/trust stems, not from their
adherence to the Law, but rather from their failure to understand
the Law rightly and so pursue it ἐκ πίστεως. In Isaiah 8, the prophet
does not set trust in God over against obedience to the Law; rather,
he claims that those who do not trust in God have stubbornly sealed
up the Law so as not to learn it (8:16). This indictment finds its
counterpart in Isaiah 28–29, where Isaiah likens the people's inability to grasp the meaning of the Law to the comic spectacle of an
illiterate person trying to read a sealed scroll. The repeated call to
rebellious Israel to listen to and learn the word of the Lord (28:12,
14, 19, 23; 29:18, 24) demonstrates that trusting in the "stone"
requires willing obedience to God's Law.[103]

Paul too claims in Romans 9:30ff. that faith and obedience to the
Law go together. He does not criticize Israel for pursuing "the Law
that leads to righteousness" (νόμος δικαιοσύνης, 9:31), nor does he
oppose this Law to "the righteousness from faith" (δικαιοσύνην ἐκ
πίστεως, 9:30). Rather, he laments Israel's failure to overtake the Law.
His point is not that Israel has pursued the wrong goal, but that
Israel has altogether failed to grasp the τέλος of the Law. Paul has
radically reconceived the nature of obedience to the Law out of the
conviction that the Law finds its true τέλος only in Christ.[104] Drawing
together the key terms of Romans 9:30–10:3—δικαιοσύνη, νόμος,
πίστις/πιστεύω—Paul claims in Romans 10:4 that the *righteousness* to
which the *Law* leads (cf. νόμος δικαιοσύνης, 9:31) is available, through

---

[102] Note that 1 Peter also interprets "stumbling" in Isaiah 8:14 as the consequence of failure to "believe/trust" in the stone (τοῖς πιστεύουσιν/ἀπιστοῦσιν,
1 Pet 2:7; οἳ προσκόπτουσιν τῷ λόγῳ ἀπειθοῦντες, 2:8).

[103] This Isaianic theme is greatly augmented by the Isaiah Targum in its para-
phrastic rendering of 28:9–13. For extensive discussion of the Targum's view that
repentance and renewed obedience to the Torah are crucial conditions for Israel's
restoration, see Chilton 1982:13–18, 37–46.

[104] In the context of Paul's metaphor of a footrace, I take τέλος to refer to the
finish line toward which the Law was leading; only in the sense of arrival at one's
destination does τέλος denote the "end" of the Law. See Cranfield 1979:522–26;
Wilckens 1978–82, 2:222–23; and especially the detailed analysis of Badenas 1985,
with references to further literature. Had Israel "caught up with" the Law instead
of stumbling, they would have ended up with righteousness in Christ (Rom 10:4).
As Romans 11 makes clear, Paul expects that Israel will recover its balance and
finish the race to its τέλος.

Christ, to everyone who *believes* (παντὶ τῷ πιστεύοντι). From the per-spective of Paul's understanding of the Law (for which he claims the authority of Isaiah 28:16/8:14), Israel has failed to perceive the goal of the Law, and so has pursued the Law in entirely the wrong man-ner, ἐξ ἔργων rather than ἐκ πίστεως. In terms reminiscent of Isaiah's indictment of Israel, Paul charges in Romans 10:2–3 that, when it comes to the Law, Israel is both ignorant and, ultimately, rebellious.

Attending to the wider contexts of Isaiah 8 and 28–29 further elu-cidates how Paul can attribute Israel's pursuit of the Law not ἐκ πίστεως but ὡς ἐξ ἔργων to their ignorance of, and indeed outright resistance to "the righteousness of God" as they seek instead to estab-lish "their own righteousness."[105] In Isaiah 8 and 28–29, trust in God entails staking one's life on God's righteousness—God's wisdom, power, and faithfulness—to rescue his people from the international crises threatening to engulf them. The antithesis of such trust is to rely for protection on foreign rulers and their gods, whether the kings of Damascus and Samaria (8:6) or Pharaoh (28:15; 30:1–7; 31:1c–3). Israel's misplaced trust stems from their inability to per-ceive God's plans vis-à-vis Israel and the nations—that God is using these nations as a tool to discipline and ultimately to deliver his peo-ple.[106] Ironically, those who refuse to submit to God's righteousness by resisting his use of these Gentile nations and who seek to estab-lish their own righteousness apart from God by entering into treaties with foreign nations suffer the very fate they sought to avert and forfeit the deliverance God promises to those who trust in him.

Admittedly, making the imaginative leap to Paul's own situation requires a bit of mental agility,[107] but reading Romans 9:30–10:4 in light of Isaiah 8 and 28–29 helps to clarify that the target of Paul's

---

[105] Paul speaks of two "righteousnesses," as he does also in Philippians 3:9. In Romans 10:3, however, he claims that "their own righteousness" (the righteousness available only to Jews who observe the distinctive markers of circumcision, Sabbath, and food laws) is precisely *not* the righteousness to which the Law is leading. See further n. 122 below.

[106] In the previous chapter I noted that the background of the potter/clay texts in Isaiah 29:16/45:9 (Rom 9:20) is similarly a protest against God's chosen means of disciplining and delivering his people, a questioning of God's wisdom and right-eousness (pp. 62–68).

[107] Though, as other befuddled explorers of Paul's thought world can attest, this chasm certainly does not require as great a leap as some of Paul's appropriations of scripture—such as his use of Leviticus 18:5 and Deuteronomy 9:4/30:12 in Romans 10:5–10 (see pp. 159–68).

polemics is not Jewish *legalism* versus some abstract principle of "faith," but rather Israel's failure to recognize and submit to God's chosen means of delivering his people (that is, "the righteousness of God").[108] At the same time, hearing Paul in counterpoint with Isaiah 8 and 28–29 highlights the radical rereading of Isaiah necessitated by Paul's conviction that God has now acted in Christ to redeem his people and the entire world and that the good news of this cosmic redemption must be proclaimed to Jew and Gentile alike. Like Isaiah before him, Paul claims that Israel is resisting God's plan of deliverance in favor of a plan of their own devising. For Paul, however, the issue is not Israel's idolatrous trust in foreign nations and their gods, but their insistence on pursuing the Law ὡς ἐξ ἔργων rather than ἐκ πίστεως. Out of a misplaced devotion to "their own righteousness" on the basis of "works," Israel refuses to recognize that God's righteousness—to which the Law, pursued ἐκ πίστεως, would have led them all along—has now come to focus in Christ and is available to everyone on the basis of faith (10:2–4).

It is crucial to see that the standpoint from which Paul criticizes Israel is his firm belief that the righteousness of Israel's God is now revealed in the gospel, through which God effects the salvation of both Jew and Gentile *apart from* observance of the markers of the covenant (cf. Rom 3:21–26).[109] Just as God's dealings with foreign nations—particularly his choice of Assyria as an instrument to discipline his own people—scandalized the majority of Israel in Isaiah's day, so now the gospel Paul proclaims to the Gentiles has caused Israel to stumble badly. Whereas Israel had long associated God's righteousness with the markers of the covenant (pursuing the Law ἐξ ἔργων),[110] Paul now proclaims the news that in Christ God's right-

---

[108] In light of the problem posed for Israel of old by God's dealings with the Gentiles, it is tempting to see Isaiah 8 and 28–29 as part of the scriptural and theological backdrop for Paul's dramatic narrative of Israel's temporary hardening and ultimate restoration in Romans 11. Paul argues that God is using the Gentiles both to judge Israel's lack of πίστις and, by provoking Israel to jealousy, ultimately to effect their salvation. Although "the righteousness of God" does not appear either in Isaiah 8 or Isaiah 28–29, this phrase is used often in Isaiah 40–55 to speak of God's deliverance of his covenant people. It is not unlikely that Paul, like many ancient readers, would have read Isaiah primarily through the lens provided by chapters 40–55 (see p. 102 n. 188 above).

[109] E. P. Sanders (1977, 1983) rightly insists on the crucial role Paul's convictions about what God has done for the world in Christ play in shaping Paul's account of Israel's present plight.

[110] It was a widespread and noncontroversial belief among Jews of the Second

eousness is extended to Jew and Gentile alike on the same basis of faith. For Israel to hang on to its covenant markers now and to refuse to recognize God's acceptance of Jews and Gentiles solely on the basis of πίστις would be to reject God's righteousness in favor of "their own righteousness."[111] Paul even dares to maintain that Israel should have known about God's plan all along (Rom 10:18–21) and so pursued the Law ἐκ πίστεως right out of the starting blocks. After all, Isaiah had warned them about the stumbling stone on the track long ago.

The Identity of the "Stone" in Romans

The foregoing discussion has prepared us to address at long last the question of the identity of the "stone" in Romans 9:32–33. The stone is clearly a symbol, but for whom or for what? As we have seen, in Isaiah 8:14 the "stone" unambiguously refers to God himself. In 28:16 LXX, however, the presence of an additional phrase, "the one who trusts ἐπ' αὐτῷ . . ." creates a measure of ambiguity. The antecedent of αὐτῷ may well be God, despite the abrupt shift from first to third person. This interpretation finds strong support from my earlier observation that Isaiah 28:16 is linked to 8:14, 17 via this very prepositional phrase (among other things) and that in Isaiah 8:14 and 17, the antecedent of αὐτῷ—and the object of trust—is God himself. Nevertheless, we have seen that the potential to identify the "stone" with someone other than God was exploited by ancient interpreters such as the translators of the Isaiah Targum, the tradents of the *Community Rule*, the poets of the *Hodayot*, and the author of 1 Peter. We should not be surprised, then if Paul has made a similar interpretive move.

In fact, this quotation offers a textbook example of the semantic ambiguity or polyvalence produced by Paul's creative transformations of scripture. In the context of Romans, the stone may be understood

---

Temple Period that God wanted Israel to keep his covenant by obeying him. On the truly radical nature of Paul's claim that one can fulfill the Law without keeping some of its commandments (such as circumcision! cf. 1 Cor 7:19), see the classic study by E. P. Sanders (1977).

[111] I.e., the righteousness available only to Jews who obey the Law. The result of Jewish adherence to "their own righteousness" is that Gentiles are excluded from God's people unless they take on the covenant markers themselves (see n. 122). It is the Gentile mission, rather than an aversion to "legalism" that drives Paul's critique of Israel here.

to be God himself, as familiarity with the original passages in Isaiah would suggest. However, the shift in person from τίθημι to ἐπ᾽ αὐτῷ is, if anything, even more jarring in Romans, making the identification of the stone with God somewhat problematic. A number of interpreters have floated the hypothesis that the stone refers to the true nature of the Law.[112] While this interpretation is buoyed by Paul's claim in 9:32 that Israel has stumbled because of their failure to pursue the Law ἐκ πίστεως, it founders on the expectation of a personal antecedent for αὐτῷ as the object of the verb πιστεύω, and it ultimately runs aground on the logic of Paul's metaphor. Israel has been chasing the Law, not tripping over it. They hadn't even caught up with it yet when they stumbled violently.

The ambiguity of the stone's identity in Romans 9:33 may well be deliberate, with Paul intending to hold his readers in suspense until a later stage in his discussion. The christological significance of the stone, adumbrated by Paul's claim in Romans 10:4 that the τέλος of the Law is Christ, comes fully into view only with the re-citation of Isaiah 28:16 in Romans 10:11.[113] Romans 10:12 points to Christ as the antecedent of αὐτῷ as it speaks of calling on the "Lord," who has been identified in 10:9 as Jesus. As Figure 3.4 shows, Paul has crafted this citation of Isaiah 28:16 to create a close parallel with the quotation of Joel 2:32 LXX in Romans 10:13.

Figure 3.4: Isaiah 28:16 (Rom 10:11) and Joel 2:32 LXX [3:5 MT] (Rom 10:13)

Isa 28:16	πᾶς	ὁ πιστεύων	ἐπ᾽ αὐτῷ	οὐ καταισχυνθήσεται
Joel 2:32	πᾶς	ὃς ἂν ἐπι-καλέσηται	τὸ ὄνομα κυρίου	σωθήσεται

The net effect is that, as Paul's exposition proceeds, Joel's "the name of the Lord [= Jesus]" not only corresponds to, but also interprets, the pronoun αὐτῷ in Isaiah 28:16.

It is instructive to compare Paul's interpretation of these "stone" texts with the use of Isaiah 28:16 in 1QS and 1QH.[114] In these Qumran texts, the community—those who trust in and remain faith-

---

[112] P. W. Meyer 1980:64; Barrett 1982. Dinter provides an incisive critique of Barrett's argument (1980:120–25).

[113] See pp. 168–70 below.

[114] See pp. 143–44 above.

ful to God—*is* the stone. For Paul, the community is made up of those who trust *in* the stone, Christ. Paul's christological reading of the stone passages fully coheres with his reinterpretation of Isaiah's call to trust in God's power and faithfulness to deliver his people (Isaiah 8:14, 28:16, and contexts) as a summons to believe that the righteousness of God is now revealed in Christ.[115]

Paul has hewn and dressed the Isaianic "stone" passages so that they fit snugly into the christological argument he is constructing. Yet his exegetical "stone cutting" does not entirely alter the shape of these passages, and his reinterpretation does not suppress the original referent of the stone in the Isaianic context—God himself. To press for a sharp distinction between a "christological" and a "theological" reading of Isaiah 28:16 would be profoundly unfaithful to the structure of Paul's own thought, in terms of which such a dichotomy is incomprehensible.[116] Significantly, Paul stops short of an explicit identification of the stone as Christ.[117] Moreover, he does not present *Jesus* as the object of belief or trust, but rather God's action in raising him from the dead and declaring him to be Lord. For Paul, to identify the stone with Christ is not to push God off center stage; it is rather to specify more exactly the manner in which God has become a stumbling stone to some in Israel. The irreducible polyvalence of Paul's metaphor is thus rooted ultimately in his theological and christological convictions.[118]

THE Τέλος OF THE LAW: ROMANS 10:4–13

From the vantage point provided by Romans 10:4, one can see that Paul has attempted an extremely bold redefinition of the Law. Contrary to his common coupling of "works" and "Law," Paul has in this passage carefully and methodically separated the two terms.[119]

---

[115] In this light, it appears that Paul's comment in 1 Cor 1:23 that the gospel of "Christ crucified" is a σκάνδαλον to Jews may well draw on the imagery of Isaiah 8:14.

[116] So, rightly, E. P. Sanders 1977:194.

[117] Contrast the direct identification of Christ with the stone in 1 Peter 2:4–8: πρὸς ὃν [τὸν κύριον, v. 3] προσερχόμενοι λίθον ζῶντα . . . (2:4).

[118] Similarly, N. T. Wright (1991:244), who views the stone as a polyvalent metaphor pointing to God, the Law, and Christ: the "stone" is *"the covenant plan of the one God,* which, expressed in Torah, was enacted in the Messiah" (emphasis original). See further Boers 1993, although he does not discuss this particular passage.

[119] Romans 9:12 prepares the reader for this move, for there Paul makes no

In Paul's metaphor, the Law is running after righteousness, and Israel is pursuing the Law, but Israel's mistaken idea that the Law is about "works" (and that the righteousness to which it leads is "their own righteousness") causes them to stumble in mid-race. What is only implicit in the contrast between "the Law of works" and "the Law of faith" in Romans 3:27[120] becomes explicit in Romans 9:32, where Paul actually sets "works" in clear *opposition* to the Law, claiming that the Law has eluded Israel because they have been pursuing it ὡς ἐξ ἔργων: "*as if* it were from works [which it is not]." For Paul, the Law is rightly pursued only ἐκ πίστεως (through faith "we establish the Law" [Rom 3:31]); only thus can Israel attain the righteousness they seek.

Thus isolated from "works," the Law has a positive valence for Paul.[121] He terms it "the Law that leads to righteousness" (νόμος δικαιοσύνης) because its τέλος is Christ. It is fully in keeping with his redefinition of the Law apart from works that Paul contrasts "God's righteousness"/"righteousness ἐκ πίστεως" not with "righteousness from the Law," but with Israel's "own righteousness."[122]

---

mention of νόμος as he contrasts ἐξ ἔργων with ἐκ τοῦ καλοῦντος. Similarly, in 11:6 the opposite of χάριτι is ἐξ ἔργων, with no reference to the Law in the context.

[120] The issue in Romans 3:27–31 is, "What is the nature of the Law?" (ποῖος νόμος;). Cf. Dunn 1988a:185–87; Rhyne 1981:25–93.

[121] Comparison of this passage with the strong dichotomy Paul draws between "faith" and "Law" in Galatians 2–3 (esp. 2:16–21; 3:10–12) raises the question of inconsistency or development in Paul's thought on the Law. While I cannot hope to add much to the debate here, it is perhaps not superfluous to reiterate that context is crucial for understanding what Paul means by terms like "Law," "works," and "faith." These terms are clearly used by Paul in somewhat idiosyncratic ways, and it is not unthinkable that their meaning might be flexible to some degree, depending on the rhetorical situation. Because in Galatians the Law is linked inextricably to "works" and absolutely opposed to "faith" does not mean that the terms must line up this way in the very different argument of Romans 9–11. We should not neglect the possibility that Paul modified his position after [because of?] his debate with the rival teachers in Galatia. See further Martyn 1997b; Wilckens 1982.

[122] E. P. Sanders rightly understands "their own righteousness" to mean "that righteousness which the Jews alone are privileged to obtain" rather than "self-righteousness which consists in individuals' presenting their merits as a claim upon God." The argument is christological and is oriented around the principle of equality of Jew and Gentile (1983:38; emphasis removed).

However, when Sanders elsewhere says that ἡ ἰδία δικαιοσύνη "becomes wrong only because God has revealed another one" (1991:122), he does not do justice to the radical claim Paul is making in Romans 9:33–10:13. The force of Paul's argument in Romans 10 is not that "God has revealed *another*" righteousness; rather, he claims that the righteousness now available in Christ has always been the *only* righteousness Israel was intended to attain through its pursuit of the Law. In Paul's

Recognition of this distinction becomes crucial to understanding Paul's interpretation of scripture—not least Isaiah 28:16 (Rom 10:11)—in the following verses. In stark contrast to Israel's "own righteousness," which is limited to those who pursue the Law "as if from works," the righteousness to which the Law leads when pursued "from faith" is the righteousness available without distinction "to everyone who believes." Indeed, it is the same "righteousness from faith" that the Gentiles have now obtained (Rom 9:30).

On the face of it, Paul's radical claim that the Law can be divorced from the "works" it commands brazenly contradicts the scriptures, certainly as they were read by most of his contemporaries (and, indeed, by the vast majority of faithful Jews throughout the ages). Recognizing this problem, Paul calls on Moses himself in order to uphold his assertion that Christ is the τέλος of the Law (Rom 10:5–10). A great deal of attention has been devoted to this passage in recent literature.[123] Although it is not possible to interact with all of these studies here, I will sketch briefly my understanding of Paul's argument, and particularly how the scriptural quotations function in it. This reading will provide the necessary context for understanding Paul's subsequent quotation of Isaiah 28:16 in Romans 10:11. At the same time, it will shed further light on Paul's interpretive techniques as he wrestles with scripture in light of the gospel he is called to proclaim.

On the Testimony of Two Witnesses: Moses and "Righteousness from Faith"

In Romans 10:5–6, Paul summons two witnesses, Moses and the personified "Righteousness from Faith" (introduced more prosaically in 9:30), to support the case he has been building.[124] Although this

---

view, Israel's "own righteousness" is emphatically *not* the righteousness to which the Law leads. In fact, Israel's quest for "their own righteousness" has actually prevented them from reaching the τέλος of the Law. Contrast Philippians 3:9, where Paul's reference to "my own righteousness" (set over against "the righteousness of God through the faithfulness of Christ") not only clearly refers to "covenant markers" such as circumcision, but also finds further specification as "the righteousness from the Law." It is just this identification of "their own righteousness" with "Law" that is significantly absent from Paul's argument in Romans 9:30–10:4.

[123] Important studies of Romans 10:5–10 include Bring 1966; Suggs 1967; Howard 1969; Rhyne 1981:95–116; Badenas 1985; Dunn 1987; Hays 1989:73–83; Bekken 1995.

[124] Note the personification of righteousness in Isaiah 41:2–4: τίς ἐξήγειρεν ἀπὸ ἀνατολῶν δικαιοσύνην ἐκάλεσεν αὐτὴν κατὰ πόδας αὐτοῦ καὶ πορεύσεται; (Isa 41:2a).

passage is often read as if Paul were contrasting "righteousness from the Law" with "righteousness from faith,"[125] I have attempted to show in the preceding paragraphs why the larger context of Paul's argument actually points in the opposite direction. Richard Hays rightly argues that Moses and "Righteousness from Faith" should be heard as offering complementary testimony.[126] In contrast to Galatians 3, where Paul explicitly identifies the Law with "doing" and isolates it completely from "faith" (ὁ δὲ νόμος οὐκ ἔστιν ἐκ πίστεως, Gal 3:12),[127] in Romans 10 Paul does not directly oppose "doing" to "believing." Rather, by using the second quotation to interpret the first, Paul *redefines* "doing" *as* "believing/trusting in what God has done in Christ." Citing the words of the Law itself, Paul argues that the Law points to Christ as its goal and thus that the "righteousness from the Law" finds its fulfillment in "the righteousness from faith."

The value of Moses and "Righteousness from Faith" as witnesses for Paul rests on the fact that their testimony agrees. In fact, they support complementary aspects of the case Paul summarizes so succinctly in Romans 10:4. First on the stand is Moses, who avers that the Law was intended to lead to *life* (Romans 10:5 [Lev 18:5]).[128] In its original setting, Leviticus 18:1–5 contrasts the laws and customs of Egypt and of Canaan with God's Law, claiming that only God's commandments lead to life.[129] In the context of Romans, "will

---

[125] See Käsemann 1980:283–92 for a particularly strong statement of this position. So also Dunn 1987.

[126] Hays 1989:76. See his detailed discussion of the entire passage, pp. 73–83. In arguing forcefully against the normal reading of this passage that drives a wedge between 10:5 and 10:6, Hays has perhaps over-emphasized the continuity between Moses and "Righteousness from Faith" in this passage. His paraphrase of 10:6 obscures the distinction Paul makes between the two characters: "In another place, *as Moses writes*, this righteousness from faith . . . speaks like this . . ." (77; italics mine). In 10:6 Paul does not mention Moses explicitly at all; a distinct, though harmonious, voice is heard. Paul's refusal to collapse the two quotations from Moses' writings into one voice creates the rhetorical effect of having two witnesses to substantiate his point.

[127] Galatians 3:10 paves the way for the citation in 3:12 by pronouncing a curse on "everyone who does not remain in all the things written in the book of the Law *in order to do them* (τοῦ ποιῆσαι αὐτά), and Galatians 3:11–12 explicitly contrasts "doing" with πίστις (cf. E. P. Sanders 1983:21–23).

[128] *Contra* Käsemann (1980:284, 287), it is unlikely that Paul's introductory phrases, "Moses writes" and "Righteousness from Faith says," are intended to set up a contrast between writing and speaking in order to devalue the former. Paul's ubiquitous citation formula, "It is written," makes it difficult to see how "Moses writes" could carry a negative valence.

[129] Cf. the continuing characterization of God's commandments as that which

live" (ζήσεται) picks up the notion elsewhere expressed by the terms "righteousness" (9:20, 31; 10:3, 4), "will not be ashamed" (9:33), and "salvation" (10:1).[130] Moses' words thus establish one of the major points Paul argues in Romans 9:30–10:4: that the Law is νόμος δικαιοσύνης, "the Law that leads to righteousness," or, in the words of Romans 10:4, "the τέλος of the Law is . . . *righteousness*."[131]

The next witness, "Righteousness from Faith," speaks in behalf of the second—and more controversial—step in Paul's argument: that this righteousness to which the Law has been leading comes to focus in Christ.[132] Her opening words are generally recognized as a quotation of Deuteronomy 8:17/9:4, with the latter text the most probably source of Paul's quotation due to the (metaleptically suppressed)

---

leads to life: Neh 9:29; Ezek 20:11, 13, 21 (all clearly echoing Lev 18:5). See also Deut 4:1; 6:25; 8:1; 11:8 (LXX); 30:2, 8, 10, 12, 13, 14.

[130] See E. P. Sanders (1977:463–72) for a perceptive analysis of terms that, in Paul's usage, belong to the same semantic field as "righteousness" language.

[131] While it is not possible to offer a full discussion here of the difficult text-critical issues surrounding Paul's quotation of Leviticus 18:5, a good case can be made for the reading adopted by NA²⁵: Μωϋσῆς γὰρ γράφει ὅτι τὴν δικαιοσύνην τὴν ἐκ [τοῦ] νόμου ὁ ποιήσας ἄνθρωπος ζήσεται ἐν αὐτῇ. In addition to finding support from important Alexandrian and Western witnesses (ℵ* D* 81. 1506. 1739), this reading has in its favor its distance both from LXX (not only Lev 18:5, but also the virtually identical phrase in Neh 9:29; Ezek 20:11, 13, 21) and from Paul's quotation in Gal 3:12. On this reading, the focus of the citation is on "*righteousness* from the Law" as a whole (the antecedent of αὐτῇ) rather than on the individual commandments (αὐτά, ἐν αὐτοῖς). At the same time, it becomes more clear that Paul's point is not "doing" the commandments versus "believing," but that the "righteousness from the Law" (cf. νόμος δικαιοσύνης) leads to life. My understanding of Paul's quotation of Leviticus 18:5 in its context would tend to support this variant's claim to be the original reading, although my interpretation does not depend on its adoption. For arguments in favor of the text adopted by NA²⁶/²⁷, however, see Dunn 1988b:599, note a.

[132] Although δέ in 10:6 is often thought to contrast the testimony of the two speakers, note that Paul uses δέ in 10:20 not to oppose Isaiah's oracle to the words of Moses, but merely to signal the change of speakers (see also pp. 92–93 n. 156). Further arguments for the connective force of δέ in 10:6 are marshalled by Badenas 1985:121–25. Sanday and Headlam suggest that Paul is not intending to interpret scripture here but only borrowing scriptural language to make his point (1902:286–90; so also Hübner 1984:85–91). This counsel of desperation reveals not only a misperception of Paul's point in Romans 10:5–13, but even more so a decidedly narrow and unimaginative understanding of Paul's interpretive practices. Sanday and Headlam cannot conceive how Paul could *possibly* have considered such a radical transformation of Deuteronomy 30 to be 'legitimate': "In the O.T. the words are used by Moses of the Law: *how can* St. Paul use them of the Gospel as against the Law?" (1902:288; emphasis mine). I hope in what follows to make the logic of Paul's rereading of scripture understandable, though not to downplay its astoundingly revisionary character (cf. Koch 1986:129–32; Hays 1989:73–83).

catchword "righteousness" (δικαιοσύνη) in 9:4–6.[133] In light of my
earlier contention that "God's righteousness" should be understood
as God's power and faithfulness to deliver his people, it is significant
to note that these texts speak of God's deliverance of Israel from
Egypt and his victory over the nations of Canaan. Both passages
warn Israel not to attribute these miraculous deeds to their own
"strength" (8:17) or "righteousness" (9:4). Rather, Deuteronomy insists
that God has acted out of faithfulness to the covenant he made with
Abraham, Isaac, and Jacob (Deut 8:18; 9:5). In view of Paul's criticism of Israel in Romans 10:3, it is surely not accidental that he
has drawn on a text that repeatedly admonishes Israel against trusting in "their own righteousness":

> Do not say in your heart, because of my righteousness (διὰ τὴν
> δικαιοσύνην μου) the Lord has lead me in to inherit this good land. . . .
> It is not because of your righteousness (οὐχὶ διὰ τὴν δικαιοσύνην σου)
> nor because of your holiness of heart that you are entering in to inherit
> their land. . . . It is not because of your righteousness (οὐ διὰ τὴν
> δικαιοσύνην σου) that the Lord your God is giving you this good land
> to inherit. . . . (Deut 9:4, 5, 6).

With Paul serving as interpreter for the court,[134] Righteousness from
Faith goes on to assert in the words of Deuteronomy 30:12–14 that
the goal of the Law has now been realized in God's sending Christ
and raising him from the dead: "the τέλος of the Law is *Christ* for
righteousness. . . ." As a result, the "doing" Moses calls for in Leviticus
18:5 is identified as the response of faith to the "word of faith" that
Paul proclaims: "the τέλος of the Law is Christ for righteousness *to
everyone who believes.*"[135]

Careful attention to Romans 10:6–8 shows just how thoroughly
Paul has reworked Deut 30:12–14 in order to interpret "doing" as
"believing/trusting in what God has done in Christ."

---

[133] Interestingly, δικαιοσύνη appears in Deuteronomy only in this passage and
in chapter 33. On a practical level, Paul's use of this phrase solves the problem of
how to introduce the words of Deuteronomy 30:12–14 as a quotation within a quotation. The anacoluthon, οὐκ ἐν τῷ οὐρανῷ ἐστὶν λέγων, renders 30:12a LXX unus-
able for this purpose. On the connections between Deuteronomy 9:4 and Paul's
interpretation of Deuteronomy 30:12–14, see further Dinter 1980:30–32.

[134] Lim convincingly argues that despite the similarities between Pauline exegesis and that of the Qumran *pesharim*, terming Paul's quotation of Deuteronomy
30:12–14 a "*pesher*" is inaccurate and misleading (1997a:124–39, 1997b); *contra* Barrett
1970:392 and Ellis 1988:696–97.

[135] I should note in passing the interesting terminological links between Leviticus

Figure 3.5: Deuteronomy 30:11–14 LXX in Romans 10:6–8[136]

Deuteronomy 30:11–14 LXX	Romans 10:6–8
[11] ἡ ἐντολὴ αὕτη ... [12] οὐκ ἐν τῷ οὐρανῷ ἐστὶν λέγων· τίς ἀναβήσεται ἡμῖν εἰς τὸν οὐρανὸν καὶ λήμψεται ἡμῖν <u>αὐτὴν</u>; καὶ ἀκούσαντες <u>αὐτὴν</u> *ποιήσομεν*. [13] οὐδὲ πέραν τῆς θαλάσσης ἐστὶν λέγων· <u>τίς</u> διαπεράσει ἡμῖν εἰς τὸ πέραν τῆς θαλάσσης καὶ λήμψεται ἡμῖν <u>αὐτήν</u>; καὶ ἀκούσαντες <u>αὐτὴν</u> *ποιήσομεν*. [14] <u>ἐγγύς σου ἐστιν τὸ ῥῆμα</u> σφόδρα <u>ἐν τῷ στόματί σου καὶ ἐν τῇ καρδίᾳ σου</u> καὶ ἐν ταῖς χερσίν σου αὐτὸ *ποιεῖν*.	[6] ἡ δὲ ἐκ πίστεως δικαιοσύνη οὕτως λέγει· μὴ εἴπῃς ἐν τῇ καρδίᾳ σου· <u>τίς ἀναβήσεται</u> εἰς τὸν οὐρανόν; τοῦτ᾿ ἔστιν <u>Χριστὸν</u> καταγαγεῖν· [7] <u>ἤ·</u> <u>τίς</u> καταβήσεται εἰς τὴν ἄβυσσον; τοῦτ᾿ ἔστιν <u>Χριστὸν</u> ἐκ νεκρῶν ἀναγαγεῖν. [8] ἀλλὰ τί λέγει; <u>ἐγγύς σου τὸ ῥῆμά ἐστιν ἐν τῷ στόματί σου καὶ ἐν τῇ καρδίᾳ σου</u>, τοῦτ᾿ ἔστιν τὸ <u>ῥῆμα</u> τῆς πίστεως ὃ κηρύσσομεν.

Paul's strategic omissions and crisp interpretive comments (displayed in Figure 3.5) deftly replace Deuteronomy's original emphasis on "doing the commandment" with the story of Christ proclaimed in Paul's gospel. Paul studiously omits every reference to "doing"[137] and substitutes for Deuteronomy's αὐτή (= ἡ ἐντολὴ αὕτη ἣν ἐγὼ ἐντέλλομαί σοι σήμερον, Deut 30:11) the name "Christ" (Rom 10:6–7).[138] He

---

18:1–5 and Deuteronomy 30: Both texts promise "life" (ζωή, ζάω; Lev 18:5; Deut 30:6, 15, 16, 19, 20) to those who "do" (ποιέω; Lev 18:4, 5; Deut 30:2, 8, 10, 12, 13, 14) God's Law. Neither of these links is evident from Paul's quotations, but they may suggest how Paul himself arrived at this particular juxtaposition of texts.

[136] The text of Deuteronomy 30:13 provided in Figure 3.5 follows the correction to the Göttingen edition suggested by Wevers 1995:484.

[137] Deut 30:12, 13, 14; for the prominence of this theme, cf. 30:2, 8, 10. This is one of the clear verbal links with Leviticus 18:5 as well. I highlight this omission in Figure 3.5 through the use of italics in the first column. S. Westerholm has noted that Paul carefully avoids the language of "doing" when speaking of the Christian's relationship to the Law (1988:201–205).

[138] In Figure 3.5, I highlight these transformations with double underlining. Behind this christological identification of "the commandment" may lie a form of "wisdom christology" (cf. Bar 3:29–30; Sir 24:1–7). For a detailed analysis, see Suggs 1967.

further identifies "the message" in the last line of the quotation (τὸ ῥῆμα = ἡ ἐντολὴ αὕτη, Deut 30:11) as "the message of faith" (τὸ ῥῆμα τῆς πίστεως, Rom 10:8, which = "the message about Christ," ῥῆμα Χριστοῦ, Rom 10:17). By reinterpreting the two questions in the quotation as references to bringing Christ down from heaven or up from among the dead, Paul demonstrates exegetically that the τέλος of the Law is Christ and that "righteousness from faith" is, first and foremost, a matter of what *God* has done in the resurrection and exaltation of Christ. When this reworked citation is placed side by side with Moses' testimony in Leviticus 18:5, it becomes clear that the "doing" that leads to "life"—to which the Law itself testifies— is none other than "believing/trusting what God has done in Christ."

Paul's own ministry of proclamation comes to the forefront in his bold claim that the "word" (ῥῆμα) of Deut 30:12–14 is the "word of faith" (τὸ ῥῆμα τῆς πίστεως) that we preach" (Rom 10:8). It is just possible in this atmosphere so charged with metaphor that Paul intends his hearers to identify the "we" who preach the word of faith as Moses, "Righteousness from Faith," and Paul.[139] In any event, Paul's interpretive gloss underscores the continuity between scripture and Christian proclamation claimed by his statement in 10:4 that Christ is the τέλος of the Law.[140] Although ῥῆμα is not Paul's usual

---

Another parallel to Paul's interpretation has been found in Targum Neofiti (cf. the Fragment Targum), which in its interpretive rendering of Deuteronomy 30:13 mentions Jonah's descent "into the depths of the great sea" (לעמקוי דימה; cf. Tg. Jonathan to Jonah 2:4, לעומקיא בליבא דימא). For this suggestion, see McNamara 1966:74–75; M. Black 1971–72:9; Evans 1993:49–50. The case for Paul's dependence on the particular tradition preserved in this targum is rather weak, however, both because of the common association of the "abyss" with the "sea" in Israel's scriptures (e.g., Gen 1:2; Ps 32:7; 76:16; 103:6; 105:9 LXX; Job 28:14; 38:16; 41:23 LXX; Isa 51:10; 63:13; Jonah 2:5; Sir 24:29; 43:23–24; cf. Pr Man 3) and because in the "three-story universe" in which Paul and his contemporaries lived, "abyss" is a natural opposite of "heaven" (e.g., Gen 7:11; 8:2; Deut 33:13; Ps 106:26; 134:6; 148:7–8 LXX; Prov 3:20; Sir 1:3; 16:18; 24:5; cf. Ps 35:7 LXX). Moreover, since the word "abyss" admirably serves Paul's interpretation of this verse as a reference to Christ's death and resurrection, we cannot rule out the possibility that Paul himself made the substitution of terms independent of prior traditions.

[139] I owe this insight to Diana Swancutt (private correspondence). Cf. Hays's paraphrase, "which we also now preach" (1989:77). This would not exclude, of course, a reference to other Christian preachers besides Paul. In his letters, Paul normally speaks of the work of proclamation (κηρύσσειν) in the plural (Rom 10:14, 15; 1 Cor 1:23; 15:11; 2 Cor 1:19; 4:5; 11:4; 1 Thess 2:9) except when emphasizing his own personal activity over against that of others (1 Cor 9:27; Gal 2:2; 5:11).

[140] This continuity is emphasized in the closing doxology, 16:25–27, which con-

designation for the gospel message, he employs it here for the sake of identifying his message with the ῥῆμα of Deut 30:12–14.[141] In Rom 10:17 he will call his message ῥῆμα Χριστοῦ. It is this word that has now come near "in your mouth and in your heart."

In speaking of the human response required to what God has done in Christ, Paul hones in on Deuteronomy's mention of "mouth" and "heart" (Rom 10:8–10). The catchword link, "heart," binds together the two halves of his quotation (Deut 8:17/9:4 and 30:14). By means of his interpretation of Deut 30:14 as a call to "confess" and "believe," Paul presents the alternative to the misguided "speech" of the heart in Deut 9:4 (Rom 10:6). At the same time, Paul omits mention of "hands" altogether (Deut 30:14).[142] This two-pronged strategy allows him not only to avoid Deuteronomy's language of "doing" but, more significantly, to redefine it as "believing" and "confessing."

Deuteronomy 30:12–14 in Context

Paul's focus on the heart echoes an important theme of Deuteronomy 30, as a brief survey of the passage will demonstrate. This chapter is written from a perspective that treats Israel's exile under the curses of the Law as a *fait accompli*:

> And it will be when all these things have come upon you—the blessings and the curses that I have set before you—and you take it to

---

nects the revelation of the "mystery" of God's redemptive purpose both with "prophetic scriptures" and with "my gospel and the kerygma of Jesus Christ." Even if these verses are a later addition to the letter, they capture well Paul's concern in Romans to demonstrate that his gospel is rooted in Israel's scriptures. For arguments that the doxology was added secondarily to a shortened, 14–chapter edition of Romans, see Gamble 1977:123; so also Lampe 1985. However, Larry W. Hurtado questions Gamble's reconstruction by showing that the doxology is closely linked to the content of 15:1–13 and may well have been added (by Paul or a later redactor) to the 16–chapter edition of Romans. He argues for a "scholarly 'agnosticism'" on the origin of 16:25–27 (1981:199). J. K. Elliott (1981), noting many similarities between the doxology in Romans and those in Ephesians, 1 Timothy, 1 Peter, and Jude, suggests a late first-century origin for Romans 16:25–27. See further Peterson 1991.

[141] The term ῥῆμα appears with this sense in the undisputed Pauline letters only in Rom 10:8 (2x), 17, 18 (ῥήματα, in Psalm 18:5 LXX). Cf. Eph 5:26; 6:17.

[142] The LXX reading ἐν ταῖς χερσίν σου is well attested; its omission in a number of mss is probably due to assimilation to MT. Although there is no equivalent in MT, Samaritan Pentateuch, Targum, Peshitta, or Vulgate, Hebrew evidence for the LXX's reading is found in 4QDeutᵇ [4Q29], frg. 3, line 18: ובידך. Even if Paul's *Vorlage* somehow lacked this phrase, my point about the *tendenz* of his citation stands, since in any case he omits the final "to do it."

heart among all the nations, wherever the Lord has scattered you . . . (Deuteronomy 30:1).

. . . the Lord cast them into another land, *as it is today* (ὡσεὶ νῦν; Deut 29:28).[143]

Deuteronomy attributes Israel's exile to the dullness and deceptiveness of their "hearts," which persists "to this day."[144] Yet God remains faithful to his covenant with the patriarchs (ὑπὲρ τοὺς πατέρας σου, 30:5). When Israel turns and again obeys "with all their heart" (ἐξ ὅλης τῆς καρδίας σου, 30:2), God will gather them from the Diaspora and bring them once again into the land (30:3–5). Moreover, this time God himself will enable Israel to obey "with all their heart" and so to inherit the promise of "life" held out by the Law (cf. Lev 18:5): "The Lord will cleanse your heart and the heart of your seed to love the Lord your God with all your heart (ἐξ ὅλης τῆς καρδίας σου) and with all your being, so that you may live" (Deut

---

[143] For the author of 4QMMT, the exile and salvation spoken of in Deuteronomy 30 are being actualized in the Israel of his own day. This halakic letter quotes Deuteronomy 30:1–2 (C 12–16 = 4Q397 frgs. 14–21, lines 12–14; 4Q398 frgs. 14–17 1.5–8). In doing so, it adds two references specifying that this text is about "the end of days": באחרית הימים (C 14); באחרית (C16). These temporal references may come from Deut 31:29, quoted (without this phrase) immediately preceding the quotation of Deuteronomy 30:1–2 (C12). This time is now: וזה הוא אחרית הימים, as C 21 makes clear (= 4Q398 frgs. 11–13, line 4 [placement of these fragments is disputed]). For the individual texts, composite text, and commentary, see Qimron and Strugnell, DJD X. See further Bernstein 1996; Brooke 1997b:77–78. N. T. Wright (1998) has independently drawn some of the same conclusions as the present study regarding 4QMMT C 12–16. Much the same perspective is adopted by the author of Baruch 2:27–3:8, who from an exilic perspective hears the words of Deuteronomy 30:1–6 as a promise for his own generation. The author claims that Deuteronomy 30:1–2 has now been realized (Bar 2:30–33; 3:7) and on this basis prays for the return from exile promised in Deuteronomy 30:3ff. (Bar 2:34–35; 3:1–8). Similarly, the pentitential prayer for the Sixth Day in *4QWords of the Luminaries* (4Q504) metaphorically places the community in "exile," petitioning God for deliverance from their present distress (4Q504 frgs. 1–2 cols. 5–7). Their confidence in their own deliverance is based on God's past faithfulness to redeem and regather his people (note especially the allusions to Lev 26:44–45 and Deut 30:1–2 in 4Q504 frgs. 1–2 5.6–14 (for the text, see p. 115 above).

[144] "To this day, the Lord has not given you a *heart* to understand, nor eyes to see, nor ears to hear" (καὶ οὐκ ἔδωκεν κύριος ὁ θεὸς ὑμῖν <u>καρδίαν</u> εἰδέναι καὶ ὀφθαλμοὺς βλέπειν καὶ ὦτα ἀκούειν ἕως τῆς ἡμέρας ταύτης, Deut 29:4). Significantly, Paul quotes from this verse in Romans 11:8 (conflated with Isaiah 29:10). Deuteronomy 29:19 refers to the deceptive speech of the heart as an enticement to rebellion: καὶ ἔσται ἐὰν ἀκούσῃ τὰ ῥήματα τῆς ἀρᾶς ταύτης καὶ ἐπιφημίσηται ἐν τῇ καρδίᾳ αὐτοῦ λέγων· ὅσιά μοι γένοιτο ὅτι ἐν τῇ ἀποπλανήσει <u>τῆς καρδίας μου</u> πορεύσομαι. . . . (See also Deut 30:17, καὶ ἐὰν μεταστῇ <u>ἡ καρδία σου</u> καὶ μὴ εἰσακούσῃς καὶ πλανηθεὶς προσκυνήσῃς θεοῖς ἑτέροις. . . .)

30:6).[145] Paul refracts Leviticus 18:5 through the twin lenses of Deuteronomy 30:12–14 and of his gospel "to the Jew first and also to the Greek" in order to show that God has now acted in Christ to realize the Law's promise of life for all who will respond with heart and mouth to the word that is near.

The content of this ῥῆμα becomes the focus of Romans 10:9, as Paul artfully weaves key terms from Deuteronomy 30:12–14 into his summary of the message he proclaims. Targeting his exegetical atomizer at the level of the phrase, Paul uncovers in Deuteronomy's "mouth" and "heart" distinct, though complementary, points. The "word of faith" calls a person to "confess with your *mouth* that Jesus is Lord" and to "believe in your *heart* that God raised him from the dead."

Beyond providing the terms "mouth" and "heart," Deuteronomy has shaped Paul's précis of the gospel at a still deeper level. Paul's two "creedal statements" in Romans 10:9 correspond closely to his interpretation of the two questions in Deuteronomy 30:12–13 (Rom 10:6–7). The confession, "Jesus is Lord," recalls the early Christian proclamation that Christ has been exalted to the right hand of God.[146] It is this event that provides the most plausible background for Paul's fanciful interpretation of Deuteronomy 30:12 as a depiction of someone attempting to ascend to heaven to bring Christ down, as if there were anything left for him to accomplish on earth (Rom 10:6).[147]

---

[145] Note the repeated emphasis in Deuteronomy 30 on the promise of "life" for those who turn to God and keep his commandments: 30:15, 16, 19, 20. Deuteronomy 30:6 echoes two key texts from earlier in the book: the command to love God with all one's heart (6:5, the *Shema*ʿ) and the command to circumcise one's heart for obedience (10:6). As D. T. Olson explains (1994:127), in 30:6 these two commands "undergo a profound transformation. The *command* has become a *promise.* . . . Commanded *human* action has now become a promised *divine* gift": God himself will supply the ability to keep the covenant (similarly, P. D. Miller 1990:207–208). Miller notes the similarity of thought here to the promise of a new heart in Jeremiah 24:6–7 (cf. 31:33–34) and Ezekiel 36:26–28 (206–207).

[146] Note especially the appearance of this confession in the exaltation scene in Philippians 2:10–11.

[147] So also Dunn 1989:184–87. Dunn (187) notes that the pairing of Jesus' death and exaltation is "a variation on the regular association in earliest Christian thought of Christ's death with his resurrection—Christ died and was raised (Rom. 4.25; 8.34; 14.9; I Cor. 15.3–5; II Cor. 5.15; I Thess. 4.14)." Cranfield defends the common reading of Romans 10:6 in terms of the incarnation, arguing that this interpretation is suggested by the order of vv. 6 and 7 and by the assumption that since "bringing Christ up" (v. 7) has already happened, so "bringing Christ down" must also have already occurred (1987:273–74). Neither of Cranfield's objections is convincing, however. First, the somewhat strange order, exaltation—death, is due to

Similarly, belief "that God has raised [Jesus] from the dead" echoes Paul's version of Deuteronomy 30:13, where he finds a reference to bringing Christ up from among the dead (Rom 10:7).[148] By linking his formulation of the gospel so closely to Deuteronomy 30:12–13, Paul supplies the answer to its insistent question: "Who?" There is no need to be chasing around heaven or the abyss, Paul responds, for by raising Christ from the dead and exalting him as Lord, *Israel's God* has already done everything necessary for salvation. The word is near. All that remains is to confess and believe.

Response to Paul's message leads to "salvation" (σωθήσῃ, 10:9). Paul explicates this connection in Romans 10:10 by drawing two soteriological axioms: (1) with the heart one believes leading to right-eousness and (2) with the mouth one confesses leading to salvation. The reappearance of the key term "righteousness" ties Paul's quotation and interpretation of Deuteronomy 30:12–14 firmly to the larger context of Romans 9:30ff. (see 9:30, 31; 10:3, 4, 5, 6). Significantly, Paul sets "righteousness" in parallel with "salvation," attesting again to the importance of the notion of deliverance in Paul's use of "righteousness" terminology.

Isaiah 28:16 in Romans 10:11

Paul proceeds in Romans 10:11–13 to construct scriptural proofs for these two soteriological axioms. In support of his claim that "believing" leads to "righteousness," he revisits Isaiah 28:16, creating an *inclusio* with the beginning of his discussion of Israel's misstep (Rom 9:30–33). Here, he draws out just one key line from the text he has already cited: πᾶς ὁ πιστεύων ἐπ᾽ αὐτῷ οὐ καταισχυνθήσεται ("Whoever believes in him will not be ashamed," 10:11).[149] As Paul sets it up, "not being ashamed" (Rom 10:11) corresponds to "righteousness"

---

the constraints of the text Paul is interpreting. Second, there is no reason to suppose that the logic of Paul's interpretation *requires* Christ to have descended from heaven. The point is that there is no reason for him to leave his exalted state, for God has already accomplished his saving work through Christ. It seems to me that the clear relationship between v. 7 and the confession of Jesus as "Lord" decisively favors finding in v. 7 an allusion to the exaltation of Christ.

[148] Note the frequent reference to Jesus' resurrection in Romans (1:4; 4:25; 6:4, 5, 9; 7:4; 8:34; 15:12) as well as Paul's characterization of God as "the one who raised Jesus from the dead" (4:24; 8:11 [2x]).

[149] On Paul's introductory formula, λέγει γὰρ ἡ γραφή, see pp. 53–54 n. 34.

(Rom 10:10); both result from believing. The appropriateness of this equation becomes clear when we recall the larger context of Isaiah 28:16, in which God's promise to the one who believes is deliverance from the disaster about to engulf Israel. This correspondence of terms further underscores the significant connection of Paul's "righteousness" language with the idea of "vindication"/"deliverance" by God.

In this second citation of Isaiah 28:16, Paul adds the word πᾶς. This is a crystal-clear example of a deliberate modification of the text by Paul.[150] Whereas he first interpreted Isaiah 28:16 with reference to Israel's manner of pursuing the Law (Rom 9:33), he now finds in Isaiah 28:16 a clear reference to the basis on which Jew *and* *Gentile* alike come within the embrace of God's righteousness. The motive for the addition is not difficult to divine: Paul has modified the text of Isaiah 28:16 under the influence of his christological convictions (Romans 10:4). Πᾶς ὁ πιστεύων echoes Paul's thesis in Romans 10:4 that Christ is the τέλος of the Law for righteousness παντὶ τῷ πιστεύοντι.

The addition of πᾶς also brings Isaiah 28:16 into line with the text that closes this stage in Paul's argument, Joel 2:32 (πᾶς ὃς ἐπικαλέσηται), drawing a tight circle around the theme of the inclusion of all who respond to the message.[151] Joel 2:32, cited in Romans 10:13, offers proof for the second of Paul's axioms, that "confessing" leads to "salvation" (Rom 10:10). It promises, "Whoever calls on the name of the Lord will be saved." Using one's mouth to "call" on the Lord corresponds to "confessing" with one's mouth in Rom 10:10; both actions lead to being "saved." From the word πᾶς shared by Isaiah 28:16 and Joel 2:32, Paul draws the conclusion that there is no distinction between Jew and Greek. Employing the wording of Rom 3:22 verbatim, "there is no distinction" (οὐ γὰρ ἐστιν διαστολή), Paul substitutes for his earlier indictment that *all* humans are under sin the good news that *all* humans have the same Lord (cf. 3:29–30), who deals generously with *all* who call on him (10:12).[152] Guided by

---

[150] The only support for πᾶς in the LXX text tradition is provided by the ninth-century MS 407. The contextual factors motivating Paul's modification of Isaiah 28:16 in Romans 10:11 are so great as to all but rule out his use of a variant text as the source of πᾶς.

[151] See Figure 3.4, p. 156 above.

[152] The equal standing of Jew and Greek before God (though not apart from acknowledgment of Israel's priority in both salvation and judgment: "to the Jew

Joel 2:32 and by his own conviction of the universality of God's action in Christ, then, Paul reads Isaiah 28:16 as a promise for Gentiles as well as for Jews, and he quotes this text in such a way as to make it say more clearly what he knows it to mean.[153]

THE HERALDS OF ISAIAH AND THE MISSION OF PAUL: ISAIAH 52:7 AND 53:1 IN ROMANS 10:14–17[154]

In Romans 10:8–13, Paul has outlined a progression from the "word of faith that we preach" to the response of a person who calls on the name of the Lord and so participates in righteousness and salvation. In 10:14–15, he retraces this progression from the opposite direction through a rapid-fire burst of rhetorical questions. These questions build on one another in stair-step fashion, culminating in the necessity for preachers to be sent out with the good news. Paul frames his questions in such a way that they interconnect with the scriptural texts he employs in the immediate context. His language not only recalls the texts he has just cited: "call" (10:12–13; Joel 2:32), "believe" (10:9–11; Isa 28:16); it also anticipates key terms from the following quotations from Isaiah 52:7 and 53:1: "preach" (10:15; Isa 52:7), "believe" (10:16; Isa 53:1), "hear" (10:16; Isa 53:1).

In response to the last of his questions, "How will they preach unless they are sent?" Paul cites Isaiah 52:7, revealing the crucial role that his own mission plays in the outworking of God's redemptive purpose.

Messengers of the Good News: Isaiah 52:7 in Romans 10:15

Although Paul's citation clearly resembles Isaiah 52:7 LXX, it stands closer to the text represented by MT at four points (see Figure 3.6 below). First, in Paul's quotation, as in MT, the subject of the sen-

---

first and equally to the Greek") must be seen as one of Paul's major concerns in Romans; it finds expression in both the thematic statement of the letter (1:16–17) and in the grand finale of the ἐπίλογος (15:7–13), as well as repeatedly at key points throughout the body of the letter (2:9–10; 3:9, 22, 29; 10:12).

[153] I borrow here Bart Ehrman's (1993) apt description of the manner in which the early church fathers handled the text of scripture—including Paul's letters. In this respect, at least, the interpretation and transmission of sacred texts by later Christian tradents bear affinities to Paul's own practice (see pp. 27–28).

[154] Portions of the following discussion of Paul's use of Isaiah 52:7 and 53:1 have been adapted from Wagner 1998a:202–11.

tence is "feet": "How beautiful . . . are the feet. . . ." In contrast, the LXX reads 52:7 as a description of God *himself* coming with the good news to Zion. The sentence actually begins with the last word of Isaiah 52:6 LXX, πάρειμι:

> *I am here* as the springtime on the mountains, as the feet of a messenger of peace, as a messenger of good tidings, for *I will make* your salvation heard, saying to Zion, "Your God shall reign."

Figure 3.6: Isaiah 52:7 (LXX and MT) in Romans 10:15

Isaiah 52:7 LXX	Romans 10:15	Isaiah 52:7 MT
⁶. . . πάρειμι ⁷ὡς ὥρα ἐπὶ τῶν ὀρέων, ὡς πόδες εὐαγγελιζομένου ἀκοὴν εἰρήνης, ὡς εὐαγγελιζόμενος ἀγαθά	καθὼς γέγραπται· ὡς ὡραῖοι οἱ πόδες τῶν εὐαγγελιζομένων [τὰ] ἀγαθά	מַה־נָּאווּ עַל־הֶהָרִים רַגְלֵי מְבַשֵּׂר מַשְׁמִיעַ שָׁלוֹם מְבַשֵּׂר טוֹב

Second, where LXX has the comparison, ὡς ὥρα, "as springtime," Paul reads an exclamation, ὡς ὡραῖοι, "how beautiful." Ὡς functions in the LXX version of this verse as a comparative particle; in contrast, Paul's exclamatory ὡς more exactly represents the sense of the Hebrew particle מַה. Furthermore, Paul's ὡραῖοι is closer to the sense of the Hebrew נָאווּ than is the rendering ὥρα of LXX.[155] Finally, neither Paul nor MT has anything corresponding to the second and third occurrences of ὡς in LXX, which probably derive from the LXX translator's own interpretation of the verse rather than from his use of a variant *Vorlage*.

If Paul's citation does not follow the LXX in its distinctive reading of Isaiah 52:7, does this mean that Paul must have quoted from a Hebrew text? Unfortunately for advocates of the view that Paul was literate in Hebrew, it does not.[156] Paul's citation closely resembles

---

[155] Cf. the later Greek versions, all of which come closer to MT: τί ὡραιώθησαν, α′; τί εὐπρεπεῖς (or εὐτρεπιζεῖς), σ′; ὡς εὐπρεπεῖς (or εὐτρεπεῖς), θ′.

[156] Of course, Paul's consistent use of Greek texts of scripture does not prove that he did *not* know Hebrew. Even if he were bi(or tri)-lingual, it would be natural for him to quote scripture in the language in which he was communicating at

the text of Isaiah 52:7 found in a number of primarily Lucianic manuscripts.[157] These manuscripts attest to a septuagintal text of Isaiah 52:7 that has been revised to bring it into greater conformity with the form of text now represented by MT (see Fig. 3.7).[158]

Figure 3.7: Isaiah 52:7 (LXX and Revised LXX) in Romans 10:15

Key: double underline   agreement between Rom 10:15
                          and Isa 52:7 (Revised LXX)
       italic   agreement among all three columns

Isaiah 52:7 LXX	Romans 10:15	Isaiah 52:7 LXX (Rev)
⁶...πάρειμι ⁷*ὡς ὥρα* ἐπὶ τῶν ὀρέων, *ὡς πόδες* *εὐαγγελιζομένου* *ἀκοὴν εἰρήνης,* ὡς εὐαγγελιζόμενος *ἀγαθά*	καθὼς γέγραπται· *ὡς* <u>ὡραῖοι</u> <u>οἱ</u> *πόδες* τῶν *εὐαγγελιζομένων* [τὰ] *ἀγαθά*	*ὡς* ὡραῖοι ἐπὶ τῶν ὀρέων [οἱ] *πόδες* *εὐαγγελιζομένου* *ἀκοὴν εἰρήνης,* εὐαγγελιζόμενου *ἀγαθά*

It is quite unlikely that all of these manuscripts have been influenced by the form of Paul's citation in Romans 10:15 since they do not share with Paul three important variants: the omission of the phrases ἐπὶ τῶν ὀρέων[159] and εὐαγγελιζομένου ἀκοὴν εἰρήνης[160] and the unique reading of a plural participle, εὐαγγελιζομένων. Significantly, none of the variants unique to Paul brings his citation closer to MT. It would be odd indeed to suppose that these manuscripts scrupulously followed Paul only insofar as his changes to LXX comported with the

the time. Nonetheless, clear evidence from Paul's own letters for his competence in Hebrew or Aramaic is wanting.

[157] See the discussion in Stanley 1992b:134–41. In Figure 3.7, I follow Stanley's reconstructed text of the revised version, which is easily defended on the basis of Ziegler's apparatus. The MSS witnessing to all or part of this reconstructed text are 22ᶜ 62 90–130–311 93 456 and Theodoret's citations (all Lucianic, according to Ziegler); 88 Qᵐᵍ Syrohexapla (Hexaplaric); 86ᶜ (Alexandrian); 403–613 (mixed).

[158] So Ziegler 1939a:59: "eine genauere Übersetzung nach 𝔐."

[159] The phrase is absent from the Hexaplaric MS 88, but otherwise appears everywhere in the manuscript tradition of the LXX.

[160] The addition of τῶν εὐαγγελιζόμενων εἰρήνην in a number of MSS of Romans represents a secondary harmonization with the LXX (cf. Metzger 1994:463).

text represented by MT. Since each of the uniquely Pauline variants plays a role in Paul's appropriation of Isaiah 52:7, it is far simpler to imagine that Paul knew a Septuagint text of Isaiah 52:7 that had already been revised toward a proto-masoretic text *and that he altered it further* to fit his purposes in Romans 10.

Three crucial modifications of this revised text of the LXX allow Paul to interpret Isaiah 52:7 as a prophecy of his own mission. First, he omits the phrase "on the mountains," a specific reference to the area surrounding Jerusalem. Paul's elimination of any reference to Zion allows him to apply the quotation to the broader geographical scope of Christian proclamation, which includes Gentiles as well as Jews.[161] Indeed, I will argue below that Paul finds in Isaiah 52:15 (Rom 15:21) explicit warrant for understanding Gentiles to fall within the larger scope of proclamation envisioned in Isaiah 52:7.[162] Second, by skipping over the phrase, "of one announcing a message of peace" (εὐαγγελιζομένου ἀκοὴν εἰρήνης), Paul facilitates his exclusive identification of the "message" (ἀκοή) with the "word of Christ" (Rom 10:16–17).[163] Finally, Paul transforms the lone herald of the LXX (πόδες εὐαγγελιζομένου) into multiple preachers of the good news (οἱ πόδες τῶν εὐαγγελιζομένων). This variant, without support in the Hebrew and Greek text traditions or in the Targum, Peshitta, or Vulgate, is almost certainly Pauline.[164] By means of this subtle

---

[161] Contrast the Targum's rendering: "how fitting on the mountains of the land of Israel . . ." (מא יאין על טורי ארעא דישראל).

[162] See pp. 332–36 below.

[163] The definite article with ἀγαθά, if original to Romans 10:15, may function anaphorically to specify the "good things" announced by the heralds as the "word of faith" Paul has been expounding. The omission of τά has strong Alexandrian and Western support (including א² A B C D* F G 1739). In favor of the originality of τά, however, is the attestation of this reading by 𝔓⁴⁶ א* D¹ and, assuming the tendency of scribes to harmonize NT quotations with the LXX, the fact that the article is nowhere found in the textual tradition of the LXX. Cf. Zuntz (1953:173 n. 4), who argues that τά is original to Romans 10:15. Koch 1986:82–83 (followed by Stanley 1992b:139) explains the omission of the phrase εὐαγγελιζομένου ἀκοὴν εἰρήνης by suggesting that Paul's copy of Isaiah 52:7 had suffered haplography. This hypothesis cannot be ruled out, particularly since one can well imagine that Paul would have found this phrase to be an apt description of his gospel (cf. Rom 5:1; I am indebted to Richard Hays for this point [private correspondence]). As I have noted previously, however, it is difficult to construct an argument about Paul's text on the basis of what he would or would not have found useful for his purposes. My attribution of the omission of εὐαγγελιζομένου ἀκοὴν εἰρήνης to Paul rather than to his *Vorlage* must therefore remain tentative.

[164] The reading εὐαγγελιζόμενων unique to Eusebius' citation of α' and θ' most likely reflects Eusebius' familiarity with Romans 10:15 rather than the actual texts

modification to the text, Paul makes explicit his identification of the heralds of Isaiah 52:7 (οἱ εὐαγγελιζόμενοι) with the Christian preachers (κηρύσσοντες) mentioned in Romans 10:8, 14–15.[165]

That Paul sees his own ministry of proclamation prefigured in Isaiah 52:7 is further supported by the parallel he draws between the message proclaimed by the heralds of Isaiah's oracle and his own gospel. Paul mentions the "evangel" (τὸ εὐαγγέλιον) in Romans 10:16 for the first time since 2:16.[166] In light of Paul's reference everywhere else in Romans 10 to his message as "the word of faith/ the word of Christ" (10:8, 17), his choice of terms in 10:16 can only be seen as a deliberate attempt to make the connection with Isaiah's "evangelists" (οἱ εὐαγγελιζόμενοι, Rom 10:15) unmistakable.

Isaiah 52:7 in Context

Echoes of the wider context of Isaiah 52:7 enrich the texture of Paul's imaginative depiction of his mission yet further. Isaiah 52:7 falls in the midst of an extended prophecy announcing God's redemption of Israel from captivity in Babylon. The long-awaited deliverance from exile, promised to God's people at various points throughout Isaiah, at last finds its realization as heralds come bounding over the mountains to Jerusalem with the triumphant cry, "Your God shall

---

of α′ and θ′. Significantly, his version of α′ shares with Romans 10:15 (against other witnesses to α′) both the omission of the phrase ἀκουτίζοντος εἰρήνην εὐαγγελιζόμενου and the LXX reading ἀγαθά (according to MS Q, α′ reads ἀγαθόν). Although two MSS (106 87*) read εὐαγγελιζόμενοι, they treat the participle as an *adjective* modifying πόδες and so do not provide attestation for Paul's interpretation of multiple messengers. The attributive *euangelizantes* found in the parallel passage, Nahum 1:15 (some MSS of the *Speculum*), fails to support Paul's variant for the same reason.

[165] In light of Paul's citation of Joel 2:32a just two verses earlier (Rom 10:13), it is interesting to note the way this verse concludes in the LXX:

καὶ ἔσται πᾶς ὃς ἂν ἐπικαλέσηται τὸ ὄνομα κυρίου σωθήσεται ὅτι ἐν τῷ ὄρει Σιων καὶ ἐν Ιερουσαλημ ἔσται ἀνασῳζόμενος καθότι εἶπε κύριος <u>καὶ εὐαγγελιζόμενοι οὓς κύριος προσκέκληται.</u>

In its LXX form, Joel 2:32 speaks of the appointing of preachers, εὐαγγελιζόμενοι, to announce the good news that "everyone who calls on the name of the Lord will be saved." This is just the role Paul ascribes to himself and his fellow preachers of the gospel. We see here yet another strand of the thick intertextual fabric Paul has woven in this section of Romans (similarly, Dinter 1980:33, who speaks of "covert sources for Paul's reflection here on the mission of preachers"). Once again, this intertextual connection depends on the LXX form of the text, for other witnesses speak not of "preachers," but of "survivors": וּבַשְּׂרִידִים, MT (so apparently MurXII); וּמְסַבְּרִין, Tg.; ܘܡܣܒܪܝ, Peshitta. The LXX apparently reads וּמְבַשְּׂרִים, but this may be the result of exegesis rather than a reflection of a variant *Vorlage*.

[166] The term does not appear again until Romans 11:28.

reign!" Their arrival fulfills the summons in 40:1–9 for messengers to announce the comforting news that the Lord is returning victorious to Zion, his redeemed people in his train.[167] Paul's frequent characterization of his message as one that leads to "salvation" (σωτηρία/σῴζω; Rom 10:9, 10, 13; cf. Rom 10:1) and his emphasis on "hearing" the good news acquire a new layer of significance when set in counterpoint with the metaleptically suppressed promise in Isaiah 52:7b, "I will make my salvation (σωτηρία) heard."

Resonances of the wider context of Isaiah 52:7 with Paul's argument in Romans suggest that his notion of the "salvation" effected by the gospel finds its conceptual home within the context of God's ancient promises to deliver his people. Viewed against the rather drab backdrop of the historical return of Israel from Babylon and its continued subjection to foreign nations, Isaiah's vivid oracle, like similar prophecies of restoration, was widely understood in the Second Temple period as a depiction of a future, eschatological deliverance.[168] By appealing to Isaiah 52:7 and the larger story of which it is a part, Paul proclaims that Israel's long-awaited redemption is now at hand.

---

[167] On the tight verbal and thematic connections between Isaiah 40 and Isaiah 52, see pp. 183–84.

[168] See the discussion of this point in Chapter 1 above. A fascinating interpretation of Isaiah 52:7 along these lines is attested by *11QMelchizedek* (11Q13), dating from the first or second century CE. For text, translations, and discussions, see: DJD XXIII, 221–241, pl. XXVII; Puech 1987; Kobelski 1981:3–23; J. A. Sanders 1973; Milik 1972:96–109, 124–26; M. P. Miller 1969; Fitzmyer 1967; de Jonge and van der Woude 1965–66; van der Woude 1965. This complex and fragmentary midrash reads Leviticus 25:8ff. and Isaiah 61:1–3, which speak of the Jubilee year, as prophecies of the eschatological redemption of God's people by the heavenly deliverer Melchizedek. Isaiah 52:7 is understood to refer to the day on which Melchizedek will take vengeance on Israel's enemies and rescue Zion (2.15–16). Especially intriguing is the identification in 2.18 of "the herald" as the "anointed of the spir[it]" (Isa 61:1) spoken of by "Dan[iel]" (Dan 9:25?), and the statement in 2.18–20 that "[the herald of] good, proclaimin[g salvation]" is the one who is sent "to comfor[t] the [mourners]" (Isaiah 61:2–3). This "comforting" is interpreted as meaning, "to [i]nstruct them in all the ages of the w[orld]." It is likely that the identification of the herald of Isaiah 52:7 with the prophetic figure of Isaiah 61:1 was suggested by the shared description of their activity as "proclaiming" (בשׂר). This *Stichwort* occurs in Isaiah only in 40:9; 41:27; 52:7; 60:6; 61:1. Note the similar interpretive move in 1QHᵃ 23[18].14, where the two texts are conflated in a description of the ministry of "your servant" (עבדכה = the poet): ל[ ] כאמתכה מבשר [ ] טובכה (Isa 52:7) לבשר ענוים (Isa 61:1) לרוב רחמיכה. While 11Q13 is important for understanding the messianic interpretation of Isaiah 61 (cf. 4Q521; Luke 4:16–30; see further J. A. Sanders 1973, 1975a; Collins 1995b:117–22, 1997; Puech 1992), Paul nowhere quotes from Isaiah 61. Furthermore, Paul does

At the same time, however, Paul has thoroughly reconfigured Isaiah's vision. For Paul, the fulfillment of Israel's hopes centers on God's act in Christ. While the message of "salvation" in Isaiah 52:7 consists in the announcement to Zion that her God reigns, Paul's gospel focuses on God's decisive act of raising Jesus Christ from the dead and exalting him as Lord. Corresponding to Isaiah's proclamation, "Your God shall reign!" is Paul's confession, "Jesus is Lord!" (Rom 10:9). Just as Christ is for Paul the τέλος of the Law "for righteousness," so, thanks to his interpretive creativity, the goods news proclaimed by Isaiah's heralds—that God has acted to deliver his people from captivity—is shown to be none other than the gospel of Christ. Imaginatively transformed into the heralds of Isaiah, Paul and his cohorts go out, bearing the message that God's righteousness has at last been revealed in the gospel for the salvation of Jew and Gentile alike.

Excursus: Blasphemed among the Gentiles: Isaiah 52:5 in Romans 2:24
Recognizing Paul's deep engagement with Isaiah's story opens the way for a clearer understanding of his quotation of Isaiah 52:5 in Romans 2:24.

> You who boast in the Law, do you through your transgression of the Law dishonor God? "For the name of God is blasphemed among the Gentiles because of you," just as it is written (Rom 2:23–24).

On the surface, Paul appears to be harsh and vindictive, completely oblivious to the original setting of Isaiah 52:5 in an oracle of comfort and assurance directed to exiled Israel (Isa 52:1–10).[169] Yet such an impression is mistaken.

Isaiah 52:1–10 opens with a call to Zion to awake and take off her bonds (52:1–3). God recounts his people's captivity at the hands of "Egypt" and "Assyria" and the scorn this has brought on God's name "among the Gentiles" (52:4–5). Therefore, God vows that he will now act to vindicate his name (52:6). Verses 7–10 depict a herald coming to Zion with the good news, the message of "salvation": "Your God shall reign!" (52:7).[170]

---

not identify the herald of Isaiah 52:7 with a messianic figure, but with missionaries who proclaim Christ (it is unclear whether the "herald" in 11Q13 is Melchizedek himself [so rightly Lim 1992:91]). There thus do not appear to be any clear points of contact between Romans 10 and 11Q13 beyond the important observation that both understand Isaiah 52:7 to refer to a future eschatological deliverance of Israel and that, on the basis of terminological and thematic links, both relate Isaiah 52:7 to other texts in Isaiah (40:9 for Paul; 61:1 for 11Q13).

[169] Fitzmyer comments on Paul's use of scripture in Rom 2:24: "Paul, writing frequently in the rhetorical style of a preacher, often fails to take into consideration the original context of the Old Testament and twists the quotation which he uses to his own purpose" (1960–61:44).

[170] The LXX ties 52:6 and 7 together syntactically, so that God himself is the

It is crucial to see that in the context of 52:1–10, the words Paul quotes in Romans 2:24 stand as a word of *judgment* on Israel, laying the blame for their exile squarely on their shoulders: God is dishonored *"because of you."*[171] The LXX, which Paul quotes here, specifies that it is "among the Gentiles" that God is blasphemed.[172] The LXX translator further intensifies the sense of blame and accusation in 52:5 by addressing Israel directly,[173] introducing a complaint by Israel against the Lord,[174] and reading a phrase absent from MT: "on account of you" (δι' ὑμᾶς). Paul actually appears to soften the blow slightly by eliminating "continually" (διὰ παντός).[175] He also draws attention to the primary issue at hand, the reputation of God, by advancing the phrase "the name of God" (LXX, "my name") to the beginning of the quotation (see Figure 3.8).[176]

Figure 3.8: Isaiah 52:5 LXX in Romans 2:24

Isaiah 52:5 LXX	Romans 2:24
δι' ὑμᾶς διὰ παντὸς τὸ ὄνομά μου βλασφημεῖται ἐν τοῖς ἔθνεσι.	τὸ γὰρ ὄνομα τοῦ θεοῦ δι' ὑμᾶς βλασφημεῖται ἐν τοῖς ἔθνεσιν, καθὼς γέγραπται.

Isa 52:5 MT: וְתָמִיד כָּל־הַיּוֹם שְׁמִי מִנֹּאָץ

---

one who brings the good news. As already noted, Paul's quotation of 52:7 more nearly approximates the reading of a number of primarily "Lucianic" manuscripts, whose syntax is closer to that of the text represented by MT. For Paul, the heralds are not to be identified with God, but with preachers such as himself.

[171] Compare the similar thought in Isaiah 48:11 (τὸ ἐμὸν ὄνομα βεβηλοῦται). Isaiah 48:1–11, like 52:1–10, emphasizes both Israel's culpability and God's determination to deliver them for the sake of his own glory (48:9, 11).

[172] This is implied, but not stated, in MT (the phrase falls under the obelus in B Q 88 Syrohexapla and is omitted in V). It appears that the LXX translator has borrowed "among the Gentiles" from Ezekiel 36:20–23 (ms 46 takes a further phrase from here, τὸ ὄνομα τὸ ἅγιον). Like Isaiah 52, Ezekiel 36:16–38 bemoans the profanation (βεβηλόω) of the Lord's name in the exile. As in Isaiah, so also in Ezekiel's oracle the Lord vows to rescue his people and restore them to the land for the sake of his name. He removes their uncleanness and iniquity, giving them a new heart and a new spirit so that they can keep his covenant (note the covenant formula in 36:28: ἔσεσθέ μοι εἰς λαόν, καὶ ἐγὼ ἔσομαι ὑμῖν εἰς θεόν). For the argument that Paul's thought in Romans 2:24 also betrays the influence of Ezekiel 36, see Berkley 2000:136–41 (cf. 90–94).

[173] καὶ νῦν τί ὧδέ ἐστε; ("Now why are you here?").

[174] ὅτι ἐλήμφθη ὁ λαός μου δωρεὰν θαυμάζετε καὶ ὀλολύζετε ("Because my people were taken away for nothing, *you marvel and you cry aloud*").

[175] The omission of this phrase in Justin, Eusebius, and Tertullian may be due to their dependence on Paul's citation (cf. Skarsaune 1987:114).

[176] No other witness to the text of Isaiah attests this word order.

Paul does not go on to quote the next verse, Isaiah 52:6, in which God vows that he will vindicate his name by redeeming his people from exile. But the role Isaiah 52:5 plays in the structure of Paul's argument in Romans suggests that he is well aware of the larger setting of 52:5 in Isaiah 52:1–10. In Romans, as in Isaiah, these words of blame serve only as a prelude to the imminent announcement that God has redeemed his people Israel. Paul quotes Isaiah 52:5 in Romans 2:24 precisely because he believes that without the gospel, Israel is, figuratively speaking, still in exile, still in bondage to the power of sin like the rest of humanity (Rom 3:9).[177] But just as the word of judgment in Isaiah 52:5 precedes the herald's announcement of the return from exile in Isaiah 52:7–10, so also Romans 2:24 precedes Paul's exposition of the gospel (the righteousness of God *for the Jew first* and also for the Greek [1:16]), in Romans 3:21ff.[178] Paul's citation of Isaiah 52:7 as a prefiguration of his own proclamation of the gospel (Rom 10:15) strongly suggests both that Paul is aware of the connection between 52:5 and 52:7 within Isaiah's oracle and that he employs each of these passages in his argument in Romans with their original setting in mind. If Paul sharply criticizes his fellow Jews, he does so not as an outsider slinging mud, but as a prophet, wounding that he may heal.[179]

Who Has Believed? Isaiah 53:1 in Romans 10:16

Although Paul and his associates have been sent to preach the good news, as Isaiah prophesied, they have met with resistance. Despite the fact that Christ is the τέλος of the Law for righteousness to *all* (πάντες) who believe (10:4), and that he is the one Lord over *all* (πάντες), Jew and Gentile alike, who offers salvation to *all* (πάντες) who believe/call on him (10:11–13), "*Not all* (οὐ πάντες) have obeyed the gospel" (10:16). Without excluding a reference to Gentile unbelief, the continued focus on Israel in Romans 10:19 suggests that in vv. 16–18, as througout Romans 9–11, Paul is primarily concerned with *Israel's* resistance to the gospel.[180] Yet just as Paul has found in Isaiah a prefiguration of his ministry of proclamation, so he discovers in Isaiah a prophecy of the rejection of the message by some: "Lord, who has believed our message?"

---

[177] See further pp. 353–54 below.
[178] Cf. the discussion of this passage in Hays 1989:44–46.
[179] Cf. Evans 1984a; J. A. Sanders 1977a.
[180] So also Gignac 1999:349.

Figure 3.9: Isaiah 53:1 LXX in Romans 10:16

Isaiah 53:1 LXX	Romans 10:16
κύριε, τίς ἐπίστευσε τῇ ἀκοῇ ἡμῶν; καὶ ὁ βραχίων κυρίου τίνι ἀπεκαλύφθη;	Ησαΐας γὰρ λέγει· κύριε, τίς ἐπίστευσεν τῇ ἀκοῇ ἡμῶν;

Isa 53:1 MT: מִי הֶאֱמִין לִשְׁמֻעָתֵנוּ וּזְרוֹעַ יְהוָה עַל־מִי נִגְלָתָה

Paul has not selected Isaiah 53:1 at random. A complex network of correspondences connects the wording of the citation to its context in Romans 10.[181] The prophet calls out to the "Lord" concerning the unbelief of his hearers, who, ironically, ought to have been the ones calling on the name of the Lord for salvation (10:13). The lament, "who has *believed*?" echoes the promise of righteousness through Christ for all who *believe* (10:4), a promise announced both by Isaiah (Isa 28:16; Rom 10:11) and by Paul and his associates (10:9–10) who preach the "word of *faith*" (10:8). Isaiah's reference to the ἀκοή that meets with disbelief recalls Paul's statement that the hearing (ἀκούειν) that leads to believing depends on preachers being sent forth (10:14–15). This ἀκοή also provides a link to the (metaleptically suppressed) ἀκοή of Isaiah 52:7b, tightening the connection between the "message" of Isaiah 53:1 and the message of those who bring good news (Isa 52:7a), with whom Paul has identified himself and other Christian evangelists.

Paul allows Isaiah to speak in his own voice about the rejection of "*our* message." It is of tremendous significance for understanding Paul's appropriation of the Book of Isaiah to recognize that this quotation assumes a fundamental correspondence between Paul's apostolic proclamation and Isaiah's message. It is not simply that

---

[181] As Figure 3.9 shows, Paul's quotation of Isaiah 53:1a exactly follows the reading of the LXX, whose own textual tradition is univocal at this point. This is a clear example of Paul's dependence on a septuagintal text, for the LXX alone explicitly makes this verse an address to God (against MT, 1QIsaᵃ, Targum, Peshitta, Vulgate). There is a lacuna in 4QIsaᶜ [4Q57] at the beginning of Isaiah 53:1, but there was probably a space here indicating the beginning of a new section (as in 1QIsaᵃ, MT) rather than anything corresponding to κύριε (see Skehan and Ulrich, DJD XV, p. 68, note on line 9).

Isaiah long ago predicted something that is now fulfilled in Paul's ministry. Rather, Isaiah remains a living voice for Paul, one who speaks alongside the apostle as an authoritative witness to the gospel.

By adducing Isaiah 53:1 as support for the claim that not all have believed "the gospel," Paul identifies the "message" of Isaiah 53:1 with Christian proclamation (Rom 10:16). He draws the same parallel in Romans 10:17, concluding from Isaiah 53:1 that faith follows "hearing the message" (ἀκοή) and that this "hearing the message" comes through the "word of Christ" (ῥῆμα Χριστοῦ), which Paul has also termed the "word of faith that we preach" (10:8). Paul's claim that Isaiah's "message" concerns the "word of Christ" raises the intriguing possibility that he understands the Servant Song of Isaiah 52:13–53:12 to refer to Christ, and, in some sense, to be Isaiah's preaching of the same "gospel" that Paul, now Isaiah's "co-worker," also preaches.[182]

Paul has marshalled an impressive array of scriptural texts to support his contention that the Christ whom he proclaims in the gospel is the true goal and completion of the Law. He enlists Moses, "Righteousness from Faith," Isaiah, and Joel as witnesses to the "word of faith" that he preaches. But Paul finds not only that the gospel is announced beforehand in the scriptures; he also uncovers in Isaiah 52–53 a prophecy of his own crucial role in God's redemptive plan. He is one of those depicted in Isaiah 52:7, a herald sent to broadcast the good news that God reigns, that Jesus is Lord. Through his apostolic ministry, people are able to hear, believe, and call upon the Lord. Tragically, he is also one who laments, "Lord, who has believed our report?" Confronted with the tragedy of Israel's resistance to the gospel, Paul finds in Isaiah 53:1 that facing the unbelief of his own people is also part of God's design for his ministry. But why should this be so?

EXPLAINING ISRAEL'S UNBELIEF: ECHOES OF ISAIAH 40 IN ROMANS 10:18–19

In Romans 10:18–19, Paul addresses the problem of Israel's unbelief by posing two questions that, due to their parallel introductory formulas (ἀλλὰ λέγω), should be heard as forming one query. Considered

---

[182] See further on this below, pp. 334–35.

by itself, the first question, "It is not that they haven't *heard*, is it?" (μὴ οὐκ ἤκουσαν;) appears as nothing more than the logical outgrowth of Paul's statement in 10:17 that faith comes through hearing. But before the reverberations of this question and its answer fade away, Paul presses his query further: "It is not that Israel hasn't *known*, is it?" (μὴ Ἰσραὴλ οὐκ ἔγνω;).[183] Heard together, these questions strikingly echo the challenge to Israel's unbelief twice issued in Isaiah 40:[184]

> Will you not know? Will you not hear?
> οὐ γνώσεσθε; οὐκ ἀκούσεσθε; (40:21)
>
> And now, have you not known? Have you not heard?
> καὶ νῦν οὐκ ἔγνως εἰ μὴ ἤκουσας; (40:28)[185]

Isaiah 40 opens with God's insistent summons for messengers to comfort his people with the news that their sins have been forgiven and that their period of humiliation is now completed (40:1–2). A voice cries out in the desert, "Prepare the way of the Lord." Israel's God is returning in victory to Zion, and the whole world will see his glory and the salvation he has wrought (40:3–5). The message that God is coming to deliver his people is reliable, for "the word (ῥῆμα) of our God endures forever" (40:6–8). Therefore, the one who brings the good news (ὁ εὐαγγελιζόμενος) to Zion is to shout boldly from the mountaintop: "Here is your God!" (40:9).[186] The Lord is returning to Zion as a triumphant warrior who gently shepherds his people on the long journey home (40:10–11).

Immediately following this exuberant proclamation of Israel's imminent salvation, however, there is a marked shift in tone. It appears

---

[183] The continued focus on Israel in Romans 10:19 suggests that in vv. 16–18, "not all" (οὐ πάντες, 10:16), "who?" (τίς, 10:16), and "they" (ἤκουσαν, 10:18) should all be understood primarily as references to Israel.

[184] Wilk (1998:314–15) considers Romans 10:19 an allusion to Isaiah 1:3 (ἔγνω βοῦς τὸν κτησάμενον καὶ ὄνος τὴν φάτνην τοῦ κυρίου αὐτοῦ· Ἰσραηλ δέ με οὐκ ἔγνω, καὶ ὁ λαός με οὐ συνῆκεν), but as the following discussion will show, on both linguistic and thematic grounds Isaiah 40:21/28 is a much more likely source text for Paul's questions in Romans 10:18–19.

[185] On εἰ μή in 40:28b, see Ottley 1906–1909, 2:301.

[186] Due to the feminine form of the participle מבשרת, there is some ambiguity in MT with regard to whether Zion is the recipient of the message or the messenger (J. D. W. Watts 1987:78 n. 9b–b). The LXX disallows the latter interpretation; even though Σιων and Ἰερουσαλημ are not inflected, they are clearly feminine (40:2; 52:8), whereas the participle εὐαγγελιζόμενος is masculine. Interestingly, the later Greek versions take just the opposite tack, employing the feminine form of the participle in order to identify Zion as the messenger.

that the good news has been received not with rejoicing, but with skepticism and unbelief. Although we are privy to only one side of the dialogue, the extended string of rhetorical questions in Isaiah 40:12–26 suggests that Israel has called into question both the wisdom and the justice of God's plan of deliverance:

> Who has known the mind of the Lord, and who has become his counselor to advise him? With whom has he taken counsel and he has advised him? Who has shown him judgment? Who has shown him the way of understanding? (40:13–14 LXX).

Isaiah's response focuses on God's incomparable wisdom and power as creator and ruler of the world (40:12, 22). The nations and their rulers—those who have been the instruments of Israel's chastisement by God—are as nothing before him (40:15–17, 23–24). There is no god like the Lord (40:18–20, 25–26). The prophet impatiently asks how long Israel intends to remain stubbornly uncomprehending: "Will you not know? Will you not hear?" (40:21).

Israel's challenge to God specifically targets God's faithfulness to his people. This becomes clear in 40:27, when Israel's complaint is finally given voice: "Do not say, O Jacob—and why have you said, O Israel—'My way is hidden from God, and my God has taken away (my) judgment and stood aloof.'"[187] Incredulous, Isaiah demands: "And now, have you not known? Have you not heard? The eternal God, the God who created the ends of the earth, never gets hungry or tired; his understanding is inscrutable" (40:28). While those who rely on themselves will hunger and grow weary, those who patiently wait on the Lord will find him faithful to sustain them (40:28–31).

The close verbal resemblance between Romans 10:18–19 and Isaiah 40:21/28 suggests that Paul deliberately framed his twin questions to recall Isaiah's challenge to unbelieving Israel. In order to incorporate these questions into the context of his argument, Paul has altered the verbs from second to third person and reversed their order.[188] He has further added μή to ensure that his words are under-

---

[187] My translation is indebted to Ottley 1906–1909, 1:223. Note the correspondence between Israel's complaint, ὁ θεός μου τὴν κρίσιν ἀφεῖλε, and Isaiah's earlier challenge to their unbelief, τίς ἔδειξεν αὐτῷ κρίσιν; (40:14).

[188] Curiously, the Peshitta has the order "hear . . . know" in 40:21, but in 40:28, "know . . . hear." The order in 40:21 is probably due to an unintentional metathesis of terms. In contrast, the way in which Paul's order fits the structure of his argument suggests that it is the product of a deliberate rhetorical strategy.

stood as questions rather than as statements.[189] Nevertheless, the correspondence of Paul's questions to Isaiah 40:21, and particularly to 40:28, is striking. Although the pairing of γινώσκω and ἀκούω is not uncommon, in the entire LXX they appear in parallel questions only in these two passages from Isaiah 40. Paul's familiarity with Isaiah 40 is well attested by his use of Isaiah 40:13 in Romans 11:34 and 1 Corinthians 2:16.[190]

That Paul would allude to Isaiah 40 in Romans 10:18–19 becomes more comprehensible in light of the close proximity of his citation of Isaiah 52:7 (Rom 10:15). These two chapters, particularly in the LXX version, share a number of strong verbal and thematic links. In both passages—and in these two passages alone in Isaiah—a messenger[191] is depicted as coming over the mountains to Zion with good news:

> Go up on a high mountain, you who bring good news to Zion. Lift up your voice in strength, you who bring good news to Jerusalem. Lift it up, do not be afraid. Say to the cities of Judah, "Here is your God."

> ἐπ' ὄρος ὑψηλὸν ἀνάβηθι, ὁ εὐαγγελιζόμενος Σιων· ὕψωσον τῇ ἰσχύι τὴν φωνήν σου, ὁ εὐαγγελιζόμενος Ιερουσαλημ ὑψώσατε μὴ φοβεῖσθε εἰπὸν ταῖς πόλεσιν Ιουδα· ἰδοὺ ὁ θεὸς ὑμῶν (40:9).

> How beautiful on the mountains are the feet of the one who brings the good news of a message of peace, who brings the good news of good things, for I will make your salvation heard, saying to Zion, "Your God shall reign."

> ὡς ὡραῖοι ἐπὶ τῶν ὀρέων [οἱ] πόδες εὐαγγελιζομένου ἀκοὴν εἰρήνης, εὐαγγελιζομένου ἀγαθά, ὅτι ἀκουστὴν ποιήσω τὴν σωτηρίαν σου λέγων Σιων· βασιλεύσει σου ὁ θεός (52:7).[192]

---

[189] In the absence of any other device to indicate punctuation, Paul's use of μή is required here to prevent a potentially devastating misunderstanding of his meaning, since the performative, ἀλλὰ λέγω, might be heard as introducing an emphatic *assertion* (cf. Rom 15:8). The use of μή also signals that these questions are to be answer negatively.

[190] Note as well the possible echo of Isaiah 40:28 in Romans 11:33, discussed below (p. 303 n. 247).

[191] The verb εὐαγγελίζω occurs in Isaiah only in 40:9; 52:7; 60:6; 61:1. Paul's use of this uncommon word to link together Isaiah 40 and 52 finds a parallel in *11QMelchizedek* [11Q13] 2.18–20, where the corresponding Hebrew verb בשׂר provides the key exegetical connection between Isaiah 52:7 and 61:1. See n. 168 above.

[192] For this reconstructed text of Paul's *Vorlage*, see Figure 3.7 above.

In both Isaiah 40 and 52, the herald announces God's triumphant return to Zion: "Here is your God" (ἰδοὺ ὁ θεὸς ὑμῶν, 40:9); "Your God shall reign" (βασιλεύσει σου ὁ θεός, 52:7). Likewise, in both passages, all people—"all flesh" (πᾶσα σάρξ, 40:5); "all the nations" (πάντα τὰ ἔθνη, 52:10); "all the ends of the earth" (πάντα τὰ ἄκρα τῆς γῆς, 52:10; cf. 40:28)—witness the saving deeds (τό σωτήριον τοῦ θεοῦ, 40:5; ἡ σωτηρία ἡ παρὰ θεοῦ; cf. 52:7, ἡ σωτηρία σου) wrought by God's "arm" (βραχίων, 40:10–11; 52:10).

This web of *intra*textual connections stretching between chapters 40 and 52 within the book of Isaiah helps to explain why Paul draws on key phrases from Isaiah 40 as he attempts to explain Israel's failure to respond to his mission, prophesied in Isaiah 52:7 and 53:1. In Isaiah 40, as in 53:1, Israel has refused to believe the herald's announcement that God is at long last coming to deliver his people. Paul's allusion to Isaiah 40:21/28 adds yet another Isaianic strand to his tightly-woven critique of Israel's unbelief, reprising once again the themes I have repeatedly noted in Paul's appeals to Isaiah in Romans 9–10. As in Isaiah 29:16/45:9, 10:22–23, and 28:16/8:14, so in Isaiah 40 Israel is seen questioning God's wisdom and resisting God's plan of deliverance.

Within the overarching framework constructed through Paul's allusion to Isaiah 40:21/28, the quotation of Psalm 18:5 in Romans 10:18 and the citation of Deuteronomy 32:21b and Isaiah 65:1–2 in Romans 10:19–21 provide explicit answers to Paul's query concerning whether Israel perhaps has not "heard" or "known" his message. In examining these quotations, I will focus on the ways in which each text is related to Paul's previous appeals to Israel's scriptures, particularly Isaiah.

ISRAEL HAS HEARD: PSALM 18:5 IN ROMANS 10:18

Paul's statement in Romans 10:17 that hearing the message leads to faith causes him to question in 10:18 whether it is possible that "they" (identified specifically as "Israel" in the next verse) have not heard. "On the contrary" (μενοῦνγε), Paul answers, quoting Psalm 18:5 (LXX): "Their voice has gone out into all the earth and their words (ῥήματα) to the ends of the world." This snippet of Psalm 18 fits smoothly into Paul's argument. The catch-word ῥῆμα links this citation to Paul's sustained use of ῥῆμα for the Christian gospel in

Romans 10, beginning with his quotation of Deuteronomy 30:14 in 10:8. Moreover, in a context where Paul has been speaking of Christian preachers in the plural,[193] the pronoun αὐτῶν most naturally refers to Paul and his fellow missionaries.

At first glance, it would appear that Paul has merely torn this sentence from its context in Psalm 18 (LXX) and forced it to say something quite different than it does in its original setting.[194] Paul's interpretation would probably have struck a person who was familiar with the psalm as extremely tendentious, since it is obvious that the "voice" and "words" spoken of by the psalmist belong not to Christian missionaries, but to the "heavens." Yet the tension between Paul's use of these words and their original sense generates a number of suggestive correspondences between the message of the gospel and the witness of the heavens to the glory of God.

Psalm 18:5 functions in Romans 10 as more than a prooftext for the wide dissemination of the gospel. Paul's appeal to this text is set within the larger framework established by Paul's quotations of Isaiah 52:7, 53:1 and by his allusion to Isaiah 40:21/28. In Isaiah 40, the prophet's focus on God as creator grounds his affirmation both of the inscrutable wisdom of God's plan to redeem his people and of the incomparable power of God to effect their deliverance. Psalm 18, with its cosmic celebration of God as creator, thus quite appropriately answers the question drawn from Isaiah 40:28: "It is not that they haven't heard, is it?" From Paul's vantage point "on the mountains" of Isaiah 52, the message that has gone out "into all the earth" and "to the ends of the world" (εἰς πᾶσαν τὴν γῆν . . . τὰ πέρατα τῆς οἰκουμένης, Ps 18:5) is seen to be none other than the message he brings, announced also by Isaiah, that Israel's God, the creator of "the ends of the earth" (τὰ ἄκρα τῆς γῆς, Isa 40:28), has now acted to bring salvation to his people.[195]

Echoes of the remainder of Psalm 18 (LXX) in Romans 10 suggest an even more damning proof that Israel *has* heard the message Paul preaches. Having shown that the heavens declare God's glory,

---

[193] κηρύσσομεν, 10:8; κηρύξωσιν, τῶν εὐαγγελιζομένων, 10:15; ἡμῶν, 10:16.

[194] So Dodd 1932:170; Käsemann 1980:295; Leenhardt 1995:155. Somewhat more sympathetically, Hays suggests that Paul has taken over the vocabulary of the psalm to give greater rhetorical weight to his assertion (1989:175; cf. Lagrange 1916:262).

[195] See also Isaiah 52:10: καὶ ὄψονται πάντα τὰ ἄκρα τῆς γῆς τὴν σωτηρίαν τὴν παρὰ τοῦ θεοῦ.

the psalmist sings the praise of Torah as a revelation of God in harmony with, but far superior to, that found in creation. In the dynamic movement of the psalm, the creator of the universe comes near through Torah, and ultimately makes himself most fully known to his servant in the personal encounter of penitent and trusting prayer (18:12–15).[196] Indeed, the entire poem comes to focus in the psalmist's closing petition, which addresses God not as creator, but as "help[197] and redeemer":

> May the words of my *mouth* (τὰ λόγια τοῦ στόματός μου) and the meditation of my *heart* (ἡ μελέτη τῆς καρδίας μου) be acceptable before you always, O Lord, my help and my redeemer. (Ps 18:15).

Echoes of Psalm 18, intermingling with the fading sounds of Deuteronomy 30:12–14, resonate with Paul's claim that the Law proclaims the "word of faith" that calls *heart* and *mouth* to acknowledge God's work of redemption through Christ (Romans 10:8–10).[198] Paul's citation of Psalm 18:5 implies, not just that messengers of the gospel have gone out all over the world, but more specifically that Israel, knowing the truth about God as creator and entrusted with the inestimable gift of God's νόμος, should have been particularly receptive to the good news of God's salvation for Jew and Gentile alike through Christ.[199]

The juxtaposition of this Psalm with Paul's story in Romans of Israel's refusal to heed his message generates an intertextual field pulsating with multiple resonances of meaning. In this environment, the phrases of Psalm 18:5 ring out with a complex polyphony: "their voice . . . their words" refer at once to the message "spoken" by creation, the message of the Law, and the message of Paul and his associates. Confronted with the harmonious testimony of these many witnesses, Israel's unbelief appears tragic and inexcusable.[200]

---

[196] For the argument that the structure of the psalm is organized around the idea of increasing intimacy with God—from God's revelation in creation to his gift of Torah and, finally, to his personal encounter with the worshipper—see Wagner 1999a.

[197] According to Staffan Olofsson, the LXX avoids a literal translation of the title "rock" (צור, סלע) for God both because of the inappropriateness of the metaphor in Greek (where "rock" does not connote "security, stability") and because of the potential association of "rock" with pagan worship (1990:35–50 [esp. 49–50], 140).

[198] Cf. Psalm 18:9, where it is said that the Law brings joy to the *heart* (τὰ δικαιώματα κυρίου εὐθεῖα, εὐφραίνοντα καρδίαν).

[199] Again, it is clear that Romans 10:4 is the keystone of the whole interpretive edifice Paul constructs in 9:30–10:21.

[200] In answer to the question, "How can Paul consider all of Israel to have heard

ISRAEL *HAS* KNOWN: DEUTERONOMY 32:21 AND ISAIAH 65:1–2 IN
ROMANS 10:19–21

The charge—evoked allusively by Paul's appeal to Psalm 18—that
Israel has known from their scriptures Paul's gospel of salvation for
the Jew first and also for the Gentile, comes to explicit expression
in Paul's follow-up question: "It is not that Israel has not known, is
it?" (μὴ Ἰσραὴλ οὐκ ἔγνω;). The immediate context makes it clear that
Paul is talking specifically about Israel's knowledge of the gospel
(10:16–17). At the same time, this question recalls his earlier claim
that Israel has zeal for God, but "not according to knowledge" (οὐ
κατ᾽ ἐπίγνωσιν, Rom 10:2).

Paul's explanation of his charge, "not according to knowledge,"
in Romans 10:3 implies that the "knowledge" Israel lacks is not
solely or even primarily a matter of the intellect, but of the heart
and will:[201]

> ἀγνοοῦντες γὰρ τὴν τοῦ θεοῦ δικαιοσύνην καὶ τὴν ἰδίαν [δικαιοσύνην]
> ζητοῦντες στῆσαι, τῇ δικαιοσύνῃ τοῦ θεοῦ οὐχ ὑπετάγησαν.

While ἀγνοέω can have a range of meanings from "be ignorant of"
to "disregard," the latter is closer to Paul's meaning here, for the
result of their ἄγνοια is that "they *did not submit* to God's righteousness." If, as I have argued, Paul's questions in Romans 10:18–19
echo Isaiah 40:21/28, the moral nature of knowing is highlighted
yet further. These are not idle inquiries, but challenges to respond

---

the gospel?" Johannes Munck argues that Paul's claim is analogous to his later declaration that he has "fulfilled" the gospel in the east (15:19, 23):
> Although [the apostles sent to the Jews] have not been everywhere or preached
> the gospel to every single Jew, yet they have finished the work as far as Israel
> as a whole is concerned. The parts to which they have preached may be taken
> as the whole, the Jewish people; and Paul may therefore assert, as he does in
> what follows, that Israel is unbelieving and hardened (1959:277).
What Munck misses, however, is the repeated claim Paul makes that *Israel's scriptures* witness to his gospel. For Paul, Israel has heard the gospel not only through
the apostolic preaching, but also through the testimony of their own sacred texts.
Munck goes well beyond the evidence in concluding that Paul or any of his associates believed that the mission to Israel had been completed; this view owes more
to a particular reading of the salvation-historical scheme of Acts than it does to
Paul's own writings.
[201] See p. 125 n. 20 above. I use these categories not because I think they were
Paul's, but because the modern tendency to divorce knowledge from character renders such a distinction necessary. For an insightful discussion of the problems posed
for the enterprise of biblical studies by this (inadequate) modern understanding of
knowledge, see Fowl and Jones 1991:4–28.

in faith and obedience: "*Will* you not know? *Will* you not hear?" (Isa 40:21).[202]

Paul argues that Israel has known, and yet, paradoxically, that they have stubbornly refused to know. Moses, "Righteousness from Faith," Isaiah, Joel—all point to Christ as the source of "righteousness for all who believe" (Rom 10:4). The problem, as Paul has variously stated it, is that "not all have *obeyed* the gospel" and "*believed* our message" (10:16). Rather, by seeking "their own righteousness" (10:3)—that is, by pursuing the Law that leads to righteousness "not by faith but as if by works" (9:32)—Israel has "not submitted to God's righteousness" (10:3).

But Paul does not merely claim that Israel has "known" that God's righteousness reaches its culmination in Christ for righteousness to everyone, Jew or Greek, who believes. Having argued—using Moses' own words—that the "righteousness from faith" obtained by the Gentiles is precisely that to which the Law has pointed all along, and having found his own ministry of proclamation to the Gentiles portrayed in Isaiah's prophecies, Paul summons Moses (Rom 10:19/Deut 32:21b) and Isaiah (Rom 10:20–21/Isa 65:1–2) yet once more. This time, their words will support Paul's astounding claim that Israel "has known" from scripture that the Gentiles would obtain righteousness *before* them!

With the mention of "Gentiles" in the quotation in 10:19, we find ourselves back once again to the problem with which this section of Paul's argument opened: Gentiles have obtained righteousness, while Israel has stumbled (9:30–32). Isaiah's characterization of Gentiles as "those not seeking me" (οἱ ἐμὲ μὴ ζητοῦσιν, Isa 65:1/Rom 10:20) evokes Paul's quasi-Isaianic description of Gentiles in Romans 9:30 as those "not pursuing righteousness" (ἔθνη τὰ μὴ διώκοντα δικαιοσύνην), while Moses' reference to "not a nation" (οὐκ ἔθνει, Deut 32:21/Rom 10:19) reaches back even further to recall the appellation "not my people" (οὐ λαός μου) from Hosea (Rom 9:25). The problem Paul faces is one posed acutely by his own missionary activity, which he understands to be a key component of God's eschatological redemption of Israel and of the world. Gentiles have responded eagerly to the gospel, but by and large, it seems, Jews have not—at least not in the sort of numbers that would imply the restoration of the nation as a whole.

---

[202] οὐ γνώσεσθε; οὐκ ἀκούσεσθε; On the volitional nuance of the future, see Porter 1989:404–16, 424–26.

Paula Fredriksen summarizes Paul's quandary with characteristic clarity: "Too many Gentiles, too few Jews, and no End in sight."[203]

Speaking with their own voices, as it were, Moses and Isaiah come forward in Romans 10:19–21 to testify that the present situation, in which Gentiles enjoy what Israel has not yet attained, far from representing a surprising development, has been part of God's plan all along. Both Moses and Isaiah have already figured prominently as named characters in Romans 9–10.[204] These two esteemed personages lend to Paul's argument the combined authority of the Lawgiver and of the chief representative of the canonical prophets. Paul's use of πρῶτος in connection with Moses is intriguing, but it is unclear whether this adverb suggests more than that Moses is the first witness to testify in the present case.[205] Interestingly, Isaiah receives the more dramatic introduction, and he ends up speaking twice as long as Moses.

It is vital to Paul's argument that he present Moses and Isaiah as witnesses whose testimony agrees.[206] Because their words are so closely conjoined in Romans 10:19–21, I cannot do justice to Paul's use of Isaiah 65:1–2 without also examining closely his quotation of Deuteronomy 32:21. As has been the case with many of Paul's citations explored thus far, the significant connections between these

---

[203] Fredriksen 1988:169. But see Stark 1996:49–71 for the argument that the early Christian movement continued to spread among Jews long after the end of the first century (see p. 4 n. 15 above).

[204] Moses: Romans 9:15; 10:5; Isaiah: Romans 9:27, 29; 10:16.

[205] The adverb could also conceivably refer to Moses' priority in history and/or in significance. In a tannaitic midrash based on the parallel between Moses' opening address to heaven and earth (Deut 32:1) and the invocation of heaven and earth at the beginning of Isaiah's prophecy (Isa 1:2), Moses is clearly seen to be the superior figure. Moses is said to be closer to heaven than to earth, while Isaiah is closer to earth than to heaven (*Sifre Deut* §306 [on Deut 32:1]). Variations on this midrash are found in Tg. Pseudo-Jonathan, the Fragment Targum, and Tg. Neofiti, all at Deuteronomy 32:1. *Mek. Pisḥaʾ* 12 (on Exod 12:25–28; Lauterbach 1933–35, 1:91) also connects Isaiah 1:2 and Deuteronomy 32:1, though without a comparison of Moses and Isaiah. See further Fraade 1991; Basser 1984.

[206] In a subsequent citation (Rom 11:8), Paul will go so far as to conflate their words without comment. Tg. Neofiti (Deut 32:1) emphasizes the role of Moses and Isaiah as witnesses against Israel:

תרין נביין קמו למסהדה בישראל משה נבייה וישעיה נבייא . . .
ותריהון על דהוו דהילין מן לשמה קדישה קמו למסהדה בישראל

Two prophets arose to testify against Israel, Moses the prophet and Isaiah the prophet . . . . And the two of them, because they feared the holy Name, arose to testify against Israel."

scriptural texts go far beyond what is evident from a superficial reading of Paul's argument. Indeed, my investigation will strongly suggest that Paul has interpreted Deuteronomy 32 and Isaiah 65 in light of one another as he attempts to understand the outworking of God's redemptive plan in his own day.

One Good Spurn Deserves Another: Deuteronomy 32:21 in Romans 10:19

First on the witness stand is Moses, whose testimony takes the form of a partial citation of Deuteronomy 32:21.[207] Paul quotes only the second half of the verse, following the LXX with but one variation. By changing the pronoun referring to Israel from third to second person,[208] Paul turns the quotation into a direct address to Israel and so heightens its rhetorical impact.[209] Of course Israel "knows," because God has informed them personally:

> So I will provoke you to jealousy with a no-nation,
> With a nation lacking understanding I will provoke you to anger.

Figure 3.10: Deuteronomy 32:21 LXX in Romans 10:19

Deuteronomy 32:21 LXX	Romans 10:19
	πρῶτος Μωϋσῆς λέγει·
αὐτοὶ παρεζήλωσάν με ἐπ᾽ οὐ θεῷ, παρώργισάν με ἐν τοῖς εἰδώλοις αὐτῶν· κἀγὼ <u>παραζηλώσω</u> αὐτοὺς <u>ἐπ᾽ οὐκ ἔθνει,</u> <u>ἐπ᾽ ἔθνει ἀσυνέτῳ παροργιῶ</u> αὐτούς	<u>ἐγὼ παραζηλώσω</u> ὑμᾶς <u>ἐπ᾽ οὐκ ἔθνει,</u> <u>ἐπ᾽ ἔθνει ἀσυνέτῳ παροργιῶ</u> ὑμᾶς

---

[207] For a detailed analysis of the "jealousy" motif in Deuteronomy 32 and its interpretation in early Judaism and Christianity, see Bell 1994.

[208] This shift in pronoun finds no support in the manuscript tradition of the LXX. Hebrew witnesses, the Targums (Onkelos, Pseudo-Jonathan, Fragment Targum, Neofiti), Peshitta, and Vulgate all likewise read the third person pronoun here.

[209] Bell (1994:96) downplays the rhetorical motive and suggests that Paul is merely attempting to distinguish Israel from "they" in his previous quotation (Rom 10:18/ Ps 18:5). While the shift in pronoun certainly does accomplish this, the explicit mention of Israel in 10:19a would appear to have sufficed were this Paul's only concern. Moreover, Paul doesn't seem to worry in 10:18 about the potential confusion between the subject of ἤκουσαν and the antecedent of "*their* voice . . . *their* words" in Psalm 18:5.

Through Moses, God proclaims to Israel, "I will provoke you to jealousy . . . I will provoke you to anger." It is not difficult to grasp the gist of Paul's quotation: Moses' words reveal that God is calling Gentiles to be a part of his people in order to make Israel jealous.[210] Because God told them about this through Moses, Israel certainly "has known" all along that God planned to pour out his mercy on Gentiles, as now is happening through the ministry of Paul.

To state the matter this way, however, does not begin to capture the polyphonic resonances of the Deuteronomic chord struck by this citation. Paul's claim that in showing mercy to the Gentiles God intends to make Israel "jealous" and "angry" can be heard in all of its rich complexity only when one perceives that Paul is drawing here on a much larger narrative about God's often tumultuous relationship with Israel. Recognizing that Paul's citation evokes this larger story, encapsulated poetically in the Song of Moses (Deuteronomy 32:1–43), makes it possible to trace the integral connections between this quotation and the analysis of Israel's plight that Paul has painstakingly developed in Romans 9–10.

Moses' Song: Deuteronomy 32:21 in Context

The Song of Moses occupies a key position in the structure, not only of Deuteronomy, but indeed of the entire Pentateuch. It stands as the last of three great blocks of poetic material[211] that anticipate with prophetic insight what will happen to Israel "at the end of days."[212] It is not surprising that Paul would turn to this portion of scripture, for there is good evidence from the Qumran finds that the Song was the focus of particular attention among at least some Jews in the Second Temple Period.[213] It appears in several collections of biblical

---

[210] How Paul understands this to work out in practice is not clear until Romans 11:11–16.

[211] The poems are found in Genesis 49; Numbers 24; Deuteronomy 32. See Sailhamer (1992:35–37) for discussion of this macro-structural feature.

[212] Hebrew, באחרית הימים; LXX, ἐπ᾽ ἐσχάτων τῶν ἡμερῶν (Gen 49:1); ἐπ᾽ ἐσχάτου τῶν ἡμερῶν (Num 24:14); ἔσχατον τῶν ἡμερῶν (Deut 31:29).

[213] According to Josephus, a copy of the Song of Moses was kept in the Temple (*Ant.* 4.303; cf. 3.38; 5.61). Thackeray took this to refer to a collection of songs used by temple singers (1929:90–91). A rabbinic tradition preserved in the Talmud recounts that the Song of Moses was recited during the *musaf* (additional service) on the Sabbath in a six-week cycle (*b. Roš Haš.* 31a; for the six-fold division of the Song, termed "the Song of the Levites," cf. *y. Meg.* 74b [3:7]).

excerpts[214] and as the sole text in one *tefillah*.[215] That this text was of special interest to Paul may be inferred from the fact that he quotes or alludes to the Song several times not only in Romans, but also in 1 Corinthians and Philippians.[216] Since Paul quotes from Deuteronomy 29:3 (Rom 11:8) and 30:12–14 (Rom 10:6–8) elewhere in Romans 9–11, it may be safely assumed that he knew the Song as part of the larger book of Deuteronomy.[217]

Within Deuteronomy, a narrative introduction (31:1–30) and epilogue (32:44–47) frame the Song of Moses and guide the reader in interpreting the poem as the story of what will happen to Israel in the future.[218] In the introduction to the Song (31:1–30), Moses makes preparations for his impending death. After exhorting the people to trust the Lord for the conquest of the Land and promising them that the Lord "will never forsake you or abandon you (οὐ μή σε ἀνῇ οὔτε μή σε ἐγκαταλίπῃ, 31:6) Moses installs Joshua as his successor (31:7–8). He then writes "the words of this Law in a scroll" (ἔγραψεν ... τὰ ῥήματα τοῦ νόμου τούτου εἰς βιβλίον, 31:9) and deposits it with the priests and levites along with instructions to teach it to future generations, so that they may "hear and learn to fear the Lord your God" (31:9–13). In the next scene, Moses and Joshua are summoned to the Tent of Meeting, where the Lord warns that after Moses has died, Israel will turn to other gods and break the covenant God has established with them (31:14–20; cf. 29). Thus, like Deuteronomy 29–30, the Song of Moses treats Israel's idolatrous

---

[214] 4QDeut^j (4Q37), 4QDeut^kl (4Q38), 4QDeut^q (4Q44). This latter text may have contained only the Song of Moses. See further J. A. Duncan, DJD XIV, 75–98; P. W. Skehan and E. Ulrich, DJD XIV, 137–42.

[215] 4Qphyl^n (4Q141). See J. T. Milik, DJD VI, 72–74. According to Milik, the original probably contained 32:1–33, although only 32:14–20, 32–33 has survived. The latter two verses are written along the left margin and run at a right angle to the main body of text. It is hard to see why the text would have been cut off at v. 33 except due to constraints of space.

[216] Explicit citations (with introductory formulas) are found in Romans 10:19 (Deut 32:21b); 12:19 (Deut 32:35); 15:10 (Deut 32:43). Among the more plausible allusions Bell discusses are the following: Romans 9:14 (Deut 32:4); 11:11–14 (Deut 32:21b); 1 Corinthians 10:20a (Deut 32:17); 10:22 (Deut 32:21a); Philippians 2:15 (Deut 32:5). J. W. Olley (1998) finds an allusion to Deuteronomy 32:19 in the language of "sons and daughters" in 2 Corinthians 6:18.

[217] Because the evidence of Paul's citations points to his use of the LXX text of Deuteronomy (Koch 1986:51–54), I will focus in what follows on the LXX version of the Song.

[218] For various proposals concerning the structure of the Song of Moses and its setting in the book of Deuteronomy, see Cassuto 1973a; Eißfeldt 1966; Labuschagne 1971, 1997; Lohfink 1962; Sonnet 1997. On the Song in LXX Deuteronomy see Harl 1993; Dogniez and Harl 1992; Wevers 1995.

rebellion against God and their subsequent experience of the curses of the Law, including exile, as a *fait accompli.*

God commands Moses to write down the words of this Song and to teach it to the people of Israel as a "witness" to them (31:19). Moses' actions of writing and teaching the song are mentioned numerous times (31:22, 28; 31:30–32:43; 32:44). The purpose of this repetition is to drive home the point that since Moses' day, Israel has known the plot their national story would follow. Clearly, Paul stands on solid narrative ground when he quotes from Moses' Song to defend his claim that Israel "has known."

There is further narrative precedent in Deuteronomy for Paul's bold appropriation of the words of this Song to speak to the plight of Israel in his own day. In both the introduction and in the poem itself, it is explicitly stated that the Song addresses events that will befall Israel "at the end of days" (31:29; 32:20),[219] the time period in which Paul believes he and his hearers are now living. The Lord commands Moses to put this Song "in their mouth" (εἰς τὸ στόμα αὐτῶν, 31:19) and promises that "it will certainly not be lost from the mouth of their seed" (οὐ γὰρ μὴ ἐπιλησθῇ ἀπὸ στόματος τοῦ σπέρματος αὐτῶν, 31:21). When these events occur, this Song will serve as a "witness" to Israel (31:19, 21)—as indeed it now does in Paul's own day as Moses once again recites its words in Romans 10:19.

The main movements of the Song in its LXX version may be sketched as follows:

Figure 3.11: Outline of Deuteronomy 32

32:1–3	• Summons of heaven and earth as witnesses
32:4–6	• Statement of the theme: Faithful God, unfaithful Israel
32:7–14	• Call to remember God's saving deeds: the election of Israel, the exodus and wilderness journey, the entrance into the Land
32:15–18	• Israel's adulterous affair with foreign gods
32:19–25	• God's jealous response—judgment and exile
32:26–27	• God relents from total destruction of Israel because of his enemies
32:28–35	• Polemic against Israel's enemies and their gods
32:36–42	• God arises as a warrior to vindicate his people and destroy his enemies
32:43	• Doxology: Israel and the nations join together with the heavenly beings to praise God

---

[219] Cf. Deuteronomy 4:30, 8:16. Note the structural importance of this phrase in the Pentateuch (p. 191 above).

There are a number of significant correspondences between Paul's account of Israel's plight in Romans 9–11 and the story of Israel as told in the Song and in its narrative framework. The Song is a witness not only to Israel's unfaithfulness, but even more importantly, to the faithfulness of the Lord, who refuses to abandon his people. Repeatedly we have seen the prominence of these two themes in the wider contexts of the scriptural texts Paul uses to address the problem of Israel's unbelief in Romans 9–10. With his citation of Deuteronomy 32:21, Paul returns yet again to these important motifs. By tapping into the Song of Moses through his quotation of 32:21, Paul sets up a suggestive intertextual relationship between this well-known poetic depiction of Israel's election, unfaithfulness, and redemption and his own account in Romans of Israel's stumbling and ultimate salvation.

The motif of Israel's unfaithfulness and lack of wisdom figures prominently throughout the Song of Moses and its narrative framework. "A people foolish and not at all wise" (λαὸς μωρὸς καὶ οὐχὶ σοφός, 32:6), they are characterized as "blameworthy children" (τέκνα μωμητά, 32:5), "not his [children]" (οὐκ αὐτῷ, 32:5), "a crooked and perverse generation" (γενεὰ σκολιὰ καὶ διεστραμμένη, 32:5; cf. γενεὰ ἐξεστραμμένη, 32:20), "sons in whom there is no faithfulness" (υἱοί, οἷς οὐκ ἔστιν πίστις ἐν αὐτοῖς, 32:20).[220]

Deuteronomy 31–32 employs two vivid metaphors to express the heinousness of Israel's unfaithfulness toward the God who chose them, brought them out of Egypt, fed them in the wilderness, and brought them safely into the Land. One image depicts Israel as a wife who abandons her husband for other lovers: "This people (ὁ λαὸς οὗτος) will rise up and go whoring after foreign gods (ἐκπορνεύσει ὀπίσω θεῶν ἀλλοτρίων) . . . and they will forsake (ἐγκαταλείπω) me" (31:16).[221] A second figure portrays Israel as children who have despised and

---

[220] In light of his argument in Romans 9–10 that Israel has stumbled as a result of pursuing the Law "not from faith," it is somewhat surprising that Paul does not draw explicitly on this particular description of Israel; instead, he evokes this characterization only metaleptically through the larger juxtaposition of his story of Israel with that found in Deuteronomy 32. Later interpreters such as Justin recognized this echo in Romans 10:19. In his supersessionist polemic against the Jews in *Dial.* 119 (cf. 20, 123), Justin employs Deuteronomy 32:20 along with the two verses cited by Paul in Romans 10:19–20 (Deut 32:21; Isa 65:1; see Bell 1994:282). Tragically, Justin appears to have taken his exegetical cues from Paul without sharing Paul's (and the Song's!) deep conviction that God remains committed to his elect people Israel.

[221] Note the similar metaphor in Hosea 1–2, a story on which Paul draws in Romans 9:25–27a.

forsaken the father who begat them and who brought them up (32:18–19; cf. 32:5–6). Israel's treachery is also described in more prosaic, but nevertheless theologically-loaded language, as the abandonment of their "savior" (σωτήρ, 32:15), the one who "made" (ποιέω, 32:6; 32:15) and "created" (κτίζω, 32:6[2x]) them.[222]

The Song and its introduction employ a number of closely-related terms to describe the gut-wrenching effects of Israel's infidelity on the Lord: "provoke" (παροξύνω, 31:20; 32:16, 19); "provoke to anger" (παροργίζω, 31:29; 32:21[2x]); "provoke to jealousy" (παραζηλόω, 32:21[2x]; cf. ζηλόω, 32:19). These words belong to the stock repertoire of terms for describing both Israel's rebellions in the wilderness (including the golden calf affair) and their subsequent flirtations with the gods of Canaan that eventually lead to exile from the Land.[223] The jealous anger they connote erupts in response to the violation of a close and exclusive relationship. Within Deuteronomy 31–32, these terms evoke the turbulent emotions appropriate to the image of God as Israel's husband, enraged to find his wife in another's arms, and to the picture of God as Israel's father, cut to the heart to see his sons and daughters ungrateful and profligate.

Israel's adulterous affairs with foreign gods ignite God's jealously and fire his anger against them. Because they have shattered the exclusive covenantal relationship that God graciously established with his people (διασκεδάσουσιν τὴν διαθήκην μου, 31:16, 20), God brings on them the curses pronounced by the covenant.[224] The narrative

---

[222] For the theological importance of God as "maker" in Isaiah, see pp. 60–67 above.

[223] Selected examples include: παροξύνω: Num 14:11, 23; 15:30; 16:30; 20:24; Deut 1:34; 9:7, 8, 18, 19, 22; Ps 77:41; 105:29; Isa 5:24; 47:6; 63:10; 65:3; Bar 4:7 (alluding to Deut 32:15–17); παροργίζω: Deut 4:25; Judg 2:12, 17; 3 Kgdms 15:30; 16:2, 7, 13, 26, 33; 20:20, 22; 22:54; 4 Kgdms 17:11, 17; 21:6, 15; 22:17; 23:19, 26; 2 Chr 28:25; 33:6; 34:25; 35:19c; Ezra 5:12; Ps 77:40, 58; *Pss. Sol.* 4:1, 21; Zech 8:14; Isa 1:4; Jer 7:18, 19; 8:19; 11:17; 25:6; Bar 4:6; Ezek 16:26, 54; 20:27 (cf. παροργισμός/παροργίσμα: 3 Kgdms 15:30; 16:33; 20:22; 4 Kgdms 19:3; 23:26; 2 Chr 35:19c; Neh 9:18, 26); παραζηλόω: 3 Kgdms 14:22; Ps 77:58.

[224] Although, the disaster that falls on Israel is described in 31:17 by the general term κακὰ πολλά, it is clear that these evils are the curses promised to the violators of the covenant in Deuteronomy 28 (cf. Lev 26). The term κατάβρωμα (31:17) recalls the use of the same word in Deuteronomy 28:26 (it occurs elsewhere in the LXX Pentateuch only in Num 14:9). In 32:21–26, links with the vocabulary of the covenantal curses are more numerous. Deut 32:24: τήκω (Deut 28:65; Lev 26:39); λιμός (Deut 28:48); βρῶσις ὀρνέων . . . ὀδόντες θηρίων (κατάβρωμα τοῖς πετεινοῖς . . . καὶ τοῖς θηρίοις, Deut 28:26; cf. θήρια, Lev 26:6, 22); θυμός (Deut 29:23, 24, 27, 28; 31:17; Lev 26:24, 28, 41). Deut 32:25: μάχαιρα (Lev 26:8, 25, 33); φόβος (Deut 28:67). Deut 32:26: διασπείρω (Deut 28:64; Lev 26:33).

introduction to the poem emphasizes that God's response is commensurate with Israel's sin. Just as they have forsaken the Lord (ἐγκαταλείπω, 31:16), so the Lord will forsake them (καταλείπω, 31:17); just as they have turned *to* other gods (ἐπιστρέφω, 31:18), so the Lord will turn *away from* them (ἐγὼ δὲ ἀποστροφῇ ἀποστρέψω τὸ πρόσωπόν μου, 31:18). The Song of Moses elegantly expresses the identical thought with two carefully-balanced couplets (32:21):

> They provoked me to jealousy with a no-God,
> They provoked me to anger with their idols.

> So I will provoke them to jealousy with a no-nation,
> With a nation lacking understanding I will provoke them to anger.

> αὐτοὶ παρεζήλωσάν με ἐπ' οὐ θεῷ,
> παρώργισάν με ἐν τοῖς εἰδώλοις αὐτῶν·

> κἀγὼ παραζηλώσω αὐτοὺς ἐπ' οὐκ ἔθνει,
> ἐπ' ἔθνει ἀσυνέτῳ παροργιῶ αὐτούς.

It is this verse that Paul puts into Moses' mouth in Romans 10:19. Although Paul quotes only the second couplet, which speaks of God making Israel jealous through a "no-nation" (οὐκ ἔθνος),[225] his citation presumes the apostasy of Israel that is the topic of the previous couplet as well as of the larger context of the Song. In keeping with a characteristic feature of the quotations in Romans 9–10 I have examined so far, Paul's citation figuratively identifies contemporary Israel with God's rebellious people of old.[226] Paul's use of scripture in these chapters projects a world in which Israel stands estranged from God, suffering under the curses pronounced by the covenant, in dire need of deliverance. It is the Israel of his own day to whom Moses' strange words of both judgment and hope are addressed.

The scandal of God's embracing an οὐκ ἔθνος depends on the earlier story Deuteronomy 32 tells of the election of Israel (32:7–9). Out of all the nations (ἔθνη, 32:8), we are told, God chose Israel as his

---

[225] This "no-nation" is clearly the focus of the second half of 32:21. The chiastic structure of the second couplet disrupts the parallelism of the verse (cf. 32:21a) and focuses attention on the "no-nation/nation lacking understanding."

[226] This undercurrent to Paul's argument begins with his allusion to the golden calf incident in Romans 9:3 and remains a relatively constant theme in the background of the texts he cites in Romans 9–11: Exod 33:19; Isa 29:16/45:9; Hos 2:23/1:10; Isa 10:22–23/28:22; Isa 1:9; Isa 8:14/28:16; 1 Kgdms 12:22; 3 Kgdms 19:10, 14; Isa 29:10.

own portion and inheritance (μερίς . . . σχοίνισμα κληρονομίας αὐτοῦ, 32:9). But now Israel has violated this exclusive relationship by bringing in a foreign party, a "no-God," provoking God to jealousy. And so, in response, God adopts a similar strategy, choosing to lavish on a foreign nation—one not even worthy of being called a nation— the favor due his own people, Israel.

The fact that the identity of the "no-nation" remains unspecified in Deuteronomy[227] facilitates Paul's use of this phrase to describe the (predominantly Gentile) church he is helping to birth. I have already noted Paul's tendency to adopt from scripture negative descriptions for Gentiles in order to highlight the reversal wrought by God's grace.[228] The similarity of the description, "no-nation," to the appellation, "not my people," quoted by Paul from Hosea in Romans 9:25–26, may well have contributed to his selection of Deuteronomy 32:21.[229]

Paul's point in quoting these words is not only to demonstrate that long ago God planned to show mercy to Gentiles, as scandalous as such a move appears to Israel in his own time. More important for his argument in Romans 9–11 is the astounding claim made in Deuteronomy 32 that God is doing this *for the sake of Israel's own salvation.*

Paul's use of Deuteronomy 32:21 adopts the same perspective as that of the poet who penned the Song of Moses, a perspective that takes as bedrock convictions the abiding election of Israel and the faithfulness of God to his covenant. In Deuteronomy 32, the jealous anger of God at Israel's unfaithfulness arises because of his commitment to Israel. It is only in the context of God's special relationship with Israel that God's jealousy or his desire to provoke Israel to

---

[227] The lack of historical specificity in the Song kept it open to contemporizing and eschatological interpretations. Targum Pseudo-Jonathan on Deut 32:21, for example, identifies the "no-nation" as Babylon (perhaps a cipher for Rome). The identity of this "no-nation" has provoked much debate among modern scholars seeking to date the Song of Moses. Proposals range from nomadic raiders (12th–11th centuries) or Philistines (11th century) in the time of the Judges to Arameans (mid-9th century), Assyrians (8th century) or Babylonians (6th century) during the monarchial period.

[228] See p. 83.

[229] In Hebrew, the word used in both Hosea 2:1, 25 and Deuteronomy 32:21 is עַם. Interestingly, the translation of Deuteronomy 32:21 in the Peshitta (ܠܐ ܥܡ; v.l. ܥܡ) appears to be modeled on Hosea 2:1, 25. Cassuto (1973b:96–100) explores the connections in the Hebrew Bible between Hosea and the Song of Moses.

jealousy becomes intelligible. Paradoxically, it is this lover's ploy to win Israel back that manifests God's fidelity and demonstrates his enduring commitment to the covenant Israel has so brazenly violated. God shows favor to another ἔθνος in order to provoke in Israel feelings of jealousy and a renewed desire for the God they have spurned.[230] His ultimate aim is the restoration of the covenant relationship.

Deuteronomy 32:21 lies embedded in a context whose principal theme is God's fidelity to Israel. The Song of Moses celebrates God's faithful character—θεὸς πιστός, καὶ οὐκ ἔστιν ἀδικία (32:4)[231]—and proclaims that despite Israel's infidelity, God stands firmly committed to the covenant he has made. Israel remains "his people" (32:36, 43), "his servants" (32:36), "his sons" (32:43). After punishing them, he has compassion on their weary, woeful state (32:36) and rises up to defend them. So closely does God identify with his people that their enemies become his enemies.[232] The Song ends with a resounding hymn of praise to the God who "avenges the blood of *his sons*" and who "will cleanse *his people's* land" (32:43). Far beyond the catchword ἔθνος, the larger context of Deuteronomy 32:21 makes it a particularly fitting text to address the burning issue that consumes Paul throughout Romans 9–11: the vindication of God's faithfulness to Israel.

The Law in nuce

Paul will return to the jealousy motif in Romans 11:11 to show how God has turned Israel's unfaithfulness into a means of saving the Gentiles and, paradoxically, has thereby ensured the ultimate deliverance of Israel as well. Nonetheless, it is crucial to recognize that already in Romans 10:19 echoes of the wider context of Deuteronomy 32:21 presage the direction Paul's argument will take. In his agonized wrestling with the question of God's faithfulness to Israel, Paul's reading of the Song of Moses has decisively shaped the deep structure of his theodicy.

---

[230] There is no explicit statement of Israel's repentance within the poem; the focus throughout is on God's initiative in redemption as in election.

[231] In light of Paul's extensive use of Deuteronomy 32, it is quite possible that Romans 9:14 (μὴ ἀδικία παρὰ τῷ θεῷ; cf. Rom 3:5) echoes this verse.

[232] This poem plays on two senses of the verb παροξύνω. Despite the fact that Israel has "provoked" the Lord with idols (31:20; 32:16, 19), the Lord vows to "sharpen" his sword in order to defeat Israel's enemies and to redeem his people for himself (32:41).

Paul argues strenuously in Romans 10:4, and indeed throughout Romans, that the Law (Israel's scriptures) bears witness to the righteousness of God now revealed in Christ.[233] It is thus highly significant that Deuteronomy forges a strong narrative link between Moses' Song and the Law he bequeaths to Israel. In Deuteronomy 31–32, the story of Moses' writing, teaching, and singing the Song is braided together with two other strands: (1) the announcement of Moses' impending death and the commission of Joshua to lead the people (M/J)[234] and (2) the account of Moses' writing, deposit, and public proclamation (together with Joshua) of the whole Law to the people one final time (Figure 3.12).[235]

Figure 3.12: The Structure of Deuteronomy 31–32

M/J (31:1–8)—	Law (31:9–13)—	
M/J (31:14–15)—		**Song** (31:16–22)—
M/J (31:23)—	Law (31:24–29)—	
[*M/J*, 44c]—	Law (32:44b–47)	**Song** (31:30–32:44a)—

Moreover, Deuteronomy narrates Moses' recording and teaching of the Song using terminology that recalls his writing and promulgation of the Law. The author employs a technical formula to describe the "publication" of both Song and Law (λαλέω εἰς τὰ ὦτα; Song: 31:30; Law: 31:11, 28; 32:44).[236] Both are proclaimed before all Israel (Song: 31:30; Law: 32:44). In both cases, Moses discharges his commission completely (ἕως εἰς τέλος; Law: 31:24; Song: 31:30), with the result that the Law and the Song alike bear the authoritative stamp of Mosaic origin. The command to place the Song "in their mouth"

---

[233] See the explicit statements in Romans 1:1–4; 3:21–22; 16:25–27.

[234] The fact that the giving of the Song is interwoven with the account of the death of Moses reinforces the nature of these words as prophecy (Moses' "testament") about "the end of days" (cf. Jacob's death-bed prophecy regarding "the end of days" in Genesis 49). On Deuteronomy 32 as Moses' "last words," see S. Weitzman 1997:37–58.

[235] Cf. the similar analysis of Deuteronomy 31 by Lohfink 1962:74–77 (adopted with minor revisions by Olson 1994:133–34).

[236] On this formula see the important observations of Orlinsky 1975.

(32:19, 21) and the promise that the Song will not be lost "from the mouth of your seed" further echo Moses' emphatic assertion concerning the Law: "The word is very near you, in your mouth" (30:14). Just as the Song will stand as a witness to Israel (εἰς μαρτύριον, 31:19; cf. 31:21), so Moses deposits "the book of this Law" with the Levites to be "a witness" to the people (εἰς μαρτύριον, 31:26). Finally, Moses calls "heaven and earth" to witness both his promulgation of the Law and his recitation of the Song (31:28; 32:1), so that Israel will be without excuse when they experience the terrible consequences of their unfaithfulness (31:29; 32:20). Through such devices, Deuteronomy presents the Song of Moses as the Law *in nuce*.[237]

The LXX translator takes this narrative strategy one step further in the epilogue to the Song, deliberately identifying "this Song" with "this Law." First, the LXX repeats at 32:44a a sentence from 31:22, "And Moses wrote this Song in that day and taught it to the sons of Israel."[238] Then, in the very next sentence, the translator substitutes "this Law" for "this Song," found in MT: "And Moses went out and spoke all the words of *this Law* in the hearing of the people—he and Joshua son of Nun" (32:44b). The net effect of these alterations is to identify the Song explicitly with the Law proclaimed publicly by Moses and Joshua in Deuteronomy 32:44b and so to "bring the Song into the Law Code as its conclusion."[239] These interpretive additions to Deuteronomy 32 suggest even more strongly that the Song of Moses functions as a poetic précis of the Law.[240]

A reader who, led by these narrative clues, took the Song as a guide to what the Law is "about" would find that the Law tells the story of God's gracious election of Israel to be his very own people. It recounts God's mighty deeds on their behalf as he delivered them from Egypt, preserved them through the wilderness, and led them to a land of abundance. It further narrates Israel's rebelliousness,

---

[237] O. Eißfeldt made similar observations regarding the juxtaposition of Song and Law, concluding, ". . . . das Lied etwa als eine eindringliche Zusammenfassung des Gesetzes verstanden wird" (1966:333).

[238] The sentence is missing at 32:44 from MT (the verse is not extant in any of the Deuteronomy mss discovered at Qumran; cf. Ulrich 1994).

[239] Wevers 1995:535. Note also that in 31:19 LXX, *both* Moses and Joshua are commanded to write and teach the Song, just as in 32:44 both proclaim the whole Law (Wevers 1995:501).

[240] Cf. the judgment of the thirteenth-century philosopher, Shem-tob ben Joseph ibn Falaquera, who maintained that the Song of Moses "includes all the principles of the Torah" (M. H. Levine 1976:83).

their unfaithfulness and idolatry, and the jealous anger of their God, who brings upon them the curses of the covenant and sends them into exile. Finally, it affirms the power and faithfulness of Israel's God, who will arise "at the end of days" to defeat his enemies and to vindicate his people, and whose glory will be celebrated by all creation—the heavens and the angelic beings, the nations together with his people.

In light of the striking affinities that Paul's theodicy in Romans 9–11 bears to the Song of Moses—and keeping in mind Paul's repeated claim that the Law bears witness to his gospel—it is perhaps not too much of a stretch to imagine that the apostle has read the Law through the hermeneutical lens provided by Deuteronomy 32. If, as Richard Hays suggests, the Song of Moses contains Romans *in nuce*,[241] might it not also be true that, from Paul's perspective, his story in Romans 9–11 of the faithfulness of God that triumphs over Israel's unfaithfulness and at the same time extends to all nations the blessings promised to Israel, encapsulates and brings to fulfillment the essential story, not only of Deuteronomy 32, but of Israel's scriptures in their entirety?[242]

On the Testimony of Two Witnesses: Connections between
Deuteronomy 32 and Isaiah 65

By introducing Moses as his "first" speaker, Paul implies that there will be at least one further witness to corroborate Moses' testimony.[243] That this second speaker is Isaiah would not surprise listeners, who have heard his voice several times already in Romans 9–10. Nevertheless, in the absence of any explicit verbal links between Paul's

---

[241] Hays 1989:164. Similarly, Bell comments, "Paul's Heilsgeschichte was similar to that of the Song of Dt. 32.1–43 and of Deuteronomy as a whole" (1994:285).

[242] Compare the remarks of a modern scholar concerning the extensive thematic connections between Deuteronomy 32 and the Prophets: "Deuteronomy 32 was a major source, the 'bible' so to speak, of the prophetic movement... [it] has extremely close ties with especially the 7th–6th century prophecy. *Virtually all the major themes of those prophets (including even the 'remnant') have their antecedents in Deuteronomy 32*" (Mendenhall 1993:171; italics mine). The relevance of Mendenhall's observations for the present study does not hinge on whether or not he is right about the historical direction of dependence between Deuteronomy 32 and the prophetic movement. Cf. G. E. Wright 1962:37.

[243] Cf. Paul's quotation of the Mosaic requirement for two or three witnesses in 2 Corinthians 13:1, where, in an interesting interpretive twist, he counts his own presence on successive visits as fulfilling this criterion.

citations of Moses and Isaiah, it is puzzling that Paul would choose to bring together precisely these two texts in order to defend his claim that Israel "has known."

Closer examination, however, reveals an impressive network of verbal and thematic connections between these two passages, connections that point to Paul's attention to the larger literary contexts from which he draws his quotations. First, Deuteronomy 32:21 shares the word ἔθνος with Isaiah 65:1b; as I will argue below, this vocabulary link may have helped Paul read Isaiah 65:1 as a reference to the calling of the Gentiles. More striking are the multiple connections between Isaiah 65:3 and the Song of Moses:

> *This people*, who *provoke me* to my face continually—they sacrifice in the gardens and offer incense on the bricks to *demons, who are not*.
>
> ὁ λαὸς οὗτος ὁ παροξύνων με ἐναντίον ἐμοῦ διὰ παντός,
> αὐτοὶ θυσιάζουσιν ἐν τοῖς κήποις καὶ θυμιῶσιν ἐπὶ ταῖς πλίνθοις τοῖς δαιμονίοις, ἃ οὐκ ἔστι·

God's pejorative reference to idolatrous Israel as "this people"[244] finds a parallel in Deuteronomy 31:16 (the introduction to the Song): "This people (ὁ λαὸς οὗτος) will rise up and go whoring after foreign gods. . . ." Like the Song of Moses (31:20; 32:16, 19), Isaiah 65:3 employs the term παροξύνω to describe the effect of Israel's idolatry on their God.[245] Moreover, both Isaiah 65:3[246] and Deuteronomy 32:17[247] speak of Israel sacrificing to *demons*, language that appears elsewhere in the LXX only in Psalm 105:37 and Baruch 4:7.[248] Finally, both Isaiah 65:3 and the Song of Moses explicitly deny that these false gods are at all comparable to Israel's God. Isaiah 65:3 immediately qualifies its reference to demons with a relative clause: ". . . who are not."[249] Similarly, Deuteronomy 32:21 deems Israel's idols a "no-God" (οὐ θεός). Not one of these connections between Isaiah 65 and

---

[244] See my earlier discussion of the covenantal connotations of this appellation, p. 139.

[245] Bell notes this link but mistakenly identifies the verb in Isaiah 65:3 as παροργίζειν (1994:279).

[246] This reference to demons has no direct counterpart in MT (ומקטרים על־הלבנים). Note also Isaiah 65:11: οἱ . . . ἑτοιμάζοντες τῷ δαίμονι (MT, לגד) τράπεζαν.

[247] ἔθυσαν δαιμονίοις καὶ οὐ θεῷ.

[248] Psalm 105:37: καὶ ἔθυσαν τοὺς υἱοὺς αὐτῶν καὶ τὰς θυγατέρας αὐτῶν τοῖς δαιμονίοις; Baruch 4:7 (a clear allusion to Deut 32:16–17): παρωξύνατε γὰρ τὸν ποιήσαντα ὑμᾶς θύσαντες δαιμονίοις καὶ οὐ θεῷ.

[249] Or, perhaps better, "who are nothing." The translator does not deny their existence, but their status and power.

the Song of Moses actually breaks the surface of Paul's argument in Romans 10:19–21. Nonetheless, like a massive reef hidden just below the waterline, this network of close verbal and conceptual links creates a solid bridge for Paul between Isaiah 65:1–2 and Deuteronomy 32:21. For listeners whose ears are attuned to the wider scriptural settings of Paul's citations, these unspoken correspondences amplify the concordance between the testimony of Paul's two witnesses.[250]

Further evidence that Paul is well aware of the larger thematic and verbal linkages between Isaiah 65 and the Song of Moses comes from a much earlier letter, 1 Corinthians. Paul alludes to both of these texts in 1 Corinthians 10:14–22 as he attempts to impress on the Corinthian Christians the absolute incompatibility of participation in pagan worship with allegiance to Christ. Recalling Moses' account of the idolatrous worship of the nations to which Israel of old joined themselves, Paul alludes to Deuteronomy 32:17 in his description of pagan sacrifice in Corinth: "What they sacrifice, they sacrifice to demons and not to God" (Fig. 3.13).[251]

Figure 3.13: 1 Corinthians 10:20 and Deuteronomy 32:17 LXX

1 Cor 10:20	ἃ θύουσιν,	δαιμονίοις	καὶ οὐ θεῷ [θύουσιν]
Deut 32:17	ἔθυσαν	δαιμονίοις	καὶ οὐ θεῷ

---

[250] At a more general level, there are in the Song of Moses some striking affinities with the language and thought characteristic of, if not exclusive to, Isaiah 40–66. In particular, note Deuteronomy 32:39ab: ἴδετε ἴδετε ὅτι ἐγώ εἰμι, καὶ οὐκ ἔστιν θεὸς πλὴν ἐμοῦ· (compare, e.g., Isa 43:10–11; 44:6; 45:5, 6, 14, 18, 21, 22; 46:9); Deuteronomy 32:39cd: ἐγὼ ἀποκτενῶ καὶ ζῆν ποιήσω, πατάξω κἀγὼ ἰάσομαι (cf. Isa 45:6–7: ... οὐκ ἔστι πλὴν ἐμοῦ· ἐγὼ κύριος ὁ θεός, καὶ οὐκ ἔστιν ἔτι· ἐγὼ ὁ κατασκευάσας φῶς καὶ ποιήσας σκότος, ὁ ποιῶν εἰρήνην καὶ κτίζων κακά); Deuteronomy 32:39e: καὶ οὐκ ἔστιν ὃς ἐξελεῖται ἐκ τῶν χειρῶν μου (cf. Isa 43:13: οὐκ ἔστιν ὁ ἐκ τῶν χειρῶν μου ἐξαιρούμενος· ποιήσω, καὶ τίς ἀποστρέψει αὐτό;). Sommer (1998:134–37; cf. Fishbane 1985:478–79) argues that Deutero-Isaiah knows and uses both of the great poems at the end of Deuteronomy (Isa 48:20–21 echoes Deut 32:1–5; Isa 58:11–14 transforms Deut 32:9–13; Isa 45:14–19 draws on Deut 33:26–29; he does not discuss the possibility of Deutero-Isaiah's use of the Song of Moses in Isaiah 65). The same evidence Sommer adduces as evidence of Deutero-Isaiah's allusions to the Song of Moses can help explain how a later reader such as Paul might discern a strong thematic coherence between Deuteronomy 32 and portions of Isaiah. *Mek. Pisha'* 12 (on Exod 12:25–28; Lauterbach 1933–35, 1:91) notes the following connections between Isaiah and the Song of Moses: Isa 1:2/Deut 32:1; Isa 40:5/Deut 32:39; Isa 24:8/Deut 32:39; Isa 58:14/Deut 32:13.

[251] For a detailed discussion of Paul's use of Deuteronomy 32 in this passage, see Hays 1989:93–94, 1999; Bell 1994:251–55.

Paul further echoes Deuteronomy 32:21a as he challenges the Corinthians: "Or shall we provoke the Lord to jealousy?" (1 Cor 10:22).[252] Between these two allusions to the Song of Moses, he insists:

> You cannot drink the cup of the Lord and the cup of demons. You cannot share the table of the Lord and the table of demons (1 Cor 10:21).
>
> οὐ δύνασθε ποτήριον κυρίου πίνειν καὶ ποτήριον δαιμονίων, οὐ δύνασθε τραπέζης κυρίου μετέχειν καὶ τραπέζης δαιμονίων.

Paul's exclamations evoke the description of Israelite idolators in Isaiah 65:11:

> You who . . . spread a table for the demon and fill a cup for Fortune.
>
> ὑμεῖς . . . ἑτοιμάζοντες τῷ δαιμονίῳ τράπεζαν καὶ πληροῦντες τῇ τύχῃ κέρασμα.[253]

The presence of interconnected allusions to Isaiah 65 and Deuteronomy 32 in 1 Corinthians 10 suggests both that Paul knew the larger context of Isaiah 65:1–2, and that, long before the composition of Romans, he recognized the thematic and verbal resonances of Isaiah 65 with the Song of Moses.[254]

---

[252] ἢ παραζηλοῦμεν τὸν κύριον; Again Paul asks the Corinthians to understand themselves in terms of ancient Israel and warns them not to recapitulate Israel's mistake. Note that it is the second half of this verse that Paul quotes in Romans 10:20.

[253] This allusion, overlooked by most commentators, is recognized by Barrett 1968:237 (cf. Conzelmann 1975:174 n. 43; NA[27] margin). Wilk (1998) does not discuss this passage. It might be possible to explain Paul's phrases, "the cup of demons" and "the table of demons," as merely reverse formulations of traditional eucharistic terminology, "the cup of the Lord" (1 Cor 11:27; cf. 1 Cor 10:16; 11:25, 26, 28) and "the table of the Lord." However, the phrase, "the table of the Lord," is otherwise unattested in the NT. In Luke 22:30, Jesus promises to his followers seats at "my table" in the kingdom of God. 1 Clement 43:2 mentions ἡ τράπεζα τοῦ θεοῦ as part of the furnishings of the Tabernacle, but does not speak of the "table of the Lord" in connection with the eucharist. In the LXX, "the table of the Lord" is found only in Malachi 1:7, 12, where it serves as a designation for the altar (cf. Ezek 41:22; 44:16), although the "table" that holds the Bread of the Presence is a key component of the Temple furnishings (Exod 25:23–30, etc.). For references to the "table" of the god in Greco-Roman literature, see Conzelmann 1975:174 n. 44; see further Gill 1974.

[254] The possibility that Paul did not link these texts together himself but rather found them joined already in some preexisting collection of excerpts is, in my view, quite unlikely given Paul's wide-ranging use of Isaiah and his close familiarity with the final chapters of Deuteronomy. In the present instance, however, it would make little difference, since it would be necessary to suppose that these excerpts included

Paul's appropriation of scripture in Romans 10:19–21 thus involves several layers of interpretation. He refracts Isaiah 65 not only through the lens of his own missionary experience, but also through the lens provided by his interpretation of Deuteronomy 32. Likewise, his reading of the Song of Moses is shaped by the way he understands Isaiah 65, as well as by his apostolic ministry to Gentiles. Before exploring the significance of these observations further, however, it will be necessary to examine closely Paul's citation of Isaiah 65:1–2.

Israel and the Gentiles in Isaiah 65:1–2

If Moses' testimony that God has chosen to show favor to the Gentiles in order to make Israel jealous is surprising, Paul warns that the deposition of his next witness is more scandalous still: "Isaiah dares to say. . . ."[255] Isaiah's shocking statement is more than matched, however, by Paul's stunning misreading of this text. What is, in Isaiah, an oracle about God's relentless pursuit of apostate Israel (65:1) becomes in Paul's hands a declaration of God's gracious acceptance of the Gentiles. As if to add insult to injury, Paul then employs the very next verse (65:2) to paint a sharply contrasting picture of contemporary Israel as a people continually resisting God's grace.

In order to make some sense of Paul's exegetical and hermeneutical transformation of this text, I will examine three types of evidence: Paul's modifications to the text of his citation, the function

---

large parts, if not the whole, of Deuteronomy 32 and Isaiah 65. In that case, Paul still would be cognizant of a larger literary setting for his citations. Evidence for an anthology containing portions of Deuteronomy 32 and Isaiah 65 might be sought in Justin's citation in *Dial.* 119:2–4 of Deuteronomy 32:16–23 followed by citations of Zechariah 2:11; Isaiah 62:12; 65:1. Skarsaune, in a thorough study of Justin's quotations, attributes Justin's citations from Deuteronomy 32 to the apologist's use of Paul: "Justin draws much quotation material from Rom 9–11. So it is rather Paul's testimony [in Romans 10:19] which has been expanded in *Dial.* 119:2" (1987:53). Likewise, Justin's subsequent quotation from Isaiah 65:1 was "suggested by the quotation sequence in Romans" (1987:116). For the view that Justin's quotations at times reflect Pauline influence, see also Prigent 1964:114.

[255] These words (ἀποτολμᾷ καὶ λέγει) form a hendiadys (BDR 442 n. 29). Although Paul also uses the more prosaic, "Isaiah says" (λέγει, 9:29; 10:16; 10:21; 15:12), he gives Isaiah more colorful introductions than any other persona who speaks in Romans: "Isaiah cries out" (9:27), "Isaiah has foretold" (9:29), "Isaiah dares to say" (10:20). In contrast, the words of other characters are introduced much less dramatically: "Moses writes" (10:5); "Moses says" (10:19); "David says" (4:6; 11:9); "Righteousness from Faith says" (10:6); "Scripture says" (4:3; 9:17; 10:11; 11:2; but cf. Gal 3:8, where Paul claims that Scripture "foresaw" and "proclaimed the good news beforehand" to Abraham).

of these verses in the context of Paul's larger argument in Romans 9–11, and the importance of the wider setting of Isaiah 65:1–2 for Paul's reading of this text. Finally, I will show how Paul's citations of Deuteronomy 32:21 and Isaiah 65:1–2 may be regarded as mutually interpreting.

Paul's Citation and Modification of Isaiah 65:1–2 in Romans 10:20–21

In attempting to discern to what extent Paul has modified his text of Isaiah 65:1–2 one must first address the question of the original text of Romans 10:20–21. The textual variants in Romans 10:21 pose little difficulty. The reading ἐπί probably arose under the influence of a variant form of the LXX,[256] while the omission of καὶ ἀντιλέγοντα is clearly secondary, bringing Paul's quotation closer to the type of text now represented by MT.[257] In Romans 10:20, however, the situation is a bit more complex. Although NA[27] brackets ἐν in the first line of Paul's quotation, there are good reasons for regarding this reading as original. It is attested by early representatives of both the Alexandrian[258] and Western[259] text families. Moreover, this reading has absolutely no basis in the LXX text tradition; its omission by the majority of witnesses can readily be viewed as the consequence of harmonization with LXX Isaiah.[260] If ἐν is, as I have supposed, the original reading in Romans 10:20, it may well be that this variant goes back to Paul himself, since there are no other witnesses to ἐν in Isaiah 65:1 besides Paul. It is less clear what the significance of the addition of ἐν might be. It may be simply a case of the pleonastic use of ἐν with the dative after εὑρίσκω.[261] Alternatively, however, ἐν may here bear its more usual locative sense, "among."[262]

---

[256] Zuntz 1953:244 n. 1. Support for ἐπί comes from the Lucianic family of manuscripts as well as from Justin and Clement.

[257] These two words fall under the obelus in B Q 88 and the Syrohexapla.

[258] 𝔓[46] B (also 1506[vid]).

[259] D* F G (it).

[260] In contrast, the second ἐν, read by B D* and apparently by 1506, is missing from 𝔓[46] F G it and the rest of the witnesses to the Alexandrian and Western textual traditions. Its inclusion in B D* 1506 may have resulted from assimilation to the first half of Paul's quotation. Zuntz, however, argues for the authenticity of both occurrences of ἐν, supposing that 𝔓[46] "omitted the second by mere inadvertance" (1953:173 n. 4).

[261] Cf. 2 Cor 12:20, κἀγὼ εὑρεθῶ ὑμῖν. BDR and BDF carefully distinguish this use of the dative after εὑρίσκω (pass) from the dative of agent: BDR §191, 2 and n. 4; §220 n. 1; BDF §191(3); §220(1).

[262] MHT 3:264. See also N. Turner 1959:119.

If so, we may find a possible motivation for Paul's addition of ἐν by recognizing that he has heretofore taken some care not to exaggerate the reception his gospel has received among the Gentiles. *Some* "from among the Gentiles" have responded to his message (9:24).[263] With ἐν in Romans 10:20, Paul may once again be carefully nuancing his claim about the status of the Gentiles. God has been found "among" those not seeking him, rather than by all who were not seeking him.

As Figure 3.14 shows, Paul's citation bears strong affinities to the LXX version of Isaiah 65:1–2.

Figure 3.14: Isaiah 65:1–2 LXX and Romans 10:20–21

Isaiah 65:1–2 LXX	Romans 10:20–21

¹ ἐμφανὴς ἐγενόμην
   τοῖς ἐμὲ μὴ ζητοῦσιν,
εὑρέθην
   τοῖς ἐμὲ μὴ ἐπερωτῶσιν·
εἶπα· ἰδού εἰμι, τῷ ἔθνει
οἳ οὐκ ἐκάλεσάν τὸ ὄνομα μου
 	
² ἐξεπέτασα τὰς χεῖράς μου
ὅλην τὴν ἡμέραν
πρὸς λαὸν ἀπειθοῦντα καὶ
ἀντιλέγοντα,
οἳ οὐκ ἐπορεύθησαν ὁδῷ ἀληθινῇ,
ἀλλ' ὀπίσω τῶν ἁμαρτιῶν αὐτῶν.
	²⁰Ἠσαΐας δὲ ἀποτολμᾷ καὶ λέγει·
	εὑρέθην
	   [ἐν] τοῖς ἐμὲ μὴ ζητοῦσιν,
	ἐμφανὴς ἐγενόμην
	   τοῖς ἐμὲ μὴ ἐπερωτῶσιν.
	
	πρὸς δὲ τὸν Ἰσραὴλ λέγει·
	²¹ ὅλην τὴν ἡμέραν
	ἐξεπέτασα τὰς χεῖράς μου
	πρὸς λαὸν ἀπειθοῦντα καὶ
	ἀντιλέγοντα.

Isa 65:1 MT: נִדְרַשְׁתִּי לְלוֹא שָׁאָלוּ נִמְצֵאתִי לְלֹא בִקְשֻׁנִי אָמַרְתִּי הִנְנִי הִנֵּנִי אֶל־גּוֹי לֹא־קֹרָא בִשְׁמִי

Isa 65:2 MT: פֵּרַשְׂתִּי יָדַי כָּל־הַיּוֹם אֶל־עַם סוֹרֵר הַהֹלְכִים הַדֶּרֶךְ לֹא־טוֹב אַחַר מַחְשְׁבֹתֵיהֶם

The pronominal object ἐμέ in the second clause of his quotation agrees with the LXX against MT. By itself, the evidentiary value of this correspondence is not great, since there is widespread evidence for the inclusion of the pronoun in other witnesses to the Hebrew text

---

[263] Similarly, in Romans 9:30, it may be significant that ἔθνη is anarthrous: Paul does not claim that *all* the Gentiles have obtained righteousness (so Cranfield 1979:506).

of Isaiah.[264] We are on firmer ground, however, in noting that Paul's citation agrees with LXX Isaiah in the verbal phrase ἐμφανὴς ἐγενόμην. This is the only time in the entire LXX that this phrase is used to render a form of דרש.[265] The later Greek versions α' and θ' stay closer to the sense of the Hebrew, translating ἐξεζητήθην.[266] The strongest evidence for Paul's use of the LXX, however, is his phrase, καὶ ἀντιλέγοντα, which appears to be a uniquely septuagintal reading.[267]

---

[264] 1QIsaᵃ (שאלוני); Targum; Peshitta; Vulgate. Noting that 1QIsaᵃ and Paul's citation happen to agree in reading a pronominal object, Lim jumps to the sweeping conclusion that we can thus no longer be sure that Paul is quoting a text of the LXX:

The contribution of IQIsaᵃ to the quotation of Isaiah 65: 1 in Romans 10: 20 raises fundamental questions about the textual characteristics of the Pauline biblical quotations and the way that they are analysed. It is no longer primarily an inner-Greek or septuagintal matter. The far-reaching implication is that biblical texts written in the Hebrew language must be given full consideration in the evaluation of Pauline citations (1997a:147).

However, closer analysis of this particular citation shows that there are two agreements between Paul's text and readings unambiguously attested only in the manuscript tradition of LXX Isaiah (see below). Unless Lim wants to propose that Paul proceeded through a passage drawing one word from this text and one word from that, these agreements strongly suggest that Paul depends *throughout* on a Greek text related closely to LXX Isaiah.

[265] Elsewhere, ἐμφανὴς γίνεσθαι translates ידע nif. (Exod 2:14); cf. ἐμφανὴς εἶναι for כון (Isa 2:2/Micah 4:1). Isaiah 65:1 is the only occurrence of דרש in the nifal in Isaiah. In other books, נדרש is rendered by ἀποκρίνομαι and by words in the same semantic field as ζητέω (ἐκζητέω, ἀκριβάζομαι, ἐπισκέπτομαι). As far as I can ascertain, ἐμφανὴς γίνεσθαι does not occur in α' (Reider 1966) or in σ' (Hatch-Redpath; cf. González Luis 1981).

[266] Compare Targum, אשתאילית; Peshitta, ܐܬܒܥܝܬ; Vulgate, *quaesierunt me*. Cf. the similar argument for Paul's use of a (revised) septuagintal text at Isaiah 28:16 based on the common occurrence of καταισχύνω for Hebrew חוש (above, p. 129).

[267] The phrase appears in no extant Hebrew text, nor in the Targum, Peshitta, or Vulgate. The omission of this phrase in Romans 10:20 by F G and Ambrosiaster probably represents a secondary harmonization with the text represented by MT. This phrase in LXX Isaiah may have arisen through the influence of Isaiah 50:5 (the only other occurrence in LXX of ἀπειθέω and ἀντιλέγω in parallel; so also Zillesin 1902:248); if so, the LXX portrays Israel in Isaiah 65 as the antithesis of the "servant" figure in Isaiah 50. It is also possible that the LXX translator was influenced here by the collocation סורר ומ(ו)רה (found in Deut 21:18, 20; Jer 5:23; Ps 78:8) or even that his *Vorlage* contained this reading (e.g., Ziegler 1934:78–79; Goshen-Gottstein 1995:285; cf. J. D. W. Watts 1987:341 n. 2a). However, this suggestion runs up against the difficulty that ἀντιλέγω is never used in the LXX to translate √מרה. Anticipating this objection, Ziegler (1934:79) suggests that the unique occurrence of ἀντιλέγω for מורה in Isaiah 65:2 could be explained by the translator's previous use of ἀντιλέγω in tandem with ἀπειθέω in Isaiah 50:5. Support for the notion that the LXX *Vorlage* read סורר ומורה is found by Brownlee in 1QIsaᵃ (1964:244). He thinks the anomalous form סורה of 1QIsaᵃ reflects an original סורר ומורה corrupted by haplography. In contrast, Kutscher (1974:269–70) speculates that

Although Paul clearly derives his citation of Isaiah 65:1–2 from a septuagintal text, his citation diverges from Isaiah 65:1–2 LXX in important ways. Paul himself is most likely responsible for quoting only a portion of each verse, since there is no support in the LXX textual tradition for the short form of text he cites. In the case of Isaiah 65:1, it is fairly clear why Paul chooses to omit the second sentence ("I said, 'Here I am,' to a nation that did not call on my name"). Just previously in Romans, he described those who "obey the gospel" and are saved as, "everyone who calls on the name of the Lord" (Joel 2:32; Romans 10:13; cf. 10:16). It would be confusing, to say the least, to speak a few verses later of Gentiles "finding" God apart from responding to Paul's gospel by "calling on the Lord's name." Paul's omission of the relative clause in 65:2 probably follows from this prior decision as he seeks to balance the two halves of his quotation.[268] It is also quite probable that Paul has advanced the adverbial phrase, "all day long" (ὅλην τὴν ἡμέραν) to the beginning of the citation of 65:2. Not only does this variant find no parallel in any other witness to the text of Isaiah, it also serves the rhetorical function of enhancing the point Paul has been developing since Romans 9:30 concerning the deep intransigence of Israel in the face of God's persistent offer of "righteousness."[269]

Whether Paul has modified his *Vorlage* further is somewhat difficult to say due to the complex nature of the LXX evidence. The problem involves both the order of the clauses and the pairing of the verbs in Isaiah 65:1. Although the text of Romans 10:20 is secure, four different combinations of verbs and clauses are represented in witnesses to the Greek text of Isaiah, as Figure 3.15 shows.

---

the form סורה results from the *indirect* influence of מורה. The reading סורה in 1QIsaᵃ may be the result of "the assimilation of words which sometimes appear in pairs," a phenomenon attested in the Hebrew Bible with respect to other word-pairs, rather than the product of an error of transcription (270). In any case, my point stands that *Paul's access* to this variant will have come via the LXX, as shown by his agreement with the collocation ἀπειθέω/ἀντιλέγω unique to the translator of LXX Isaiah.

[268] It is not clear that Paul's criticism of Israel is any less harsh as a result of his truncated quotation.

[269] Paul's contention that God's righteousness is being offered to Israel through messengers like himself, an argument developed in Romans in large part through reliance on Isaianic texts, finds an interesting counterpart in the Targum's interpretation of Isaiah 65:2. The targumist understands God's continual spreading out of his hands to Israel (Hebrew, ידי פרשׂתי) to consist in his persistent sending of prophets to his people (שלחית נבי״). On the importance of the prophets for the targumist, see Chilton 1982:52–56.

Figure 3.15: Isaiah 65:1 LXX and Variants

1. ἐμφανὴς ἐγενόμην εὑρέθην	τοῖς ἐμὲ μὴ ζητοῦσιν τοῖς ἐμὲ μὴ ἐπερωτῶσιν	1. LXX (Ziegler): The Alexandrian text
2. ἐμφανὴς ἐγενόμην εὑρέθην	τοῖς ἐμὲ μὴ ἐπερωτῶσιν τοῖς ἐμὲ μὴ ζητοῦσιν	2. Hexaplaric and most Lucianic mss = MT
3. εὑρέθην ἐμφανὴς ἐγενόμην	τοῖς ἐμὲ μὴ ἐπερωτῶσιν τοῖς ἐμὲ μὴ ζητοῦσιν	3. Some Lucianic witnesses
4. εὑρέθην ἐμφανὴς ἐγενόμην	τοῖς ἐμὲ μὴ ζητοῦσιν τοῖς ἐμὲ μὴ ἐπερωτῶσιν	4. Origen, Clem. Alex = Rom 10:20

It is not certain whether the pairing of verbs and ordering of clauses found in Romans 10:20 is to be attributed to Paul himself or to a pre-Pauline revision of LXX Isaiah.[270] The pairing of εὑρέθην with ζητοῦσιν (Fig. 3.15, versions 2 and 4) can be understood either as a move to bring the LXX in line with the text represented by MT or as an inner-Greek improvement (i.e., matching "finding" with "seeking") without reference to a non-Septuagintal text.[271] If it is an inner-Greek phenomenon, it is conceivable that Paul made this improvement independent of other tradents.[272] Two further possibilities then present themselves: Paul might have had a *Vorlage* in agreement with the LXX (Fig. 3.15, version 1) and merely switched the initial verbs; alternatively, his *Vorlage* might have agreed with version 3, in which case Paul would have switched the second pair of verbs.

---

[270] Both Origen (*Contra Celsum* II. 78) and Clement (*Stromata* 2.9.43.2) are clearly dependent on Paul, for both also quote Deuteronomy 32:21 in the immediate context (*Contra Celsum* II. 78; *Stromata* 2.9.43.1). Furthermore, in the same passage Origen alludes to Romans 11:11, while Clement cites Romans 10:2–4 (*Stromata* 2.9.42.4–5) and Romans 11:11 (*Stromata* 2.9.43.4).

[271] While the pairing ἐπερωτάω/εὑρίσκω occurs nowhere else in the LXX (or in the NT, for that matter), the words ζητέω/εὑρίσκω appear together 42 times in the LXX (Deut 4:29; Josh 2:22; 1 Kgdms 10:2, 21; 2 Kgdms 17:20; 3 Kgdms 1:3; 18:10; 4 Kgdms 2:17; 2 Chr 15:2, 15; 1 Esd 5:39; Ezra 2:62; Neh 7:64; Tob 1:18; 5:4; 1 Macc 4:5; Ps 36:10, 36; Prov 1:28; 8:17; 14:6; 16:8 [2x]; Eccl 7:28; 8:17; 12:10; Song 3:1, 2; 5:6; Wis 6:12; 13:6; Hos 2:9; 5:6; Amos 8:12; Isa 41:12; 55:6; Jer 2:24; 5:1; 27:20; 36:13; Lam 1:19; Ezek 22:30). The pairing ζητέω/εὑρίσκω occurs 21 times in the NT, including Rom 10:20 (Matt 7:7, 8; 12:43; Mark 14:55; Luke 2:44–45; 11:9, 10; 11:24; 13:6, 7; 15:8; John 7:34, 36; Acts 12:19; 17:27; Rom 10:20; 1 Cor 4:2; Gal 2:17; 2 Tim 1:17; Heb 12:17; Rev 9:6).

[272] The wide diffusion of version 2, however, makes it impossible to be certain that Paul did not have access to a text that had already made this move.

The simplest explanation, however, would be to suppose that Paul knew version 2, a text of the LXX that had been revised toward the form of text represented by MT. I suggested above in discussing Paul's citations of Isaiah 28:16/8:14 and Isaiah 52:7 that Paul had access at some point to this type of text.[273] In the present instance, Paul would simply have reversed the order of the clauses.[274] Such a move may have communicated more dramatically the new status of the Gentiles and clarified the meaning of God's "appearing" to them: they have not just been given some sort of revelation about God, they have "found" him and been incorporated into the people he is redeeming for himself. At the end of the day, however, the evidence remains ambiguous enough that in what follows I will refrain from placing undue weight on my hypothesis that Paul has altered his *Vorlage* at this particular point.

The Function of Isaiah 65:1–2 in Romans and in the Book of Isaiah
The most notorious feature of Paul's quotation does not depend on an actual alteration of the words of his *Vorlage*, but rather on his interpretive comments. By means of his second introduction, "But to Israel he says," Paul takes Isaiah's words of reproof in 65:1–2— all of which are clearly addressed to Israel—and boldly bisects the quotation so that the first verse speaks of Gentiles, while only the second verse refers to Israel. Simultaneously, Paul transforms 65:1 from a declaration of condemnation for Israel into a proclamation of salvation for Gentiles, all the while continuing to read 65:2 as a severe censure of Israel's constant rebelliousness. It is not enough to label Paul's reading here as a rather notable example of contemporary Jewish "atomistic" exegesis without pressing on to ask the deeper hermeneutical question: What exegetical warrant, what interpretive reasoning, could have led Paul to such a brazen misreading of the prophet?

In Romans 10:20–21 we find arguably the clearest example of the extent to which Paul's reading of Isaiah is shaped by his context and convictions as apostle to the Gentiles. Paul's "missionary theology"—which itself arises in large part out of his reading of Israel's scriptures—here exercises a profound influence on his interpretation of the prophetic text. The apostle's deep conviction that God is calling Gentiles as well as Jews to be his redeemed people in Christ

---

[273] See pp. 126–34.
[274] See the similar move in Paul's quotation of Hosea 2:23 in Romans 9:25 (cf. Beentjes 1982:517).

becomes a hermeneutical lens that allows (dare I say, constrains?) him to find Gentiles in the midst of divine oracles to or about Israel.

I have already had more than one occasion to note what appears to be Paul's most common interpretive strategy for doing this, namely his penchant for locating Gentiles in negatively-phrased descriptions of people (often Israelites!) who are estranged from God.[275] Accordingly, as Paul trolled the scriptures for insight into God's purpose for his ministry, Isaiah's phrases, "those not seeking me . . . those not inquiring of me," would have set Paul's hermeneutical "Gentile-finder" ringing.[276] Though not part of the text he cites explicitly (for reasons discussed above), the term ἔθνος itself in Isaiah 65:1 would have reinforced Paul's identification of the previous two clauses as references to Gentiles.[277] Moreover, ἔθνος forms an important verbal link with Deuteronomy 32:21, a text Paul has just cited in Romans 10:19. In light of the extensive network of connections between these two passages, it may be that οὐκ ἔθνος in Moses' Song emboldened Paul to read ἔθνος in Isaiah 65:1 as a description of Gentiles.

As tendentious as such an exegetical move may appear to us, Paul defends his claim that Israel "has known" from scripture that the Gentiles would find mercy before most of Israel by exploiting a further feature of Isaiah 65:1–2. These verses place two different words for Israel in synonymous parallelism: 65:1 has ἔθνος (גוי), while 65:2 employs λαός (עם). Latching on to this terminological feature of Isaiah 65:1–2, Paul interprets ἔθνος and λαός as two completely *different* entities.[278] Having identified ἔθνος as (believing) Gentiles, Paul takes λαός in its contextual sense as a reference to Israel. In this way, he is able to identify Gentiles with those who have "found" God, while employing the very next verse in Isaiah to emphasize—this time in keeping with the Isaianic context—the refusal of Israel to respond to God's persistent pursuit of his people.

---

[275] The Gentiles are "not my people . . . not loved" (9:25–26; Hos 2:23/1:10); "no nation at all . . . a nation without understanding" (10:19; Deut 32:21), "those not seeking me . . . those not asking for me" (10:20; Isaiah 65:1), "those to whom it was not announced concerning him . . . those who have not heard" (15:21; Isaiah 52:15). We saw that Paul even creates one of his own according to this pattern: "Gentiles, who were not pursuing righteousness" (Rom 9:30; cf. Isa 51:1).

[276] This word-picture may be thought ironically appropriate by those who are certain there is something fishy about Paul's use of scripture.

[277] Paul never uses the term ἔθνος of Israel.

[278] A similar exploitation of originally synonymous terminology takes place in an early Christian interpretation of Psalm 2:1–2:

Paul's "discovery" of Gentiles in a text originally concerned only with Israel is not the only stunning reversal wrought by his reinterpretation, however. What marks Paul's rereading of Isaiah 65:1 as especially radical is the fact that Paul's recontextualization of these words within Romans 9–11 entirely transforms the meaning of Isaiah's oracle. In Isaiah 65:1, there is bitter irony in the statement that God has been "found by" or has "appeared to" those not seeking or asking for him, since the next verse makes it clear that despite God's gracious self-revelation and his continued pleading with Israel to respond to him, Israel continues stubbornly to go their own way.[279] God's being "found" by them only compounds the tragedy of their disobedience and rebelliousness.[280]

When Paul splits Isaiah 65:1 off from the following verse, however, Isaiah's words take on a quite different sense.[281] Now set in *opposition* to Israel's intransigence, described in the words of 65:2 (Romans 10:21), the statement in 65:1 that God has been "found" by those not seeking him becomes a *positive* claim that *Gentiles* have obtained righteousness (Romans 10:20; cf. Rom 9:30). As quoted by Paul, Isaiah's words are still fraught with irony, but now the irony involves the fact that while God has been received readily among the Gentiles, his own people Israel continue to resist him. Paul's reinterpretation of Isaiah 65:1 thus involves two distinct, though related moves: first, finding the Gentiles in a text originally dealing with disobedient Israel; second, turning an ironic lament over Israel's

---

ἱνατί ἐφρύαξαν <u>ἔθνη</u> καὶ <u>λαοὶ</u> ἐμελέτησαν κενά;
παρέστησαν οἱ βασιλεῖς τῆς γῆς καὶ οἱ ἄρχοντες συνήχθησαν ἐπὶ τὸ αὐτὸ
κατὰ τοῦ κυρίου καὶ κατὰ τοῦ χριστοῦ αὐτοῦ (Acts 4:25–26).
The interpretive gloss on the passage identifies the "kings" as Herod, the "rulers" as Pontius Pilate, ἔθνη as the Gentiles (especially the Romans), and λαοί as Israel: (λαοῖς Ἰσραήλ, Acts 4:27). Paul may thus be drawing on an early Christian interpretive convention regarding the meanings of ἔθνος and λαός, although the atomizing interpretation of a verse based on differences in vocabulary is a common exegetical strategy found in many strands of ancient Jewish exegesis.

[279] Compare the lament in Isaiah 64:7, καὶ οὐκ ἔστιν ὁ ἐπικαλούμενος τὸ ὄνομά σου καὶ ὁ μνησθεὶς ἀντιλαβέσθαι σου.

[280] The same irony is present in the Hebrew text, although the NRSV waters it down by translating, "I was *ready to be* sought out ... found" (italics mine).

[281] Wisdom 1:2 similarly separates Isaiah 65:1 from the following verses and in so doing transforms its meaning. In Wisdom, these words become a general maxim concerning the right way to seek God, and "finding" God takes on entirely positive connotations: ὅτι εὑρίσκεται [ὁ κύριος, verse 1] τοῖς μὴ πειράζουσιν αὐτόν, ἐμφανίζεται δὲ τοῖς μὴ ἀπιστοῦσιν αὐτῷ.

obduracy into a positive celebration of Gentile inclusion in the people of God.

Paul's reading of Isaiah 65:2 keeps much closer to the sense of this verse in its Isaianic context. By drawing on Isaiah 65:2 to answer the question, "It is not that Israel hasn't heard, is it?" Paul models his response after God's own response to a similar challenge. In the passage immediately preceding Isaiah 65:1–2, Israel accuses God of maintaining an indifferent silence in the face of the destruction of Jerusalem and its Temple:

> Yet while all these things happened you stood aloof, Lord. You kept silent, and you humbled us greatly (64:12).[282]

Isaiah 65:1–2 offers God's vigorous response to this outrageous charge. God has not been silent or indifferent; God has been pursuing his people passionately: "I have stretched out my hands all day long" (65:2). The problem is not God's silence, but Israel's intransigence.

It is enlightening to compare Isaiah's characterization of Israel as disobedient and rebellious, preferring to walk in their own ways rather than in God's, with Paul's criticism of Israel in Romans 10. Isaiah terms Israel

> . . . a people disobedient and contrary, who do not walk in the way of truth, but [who walk] after their sins.
>
> λαὸν ἀπειθοῦντα καὶ ἀντιλέγοντα, οἳ οὐκ ἐπορεύθησαν ὁδῷ ἀληθινῇ, ἀλλ᾽ ὀπίσω τῶν ἁμαρτιῶν αὐτῶν (65:2).

Paul charges that, determined to seek "their own righteousness," Israel has disregarded (ἀγνοοῦντες) and refused to submit (οὐχ ὑπετάγησαν) to "God's righteousness" (Rom 10:1–3).[283] Twice in Isaiah 65–66 God says to the unfaithful in Israel, "I called you, and you didn't obey" (ἐκάλεσα ὑμᾶς καὶ οὐχ ὑπηκούσατε, 65:12; cf. 66:4). In Romans 10:16, Paul laments along with Isaiah that many in Israel have not "obeyed" (ὑπήκουσαν) the gospel or "believed our message." The similar depictions of Israel in Romans and Isaiah 65:2 result not from Paul's direct borrowing of Isaiah's words, but rather from his much broader appropriation of the story of Israel told in Isaiah as he attempts to understand the plight of Israel in his own day.

---

[282] καὶ ἐπὶ πᾶσι τούτοις ἀνέσχου, κύριε, καὶ ἐσιώπησας καὶ ἐταπείνωσας ἡμᾶς σφόδρα.
[283] Paul's comment regarding Israel's pursuit of "their own righteousness" becomes tragically ironic when heard in conjunction with Isaiah's confession in the prayer leading up to Isaiah 65: ὡς ῥάκος ἀποκαθημένης πᾶσα ἡ δικαιοσύνη ἡμῶν (64:6).

Paul's account of Israel in Romans 9–11 corresponds at a deep level to the depiction of Israel in Isaiah 65–66 as a nation profoundly divided.[284] Although Isaiah 65:1–2 speaks of the "nation" (ἔθνος) and the "people" (λαός) as a whole and Isaiah 65:3–7 decries the idolatry of "this people" (ὁ λαὸς οὗτος),[285] beginning in 65:8 a second group steps into view, God's "servant" (ὁ δουλεύων μοι), on whose account God will not destroy all of Israel (65:8). The remainder of Isaiah 65–66 draws a sharp distinction between these two groups. While those who forsake Israel's God for other gods will be annihilated,[286] those who remain faithful to the Lord will return to the Land and enjoy the Edenic bliss of the new heaven and new earth in which "all flesh" will worship Israel's God alone.[287]

Although Paul's use of the term "Israel" in Romans 10:21 could imply that he employs Isaiah 65:2 as a depiction of all Jews, he immediately attempts to head off such an interpretation of his words by reintroducing the concept of the remnant in Romans 11:1. Paul insists on his own identity as "an Israelite of the seed of Abraham"

---

[284] As noted earlier, a similar situation of division within Israel forms the background for the texts Paul cites in Romans 9:33 and 10:11 (Isaiah 8:14 and 28:16).

[285] This appellation, laden with connotations of a ruptured covenant relationship, occurs also in the wider contexts of Isaiah 28:16/8:14 (cited in Rom 9:33).

[286] The wicked are those who have forsaken God and his Temple in order to participate in idolatrous worship; as a result, even the sacrifices they do offer to Israel's God are detestable (65:3–7, 11; 66:3–4, 15–18a). Repeatedly God vows to repay them for their evil deeds with everlasting shame and destruction (65:6–7, 11–16; 66:4, 5b, 15–18a, 24).

[287] "I will lead out [from exile] seed (σπέρμα) from Jacob and from Judah, and they will inherit my holy mountain; my elect (οἱ ἐκλεκτοί μου), my servants (οἱ δοῦλοί μου), will inherit it, and they will dwell there" (65:9). Other descriptions of the faithful emphasize their fear of God and exclusive loyalty to him: "my servants" (οἱ δουλεύοντες, repeated five times in vv. 13–15), "the humble and quiet one who trembles at my word" (66:2; cf. 66:5). These constitute the true Israel and are called by the covenant name, "my people" (65:19); it is they who will enjoy the eschatological blessing of the new heavens and new earth (65:17–25). "In a day ... in a moment" Zion will give birth to her children (66:7–14). God's people will be gathered from among all the nations into Jerusalem to serve him, and they will be joined in worship by "all flesh" (66:18b–23). As long as the new creation remains, God promises them, "your seed and your name will endure" (66:22). While it is intriguing to speculate about the extent to which Paul's eschatology may have been formed by these chapters, such an inquiry goes beyond the bounds of this study since there are no explicit citations or even strong allusions to the remainder of Isaiah 65–66 in Paul's letters (I remain skeptical of the proposal by S. G. Brown 1993). Many have speculated that the depiction of missionaries being sent out to the nations in Isaiah 66:19 strongly influenced Paul's apostolic self understanding (see especially Aus 1979 and Riesner 1998:245–53). If this verse indeed played such a role, it is curious that Paul nowhere cites or alludes to it, as he does, for example, Isaiah 49:1ff. (e.g., Gal 1:15; 1 Cor 15:10).

(11:1) and differentiates between "a remnant [of Israel] according to the election of grace" (λεῖμμα κατ᾽ ἐκλογὴν χάριτος, 11:5; cf. 11:7) and "the rest" of Israel (οἱ λοιποί, 11:7). Paul turns to portions of scripture other than Isaiah to make this move in Romans 11:1. Nevertheless, in light of what follows it is clear that in Romans 10:21 Paul understands Isaiah 65:2 to refer to the majority, but by no means the whole, of Israel. In a manner that does justice to the larger context of Isaiah 65–66, Paul exempts from the condemnatory words of Isaiah 65:2 not only Gentiles, but also the "remnant" God has chosen in the present time.[288] Even here, where Paul most brazenly reads Gentiles into texts originally addressed to Israel, he does not thereby disinherit his own people of the salvation promised them in scripture.

Hearing Deuteronomy 32 and Isaiah 65 in Concert

I argued earlier that Paul understands Deuteronomy 32:21 and Isaiah 65:1–2 to be mutually interpreting and that he introduces these citations in such a way as to suggest they must be heard together. It is now possible to summarize the implications of this claim. Paul sets up the two citations rhetorically so that Moses' words still ring in the ear as Isaiah steps forward to speak: it is the message they bring collectively that is important for Paul's argument. Isaiah supports and supplements the outline of God's plan sketched by Moses.[289] Isaiah 65:2 clarifies that it is because Israel continually rebuffs God's overtures that God is driven to provoke his people to jealousy and anger. Isaiah 65:1 reveals that the Lord will arouse Israel's jealousy by graciouly making himself known to those who were not seeking him. Conversely, Paul's reading of the Song of Moses proves crucial for his radical reinterpretation of Isaiah 65:1–2. The reference in Romans 10:20 to the "no-nation" (Deut 32:21) helps Paul in the

---

[288] The use of Isaiah 65:2 in 1QHᵃ 7.20–21 [15.17–18] (לא הלכו בדרך . . . ורשעים טוב) is broadly parallel to the way Paul uses this text. The poet of the *Hodayot* understands Isa 65:2 as a reference to the wicked *within* Israel rather than to Israel *in toto*.

[289] Paul's technique is similar to the use in *Sifre Deut* §306 of a citation from Isaiah to support a statement of Moses. The prophet's words are introduced by the comment, בא ישעיה וסמך לדבר, "Isaiah came and confirmed the matter." Fraade comments, "The sense is that Isaiah, in adding his language to that of Moses, supported or expanded the significance of Moses' choice of words" (1991:270 n. 65).

following verse (Rom 10:21) clearly to identify "those not seeking me . . . those not asking for me" (Isa 65:1) as Gentiles, an interpretation that cuts against the grain of Isaiah 65 considered on its own terms. Moreover, although in Romans 10:21 Isaiah decries Israel's chronic resistance to God's offer of redemption in the gospel, the hopelessness of his depiction of Israel's plight is tempered by Moses' claim that God's ultimate intention in showing favor to Gentiles is to win Israel back to himself.

For Paul, both Moses and Isaiah witness to the same story of God's faithful love for Israel. Both also testify that the Gentiles have an important part to play in the drama of God's redemption of his people, even if their exact role—not to mention that of the "apostle to the Gentiles" himself—has not yet been made clear. Significantly, as he fills in the details in the following chapter, Paul appeals once again to the jealousy motif of the Song of Moses (Rom 11:11–14) and to Isaiah's oracles (Rom 11:26–27) to insist that the God who can be found by Gentiles who were not even seeking him is both willing and able to reverse the unbelief of his people Israel as well.

CHAPTER FOUR

"THE REDEEMER WILL COME FROM ZION"
ISAIAH IN ROMANS 11

> I say, then: "God has not rejected
> his inheritance, has he?"
>
> *Romans 11:1*

The rhetorical question in Romans 11:1 marks the beginning of a new stage in Paul's argument. His astounding claim that Israel has both "heard" and "known" of God's gracious plan to call the Gentiles to himself in Christ has been sustained by two important witnesses, Moses and Isaiah, who stood forth, as it were, to testify against Israel with their own voices (10:19–21). But having emphasized Israel's stubborn refusal to respond to the God who "all day long" stretches forth his hands to "a disobedient and contrary people" (Isa 65:2/Rom 10:21), Paul now asks whether Israel's chronic infidelity will finally overcome God's own faithful character (cf. Rom 3:3) and render null and void the promises God made to his people: "God has not rejected his inheritance, has he?" Could the election of Gentiles be a sign that God has now cast off Israel, the people he once chose to be his very own?[1]

Although it will be some time before we encounter another quotation from Isaiah (Rom 11:8), it is crucial that we continue to follow Paul's argument as it unfolds, for in Romans 11:1–7 Paul begins to

---

[1] Note once again *Dial.* 119, where, in dependence on the very texts Paul cites in Romans 10:19–21, Justin arrives at the conclusion, all too common among Christian interpreters, that God has indeed chosen the church *in place of* Israel:

> [We are] the nation that long ago God promised to Abraham.... God promises to him a certain nation, of like faith, both god-fearing and righteous, pleasing to the Father—but it is not you, in whom there is no faith (119.4, 6).
>
> [ἡμεῖς] τὸ ἔθνος, ὃ πάλαι τῷ Ἀβραὰμ ὁ θεὸς ὑπέσχετο.... Ὁμοιόπιστον οὖν τι ἔθνος καὶ θεοσεβὲς καὶ δίκαιον, εὐφραῖνον τὸν πατέρα, ὑπισχνεῖται αὐτῷ, ἀλλ' οὐχ ὑμᾶς, οἷς οὐκ ἔστι πίστις ἐν αὐτοῖς.

In drawing this conclusion, of course, Justin directly controverts Paul's explicit statement in Romans 11:1–2 (Greek text of Justin's *Dialogue* from Marcovich 1997:275–76).

deconstruct his earlier "misreading" of passages of scripture such as Hosea 2:23/1:10, Isaiah 52:7, and Isaiah 65:1–2. The original contexts of these biblical texts promising Israel's restoration—texts that Paul has brazenly subverted into prophecies of God's redemption of *Gentiles*—have, below the surface, exerted a subtle, but steady pull on the direction of Paul's reasoning. In Romans 11:1–7, this undertow finally gains enough strength to sweep the argument out into the powerful scriptural current testifying to God's abiding faithfulness to Israel. If God has extended his grace to those "not his people," how much more will he remain faithful to his promises to redeem the people he has chosen as his very own inheritance? Careful attention to Romans 11:1–7 will also enable us to properly contextualize the Isaianic quotations that follow. The opening verses of Romans 11 reveal the theological convictions that shape Paul's appropriation of the Isaianic motif of Israel's spiritual blindness (Rom 11:8) and that support his unwavering confidence, expressed in Isaiah's words, that God will ultimately act to save "all Israel" (Rom 11:26–27).

The opening words of Romans 11:1, λέγω οὖν, draw attention to the importance of the following question for Paul, who has taken pains throughout these chapters to keep before his hearers his own intense grief over the plight of his kinspeople (9:1–5, 10:1). The apostle offers here his most explicit challenge yet to the notion of God's faithfulness to Israel. And yet, even now, his very manner of framing the question—"God hasn't rejected his inheritance, has he?"—anticipates the answer, a resounding μὴ γένοιτο![2] However, Paul does more than merely protest in a shrill voice that, despite all appearances, God can be trusted. He supports his all-important denial that God has forsaken Israel both with empirical data and with an elaborate and densely-allusive scriptural argument.

Empirical Evidence: Romans 11:1

At an earlier stage in the discussion, Paul could take for granted the fact that the "vessels of mercy" whom God has called include those "from among the Jews" (ἐξ Ἰουδαίων, 9:24). Now, as living proof that God has not forsaken Israel, he offers himself: Paul, an Israelite from Abraham's seed, one of Benjamin's tribe (Rom 11:1). Paul has

[2] For the textual variant, "inheritance," adopted here, see below, p. 222.

not chosen these self-designations carelessly. "Israelite" evokes his earlier affirmation of the privileges that belong to the "Israelites" by God's grace:

> Theirs is the adoption as sons, the glory, the covenants, the giving of the Law, the worship, and the promises. Theirs are the fathers, and from them, according to the flesh, is the Christ . . . (9:4).

The clear implication of Paul's self-identification as an Israelite in Romans 11:1 is that Israel has not forfeited these gifts.[3]

The phrase "ἐκ σπέρματος Ἀβραάμ" recalls God's free and gracious promise to call "seed" for Abraham from among his children (9:6–9), evoking once again the whole complex of ideas accompanying the term "seed," a term which has proven so crucial in Paul's argument thus far.[4] As this letter is read out, one from Israel's "seed" stands before the Roman congregation, a tangible reminder of the hope latent in Isaiah's dark oracle: "the Lord Sabaoth left us seed" (κύριος σαβαὼθ ἐγκατέλιπεν ἡμῖν σπέρμα, Isa 1:9/Rom 9:29).

It is somewhat curious that Paul bothers to identify himself further as one "from the tribe of Benjamin." Apparently, he intends to press home his point by linking himself with a particular descendant of Jacob, the chosen son of Isaac, to whom the blessing of Abraham was granted (Rom 9:10–13). One wonders, however, if there is more to the reference to "Benjamin" than first meets the ear, especially since Paul has already identified himself as Jacob's descendant by means of the term "Israelite."[5] Consideration of this matter requires attention to the complex scriptural argument within which Paul situates his appeal to himself as empirical evidence of God's faithfulness.

ECHOES OF SCRIPTURE: ROMANS 11:1–2A

In Romans 11:1, Paul asks, "God hasn't rejected his inheritance, has he?" His answer in 11:2 employs virtually the same wording: "God has not rejected his people whom he foreknew." It has long been

---

[3] This is stated explicitly in Romans 11:29, "The gifts and the call of God are irrevocable (ἀμεταμέλητα γὰρ τὰ χαρίσματα καὶ ἡ κλῆσις τοῦ θεοῦ)."

[4] See the extended discussion of "seed" above, pp. 110–16.

[5] That the reference to the tribe of Benjamin (cf. Phil 3:5) is the result of Paul's pride in his particular genealogy (Käsemann 1980:299) seems an overly psychological explanation.

recognized that a scriptural allusion is embedded in Paul's question and answer, although a textual difficulty has often obscured the full import of Paul's allusion for his argument in Romans 11. Whereas the majority of early manuscripts read λαόν in Romans 11:1, 𝔓⁴⁶ (joined by F G it^{b,f,g,x} Ambrose, Ambrosiaster, Pelagius, and the Gothic) has κληρονομίαν. In a recent article, Mark Given has shown that despite the decision of NA²⁷ to "incline after the majority," a strong case can be made that κληρονομίαν is the better reading.[6] It is far more plausible that a scribe changed an original κληρονομίαν to λαόν under the influence of the parallel phrase in v. 2 than that the reverse movement occurred,[7] especially when it is remembered that the term κληρονομία is not part of Paul's normal vocabulary.[8] It appears elsewhere in Paul's undisputed letters only once[9] and, in all of Pauline literature, only one other time does it refer to *God's* inheritance (Eph 1:18).[10] As in the case of Romans 9:26, discussed above, 𝔓⁴⁶ and a few Western witnesses preserve the original text of a quotation or allusion to scripture.[11]

Restoring the reading κληρονομίαν brings into clearer focus both the identity of Paul's scriptural precursors and the significance of this allusion for Paul's larger argument in Romans 9–11 concerning God's faithfulness to Israel. As to the source of Paul's language, it is widely recognized that Paul's question and answer closely mirror the wording of an assertion found twice in the LXX, "The Lord will not reject his people" (οὐκ ἀπώσεται κύριος τὸν λαὸν αὐτοῦ, 1 Kgdms 12:22; Ps 93:14). In order to fit these words into the context of his argument, Paul changes ἀπωθέω from the future to the aorist (see Fig. 4.1).[12] He further substitutes ὁ θεός for κύριος, in keeping with

---

[6] Given 1999. Zuntz 1953 does not discuss this passage.

[7] Note that 𝔓⁴⁶ ℵ² A D* have added ὃν προέγνω to 11:1 from the parallel phrase in 11:2.

[8] Metzger (1994:464) considers κληρονομίαν to be "a Western assimilation to Ps 94:14 [= LXX 93:14]." However, as I will show below, there are good reasons to think that the allusive appeal to Psalm 93:14 is part of Paul's own argument. On the importance of 𝔓⁴⁶ and of Western witnesses for the text of Paul's epistles, see p. 84 n. 126.

[9] Gal 3:18.

[10] Cf. Lincoln 1990:59–60. The word is found also in Eph 1:14, 18; 5:5; Col 3:24. Given is thus mistaken in asserting that nowhere in the NT (besides Rom 11:1) does κληρονομία refer to the people of God (1999:92).

[11] On Romans 9:26, see pp. 84–85. See also the discussion of Romans 10:20, pp. 206–207.

[12] The variant ἀπώσατο in 1 Kingdoms 12:22, found in the tenth-century minus-

his normal practice of reserving κύριος to refer to Christ.[13] Finally, Paul adds the descriptive clause—brief, but pregnant with meaning—"whom he foreknew."

Figure 4.1: 1 Kingdoms 12:22, Psalm 93:14 LXX, and Romans 11:1–2

Key: *italic*   agreement among all three columns
     double underline   agreement between Rom 11:1–2 and Ps 93:14 only

1 Kgdms 12:22	Romans 11:1–2	Psalm 93:14 LXX
ὅτι οὐκ *ἀπώσεται* *κύριος τὸν λαὸν αὐτοῦ* διὰ τὸ ὄνομα αὐτοῦ τὸ μέγα, ὅτι ἐπιεικέως κύριος προσελάβετο ὑμᾶς αὐτῷ εἰς λαόν.	[2] οὐκ *ἀπώσατο* ὁ θεὸς *τὸν λαὸν αὐτοῦ* ὃν προέγνω. [1] Λέγω οὖν, μὴ ἀπώσατο ὁ θεὸς <u>τὴν κληρονομίαν αὐτοῦ;</u>	ὅτι οὐκ *ἀπώσεται* *κύριος τὸν λαὸν αὐτοῦ* καὶ <u>τὴν κληρονομίαν αὐτοῦ</u> οὐκ ἐγκαταλείψει.

In seeking to pinpoint which of these two biblical passages Paul had in mind, it must be noted that Paul frequently quotes from or alludes to the Psalms,[14] while he draws on the historical books far less often.[15] Moreover, Paul's use of κληρονομία in v. 1 followed by λαός in v. 2 neatly brings together both halves of Psalm 93:14, making a reference to this verse in Romans 11:1–2 virtually certain. On the other hand, the fact that immediately following this allusion Paul takes up a narrative from 3 Kingdoms about Elijah (Romans 11:2b–6) suggests that an allusion to 1 Kingdoms 12 may not be as unlikely as it first appears. Furthermore, in view of the stress laid on Saul's descent from the tribe of Benjamin in the narrative of 1 Kingdoms 8–12,[16] one wonders whether Paul's own reference to his Benjaminite

---

cule 121 (= Brooke-McLean's MS y), almost certainly reflects a secondary harmonization with Romans 11:1–2.

[13] According to the collations of Holmes-Parsons, there are no texts of the LXX showing the variant reading ὁ θεός in either Psalm 93:14 or in 1 Kingdoms 12:22. Likewise, there is no Hebrew evidence for a reading other than יהוה in these verses.

[14] Paul quotes the Psalms about twenty times, more than any other single biblical book except Isaiah (about twenty-eight times). See further Koch 1986:21–24.

[15] Rom 11:3–4 (3 Kgdms 19:10/14, 18); 1 Cor 1:31 and 2 Cor 10:17 (1 Kgdms 2:10/Jer 9:23–24); 2 Cor 6:18 (2 Kgdms 7:14; 7:8). Cf. Rom 15:9 (Ps 17:50 = 2 Kgdms 22:50).

[16] 1 Kgdms 9:1, 16, 21; 10:20–21. Cf. ἀνὴρ Ιεμιναῖος, 9:1; υἱὸς Ιεμιναίου, 9:21.

lineage represents a subtle nod in the direction of this story concerning his illustrious namesake.[17]

It may in fact be rather flat-footed to attempt to pin Paul's allusion down to one of these two biblical passages to the exclusion of
the other. The preceding chapters have offered abundant evidence
of Paul's intimate acquaintance with Israel's scriptures and his ability to bring together quite distant passages on the basis of shared
terminology and themes. It would not be at all remarkable if Paul
were aware that the phrase he borrowed belonged to *both* Psalm 93
and 1 Kingdoms 12 and if his allusion were intended to evoke *both*
contexts to some degree. For, as we will see, the two passages are
rooted in the same foundational narrative of God's relationship to
Israel.

God's Inheritance: Psalm 93

Like so many of the scriptural texts on which Paul draws in Romans
9–11,[18] Psalm 93 portrays a state of division and conflict within
Israel. In such a situation, God's vindication of the righteous is understood by the biblical author to entail judgment on those among
God's people who have been unfaithful. The psalmist cries desperately for God to rise up and judge the wicked within Israel[19] who
are destroying the righteous (Ps 93:1–7). The extent of their law-
lessness comes to light in their outrageous treatment of the weak and
the defenseless, those singled out in Deuteronomic tradition for special protection: the widow, the stranger, and the orphan.[20] The poet
urges God to take action by reminding him that it is *God's* inheritance, *God's* people, that the unrighteous are ravaging (93:5). Yet
through his lament, the psalmist attains a renewed assurance that
God will act to vindicate the righteous ones who hold faithfully to

---

Note also the identification of Saul as ἄνδρα ἐκ φυλῆς Βενιαμίν in Acts 13:21, part
of a speech attributed by the author of Luke-Acts to Paul.

[17] N. T. Wright comments, "We should not miss the deliberate 'echo' in 11.2
of 1 Sam 12.22, in which another Saul, from the tribe of Benjamin, was in himself the evidence that 'God had not forsaken his people'" (1991:247 n. 39).

[18] E.g., Isa 8, 28–29, 65; 3 Kgdms 19; Ps 68.

[19] The psalmist terms them "the proud," v. 2; "sinners," v. 3; "workers of law-
lessness," vv. 4, 16; "fools," v. 8; "evildoers," v. 16; "a lawless throne," v. 20. Verse
8 (ἄφρονες ἐν τῷ λαῷ) makes it clear that they are Israelites rather than foreign
oppressors.

[20] See Deut 10:18; 14:29; 16:11, 14; 24:17, 19, 20, 21; 26:12–13; 27:19;
Ps 145:9 LXX; Zech 7:10; Mal 3:5; Jer 7:6; 22:3; Ezek 22:7.

God's law (vv. 12–13), and he emphatically affirms: "God will not reject his people; his inheritence he will not abandon."[21] God will ensure that "all those right in heart" will be delivered by his righteous judgment.[22]

The designation of Israel as God's personal "inheritance" (κληρονομία, Ps 93:5, 14), a metaphor that appears frequently throughout Israel's scriptures,[23] is particularly significant for Paul's argument in Romans 11. In calling Israel God's "inheritance," Paul, like the psalmist, taps into one of the cultural narratives that shaped Israel's understanding of its special relationship to God: the story that out of all the nations, God chose Israel to be his own particular possession.[24] Indeed, this is not the first time Paul's argument has presumed this foundational narrative. It is the vivid retelling of this story in Deuteronomy 32:8–9, which pictures God parcelling out the nations among the heavenly court, but reserving Israel for himself as his own portion,[25] that accounts for the scandalous nature of the announcement that God has now chosen Gentiles in order to make Israel jealous (Deut 32:21 in Rom 10:19). In employing the designation κληρονομία for Israel in Romans 11:1, Paul once again draws on the foundational convictions that underlie Moses' Song, this time in

---

[21] ὅτι οὐκ ἀπώσεται κύριος τὸν λαὸν αὐτοῦ καὶ τὴν κληρονομίαν αὐτοῦ οὐκ ἐγκαταλείψει (v. 14).

[22] ἕως οὗ δικαιοσύνη ἐπιστρέψῃ εἰς κρίσιν καὶ ἐχόμενοι αὐτῆς πάντες οἱ εὐθεῖς τῇ καρδίᾳ (v. 15).

[23] In the LXX, κληρονομία occurs numerous times as a term for Israel, often in parallel with λαός: Deut 32:9; 1 Kgdms 10:1; 3 Kgdms 8:51, 53; 4 Kgdms 21:14; Esther C8 [13:15]; C16 [14:5]; C20 [14:9]; F9 [10:12]; Jdt 13:5; Ps 27:9; 32:12; 77:62, 71; 93:5, 14; 105:4–5, 40; Sir 24:12; Micah 7:14; Joel 2:17; 3:2; Isa 19:25 (LXX!); 47:6; 63:17; Jer 12:7–9. Note the employment of similar expressions for Israel as God's portion or possession: κλῆρος (Deut 9:29; Esth C10 [13:17]); μερίς (Deut 9:26; 32:9; Esth C9 [13:16]; 2 Macc 1:26; 14:15; 3 Macc 6:3; Sir 17:17; 24:12; Zech 2:8; Jer 12:10; 28:19 [51:19 MT]); λαὸς περιούσιος (Exod 19:5; 23:22; Deut 7:6; 14:2; 26:18); περιουσασμός (Ps 134:4); περιποίησις (Mal 3:17).

[24] E.g., Exod 19:5; 23:22 [LXX]; 33:16; Lev 20:24, 26; Deut 7:6, 14; 10:15; 14:2; 26:19; 28:1. Several texts explicitly identify God's apportioning Israel to himself with the calling of the patriarchs or with the exodus (cf. Deut 9:26–29): 3 Kgdms 8:53; Esth C9 [13:16]; C16 [14:5]. Zechariah 2:12 describes the eschatological restoration of Israel as the reenactment of God's original selection of Israel to be his portion. Meyers and Meyers (1987:187) note that the echo of Deuteronomy 32:8–9 in Zechariah 2:12 is amplified by a further connection between Zechariah 2:8 and Deuteronomy 32:10 (in LXX, κόρη ὀφθαλμοῦ).

[25] ὅτε διεμέριζεν ὁ ὕψιστος ἔθνη, ὡς διέσπειρεν υἱοὺς Ἀδάμ, ἔστησεν ὅρια ἐθνῶν κατὰ ἀριθμὸν υἱῶν θεοῦ, καὶ ἐγενήθη μερὶς κυρίου λαὸς αὐτοῦ Ἰακώβ, σχοίνισμα κληρονομίας αὐτοῦ Ἰσραήλ. Clear echoes of this story are found in Sirach 17:17 and Jubilees 15:31–32 (cf. Dan 10:13, 20, 21; 12:1).

order to emphasize God's immutable commitment to Israel. Thus, as his argument moves on to a new stage in Romans 11, Paul's thought continues to be shaped at a deep level by the grand story he finds in Deuteronomy 32 of God's unshakeable fidelity to Israel.

Even a cursory examination of Second Temple texts reveals that the metaphor of Israel as God's own "inheritance" was a vital component of Israel's self-conception up to and beyond the time of Paul.[26] The significance of the inheritance metaphor is found in the conviction that God has a vested interest in the welfare of Israel and that he will act to redeem and preserve the people he has called to be his own. Moses' final prayer for Israel in Pseudo-Philo's *Liber Antiquitatem Biblicarum* expresses this perspective eloquently:

> And now I beg, may your mercy toward your people and your pity toward your portion (*hereditas*), Lord, be firm; may your long-suffering be directed toward your place upon the chosen nation, because you love them beyond all others. . . . Unless your patience abides, how will your portion (*hereditas*) be secure, unless you be merciful to them? Who will yet be born without sin? Chastize them for a time, but not in anger (*LAB* 19.8–9).[27]

In penitential prayer, the fact that God has chosen Israel as his inheritance allows the plea for restoration and deliverance to be grounded in an appeal to God's commitment to his own glory. So Moses pleads in *LAB* 12:9 after Israel's sin with the golden calf:

> Therefore, if you do not have mercy on your vine, all things, Lord, have been done in vain, and you will have no one to glorify you. . . . And now let your anger be kept from your vine. . . . let not your labor be in vain, and let not your portion (*hereditas*) be sold cheaply.[28]

Likewise, in *LAB* 39:6–7, the Israelites affirm, "Although our sins be abundant, nonetheless his mercy fills the earth," and they pray for deliverance in words that remind God that it is in his own interest to preserve his inheritance, Israel:

---

[26] See *Pss. Sol.* 14:5; *Jub.* 16:8, 17–18; 22:9–10, 15; 33:20; *LAB* 12:9; 19:8–9; 21:2, 4; 27:7; 28:2; 30:4; 39:7; 49:6; *4 Ezra* 8:15–16, 45. Among the Dead Sea Scrolls, note 1QH[a] 14[6].8; 4Q501 line 2; 4Q511 frg. 2 1.5–6; 11QMelch (11Q13) 2.5 (the returnees are "the inheritance of Melchizedek"). Early Christian texts appropriate this metaphor as a description of the church (including Gentiles!): Eph 1:18; Titus 2:14; 1 Pet 2:9.

[27] Jacobson 1996:121–22.

[28] Jacobson 1996:112.

Lord, pay attention to the people that you have chosen, and do not destroy the vine that your right hand has planted, in order that this nation, which you have had from the beginning and always preferred and for whose sake you made the habitable world and which you brought into the land you promised them, should be before you as a portion (*hereditas*); and do not deliver us up before your enemies, Lord.[29]

The inheritance motif, with its confidence that God will protect his special interest in Israel, comprises but a part of a much larger set of convictions widespread in Second Temple Judaism concerning the abiding election of Israel. Thus, even where God's rejection of his people is threatened[30] or lamented,[31] this sense of abandonment eventually leads to renewed hope and trust that despite Israel's sins, God will ultimately turn back and redeem his people.[32] I mention here only a few of the many explicit statements found in post-biblical writings that God will not forsake his people forever:[33]

You will have mercy on the race of Israel forever and you will not reject [them] (*Pss. Sol.* 7:8).[34]

You chose the seed of Abraham above all the nations; you placed your name upon us, Lord, and you will not reject them forever (*Pss. Sol.* 9:9).[35]

I surely know that they will corrupt their ways, and I will abandon them, and they will forget the covenants that I have established with their fathers; but nevertheless I will not forget them forever (*LAB* 13:10).[36]

---

[29] Jacobson 1996:159. See further *LAB* 30:4; 49:6; *4 Ezra* 8:15–16, 45.

[30] Cf. Hos 4:6; Jer 7:29; Ezek 5:11; 11:16; *LAB* 12:4; 13:10; 19:2, 6; 21:1.

[31] Note the frequent complaint in laments that God has "rejected" (ἀπωθέω) his servant or his people: Judg 6:13; LXX Ps 42:2; 43:10, 24; 59:3, 12; 73:7; 76:8; 77:60; 87:15; 88:39; 107:12; Lam 2:7; 5:22; Jonah 2:5; *LAB* 49:3, 6; 54:4.

[32] Texts such as 4 Kgdms 17:20; 21:14; 23:27; 2 Chr 35:19*d* are striking because their announcements that God has rejected his people are followed by no mitigating words of hope. As a result, they completely controvert the expectation that God will preserve his own possession from complete annihilation. In their larger literary settings, however, even these dire pronouncements ultimately give way to hope for a future for Israel (see 4 Kgdms 25:27–30; 2 Chr 36:22–23).

[33] Cf. the conviction expressed in Lamentations 3:31: οὐκ εἰς τὸν αἰῶνα ἀπώσεται κύριος.

[34] σὺ οἰκτιρήσεις τὸ γένος Ισραηλ εἰς τὸν αἰῶνα καὶ οὐκ ἀπώσῃ.

[35] σὺ ᾑρετίσω τὸ σπέρμα Αβρααμ παρὰ πάντα τὰ ἔθνη καὶ ἔθου τὸ ὄνομά σου ἐφ᾽ ἡμᾶς, κύριε, καὶ οὐκ ἀπώσῃ εἰς τὸν αἰῶνα (Rahlfs 1935, following von Gebhardt's emendation).

[36] . . . *et ego tamen non in sempiternum obliviscar eos* (ET, Jacobson 1996:114).

Behold now the Lord will be favorably disposed to you today, not because of you but because of his covenant that he established with your fathers and the oath that he swore not to abandon you forever (*LAB* 30:7).[37]

I know that God will not reject us forever, nor will he hate his people for all generations. . . . For even if our sins are many, nevertheless his long-suffering will not fail (*LAB* 49:3).[38]

You made an everlasting covenant with [Abraham] and promised him that you would never forsake his seed (*4 Ezra* 3:15).[39]

This brief survey has revealed only the tip of the iceberg; nevertheless, the implications for our reading of Romans 11:1–2 are as clear as they are profound. When set against the broad backdrop of contemporary Jewish understandings of Israel's election and heard in concert with the scriptural citations Paul has repeatedly employed in Romans 9–10—citations whose wider contexts reverberate with the motif of God's unshakeable commitment to Israel—Paul's question, "God hasn't rejected his *inheritance*, has he?" all but answers itself before μὴ γένοιτο escapes his lips.

Israel's King: 1 Kingdoms 8–12

While the term κληρονομία and its associated ideas constitute the primary point of contact between Romans 11 and Psalm 93, it is the depiction of Israel's unfaithfulness in the larger narrative surrounding 1 Kingdoms 12:22 that provides a number of interesting parallels with Paul's portrayal of Israel in Romans. Taken in conjunction with the verbal link between Romans 11:1–2 and 1 Kingdoms 12:22, these parallels strengthen the case for hearing in Paul's question and answer a recollection of this scriptural story of Israel's misguided quest for deliverance apart from exclusive reliance on God's righteousness.

Chapters 8–12 of 1 Kingdoms (1 Samuel, MT) narrate the monumental transition of leadership from Samuel, the last of the judges, to Saul, the first king. The rather tortuous fashion in which the tale

---

[37] . . . *pro . . . iuramento quod iuravit, ut non desereret vos usque in finem* (ET, Jacobson 1996:146).

[38] *Scio enim quia non in finem nos abiciet Deus, neque in generationem odiet populum suum . . .* (ET, Jacobson 1996:174).

[39] *Et disposuisti ei testamentum aeternum et dixisti ei, ut non umquam derelinquas semen eius* (ET, Metzger 1983:528, slightly altered).

is told betrays a deep ambivalence about the inauguration of the kingship in Israel.[40] In its final form,[41] the narrative depicts Israel's desire for a king as a great evil; it is an idolatrous rejection of the Lord as their rightful king and sole deliverer (1 Kgdms 8:7). It is also an implicit denial of their status as God's elect people: "We too will be like all the nations" (8:20).[42]

The narrative of 1 Kingdoms 8–12 stresses that the cause of Israel's unfaithfulness is their chronic failure to trust God alone for deliverance. As Samuel's climactic recitation of God's "righteousness" shows, God has always been faithful to save his people from their enemies (1 Kgdms 12:6–11).[43] Yet despite these great deeds of deliverance, Israel has repeatedly abandoned God and turned to deliverers of their own choosing, whether the gods of the nations around them or, in the present instance, a human king (1 Kgdms 8:8; 12:9–10).[44] In this light, Paul's claim that by striving to establish "their own righteousness," Israel has resisted God's "righteousness," effected through his chosen deliverer, Christ (Rom 10:3–4), bears a striking resemblance to the charge leveled by Samuel that in seeking a king for themselves, Israel has rejected the Lord as their king and only savior (1 Kgdms 10:19; cf. 8:7).[45]

---

[40] The epic account of Samuel's secret anointing of Saul to be king (9:1–10:16), of the selection of the reluctant Saul by lot in the presence of all the tribes of Israel (10:17–27), of the new king's first great victory (11:1–13), and of the celebratory reaffirmation of Saul's kingship (11:14–15) is bounded and punctuated by bitter remonstrances against Israel for seeking a king in the first place (8:6–18; 10:18–19; 12:7–18).

[41] I.e., the form of the narrative that a first-century audience would have known. For analysis of the manner in which the canonical narrative juxtaposes and finally reconciles these conflicting perspectives on the kingship, see McCarthy 1973; Clements 1974; Mayes 1978; Birch 1976.

[42] καὶ ἐσόμεθα καὶ ἡμεῖς κατὰ πάντα τὰ ἔθνη. Cf. 8:5, καθὰ καὶ τὰ λοίπα ἔθνη.

[43] It is clear from the relative clause modifying "righteousness" in 12:7 that δικαιοσύνη carries the connotation, "power and faithfulness to deliver," for "all the Lord's righteousness" (τὴν πᾶσαν δικαιοσύνην κυρίου) refers to "the things he did among you and your ancestors" (ἃ ἐποίησεν ἐν ὑμῖν καὶ ἐν τοῖς πατράσιν ὑμῶν). Samuel's proclamation of the Lord's δικαιοσύνη recalls the Lord's own two earlier brief narrations of Israel's history (1 Kgdms 8:8; 10:18). As in these earlier accounts, so here the exodus from Egypt and the conquest of the Land stand as the foremost examples of the Lord's power and faithfulness to deliver the people he chose for himself (12:8). So pivotal is the exodus for establishing the nature of the Lord's relationship to Israel that Samuel appeals to this event as revelatory of God's very character (12:6).

[44] McCarter (1980:214) notes that the Deuteronomist punctuates his larger narrative with a series of speeches limning Israel's long history of apostasy (e.g., Josh 23–24; 1 Kgs 8:12–61).

[45] It is interesting to note the ironic inversion in Romans 9–11 of Israel's desire

Paul's stubborn insistence that despite Israel's resistence to the righteousness of God as revealed in the gospel, God remains committed to redeem his people also finds an important parallel in the narrative of 1 Kingdoms 8–12. In the face of Israel's outright rejection of God as king and deliverer, Samuel amazingly reaffirms the Lord's continuing faithfulness to Israel. In words later appropriated by Paul, the prophet avows, "God will not reject his people" (1 Kgdms 12:22). Undergirding Samuel's confidence that God remains committed to Israel is the same foundational narrative that lies behind Psalm 93, that God has freely chosen Israel to be his own special possession: "God will not reject his people for the sake of his great name,[46] for in kindness the Lord brought you near to be his own people" (1 Kgdms 12:22; cf. 10:1). Heard in concert with 1 Kingdoms 12:22, Paul's additional modifier, ". . . his people *whom he foreknew*" (ὃν προέγνω), takes on rich scriptural resonances, for it corresponds to the reasons given by Samuel for God's unquenchable love for Israel. Like his scriptural predecessors, Paul is unshakeable in his conviction that God's election of Israel depends ultimately not on Israel's faithfulness, but only on God's grace and mercy—which never fail.

Did Paul expect that his listeners would catch his allusion to the kingship narrative of 1 Kingdoms 8–12? It is difficult to express much confidence on this point, given what little we know about Paul's audience in Rome. Paul himself does not seem to have made extensive use of this narrative in his teaching; at least, it appears nowhere else in his extant writings.[47] Those whose early training included immersion in Israel's scriptures may well have recognized the narrative source of Paul's wording and, upon reflection, appre-

---

to be like the other nations in having a human king—a request tantamount to denying their elect status as God's own special people (1 Kgdms 8:5, 20). Paul's argument in Romans insinuates that Israel's resistance to the gospel is due in large part by a desire *not* to be like the ἔθνη in depending on God's righteousness offered in Christ to all who believe. Instead, they prefer "their own righteousness," that is, the distinctive observances of the Law that effectively isolate Jews from the ἔθνη and keep the non-observant outside the bounds of the people of God.

[46] That Israel's hope of redemption rests on God's commitment to the glory of his name, rather than on their own worthiness, is a common theme in prayers and in prophetic texts: E.g., Ps 25:11; 31:4; 43:27 [LXX]; 79:9; 106:8; 109:21; 143:11; Pr Azar 11; Isa 43:25; 48:9, 11; Jer 14:21; Ezek 20:44; 36:21–23; 39:25; Dan 9:19.

[47] NA[27] suggests an echo of 1 Kingdoms 12:5–6 (μάρτυς κύριος) in Romans 1:9 (μάρτυς γάρ μού ἐστιν ὁ θεός), but surely, in the absence of further evidence, the use of such a common oath formula makes a link with a particular text extremely tenuous.

ciated the figurative possibilities latent in Paul's allusion. Others with less knowledge of Israel's scriptures, but who were familiar with the stories Jews told about their election as God's special people may have recognized a scriptural-sounding affirmation of that election. In any case, it is not necessary to suppose that Paul's words would have been readily comprehended as an allusion to scripture or that their source would have been widely recognized in order to think it possible that Paul's own confidence in God's immutable commitment to Israel and his understanding of his apostolic role have been shaped by careful reflection on this pivotal episode in the narrative of God's past dealings with Israel.

Elijah and the Chosen Remnant of Israel: Romans 11:2b–6

I have suggested thus far that in Romans 11:1–2 Paul frames his question and presents his initial answer in terms that recall two particularly strong statements (1 Kgdms 12:22; Ps 93:14) of a conviction that permeates Israel's scriptures and traditions: that God remains faithful to his people despite their unfaithfulness. Paul's denial that God has rejected his people thus carries the full weight of a foundational and widely-disseminated narrative of the election of Israel. We saw that in Romans 11:2 Paul modifies "his people" with a relative clause, "whom he foreknew," a clause that conveys the notion of Israel's gracious election by God. In the context of Romans, however, these words bear an even deeper significance, for they echo Paul's stirring affirmation that those who trust in Christ will, despite present suffering (Rom 8:18), finally share in God's glory:[48]

> The ones *whom he foreknew* he also predestined to become conformed to the image of his son, so that he would be the firstborn among many siblings. And whom he predestined, these he also called; and whom he called, these he also righteoused; and whom he righteoused, these he also glorified.
>
> οὓς προέγνω, καὶ προώρισεν συμμόρφους τῆς εἰκόνος τοῦ υἱοῦ αὐτοῦ, εἰς τὸ εἶναι αὐτὸν πρωτότοκον ἐν πολλοῖς ἀδελφοῖς· οὓς δὲ προώρισεν, τούτους καὶ ἐκάλεσεν· καὶ οὓς ἐκάλεσεν, τούτους καὶ ἐδικαίωσεν· οὓς δὲ ἐδικαίωσεν, τούτους καὶ ἐδόξασεν (Rom 8:29–30).

---

[48] These are the only two occurrences of προγινώσκω in all of Pauline literature. The noun πρόγνωσις never appears in Paul.

As part of an address to a congregation that has put its hope for deliverance in what God has done in Christ, the implication of the little clause "whom he foreknew" in Romans 11:2 is inescapable. The confidence of Paul's hearers in God's mercy toward them in Christ rests on precisely the same foundation as does Israel's assurance of its abiding election—the faithfulness of God. Thus, God's unshakeable commitment to Israel constitutes a crucial underpinning of the eschatological hope of those who trust in Christ. The question Paul poses in Romans 11:1 is one of as much urgency for Paul's hearers as it is for those about whom he writes, for if God cannot be trusted to keep his promises to Israel, Paul's firm conviction that "nothing ... can separate us from the love of God in Christ Jesus our Lord" is no more than a tragic delusion.[49]

Given the immense importance of God's enduring faithfulness to Israel for Paul's entire argument in Romans, it is not surprising that he does not rest content with a bald assertion that God has not forsaken his people—as rich with scriptural and theological resonances as that asseveration may be—but immediately makes an *explicit* appeal to scripture (Rom 11:3–6). In so doing, Paul also anticipates a possible objection to his appeal to himself as empirical evidence of Israel's continuing election: the simple retort that Paul is the only one of his kind, an anomaly whose existence does not refute the charge that God has abandoned Israel as a whole. With these concerns in mind, Paul turns to the episode in the story of Elijah where, after Elijah's dramatic victory over the prophets of Baal and his subsequent ignominious flight to the desert in fear and despair, the prophet encounters God on Mt. Horeb.[50] Paul treats the story as one familiar to his hearers,[51] one whose relevance to his present

---

[49] The problem is eloquently stated in *LAB* 12:9. Pleading with God to forgive Israel their idolatrous worship of the golden calf, Moses reasons:

> Therefore, if you do not have mercy on your vine, all things, Lord, have been done in vain, and you will have no one to glorify you. *For even if you plant another vine, it will not trust you, because you destroyed the former one* (Jacobson 1996:112; emphasis mine).

[50] 3 Kingdoms 19:1–18.

[51] While Paul may be mistaken with regard to the "hearer competence" of some in his audience, it is doubtful that his introduction is merely for rhetorical effect. Paul certainly shapes the audience's perspective on the narrative through his selective retelling, but much of the impact of his appeal to the Elijah story depends on a prior knowledge of its general outline. Cf. my similar observation above with regard to Paul's use of the exodus story in Romans 9:14–18 (p. 54).

argument requires no explanation, and he invites them by his mild rebuke to reflect on the narrative and to draw from it the same conclusions he has drawn: "Or don't you know what the scripture says in the Elijah story, when he petitions God against Israel?" (Rom 11:2).[52]

Nevertheless, Paul's retelling of this story is quite selective.[53] Neglecting many of the details of the narrative, he hones in on Elijah's exchange with the divine voice. Paul's introduction emphasizes the accusatory nature of Elijah's speech, characterizing it as a petition *against* Israel.[54] Elijah complains that all of Israel has turned against God, slaying his prophets and destroying his altars; Elijah is left alone, and they are seeking to kill him.[55] The emphasis of Paul's citation falls on Elijah's claim that because of Israel's apostasy, he alone now constitutes the faithful remnant.[56] The verb ὑπελείφθην recalls Paul's earlier discussion of the remnant (ὑπόλειμμα) God has graciously left (ἐγκατέλιπεν) to Israel (Rom 9:27–29), a remnant that,

---

[52] ἢ οὐκ οἴδατε ἐν Ἠλίᾳ τί λέγει ἡ γραφή, ὡς ἐντυγχάνει τῷ θεῷ κατὰ τοῦ Ἰσραήλ;

[53] Paul quotes from 3 Kingdoms 19:10–18 in Romans 11:3 and from 3 Kingdoms 19:18 in Romans 11:4. It is extremely difficult to reconstruct Paul's *Vorlage* here, in part because of the confusion in the manuscript tradition caused by the nearly (but not quite) parallel complaints of Elijah in 3 Kingdoms 19:10 and 19:14. Paul's citations share a significant number of variants with the readings of certain "Lucianic" minuscules (19–108 127 93 [= Brooke-McLean, bc₂e₂]) in 19:10, 14 and 18. Paul may well depend for his text on a septuagintal text similar to that attested by these manuscripts, although certainty on this point is not possible (see further Stanley 1992b:147–58; 1993b). As a result, I will avoid placing undue weight here on arguments that Paul has altered his *Vorlage*.

[54] ὡς ἐντυγχάνει τῷ θεῷ κατὰ τοῦ Ἰσραήλ. The phrase ἐντυγχάνω κατά τινος is used to describe complaints levelled against the Maccabean ruler Jonathan before king Ptolemy VI (1 Macc 10:61–64) and before Demetrius II (1 Macc 11:25). Similarly 1 Macc 8:32, which envisions an accusation by the Jews against Demetrius I before the Roman Senate. Contrast the very different meaning of the phrase, ἐντυγχάνω ὑπέρ τινος, "to intercede *for* someone" (Rom 8:27, 34; Heb 11:25).

[55] Paul omits "with the sword" (the omission of this phrase by Origen, Justin, and Priscillian most probably reflects dependence on Paul). In addition, Paul alone has the order: kill prophets/destroy altars (again, Origen and Justin likely follow Paul here). If there is any significance to this transposition, it may be that it avoids the implication that Elijah is the sole *prophet* left. In Paul's version, the claim is much broader—Elijah is the sole *Israelite* who remains faithful to the Lord.

[56] Contrast Josephus' retelling of the story (*Ant.* 8.347–54), which emphasizes that Elijah has convinced the people to return to exclusive allegiance to the Lord (πεῖσαι δὲ τὸν λαὸν ὅτι μόνος εἴη θεὸς ὁ ὤν) and that it is Jezebel who is seeking to kill the prophet (350). Later he mentions "the ungodly crowd" (ὁ ἀσεβὴς ὄχλος), but this clearly refers to a minority within Israel (352). Tellingly, Josephus omits Elijah's repeated complaint that he alone remains faithful to the Lord.

although it is the product of divine judgment, yet holds out the hope of Israel's continued survival. The urgency and pathos of Elijah's complaint arises from his belief that the faithful of Israel have been cut down to a remnant of one and that the elimination of the sole survivor—and thus the extinction of all Israel—is imminent.

It is tempting to find in this passage a self-reference by Paul to his own isolated and persecuted state (cf. Rom 15:31).[57] Such an "Elijah complex," however, is far from evident in the way Paul actually employs this passage in Romans 11. Rather than identifying with Elijah's view of the remnant, Paul emphatically rejects it as a profound misperception of the depth of God's commitment to preserve his people. In 11:4, he appeals to the divine response to Elijah precisely to insist that he himself is *not* the sole Israelite who has believed the gospel, but that by God's grace there exists even now a significantly larger "remnant" of Israel. Passing over the commissioning of Elijah to anoint rulers over Syria and Israel and to appoint a prophetic successor (the purpose of which is to ensure the destruction of the idolators in Israel, 3 Kgdms 19:15–17), Paul zeroes in on the divine rebuttal of Elijah's charge that he alone has remained faithful to the Lord: "I have reserved for myself seven thousand who have not bowed the knee to Baal" (3 Kgdms 19:18/Rom 11:4).

Paul shapes the wording of the divine reply[58] so as to emphasize God's own deep commitment to preserving Israel as his very own people. Several points are worth noting. First, the crucial pronoun, ἐμαυτῷ ("for myself"), which in all likelihood represents a Pauline addition to the text, reprises the powerful motif of Israel as God's personal inheritance sounded just previously by Paul's scriptural allusions in Rom 11:1–2.[59] Although Elijah accuses Israel before God of heinous deeds, God affirms that he has not cast off the people he has chosen for himself. Moreover, it is clear from Paul's retelling that God has not waited for Elijah to persuade him to act; he does not need to be encouraged to deliver his people. The phrase, "I have reserved for myself," stresses God's own initiative in preserv-

---

[57] So Käsemann 1980:301; Dunn 1988b:637; Wright 1996.

[58] Paul's word choice, ὁ χρηματισμός (a NT *hapax*; though cf. Rom 3:2), may reflect the marked reticence of the narrative in 3 Kingdoms to specify the nature of the Lord's appearance to Elijah (cf. Hanson 1972–73; Dunn 1988b:637).

[59] B. N. Fisk notes, "It is just possible that Paul's addition of ἐμαυτῷ was influenced by the final phrase of 1 Sam 12:22: ὅτι ἐπιεικέως προσελάβετο ὑμᾶς αὑτῷ εἰς λαόν" (1997:330 n. 38).

ing a remnant who have not succumbed to idolatry. Unbeknownst
to the prophet, God has *already* taken steps to ensure Israel's survival as the people of God.[60] Finally, it is hardly insignificant for
Paul's argument that the remnant in 3 Kingdoms 19:18 is fairly substantial in number. Elijah fears that he alone is left; God reveals to
him that there are seven thousand whose existence Elijah has not
even imagined. Echoes in Romans 11 of the "still, small voice" that
spoke to Elijah imply that even though Paul may not be able to
point to a great multitude of Jews who have confessed Jesus as Lord,
the "remnant in the present time" is far more numerous than Paul
himself knows.

In his interpretive comments on the narrative (οὕτως οὖν, v. 5),
Paul explicitly draws attention to the first two of the three points I
have just noted. First, he emphasizes that this "remnant" is not a
future expectation, but a present reality (ἐν τῷ νῦν καιρῷ) testifying
to God's unbroken commitment to Israel. Paul's resumption of "remnant" language in Romans 11:3–5 recalls the words of Isaiah he
quoted earlier (Rom 9:27–29), which speak of God's preservation of
a "remnant" and "seed" for Israel. It is clear that Paul understands
Isaiah's words to refer to the present time: Isaiah's τὸ ὑπόλειμμα
σωθήσεται, "a remnant *will* be saved," is realized in Paul's own day
as λεῖμμα κατ' ἐκλογὴν χάριτος γέγονεν.

As we have already seen, the concept of a remnant in post-exilic
Judaism was one that normally held out hope for the future restoration of the entire nation of Israel.[61] I argued earlier that, when heard
in this cultural and historical context, Isaiah's promise of a "remnant" and "seed" in Romans 9:27–29 adumbrates Paul's conclusion
in Romans 11:26 that "all Israel will be saved." In Romans 11, the
link between the remnant and the restoration of "all Israel" in Paul's
thought becomes much clearer. While it still remains an open question

---

[60] The majority of manuscripts read καταλείψεις (cf. καταλείψῃς, jxy). The first
person future, καταλείψω (which corresponds to MT, וְהִשְׁאַרְתִּי), appears in the
"Lucianic" minuscules bc₂e₂, while only one minuscule, i, reads the first person
aorist form found in Paul, κατέλιπον. If Paul is not responsible for the first-person
verb, it is still quite possible that he has changed the verb to the aorist (as with
ἀπώσατο, 11:1–2) in order to portray the action as a *fait accompli* rather than a
future expectation (cf. Paul's interpretive comment, "in the present time," 11:5).

[61] See pp. 108–16 and the literature cited there. In the context of God's reply
to Elijah in 3 Kingdoms 19, the remnant must be seen ultimately as a sign of the
nation's restoration. The Lord commissions Elijah to appoint rulers and a prophetic
successor who will destroy the idolators and turn Israel back to their God.

at this point in Paul's argument whether the existence of the remnant is a temporary condition or a permanent one, it will not be long before the apostle's expectation of a renewal of Israel as a whole begins to surface in his argument in more explicit terms (11:11ff.).

The second point to which Paul directs his hearers' attention concerns the gracious initiative of God in preserving this remnant. Although one might suggest that the seven thousand were saved *because* they did not bow the knee to Baal, Paul forecloses this interpretive option by taking the words, "I have reserved for myself," to mean that the existence of the remnant depends on God's sovereign and gracious election alone. It is a remnant κατ᾽ ἐκλογὴν χάριτος (11:5). Since it is by grace, Paul argues, election cannot be based on "works" at all, else grace would cease to be grace (11:6).[62]

Significantly, rather than employing his more usual pair of opposites, "works" versus "faith," Paul here contrasts "works" with "grace." It is widely agreed that where Paul opposes "works of the Law" to "faith," his primary target is the particular covenant practices distinctive to Israel that functioned (wrongly, in his view) to exclude Gentiles from full membership in the people of God.[63] By exalting "faith" over "works of the Law," Paul seeks the inclusion of Jews and Gentiles in the people of God on the same basis.

In Romans 11:5-6, however, the focus has shifted to a more radical denial that human works of *any* kind (not just "works of the Law") can serve as the basis for God's election.[64] The apostle appeals again to the principle enunciated earlier by means of the story of Jacob and Esau in Romans 9:11-13. Indeed, there are unmistakable similarities between these two passages in language as well as in thought:

> When they were not yet born, and they had not done anything good or evil, so that the purpose of God according to election (ἡ κατ᾽ ἐκλογὴν πρόθεσις τοῦ θεοῦ) might stand—not from works (ἐξ ἔργων) but from

---

[62] Compare Paul's line of reasoning in Romans 4:3-5.

[63] The opposition of ἔργα νόμου to πίστις/πιστεύω occurs in Gal 3:7-10, Rom 3:20-22b, and Rom 3:28; in addition, ἔργα in Rom 4:2, 6 should probably be understood as shorthand for ἔργα νόμου (cf. Moo 1983a:94-96). In Gal 3:2 and 5, Paul contrasts ἔργα νόμου with ἀκοὴ πίστεως. In several texts, the contrast is between ἔργα νόμου and πίστις Ἰησοῦ Χριστοῦ (Gal 2:16 [2x]); Rom 3:20-22a; cf. Philippians 3:9 (νόμος v. πίστις Χριστοῦ). Elsewhere, ἔργα and πίστις describe two understandings of or approaches to the Law (Rom 3:27; 9:32).

[64] Cf. E. P. Sanders 1983:166 n. 40. See further I. H. Marshall 1996:356-58.

the one who calls—it was said to her, "The older will serve the younger" (Rom 9:11–13).

So now in the present time a remnant has come into being according to the election of grace (λεῖμμα κατ' ἐκλογὴν χάριτος γέγονεν)—and if by grace, then no longer from works (ἐξ ἔργων), otherwise grace would no longer be grace (Rom 11:5–6).

In Paul's view, the grace shown to the remnant of Israel—like Israel's election in the first place—depends on nothing but God's own good pleasure.

It is absolutely crucial to note what Paul does *not* do, at this point, however. Having emphasized again the sovereign freedom of God in election, Paul does not return here to his opening move, "not all from Israel are Israel," in order to claim that "the remnant at the present time" is coterminous with "Israel." Although he proceeds to speak of the remnant as "the elect" of Israel, as opposed to "the rest" who were "rendered insensible" (11:7), Paul does not ultimately collapse Israel into the remnant or call "the elect" by the name "Israel."[65] Rather, as the rest of the chapter will make clear, "Israel" is an eschatological category for Paul. The remnant is the "offering of firstfruits," the earnest of a much greater harvest to come (11:16). The existence of an elect remnant (ἡ ἐκλογή) in the present is thus for Paul a sign of God's continuing election of Israel, for ultimately, God's redemptive purpose encompasses "all Israel" (11:26). Even those who now, in God's mysterious design, are considered "enemies with respect to the gospel for the sake of you [Gentiles]" are yet "beloved with respect to election (κατὰ δὲ τὴν ἐκλογὴν ἀγαπητοί) for the sake of the patriarchs" (11:28).

Before leaving the Elijah narrative, it is important to note how the depiction of Israel in this story fits with the portrait of his kinspeople that Paul has been painting throughout Romans 9–11 by means of scriptural quotations. As in earlier texts from Isaiah 8,

---

[65] Note that from here until 11:25, Paul does not use the term "Israel," but instead refers to "them." Having made a distinction within "Israel" between "the remnant" and "the rest" (11:7), he does not disinherit either group by employing the term to refer exclusively to one party or the other. This observation will prove crucial for understanding what Paul means by "all Israel" in 11:26. Like Paul, the Qumran covenanters did not consider themselves the sum total of eschatological Israel. They were reluctant "to deny to the unconverted the title 'Israel' and to appropriate it for a new group or sub-group" (E. P. Sanders 1983:176). Moreover, the covenanters expected many Israelites not currently part of the sect to join them in the last days (see further E. P. Sanders 1977:244–55; Huebsch 1981).

28–29, 65, and Psalm 93, so in 3 Kingdoms 19 Israel is a nation profoundly divided. A small band of those who have remained faithful to Israel's God stand in opposition to the majority, who have placed their hope in other gods. The denunciation of Israel as idolatrous is a curiously persistent motif in many of the texts appropriated by Paul in Romans 9–11 to explain Israel's current plight. The sin of idolatry is particularly prominent in the Elijah story. But for the remnant, Israel has forsaken the Lord and gone over to Baal. Interestingly, idolatry appears as an important theme in all three of the texts that Paul has most recently quoted or evoked by allusion: 1 Kingdoms 8–12, Isaiah 65, and Deuteronomy 32.[66]

All of this remains just below the surface of Paul's argument, however. Paul never openly accuses his own people of idolatry, and certainly his contemporaries scrupulously avoided and despised the gross idolatries of the pagan world into which Paul's Gentile converts were prone to relapse. If the charge of idolatry surfaces at all in Romans 9–11, it does so having been transposed into another key, in the form of Paul's critique that in pursuing "their own righteousness," Israel has refused to submit to "God's righteousness" (10:1–4). Israel of old sought deliverance in other gods, rather than trusting in and submitting to God's righteousness—that is, God's power and faithfulness to deliver his people. The new idol, from Paul's perspective, is Israel's blind devotion to its version of Law observance, which prevents them from perceiving in Christ the revelation of "the righteousness of God" to which the Law has been pointing all along.

"The Remnant" and "The Rest": Romans 11:7

Although Israel, pursuing the Law "as if from works" (ὡς ἐξ ἔργων, 9:32), has stumbled and so has failed to attain the promise of righteousness that is their inheritance, a remnant within Israel, by God's grace, *has obtained* in Christ the righteousness that is the τέλος of the Law (10:4). Paul earlier marveled at the paradox that the righteousness for which Israel is so zealously, though misguidedly, striving has been granted to outsiders—Gentiles who were not even pursuing

---

[66] Israel's idolatrous past has also come into view through Paul's allusion to the golden calf episode at the opening of Romans 9 (9:3; cf. 9:15) and through his subsequent quotations from Hosea 1–2 and Isaiah 1, 8, 10, 28.

Figure 4.2: Romans 9:30–31 and Romans 11:7

Romans 9:30–31	Romans 11:7 (altered)
³⁰ Τί οὖν ἐροῦμεν; ὅτι ἔθνη τὰ μὴ διώκοντα δικαιοσύνην κατέλαβεν δικαιοσύνην, δικαιοσύνην δὲ τὴν ἐκ πίστεως, ³¹ Ἰσραὴλ δὲ διώκων νόμον δικαιοσύνης εἰς νόμον οὐκ ἔφθασεν.	Τί οὖν; ἡ δὲ ἐκλογὴ ἐπέτυχεν (ὃ ἐπιζητεῖ Ἰσραήλ)· ὃ ἐπιζητεῖ Ἰσραήλ, τοῦτο οὐκ ἐπέτυχεν . . . οἱ δὲ λοιποὶ ἐπωρώθησαν

righteousness in the first place (9:30–31). Now, with Gentiles entirely out of the picture, Paul portrays a strikingly parallel state of affairs *within* Israel: "What then? That which Israel is seeking, they did not attain; the elect (ἡ ἐκλογή), however, did attain it. The rest were rendered insensible" (11:7).

The parallels between these two passages (Fig. 4.2) are neither accidental nor insignificant. Seen from the vantage point of Romans 11:7, it becomes clear that the situation Paul described in Romans 9:30–31, in which some Gentiles have now laid hold of the righteousness Israel has failed to grasp, is for Paul but a part of a much larger theological problem: namely, that only a remnant of Israel has thus far attained the righteousness that all of Israel has been seeking. As Paul tracks the outworking of God's design to redeem the entire cosmos, the division that is most problematic for him is not that between "some Gentiles" and "Israel," but the more fundamental rift between "the remnant of Israel in the present time" and "the rest of Israel." Although Gentiles do enter into the saga of God's relationship to Israel, they do so in a supporting role. The main plot line in Romans 9–11 remains the suspenseful story of how God is going about making good on his promises to redeem his people Israel.

Hearing Romans 11:7 and Romans 9:30–31 together further supports the view I advocated throughout my earlier analysis of Paul's use of scripture in Romans 9–10, that in Paul's rereading of texts such as Hosea 1:10; 2:23 and Isaiah 65:1–2, the Gentiles whom God has called never displace Israel as the recipients of God's promises of redemption. Because God's promises to Israel remain valid, though as yet unfulfilled, it is not enough for Paul to identify the present remnant with Israel and dismiss the rest as hopelessly reprobate. In order to maintain God's faithfulness to Israel, he must first explain what has happened to the majority of God's people in the present time and then show that God has intended even this tragic event to result in the ultimate salvation of "all Israel."

THE DIVINE BLINDING OF "THE REST" OF ISRAEL: ROMANS 11:7–10

In explaining what has happened to "the rest" of Israel, Paul does not shrink from the implications of the high view of God's sovereignty that he developed in Romans 9.[67] Why have "the rest" of Israel failed to attain what they were seeking? It is because *God* has made them insensible.[68] But as was the case in the elaborate blend-

---

[67] See, for example, the language of "will," "authority," and "power" in Romans 9:14–23, and particularly the metaphor of potter and clay as a way of speaking about God's relationship to Israel.

[68] Although πωρόω is frequently translated, "to harden" (e.g., RSV, NRSV, NASB, NIV), J. A. Robinson demonstrated nearly a century ago in his careful study of the word group that "in the New Testament obtuseness or intellectual blindness is the meaning indicated by the context; and this meaning is as a rule assigned by the ancient translators and commentators" (1902:92). Although the technical sense of πωρόω, "cover with a callus," is common in medical writers, the word also developed an extended sense, "to deaden or dull." By the time the word appears in LXX Job 17:7,

> πώρωσις, losing its first sense of petrifaction or hardness, comes to denote the result of petrifaction as metaphorically applied to the organs of feeling, that is, insensibility, and more especially in reference to the organs of sight, obscuration or blindness (Robinson 1902:82).

Compare the glosses offered by ancient commentators (collected in Schleusner 1822): πεπωρωμένοι = ἐσκληρωμένοι, τετυφλωμένοι; ἐπωρώθησαν = ἐτυφλώθησαν (Hesychius); πεπώρωται = τετύφλωται; πωρός, ὁ τυφλός, καὶ πώρωσις, ἡ τύφλωσις (Suidas). The meaning "insensibility" is recognized by LSJ (s.v. πωρόω, III; πώρωσις, II) and BDAG (s.v. πωρόω, πώρωσις). Despite the impression left by Cranfield's (1979:549) dismissal of Robinson, the latter's argument does not depend primarily on the meaning assigned to πωρόω by ancient translators and commentators. Cranfield fails to engage Robinson's detailed and persuasive discussions of the biblical and secular hellenistic texts themselves, on which Robinson founds his thesis. It would be possible for ἐπωρώθησαν to have the active, intransitive sense, "become insensible" (so LSJ, s.v. πωρόω, III), but this is unlikely in Romans 11:7 in view of the following quotation, which has God as the agent blinding Israel (see below, pp. 242–51). The conceptual parallel with Romans 9:18 would also favor seeing God as the agent of ἐπωρώθησαν.

ing of scriptural quotations with the potter/clay metaphor in Romans 9:14–23, Paul's conception of God's sovereignty is not one of raw power exercised arbitrarily. Rather, the larger context in which Paul understands God's sovereignty is the story of God's gracious commitment to create Israel as a people for himself and through them to bless the Gentiles as well. For Paul, God's sovereignty is inseparable from his righteousness, his absolute faithfulness to the covenant he has freely made with his people. Because God is sovereign, nothing—not even Israel's unfaithfulness—can nullify God's election of Israel or frustrate his plan for their redemption and, with them, the redemption of the cosmos.

That Paul conceives of God's sovereignty within a covenantal context is clearly evidenced by the fact that as Paul fleshes out his statement that "the rest" have been made insensible, he does so by appealing to a larger scriptural narrative of God's dealings with his people (Rom 11:8–10). Paul's quotations here cluster around the motif of the divine blinding of Israel. Significantly, this motif is prominent in Isaiah; as well, it is an important part of the story of Israel told in the latter chapters of Deuteronomy. Paul's first quotation combines elements from Isaiah 29:10 and Deuteronomy 29:4.[69] This conflation becomes particularly noteworthy in light of Paul's previous appeal to Moses and Isaiah in Romans 10:19–21 as witnesses testifying together against Israel. As in the latter passage, so also in Romans 11:8 Paul reads the two scriptural texts together so that they interpret one another. As before, the literary and theological contours of their original settings shape Paul's creative appropriation of these texts to speak of contemporary events. In both Isaiah and Deuteronomy, the blinding of Israel is not God's final word, but rather a solemn act of judgment on disobedient Israel that ultimately leads to God's gracious redemption of his people for his name's sake alone.

In order to appreciate fully Paul's reading of these texts as an explanation of the present insensibility of "the rest" of Israel, we must first explore the manner in which Paul has woven these passages together in order to form a single quotation. Close attention to the details of this conflated citation will shed valuable light on

---

[69] I will also suggest that Isaiah 6:9–10 lies not far beneath the surface of Paul's argument here.

Paul's strategy as a reader of scripture and will result in a clearer understanding of how this quotation fits within the larger argument of Romans 11.

Paul introduces his citation with the simple phrase, "just as it is written." Given the absence of a more specific reference, it is likely that many of his hearers in Rome would have had difficulty pinpointing the precise sources. Nonetheless, from the standpoint of this study, which focuses on Paul as interpreter of scripture, it is crucial to note that the reading strategy commended by Paul's rhetoric in Romans 10:19–21—that Moses and Isaiah are to be heard testifying in concert against Israel—now comes into play as Paul conflates the words of these two witnesses into a single scriptural voice. As important as Isaiah and Moses are rhetorically in Romans 9–11 as "characters" testifying *viva voce*, they are ultimately significant for Paul as part of the larger voice of scripture.[70]

As Figure 4.3 shows, Paul's quotation owes more verbally to Deuteronomy 29:4 than to Isaiah 29:10.[71]

The final temporal phrase, "to the present day," taken from Deuteronomy 29:4,[72] is particularly important, for it affords Paul the hermeneutical leverage to treat the citation as a diagnosis of the condition of "the rest" of Israel in his own day. The only explicit trace

---

[70] Cf. J. M. Baumgarten 1992 for a striking formal parallel (and possibly a hermeneutical parallel as well) to Paul's interpretive conflation of texts in Romans 11:8. In 4Q266 frg. 11, lines 3–4 (= 4Q270 frg. 7 1.17–18) we find a citation formula (ועל ישראל כתוב) introducing what is actually a conflated citation of Deuteronomy 30:4 and Leviticus 26:31 (interestingly, the texts come from the two major "curse" sections of the Pentateuch).

[71] The chart is self-explanatory; however, two notes are in order: (1) The divine name probably comes from Deuteronomy 29:4 (the reading ὁ θεός in the Speculum and κύριος ὁ θεός in the Syrohexapla at Isaiah 29:10 are likely due to assimilation to Romans; the reading יהוה אלהיך in the quotation of Isaiah 29:10 in *Sifre Deut* [MS א] §41 is almost certainly a secondary expansion and cannot be used as evidence for Paul's *Vorlage*). (2) The pronoun, which Paul changes from second to third person to fit the context in Romans, could come from either text; in position it corresponds to Isaiah 29:10.

[72] Paul's phrase ἕως τῆς σήμερον ἡμέρας is virtually synonymous with the phrase found in Deuteronomy 29:4, ἕως τῆς ἡμέρας ταύτης. Although the latter formulation is much more common (78x, versus 20x for the former), both occur in the LXX as a translation of the Hebrew that underlies Deuteronomy 29:4, עד־היום הזה. Moreover, in a number of places the two phrases occur in close proximity as alternate translations of the same Hebrew text (e.g., Deut 10:8; 11:4; Josh 22:3, 7; 1 Kgdms 29:3, 6, 8). Paul's version may well be due to his saturation with biblical diction rather than to his use of a variant Greek *Vorlage* or to independent translation from a Hebrew text.

Figure 4.3: Deuteronomy 29:4 LXX and Isaiah 29:10
LXX in Romans 11:8

Key:
single underline	agreement between Rom 11:8 and Deut 29:4
double underline	agreement between Rom 11:8 and Isa 29:10
italic	agreement among all three columns

Deuteronomy 29:4 LXX	Romans 11:8	Isaiah 29:10 LXX
καὶ οὐκ <u>ἔδωκεν</u> κύριος <u>ὁ θεὸς</u> ὑμῖν καρδίαν εἰδέναι	καθὼς γέγραπται· <u>ἔδωκεν</u> αὐτοῖς <u>ὁ θεὸς</u> <u>πνεῦμα</u> <u>κατανύξεως</u>,	ὅτι πεπότικεν ὑμᾶς κύριος <u>πνεύματι</u> <u>κατανύξεως</u> καὶ καμμύσει
καὶ *ὀφθαλμοὺς* <u>βλέπειν</u> <u>καὶ ὦτα</u> <u>ἀκούειν</u> *ἕως τῆς ἡμέρας* ταύτης	*ὀφθαλμοὺς* τοῦ μὴ <u>βλέπειν</u> <u>καὶ ὦτα</u> τοῦ μὴ <u>ἀκούειν</u>, *ἕως τῆς* σήμερον *ἡμέρας*	τοὺς *ὀφθαλμοὺς* αὐτῶν καὶ τῶν προφητῶν αὐτῶν καὶ τῶν ἀρχόντων αὐτῶν οἱ ὁρῶντες τὰ κρυπτά

Deut 29:3 MT: וְלֹא־נָתַן יְהוָה לָכֶם לֵב לָדַעַת וְעֵינַיִם לִרְאוֹת וְאָזְנַיִם לִשְׁמֹעַ עַד הַיּוֹם הַזֶּה

Isa 29:10 MT: כִּי־נָסַךְ עֲלֵיכֶם יְהוָה רוּחַ תַּרְדֵּמָה וַיְעַצֵּם אֶת־עֵינֵיכֶם אֶת־הַנְּבִיאִים וְאֶת־רָאשֵׁיכֶם הַחֹזִים כִּסָּה

of Isaiah 29:10 is found in the words πνεῦμα κατανύξεως, a phrase unique to this passage in the LXX.[73] Following the lead of this telling clue, however, it is fairly easy to detect the more pervasive influence of Isaiah 29:10 on the shape of Romans 11:8. With Isaiah 29:10 as catalyst, Moses' lament that God has not intervened to cure Israel's obtuse rebelliousness—"God has not given you a heart to understand and eyes to see and ears to hear"—is transmuted into the much

---

[73] The noun κατάνυξις appears elsewhere only in Psalm 59:5, where the psalmist likens God's judgment on Israel to making them drink strong wine: ἐπότισας ἡμᾶς οἶνον κατανύξεως. Moo's reference to the appearance of this noun in Isaiah 60:3 (1996:682 n. 58) is an error for *Psalm* 60:3 (English numbering for Ps 59:5 LXX). Although it appears more likely that Paul has altered πνεύματι to πνεῦμα in order to go along with the verb δίδωμι, it is just possible that Paul's *Vorlage* read πνεῦμα, as do several extant mss of LXX Isaiah (S 93 309 301 538). It is not clear that these witnesses have all been influenced by Romans, for the double accusative with ποτίζω is found in Gen 19:32 and Sir 15:3 (the accusative-dative pattern occurs in 3 Macc 5:2 as well as in most witnesses to Isaiah 29:10).

stronger claim that Israel's insensibility has been directly *caused by* God: "God has given them a spirit of stupor, eyes such as do not see and ears such as do not hear."[74] God has not merely withheld spiritual insight, he has actively dulled their perception, afflicting them with blind eyes and unhearing ears.

Paul's phraseology (ὀφθαλμοὺς τοῦ μὴ βλέπειν καὶ ὦτα τοῦ μὴ ἀκούειν), though a bit odd, may result simply from negating the infinitives of Deuteronomy 29:4 (and substituting the genitive of the articular infinitive for the anarthrous infinitive). It appears, however, that Paul's syntax was influenced by the phrase, ὀφθαλμοί . . . τοῦ μὴ βλέπειν, in Psalm 68:24, the text that he cites in the very next sentence (Rom 11:10).[75] I will explore the tight network of connections between Paul's citation in Romans 11:8 and that in Romans 11:9–10 shortly. For now, it is enough to note that both quotations attribute the blinding of "the rest" of Israel to God's personal intervention.

Although it is clear that Paul has drawn together Deuteronomy 29:4 and Isaiah 29:10 in Romans 11:8, it is not immediately evident why Paul would have chosen to conflate these two passages in particular. After all, they share only one word in common (ὀφθαλμούς), and the conceptual parallels are not especially striking, particularly since Deuteronomy 29:4 does not attribute Israel's insensibility to God's direct agency. To solve this riddle will require two steps. First, in a bit of "exegetical archaeology," I will unearth the interpretive bridge that may have led Paul from Isaiah 29:10 to Deuteronomy 29:4. Second, I will suggest how Paul's use of these two texts together in Romans 11:8 springs from his reading of the wider literary contexts from which they are excerpted.[76]

Isaiah 6:9–10: Bridge Between the Texts

Although it is nowhere cited explicitly by Paul,[77] Isaiah 6:9–10 serves him as a strategic hermeneutical hub with important verbal and conceptual connections to both Deuteronomy 29:4 and Isaiah 29:10.

---

[74] For the sense of these infinitives, see BDF §400[2]; MHT 3:141.

[75] Moo's claim (1996:681 n. 57) that Paul's syntax has not been shaped at this point by any of the scriptural texts that influence him depends on the commentator's atomistic approach to Paul's use of scripture that overlooks significant interconnections among discrete citations.

[76] The objection that Paul has merely borrowed a pre-formed citation will be answered in what follows by presenting the positive case for Paul's exegetical work as the source for the conflated quotation in Romans 11:8.

[77] Isaiah 6:9–10 figures prominently in several strands of early Christian exege-

⁹And he said, "Go and say to this people: 'Hear a message, and do not understand; see indeed, but do not perceive.' ¹⁰For the heart of this people has grown fat; they hardly hear with their ears, and they have covered their eyes, lest they see with their eyes and hear with their ears and understand with their heart and turn, and I heal them."

⁹ καὶ εἶπε· πορεύθητι καὶ εἶπὸν τῷ λαῷ τούτῳ· ἀκοῇ ἀκούσετε καὶ οὐ μὴ συνῆτε καὶ βλέποντες βλέψετε καὶ οὐ μὴ ἴδητε· ¹⁰ ἐπαχύνθη γὰρ ἡ καρδία τοῦ λαοῦ τούτου, καὶ τοῖς ὠσὶν αὐτῶν βαρέως ἤκουσαν καὶ τοὺς ὀφθαλμοὺς αὐτῶν ἐκάμμυσαν, μήποτε ἴδωσι τοῖς ἰφθαλμοῖς καὶ τοῖς ὠσὶν ἀκούσωσι καὶ τῇ καρδίᾳ συνῶσι καὶ ἐπιστρέψωσι καὶ ἰάσομαι αὐτούς.

The verbal affinities of Isaiah 6:9–10 with Deuteronomy 29:4 are striking. In the entire LXX, the combination "heart-eyes-ears" occurs a mere six times;[78] of these, only Isaiah 6:9–10 and Deuteronomy 29:4 speak of the failure to perceive with heart, eyes, and ears.[79]

Isaiah 6:9–10 shares with Isaiah 29:10 the reference to ὀφθαλμοί as well as the rare verb, καμμύω.[80] More importantly, both texts explicitly attribute the blinding of Israel to God's judgment on the nation.[81] As we have seen, this theological perspective is crucial to Paul's argument, and it is at just this point that Isaiah 29:10 most powerfully shapes Paul's interpretive citation of Deuteronomy 29:4.

---

sis. It is quoted, in whole or in part, in Mark 4:12//Matthew 13:13//Luke 8:10; Matthew 13:14–15; John 12:40; Acts 28:29. See the study of this passage in Jewish and Christian traditions from the perspective of "comparative midrash" in Evans 1989.

[78] Deut 29:4; Isa 6:10; Ezek 40:4; 44:5; Sir 17:6; 38:28.

[79] Close parallels to these two texts are found in Jeremiah 5:21 and Ezekiel 12:2:

ἀκούσατε δὴ ταῦτα, λαὸς μωρὸς καὶ ἀκάρδιος, ὀφθαλμοὶ αὐτοῖς καὶ οὐ βλέπουσιν, ὦτα αὐτοῖς καὶ οὐκ ἀκούουσιν (Jer 5:21).

υἱὲ ἀνθρώπου, ἐν μέσῳ τῶν ἀδικιῶν αὐτῶν σὺ κατοικεῖς, οἳ ἔχουσιν ὀφθαλμοὺς τοῦ βλέπειν καὶ οὐ βλέπουσιν καὶ ὦτα ἔχουσιν τοῦ ἀκούειν καὶ οὐκ ἀκούουσιν, διότι οἶκος παραπικραίνων ἐστίν (Ezek 12:2).

Although it is widely agreed that Ezekiel borrowed heavily from Jeremiah, it is perhaps less clear whether or not Jeremiah 5:21 derives from Isaiah of Jerusalem (so Jack Lundbom, private communication); it may be that the *topos* of Israel's blindness was fairly widespread in prophetic circles in pre-exilic Jerusalem and that Jeremiah's use of the figure is not directly dependent on Isaiah. Williamson, however, thinks it likely that Jeremiah 5:21 *has* been influenced by Isaiah 6 (1994:50).

[80] Apart from these two passages, καμμύω occurs in the LXX only in Isaiah 33:15 and Lamentations 3:45.

[81] A further verbal link between the two texts is found only in Hebrew, where Isaiah 6:10 and 29:9 share the rare root שעע, "to blind."

Within the book of Isaiah, 29:10 is one link in a chain of texts, anchored in Isaiah 6:9–10 and extending as far as chapter 61, that depict Israel's alienation from God as blindness and deafness and that correspondingly picture Israel's redemption as the opening of eyes and ears.[82] Indeed, Isaiah 29:10 is the first time after 6:9–10 that God's blinding of the people is mentioned. It would not be at all surprising, then, if Paul recognized the link between 29:10 and 6:9–10.[83] Given its close affinities with both Deuteronomy 29 and Isaiah 29, Isaiah 6:9–10 may well have served as the exegetical bridge by which Paul spanned the gap between the two texts.[84]

The hypothesis that Isaiah 6:9–10 stands behind Paul's conflation of Deuteronomy 29:4 and Isaiah 29:10 does not depend entirely on probing below the surface of the text, however. A distinct trace of Isaiah 6:9–10 can be found in the comment that calls forth the conflated citation in the first place: οἱ δὲ λοιποὶ ἐπωρώθησαν, "but the rest were made insensible" (Rom 11:7).[85] The verb πωρόω and its related noun, πώρωσις, appear only once in the LXX and a mere eight times in the NT.[86] Aside from the two occurrences of this word-group in Romans 11:7 and 25, πωρόω is found in Paul's writings only in 2 Corinthians 3:14.[87] Significantly, however, πωρόω twice appears in the gospels in connection with a citation or allusion to Isaiah 6:9–10. In Mark 8:17–21, Jesus, exasperated at his disciples' repeated failure to comprehend, upbraids them in terms that liken them to the spiritually imperceptive Israelites to whom Isaiah was sent:

---

[82] Isaiah 6:9–10; 29:10, 18; 32:3–4; 35:5; 42:7, 16, 18–20; 43:8; 56:10; 59:10; 61:1. From a diachronic perspective, Isaiah 29:9–10 "clearly reflects a development of the theme of 6:9–10" (Williamson 1994:48).

[83] Further links bind the wider context of Isaiah 29:10 closely to Isaiah 6, increasing the probability that an ancient reader would pick up on the connections between the passages. Williamson (1994:48, 50, 60) finds a significant number of texts in Isaiah 28–29 that appear to reflect the vocabulary and themes of Isaiah 6 (28:9, 19; 29:9–10, 13–14, 15–16, 18, 23–24). See the similar analysis in Stansell 1996:85–86.

[84] Cf. Lindars 1961:164, 241–42; Moo 1996:682 n. 59.

[85] C reads ἐπηρώθησαν; on the common confusion in manuscripts between πωρόω/πηρόω and πώρωσις/πήρωσις, see Robinson 1902:89–90; Schmidt and Schmidt 1967:1027–28.

[86] Affecting the "heart": Mark 3:5; 6:52; 8:17; John 12:40; Eph 4:18; the "mind" (νόημα): 2 Cor 3:14; cf. "eyes": Job 17:7 LXX. With no part of the body specified: Rom 11:7, 25.

[87] ἀλλὰ ἐπωρώθη τὰ νοήματα αὐτῶν. Here too the subjects are Jews who reject Paul's gospel. Cf. Eph 4:18, which attributes insensibility of heart to "the Gentiles."

¹⁷... Do you not yet perceive or understand? Is your heart insensible? ¹⁸Having eyes, do you not see? Having ears, do you not hear? Do you not remember?.... ²¹... do you not yet understand?

¹⁷... οὔπω νοεῖτε οὐδὲ συνίετε; πεπωρωμένην ἔχετε τὴν καρδίαν ὑμῶν; ¹⁸ ὀφθαλμοὺς ἔχοντες οὐ βλέπετε καὶ ὦτα ἔχοντες οὐκ ἀκούετε; καὶ οὐ μνημονεύετε ... ²¹... οὔπω συνίετε;⁸⁸

Likewise, πωρόω appears in the citation of Isaiah 6:10 in John 12:39–41,⁸⁹ as the evangelist explains why Jesus was rejected by so many of his fellow Jews:

> For this reason they were not able to believe, for again Isaiah said: "He has blinded their eyes, and he has *rendered* their heart *insensible*, so that they may not see with their eyes and perceive with their heart and turn, and I heal them." These things Isaiah said because he saw his glory, and he spoke concerning him.

> ³⁹ διὰ τοῦτο οὐκ ἠδύναντο πιστεύειν, ὅτι πάλιν εἶπεν Ἡσαΐας· ⁴⁰ τετύφλωκεν αὐτῶν τοὺς ὀφθαλμοὺς καὶ ἐπώρωσεν αὐτῶν τὴν καρδίαν, ἵνα μὴ ἴδωσιν τοῖς ὀφθαλμοῖς καὶ νοήσωσιν τῇ καρδίᾳ καὶ στραφῶσιν, καὶ ἰάσομαι αὐτούς. ⁴¹ ταῦτα εἶπεν Ἡσαΐας ὅτι εἶδεν τὴν δόξαν αὐτοῦ, καὶ ἐλάλησεν περὶ αὐτοῦ.

What is most intriguing about this citation—and most significant for an investigation of Romans 11:8—are the important ways in which the citation in John 12:40 differs from the version of Isaiah 6:10 found in the LXX.⁹⁰ The lexical and syntactical variances can be seen clearly in Figure 4.4.

Both John 12:40 and Isaiah 6:10 LXX are acceptable translations of Isaiah 6:10 into Greek, yet they differ in important ways.⁹¹ Most noticeably, John 12:40 has different Greek equivalents for a number of Hebrew verbs (Figure 4.5).

---

⁸⁸ Cf. Guelich 1989:425; Hooker 1991:195–96. This text also recalls the characterization of Israel in Jeremiah 5:21 and Ezekiel 12:2, both of which appear to be related to Isaiah 6:9–10 (see n. 79 above). Surprisingly, the marginal notes to Mark 8:17–21 in NA²⁷ do not refer the reader to Isaiah 6:9–10 (or, for that matter, to Mark 4:12).

⁸⁹ Several mss read πηρόω (𝔓⁶⁶.⁷⁵ ℵ K W). See n. 85 above, and cf. Metzger 1994:203.

⁹⁰ The quotations of Isaiah 6:10 in Matthew 13:14–15 and Acts 28:27 follow the LXX nearly verbatim.

⁹¹ John 12:40 transposes a number of clauses and cola and also omits the reference to ears and deafness. It is impossible to know whether these represent the original translation or a Johannine modification of a pre-existing translation that itself more closely followed the Hebrew represented by MT.

Figure 4.4: John 12:40, Isaiah 6:10 MT, and Isaiah 6:10 LXX

	single underline	Agreement with MT but not with LXX (i.e., a different Hebrew-Greek equivalency)
Key:	*italic*	Agreement with MT (consonants) *against* LXX
	double underline	Agreement with LXX *against* MT

Isaiah 6:10 MT	John 12:40	Isaiah 6:10 LXX
הֵשַׁמֵן	ᵇ [καὶ ἐπώρωσεν	ἐπαχύνθη γὰρ
לֵב־הָעָם הַזֶּה	αὐτῶν τὴν καρδίαν,]	ἡ καρδία τοῦ λαοῦ τούτου
וְאָזְנָיו		καὶ τοῖς ὠσὶν αὐτῶν
הַכְבֵּד		βαρέως ἤκουσαν
וְעֵינָיו	ᵃ [τετύφλωκεν <u>αὐτῶν</u>	καὶ τοὺς ὀφθαλμοὺς <u>αὐτῶν</u>
הָשַׁע	τοὺς ὀφθαλμοὺς]	ἐκάμμυσαν
פֶּן־יִרְאֶה	ᶜ ἵνα μὴ ἴδωσιν	μήποτε ἴδωσιν
בְעֵינָיו	τοῖς ὀφθαλμοῖς	τοῖς ὀφθαλμοῖς
וּבְאָזְנָיו יִשְׁמַע		καὶ τοῖς ὠσὶν ἀκούσωσιν
וּלְבָבוֹ	καὶ <u>νοήσωσιν</u>	καὶ τῇ καρδίᾳ
יָבִין	τῇ καρδίᾳ	συνῶσιν
וָשָׁב	καὶ <u>στραφῶσιν</u>,	καὶ ἐπιστρέψωσιν
וְרָפָא לוֹ	καὶ ἰάσομαι αὐτούς.	καὶ ἰάσομαι αὐτούς

Figure 4.5: Variant Lexical Equivalents in John 12:40
and Isaiah 6:10 LXX

Hebrew	John 12:40	Isaiah 6:10 LXX
שָׁמֵן	πωρόω	παχύνω
שָׁעַע	τυφλόω	καμμύω
בִין	νοέω	συνίημι
שׁוּב	στρέφω	ἐπιστρέφω

In addition, John 12:40 uses ἵνα μή + Subjunctive to translate Hebrew פֶּן + Imperfect, while LXX Isaiah chooses an alternate method for rendering the construction into Greek: μήποτε + Subjunctive. Despite the fact that John's quotation agrees with LXX against MT in reading the first person singular verb and third plural object, ἰάσομαι αὐτούς, it is not easily explained as a revision of LXX.[92] The evidence suggests rather that the citation in John 12:40 represents an

---

[92] The agreement between John 12:40 and Isaiah 6:10 LXX is less impressive than it first appears: ἰάομαι is an obvious Greek equivalent for רָפָא, and the plural pronoun is found also in the Targum. Still, only John 12:40 and LXX read the first person singular for the final verb.

independent translation of Isaiah 6:10 into Greek from a Hebrew *Vorlage*.[93] Mark 8:17 provides indirect support for the circulation in Christian circles of this alternate Greek translation of Isaiah 6:10, for it shares with John 12:40 two key terms not found in Isaiah 6:10 LXX: νοέω and πωρόω.[94]

The differences between John 12:40 and Isaiah 6:10 LXX at the linguistic level are matched by a striking divergence in theological perspective. The LXX quite noticeably softens the troublesome theological implications of Isaiah 6:10, which in the Hebrew text unapologetically attributes Israel's torpor to God's own agency through his prophet. In the Hebrew, Isaiah's commission is to *make* Israel blind and unheeding.[95] The LXX translator removes God as agent by employing the passive verb, ἐπαχύνθη, which in context probably carries its intransitive (active) meaning: "their heart has grown fat."[96] Furthermore, he makes the Israelites the subjects of ἀκούω and καμμύω: *they* are hard of hearing; *they* have closed their eyes. Thus, in the LXX, Isaiah is commissioned to intensify an obduracy that already exists, rather than to cause Israel's blindness.[97] Similar reservations about the theology of Isaiah 6:10 probably account for the uncharacteristically free translation of Symmachus at this point;[98] such concerns may have influenced the renderings of the Targum

---

[93] An extended discussion (with copious references to previous studies) may be found in Menken 1988. For the suggestion that the author of the Fourth Gospel found this traditional Christian testimony already incorporated into his source, see Smith 1984:91–92.

[94] So also Lindars 1961:162, though he does not note the shared use of νοέω.

[95] With the vast majority of scholars, I assume that MT has substantially preserved the original form of Isaiah 6:9–10 (see Evans 1989:170–71, n. 2; de Waard 1997:28–29). For the argument (*contra* Brownlee 1964 and Evans 1984b) that the meaning of these verses in 1QIsaᵃ is essentially the same as in MT, see Wagner 1999b:313–17.

[96] *Contra* LEH (s.v. παχύνω) but with BDAG (s.v. παχύνω, 2; cf. LSJ s.v. παχύνω, II). See Isaiah 34:6 and Deuteronomy 32:15. Ziegler (1934:108–109) suggests that the latter text has influenced the translation of Isaiah 6:10 LXX.

[97] While the LXX translator clearly attempts to modify the theology of Isaiah 6:10, the contrast between LXX and MT can be overdrawn. Even in MT, the position of the call narrative within the book of Isaiah suggests that God's command to Isaiah to make the people insensible is itself an act of judgment on their stubborn refusal to hear and obey God's words (a major theme of the book since Isaiah 1:2).

[98] ὁ λαὸς οὗτος τὰ ὦτα ἐβάρυνε καὶ τοὺς ὀφθαλμοὺς αὐτοῦ ἔμυσε... (so Theodoret; cf. 710, σ´ καὶ τὰ ὦτα ἐβάρυνε). Interestingly, by putting "this people" in the nominative, Symmachus states even more strongly than LXX that the people are the cause of their own obtuseness.

and Peshitta as well.[99] To a greater or lesser extent, all of these versions attempt to minimize the awful theological implications of Isaiah 6:9–10.[100]

Whereas LXX, Symmachus, Targum, and Peshitta attempt to downplay God's responsibility for Israel's spiritual stultification, John 12:40 actually lays greater stress on God's agency than does the Hebrew, dispensing with Isaiah's mediatory function altogether in accounting for Israel's stubborn obtuseness. In the main clause of the sentence, John 12:40 employs two active, transitive verbs, ἐπώρωσεν and τετύφλωκεν.[101] In the context, the subject can be none other than God himself. According to this interpretation, God has already

---

[99] As does LXX Isaiah, the Isaiah Targum also places Israel's resistance prior to God's decree:

ואמר איזיל ותימר לעמא הדין דַשמעִין משמע ולא מסתכלין וחזן מחזא ולא ידעין

And he said, "Go and speak to this people *who hear* indeed but do not understand and who see indeed but do not perceive.

The Peshitta, like the LXX and Symmachus, makes "this people" the agents of their own insensibility in 6:10:

[v.l. ܂ܬ] ܂ܟ݂ܕ ܂ܟ݂ܐܘܢ ܂ܟ݂ܐܢܘܢ ܂ܟ݂ܐ ܂ܟܒ݂ ܂ܟ݂

For the heart of this people has become thick, and it has made its ears dull and closed its eyes lest it see with its eyes and hear with its ears and understand with its heart and turn and it be forgiven it.

Evans's rendering (1989:77–78) actually misses the force with which the Peshitta depicts Israel's blindness and deafness as *active* rebellion against God. His translation, "their ears are heavy and their eyes are closed" (apparently following Lamsa 1957: 704), implausible, in context, the verbs ܂ܟ݂ (Evans mistranscribes this as 'wwr) and ܂ܬ (the v.l. he adopts) are most naturally read as singular. The plural nouns "eyes" and "ears" must be the *objects* of their respective verbs, not the subjects, and consequently the verbs each have a transitive, rather than an intransitive, sense. It is possible—though unlikely in the context—that ܂ܟ݂ and ܂ܟ݂ should be read as imperatives à la MT (the v.l. ܂ܬ, however, can only be read as a perfect). It is even less likely that the subject of these (perfect) verbs would be understood to be God. Rather, the subject is "this people" (to whom reference is made by means of singular pronouns throughout 6:10).

[100] See further Evans 1989, whose study suggests that quite a bit of interpretive energy was expended on Isaiah 6:9–10 in both early Jewish and early Christian communities.

[101] If John 12:40 derives from a Hebrew text similar to that preserved in MT, the translator would have understood the verbs not as imperatives (הַשְׁמֵן, הָשַׁע), but as (defectively-written) perfects (הַשְׁמֵן, הֵשַׁע). The same ambiguity of form would pertain if we hypothesized an Aramaic *Vorlage*. In this case, the imperative singular and perfect third masculine singular share exactly the same consonants: טַמְטֵם, יַקַּר, טַפֵּשׁ.

acted to render Israel insensible (*God* blinded their eyes . . . *God* made their heart insensible) *before* he commissions Isaiah. Thus, John 12:40 not only maintains the strong predestinarian tone of Isaiah 6:9–10 in the Hebrew text, it actually cranks the volume up a notch on this crucial Isaianic theme.

The affinity of Paul's argument in Romans 11:8 with the interpretation of Israel's insensibility offered in John 12:39–41 is striking. Considering Paul's use of the rare term πωρόω in conjunction with the network of verbal and thematic relationships anchored in Isaiah 6:9–10 and extending to encompass both Deuteronomy 29:4 and Isaiah 29:10, it is quite possible that in Romans 11:8 Paul has made use of a Greek translation[102] of Isaiah 6:9–10 similar to that attested in the Fourth Gospel and possibly also in Mark 8:17.[103] In stark contrast to the tendency of the versions, particularly the LXX, to mitigate God's direct responsibility for Israel's spiritual torpor, John 12:40 attests to an alternative tradition of interpretation—in Greek—of Isaiah 6:9–10, one that maintains the strong emphasis of the Hebrew text on divine sovereignty.[104] Although Paul nowhere quotes explicitly from Isaiah 6:9–10, it is evident that he stands within a broader stream of early Christian interpretation that found in Isaiah's blindness motif a clear, if difficult, answer to the troubling refusal of many fellow Jews to embrace the gospel: *God* has rendered them unable to hear and believe.

---

[102] Once again, there is no evidence suggesting that Paul relied on a *Hebrew* text for this particular interpretation of scripture.

[103] There are other intriguing similarities between Romans 9–11 and John 12— such as the use in both passages (and only here in the NT) of Isaiah 53:1 to lament Israel's refusal to believe the gospel (Romans 10:16; John 12:37–38)—which may provide further evidence of a relationship of some sort between the Pauline and Johannine traditions. On the question of Pauline traditions in the Fourth Gospel, see Smith 1996 and the literature cited there. In an earlier essay, Smith suggested that the Isaiah quotations in John 12:37–40 may be traced to an early stratum of the Fourth Gospel (1984:90–93).

[104] This theological perspective is also evident in Mark's explicit quotation from Isaiah 6:9–10 in Mark 4:12, and, indirectly, in Matthew's attempt to soften Mark's emphasis on divine sovereignty as the explanation for Israel's blindness (Matt 13:13). Significantly, Matthew goes on to quote in full the LXX version of Isaiah 6:9–10 (Matt 13:14–15), which lays responsibility for failing to understand squarely on the shoulders of the people.

The Larger Story: Isaiah 6 and Isaiah 29 in the
Book of Isaiah

For Paul, however, the imposition of spiritual insensibility is not
God's final word to Israel. Within the flow of his larger argument
in Romans 11, Paul lays emphasis on God's sovereign choice to
blind "the rest" of Israel precisely in order to insist that God intends
the ultimate effect of this blinding to be the outpouring of mercy
on "all," Gentile *and Jew* alike. At this point it becomes crucial to
note the ways in which the wider theological and literary contexts
of Deuteronomy 29:4, Isaiah 29:10, and Isaiah 6:9–10 shape Paul's
appropriation of these texts.

Isaiah 6 stands as a pivotal passage within the book of Isaiah. It
sets up a profound theological problem with which much of the rest
of the book must deal,[105] namely, that God himself has determined
to judge his people for their rebellion against him. In order to ensure
the inevitability of their punishment, God commissions Isaiah to make
them yet more stubborn and unresponsive to his word. Faced with
such an awful task, Isaiah cries out on behalf of his people, "How
long, Lord?" (6:11). The answer he receives is not at all comforting,
for it foretells in vivid terms the devastation of the land and the
exile of the nation. On this dark scene beams a solitary ray of hope:
the cryptic promise that out of the decimation of Israel "the holy
seed" will survive as a stump from which the nation may one day
sprout again. In the LXX, even this hopeful word is absent; the
remnant that remains (6:12 LXX) will lie helpless, open to plundering by any who pass by (6:13 LXX).[106]

---

[105] For the influence of Isaiah 6 in Deutero-Isaiah, see Carroll 1997; McLaughlin
1994; Clements 1985:101–104; Williamson 1994:30–56; Rendtorff 1989:175–79;
Gosse 1991. Clements comments that the theme of Israel as blind/deaf/uncom-
prehending "is clearly of central importance to Isa. 40–55" (1985:102). Sommer
(1994:139–40, 164–69; cf. Sommer 1998:93–96, 242 n. 14, 258 n. 95) notes the
following texts in Deutero-Isaiah (defined in his study as Isa 40–66) that reuse (and
often reverse) the oracle of judgment in Isaiah 6: Isa 40:21–28; 42:7, 16, 18–20,
25; 43:8; 44:9–19; 49:6, 8, 19–20; 52:8, 52:13–53:12; 61:1. Williamson (1994) suggests a number of additional allusions to Isaiah 6: Isa 41:20; 56:10–11; 57:1.

[106] It appears that the LXX translator introduces a message of hope into Isaiah
6:12 by predicting that some will not go into exile but remain in the land and
multiply (καὶ μετὰ ταῦτα μακρυνεῖ ὁ θεὸς τοὺς ἀνθρώπους, καὶ οἱ καταλειφθέντες
πληθυνθήσονται ἐπὶ τῆς γῆς). However, the following verse suggests that those left
in the land will continue to suffer oppression (καὶ ἔτι ἐπ᾽ αὐτῆς ἔστι τὸ ἐπιδέκατον,
καὶ πάλιν ἔσται εἰς προνομὴν ὡς τερέβινθος καὶ ὡς βάλανος ὅταν ἐκπέσῃ ἀπὸ τῆς θήκης
αὐτῆς, Isaiah 6:13 LXX). The best witnesses to LXX Isaiah lack the final line, "the

Within LXX Isaiah as a whole, however, this dire pledge of inevitable and unrelenting destruction is not God's final verdict on Israel. Subsequent oracles continue to sound the dark notes of Isaiah 6, but running alongside this somber motif is a countermelody that grows in strength and eventually swells to become the dominant strain of Isaiah's prophecy. Israel's God, who has afflicted his wayward people with blindness and insensibility, promises in due time to heal and to comfort them. It is no mere coincidence that Isaiah frequently pictures God's deliverance of his people as the restoration of sight to the blind and the recovery of hearing by the deaf.[107] In Isaiah 29, this movement from judgment as blindness to redemption as recovery of sight takes place within the space of a few verses. In 29:9–12, Israel staggers under a spirit of stupor and of blindness. The prophet likens their inability to understand God's message to the predicament of a person attempting to read a sealed book or, worse yet, to the confusion of a person called on to read who doesn't even know letters.[108] And yet, on the other side of exile (29:17) awaits the amazing eschatalogical reversal of Israel's deafness and blindness:

> And in that day the deaf will hear the words of a book, and the darkened and befogged eyes of the blind will see; the poor will rejoice with gladness on account of the Lord, and those without hope will be filled with gladness.
>
> καὶ ἀκούσονται ἐν τῇ ἡμέρᾳ ἐκείνῃ κωφοὶ λόγους βιβλίου, καὶ οἱ ἐν τῷ σκότει καὶ οἱ ἐν τῇ ὁμίχλῃ ὀφθαλμοὶ τυφλῶν βλέψονται· καὶ ἀγαλλιάσονται πτωχοὶ διὰ κύριον ἐν εὐφροσύνῃ, καὶ οἱ ἀπηλπισμένοι τῶν ἀνθρώπων ἐμπλησθήσονται εὐφροσύνης (Isaiah 29:18–19).

By drawing on the blindness motif, Paul clearly seeks to liken "the rest" of Israel in his own day to the rebellious and sinful Israelites

---

holy seed is its stump" (= MT); it is found in α', σ' and θ', as well as in Hexaplaric manuscripts. Contrast the Isaiah Targum, which, in addition to offering the promise concerning the "holy seed," further mollifies the harshness of Isaiah 6:13 with an explicit promise of return from exile: כין נלוותא דישראל יתכנשון ויתובון לארעהון. On the textual and tradition-historical problems of Isa 6:13, see Emerton 1982; de Waard 1997:29–31.

[107] E.g., Isaiah 9:2; 29:18–19; 32:3–4; 35:5; 42:7; 61:1 LXX.

[108] See above, p. 148 for the argument that in LXX Isaiah "this sealed book" (29:11) refers to the Law (Isaiah 8:16 LXX). Compare Paul's statement in 2 Corinthians 3:14 that Israel cannot understand the reading (ἀνάγνωσις) of the "old covenant" because their minds have been "rendered insensible" (ἐπωρώθη τὰ νοήματα αὐτῶν).

against whom Isaiah spoke his words of judgment and reproof.[109] For Paul, the refusal of fellow Jews to believe the gospel is a tragic rejection of Israel's God, and God has poured out judgment on them in the form of blindness and spiritual insensibility. Yet, like Isaiah, Paul is convinced that God's fidelity to his people will finally overcome Israel's unfaithfulness. Just as in Isaiah Israel's blindness will one day give way to sight, its deafness yield to hearing, so in Paul's eschatological vision the spiritual stupor of "the rest" of Israel is only temporary. As in Isaiah, so too in Paul's theodicy, God will be faithful to redeem and restore those whom he has rendered insensible.[110]

The Larger Story: From Deuteronomy 29 to
Deuteronomy 30

The latter chapters of Deuteronomy, from which Paul draws several of his quotations in Romans, including Deuteronomy 29:4, exhibit a similar pattern of present blindness alleviated by the eschatological intervention of God.[111] Following the awesome scene in Deuteronomy 28 in which Moses pronounces the covenantal blessings and curses (which include blindness),[112] Deuteronomy 29 narrates Moses' concluding exhortation to the generation about to enter the land.[113] He swiftly recaps the mighty deeds of the Lord in delivering them from

---

[109] Compare Paul's reading of Isaiah 29:16 in Romans 9:20 and his use of Isaiah 28:16 in Romans 9:33; 10:11. It is interesting to note the connection of blindness to idolatry in Isaiah (e.g., 44:9–20, which Clements [1985:102] thinks is indebted to 6:9–10), particularly in light of Paul's employment elsewhere in Romans 9–11 of texts that picture Israel as idolatrous (Deut 32; Hos 1–2; Isa 8, 28, 65; 1 Kgdms 8–12; 3 Kgdms 19). Cf. Beale 1991.

[110] We saw in Romans 10:15–16 the importance of the motif of "hearing" in Paul's appropriation of Isaiah 52:7 and 53:1. In Romans 15:21, Paul finds in the words of Isaiah 52:15 a prophecy of the reception of the gospel by Gentiles: "those to whom it was not announced concerning him him will see, and those who have not heard will understand" (see below, pp. 329–36). Having picked up on Isaiah's promise that those who have not seen or heard will receive God's grace, it would be strange indeed if Paul did not also note the reiterated Isaianic promise that blind and deaf Israel too will one day see and hear again.

[111] Paul quotes Deuteronomy 30:12–14 (Rom 10:6–8); 32:21 (Rom 10:19); 32:35 (Rom 12:19); 32:43 (Rom 15:10). Lohfink argues from a redaction-critical perspective that Deuteronomy 29:1[28:69]–32:47 is "eine umfassende Komposition" (1962:51; similarly, P. D. Miller 1990:199).

[112] Deut. 28:28–29: πατάξαι σε κύριος παραπληξίᾳ καὶ ἀορασίᾳ καὶ ἐκστάσει διανοίας, καὶ ἔσῃ ψηλαφῶν μεσημβρίας, ὡσεὶ ψηλαφήσαι ὁ τυφλὸς ἐν τῷ σκότει... (cf. Deut 28:65).

[113] As 29:14–15 makes clear, the covenant and its curses apply to future descendants of Israel as well.

Egypt, reminding his listeners that they saw all of those signs and
wonders with their own eyes.[114] And yet, after all this, Moses laments
that "to this day," God has not given them eyes, ears, or heart to
perceive and obey (29:4). Within the larger story told by Deuteronomy,
this statement of Moses is crucial, for it explains how, even as Israel
has yet to cross over the Jordan, their future exile can be repeatedly spoken of as an inevitable occurence.[115] According to Deuteronomy
29:4, Israel lacks the ability to keep the covenant that they have just
ratified.[116] Only on the other side of exile, "when all of these words
have come upon you, the blessing and the curse," will Israel be able
to keep the covenant. And this will be, not the consequence of Israel's
own moral exertion, but the gracious gift of God, who will heal
them,[117] restore them to the land, and guarantee their security there
by supplying himself what Israel now lacks: the capacity to keep the
covenant blamelessly:

> And the Lord will cleanse your heart and the heart of your seed so
> that you will love the Lord your God with all your heart and with all
> your soul, so that you will live. . . . And you will turn and hearken to
> the voice of the Lord and you will do his commandments, as many
> as I am commanding you today.
>
> καὶ περικαθαριεῖ κύριος τὴν καρδίαν σου καὶ τὴν καρδίαν τοῦ σπέρματός
> σου ἀγαπᾶν κύριον τὸν θεόν σου ἐξ ὅλης τῆς καρδίας σου καὶ ἐξ ὅλης τῆς
> ψυχῆς σου, ἵνα ζῇς σύ. . . . καὶ σὺ ἐπιστραφήσῃ καὶ εἰσακούσῃ τῆς φωνῆς
> κυρίου τοῦ θεοῦ σου καὶ ποιήσεις τὰς ἐντολὰς αὐτοῦ, ὅσας ἐγὼ ἐντέλλομαί
> σοι σήμερον (Deuteronomy 30:6–8).

We observed in the previous chapter that this Deuteronomic story
of exile and restoration, in which Israel is endowed by God with
the ability to obey the covenant fully, shaped the self-understanding
and hopes of at least some post-exilic Jewish groups.[118] Paul's own
narrative of God's dealings with Israel appears to have been similarly

---

[114] ὑμεῖς ἑωράκατε πάντα, ὅσα ἐποίησεν κύριος ἐν γῇ Αἰγύπτῳ ἐνώπιον ὑμῶν Φαραω
(29:2) . . . τοὺς πειρασμοὺς τοὺς μεγάλους, οὓς ἑωράκασιν οἱ ὀφθαλμοί σου, τὰ σημεῖα
καὶ τὰ τέρατα τὰ μεγάλα ἐκεῖνα (29:3).

[115] I am speaking, of course, not of the historical circumstances in which
Deuteronomy was composed and redacted, but of the literary perspective adopted
by the work.

[116] "The only covenant known in Deuteronomy is a broken covenant" (G. E.
Wright 1962:60).

[117] Deuteronomy 30:3: καὶ ἰάσεται κύριος τὰς ἁμαρτίας σου. Compare Isaiah 6:10,
μήποτε . . . ἐπιστρέψωσι καὶ ἰάσομαι αὐτούς.

[118] See the discussion of *4QWords of the Luminaries*, 4QMMT, and Baruch 2:27–3:8
above, p. 166 n. 143.

molded in a profound way by the sequence of events recounted in
Deuteronomy 29–30. As his interpretive rendering of Deuteronomy
30:12–14 in Romans 10:6–13 shows, Paul believes that God has now
acted in Christ to realize the promise of life held out by the Law
(cf. Deut 30:6) for all who will respond with heart and mouth to
the word that is near. Those who, metaphorically speaking, inhabit
Deuteronomy 30 include the present-day "remnant" of Israel, chosen
by grace, and—surprisingly—some Gentiles. Paradoxically, "the rest"
of Israel remains mired in Deuteronomy 29; they have yet to receive
the promise of a renewed heart, of eyes that can see and ears that
can hear.[119] Paul must turn to the parallel version of Israel's story
in Deuteronomy 32 to explain this unexpected twist in the plot, but
he remains convinced that the happy ending common to both versions of the tale awaits "the rest" of Israel as well.

In light of the preceding discussion, it appears fairly certain that
Paul himself is responsible for conflating Deuteronomy 29:4 and
Isaiah 29:10 in Romans 11:8, perhaps through the mediating influence
of Isaiah 6:9–10. The manner in which Paul employs these texts
accords well with his use elsewhere in Romans of Deuteronomy 30
and 32 and of Isaiah 28–29 to describe Israel's present alienation
from God. Having read Deuteronomy 32 and Isaiah 65 together in
Romans 10:19–21 to show that Israel has indeed known of God's
intention to welcome Gentiles into the people of God, Paul once
again presents Moses and Isaiah in concert to explain the present
insensibility of "the rest" of Israel.[120] Moreover, as in the case of so
many of the citations and allusions we have examined, Paul's appeal
to these texts adumbrates the conclusion toward which his entire
argument in Romans 9–11 steadily flows: that God himself will per-

---

[119] A similar sequential reading of Deuteronomy 27–30 may be evident among
the Dead Sea sectarians. In CD-A 1:8–10, the image of people groping in the dark
like those who are blind (common to Isaiah 59:9–10 and Deuteronomy 28:28–29)
describes the community in the days before the coming of the Righteous Teacher
(cf. J. G. Campbell 1995:56, 59, 62). In 4QMMT, the author claims, "We know
that some of the blessings and curses have (already) been fulfilled as it is written
in the bo[ok of Mo]ses": ואנחנו מכירים שבאו מקצת הברכות והקללות שכתוב בס[פר
מש[ה (C 20–21 = 4Q398 frgs. 11–13, lines 3–4; translation by Qimron and Strugnell,
DJD X, 61). Situating himself and the recipients of the letter amidst the curses of
Deuteronomy 27–29, the author nevertheless insists that they stand on the cusp of
the fulfillment of the restoration of Israel promised in Deuteronomy 30 (cf. C 12–16).

[120] Some of the most intriguing implications of listening to Deuteronomy 29:4,
Isaiah 6:9–10, and Isaiah 29:10 in concert remain unexploited by Paul, such as the
possibility of hearing Isaiah's question, "ἕως πότε κύριε;" answered by Moses: "ἕως
τῆς ἡμέρας ταύτης."

sonally intervene to remove Israel's blindness and restore them to himself.

Messianic Maledictions: Psalm 68:23–24 LXX in Romans 11:9–10

The echoes of Paul's conflated citation of Deuteronomy 29:4 and Isaiah 29:10 have not yet faded when a second scriptural voice rings out testifying to the divine blinding of Israel (Rom 11:9–10). Paul has selected and shaped this excerpt from Psalm 68:23–24 LXX with some care. His citation shares a number of significant thematic and verbal connections not only with the two texts he has quoted in the preceding verse, but also with passages that have figured prominently in earlier stages of his argument. It will be useful to examine the quotation itself more closely before tracing the various strands that anchor it firmly to Paul's larger discussion in Romans 9–11.

Paul's introduction—καὶ Δαυὶδ λέγει (Rom 11:9; cf. 4:6)—identifies these words as an excerpt from the Psalms, and thus from holy scripture.[121] At the same time, his presentation of David "in person" as speaker lends considerable rhetorical weight to the dreadful words of malediction that follow. David now joins Moses and Isaiah as a third witness who steps forward in Romans 9–11 to testify *viva voce* regarding God's dealings with Israel.[122]

---

[121] In both MT and LXX, this psalm bears a superscription attributing it to David (לדוד; τῷ Δαυιδ). *11QMelchizedek* (11Q13) 2.9–10 introduces a quotation from Psalm 82 (MT, לאסף!) with the words כאשר כתוב עליו בשירי דויד. For "David" used alongside Torah and Prophets, see 4QMMT C 10 (4Q397 frgs. 14–21, line 10; cf. Luke 24:44). See further Evans 1997.

[122] Paul has previously drawn together Psalm 18, Deuteronomy 32, and Isaiah 65 in Romans 10:18–21, and the climactic catena of citations in Romans 15:9–12 will similarly weave together citations from Deuteronomy 32, Isaiah 11, and Psalms 17 and 116 (see pp. 310–29). While Paul once mentions "the Law and the prophets" (Rom 3:21), he never betrays consciousness of a tripartite division of scripture. J. G. Campbell (2000) buttresses Barton's argument (1986) for a bipartite conception of scripture in this period: Torah and a (somewhat fluid) collection of "Prophets." The book of Psalms (ספר התהלים, 4Q491 frg. 17, line 4; ἐν βίβλῳ ψαλμῶν, Acts 1:20) would have been included in this latter group (note the emphasis on David as a prophet in 11QPsalmsᵃ [11Q5] 27.2–11; Acts 2:30). See DJD IV; see further Flint 1998. For a defense of a tripartite canon in this period, see Beckwith 1985:110–80; Leiman 1976. At the same time, Paul's pattern of conjoining excerpts from Deuteronomy, Isaiah, and the Psalms points to his recognition of some sort of "canon within the canon" that spanned the range of scriptural genres. Psalms, Isaiah, and Deuteronomy are among the books Paul quotes most frequently (in addition to these, only Genesis receives anything like the same amount of attention; it is quoted approximately as often as Deuteronomy, particularly in connection with the Abraham

Figure 4.6: Psalm 68:23–24 LXX in Romans 11:9–10

Psalm 68:23–24 LXX	Romans 11:9–10
²³ γενηθήτω ἡ τράπεζα αὐτῶν ἐνώπιον αὐτῶν εἰς παγίδα καὶ εἰς ἀνταπόδοσιν καὶ εἰς σκάνδαλον· ²⁴ σκοτισθήτωσαν οἱ ὀφθαλμοὶ αὐτῶν τοῦ μὴ βλέπειν καὶ τὸν νῶτον αὐτῶν διὰ παντὸς σύγκαμψον.	⁹ καὶ Δαυὶδ λέγει· γενηθήτω ἡ τράπεζα αὐτῶν εἰς παγίδα καὶ εἰς θήραν καὶ εἰς σκάνδαλον καὶ εἰς ἀνταπόδομα αὐτοῖς, ¹⁰ σκοτισθήτωσαν οἱ ὀφθαλμοὶ αὐτῶν τοῦ μὴ βλέπειν καὶ τὴν νῶτον αὐτῶν διὰ παντὸς σύγκαμψον.

Ps 69:23–24 MT: ²³ יְהִי־שֻׁלְחָנָם לִפְנֵיהֶם לְפָח וְלִשְׁלוֹמִים לְמוֹקֵשׁ

²⁴ תֶּחְשַׁכְנָה עֵינֵיהֶם מֵרְאוֹת וּמָתְנֵיהֶם תָּמִיד הַמְעַד

As Figure 4.6 shows, Paul's citation corresponds closely to the LXX version, with only a few minor variations.[123] For ἀνταπόδοσις, found in LXX, α΄, σ΄, and θ΄, Paul has the related word ἀνταπόδομα; both readings, however, represent a common understanding (shared also by the Peshitta and Syrohexapla) of the underlying Hebrew word שלומים, in contrast to the different meanings given to שלומים in the MT and the Targum.[124]

---

narratives). Interestingly, though all of the books of the Hebrew Bible except Nehemiah and Esther are represented among the Dead Sea Scrolls, the books with the greatest number of surviving manuscripts are Psalms (36), Deuteronomy (29), Isaiah (21), Exodus (17), and Genesis (15). See further VanderKam 1994:30–31, 1998; Brooke 1997a.

[123] The absence of a truly critical text of the Septuagint Psalter continues to handicap efforts to study Paul's quotations from the Psalms. On the shortcomings of Rahlfs's edition in the Göttingen Septuagint (1979), see Jellicoe 1993:297–98 and Flint 1997:228–36, esp. 229–30.

[124] LXX, Paul, the later Greek versions, Peshitta (ܘܠܦܘܪܥܢܐ), and Syrohexapla (ܠܦܘܪܥܢܐ) presuppose וּלְשִׁלּוּמִים or וְשִׁלּוּמָם, "recompense, retribution" (for the Syrohexapla, see Hiebert 1989). In contrast, MT points the word, וְלִשְׁלוֹמִים, "those at peace" (cf. Dahood's repointing as a qal passive participle [וְלִשְׁלוּמִים], "even their companions/allies" [1968:162; 1965:42–43; cf. Tate 1990:190 n. 23a), while the Targum (וּנְכַסְתְּהוֹן; P. de Lagarde 1967) apparently reads וְשַׁלְמֵיהֶם, "fellowship sacrifices." Psalm 69:22–23 (= LXX 68:23–24) is not found among the Qumran Psalms scrolls, although, presumably, these verses were originally part of 4QPsᵃ [4Q83], which breaks off now after 69:1–19 (Flint 1997:257, 267).

Four times, however, Paul's text varies from all other known witnesses to the Psalm.[125] The absence of the prepositional phrase, ἐνώπιον αὐτῶν, and the presence of the pronoun αὐτοῖς do not noticeably affect the meaning of the quotation.[126] Of greater significance, however, are two other variants, namely, the different order of the phrases καὶ εἰς σκάνδαλον and καὶ εἰς ἀνταπόδομα, and the additional phrase καὶ εἰς θήραν. Closer examination of these divergences from LXX suggests that Paul's version of Psalm 68:23–24 in Romans 11:9–10 has been shaped by his reading of other passages of scripture, including, not surprisingly, a passage from Isaiah. I will treat these variants in reverse order.

David in Stereo: Psalm 34 and Psalm 68 in Romans 11:9
The most likely source for Paul's additional phrase καὶ εἰς θήραν in Romans 11:9 is Psalm 34:8 LXX, where the collocation of παγίς and θήρα occurs for the first and only time in the LXX.[127] An intricate web of thematic and verbal connections stretches between Psalm 68 and Psalm 34. In both songs—each of which is attributed to David—the psalmist laments the shame and injustice he suffers at the hands of the wicked and calls upon God for deliverance. Though other psalms also develop this theme of "the righteous sufferer,"[128] Psalm 68 and Psalm 34 share a number of striking verbal parallels. Both suppliants cry out against "those who hate me without cause" (οἱ μισοῦντές με δωρεάν).[129] Both recall their own piety and humility in the face of persecution:[130]

> I bowed *my soul with fasting*, and it became a reproach to me; I made my *clothing sackcloth*, and I became a byword for them.

---

[125] The identical reading, καὶ εἰς θήραν καὶ εἰς σκάνδαλον καὶ εἰς ἀνταπόδομα αὐτοῖς, in LXX MS 55 most likely depends on Rom 11:9 (so Rahlfs 1979).

[126] An old latin MS (Rahlfs's La^G), the Targum, and the Peshitta (but not LXX, α′, σ′, θ′, MT, Syrohexapla) suggest a *Vorlage* in which ולשלומים carries a third person plural pronoun. Thus, it is just possible that αὐτοῖς represents the reading of Paul's *Vorlage* rather than an authorial adaptation.

[127] So also Dunn 1988b:642.

[128] E.g., Psalms 6, 22, 31, 35, 41, 42, 43, 55, 56, 69, 70, among others.

[129] Psalm 68:5; Psalm 34:19. This phrase is found nowhere else in the Psalter. Note also in both verses the adverb, ἀδίκως, used of the enemies' hostility toward the psalmist.

[130] "Fasting" and "sackcloth" appear together only in these two places in the LXX Psalter.

καὶ συνέκαμψα ἐν νηστείᾳ τὴν ψυχήν μου, καὶ ἐγενήθη εἰς ὀνειδισμὸν ἐμοί·
καὶ ἐθέμην τὸ ἔνδυμά μου σάκκον, καὶ ἐγενόμην αὐτοῖς εἰς παραβολήν (Ps
68:11–12).

But while they troubled me, I *clothed* myself in *sackcloth*, and I hum-
bled *my soul with fasting*. . . .[131]

ἐγὼ δὲ ἐν τῷ αὐτοὺς παρενοχλεῖν μοι ἐνεδυόμην σάκκον καὶ ἐταπείνουν ἐν
νηστείᾳ τὴν ψυχήν μου . . . (Ps 34:13).

Most strikingly, both suppliants invoke terrible curses on their tormentors (Ps 68:23–29; Ps 34:6–8). Each of these imprecations calls
down darkness upon the oppressors and bids them be caught like
hapless animals in the hunter's snare:

Let their table become before them a *snare* and a retribution and an
offense. Let their eyes *be darkened* so that they cannot see. . . .

γενηθήτω ἡ τράπεζα αὐτῶν ἐνώπιον αὐτῶν εἰς παγίδα καὶ εἰς ἀνταπόδοσιν
καὶ εἰς σκάνδαλον· σκοτισθήτωσαν οἱ ὀφθαλμοὶ αὐτῶν τοῦ μὴ βλέπειν . . .
(Ps 68:23–24).

Let their way become *darkness* and stumbling. . . . Let a *snare* of which
they were not aware confront them. Let the trap that they hid seize
them, and they will fall in the *snare*.

γενηθήτω ἡ ὁδὸς αὐτῶν σκότος καὶ ὀλίσθημα. . . . ἐλθέτω αὐτοῖς παγὶς ἣν οὐ
γινώσκουσιν καὶ ἡ θήρα ἣν ἔκρυψαν συλλαβέτω αὐτοὺς καὶ ἐν τῇ παγίδι
πεσοῦνται ἐν αὐτῇ (Ps 34:6, 8).

In Romans 11:9, Paul has apparently mingled the words of these
two similar Davidic maledictions. Whether the conflation was deliberate or unconscious,[132] it betrays the apostle's familiarity with the
diction and cadences of the psalms of the righteous sufferer.[133]
Moreover, this conflation may offer a glimpse of the interpretive
logic that lies behind Paul's appeal to David in Romans 11:9–10. It
is notable that Paul, like other early Christian interpreters, appeals

---

[131] Note also the shared focus on the enemies' taunts (Ps 68:11–13; Ps 34:16)
and on the shame the psalmist endures because of his faithfulness to God (Ps
68:8–11, 20–21; Ps 34:7; compare the terminology in 68:7 and 34:4 and the identical set of parallel verbs in 68:7 and 34:26: αἰσχυνθείησαν . . . ἐντραπείησαν).

[132] If the latter, we should probably suppose Paul is quoting here from memory
rather than from a written exemplar.

[133] In employing this designation, I do not claim that early Jewish or Christian
interpreters recognized this to be a genre, let alone a fixed collection, of psalms. I
suggest only that they would have recognized the similarity of outlook and concern
among prayers such as LXX Psalms 21, 34, 40, 68.

to psalms of the righteous sufferer in order to elaborate the story of Jesus. In Romans 15:3, in fact, Paul quotes Psalm 68:10b as Jesus' very own words. Christological interpretations of portions of Psalm 68 appear several times in the Fourth Gospel,[134] as well as in the synoptic Passion narratives.[135] One may reasonably infer that a christocentric reading of the psalms of the righteous sufferer was an interpretive convention widely diffused among early Christians.[136]

Paul's use of Psalm 68 in Romans 15:3 presupposes such a christological reading of the psalm. In Romans 11:9–10, however, attention is focused on the psalmist's persecutors. According to Psalm 68:9, among these tormentors are found the speaker's own relatives.[137] It does not take a great leap of the imagination to envision how, given a christological interpretation of the psalm, Paul found in these hostile kinspeople a prefiguration of those among the Jews who continued to reject his gospel proclaiming Jesus as Lord.[138] Paul's quotation of Psalm 68:23–24, then, evokes a larger story in which "the rest" of Israel stands in a hostile relationship to God's suffering righteous one; as a result, they suffer the curse of darkness and insensibility invoked by "David."[139]

Psalm 68 and the Blinding of Israel

That a larger story about Israel informs Paul's reading of Psalm 68 finds further confirmation when we observe the significant verbal and thematic connections between Psalm 68:23–24 and several other texts to which Paul has already appealed in Romans 9–11. Most

---

[134] Ps 68:5 (John 15:25; cf. Ps 34:19); Ps 68:10a (John 2:17); Ps 68:22 (John 19:28–29).

[135] Ps 68:22 (χολή, ὄξος) in Mark 15:36; Matt 27:34, 48; Luke 23:36; Jn 19:28–29.

[136] See further Dodd 1952a:57–59, 96–106; Vis 1936:49–54; Lindars 1961:99–108; Moo 1983b:225–300; Juel 1988:89–117; Marcus 1992:172–86; Hays 1993a.

[137] ἀπηλλοτριωμένος ἐγενήθην τοῖς ἀδελφοῖς μου καὶ ξένος τοῖς υἱοῖς τῆς μητρός μου.

[138] The use of Psalm 68:26 in Acts 1:20 reveals a similar hermeneutic at work. It is because the psalm was read christologically that the psalmist's curse can be applied to Jesus' betrayer. C. K. Barrett's comment regarding Acts 1:20, "It cannot be said that any attention is given to the context, still less to the original meaning and reference, of the passages cited" (1994:100), reveals the lamentable tendency (that has long dominated modern study of the NT) to measure the use of scripture by the early church against the canons of historical criticism rather than to investigate it in terms of its own internal logic.

[139] The identification of "the rest" of contemporary Israel with the opponents of God is implicit in Paul's reading of other texts (e.g., Isaiah 8:14/28:16; Ps 93:14) that presuppose a division *within* Israel.

prominent is the verbal link that Paul has created between the psalm (ὀφθαλμοί . . . τοῦ μὴ βλέπειν) and the composite citation in Romans 11:8 (Isa 29:10/Deut 29:4/Isa 6:9–10) by altering the latter to read ὀφθαλμοὺς τοῦ μὴ βλέπειν.[140] Just as in Deuteronomy 29:4 Israel's blindness persists "to this day" (ἕως τῆς σήμερον ἡμέρας), so in Psalm 68:24 David prays for his enemies to suffer God's judgment "continually" (διὰ παντός).[141] Isaiah 29:10 attributes Israel's insensibility to God's direct action. Similarly, David asks God to intervene personally to bring retribution on the wicked. David calls down on his persecutors the same spiritual stupor as that poured out by God upon those who rejected Isaiah's message. Taking the two quotations together (Rom 11:8 and 9–10), it is clear that God's sovereign blinding of "the rest" of Israel represents for Paul yet another instantiation of this scriptural pattern of judicial blinding, just as the refusal of so many of his contemporaries to believe the gospel is of a piece with Israel's earlier history of rebellion against their God.

Psalm 68 and the Stone of Stumbling

Equally significant for understanding Paul's thought is the more subtle connection between the imprecation of Psalm 68:23–24 and the threat of judgment for those who do not put their trust in the "stone" of Isaiah 8:14. This latter text (conflated with Isaiah 28:16) played an important role at an earlier stage of Paul's discussion in Romans 9–11, where it helped Paul argue that Israel has failed to attain righteousness because they have not been pursuing the Law ἐκ πίστεως.[142]

> And if you trust in him, he will be for you a sanctuary, and you will not encounter him as the obstruction of a stone or as the obstacle of a rock. But the house of Jacob is in a snare, and they are lying in a trap in Jerusalem.

---

[140] See p. 244 above on the likely Pauline origin of this reading in Romans 11:8.

[141] Note the shared motifs of "darkness" and "blindness" in Psalm 68:24 and in the context of Deut 29:4 (i.e., the curses threatened in Deuteronomy 28:29). For the "bowed back" as a metaphor for oppression or affliction, see Gen 49:8; Ps 80:7 LXX; particularly notable as a parallel to Ps 68:24 is Ps 65:11: εἰσήγαγες ἡμᾶς εἰς τὴν παγίδα, ἔθου θλίψεις ἐπὶ τὸν νῶτον ἡμῶν. Cf. LXX Ps 37:7; 56:7; Isa 58:5; Pr Man 10; Sir 33:27.

[142] See the extended treatment of this passage above, pp. 127–57.

καὶ ἐὰν ἐπ' αὐτῷ πεποιθὼς ᾖς, ἔσται σοι εἰς ἁγίασμα, καὶ οὐχ ὡς λίθου προσκόμματι συναντήσεσθε αὐτῷ οὐδὲ ὡς πέτρας πτώματι· ὁ δὲ οἶκος Ιακωβ ἐν παγίδι, καὶ ἐν κοιλάσματι ἐγκαθήμενοι ἐν Ιερουσαλημ (Isaiah 8:14).

The overt link between Psalm 68:23 and Isaiah 8:14 consists in the word pair, παγίς and σκάνδαλον.[143] However, there is more to the relationship between these two texts in Paul's thought than simply this terminological connection.[144] The echo of Isaiah 8:14 in the diction of Paul's quotation of Psalm 68:23 suggests that for Paul the two passages fit within the same underlying story he has been telling about Israel throughout Romans 9–11, a story whose plot line he finds laid out in Israel's own scriptures.[145] Isaiah 8 draws a line in the sand through the very midst of Israel, separating those who put their trust for deliverance in YHWH alone, and those who, doubting YHWH's righteousness—his power and faithfulness to rescue his people—turn elsewhere for security. According to Isaiah, those who do not trust YHWH find him to be a stumbling stone blocking their path, a snare into which they fall and are caught (8:14–15). Heard in concert with Isaiah 8:14, David's imprecatory prayer that their

---

[143] Although σκάνδαλον does not appear in the LXX version of Isaiah 8:14, I have argued that there are good reasons to suppose that Paul knew another Greek text that did employ this term. The Hebrew terms in Psalm 68:23 and Isaiah 8:14 are identical: לְמוֹקֵשׁ and לְפַח. In the LXX, they are rendered as εἰς παγίδα and εἰς σκάνδαλον (Ps 68:23) and ἐν παγίδι and ἐν κοιλάσματι (Isa 8:14). However, σ' and θ' use σκάνδαλον as a lexical equivalent for מוֹקֵשׁ in Isaiah 8:14.

Ps 69:23; Isa 8:14 MT	Ps 68:23 LXX	Isa 8:14 LXX	Isa 8:14 σ' θ'
לְפַח	εἰς παγίδα	ἐν παγίδι	εἰς παγίδα (σ')
לְמוֹקֵשׁ	εἰς σκάνδαλον	ἐν κοιλάσματι	εἰς σκάνδαλον (σ' θ')

We saw earlier that Paul's citation of Isaiah 8:14 in Romans 9:33 shows lexical affinities with the later Greek versions and probably reflects a septuagintal text revised toward a proto-masoretic exemplar (pp. 126–31). The variant order of clauses in Paul's quotation (εἰς παγίδα . . . καὶ εἰς σκάνδαλον καὶ εἰς ἀνταπόδομα) may be a reflex of the order of the two terms, παγίς . . . σκάνδαλον, in Isaiah 8:14 LXX (revised).

[144] This collocation of terms is fairly rare in the LXX: Josh 23:13; Ps 68:23; 139:6; 140:9; [Isa 8:14]; Wis 14:11; 1 Macc 5:4. Of these texts (apart from Psalm 68:23), Paul quotes only from Isaiah 8:14 (see previous note).

[145] I am deliberately choosing to speak at this point about Paul's thought rather than about "echoes" of scripture in the text of Romans. In light of the picture of Paul as interpreter of scripture that has been emerging from this study, I find it quite plausible that Paul recognized the relationship between Psalm 68:23 and Isaiah 8:14 that I have uncovered. It is much more difficult to suppose that any of his hearers would have caught the connection of language and thought between the two passages, especially since they are separated so widely in Paul's argument.

table become "a snare and a trap and a stumbling stone and retribution" becomes a plea for God to visit on the wicked the fate threatened in Isaiah's oracle. For Paul, "the rest" of Israel suffers the effects of the Davidic curse precisely because they have not put their trust for deliverance in the "stone"—the God who has now acted in Jesus Christ to effect Israel's redemption.[146]

The numerous interconnections noted among Psalm 68, Deuteronomy 29, Isaiah 6, and Isaiah 29 and between Psalm 68 and Isaiah 8 offer a tantalizing glimpse of a larger story about God and Israel that provides coherence to Paul's explicit as well as allusive appeals to scripture throughout Romans 9–11.[147] Paul's explanation for the spiritual insensibility of "the rest" of Israel in Romans 11:7–10 is grounded in a scripture-shaped narrative that emphasizes not only Israel's continued failure to trust in the God who has promised to deliver them, but also God's own unremitting faithfulness to the covenant he has made with his people. It cannot be insisted too strongly that in Romans 9–11 Paul does not conceive of God's sovereignty over Israel apart from this larger covenantal narrative. The divine blinding of Israel is emphatically not God's last word to "the

---

[146] It is unclear what importance to give to the reference to "their table" (Ps 68:23) in the context of Paul's argument. Dinter (1980:154) notes an ancient Christian interpretation that finds in this phrase a reference to the tables used for reading in the synagogue and understands Paul to be alluding to the failure of many Jews to understand scripture properly (cf. 2 Cor 3:14–15). Dinter further suggests (361–63) that Paul alludes to the false prophets' tables full of filth (Isaiah 28:8). Even though a reference to "tables" does not appear in the LXX version of Isaiah 28:8, the word is found in α', σ', θ', as well as in Hebrew, so the possibility of an allusion to Isaiah 28:8 cannot be completely excluded. However, I find this—together with the few other examples Dinter offers—very slim evidence for his conclusion that "Paul was a multi-lingual midrashist, cullying [sic] and tallying texts on the basis of both the Hebrew and Greek textual witnesses, enriching his Greek texts with terms whose connotation is only to be found in the Hebrew substratum of Scripture" (366). If we are to press the question of the significance of "table," I find more plausible the idea that it is a cultic reference (see Isaiah 65:11 and the discussion of this passage above, p. 204; cf. Dunn 1988b:642–43). While Paul never explicitly accuses his contemporary Jews of idolatrous worship, he has repeatedly drawn on passages that speak of Israel's abandonment of God for some other object of trust and devotion (e.g., Exod 32–33; Deut 32; Hos 1–2; Isa 8/28, 65; 1 Kgdms 12; 3 Kgdms 19).

[147] At the same time, these interconnections offer further evidence that the combination of citations in Romans 11:8–10 derives from Paul's own exegetical creativity rather than from some pre-Pauline collection of testimonies. This complex network of intertextual relationships contributes yet another important datum to the inductive case I have been assembling in this study that Romans 9–11 represents a carefully-planned and intricately-woven argument.

rest" of his covenant people. Perhaps for this reason Paul reiterates David's curse only through Psalm 68:24. Certainly the grim finality of the maledictions in Psalm 68:25–29[148] does not suit Paul's personal attitude toward his fellow Jews;[149] nor does it comport with his emphatic denial in the very next verse that Israel has taken a fatal fall (Rom 11:11). Rather, in Paul's view, the profound stupor that has been poured out on "the rest" of Israel represents an intermediate stage in God's plan to redeem Israel. But to show how this is so, Paul must once again turn to Isaiah and to Deuteronomy for assistance.

THE PURPOSE OF ISRAEL'S STUMBLING:
ROMANS 11:11–24

In response to the crucial question, "Has God rejected his inheritance?" Paul has argued vigorously that despite Israel's rejection of the gospel, God remains faithful to his chosen people (11:1–2). God's enduring commitment to Israel is proven by the fact that "at the present time" God is reserving for himself a remnant of Israel, one of whom—but by no means the only one—is Paul himself (11:3–6). "The rest" of Israel, however, God has made insensible, just as scripture testifies (11:7–10). Paul's analysis of the situation naturally gives rise to a further query concerning the fate of those who have been divinely anaesthetized. Do Paul's statements in Romans 11:1–10 imply that the "remnant" has effectively *become* "Israel," or does there remain a future for "the rest" as well?

In Romans 11:11a, the apostle resumes the athletic metaphor

---

[148] Psalm 68:25–29 (LXX):
   [25] ἔκχεον ἐπ' αὐτοὺς τὴν ὀργήν σου, καὶ ὁ θυμὸς τῆς ὀργῆς σου καταλάβοι αὐτούς.
   [26] γενηθήτω ἡ ἔπαυλις αὐτῶν ἠρημωμένη, καὶ ἐν τοῖς σκηνώμασιν αὐτῶν μὴ ἔστω ὁ κατοικῶν· [cf. Acts 1:20]
   [27] ὅτι ὃν σὺ ἐπάταξας, αὐτοὶ κατεδίωξαν, καὶ ἐπὶ τὸ ἄλγος τῶν τραυματιῶν σου προσέθηκαν.
   [28] πρόσθες ἀνομίαν ἐπὶ τὴν ἀνομίαν αὐτῶν, καὶ μὴ εἰσελθέτωσαν ἐν δικαιοσύνῃ σου·
   [29] ἐξαλειφθήτωσαν ἐκ βίβλου ζώντων καὶ μετὰ δικαίων μὴ γραφήτωσαν.

[149] Compare the curse in Psalm 68:28–29 with Paul's asseveration, "I could wish myself accursed from Christ" (Rom 9:3; cf. 10:1), and the echo there of Moses' plea with God on behalf of Israel after the sin of the golden calf (Exod 32:32: καὶ νῦν εἰ μὲν ἀφεῖς αὐτοῖς τὴν ἁμαρτίαν, ἄφες· εἰ δὲ μή, ἐξάλειψόν με ἐκ τῆς βίβλου σου, ἧς ἔγραψας). In Romans 11:14, Paul claims that his labors on behalf of the Gentiles are also an effort to save some of his fellow Jews.

introduced in 9:30 (and reprised as recently as 11:7): "I say, then, they haven't stumbled so as to fall, have they?" (Rom 11:11). Having run up against the "stone of stumbling" (9:33; 11:9), "the rest" of Israel have failed to reach the τέλος of their race—righteousness (9:31; 10:4; 11:7). But has this misstep knocked them out of the contest altogether? The answer Paul gives to this question is crucial for understanding the entire argument of Romans 9–11.[150]

Once again, Israel's scriptures ground Paul's adamant denial that God has forsaken the people he called to be his own. Although Paul does not quote scripture explicitly at this point in his argument, his explanation of God's plan for Israel has been hammered out in conversation with passages cited previously in Romans, particularly Deuteronomy 32 and Isaiah 65. These texts provide the conceptual and temporal framework for Paul's sweeping account of God's design to redeem Israel and, with them, the entire cosmos. This plan is captured succinctly in verses 11b–12:

> Through their misstep,[151] salvation [comes] to the Gentiles, in order to provoke [Israel] to jealousy. And if their misstep [brings] wealth for the cosmos, and their defeat [brings] wealth for the Gentiles, how much more [will] their fullness!
>
> τῷ αὐτῶν παραπτώματι ἡ σωτηρία τοῖς ἔθνεσιν εἰς τὸ παραζηλῶσαι αὐτούς. εἰ δὲ τὸ παράπτωμα αὐτῶν πλοῦτος κόσμου καὶ τὸ ἥττημα αὐτῶν πλοῦτος ἐθνῶν, πόσῳ μᾶλλον τὸ πλήρωμα αὐτῶν.

Paul will spend the rest of the chapter unpacking the full import of these lines, but already the contributions of Deuteronomy 32 and Isaiah 65 to his conception of the divine economy is evident. The language of "provoking to jealousy" recalls Paul's earlier quotation of Deuteronomy 32:21 (Rom 10:19), where God vows to make Israel jealous by means of a "no-nation."[152] As we have seen, Paul interprets Deuteronomy 32:21 in light of the passage he quotes alongside it, Isaiah 65:1 (Rom 10:20). It is by means of this latter text that Paul identifies God's "provoking Israel to jealousy" with his

---

[150] Note the introductory performative λέγω οὖν in Romans 11:11, which stands parallel to the formula used in 11:1. The question in 11:11 is no less vital for Paul's defense of the trustworthiness of God than is his query in 11:1. For Paul, the preservation of a "remnant" apart from "all Israel" is not sufficient to secure the vindication of God's fidelity to Israel.

[151] It is impossible to capture in English Paul's clever play on words, in which παράπτωμα means both "false step" and "transgression."

[152] See the discussion of this passage above, pp. 190–217. See also Bell 1994:271–75.

astonishing decision graciously to call the Gentiles into his people by extending to them the "salvation" promised to Israel.

Yet, for Paul, the drama does not end here; he speaks not only of Israel's "misstep" and "loss," but also of their "fullness." This conception too coheres with the plot line of Israel's story disclosed in Moses' Song. As I argued earlier, Paul's interpretation of Deuteronomy 32:21 hinges on its context in the larger ballad of God and Israel sung by Moses in Deuteronomy 32. There, YHWH's abandonment of Israel is only temporary. Having provoked his people to jealousy, Israel's God once again arises to rescue them by defeating their enemies (Deut 32:34–42). As Paul understands it, the jealous rage into which God seeks to drive Israel by embracing Gentiles will be what eventually leads to the full reconciliation of their estranged relationship (Rom 11:12) and, ultimately, to the renewal of all creation (Rom 11:15).[153] Or, to continue the athletic metaphor, the sight of Gentiles crossing the finish line will be what inspires Israel to regain their feet and run with renewed zeal toward the goal[154]—the righteousness of God revealed in Christ.[155]

---

[153] Cf. Paul's quotation in Romans 15:10 of the doxological conclusion to Moses' Song (32:43), which calls all creation—Israel and the nations *together*—to praise God for the deliverance he has wrought.

[154] One is reminded of the gripping scene in the film *Chariots of Fire* (20th Century Fox, 1981) in which the Scottish sprinter Eric Liddell takes a bad fall in a footrace. As the film rolls in (painfully) slow motion, Liddell picks himself up, steps back on the course, and in a tremendous display of athletic prowess and sheer force of will overtakes the pack of runners to win the race.

[155] While Stowers is keenly aware of the significance of the race metaphor in Romans 9–11, he is surprisingly tone deaf when it comes to the clear echoes in Paul's argument of the story of Israel as told in Deuteronomy 32:

> Paul finds a bit of the sacred Jewish writings (Deut 32:21) meaningful because it fits within an illuminating scenario derived from a most essentially Greek practice. Deut 32:21 says that God will make Israel jealous of gentile nations. Because the same word is central to the Greek conception of athletic competition, Paul can interpret Deut 32:21 through the athletic metaphor. Paul explicitly cites the scriptural text, appealing to its authority, but the allusive background metaphor from the discourse of Greek culture provides the framework of meaning for Deut 32:21 (1994:316).

Stowers's contention that although Paul "privileges the scriptures and situates his Greek texts [i.e., cultural codes] in the background . . . the Greek texts often control the scriptures" is entirely unpersuasive (316). The account I have offered here of Paul's use of Deuteronomy 32 suggests that Paul's thought moves in exactly the opposite direction: Deuteronomy 32 provides the basic story line that Paul then illustrates for his Gentile hearers by using the familiar terminology of a footrace. This is not to deny the importance of hearing Paul's metaphor in the context of hellenistic athletic contests. Stowers has shown how essential this is for understanding Paul's argument. His reading is inadequate not because of what it includes, but because of what it excludes. Since Paul's mission led him to transmit a basically

Paul's Provocative Mission: Deuteronomy 32:21
in Romans 11:13–14

Not surprisingly, Paul sees himself playing a crucial role in the outworking of this scriptural vision. He details his part in the divine
drama in vv. 13–14. Although Paul turns in v. 13 to address his
remarks specifically to the Gentiles in his audience, we must be wary
of naively reading this rhetorical move as evidence that Paul envisions his audience to be composed entirely of Gentiles. The hypothesis of a mixed Jewish/Gentile audience or of multiple intended
audiences may actually make better sense of Paul's decision to single out the Gentiles among his listeners.[156] In any case, it is quite
likely that Paul counts on his exhortation to the Gentiles being "overheard" by Jewish Christians as well (whether in Rome or elsewhere).[157]

Though his calling as an apostle is "to bring about the obedience
of faith among all the Gentiles" (Rom 1:5), Paul avers that his ultimate aim is none other than to provoke his own kindred ("my flesh")
to jealousy and thereby to effect their salvation.

> But I tell you Gentiles, inasmuch as I am an apostle to the Gentiles,[158]
> I make much of my ministry, if somehow I may provoke my kindred
> to jealousy and save some of them.

Jewish message across cultural boundaries, it is necessary when interpreting his letters to allow for important influences from a *variety* of cultural contexts (Stowers
acknowledges this point [316]; he simply fails to follow through on his own insight).
Thus, when studying Paul's metaphors, we have to allow for a number of meaning effects, not only on account of the diversity of Paul's hearers, but also because
of Paul's own social location as a cross-cultural missionary. Only a failure of historical and literary imagination will lead us to insist on a single meaning for Paul's
metaphorical language.

[156] Cf. Paul's similar rhetorical moves in 7:1 ("you who know the Law") and 15:1
("we who are strong"). This latter phrase (and possibly the former) is targeted at a
subgroup within the congregation, but those who are not "strong" (not necessarily
to be identified as *Jewish* Christians) obviously are intended to "overhear" Paul's
exhortation.

[157] See pp. 35–36.

[158] I see no reason to assume that Paul claims here to be *the* (sole) apostle to the
Gentiles (as does Tatum 1997:32–33). Finding this connotation here, where it is
not required grammatically, owes more to a reading of Galatians 2:1–10 (presumably not known to the Roman churches) than to the particular argument of Romans.
Within the context of Romans, it is more plausible to see in 11:13 a reference to
Paul's self-description in 1:5 than to read between the lines and find a reflection
of the "Jerusalem accord" described in Galatians. I have great difficulty hearing
Romans 11:13–14 (or, for that matter, even Gal 2:1–10) as a renunciation on Paul's
part of any desire to preach directly to Jews or as a claim to exclusive authority
to plant churches among the Gentiles (Tatum 1997:110–17).

ὑμῖν δὲ λέγω τοῖς ἔθνεσιν· ἐφ᾽ ὅσον μὲν οὖν εἰμι ἐγὼ ἐθνῶν ἀπόστολος, τὴν διακονίαν μου δοξάζω, εἴ πως παραζηλώσω μου τὴν σάρκα καὶ σώσω τινὰς ἐξ αὐτῶν (Romans 11:13-14).

Historical debates concerning Paul's actual missionary practice, such as the extent to which he actually proclaimed his gospel in Jewish contexts, should not be allowed to blunt the force of what Paul claims here.[159] In this description of his apostolic service (διακονία), Paul asserts that scripture (Deuteronomy 32/Isaiah 65:1) is finding its fulfillment in and through his ministry. This hermeneutic accords fully with his appeals in Romans 10 to Deuteronomy 30:12-13, Isaiah 52:7, and Isaiah 53:1 as descriptions of the apostolic preaching of the gospel and its reception among Gentiles and Jews.[160]

The Dialectic of Scripture and Mission in Paul's Thought
Paul's reading of Deuteronomy 32:21 as a charter for his mission to Gentiles reveals a dynamic dialectic in which the apostle's interpretation of scripture and his practice of ministry continually shape and reshape one another. Paul insists that his own focus on the Gentile mission reflects his deepest conviction that God's intention is ultimately to save Israel along with the entire cosmos, a conviction that has been shaped by his attentiveness to the living voice of Israel's scriptures. Rather than supposing that Paul had a comprehensive and definitive vision of his ministry from the outset, I consider it much more likely that Paul's reading of scripture continued to form and deepen his understanding of God's calling on his life as his circumstances changed.[161] Romans 11:13-14 may well represent an

---

[159] This is not to deny the relative importance of historical reconstruction, only to insist that it not function to prevent us from attending closely to what Paul actually says in the letter. E. P. Sanders has argued that Paul did not attempt to preach to Jews (1983:179-90). Although the evidence of the letters tends to support this view (and the narrative of Acts is schematized enough to arouse suspicion), Paul's claim to have received 39 lashes not once, but five times (2 Cor 11:24), suggests a dogged determination to bring his gospel into the synagogue over a considerable period of time. Sanders recognizes that 2 Cor 11:24 implies Paul's "continuing commitment to Judaism," but he curiously limits this to "attending the synagogue" (192). Apparently Sanders imagines that Paul would have refrained from proclaiming his gospel to his fellow worshippers—despite Paul's insistence in Romans that the gospel is "for the Jew first" and his emotional avowal of his "unceasing grief" over the alienation of his kinspeople from their God.
[160] As we shall see in the next chapter, Paul continues this reading strategy with his quotation of Isaiah 52:15 in Romans 15:21.
[161] I am skeptical of S. Kim's thesis that the main lines of Paul's thought can

understanding of his apostolic role reached by Paul rather late in his career.[162] This interpretation of Deuteronomy 32:21 allows him to locate the ongoing effort to plant churches among the Gentiles in the context of a growing realization that the mission of other apostles directly to Israel has been much less successful than once hoped. Paul throws himself into the task of planting churches among the Gentiles not because he believes God has chosen Gentiles *in place of* Israel, but because he is convinced that the Gentile mission itself will finally lead to Israel's full restoration to their God. It is this scripture-shaped conception of his unique role in the divine plan that Paul now commends to the Roman Christians as he solicits their assistance for a major new thrust into the western Mediterranean.

While Israel's scriptures thus help to form Paul's sense of his own vocation, it is also clear that Paul's understanding of the gospel revealed to him by God and his actual experiences as an apostle to the Gentiles shape his interpretation of Israel's scripture in decisive ways.[163] This is manifestly so in the case of his rereading of Deuteronomy 32:21 in Romans 10–11. In the Song of Moses, the role of the nations is to punish Israel. It is their victories over God's people—attributed to God's transferral of favor from Israel to the nations—that make Israel jealous (Deut 32:21). But these nations themselves do not come to put their trust and allegiance in Israel's God; on the contrary, they remain reprehensible idolators (Deut 32:27–33).[164] Consequently, God reaffirms his election of Israel by rising up to defeat the nations whom he has temporarily allowed to plunder his people (Deut 32:34–42).[165]

---

all be traced back to his conversion experience (1981; Kim conveniently summarizes his argument concerning Paul's understanding of his mission in 1997:412–15). It does not follow, however, that Paul is just making up arguments on the spot as he writes Romans. The truth of the matter probably lies somewhere between: "Paul thought this way from the time of his calling on," and: "in the heat of dictation, Paul just happened to light upon a clever argument he'd never considered before." I would propose that in most cases, Paul has thought fairly deeply and at length about what he writes in Romans (I grant that Galatians has much more the flavor of being composed in the heat of battle). My reading of Paul's use of scripture in Romans 9–11 would appear to sustain this hypothesis, at least for these chapters.

[162] He certainly does not write anything like this in earlier letters (see Tatum 1997:110–17).

[163] B. Lindars notes, "the creative aspects of Paul's thought are the result of grappling with problems arising in the course of his mission" (1985:781 n. 28).

[164] Deuteronomy 32:43 does envision Gentiles joining in the praise of Israel's God, but only after Israel's enemies have been defeated and Israel itself has been reconciled to God.

[165] Cf. the similar idea in Isaiah 10:5–34, discussed above, pp. 100–101.

Paul's recontextualization of Deuteronomy 32:21 presents a quite different scenario, however. As Paul would have it, God is making Israel jealous not by allowing the Gentiles to oppress them, but by graciously embracing these strangers as his own and thereby stirring up in Israel a zeal to resume their proper place as God's people. In Romans 11, the Gentiles appear not as a divine scourge to be wielded for a time and then cast aside, but as objects of divine mercy and instruments through whom God will ultimately bring salvation to Israel. Paul unabashedly claims that Israel "has known" that their God would extend his grace to the Gentiles while most of Israel remained unmoved by his arms outstretched in reconciliation (Rom 10:19–21). In reality, Paul's interpretation of Deuteronomy 32:21 is a radical re-reading of Moses' Song plausible only when seen through the eyes of one fully committed to the Gentile mission. That Paul accomplishes this remarkable reinterpretation of scripture by means of another verse of scripture (Isaiah 65:1) only reveals further the complexity of this dialectic, for Paul's reading of Isaiah 65:1–2 is itself inconceivable apart from his prior convictions and experiences as an apostle to Gentiles.[166]

Israel's "Fullness" and Cosmic Redemption

Paul's version of the drama of redemption, shaped both by his reading of Israel's scriptures and by his concrete experiences as an apostle, finds no parallel among his predecessors or contemporaries—Jewish or Christian—for the scope and importance of the part it assigns to Gentiles in the salvation of Israel. Nonetheless, for Paul, Israel still plays the crucial role in the redemption of the cosmos. It is their refusal to respond to the gospel that has opened the way for the mission to the Gentiles. Moreover, the inclusion of "the rest" of Israel will be the event that ushers in the restoration of the entire created order.[167]

These convictions rise to the surface in the form of two somewhat

---

[166] See below on Paul's use of Deuteronomy 32:43 in Romans 15:11 for further evidence of the effects of the Gentile mission on his reading of the Song of Moses (pp. 315–17, 328). Note the tension in Romans 16:25–26 (which, if not by Paul, captures remarkably well many of the key emphases of the letter; see pp. 164–65 n. 140) between the claim that this "mystery" has been hidden for long ages and the statement that it is now being made known "through the prophetic scriptures." The scriptures have not changed; rather, God has finally granted eyes to read and minds to grasp them aright (cf. 2 Cor 3:12–18).

[167] See further Allison 1980, 1985.

cryptic *qal va-ḥomer* arguments that frame Paul's discussion of his own role in the divine plan to redeem Israel.

> And if their misstep [brings] wealth for the cosmos, and their defeat [brings] wealth for the Gentiles, how much more [will] their fullness!
>
> εἰ δὲ τὸ παράπτωμα αὐτῶν πλοῦτος κόσμου καὶ τὸ ἥττημα αὐτῶν πλοῦτος ἐθνῶν, πόσῳ μᾶλλον τὸ πλήρωμα αὐτῶν (Romans 11:12).

> For if their rejection [brings about] the reconciliation of the world, what will be their acceptance if not life from the dead?
>
> εἰ γὰρ ἡ ἀποβολὴ αὐτῶν καταλλαγὴ κόσμου, τίς ἡ πρόσλημψις εἰ μὴ ζωὴ ἐκ νεκρῶν; (Romans 11:15).

In Paul's view, Israel's own stumbling and apparent defeat—its failure to attain the righteousness of God to which the Law was leading (now revealed to be none other than Christ)—has had cosmic consequences. Their misstep has brought a wealth of benefits to the rest of the world,[168] as the Gentiles have astonishingly, by God's grace, been awarded the prize Israel sought.[169] Israel has been the agent of blessing for all the nations,[170] though, tragically, God's people have largely failed to realize the blessing themselves. At this point, however, Paul's foundational conviction that God has not rejected his people Israel kicks in. If their exclusion has brought salvation to the Gentiles, he reasons, Israel's eventual "fullness," their "acceptance"[171] by God, will mean nothing less than the resurrection of

---

[168] For an Isaianic "spin" on πλοῦτος κόσμου and πλοῦτος ἐθνῶν, see below, p. 292.

[169] To return for a moment to the introduction of this athletic metaphor in Romans 9:30, it is crucial to Paul's figure that the Gentiles were never competing for the prize in the first place. It is not that they have somehow beaten Israel at its own game. Rather, they have received the prize solely ἐκ πίστεως. Likewise, it is no accident that, according to Paul, Israel will attain its goal not by dint of its own efforts, but through the mercy of God (11:32).

[170] Note the repeated statement in Genesis that Abraham and his offspring will bring blessing to all nations: 12:3; 18:18; 22:18; 26:4. The promise is recalled by later writers as well (e.g., Jer 4:2; Sir 44:21; cf. Isa 19:24–25), including Paul (Gal 3:8–9, 14). Although Paul labors to detach these texts from an interpretation that requires Gentiles to join ethnic Israel through circumcision and observance of Torah, he remains convinced that it is by becoming united with Abraham's descendants through faith that Gentiles are saved (Gal 3:23–29; cf. Rom 4:11, 16–17; 11:17–24).

[171] The noun πρόσλημψις occurs only here in the NT. Although the noun form is not found in the LXX, the related verb appears, interestingly enough, in 1 Kingdoms 12:22b. Paul appropriates the first half of this verse to insist that God has not forsaken Israel (11:1–2): οὐκ ἀπώσεται κύριος τὸν λαὸν αὐτοῦ διὰ τὸ ὄνομα αὐτοῦ τὸ μέγα, ὅτι ἐπιεικέως κύριος προσελάβετο ὑμᾶς αὐτῷ εἰς λαόν.

the dead, the consummation of the long-awaited renewal of the entire cosmos.[172]

Paul's veiled references here to Israel's eschatological redemption presage the climax of his entire argument in Romans 11:25–36. Yet it is crucial to recognize that this promise of future "fullness" and "acceptance" is not a *deus ex machina* hurriedly thrust on stage just at the point where the implications of Paul's logic finally become too terrible for him to bear. As I have argued throughout this study, Israel's ultimate reconciliation to God is a conviction that undergirds Paul's theodicy in Romans 9–11 from the very beginning. The concept of a "remnant," introduced first in Romans 9:27, does not function to exclude "the rest" of Israel from the scope of God's redemptive activity, as if "remnant" and "Israel" were coterminous entities in Paul's conceptual universe. Rather, the existence of a remnant "at the present time" (Rom 11:5) vouchsafes for Paul the fuller redemption of "all Israel" in the future.

Paul explicates this connection between the "remnant" and the ultimate salvation of "all Israel" by means of two metaphors. The first draws on the commandment to offer to God the first portion of dough (Num 15:18–21, ἀπαρχὴ φυράματος):[173] "If the first portion [of dough] is holy, then so is the entire lump" (εἰ δὲ ἡ ἀπαρχὴ ἁγία, καὶ τὸ φύραμα, Rom 11:16a). By giving to the Lord the first portion, one acknowledges that all of one's sustenance belongs to God and represents God's gracious gift.[174] In the same way, "the remnant in the present time, chosen by grace" from Israel, is a sign and seal that "all Israel" is the Lord's, the earnest of the full harvest of redemption yet to come.[175]

---

[172] See Romans 8:18–25, especially 8:23; cf. 1 Corinthians 15:23–28.

[173] This offering is mentioned again in Ezekiel 44:30 and in Nehemiah 10:37. The rabbis call it *ḥallah* (see *m. Ḥal.*).

[174] So Milgrom 1990:121–22 and Budd 1984:171. Note the solemn "confession" at the offering of first fruits in Deuteronomy 26:1–11. It is in the extended sense of "belonging to God" that Paul is using the term "holy." Once the firstfruits were consecrated to God and offered to the priest, the rest of the dough was available for normal use (cf. *m. Ḥal.* 1:9); it was not "holy" in the technical cultic sense that it could be eaten only by a priest in a state of purity (Num 18:8–19, 32; cf. Jdt 11:10–15).

[175] In Romans 8:23, the metaphor ἀπαρχή indicates that the present experience of the Spirit's presence is a foretaste of the resurrection and cosmic restoration yet to come. Note also Paul's use of ἀπαρχή to designate the first converts from a region, who are the pledge of a much greater harvest there (Rom 16:5; 1 Cor 16:15). Similarly, Christ's resurrection is the guarantee that those who belong to him will also be raised in him (1 Cor 15:20, 23).

Paul's second metaphor, that of root and branches (11:16b–24), similarly finds in the preservation of "the remnant" a sure hope for the restoration of "the rest." Because Israel—the root—has been chosen to be God's own possession, those who belong to Israel—the branches—are also God's (11:16b). Paul concedes that *some* of the branches have been cut off (11:17). Nevertheless, despite the severe pruning, the root remains firmly planted, and the remaining branches continue to flourish. The apostle to the Gentiles takes pains to point out to his Gentile listeners that God, in defiance of all horticultural logic, has grafted them, wild olive branches that they are, onto this very root.[176] They must not forget that it is this root that makes them holy and that continues to support and nourish them as well as its natural branches.[177]

Paul's earlier contention that Israel has stumbled in order to bring salvation to the Gentiles (11:11) finds figurative expression in his statement that natural branches were cut off *so that* wild branches could be grafted in (11:19). Yet God's unconventional husbandry does not reflect the superiority of the uncultivated branches. Instead, it displays both the incredible wideness of God's mercy, which embraces even those who had no reason to expect his blessing, and the sobering severity of his judgment, which does not overlook the unbelief of God's own people. The proper response to such a combination of grace and impartiality is not boasting,[178] but holy fear and a fixed determination to hold fast to God's goodness. The Gentiles stand "by faith" (11:20), which in the context of Romans refers first and foremost to God's own faithfulness, embodied and enacted in and through Jesus Christ. If they fail to remain in God's goodness, however, they too will find themselves severed from the root.[179]

Although Paul clearly intends by means of this extended metaphor to call his Gentile listeners to humility and perseverance in faith, the

---

[176] See Hartung 1999; Rengstorff 1978.

[177] See further Davies 1984b.

[178] Paul evidences a pronounced concern with Gentile pride in this section (11:18, 20, 25). It is difficult not to think that he is alluding to strained relations between Gentile believers and Jews in Rome, though whether this tension is real or simply imagined by Paul on the basis of his experience elsewhere is perhaps less clear.

[179] It is not insignificant from a pastoral perspective that Paul exhorts them to hold fast to God's goodness rather than to keep believing. The focus remains on God and not on an introspective obsession with one's spiritual "temperature." Nevertheless, the possibility of being cut off is real, and Paul regularly exhorts his converts to stand steadfast in their faith. See further Gundry-Volf 1990.

central theme of his trope is God's continuing commitment to Israel even in the face of Israel's unfaithfulness. It is Israel's refusal to embrace the gospel of Christ, in which God's righteousness is now fully revealed, that has led to their being cut off.[180] But Paul does not believe that Israel's unbelief is the end of the story. The branches God has pruned away have not been thrown on the trash heap and burned.[181] Instead, Paul argues, these natural branches may yet be regrafted onto the tree from which they have been cut if they do not remain in their unbelief (11:23).[182]

Although Paul does insist that regrafting entails the abandonment of unbelief for a response of faith and trust in what God has done in Christ (11:20a, 23a), his hope for Israel does not rest primarily on Israel's own ability to change its heart, but on *God's power* to regraft them and on *God's faithfulness* to his prior election of Israel. Paul alludes to the election of Israel by reminding his hearers that the lopped off branches belong to the cultivated olive tree; it is "their own olive tree" (τῇ ἰδίᾳ ἐλαίᾳ). The point is not so much that the branches have a claim on the root, but rather that the root has a claim on the branches. We have thus come full circle to the statement with which Paul began this parable: "If the root is holy, so are the branches" (11:16b). By virtue of his election of Israel, God has chosen this root and these branches for his own and committed himself in turn to care for them.

Moreover, God not only remains faithful to "the rest" of Israel, he is also fully *able* to fulfill that commitment by securing their redemption. Again Paul resorts to *qal va-ḥomer* reasoning: If God is

---

[180] Note the echo in 11:20, 23 (ἀπιστία) and in 11:30–31 (ἀπείθεια/ἀπειθέω) of Isaiah 65:2, λαὸς ἀπειθῶν (Rom 10:21). I noted above the crucial role that πίστις plays in Isaiah 8:14/28:16 (quoted in Romans 9:33) and their wider narrative contexts in Isaiah, where Israel's failure to trust in God's righteousness—God's power and faithfulness to deliver them—leads to their stumbling. Similarly, in Deuteronomy 32:21, God's provoking his people to jealousy is a response to their prior unfaithfulness in embracing other gods (32:20: ὅτι γενεὰ ἐξεστραμμένη ἐστίν, υἱοί, οἷς οὐκ ἔστιν πίστις ἐν αὐτοῖς).

[181] Contrast the figure in John 15:1–8 (v. 6); cf. John the Baptist's metaphor for judgment in Matthew 13:10//Luke 3:9.

[182] Bell argues that "Israel comes *to the Church* through jealousy" (1994:275 n. 323, emphasis mine; cf. 134 n. 153). However, this completely inverts Paul's figure, in which it is Gentiles who join Israel (the "root"). "The rest" of Israel are still "natural branches" who will be regrafted to their own root, not joined to another entity. In Romans 11, the Church does not supersede Israel; rather, Gentiles have been joined *to Israel*, who remain God's one people.

mighty enough to go against nature, as it were, by grafting wild branches onto a cultivated olive tree, how much more is he able to regraft the natural branches onto their own tree?[183] God's power (δυνατός, 11:23b), displayed in his exercise of wrath toward vessels of dishonor (ἡ δύναμις, 9:17; τὸ δυνατόν, 9:22), now shows itself most gloriously in the redemption of the people he chose to be his very own.

"ALL ISRAEL WILL BE SAVED": ROMANS 11:25–27

Paul is convinced both that God is able to take away Israel's unbelief and that God has committed himself to doing this very thing. Consequently, what in vv. 23–24 Paul entertains as a possibility, in vv. 25ff. he immediately depicts as a certain future reality. Once again, a quotation from Isaiah plays a crucial role in the apostle's exposition of God's redemptive design:

Οὐ γὰρ θέλω ὑμᾶς ἀγνοεῖν, ἀδελφοί, τὸ μυστήριον τοῦτο, ἵνα μὴ ἦτε [παρ'] ἑαυτοῖς φρόνιμοι, ὅτι πώρωσις ἀπὸ μέρους τῷ Ἰσραὴλ γέγονεν ἄχρι οὗ τὸ πλήρωμα τῶν ἐθνῶν εἰσέλθῃ καὶ οὕτως πᾶς Ἰσραὴλ σωθήσεται. . . .

Lest his Gentile listeners regard themselves too highly in view of the favor God has shown them at Israel's expense,[184] Paul reveals to them that their inclusion is but one act in a drama whose culmination is the redemption of "all Israel."[185] In employing the term μυστήριον, Paul implies that what follows has been revealed to him by God.[186] At the same time, in the very next verse, he emphasizes

---

[183] Cf. Hosea's image of restored Israel as an olive tree sprouting new branches and bearing abundant fruit (Hos 14:7): πορεύσονται οἱ κλάδοι αὐτοῦ καὶ ἔσται ὡς ἐλαία κατάκαρπος.

[184] I take εἶναι ἑαυτοῖς φρόνιμοι to refer to the same attitude of superiority mentioned previously in 11:18–20 (κατακαυχᾶσθαι, ὑψηλὰ φρόνειν).

[185] The phrase, "I do not want you to be ignorant," introduces new information in Romans 1:13, 2 Corinthians 1:8, and 1 Thessalonians 4:13. In 1 Corinthians 10:1, it introduces a novel interpretation of what is most likely a familiar scriptural narrative.

[186] The term μυστήριον is often associated in Paul's writings with "gospel" (Rom 16:25; 1 Cor 2:1, 7; 4:1; cf. Eph 1:9; 3:3, 4, 9; 6:19; Col 1:26–27). The closest parallel to Romans 11:25 may be 1 Cor 15:51, where the "mystery" also refers to an eschatological event—the resurrection "at the last trumpet." On the term "mystery" as "virtually a technical term in early Jewish and early Chrstian apocalyptic and prophetic texts," see Aune 1983:250–53, 333 (quotation from 333); Bornkamm 1967; R. E. Brown 1968; Coppens 1968; Bockmuehl 1990.

that this "mystery" is consonant with the witness of the scriptures to God's eschatological redemption of Israel (Rom 11:26–27). What is new in Paul's statement is not the belief that "all Israel" will be saved; Paul grounds this conviction in the scriptural quotation that follows, and it has been implicit in his previous citations and allusions to Israel's scriptures. What is new is the idea that the full redemption of Israel *awaits the completion of the Gentile mission.*[187] Romans 11:25–26a states in explicit terms the temporal scheme that Paul's reference to the remnant "in the present time" (11:5) and his veiled allusions to Israel's future "fullness" (11:12) and "acceptance" (11:15) have presupposed.[188] The "insensibility" (πώρωσις) that has come upon "the rest" of Israel will last only until (ἄχρι οὗ) the "fullness" of the Gentiles comes in to God's people. When this full number is attained,[189] God will act to save "all Israel," just as the scriptures promise.

Paul's reference to "all Israel" continues to engender debate,[190] but

---

[187] Where the redemption of the Gentiles was considered at all in Second Temple Jewish texts, it was normally subsequent to and peripheral to the restoration of Israel (see Donaldson 1997:51–78; Goodman 1994a; McKnight 1991; Fredriksen 1991; E. P. Sanders 1985:213–18, 1992:291–92). However, Donaldson argues that one important school of thought, holding that Gentiles could only join Israel *before* the eschatological consummation, actively sought proselytes (see below, p. 293 n. 227; see also Feldman 1993, an important study of various ways in which Gentiles in the ancient world were attracted to Judaism). Paul's statements in Gal 2:1–10 would suggest that the Jerusalem "pillars" viewed the mission to the Gentiles as secondary to, if not subsequent to, the mission to the Jews. According to the narrative of Acts, there was only a gradual recognition by many in the early church that God was at the present time calling Gentiles as well as Jews. In contrast, the "apocalyptic discourse" in Mark and Matthew places the preaching of the gospel to the Gentiles *before* the final redemption of Israel (Mark 13:10; Matt 24:14).

[188] The same temporal scheme underlies Paul's subsequent remarks in 11:30–31.

[189] Paul gives no indication as to when this condition might be fulfilled, though he may well have hoped to see it in his lifetime. Presumably he believed that the "fullness" of the Gentiles was a group whose number was known only to God. Romans 15:19 has been taken as Paul's claim already to have brought in the full number of Gentiles in the eastern Mediterranean (notably by Munck 1959:47–49, 1967:132–35; cf. Aus 1979; E. P. Sanders 1983:189), but this is by no means the most natural interpretation of Paul's words. Certainly he does not think that all preaching of the gospel should now cease in those regions. Rather, Paul is speaking in Romans 15:19 with reference to the fulfillment of his own particular commission as an apostle to preach where Christ is not yet known.

[190] A full discussion and evaluation of the literature on this question is, for obvious reasons, impossible here. Recent treatments of this text include Davies 1984a; Hahn 1982; Harding 1998; Harrington 1992; Holtz 1990; Hvalvik 1990; Keller 1998; S. Kim 1997; Mußner 1976; Nanos 1996:239–88; Ponsot 1982; Refoulé 1984; E. P. Sanders 1978, 1983:192–98; Schaller 1984; Sievers 1997; C. D. Stanley 1993a.

it is probably best understood in light of his earlier division of "Israel" into "the elect" (ἡ ἐκλογή) and "the rest" who have been rendered insensible (οἱ λοιποὶ ἐπωρώθησαν, 11:7). Paul's statement in 11:25 that a "partial insensibility has come upon Israel" (πώρωσις ἀπὸ μέρους τῷ Ἰσραὴλ γέγονεν) clearly alludes to this bifurcation of Israel and creates an *inclusio* around the whole section.[191] In the intervening verses, "the rest" of Israel are the primary object of Paul's concern. It is they who have stumbled, but not fallen completely (11:11a). It is they whom God has made jealous by embracing Gentiles (11:11b). When Paul speaks of "their fullness" and "their acceptance," it is to this group that he refers (11:12, 15). When Paul talks about "some of the branches" that were broken off but that can be regrafted onto their own olive tree by God (11:17–24), it is "the rest" whom he has in mind. Paul's refusal to employ the term "Israel" as a name for either "the elect" or "the rest" in Romans 11:8–24 suggests that "all Israel" in 11:25 includes both groups—"the elect," who have already obtained what "Israel" sought, and "the rest," who have been temporarily rendered insensible but whose future "fullness" and "acceptance" Paul can anticipate with confidence.[192]

Although "all Israel" may also include those Gentiles who have "come in" (11:25),[193] Paul's attention in the following verses remains focused

---

[191] Although it is strictly true that ἀπὸ μέρους modifies πώρωσις rather than "Israel," the clear terminological link with 11:7 requires that "partial insensibility" mean that some Israelites have been blinded while others have not. The Peshitta takes ἀπὸ μέρους as temporal (cf. Rom 15:24), but this makes ἄχρι οὗ somewhat redundant. In addition, the verbal link with 11:7 favors the partitive sense (for partitive ἀπὸ μέρους, see Rom 15:15; 2 Cor 1:14; 2:5).

[192] So also Dinter 1980:53.

[193] This view, argued recently by N. T. Wright (1991:250), is certainly a plausible inference from Paul's language of the Gentiles "coming in," particularly when it is heard in conjunction with the olive tree metaphor, where Gentile "branches" are grafted into the "root," which is Israel (cf. Donaldson 1997:215–48, who argues that for Paul, Gentiles become full members of an Israel reconfigured around Christ). While I follow Wright in seeing Gentiles included implicitly in the phrase "all Israel," I would stress that Paul's focus in the following verses remains on "the rest" of ethnic Israel. It must be admitted, however, that even though Paul can refer to his converts' past lives as "when you were Gentiles"—implying that they are something else now (1 Thess 4:5; 1 Cor 12:2; cf. Eph 2:11; 4:17)—and although he can talk of the exodus generation as the Gentile Corinthians' "fathers" (1 Cor 10:1) and speak of Gentiles as children of Abraham, Isaac and of "Jerusalem above" (Gal 3–4; Rom 4), Paul still curiously refrains from explicitly denominating them "Israel." Galatians 6:16, καὶ ἐπὶ τὸν Ἰσραὴλ τοῦ θεοῦ, may be the sole exception (Martyn suggests that Paul's more nuanced definition of "Israel" in Romans reflects the apostle's response to a backlash against his statement in Galatians 6:16 [1997a:32–34, 567 n. 13; cf. 1997b:43–45]. If this καί is epexegetic, then Paul is here equating the "Israel of God" with those who define membership in God's people not on the

on the full inclusion of "the rest" who have in the present time been rendered insensible.[194] As the pairing of adverbs, οὕτως . . . καθώς indicates,[195] Paul bases his confidence in their ultimate redemption

---

basis of circumcision, but in light of God's act of cosmic redemption in Christ (καινὴ κτίσις; see further Martyn 1997a:567; E. P. Sanders 1983:173–74). At the same time, there are indications that Paul's thought tends toward the identification of the Church as a third entity (1 Cor 10:32; Gal 3:28—though, significantly, he speaks in these passages not of Ἰσραήλ, but of Ἰουδαῖοι). See the careful and nuanced discussion in E. P. Sanders 1983:171–79; see further Harvey 1996. The tensions inherent in Paul's use of the term "Israel" can be resolved only by recognizing the eschatological substructure of his thought (as Daniel Boyarin fails to do in his brilliant misreading of Paul [1994]). For Paul, "Israel" will be a complete entity only when "the fullness of the Gentiles" comes in and "the Redeemer" comes from Zion to take away "Jacob's" sins.

[194] N. T. Wright argues that, in Paul's view, the completion of the Gentile mission *is* the salvation of "all Israel" without remainder (1991:246–51). Wright contends that Paul has "polemically redefined" the term "Israel" so that in Romans 11:26 "all Israel" refers to Jews and Gentiles being won to the gospel now (cf. νῦν, 11:31 א B D) through Paul's (and the church's) missionary efforts, *rather than* to ethnic Israel. According to Wright, Paul envisions the salvation of this newly delimited "Israel" as taking place currently, as he and others preach the gospel (cf. Rom 11:13–14). Thus, the "fullness" of the Gentiles will *complete*, rather than lead to, the salvation of "all Israel." There is for Paul no eschatological turning of Israel to God subsequent to the Gentile mission. Not only does this interpretation demand that "Israel" in 11:25 refer to a group (i.e., the "rest") not included in "all Israel" in 11:26, it requires Wright to hear the subsequent quotation from Isaiah, which speaks of God's removal of "Jacob's" sins, as well as Paul's previous statements in 11:12, 15, as descriptions of the salvation of *individual* Israelites: "The ὅταν ἀφέλωμαι in 11.27b enables Paul to include the idea of a recurring action. 'Whenever' God takes away their sins, i.e. whenever Jews come to believe in Christ and so enter the family of God, in that moment the promises God made long ago to the patriarchs are being reaffirmed" (251). Similarly, he comments on 11:15, "When a Gentile comes into the family of Christ, it is as it were a *creatio ex nihilo*, but when a Jew comes in it is like a resurrection (compare 4.17, in context)" (248). This individualization of "Israel" strikes me as quite out of step with Paul's usage elsewhere in Romans 9–11 (9:6 notwithstanding). The strongest objection to Wright's reading, however, is that by denying that the solution Paul offers to the problem of Israel's rejection of the gospel is essentially a *temporal* one—partial hardening now, fullness later—Wright leaves out "the rest" of Israel who have temporarily been rendered insensible: once "the fullness of the Gentiles comes in," the show is over; those who are hardened can expect only judgment (249; in n. 44, Wright claims that Romans 11:25ff. is closely linked in thought to 1 Thess 2:14–16). It would seem that God has indeed rejected his people by inflicting them with spiritual insensibility, if he does not also intend to remove their blindness in the future (11:7–10). There is not space here to offer a full critique of Wright's reading of Paul in terms of an essentially "realized" eschatology. However, Allison (1999) makes a convincing case that in his reconstruction of Second Temple Jewish eschatological expectations, Wright dramatically misreads the evidence in attempting to downplay the importance of future eschatology. As will become clear in the ensuing discussion, I hold the view that in Romans 11 Paul anticipates a massive turning of Jews to Christ *as a result of* and *subsequent to* the entrance of the full number of Gentiles.

[195] Wright (1991:249–50) argues that οὕτως in Romans 11:26 refers backward

on scripture's testimony that God himself will come to deliver his people:

> . . . and thus all Israel will be saved, just as it is written: "The redeemer will come from Zion; he will remove ungodliness from Jacob. And this [will be] my covenant with them, when I take away their sins."

Paul's quotation is interesting in its own right as a rather deft conflation of two texts widely separated from one another within the book of Isaiah, Isaiah 59:20–21 and Isaiah 27:9. In addition, closer investigation of the larger literary contexts from which these verses are drawn reveals Paul's deep indebtedness in Romans 9–11 to the larger story Isaiah tells about God's passionate commitment to restore Israel to himself. We turn first to examine the quotation itself.

Isaiah 59:20–21 and Isaiah 27:9 in Romans 11:26–27: The Text

As Figure 4.7 shows, Paul's combined citation follows Isaiah 59:20–21 closely through the end of the first clause of 59:21, "and this [will be] my covenant with them." At this point, a line from Isaiah 27:9 completes the sentence. Although the two texts share only a few words in common, there is a remarkable correspondence between Isaiah 59:20–21 and Isaiah 27:9 both in theme and in syntactical structure. This double similarity would have made conflation—whether intentional or not—a simple matter.[196]

---

and means that all Israel is saved *as* (not after) the fullness of the Gentiles comes in (see the previous note). The pairing of οὕτως and καθώς occurs two other times in the NT (Luke 24:24; Phil 3:17); in both cases, οὕτως points forward to the clause introduced by καθώς. (So also in the LXX: Gen 18:5; Neh 5:12; Jer 19:11; Dan 6:12a. In Judg 5:31 and 2 Kgdms 9:11, οὕτως refers backward, rather than pointing forward to a following καθώς, but the two adverbs occur in clauses separated by καί). If καθώς in Romans 11:26 is understood solely as part of the citation formula καθώς γέγραπται, it is certainly possible to take οὕτως as a reference to what precedes. This still does not require Wright's interpretation, however. E. P. Sanders, who thinks οὕτως points backwards, understands the sense of the clause to be: "and thus—in that manner—all Israel will be saved: as a *consequence* of the Gentile mission, as Paul had already said (11:13–16)" (1983:193; emphasis mine).

[196] Stanley argues that Paul has taken over a pre-formed citation (1992b:166–71; expanded in Stanley 1993a). His reasons in favor of a non-Pauline origin for this conflated citation are less than compelling, however. Stanley claims both that there is nothing clearly "Pauline" or "Christian" about this conflation of texts and that none of the variants from the LXX may be traced with confidence to Paul. This appeal to the "criterion of dissimilarity" carries little weight, however, since it unfairly requires that Paul be un-Jewish or distinctively "Pauline" (whatever that might mean)

Figure 4.7: Isaiah 59:20–21 LXX and Isaiah 27:9a LXX in
Romans 11:26–27

Key:
single underline	agreement between Isa 59:20–21 and Rom 11:26–27
double underline	agreement between Isa 27:9a and Rom 11:27
italic	agreement among all three columns

Isaiah 59:20–21 LXX	Romans 11:26–27	Isaiah 27:9a LXX
²⁰ *καὶ* ἥξει ἕνεκεν Σιων ὁ ῥυόμενος καὶ ἀποστρέψει ἀσεβείας ἀπὸ Ιακωβ. ²¹ *καὶ αὕτη αὐτοῖς ἡ παρ' ἐμοῦ διαθήκη,*	²⁶ καθὼς γέγραπται· ἥξει ἐκ Σιὼν ὁ ῥυόμενος, ἀποστρέψει ἀσεβείας ἀπὸ *Ἰακώβ.* ²⁷ *καὶ αὕτη αὐτοῖς ἡ παρ' ἐμοῦ διαθήκη,* ὅταν ἀφέλωμαι τὰς ἁμαρτίας αὐτῶν.	διὰ τοῦτο ἀφαιρεθήσεται ἡ ἀνομία *Ἰακωβ,* καὶ τοῦτό ἐστιν ἡ εὐλογία αὐτοῦ, ὅταν ἀφέλωμαι αὐτοῦ τὴν ἁμαρτίαν.

Isa 59:20–21 MT:

²⁰ וּבָא לְצִיּוֹן גּוֹאֵל וּלְשָׁבֵי פֶשַׁע בְּיַעֲקֹב נְאֻם יְהוָה
²¹ וַאֲנִי זֹאת בְּרִיתִי אוֹתָם אָמַר יְהוָה רוּחִי אֲשֶׁר עָלֶיךָ
וּדְבָרַי אֲשֶׁר־שַׂמְתִּי בְּפִיךָ

Isa 27:9a MT:

לָכֵן בְּזֹאת יְכֻפַּר עֲוֹן־יַעֲקֹב וְזֶה כָּל־פְּרִי הָסֵר חַטָּאתוֹ

every time he quotes a text. Stanley further argues (1) that Paul would have been unlikely to give such emphasis to the word διαθήκη in a citation, since the word hardly figures elsewhere in his writings, and (2) that had Paul known the full context of Isaiah 59:20–21, he would not have passed by the opportunity to link διαθήκη with τὸ πνεῦμα τὸ ἐμόν. Apart from the problems inherent in attempting to predict what Paul "would have done" as an interpreter of scripture, Stanley's second argument actually works against the first. Given the fact that the term διαθήκη plays so little a role in Paul's writings and that nowhere else does he explicitly link the two words διαθήκη and πνεῦμα, it is hardly the case that by choosing to end the quotation of Isaiah 59:21 where he does, Paul would have passed over "an association that seems tailormade for Paul's theology" (1993a:124). The observation concerning Paul's infrequent use of the term διαθήκη is itself of dubious value, however, for even if Paul took this conflated citation over pre-formed, the word is still there. Why it would have been more appealing to Paul in the context of a non-scriptural source than in Isaiah is never explained. (On Paul's infrequent use of the term "covenant," see p. 46 n. 9 above; the infrequency of the *term* "covenant" in Paul's writings should not obscure the fact that foundational to Paul's thought is the conviction that God remains faithful to his covenant with Israel.) Given that Paul is quite familiar with the book of Isaiah, it is far simpler to suppose that he has made the conflation himself. In what follows, I will assume that the combined citation in Romans 11:26–27 originated with Paul (so Koch 1986:177) and attempt to understand its use in that light.

For the most part, Paul cites each text in a form identical to the reading of LXX Isaiah.[197] The high degree of verbatim agreement is even more impressive when one notes the points at which Paul and LXX agree together against other witnesses (notably MT). In the case of Isaiah 59:20–21, both have a transitive finite verb, ἀποστρέψει, where MT and 1QIsaᵃ have an intransitive participle (+ ל) functioning as indirect object, לשבי.[198] Paul and LXX both read ἀπὸ Ἰακώβ where MT, 1QIsaᵃ, and most of the versions attest to the preposition ב.[199] Moreover, Paul and LXX agree against all other witnesses in the plural ἀσεβείας, in the absence of any phrase comparable to נאם יהוה, and in the order αὐτοῖς . . . διαθήκη.[200] The

---

[197] The omission of the two occurrences of καί in Paul's citation of 59:20 is insignificant (cf. Stanley 1993a:122–23).

[198] Cf. α′ σ′ θ′ (τοῖς ἀποστρέψασιν/ἀποστρέφουσιν). At this point, the Targum and Peshitta also select a transitive verbal form, though the Targum has an infinitive while the latter has a participle:

Targum Isaiah 59:20:

וייתי לציון פריק ולאהבא מרודיא דבית יעקב לאוריתא אמר יוי

And he will come to Zion as a redeemer and to turn back the rebels of the house of Jacob to the Law, says the Lord.

Peshitta Isaiah 59:20:

ܘܢܐܬܐ ܠܨܗܝܘܢ ܦܪܘܩܐ ܘܠܐܝܠܝܢ ܕܡܗܦܟܝܢ ܥܘܠܐ ܡܢ ܝܥܩܘܒ ܐܡܪ ܡܪܝܐ

And the redeemer will come to Zion, along with those who turn iniquity away from Jacob, says the Lord.

[199] MT: ביעקב; 1QIsaᵃ: ביעקוב. According to Procopius, α′ and σ′ have ἐν Ἰακώβ, while ms 86 attributes ἐν Ἰακώβ to σ′ and θ′. The Targum appears to support ב; the Peshitta, however, has מי. The frequent self-characterization, שבי פשע, in the Dead Sea Scrolls is probably to be understood as an allusion to Isaiah 59:20 as found in 1QIsaᵃ and MT (e.g., 1QS 10.20; CD-A 2.5; 1QHᵃ 10[2].9; 14[6].6; 6[14].24; 4QShirShabb [4Q400] frg. 1 1.16; 4Q512 frgs. 70–71 1.2. The even closer parallel to Isaiah 59:20, שבי פשע יעקב, in CD-B 20.17). The appellation reflects the sectaries' claim that they are "those who turn from wickedness" and to whom God will come with deliverance. The title שבי ישראל may be a development of שבי פשע (CD-A 4.2; 6.5; 8.16 = CD-B 19.29; 4QpPsᵃ [4Q171] frgs. 1–10 4.24). Note the allusion to Isaiah 8:14 in the description of this group as those who "turned from the way of the people" (CD-A 8.16 = CD-B 19.29): שבי ישראל סרו מדרך העם (cf. p. 139 n. 66). In a similar vein, CD-B 20.17 speaks of שבי פשע יעקב who keep God's covenant, but then laments several lines later (20.24) that others "turned back to the way of the people in a few matters": ושבו עוד אל דרך העם בדברים מעטי]ם.

[200] In support of his claim that "biblical texts written in the Hebrew language must be given full consideration in the evaluation of Pauline citations," Lim (1997a:147 and n. 19) notes that αὐτοῖς (the reading of LXX as well as of Paul) probably reflects אתם (1QIsaᵃ; many masoretic mss; cf. Targum, Peshitta, Vulgate) rather than אותם (Leningradensis; Aleppo Codex). This is possible, but not certain. Confusion in mss between suffixed forms of the accusative particle and suffixed forms of the preposition את is not uncommon (Joüon and Muraoka 1993, §156b, §103j; Kutscher 1974:405), but it does not appear to have proven a barrier to understanding. It is

fact that both Paul and LXX read ἡ παρ' ἐμοῦ διαθήκη, certainly not an obvious translation for אני ... בריתי, further strengthens the case for Paul's dependence on Isaiah 59:20–21 LXX.[201] Similarly, in the case of Isaiah 27:9, Paul agrees with the LXX against all other witnesses in rendering Isaiah 27:9b with a temporal clause, ὅταν ἀφέλωμαι κτλ. The few variations from LXX Isaiah 27:9 appear to be of little consequence.[202] The plural form ἁμαρτίας in Paul's quotation probably reflects normal Pauline usage (and perhaps a desire for parallelism with ἀσεβείας) rather than any substantive interpretive move.[203]

---

difficult to imagine how a Greek translator could have taken אותם in Isaiah 59:21 to mean anything other than "with them" or "for them" (see Ezek 16:8; 37:26 for other occurrences in MT of ברית + nota accusativi with suffix; in both cases, the LXX reads μέτα + pronoun). In any case, Paul's reading αὐτοῖς is fully explicable on the basis of his use of the LXX alone. Unless one is convinced on other grounds that Paul knew Hebrew and/or Aramaic and is prepared to argue that Paul meticulously compared texts across several languages, it is not apparent that the reading of 1QIsaᵃ is relevant to the question of Paul's text in the present instance, since elsewhere in Romans 11:26–27 Paul is so obviously dependent on LXX Isaiah.

[201] The variant reading in 𝔓⁴⁶, παρ' ἐμοῦ ἡ διαθήκη, if original, does not diminish the force of this point; neither does it affect the meaning of the citation.

[202] The variant order of noun and pronoun—τὰς ἁμαρτίας αὐτῶν (Rom 11:27)/αὐτοῦ τὴν ἁμαρτίαν (LXX)—does not affect the meaning (Paul's order is attested by several witnesses to the LXX, but these may be dependent on Rom 11:27). The plural pronoun αὐτῶν in Romans 11:27 is likely due to the influence of αὐτοῖς in the first half of the verse (from Isa 59:21 LXX).

[203] Stanley maintains that the switch from the singular to the plural form of ἁμαρτία is "hardly Pauline," noting that the plural form is "uncommon in Paul's letters" (1993a:123). On closer examination, however, the practice both of Paul and of the NT writers in general invalidates Stanley's line of reasoning. Given Paul's distinctive use of ἁμαρτία in the singular (particularly in Romans) as a quasi-hypostatized cosmic power, it is more likely than not that he would have changed ἁμαρτίαν in Isaiah 27:9 to a plural form, since he is here speaking not of "Sin," but of Israel's transgressions. Apart from this consideration, the variant ἁμαρτίας conforms to the normal usage of the singular and plural forms of ἁμαρτία elsewhere in Paul and in the rest of the NT. In the overwhelming number of cases, ἁμαρτία occurs in the plural when either it is modified by a possessive of some sort or it is the object of a verb or noun denoting forgiveness, removal, and the like. (1) Modification by a possessive noun, pronoun, or the equivalent: Paul uses the singular ἁμαρτία 52 times in his undisputed letters. Of these, only once is the singular noun modified by a possessive of any type (Rom 4:8, in a verbatim quotation of Ps 31:2 LXX). In contrast, Paul uses the plural ἁμαρτίαι 7 times; of these, only once is ἁμαρτίαι not modified by a possessive (Rom 7:5; here, τῶν ἁμαρτιῶν is a qualitative genitive, modifying παθημάτων). In the rest of the NT, about half of the occurrences of ἁμαρτία in the plural are modified by a possessive of some sort. Of those not so modified, over half appear in some sort of stock expression such as ἀφέσις ἁμαρτιῶν (see point 2 below). The singular form of ἁμαρτία occurs 45 times outside Paul's undisputed letters, but only in John's gospel does it appear with a modifier indicating possession, and then only in five of eight occurrences (Jn 1:29; 8:21; 9:41; 15:22, 24). Similarly, in LXX Isaiah it is usual to speak of

Of greater significance, however, is Paul's departure from Isaiah 59:20 LXX in reading ἐκ Σιων. With the exception of a few witnesses to the Greek text that may well depend on Paul's quotation, no other ancient version of Isaiah 59:20 supports this reading.[204] The variant ἐκ Σιων reflects a fundamental interpretive shift, in which the events narrated in these verses are viewed from the standpoint of the Diaspora.[205] Rather than focus on the Lord's victorious return *to* Zion, as does LXX Isaiah 59:20, Paul's quotation depicts the Lord's coming in person *from* a restored Zion to bring deliverance to his people who are scattered among the nations.

In this form, Paul's citation resonates with a significant number of scriptural texts that also adopt a narrative standpoint outside Jerusalem as they depict God's eschatological deliverance of his people and/or God's cosmic rule ἐκ Σιων. A striking example comes from Isaiah 2:3–4 // Micah 4:2–3:

---

someone's sin*s* (ἁμαρτίαι, 22x); the singular form of ἁμαρτία is found modified by a possessive only in Isaiah 27:9 and 40:2. (2) With verbs (and related nouns) of forgiving/removing sin(s), the plural form of ἁμαρτία is clearly the norm in the NT (ἀφίημι ἁμαρτίας: Mt 9:2, 5, 6; Mark 2:5, 7, 9, 10; Luke 5:20, 21, 23, 24; 7:47, 48, 49; 11:4; John 20:23; 1 John 1:9; 2:12; Jas 5:15; ἄφεσις ἁμαρτιῶν: Matt 26:28; Mark 1:4; Luke 1:77; 3:3; 24:47; Acts 2:38; 5:31; 10:43; 13:38; 26:18; Col 1:14; αἴρω ἁμαρτίας: 1 John 3:5; ἀναφέρω/εἰσφέρω ἁμαρτίας: 1 Pet 2:24; Heb 9:28; ἐπικαλύπτω ἁμαρτίας, Rom 4:7; καθαρισμὸς ἁμαρτιῶν: Heb 1:3; 2 Pet 1:9; καλύπτω πλῆθος ἁμαρτιῶν: Jas 5:20; 1 Pet 4:8; περιαιρέω ἁμαρτίας: Heb 10:11; σῴζω ἀφ' ἁμαρτιῶν: Matt 1:21). The particular collocation found in Romans 11:27, ἀφαιρέω ἁμαρτίας, appears only one other time in the NT, also with the plural ἁμαρτίας, in Heb 10:4. The following cases are the only exceptions I found to this tendency to use the plural form of ἁμαρτία with verbs of forgiving: Matt 12:31 (N.B., πᾶς); John 1:29; Heb 9:26; 1 John 1:7 (N.B., πᾶς). While the foregoing does not prove that Paul himself was the source of ἁμαρτίας in the quotation of Isaiah 27:9, it does show that this variant is quite understandable in terms of Pauline usage and thus that it does *not* point to a non-Pauline origin for this combined citation. I doubt that the Targum's use of the plural noun (חובוהי) is relevant in any direct way to the question of this aspect of Paul's wording. Incidentally, J. D. W. Watts's comment (1985:347 n. 9a) that with חטמאו, 1QIsaᵃ 27:9 turns the noun (MT, חטאתו) into a verb ("they sinned") is mistaken; חטמאו is a suffixed form of the noun חטא (so Kutscher 1974:374—whom Watts cites in support of his remark!).

[204] The witnesses to the Greek text that read ἐκ instead of ἕνεκεν are 22ᶜ⁻93 564* 407 534 Bohairic; Epiphanius; Hilary; Jerome. α′ σ′ translate τῇ Σιων; MT, Targum, and Peshitta attest לציון; 1QIsaᵃ has אל ציון.

[205] So Stanley 1993a:135–36. De Waard's proposal (1965:12–13) that ἐκ may be understood here in the sense, "because of," appears to be a desperate measure to link Paul's citation with a known textual precursor (in this case, de Waard suggests that ἐκ translates אל [= על], as in 1QIsaᵃ). Although causal ἐκ is not unknown (cf. BDF § 212), it would be very surprising to find it used with a place-name (note that LXX uses ἕνεκεν).

The Law will go out from Zion and the word of the Lord from Jerusalem (ἐκ γὰρ Σιων ἐξελεύσεται νόμος καὶ λόγος κυρίου ἐξ Ιερουσαλημ). And he will judge between nations and reprove a great people. . . .[206]

Joel 3:16 LXX [4:16 MT] depicts God judging the nations and rescuing his people from his throne in Zion (cf. Amos 1:2):

The Lord has cried out from Zion (ἐκ Σιων), and he will give voice from Jerusalem, and the heaven and earth will be shaken. But the Lord will spare his people, and the Lord will strengthen the children of Israel.

Similarly, Psalm 13:7 LXX speaks of Israel's deliverance from exile as originating from God's reestablished rule in Zion:

Who will give from Zion (ἐκ Σιων) the salvation of Israel? When the Lord turns back the captivity of his people, let Jacob be glad, let Israel rejoice!

Psalm 109:2 LXX emphasizes that God's rule extends from Zion over the entire world:

The Lord will send forth the rod of your power from Zion (ἐκ Σιων). Rule in the midst of your enemies![207]

Such a change of perspective in this text would not necessarily have been made first by Paul,[208] but it coheres admirably with the similar

---

[206] In Romans 11:26–27, it is the salvation of Israel that is the object of the redeemer's mission. It is possible, however, that Paul would have read Isaiah 2:3–4 not only as a prophecy of an eschatological mission to Gentiles, but also as a promise that God's word would go forth to reprove and correct Israel (= λαός; on this interpretive move elsewhere in Paul, see pp. 212–13 and 314–15). This remains highly speculative, of course (*contra* Wright 1995:61), since Paul never cites or otherwise alludes to Isaiah 2:3–4. Isaiah 37:32 MT (//2 Kings 19:31) speaks of a remnant going out from Jerusalem to repopulate the Land after its devastation by Assyria, but this seems less apposite to Paul's point, particularly since Isaiah 37:32 LXX reads, "those remaining *will be from Jerusalem*" (ἐξ Ιερουσαλημ ἔσονται οἱ καταλελειμμένοι).

[207] Cf. Psalm 127:5; 133:3: "May the Lord bless you from Zion". Paul quotes Psalm 109:1 to speak of Christ's present reign over the cosmos that will culminate in the eschatological rule of God over all of creation (1 Cor 15:23–28).

[208] Stanley traces this combined citation to an (anonymous) Jewish community in the Diaspora (1993a:135–36), but this hypothetical reconstruction does not account for the shift in perspective any better than the view that the variant originates with Paul (who was himself, after all, a Diaspora Jew). Moreover, Stanley's hypothesis suffers from the lack of any evidence for the reading ἐκ Σιων other than Paul's own citation (and LXX mss that are quite possibly dependent on Romans 11:26 [cf. Stanley 1992b:167]).

alterations made to his citations of Isaiah 52:7 (Rom 10:15)[209] and
Hosea 1:10 (Rom 9:26)[210] as well as with Paul's comparative lack of
interest elsewhere in his letters in Jerusalem or the Land of Israel.[211]

The Restoration of Israel and Forgiveness of Sins: Isaiah 59–60

Beyond the striking resemblance that Isaiah 59:20–21 and 27:9 bear
to one another, their larger literary settings tell remarkably similar
stories about Israel's future deliverance by God. Attention to these
wider contexts will suggest a possible reason for the particular combination of texts found in Romans 11:26–27 as well as reveal the
extent to which Paul's argument throughout Romans 9–11 resonates
with the moving accounts of the Lord's restoration of Israel found
in Isaiah.[212] It is difficult to be dogmatic about the exact extent of
the "wider contexts" of these verses, but my argument does not
depend on the precise delineation of boundaries. Indeed, my con-

---

[209] Paul's citation of Isaiah 52:7 lacks the phrase "on the mountains," a geographical reference to the environs of Jerusalem (see above, p. 173).

[210] See the discussion of this text (ἐν τῷ τόπῳ οὗ ἐὰν κληθήσονται) above,
pp. 84–85.

[211] One may profitably contrast the crucial role Jerusalem plays in the narrative
of Luke-Acts—and particularly in Luke's account of Paul's career—with the relative silence of Paul's letters on this point. It is curious, for example, that Paul never
specifies the holy city as the locus of Jesus' *parousia*. Interestingly, one of the few
references to Jerusalem in Romans suggests a parallelism of sorts between Paul's
ministry and the future mission of "the redeemer": Paul's apostolic mission has
extended "*from Jerusalem* in a circle as far as Illyricum" (15:19). On this whole topic,
see Davies 1974:164–220.

[212] The hope for Israel's future restoration is not limited to the oracles of Isaiah,
of course. Other prophetic texts tell similar stories about God's coming to redeem
his people. These stories were told and retold in new and various ways in the
Second Temple Period (see above, pp. 29–31). Nevertheless, this theme is particularly characteristic of the book of Isaiah. Consequently, I will focus on the possible influences of Isaiah on Paul's conception of Israel's redemption without claiming
by any means that this was the only source for his eschatological vision. Recognizing
the cultural currency in the Diaspora of prophecies of Israel's restoration, Stanley
curiously draws the conclusion that if Paul took over this conflated citation from a
source, he would probably have been unaware of the location and wider setting of
these particular oracles in the book of Isaiah (1992b:253, n. 2). There is no reason to set Paul's familiarity with Jewish tradition over against his own knowledge
of scripture, however. Time and again in the present study, we have found Paul's
reading of the prophet to be shaped by his larger cultural context as well as by
features of the wider literary and theological contexts of Isaiah. In view of Paul's
deep intimacy with Isaiah, it is difficult to imagine that he would have been unaware
of the contexts from which these excerpts were taken, even if the actual conflation
of texts did not originate in Paul's own study of Isaiah.

tention that Paul is influenced not only by particular verses from
Isaiah, but even more by Isaiah's larger "story" about Israel, depends
to a great extent on the fact that, much like a musical "theme and
variations," the motif of God's deliverance of Israel from foreign
oppression is continually reprised in new and different forms throughout much of the book of Isaiah.

Isaiah 59 opens with a sarcastic question.[213] Does Israel's salvation tarry because God is too weak or too unconcerned to deliver
them? "It is not the case that the Lord's arm is not strong enough
to save, is it? Or that his ear is deaf so that he cannot hear?" (59:1).[214]
In response, the prophet lays the blame for Israel's continued suffering
of oppression squarely on the people's shoulders. The problem is
their sins (59:2):

> Your sinful deeds (τὰ ἁμαρτήματα ὑμῶν) are separating you from God,
> and on account of your sins (διὰ τὰς ἁμαρτίας ὑμῶν) he has turned his
> face from you so as not to show mercy (τοῦ μὴ ἐλεῆσαι).[215]

An extensive indictment cataloging Israel's sinfulness follows in 59:3–8,
organized around parts of the human body. Interestingly, an excerpt
from this catalog (59:7–8) appears in Paul's lengthy charge in Romans

---

[213] Although there is a clear break at 58:14 with, "For the mouth of the Lord
spoke these things" (cf. 57:21, "said the Lord God"), there are important continu-
ities between the oracles in Isaiah 58 and 59, not least of which is the emphasis
laid on the idea that it is Israel's "sins" that prevent God from delivering them.
Interestingly, that deliverance is portrayed in terms strikingly reminiscent of the
account of Israel's first entrance into the land in the Song of Moses (cf. Fishbane
1985:477–79; Sommer 1998:134–35):

> Isaiah 58:14: ἀναβιβάσει σε ἐπὶ τὰ ἀγαθὰ τῆς γῆς καὶ ψωμιεῖ σε τὴν κληρονομίαν
> Ιακωβ τοῦ πατρός σου . . .

> Deuteronomy 32:13: ἀνεβίβασεν αὐτοὺς ἐπὶ τὴν ἰσχὺν τῆς γῆς, ἐψώμισεν αὐτοὺς
> γενήματα ἀγρῶν . . .

[214] Μὴ οὐκ ἰσχύει ἡ χεὶρ κυρίου τοῦ σῶσαι; ἢ ἐβάρυνε τὸ οὖς αὐτοῦ τοῦ μὴ εἰσακοῦσαι;
The first question evokes God's earlier rebuke of Israel for doubting his power to
save them (Isa 50:2): μὴ οὐκ ἰσχύει ἡ χείρ μου τοῦ ῥύσασθαι; The query is particularly ironic in view of Isaiah's frequent celebration of the saving might of God's
"hand" (χείρ: e.g., 11:11, 15; 41:20; 43:13; 49:22; 50:2; 60:21; 64:8) or "arm"
(βραχίων; e.g., 26:11; 30:30; 40:10; 51:5, 9; 52:10; 53:1; 59:16; 62:8; 63:5, 12). The
second question attributes to the Lord the same deafness with which Israel is charged
(Isa 6:10).

[215] Cf. Isa 1:15: "When you stretch your hands to me, I will turn my eyes from
you; if you pray all the more, I will not listen to you. For your hands are filled
with blood . . . (ὅταν τὰς χεῖρας ἐκτείνητε πρός με, ἀποστρέψω τοὺς ὀφθαλμούς μου
ἀφ᾽ ὑμῶν, καὶ ἐὰν πληθύνητε τὴν δέησιν, οὐκ εἰσακούσομαι ὑμῶν· αἱ γὰρ χεῖρες ὑμῶν
αἵματος πλήρεις).

3:15–17 (also structured around parts of the body) that all humans are under sin, an accusation aimed particularly at his Jewish interlocutor.[216] Isaiah's indictment of Israel is answered by the subsequent confession of the people themselves that they are in dire straits due to their sins.

> Our lawlessness is great before you, and our sins have risen up against us. Our sins are among us, and we know our unrighteous deeds. We have acted impiously, we have lied, and we have turned away from following our God. We have spoken unjust things, and we have acted disobediently. . . .
>
> πολλὴ γὰρ ἡμῶν ἡ ἀνομία ἐναντίον σου, καὶ αἱ ἁμαρτίαι ἡμῶν ἀντέστησαν ἡμῖν· αἱ γὰρ ἀνομίαι ἡμῶν ἐν ἡμῖν, καὶ τὰ ἀδικήματα ἡμῶν ἔγνωμεν· ἠσεβήσαμεν καὶ ἐψευσάμεθα καὶ ἀπέστημεν ἀπὸ ὄπισθεν τοῦ θεοῦ ἡμῶν· ἐλαλήσαμεν ἄδικα καὶ ἠπειθήσαμεν . . . (Isa 59:12–13).

Isaiah's oracle laments both the absence of justice on the human plane and the failure of God to deliver his people, as κρίσις, δικαιοσύνη, σωτηρία, and ἀλήθεια have fled away (59:9, 11, 14). The prophet depicts the desperate condition of his people in terms that suggest the fulfillment of God's judgment pronounced against Israel in the crucial Isaianic passage, 6:9–10:[217]

> Although they were waiting for light, it became for them darkness; though they were expecting brightness, they walked in night. They will grope along the wall like those who are blind, and like those who have no eyes they will fumble around. They will stumble in midday as at midnight.
>
> ὑπομεινάντων αὐτῶν φῶς ἐγένετο αὐτοῖς σκότος, μείναντες αὐγὴν ἐν ἀωρίᾳ περιεπάτησαν. ψηλαφήσουσιν ὡς τυφλοὶ τοῖχον καὶ ὡς οὐχ ὑπαρχόν-

---

[216] "Whatever the Law says, it says to those under the Law (τοῖς ἐν τῷ νόμῳ)" (Rom 3:19; cf. Rom 2:12). It is unclear to me whether Romans 3:10–18 is a Pauline composition or whether Paul took it over pre-formed (cf. the use made of Isa 59:5 in CD-A 5:13–14 to describe the opponents of the sect). Keck 1977 argues for the latter option; so also Albl 1999. Even if Paul did not compose it himself, however, it is significant that the use made of Isaiah 59:7–8 in Romans 3 is consonant with Paul's larger pattern of reading Isaiah. For Paul, the majority of Israel in his own day are still rebellious and in need of God's deliverance. They are stuck, as it were, in Isaiah 59:7–8, and the redemption promised in Isaiah 59:20–21 remains as yet a hope unfulfilled. For further discussion of technical aspects of Paul's citation of Isaiah 59:7–8, see Koch 1986:106, 118–19, 143–44; Stanley 1992b:87–99, esp. 95–98. Wilk decides not to treat Isaiah 59:7–8 because he considers it doubtful that Paul took this text directly from Isaiah (1998:9).

[217] Compare also with Isaiah 6:10 the statement in 59:15: "They turned their mind away from understanding" (μετέστησαν τὴν διάνοιαν τοῦ συνιέναι).

τῶν ὀφθαλμῶν ψηλαφήσουσι· καὶ πεσοῦνται ἐν μεσημβρίᾳ ὡς ἐν μεσονυκτίῳ (Isa 59:9–10).

This description of Israel's plight resonates with the diagnosis offered by Paul in Romans 11:8–10, which also draws on Isaiah 6:9–10 and related texts.[218] Paul would have found in Isaiah 59:9–10 further confirmation of his analysis that "the rest" of Israel have been rendered insensible as a judgment from God, even as he looked forward to 59:20–21 for the solution to their predicament.

The turning point in Isaiah's story comes after Israel's confession and lamentation, as the Lord surveys the scene and finds Israel utterly helpless to deliver themselves, totally bereft of anyone to redeem them from their plight: "[The Lord] looked, and there was no man; he observed carefully, and there was no one to help" (59:16a). Israel's helplessness arouses God's wrath and his zeal for his people, and he determines to show them mercy (ἐλεημοσύνη, 59:16b) by delivering them from their enemies. God girds himself as a warrior with δικαιοσύνη, σωτηρίον, and ἐκδίκησις and strides forth to vindicate his people (59:17–18).[219]

At this point, Isaiah's oracle shifts into the future tense, as he describes a deliverance that is as yet unrealized. When the Lord marches out to rescue Zion, the whole world will see and fear his glorious name (59:19). The Lord will come on Zion's behalf as "the redeemer" (ὁ ῥυόμενος), a frequent title for Israel's God in Isaiah's oracles of salvation.[220] Just as Isaiah's oracles in chapters 58–59 have emphasized that Israel's sinful deeds keep their God far from them,

---

[218] Isaiah 29:10; Deuteronomy 29:4. In light of Paul's juxtaposition of blindness texts from Isaiah and Deuteronomy, it is interesting to note that there is a significant allusion in Isaiah 59:8–10 to the curse formula of Deuteronomy 28:28–29:

πατάξαι σε κύριος παραπληξίᾳ καὶ ἀορασίᾳ καὶ ἐκστάσει διανοίας, καὶ ἔσῃ ψηλαφῶν μεσημβρίας ὡσεὶ ψηλαφήσαι ὁ τυφλὸς ἐν τῷ σκότει.

Sommer comments that, from Deutero-Isaiah's perspective, "the curses Moses anticipated have been put into effect" (1998:140). CD-A 1:8–10 also echoes Isaiah 59:9–10 (נששו, כעורים; cf. Deut 28:28–29, משוש) in its account of the plight of the community before the coming of the righteous teacher: they were *groping* (נששו) for the way like blind people (כעורים) on account of *their sins* (עונם):

8 ... ויבינו בעונם וידעו כי 9 אנשים אשמים הם ויהיו כעורים וכימגששים דרך 10 שנים עשרים.

[219] Note once again the association of "righteousness" in Isaiah with the idea of God's vindication and deliverance of his people.

[220] Isaiah 5:29; 44:6; 47:4; 48:17; 49:7, 26; 54:5, 8. It is found also as a title or description for God in LXX Judg A & B 8:34; Ps 34:10 LXX; Wis 16:8; 19:9.

so now the Lord's deliverance of Israel is said to consist in taking away their ungodliness (59:20). The Lord promises to make a "covenant" with his redeemed people. This covenant bears a striking affinity to the "new covenant" promised in Jeremiah 38:31–37 LXX (31:31–37 MT), for in both cases it is God himself who guarantees Israel's ability to keep faith.[221] While Jeremiah speaks of God's laws written indelibly on the people's hearts,[222] Isaiah promises that God's Spirit will remain upon them and God's words abide in their mouths forever:

> And this [will be] my covenant with them, says the Lord: my Spirit, which is upon you, and the words that I have placed in your mouth will surely not depart from your mouth or from the mouth of your seed, says the Lord, from this time and forever.
>
> καὶ αὕτη αὐτοῖς ἡ παρ᾽ ἐμοῦ διαθήκη, εἶπε κύριος· τὸ πνεῦμα τὸ ἐμόν, ὅ ἐστιν ἐπὶ σοί, καὶ τὰ ῥήματα, ἃ ἔδωκα εἰς τὸ στόμα σου, οὐ μὴ ἐκλίπῃ ἐκ τοῦ στόματός σου καὶ ἐκ τοῦ στόματος τοῦ σπέρματός σου, εἶπε γὰρ κύριος, ἀπὸ τοῦ νῦν καὶ εἰς τὸν αἰῶνα (Isa 59:21b).

The promise of imminent deliverance in Isaiah 59:19–21 gives way to the vivid depiction in Isaiah 60 of redemption realized. Bright light suddenly pierces the darkness and floods the terrain over which Israel has been stumbling blindly: "Shine, shine, Jerusalem, for your light has come, and the glory of the Lord has risen upon you!" (60:1). Though thick darkness covers the nations, the Lord's glory gives light to Israel, just as during the exodus long ago.[223] The nations

---

[221] Noting that "Jeremiah 30–31 and 33 provide the richest mine for Deutero-Isaiah as he restates positive prophecies from Jeremiah," Sommer (1998:46) finds in Isaiah 59:21 "another occurrence of Jeremiah's idea of an inevitable covenant" (49). See also Isaiah 51:7, which speaks of God's Law located in the heart of the people. There may be an echo of one or both of these texts in Romans 2:15. However, Wright (1995:61) goes well beyond the evidence in speaking of "the quotation from Jer 31:33 that appears in [Rom] 11:27."

[222] Jeremiah's oracle reads (Jer 38:33 LXX):
For this [is] the covenant that I will make with the house of Israel after those days, says the Lord: I will surely put my laws in their minds, and I will write them on their hearts. I will be their God, and they will be my people.
ὅτι αὕτη ἡ διαθήκη ἣν διαθήσομαι τῷ οἴκῳ Ισραηλ μετὰ τὰς ἡμέρας ἐκείνας, φησὶ κύριος· διδοὺς δώσω νόμους μου εἰς τὴν διάνοιαν αὐτῶν καὶ ἐπὶ καρδίας αὐτῶν γράψω αὐτούς, καὶ ἔσομαι αὐτοῖς εἰς θεὸν καὶ αὐτοὶ ἔσονταί μοι εἰς λαόν.

[223] Isaiah 60:2 (ἰδοὺ σκότος καὶ γνόφος καλύψει γῆν ἐπ᾽ ἔθνη· ἐπὶ δὲ σὲ φανήσεται κύριος) echoes the language used to narrate the plague of darkness (Exod 10:21–23) and to describe the Lord's protection of Israel from the Egyptian army at the crossing of the Sea (Exod 14:19–20).

of the world stream to Zion's light, bearing her scattered children home on their shoulders (60:3–4, 9) and bringing their wealth as tribute and as an offering to the Lord (60:5–9).[224] As they come, the nations themselves announce the good news of the salvation the Lord has wrought (τὸ σωτήριον κυρίου εὐαγγελιοῦνται, 60:6).[225] Jerusalem will be rebuilt gloriously, and the nations' kings will submit to God's people or be destroyed (60:10, 12). All of this will be a sign of God's mercy and love for Israel:

> On account of my wrath I struck you, but on account of mercy I have loved you.
>
> διὰ γὰρ ὀργήν μου ἐπάταξά σε καὶ διὰ ἔλεον ἠγάπησά σε (Isa 60:10b).

When they experience this lavish redemption, Israel will know that the Lord alone is their savior, the one who has graciously chosen to be their God:

> And you will know that I, the Lord, am the one who saves you, and that the one who delivers you is the God of Israel.
>
> καὶ γνώσῃ ὅτι ἐγὼ κύριος ὁ σῴζων σε καὶ ἐξαιρούμενός σε θεὸς Ισραηλ (Isa 60:16).

Paul's quotation of Isaiah 59:20–21 taps into this larger story of God's restoration of Israel, drawing both on its depiction of Israel as blinded and helpless in their estrangement from God and on its

---

[224] Isaiah 60:6–7 MT speaks of the nations' wealth being offered in God's temple. The LXX translator has rendered Isaiah 60:7 in such a way ("house of prayer," οἶκος τῆς προσευχῆς, for MT, "house of glory," בית תפארתי) as to recall the promise in Isaiah 56:7–8 that God will gather Gentiles to himself along with "the outcasts of Israel" and accept their worship in his "house of prayer":

> I will bring them to my holy mountain, and I will make them rejoice in my house of prayer (ἐν τῷ οἴκῳ τῆς προσευχῆς μου). Their whole burnt offerings and sacrifices will be acceptable on my altar, for my house will be called a house of prayer (οἶκος προσευχῆς) for all nations, says the Lord, who gathers the scattered ones of Israel: for I will gather to [Israel] an assembly.

In addition, Isaiah 60:1–5 reuses material from Isaiah 2:1–4 (a text that Paul never quotes, but one that tells a similar story of Gentiles giving allegiance to Israel's God); Isaiah 5:30; and Isaiah 8:22–9:5 (see Sommer 1998:80–82, 154–55, 251–52 n. 57).

[225] As Munck saw long ago, this text provides an intriguing background to Paul's collection for the saints, borne in person to Jerusalem by Gentile delegates from the churches he has planted (1959:301–305; cf. Aus 1979; Riesner 1998:249–50). If Paul could view himself as one of the heralds spoken of in Isaiah 52:7, it is not too difficult to imagine that he thought of the Gentile delegates as a proleptic realization of Isaiah's prophecy in 60:3–9.

foundational conviction that because God's commitment to Israel never fails, God will show himself faithful to deliver his people. For Paul, as for Isaiah, God's election of Israel is irrevocable. Even when Israel experiences God's wrath, they remain his beloved (Isa 60:10; Rom 11:28–29). Moreover, both Paul and Isaiah are convinced that it is God's power alone that will ultimately overcome his people's apostasy. In the Isaianic vision, Israel's hope for salvation rests entirely on God's initiative and action. Seeing the helplessness of his people and motivated by his mercy rather than by Israel's deserts (Isa 59:16; 60:10), the Lord himself ventures forth to remove Israel's ungodliness and to restore their fortunes. Similarly, in Romans 11, Paul depicts the salvation of "all Israel" as a divine act prompted by God's mercy and accomplished by God himself (Rom 11:26–27, 31–32).

At the same time, it is clear that Paul has transmuted important elements of this Isaianic saga. According to Paul, God has revealed his righteousness in Christ for Jew and Gentile alike, and even now messengers are abroad spreading the glad tidings (Rom 10:15/Isa 52:7; cf. 60:6). Astonishingly, however, only an elect remnant of Israel have responded to the good news that God has acted to redeem his people. The rest remain blinded, locked up in their disobedience, stuck in Isaiah 59:1–15, as it were, while the nations come streaming in to embrace Israel's God ahead of God's own people. Ironically, while Isaiah envisions the salvation of Israel resulting in the "wealth of the sea and of the nations and of the peoples" (πλοῦτος θαλάσσης καὶ ἐθνῶν καὶ λαῶν, Isa 60:5) being brought into Jerusalem, it is the disobedience of most of Israel that has resulted in "wealth for the nations" (πλοῦτος ἐθνῶν, Rom 11:12) as the riches of the gospel are offered to them first. And whereas Isaiah imagined Gentiles carrying the scattered children of Israel home to Zion on their shoulders (Isa 60:3–4, 9), Paul avers that the Gentiles will indeed bring Israel back to God, but only by provoking them to jealousy for their rightful inheritance (Rom 11:13–14).[226]

Clearly, Paul's revision of the Isaianic storyline is guided by the novel interpretation he has already given to Deuteronomy 32:21 and Isaiah 65:1–2. As I suggested previously, this radical rereading of

---

[226] Paul's move is perhaps not completely unparalleled in Isaiah, however. Commenting on Isaiah's revisionist interpretation of "Zion theology," Seitz notes: "The ironic twist in the Book of Isaiah is that the nations finally turn and seek Zion (2:1–3), leaving the house of Jacob to follow their lead (2:5)" (1993:72).

scripture grows out of Paul's own struggle to reconcile the surprising receptivity of Gentiles to his message with the continued resistance of his fellow Jews to the gospel. Unwilling to abandon Isaiah's story of the restoration of Israel, Paul boldly reinterprets the prophet's vision in light of the events of his own day.[227]

One further transformation of Isaiah's oracle by Paul is more difficult to explain. In explicating the nature of God's covenant with Israel (Rom 11:27/Isa 59:21), Paul curiously substitutes for Isaiah 59:21b[228] a clause from Isaiah 27:9.[229] At first glance, Isaiah 59:21b would appear to have been an ideal text for Paul to use to describe the blessings enjoyed by redeemed Israel. The promise of the Spirit's presence would have recalled Paul's discussion in Romans 8 of the Spirit as witness to the community's status as children of God. Likewise, Isaiah's statement that God's words (ῥήματα) will not depart from their mouth would have melded nicely with Paul's interpretation

---

[227] T. L. Donaldson has recently argued that the tradition of the eschatological pilgrimage of the Gentiles cannot be invoked to explain Paul's convictions regarding the Gentile mission, particularly because for the most part Israel's restoration is still *future* for Paul (a reversal of his earlier position, Donaldson 1986). He suggests instead that Paul was influenced by a school of thought holding that Gentiles could only be saved if they became proselytes to Israel *before* the eschatological consummation (at which time the remaining Gentiles would be destroyed). See Donaldson 1993; 1997:69–78, 187–97, 215–230. Donaldson rightly observes that in Romans 11 the full restoration of Israel comes *after* the "fullness" of the Gentiles and does not lead to the salvation of the nations. In this respect, Paul's eschatological scenario is closer to the proselyte tradition than to the pilgrimage tradition. However, although he points out that Paul never quotes directly from so-called "pilgrimage passages" (i.e., Isa 2:1–4), Donaldson does not reckon with the evidence that larger narrative patterns from Isaiah have shaped the apostle's reading of the book. Moreover, Donaldson's reading does not allow sufficient weight to Paul's claim that Israel's restoration *has begun*, and that there is *in the present time* a remnant who *already* enjoy the promised deliverance. Perhaps it is unnecessary to locate Paul's convictions regarding the Gentiles within one distinct strand of Jewish eschatological expectation. But it certainly is not necessary to insist that Paul's earlier eschatological "story" was based on a pilgrimage tradition to appreciate that *in Romans* he is rereading and transforming Isaiah's narrative of the pilgrimage of the Gentiles. In fact, if Donaldson is correct in arguing that Paul, before his calling as an apostle of Christ, held to the belief that the only chance for Gentiles to be saved was *prior to* the restoration of Israel, this would mean that Paul's inversion of Isaiah's story of the restoration of Israel was supported not only by the "brute facts" of the early Christian mission and by his rereading of Isaiah through the lens of Deuteronomy 32:21, but also by a wider Jewish tradition that had previously shaped his thought in significant ways.

[228] ". . . my Spirit, which is upon you, and the words that I have placed in your mouth will surely not depart from your mouth or from the mouth of your seed, says the Lord, from now on and forever."

[229] ". . . when I take away their sins."

of Deuteronomy 30:14 in Romans 10:8–10, where he identifies this "word" (ῥῆμα) that is "in your mouth" with "the word (ῥῆμα) of faith" that he preaches.

If Paul's substitution of clauses is not to be attributed simply to an unintentional slip of memory (which is not inconceivable, given the high degree of thematic and, especially, structural similarity between Isaiah 59:20–21a and Isaiah 27:9), the reason for this textual alteration is far from clear. However, I will hazard a guess— although such an explanation must, in the nature of the case, remain quite tentative. I noted in my brief synopsis of Isaiah 59 that Isaiah fixes the blame for Israel's plight squarely on Israel's "sins" (59:2–8, 12–15). While Isaiah 59:20 specifies that God's deliverance of his people will entail the removal of their ungodliness, Paul's introduction of the clause from 27:9, "when I take away their sins," lends further weight to this point. Thus, Paul's substitution makes sense within the larger context of Isaiah 59:21.[230]

At the same time, by replacing the last half of Isaiah 59:21, Paul keeps the focus on the *fact* of Israel's redemption rather than pausing to consider its *effects*.[231] It is this simple fact that all Israel will indeed be saved that is important for Paul's argument, and it is this fact that he emphasizes in the following verses. From a rhetorical point of view, then, Paul's substitution of clauses allows him to highlight a single crucial point in the quotation and then move quickly to his summary remarks and his concluding doxology. Finally, if we are to discern here the figure of metalepsis, it is not unthinkable that those with ears attuned to Israel's hopes for future restoration may have just caught in the mention of a covenant that takes away sins the faint echoes of Isaiah's pledge of God's abiding Spirit and words and—perhaps—even a whisper of Jeremiah's promise of God's laws inscribed on heart and mind.

The Restoration of Israel and Life from the Dead: Isaiah 24–27

I suggested above that the close structural and thematic correspondences between Isaiah 59:20 and Isaiah 27:9 probably led to their

---

[230] Note that for Jeremiah, too, the new covenant entails the forgiveness of Israel's sins: ἵλεως ἔσομαι ταῖς ἀδικίαις αὐτῶν καὶ τῶν ἁμαρτιῶν αὐτῶν οὐ μὴ μνησθῶ ἔτι (Jer 38:34 LXX).

[231] Paul also avoids the implication that the salvation of "all Israel" will result in any special benefits other than the blessings all believers in Christ enjoy.

combination by Paul into a single citation. Having seen evidence that Paul's belief in Israel's ultimate redemption by God has been shaped by the larger story told in Isaiah 59–60, it remains to ask whether the wider setting of Isaiah 27:9 may have also played some role in the development of his convictions concerning the future of God's people.

Isaiah 24–27, known to many modern students of the Book of Isaiah as the "Little Apocalypse," offers a series of tableaux depicting God's redemption of Israel and, with Israel, the entire cosmos. The basic story-line is much the same as in Isaiah 59–60. God comes in person to reign in Zion (24:23; 25:6–10), cleansing his people from their wickedness (26:16–19; 27:9–11), delivering them from their oppressors, and gathering together to Zion those who are scattered among the nations (27:12–13). As in Isaiah 60, the Gentile nations are depicted as either joining in Israel's worship of God and sharing in Israel's blessings (24:14–16a; 25:6–10a) or opposing the Lord and suffering his wrath (24:1–13, 17–22; 25:10b–12; 26:11, 21). In both Isaiah 24–27 and Isaiah 59–60, God's victory is complete. Israel is finally reconciled to their God, nevermore to stray, never again to suffer the judgment of foreign oppression and exile.

At two points in particular, Paul's conception of the future restoration of Israel resonates strongly with distinctive characteristics of the story of Israel's redemption as it is narrated in Isaiah 24–27. First, these prophetic visions emphasize the cosmic consequences of Israel's redemption. In Isaiah 24–27, the restoration of Israel issues in the reconciliation of all nations to God (25:6–7) and the defeat of death (25:8),[232] the resurrection of the dead (26:19). Whatever Isaiah may have understood by "resurrection," there is little doubt that a first-century Pharisee such as Paul would have heard in these grand prophecies the promise of the resurrection of dead corpses to new life.[233] For Paul, this event is the sign of the consummation of God's

---

[232] The text of Isaiah 25:8 LXX is difficult, but, as 1 Corinthians 15:54 attests, Paul knows another version that clearly reads this as a prediction of the death of death (cf. α', σ', θ'):

ὅταν δὲ τὸ φθαρτὸν τοῦτο ἐνδύσηται ἀφθαρσίαν καὶ τὸ θνητὸν τοῦτο ἐνδύσηται ἀθανασίαν, τότε γενήσεται ὁ λόγος ὁ γεγραμμένος·
κατεπόθη ὁ θάνατος εἰς νῖκος (1 Cor 15:54).
P. W. Skehan (1969:99) suggests that Paul's quotation is drawn from a (pre-Aquilanic) revision of the LXX.

[233] Cf. the clear statement of this hope in 2 Macc 7:9–14, 23, 29; 14:46. Belief

kingdom, the culmination of God's cosmic triumph over every enemy.[234] An echo of Isaiah's vision may be heard in Paul's statement that the "acceptance" of Israel will be nothing less than "life from the dead" (Rom 11:15b). At the same time, however, in keeping with his radical revision of Isaiah's chronology, Paul sees the reconciliation of the nations taking place at the present time, not through Israel's restoration, but, prior to that restoration, through Israel's disobedience to the gospel, as "their rejection [brings about] the reconciliation of the world" (Rom 11:15a).

Second, Isaiah 27 explicitly teaches that Israel's restoration will entail the eradication of idolatry from the midst of God's people. Isaiah 27:9 depicts the removal of Israel's "sin" in vivid terms: they will pulverize the stones of their pagan altars, cut down their sacred groves, and shatter their idols. We have seen that many of the scriptural texts employed by Paul in Romans 9–11 depict Israel as idolatrous, placing their hope for deliverance in the gods of other nations. The theme appears both subtly, as when Paul likens himself to Moses pleading with God for mercy after Israel's sin with the golden calf (Rom 9:3; cf. 9:15), and more overtly, as in Paul's remarkable comparison of his own situation to that of Elijah confronting Israel's apostasy to Baal. Now, at the conclusion of his theodicy, Paul draws on a text that depicts God healing Israel of their idolatry and unfaithfulness once and for all.[235] The branches once pruned from the olive

---

in the resurrection was characteristic of (but not exclusive to) the Pharisees (Acts 23:6–8, Josephus, *J.W.* 2.164; *Ant.* 18.14; cf. *J.W.* 3.374–75; *Ag. Ap.* 2.218). See further E. P. Sanders 1992:298–303.

[234] See 1 Corinthians 15:23–28 (ἔσχατος ἐχθρὸς καταργεῖται ὁ θάνατος, v. 26). There is perhaps a further connection between Paul's eschatology and this section of Isaiah, although the mediation of tradition is much more likely in this case. Isaiah 27:12–13 associates God's eschatological gathering of Israel with the sounding of a "trumpet" (cf. the "trumpet" heralding the Day of the Lord in Joel 2:1; Zeph 1:16; Zech 9:14; and the "trumpet" announcing the Year of Jubilee in Lev 25:9. See also *Pss. Sol.* 11:1; the whole psalm, appropriately entitled εἰς προσδοκίαν, is replete with Isaianic imagery). Likewise, Paul twice speaks of a trumpet blast in connection with the resurrection of believers at Jesus' parousia (1 Cor 15:52; cf. 15:23; 1 Thess 4:16). E. P. Sanders has argued convincingly that in 1 Thessalonians 4:16, at least, Paul preserves a dominical tradition also attested in Matthew 24:31 (1985:144–46). Perhaps in dependence on a saying of Jesus, then, Paul adopts a motif belonging to the wider tradition of Jewish eschatology and attested, among other places, in the story of Israel's redemption in Isaiah 24–27.

[235] The collocation ἀφαιρέω ἁμαρτίαν/ἀνομίαν is actually fairly rare in the LXX, occurring fewer than 10 times. In light of Paul's earlier allusions in Romans 9 to the episode of the golden calf, it is interesting to note that this collocation occurs

tree due to their unfaithfulness (ἀπιστία, Rom 11:20) have been grafted in again by God, who in removing their sins has *ensured* that they do not remain in ἀπιστία (Rom 11:23).

Paul's quotation in Romans 11:26–27 depicts the ultimate restoration of "all Israel" as the gracious work of their God, who comes in person to remove their sins and reconcile them to himself.[236] In claiming that God will be faithful to redeem all Israel, Paul does not lean on the isolated testimony of a few verses from Isaiah. Rather, he taps into a broad and deep stream of thought that is characteristic of Isaiah's vision—a stream of thought, moreover, that is shared by numerous other prophetic texts and that is kept vigorously alive in later Jewish literature.[237] Paul could probably assume that many of his listeners in Rome would be familiar with the broad outlines of this widely-diffused eschatological hope for God's coming to deliver his people and to establish his reign over the cosmos. For some, his quotation might even evoke these particular oracles in Isaiah, whose themes resonate with motifs found elsewhere in Paul's own letter: the promise of the Spirit's presence, God's words deposited in the mouth and inscribed on the heart, the resurrection of the dead.

---

twice in the conclusion to this narrative: first as the Lord reveals himself to Moses as the one ἀφαιρῶν ἀνομίας καὶ ἀδικίας καὶ ἁμαρτίας (Exod. 34:7) and then as Moses prays in response, ἀφελεῖ σὺ τὰς ἁμαρτίας ἡμῶν καὶ τὰς ἀνομίας ἡμῶν καὶ ἐσόμεθα σοι (34:9). In the very next verse, the Lord signifies to Moses that he has indeed taken away the people's sins by making a covenant (διαθήκη) with him to perform marvelous deeds on Israel's behalf.

[236] "The redeemer" is commonly identified with Christ (e.g., Davies 1984a:25–27; Zeller 1973:259; Käsemann 1980; E. P. Sanders 1983:194), although there is nothing in the context of Romans 11 to suggest a specifically christological referent for the appellation, which in Isaiah refers to Israel's God. Against those who read a great deal into Paul's failure to specify "the redeemer" as Christ (e.g., Stendahl 1976:40; Gager 2000:141–42), however, E. P. Sanders rightly emphasizes that

> it matters little whether [Paul] understands "the Deliverer" to be God or Christ; for it is incredible that he thought of "God apart from Christ," just as that he thought of "Christ apart from God." This is where the interpretation of Rom 11:25f. as offering two ways to salvation seems to me to go astray. It requires Paul to have made just that distinction. By the time we meet him in his letters, however, Paul knew only one God, the one who sent Christ and who "raised from the dead Jesus our Lord" (Rom 4:24). . . . There should be no hard distinction between "theocentric" and "christocentric" strains in Paul's thought (1983:194).

[237] For this reason, I see no justification for tying Paul's statement in Romans 11:26 that "all Israel will be saved" to one scriptural text in particular (*contra* numerous interpreters who find here an allusion to Isaiah 45:17 and/or 45:25, including Hübner 1984:113, 121–22; Mußner 1976:254–55; Wilk 1998:328–29).

When it comes to Paul's own interpretation of scripture, however, there should be no doubt that Paul's vision of Israel's restoration has been shaped in crucial ways by these particular Isaianic narratives. Paul finds in Isaiah's oracles the assurance that God, on account of his abundant mercy and enduring faithfulness to Israel, will do what "the rest" of Israel cannot do for themselves. God will heal their spiritual blindness and insensibility. God himself will remove their ungodliness and take away their sins, cleansing them of their infidelity and empowering them to keep his covenant.

Paul's focus in Romans 11:25–27 remains fixed on *God's* action in the redemption of Israel. As a result, just what Israel's response to God will entail is left rather fuzzy. Yet, in view of the fact that all of Romans leading up to this point has insisted that God's righteousness has now been definitively revealed in Jesus Christ for the salvation of *all*, the Jew first and also the Greek, it is virtually inconceivable that Paul envisions Israel's reunion with God taking place on any other basis than what God has done for the world in Christ. According to Paul, that reconciliation entails the willing response of mouth and heart, confessing Jesus as Lord and believing that God has raised him from the dead. A remnant of Israel and a great number of Gentiles have already received the grace to make this confession (cf. Rom 9:24). And Paul trusts, with absolute confidence in the mercy and faithfulness of God, that "the rest" of Israel too will one day be delivered from their ἀπιστία and embrace their God, who has acted in Christ for their deliverance as well as for the salvation of the Gentiles.[238]

---

[238] Paul's statements in Romans 11:20 and 23 (and in his summary of the entire letter, Romans 15:7–13) obviate every effort to find in Romans a redemption for Israel that is not christocentric (as, for example, Stendahl 1976 attempts to do; see most recently Stendahl 1995:38–40; cf. Nanos 1996; Gager 2000). Though Paul remains vague on the details of how Israel's salvation will come about, he does not envision Israel's reconciliation with God apart from πίστις Ἰησοῦ Χριστοῦ (see the succinct and forceful defense of this point by E. P. Sanders 1978:180–83; 1983:194). Whether Christian theology should follow Paul's view on this issue is another topic, but modern theologians who decide otherwise should at least own that they genuinely disagree with Paul at this point. Wasserburg 2000 and Nickelsburg 1991 are models in this respect, illuminating the christocentric logic of Pauline soteriology even as they decline to adopt Paul's conceptual framework as their own. Noting that Paul's entire argument in Romans implies that "the justification of the Jews . . . depends on their transforming faith in Christ, which appears to be exactly what Rom 11:23 states," Nickelsburg concludes his study: "As twentieth-century Christians wrestle with this theological problem, they need to affirm Paul's view of the universal grace of God while recognizing that time has belied the exclusivism of his

THE TRIUMPH OF GOD'S WISDOM AND MERCY:
ROMANS 11:28–32

In Romans 11:28–32, Paul restates his understanding of God's plan for Israel in a way that emphasizes both the enduring faithfulness of God to his promises to Israel and the boundless mercy of God that embraces Jew and Gentile alike. The carefully balanced sentence of v. 28 reveals the divine logic behind the "mystery" of Romans 11:25–26. On the one hand, it is for the sake of the salvation of the Gentiles that Israel is now found to be hostile and resistant to the righteousness of God revealed in the gospel. Israel's disobedience opens the door for Gentiles to receive mercy (11:30–31). On the other hand, as Paul has explained through his rereading of Deuteronomy 32:21 and Isaiah 65:1–2, God's intention in embracing the Gentiles is to provoke his people to jealousy and so win them back to himself.

Paul highlights God's continuing commitment to Israel by loading Romans 11:28–29 with the terminology of election. "With respect to election" (κατὰ τὴν ἐκλογήν) picks up Paul's earlier discussion of the present "remnant according to [God's] gracious election" (λεῖμμα κατ' ἐκλογὴν χάριτος, 11:5; ἡ ἐκλογή, 11:7) and extends the referent of ἐκλογή beyond the remnant to embrace "all Israel." The affirmation that the people of Israel—"Jacob" in the quotation from Isaiah in

formulation" (357). There is, however, a profound irony in Nickelsburg's attempt to "affirm *Paul's view* of the universal grace of God" while abandoning the larger narrative that alone makes Paul's conception of God's grace, offered to all without distinction, intelligible. The observation of B. Lindars (1985:767) is apposite here:

> If it is the case that Paul was constrained to impose the Christian form of Jewish eschatology on his Gentile converts, it cannot be true that he regarded it merely as the symbolic expression of a truth that could be stated in less offensive words.

Nickelsburg treats it as self-evident that, nearly twenty centuries after Paul, eschatology can no longer serve as a plausible framework for Christian theological reflection on the relationship between Israel and the Church. It is far from evident, however, that this must be the case. In fact, a strong argument can be made that it is just such an exchange of a live eschatological hope for some version of realized eschatology that has opened the door to Christian supersessionism throughout the centuries (see further Reuther 1974:226–61; Pawlikowski 1979:151–66). Robert Jenson, among others, has begun to address the problem (for Christian theology) of Israel and the Church in an eschatological framework (1999). Other recent works that struggle with the issue of Israel and the Church from within the Christian tradition include Soulen 1996; B. D. Marshall 1997; Bader-Saye 1999. Responding appreciatively to these efforts, a number of Jewish theologians have made significant contributions of their own to this ongoing dialogue (see Frymer-Kensky 2000).

v. 26—are "beloved" by God (ἀγαπητοί) echoes the declaration of God cited by Paul in Romans 9:13, "Jacob I have loved" (τὸν Ἰακὼβ ἠγάπησα, Mal 1:2–3).[239] The language of "gifts" (χαρίσματα) and "calling" (κλῆσις) in 11:29 further recalls the conclusion Paul draws from Malachi's oracle (Rom 9:11–12), that the election of Israel is due not to "works," but to God's "purpose in accordance with [his] choice" (ἡ κατ᾽ ἐκλογὴν πρόθεσις), a purpose which issues in God's gracious "calling" of people to salvation (ἐκ τοῦ καλοῦντος).[240] Moreover, the phrase, "on account of the fathers," evokes the narrative of God's election of the patriarchs, recounted briefly by Paul in Romans 9:6–13.[241] Seen in the light of Romans 11:26–28, this earlier passage takes on new significance: whatever Paul's caveat, "not all from Israel are Israel," means (9:6), it is clear by this point in Paul's argument that "Israel" encompasses a number far greater than those Jews who have presently embraced the gospel. Even "the rest" who have temporarily been rendered insensible remain "beloved" on account of God's gracious election of their ancestors. Regarding this gracious choice of Israel, God cannot and will not change his mind (cf. ἀμεταμέλητα, 11:29).

Ultimately, the drama of redemption is for Paul the grand cosmic display of the mercy of God, lavished on Jew and Gentile alike. Israel's disobedience has opened the floodgates for this mercy to flow to Gentiles, who were formerly disobedient to God; likewise, Israel—though presently disobedient and estranged from God—will one day in turn find themselves the joyful recipients of God's incomparable mercy. "God has locked up all people in disobedience," Paul concludes, "so that he may have mercy on all people" (11:32).

It is vital to attend to the way in which Paul's confidence in the ultimate victory of God's mercy over human disobedience actually shapes his practice of mission. The apostle's belief in the cosmic triumph of God does not lead him to stop proclaiming the gospel where Christ is not yet named or to stop praying ceaselessly for Israel's salvation. On the contrary, Paul sees himself as one of the

---

[239] One might also hear in Romans 11:28 an echo of the promise of redemption in Hosea 2:23 (quoted in Rom 9:25), where God once again calls his people, "beloved."

[240] Compare the similar statement in 11:5–6 that God has chosen a remnant in the present time on the basis of "grace" (χάρις) rather than "works."

[241] See also the reference to "the promises made to the patriarchs" in the important concluding affirmation of Romans 15:8–9.

principal instruments through whom God is presently carrying out his plan to reconcile the world to himself in Christ.[242] Paul's tireless labors to see the reality and power of the gospel embodied in living communities are sustained by the conviction that in, with, and under all of his own efforts lies God's fixed purpose to shower mercy on Jew and Gentile alike. Conversely, his emphasis on salvation as the gracious gift of a sovereign God does not in any way inhibit him from insisting that Jews and Gentiles alike are called to respond to the gospel with faith and to confess Jesus as Lord; neither does it prevent him from warning in the strongest terms of the disastrous consequences of resisting God's grace. If there exists a tension for Paul between his absolute confidence in the sovereignty and mercy of God and his own fervent plea for people to be reconciled to God through Christ, he lets the tension stand without attempting to resolve it—and without diminishing either his trust in God or his christo-centric missionary zeal.[243]

From Theodicy to Doxology: Job and Isaiah in Romans 11:33–36

In the end, theodicy gives way to doxology. The carefully-reasoned argument of Romans 9–11 culminates in a thundering chorus of scriptural voices extolling the incomprehensible goodness, wisdom, and mercy of God. Here again, Paul betrays his deep indebtedness to the language and thought of Isaiah.

Paul's paean of praise resounds with *topoi* common to apocalyptic and wisdom traditions.[244] Not surprisingly, given the constraints of genre, this hymn contains no explicit citation markers. Nevertheless,

---

[242] Paul's understanding of God's plan to provoke Israel to jealously through calling the Gentiles actually motivates him to *intensify* his missionary efforts (Rom 11:13–14).

[243] D. A. Carson (1981) shows that this stubborn affirmation of *both* divine providence *and* human freedom pervades Israel's scriptures and Second Temple Jewish texts, as well as the New Testament writings. See the perceptive analysis of these themes in the Dead Sea Scrolls by E. P. Sanders 1977:257–70, 282–83 (on Paul, see 446–47). Sanders 1992:250–51, 418–19 addresses the views of the Pharisees on providence and free will.

[244] Compare the vocabulary and motifs found, for example, in Job 5:9; 9:10; 28; Bar 3:29–32; Wis 17:1; Sir 1:1–10; 18:4–6; *2 Bar* 14:8–10; *1 En* 93:11–14; 1QH^a 15[7].26–33; 1QH^a 18[10].3–7. For a detailed analysis of traditional elements in Romans 11:33–36, see E. E. Johnson 1989:164–74.

at two points there are sufficient verbal correspondences to make
the identification of particular scriptural sources for Paul's language
virtually certain. Romans 11:34 is a nearly verbatim citation of Isaiah
40:13 LXX, while Romans 11:35 appears to be a quotation of Job
41:3, though in a version quite different from the LXX.[245]

The words of Job derive, fittingly enough, from Job's climactic
encounter with God. Having spent most of the book questioning
God's wisdom, justice, and goodness, Job finally receives his wish to
confront God in person. But now, beholding the Lord face to face,
Job acknowledges God's righteousness and confesses that no creature has a claim on the Creator: "Who has first given to [God] that
it should be repaid him?" His questions still unanswered,[246] Job bows
in worship before a God whose ways he cannot comprehend, but
whose faithfulness he has learned to trust unreservedly.

The rhetorical question in Isaiah 40:13 also arises in the course
of a dispute over God's wisdom, power, and goodness. Isaiah proclaims the glorious message that the Lord is returning in victory to
Zion and, like a gentle shepherd, is leading her captives home
(40:1–11). But as the sudden and drastic change in of tone in v. 12
indicates, the prophet's news has been greeted with skepticism and
disbelief. Isaiah's half of the conversation (40:12–31) implies that
Israel has responded by calling into question God's wisdom and
power—even God's desire—to rescue them from the gods of their
oppressors. When their complaint is finally given voice, it is full of
hurt and bitterness: "My way is hidden from God; my God has
taken justice away and has stood aloof" (40:27).

In response to their doubts concerning the Lord's wisdom, power,
and faithfulness to deliver them, the prophet remonstrates with his
listeners by reminding them that it is their God who in his wisdom

---

[245] B. Schaller (1980) argues convincingly that in Romans 11:35 and in 1 Corinthians
3:19 Paul employs a text of Job LXX that has been revised toward the text now
represented by MT. A. T. Hanson (1980:85–89) suggests that Paul's association of
Isaiah 40:13 and Job 41:3 in Romans 11:34–35 derives from a Jewish exegetical
tradition (cf. *Pesiq. R.* 25.2; *Pesiq. R. Kah.* 9.2). Advancing several arguments for the
traditional origin of the hymn in 11:33–36, E. E. Johnson (1989:172–73) asserts
that Paul has taken over a prayer used in the synagogue. Whatever the origin of
the hymn, it is likely that Paul recognized the allusion to Isaiah embedded within
it; as I will argue below, the force of this allusion accords with the interpretation
Paul gives to the prophet's words elsewhere in Romans.

[246] I noted earlier (pp. 56–57) a number of intriguing resemblances between
Romans 9:19–20 and several passages in Job where the suffering protagonist questions God's justice.

Figure 4.8: Isaiah 40:13 LXX in Romans 11:34 and 1 Corinthians 2:16

Key:
single underline	agreement between Isa 40:13 and Rom 11:34	
double underline	agreement between Isa 40:13 and 1 Cor 2:16	
italic	agreement among all three columns	

Romans 11:34	Isaiah 40:13 LXX	1 Corinthians 2:16
τίς γὰρ ἔγνω νοῦν κυρίου; ἢ τίς σύμβουλος αὐτοῦ ἐγένετο;	¹³ τίς ἔγνω νοῦν κυρίου, καὶ τίς σύμβουλος αὐτοῦ ἐγένετο ὃς συμβιβᾷ αὐτόν;	τίς γὰρ ἔγνω νοῦν κυρίου, ὃς συμβιβάσει αὐτόν;

Isa 40:13 MT: מִי־תִכֵּן אֶת־רוּחַ יְהוָה וְאִישׁ עֲצָתוֹ יוֹדִיעֶנּוּ

and power created heaven and earth (40:12–14; 21–22, 28). Before
him, the nations who oppress Israel and the gods in whom they trust
amount to nothing (40:15–20; 23–26). The Lord strengthens the hungry, but he uproots the powerful and afflicts those who are in comfort (40:23–24; 29 LXX). Those who trust in their own might become
weak, but the ones who hope in the Lord find in him strength and
deliverance (40:30–31). Surely Israel can trust their God's wisdom
and might and faithfulness to rescue them from exile!

It is from Isaiah's defense of God's unparalleled wisdom as Israel's
creator and redeemer that Paul draws his words in Romans 11:34:
"Who has known the mind of the Lord, or who has been his counselor (Isa 40:13)?"[247]

---

[247] Note as well the thematic correspondences between Romans 11:33b and two
other verses from Isaiah 40:

Rom 11:33b: ὡς ἀνεξεραύνητα τὰ κρίματα αὐτοῦ καὶ ἀνεξιχνίαστοι αἱ ὁδοὶ
αὐτοῦ.
Isaiah 40:14: τίς ἔδειξεν αὐτῷ κρίσιν ἢ ὁδὸν συνέσεως τίς ἔδειξεν αὐτῷ;
Isaiah 40:28b: οὐδὲ ἔστιν ἐξεύρεσις τῆς φρονήσεως αὐτοῦ.
The motif of human inability to understand God's ways is a common topos both
of wisdom literature and of theodicy (e.g., Wis 9:13–17; Sir 42:21; *1 En.* 93:11–14;
2 En 33:4; *2 Bar* 75:3–5; *4 Ezra* 4:1–12). Isaiah 40:13 may well have influenced
some of these texts, although none evidences the degree of verbal correspondence
with Isaiah shown by Romans 11:34 and 1 Corinthians 2:16. I noted earlier a
possible echo of Isaiah 40:13 (linked with an allusion to Isa 29:16) in 1QS 11.22
(p. 70 n. 87).

304   CHAPTER FOUR

Interestingly, Paul quotes the same verse (again without an explicit
citation formula) in an earlier letter, 1 Corinthians 2:16. Whereas in
Romans 11:34 he cites the first two clauses of Isaiah 40:13, in
1 Corinthians he cites the first and third.[248] Although Lim treats this
as a case in which Paul knew two different forms of a verse,[249] it
would be more accurate to say that Paul knew one form (quite close
to the LXX) and quoted it in two different ways (see Figure 4.8).[250]

Paul's appropriation of Isaiah 40:13 is of a piece with his use of
other Isaianic texts in Romans to speak about contemporary Israel,
particularly Isaiah 29:16/45:9 (Rom 9:20), Isaiah 28:16/8:14 (Rom
9:33), and Isaiah 40:21/28 (Rom 10:18, 19). In each case, the wider
context in Isaiah portrays Israel challenging God's wisdom and doubting God's power and faithfulness to save them. Paul appears to have
found in these Isaianic oracles an analogue to the resistance his message now faces from his contemporaries, as they question how Paul's
gospel could be the announcement of their long-awaited deliverance.
In his concluding doxology, the apostle takes refuge in the incomprehensible wisdom of God who has in his hands the redemption

---

[248] In 1 Corinthians 2:16, the issue under discussion is the source of true wisdom. Paul claims that wisdom belongs to God but has been made available through
the Spirit to believers in Christ. Cf. Stuhlmacher 1987.

[249] Lim 1997a:158–60.

[250] As Figure 4.8 shows, apart from his insertion of the particle γάρ, Paul's citation varies from the LXX at only two points. In the second clause, he has ἤ for
καί, while in the third clause he has a different future form for the same verb (Paul
takes the future form as συμβιβάσω, while LXX has the form, συμβιβάω). For both
variants there are a number of LXX mss that agree with Paul. Although in both
cases Paul's text differs from Ziegler's reconstruction of LXX Isaiah, it is not necessary to suppose that the variants originated with Paul rather than with his *Vorlage*.
This is particularly so in the case of συμβιβάσει, where the variant reflects a larger
grammatical shift underway in hellenistic Greek. The contracted ("Attic") future of
verbs in -άζω becomes less common in hellenistic Greek in general and is replaced
in the NT entirely by the future form -άσω (see Thackeray 1909:228–31; BDF §74).
Lim (1997a:159–60) is simply mistaken when he argues that Paul's citation in 1
Corinthians 2:16 (which omits the phrase, τίς σύμβουλος αὐτοῦ ἐγένετο) agrees with
the original (uncorrected) reading of 1QIsaᵃ, מי תכן את רוח יהוה ועצתו יודיענה,
which instead of a reference to a "counsellor" (אִישׁ עצתו, corrected reading = MT,
LXX) takes "his counsel" as the object of יודיענה. The fact of the matter is, however, that Paul's citation in 1 Corinthians 2:16 not only does not mention a "counsellor" (אִישׁ עצתו), it has no equivalent whatsoever to the word ועצתו, which is found
in *both* the corrected and the uncorrected readings of 1QIsaᵃ. Moreover, Paul's citation does *not* agree with 1QIsaᵃ in reading a feminine suffix on יודיענה (cf. MT,
יודיענו; LXX, ὃς συμβιβᾷ αὐτόν). Once again, *contra* Lim, there is no reason to suppose that Paul's citations have been influenced by a Hebrew *Vorlage*. The hypothesis that Paul modifies LXX Isaiah here explains the data more fully and more
economically.

of his people Israel, and indeed, of the entire world: "For from him and through him and to him are all things. To him be the glory forever! Amen."

Concluding Reflections: Isaiah among the Chorus of Witnesses

In Romans 9–11, we enter a "cave of resonant signification,"[251] in which echoes of the many voices invoked by Paul ricochet off the cavern walls, commingling with Paul's own words and with one another to create a complex choral symphony. Paul has composed this masterpiece out of his own agonized wrestling with the question of God's faithfulness to Israel—a question raised, ironically enough, by his own successful mission to the Gentiles. Within this symphonic theodicy, Isaiah stands out, not only as a solo voice (9:20, 33; 10:15–16; 11:26–27), but also as a prominent member of duets, trios and quartets: Hosea and Isaiah (9:25–29); Moses, Righteousness from Faith, Isaiah, and Joel (10:5–13); Isaiah and the psalmist (10:18); Moses and Isaiah (10:19–21); Moses, Isaiah, and David (11:8–10); Isaiah and Job (11:34–35). The part Isaiah sings is distinctively his, and yet, under Paul's direction, it blends harmoniously with this multiplicity of potentially discordant scriptural voices. It is fitting, then, that in the final movement of the symphony, Isaiah's voice should merge almost imperceptibly with Paul's in a triumphant celebration of the inscrutable wisdom of Israel's God, the God who, through Paul's apostolic activity, is now accomplishing his gracious purpose to redeem Jew and Gentile together in Christ.

---

[251] For this phrase, see Hollander 1981:65, quoted in Hays 1989:21.

CHAPTER FIVE

"IN HIM WILL THE GENTILES HOPE"
ISAIAH IN ROMANS 15

> Those to whom it has not been
> announced concerning him will see,
> and those who have not heard will
> understand.
>
> *Romans 15:21*

We turn in this final chapter of analysis to the concluding sections
of Romans, where Paul provides a summary restatement of the principal themes of his letter (15:7–13) followed by a direct appeal to
the Roman churches to support his ongoing mission to the Gentiles
(15:14–33). A citation from Isaiah figures prominently in each of
these sections of the letter (15:12, 21). As before, my investigation
will attend both to the function of these quotations in their immediate contexts in Romans and to the larger patterns of interpretation that undergird Paul's reading of Isaiah.[1]

THE CHRIST, SERVANT OF JEW AND GENTILE: ROMANS 15:7–13[2]

Romans 15:7–13 functions both as a conclusion to the exhortations
of 12:1–15:6[3] and as a summation of the principal themes of letter
as a whole. Arguably, these verses represent the climax of the entire
epistle.[4] This rhetorical ἐπίλογος reprises many of the themes which
figured prominently in Romans 9–11: God's abiding faithfulness to
Israel, the inclusion of Gentiles in the people of God, and the centrality of Christ in God's work of redemption.[5] Significantly, at this
climactic moment in Paul's argument, Isaiah steps forward once again
to testify "in person" to Paul's gospel (15:12).

---

[1] The remaining quotation from Isaiah found in Romans (Isa 45:23/Rom 14:11)
is the subject of an excursus at the end of this chapter.

[2] Portions of the following discussion are adapted from Wagner 1997a.

[3] Note the verbal links: "therefore accept one another . . ." (15:7/14:1, 3); "peace,"
(15:13/14:17, 19).

[4] So Wright 1991:235. Similarly, Saß 1993:514; Keck 1990:85; Hays 1989:71.

[5] A number of important verbal links bind this passage closely to chapters 9–11:

The structure of Rom 15:7–13 is fairly simple (Figure 5.1).[6]

Figure 5.1: Outline of Romans 15:7–13

15:7a	• Exhortation
15:7b	• Appeal to the example of Christ
15:8–12	• Amplification from scripture
15:13	• Prayer that the community may embody the pattern of Christ's life and the teaching of scripture

Paul grounds his opening exhortation, "receive one another," in the example of "the Christ,"[7] who "received you to the glory of God" (15:7).[8] He then unpacks the meaning of this christological statement in a sentence that epitomizes the significance of Christ's ministry both for Jews and for Gentiles:[9]

> [8] For I say that the Christ has become a servant of the circumcision on behalf of the truthfulness of God, in order to confirm the promises made to the patriarchs, [9]and [a servant] with respect to the Gentiles on behalf of the mercy [of God] in order to glorify God.

• "patriarchs":   15:8   9:5; 11:28
• "promises"   15:8   9:4, 8–9
• "mercy" (linked with "glory")   15:9   9:23; 11:23
(ἐλεέω occurs six times in Rom 9–11)
• the inclusion of Gentiles   15:8–12   9–11, passim
(ἔθνη appears 9x in Rom 15, 9x in Rom 9–11, out of 28 occurrences in the letter as a whole).

That the climax of the letter bears such striking thematic and verbal affinities to Romans 9–11 is an argument for the centrality of 9–11 to the concerns and purposes of the letter as a whole.

[6] The structure of 15:7–13 mirrors that of 15:1–6: Exhortation (15:1–2); Appeal to the example of Christ (15:3a); Amplification from scripture (15:3b–4); Prayer (15:5–6). For similar analyses, see Keck 1990:86 and Zeller 1984:231.

[7] Following Dunn 1998b, I take ὁ Χριστός in Romans 15:7 in its full titular sense. For the significance of "the Messiah" in Paul's thought, see N.T. Wright 1991:41–55. In light of Paul's emphasis in this section on the example of the Christ (15:3; 15:5, κατὰ Χριστόν), καθώς should be read here with its normal comparative force (contra Cranfield and Käsemann, who understand the adverb as causative).

[8] Paul here follows the pattern he established in the immediately preceding section 15:1–3a, where he supports an exhortation by an appeal to something the Christ did. On the importance of the story of Jesus for Paul, see Thompson 1991; Fowl 1990; R. Penna 1989; Wedderburn 1989.

[9] I have argued at length elsewhere for the translation adopted here (Wagner 1997a). Baumert 2000 and Whitsett 2000 both support my understanding of Paul's syntax and go on to develop further insights concerning the significance of these verses for Paul's argument in Romans.

⁸ λέγω γὰρ Χριστὸν διάκονον γεγενῆσθαι περιτομῆς ὑπὲρ ἀληθείας θεοῦ, εἰς τὸ βεβαιῶσαι τὰς ἐπαγγελίας τῶν πατέρων, ⁹τὰ δὲ ἔθνη ὑπὲρ ἐλέους δοξάσαι τὸν θεόν (15:8–9).

In the first half of this carefully-balanced declaration (15:8), the clause, "the Christ has become a servant to the circumcision,"[10] is modified by two prepositional phrases. The first, ὑπὲρ ἀληθείας θεοῦ, indicates that Christ serves the Jews on behalf of (or for the sake of) the "truth of God," evoking the recurrent theme in Romans that the gospel is the vindication of God's righteousness or faithfulness (1:18, 25; 3:4, 7; 9:14). The second prepositional phrase, εἰς τὸ βεβαιῶσαι κτλ., reveals the purpose of Christ's service to the Jews: "to confirm the promises made to the patriarchs." This phrase once again sets Paul's gospel within the larger narrative of God's election of Abraham and his descendents to be God's own people (Rom 4:13, 16, 20; 9:4, 8–9).[11] "Confirm" here has the sense not only of "reaffirming," but also of "realizing" the promises.[12] In Romans 15:8, then, Christ is envisioned as God's servant, carrying out his commission with reference to the Jews by ministering on behalf of God's faithfulness to the promises made to Israel's ancestors.

The second half of Paul's sentence focuses on Christ's ministry to the Gentiles (15:9a).[13] Just as Christ has become a servant to the

---

[10] "Circumcision" (περιτομή) here stands in opposition to "the Gentiles" (15:9a) and should be understood as a reference to "the Jews," as in Romans 3:30; 4:12 (so Cranfield 1979:740).

[11] The description of Christ in 15:8–9 is reminiscent of Paul's portrait of Abraham in Romans 4. Both figures unite Jew and Gentile (see esp. 4:9–12, 17–18), both are related to the confirmed promises (4:13, 16; 15:8), both give glory to God (4:20; 15:9), and that which was written about each of them is meant for our benefit (4:23–24; 15:4). Paul's use of similar language to depict Christ and Abraham suggests that he saw a typological relationship between the faithfulness of Abraham and the faithfulness of Christ. Such a relationship in Paul's thought might help explain the surprising "absence" of Christ in the argument of Romans 4 on righteousness ἐκ πίστεως (cf. Hays 1985:97–98).

[12] Michel 1966:359.

[13] It might be objected that Paul would not have spoken of the Messiah as a servant to the Gentiles. Several commentators appeal to Matthew 15:24, "I was sent only to the lost sheep of the house of Israel," to explain Paul's statement in v. 8 as a reference to the restriction of Jesus' ministry to the Jewish people (e.g., Fitzmyer 1993:706; Murray 1959–65, 2:205; Thompson 1991:233). In my opinion, this objection is invalid. First, it is not at all clear that any such tradition as that preserved in Matthew 15:24 lies behind Paul's thought in the present passage. Second, Wilckens is certainly right in observing that it is Christ's ministry as a whole that is in view here rather than one aspect of that ministry—incarnation, death, or resurrection—in particular (Wilckens 1978–82, 3:105). It is perfectly

Jews on behalf of the truthfulness of God—thereby vindicating God's faithfulness to his promises—so also he has become a servant to the Gentiles on behalf of God's mercy—thus bringing yet greater glory to God for lavishing his grace on those outside the covenant people.[14] The parallel structure of Paul's sentence reflects his conviction that Christ's ministry is good news for the Jew first, and equally for the Gentile. Throughout Romans, Paul has been concerned to show that God's redemptive purpose, realized in and through Christ's ministry, encompasses Jew and Gentile alike in such a way that God remains faithful to his promises to Israel even as God reaches out in mercy to embrace the Gentiles, to whom he had formerly made no promises.[15]

Paul supports his declaration in Romans 15:8–9a with a catena of scriptural excerpts, summoning Torah (Deut 32:43), Prophets (Isa 11:10), and Psalms (Ps 17:50 LXX; Ps 116:1 LXX) to testify that

---

plausible that Paul envisions Christ's ministry to the Gentiles as being carried out, not during Jesus' earthly ministry, but primarily through the apostolic mission. Indeed, in Romans 15:18, Paul speaks of "that which Christ worked through me for the obedience of the Gentiles. . . ."

[14] There is a clear parallelism in Paul's sentence between "Jew" and "Gentile" and between "truth" and "mercy," all of which function as key terms in Romans. That Paul intended ἀλήθεια and ἔλεος to balance one another finds support from the observation that these two terms regularly occur together in the LXX as the translation of the common scriptural attribute of God, חסד ואמה (Michel 1966:359 n. 3). These two words appear in parallel lines in Ps 116:2 LXX, the first verse of which Paul quotes in Romans 15:11, increasing the likelihood that the close relationship between these terms did not escape his notice. For the connection of "mercy" with "the glory of God" in Romans, see especially 9:23: καὶ ἵνα γνωρίσῃ τὸν πλοῦτον τῆς δόξης αὐτοῦ ἐπὶ σκεύη ἐλέους ἃ προητοίμασεν εἰς δόξαν, "and so that he might make known the wealth of his *glory* for vessels of *mercy* that he prepared for *glory*." Note further the progression in Romans 11 from Paul's summary statement, "God has imprisoned all in disobedience so that he might have *mercy* on all," (11:32) to his outburst of praise (11:33–36) that ends with the benediction, "to him be the *glory* forever. Amen!"

[15] Romans 9:23; 11:30–32. Cf. the description of Gentiles as those "by nature not having the Law" (Rom 2:14). It is important to note that the contrast between ὑπὲρ ἀληθείας and ὑπὲρ ἐλέους is not absolute: Paul is concerned in Romans to argue that the *promises* of scripture envision the eventual inclusion of the Gentiles (e.g., 4:13–25; 15:9b–12); he likewise takes pains to emphasize that God's dealings with Israel are characterized above all by *mercy* (11:31–32). Rather, the contrast set up by the two ὑπέρ phrases reflects the priority of Israel in God's saving purposes ("to the Jew first, and equally to the Greek," 1:16) and God's different methods of working with each party. The promises have *primary* reference to Israel, while God's free mercy is seen most vividly in his inclusion of the Gentiles, with whom he had previously made no covenant (cf. Lagrange 1916:346–47). This distinction between Jews and non-Jews in the divine economy appears in Paul's metaphor of the olive tree, where Israel and the Gentiles are designated, respectively, "root/natural branches" and "wild branches" (Rom 11:17–24).

the divine purpose in the Messiah's ministry is the creation of a community of Jews and Gentiles glorifying God together.[16] Paul forges this chain of testimonies by exploiting a number of strong verbal and conceptual links among the texts. Each of these four scriptural texts depicts Gentiles joining together with Israel in the worship of YHWH. The first three employ various terms for worship and praise, while the fourth uses the language of "hope" to speak of Gentile adherence to the "shoot of Jesse" and to his God.[17]

A striking network of intertextual connections links these scriptural citations to one another and to their wider rhetorical setting in Romans (15:7–9a, 13), attesting to the care with which Paul has constructed this catena. These connections reveal just how deeply enmeshed in the conceptual and linguistic world of scripture is Paul's gospel that in Christ God has revealed his righteousness for Jew and Gentile alike. In attempting to unravel this web of intertextual relationships, I will first note significant points of contact among the first three texts Paul cites. Then I will consider in greater detail Paul's appropriation of Isaiah 11:10. Of particular interest here is the "fit" of Isaiah 11:10 with Paul's previous quotations of Isaiah in Romans as well as with with the larger "narrative" of God's redemption of Israel and the Gentiles that lies behind Paul's reading of the prophet in this letter.

Eschatological Praise:
Psalm 17:50 LXX and Psalm 116:1 LXX

Paul opens the catena with a citation of Psalm 17:50 LXX (Rom 15:9b):[18]

---

[16] In a real sense, this catena represents Paul's "canon within the canon." Of the four books Paul cites most frequently (Isaiah [28x]; Psalms [20x]; Deuteronomy [15x]; Genesis [15x]), three are represented in this chain of quotations (numbers based on Koch 1986:21–24). Though one might quibble about including or excluding a citation here or there (particularly since Koch treats 2 Cor 6:14–7:1 as non-Pauline [but see Dahl 1977a]), the general picture is sound.

[17] Note the prominence of "hope" in Paul's statements on either side of the catena (Rom 15:4; 15:13). On this term, see n. 48 below.

[18] A slightly different version of this psalm is found in 2 Kingdoms 22, just prior to the last words of David (2 Kgdms 23:1–7). The particular verse Paul quotes is identical in the two versions. I assume in what follows Paul's use of the version found in the Book of Psalms, though it makes little difference to the argument. Paul may well have known both versions or even have conflated the two in his own memory.

διὰ τοῦτο ἐξομολογήσομαί σοι ἐν ἔθνεσιν καὶ τῷ ὀνόματί σου ψαλῶ.

For this reason I will confess you among the nations, and to your name I will sing.

The superscription to Psalm 17 (Ps 18 MT) attributes this lengthy song of thanksgiving to "the Lord's servant, David,"[19] and the final verses of the poem make it clear that the speaker is none other than God's anointed king (17:51). The psalmist gives thanks to YHWH for deliverance from mortal danger and for victory over all of his enemies.[20] He rejoices in God's gift of dominion over Israel and the nations, and he celebrates God's faithfulness to his promise to show mercy to "David and his seed forever."[21] This last line helped to hold Psalm 17 open to interpretation in terms of later historical monarchs and, after the fall of the house of David, in terms of an eschatological king.[22] That Paul has read this psalm as words of the Christ is therefore not terribly surprising.[23]

---

[19] τῷ παιδὶ κυρίου τῷ Δαυιδ; לעבד יהוה לדוד.

[20] The superscription to the LXX version of the psalm reads, εἰς τὸ τέλος· τῷ παιδὶ κυρίου τῷ Δαυιδ, ἃ ἐλάλησεν τῷ κυρίῳ τοὺς λόγους τῆς ᾠδῆς ταύτης ἐν ἡμέρᾳ, ᾗ ἐρρύσατο αὐτὸν κύριος ἐκ χειρὸς πάντων τῶν ἐχθρῶν αὐτοῦ καὶ ἐκ χειρὸς Σαουλ.

[21] μεγαλύνων τὰς σωτηρίας τοῦ βασιλέως αὐτοῦ καὶ ποιῶν ἔλεος τῷ χριστῷ αὐτοῦ, τῷ Δαυιδ καὶ τῷ σπέρματι αὐτοῦ ἕως αἰῶνος (Ps 17:51). As we will soon see, the second psalm quoted by Paul also celebrates God's "mercy" (Ps 116:2 LXX). The relevance of the motif of God's mercy to Paul's argument in Romans 15:8–9a needs no explication.

[22] 2 Samuel may already point in this direction by locating David's recitation of this psalm just before his Spirit-inspired "last words" (23:1–7), where, in a scene reminiscent of the later genre of "testament," David recalls God's everlasting covenant with his house (see further S. Weitzman 1997:117–20). For readers of the LXX Psalter, the superscription εἰς τὸ τέλος (MT, למנצח) may have signalled that the psalm was to be read eschatologically (cf. Bornhäuser 1921:212–15). Curiously, J. Schaper does not consider this possibility in his study, *Eschatology in the Greek Psalter*; he mentions the phrase εἰς τὸ τέλος only as an example of the limitations of the translators' knowledge of Hebrew vocabulary (1995:31–32). Portions of Psalm 18 [17 LXX] are quoted in fragments of a non-canonical psalm found at Qumran (4Q381 frg. 24, lines 7–11 [Ps 18:3–9]; frg. 28, lines 1–2 [Ps 18:13–15]; frg. 29, line 3 [Ps 18:16]). The Qumran composition bears the superscription, תהלה לאיש האל[ה]ם ("Praise of the man of God"). For David as "the man of God," see Nehemiah 12:24, 36; 2 Chronicles 8:14 (Schuller 1986:27–29). On these fragments, see further Schuller 1986:34–38, 111–22, 124–27; 1997:1–3, 18–21; 1992:90–100.

[23] It is widely recognized that Paul understands the speaker of these words from Psalm 17:50 to be Christ (so Cranfield, Hays, Keck, Lagrange, Michel, Sanday and Headlam, Wilckens; compare the picture of Christ praising God in the midst of the Christian community in Hebrews 2:12 [Ps 21:23 LXX]). This interpretation is virtually certain in light of Paul's previous use of Psalm 68:10 (LXX) as a word of Christ in Romans 15:3 (cf. Hays 1993a). That Christ is the speaker in Romans

What *is* remarkable about Paul's "messianic exegesis" of the psalm is that he focuses almost entirely on the messiah's mission to the Gentiles: "Therefore I will confess you among the Gentiles." Significantly, the psalmist's interest in the nations is not confined to the verse Paul quotes. Earlier, the psalmist celebrates his God-given dominion over the nations in phrases that leap off the page when seen through the 3-D glasses supplied by Paul:

> You will save me from the arguments of the people, you will establish me as the leader of the Gentiles. A people whom I did not know has become subject to me; they have become obedient to me so as to listen with the ear (Ps 17:44–45a).
>
> ῥύσῃ με ἐξ ἀντιλογιῶν λαοῦ, καταστήσεις με εἰς κεφαλὴν ἐθνῶν· λαός, ὃν οὐκ ἔγνων, ἐδούλευσέν μοι· εἰς ἀκοὴν ὠτίου ὑπήκουσέν μοι.

The Gentiles, once outsiders and strangers to God's people,[24] now obey the messiah[25] whom God has raised up to be their leader.[26] The wider context of Paul's excerpt from Psalm 17 thus anticipates the clear statement of Isaiah a few verses later concerning the descendant of David who "rises to rule the Gentiles." Likewise, the affirmation of the messiah in Psalm 17:31 that God is "a shield for all who hope in him" (ὑπερασπιστής ἐστιν πάντων τῶν ἐλπιζόντων ἐπ᾽ αὐτόν) resonates with Isaiah's prophecy concerning David's scion, in whom "the Gentiles will hope."

Psalm 116 LXX, whose first verse Paul quotes in Romans 15:11,[27] shares impressive verbal and thematic links with Psalm 17. As part of the important liturgical cycle of psalms known as the *Hallel* (Ps

---

15:9b would also explain the omission of the vocative κύριε at the end of the first line of the quotation, since Paul normally reserves the title κύριος for Christ. Read from this christological perspective, the psalmist's celebration of deliverance from the "pains of death and of Hades" (17:5–6) takes on new significance (cf. the echo of Psalm 17:5 in Acts 2:24 in conjunction with Peter's interpretation of Psalm 15:8–11 LXX as a prophecy of Jesus' death and resurrection).

[24] The phrase, λαός, ὃν οὐκ ἔγνων, is similar to other negative statements in scripture that Paul reads as descriptions of the Gentiles (see pp. 83 and 335–36).

[25] Cf. Paul's statement of his goal: "to bring about the obedience (ὑπακοή) of the Gentiles" (Rom 15:18; cf. 1:5; 16:26). He does this by means of the ἀκοή that he preaches (Rom 10:16–17; cf. Gal 3:2, 5).

[26] The messiah's thanksgiving for deliverance ἐξ ἀντιλογιῶν λαοῦ provides a suggestive context for hearing Paul's description of Israel in the words of Isaiah 65:2 as λαὸς ἀπειθῶν καὶ ἀντιλέγων (Rom 10:21).

[27] αἰνεῖτε, πάντα τὰ ἔθνη, τὸν κύριον καὶ ἐπαινεσάτωσαν αὐτὸν πάντες οἱ λαοί (All you Gentiles—praise the Lord! And let all the peoples praise him!).

111–117 LXX, 113–118 MT), Psalm 116 would have been well known not only in the land of Israel, but also throughout the Diaspora. Its incorporation into the *Hallel* imbued the psalm with strong eschatological overtones of Israel's national restoration.[28] The capstone of the *Hallel*, Psalm 117 LXX (118 MT), functions as an important source for christological testimonies in early Christian circles[29] and raises the question of whether the whole cycle might have been read by the first Christians in connection with Jesus' death and resurrection.[30]

Like Psalm 17, this song also envisions the nations joining in Israel's praise of YHWH. I argued above with regard to Paul's startling interpretation of Isaiah 65:1–2 that the apostle there treats ἔθνη and λαοί, not as synonyms, but as references to distinct groups: Gentiles and Israel, respectively.[31] Similarly, in view of Paul's emphasis in Romans 15:7–13 on the fact that Christ has united Jew and Gentile in himself for the glory of God, it is quite possible that he understands λαοί in Psalm 116:1 to refer to Israel. Such an interpretation would have been facilitated both by the wider context of

---

[28] I assume here that liturgical practice is relatively more stable than exegetical practice and thus that there is no reason to doubt the general reliability of the witness of the Mishnah and Tosefta to the use of the *Hallel* at major feasts during the Second Temple Period. According to the Mishnah, Psalm 118 was sung as part of the *Hallel* at Tabernacles (*m. Sukk.* 3:9, 4:1, 4:5), Hanukkah (*m. Taʿan.* 4:4–5) and at Passover, both at the sacrifice (*m. Pesaḥ.* 5:7) and at the meal (*m. Pesaḥ.* 10:5–7; cf. *t. Pesaḥ.* 10:8–9; Mark 14:26/Matt 26:30). The Tosefta adds that the *Hallel* was also sung on the first day of the Feast of Weeks (*t. Sukk.* 3:2). The association of the *Hallel* with the acts of divine deliverance commemorated at Tabernacles, Hanukkah, and Passover may have inspired the interpretation of these psalms as celebrations of God's *future* deliverance of Israel as well.

[29] Paul echoes Psalm 118:6 MT in Rom 8:31, but without an explicitly christological reference. Quotations from Psalm 118 in reference to Jesus are found in the following NT texts: Luke 20:17; Acts 4:11, 1 Pet 2:7 (Ps 118:22); Mark 12:10–11// Matt 21:42 (Ps 118:22–23); Mark 11:9// Matt 21:9, John 12:13 (Ps 118:25–26); Matt 23:39// Luke 13:35, Luke 19:38 (Ps 118:26). Wagner 1997b explores the importance of this psalm for the narrative of Luke-Acts.

[30] Paul's quotation of Psalm 115:1 LXX in 2 Corinthians 4:13 to express his confidence in God even in the face of death (cf. LXX Ps 114:1–9; 115:6) accrues a whole new layer of meaning if the speaker of the psalm is understood to be Christ (cf. Hanson 1963:11–13, 1974:17–18; Hays 1983:189 n. 125, 1993a:128). This quotation would then be another example of the theme, so prominent in 2 Corinthians, that in his ministry Paul participates in "the death of Jesus" (2 Cor 4:10–12; cf. Hafemann 1990:63 and n. 58; 66 and n. 63).

[31] See pp. 212–13. We saw yet another instance of this very same exegetical move in Luke's interpretation of Psalm 2:1–2 in Acts 4:25–26 (see pp. 212–13 n. 278; cf. p. 285 n. 206).

Psalm 116 in the psalter[32] and by the preceding quotation from Deuteronomy 32:43 in Romans 15:10, which speaks of Gentiles rejoicing together with "his people (λαός)." If Paul does intend λαοί as a reference to Israel, his quotation of Psalm 116:1 serves as a call to Jew and Gentile to worship God *together*.

The reason for this universal call to praise appears in the second verse of the psalm:

> For his *mercy* has conquered us, and the *truthfulness* of the Lord endures forever.
>
> ὅτι ἐκραταιώθη τὸ <u>ἔλεος</u> αὐτοῦ ἐφ᾽ ἡμᾶς, καὶ ἡ <u>ἀλήθεια</u> τοῦ κυρίου μένει εἰς τὸν αἰῶνα (Ps 116:2).

These words resonate deeply with Paul's consise summation of Romans in 15:8–9a, where he states that it is for the sake of the "truthfulness" (ἀλήθεια) and "mercy" (ἔλεος) of God that Christ has become a servant to Jew and Gentile, as well as with the triumphant conclusion of Romans 9–11 that God will "show mercy (ἔλεος) to all" (11:32). Although in the recitation of the *Hallel* Psalm 116 was probably understood as a call to the nations to praise YHWH for God's mercy shown to *Israel*,[33] it is clear that for Paul, the word "us" in Psalm 116:2 would signify "Jews and Gentiles together."[34]

"Rejoice, Gentiles, with His People": Deuteronomy 32:43

Nestled between these two psalm citations is an excerpt from the doxological conclusion to the Song of Moses, a text that has already figured prominently in Romans:[35]

---

[32] At the end of the preceding psalm, the speaker vows to give thanks to the Lord "before all his people (λαός), in the courts of the house of the Lord—in your midst, O Jerusalem" (115:9–10). The following psalm calls on "the house of Israel" to praise the Lord (117:2).

[33] "The world has witnessed the blessings that God has given his people, but derives no direct benefit of itself" (Allen 1983:116 n. 1a; similarly, Kraus 1993:391; Dahood 1970:153).

[34] Similarly, it is not hard to imagine that Paul would have heard in the following psalm (Ps 117:1–4) a call, not only for "the house of Israel" (v. 2) and "the house of Aaron" (v. 3), but also for the Gentiles to acknowledge YHWH's goodness and unfailing mercy: "*Let all those who fear the Lord* say, 'He is good; his mercy [endures] forever'" (εἰπάτωσαν δὴ <u>πάντες οἱ φοβούμενοι τὸν κύριον</u> ὅτι ἀγαθός, ὅτι εἰς τὸν αἰῶνα τὸν ἔλεος αὐτοῦ, v. 4).

[35] Paul quotes Deuteronomy 32:21 in Romans 10:19 and subsequently alludes to the same text in Romans 11:11–14. Further echoes of the Song of Moses may be heard in Romans 9:14 (Deut 32:4) and possibly in Romans 11:1 (Deut 32:8–9). In addition, Paul quotes Deuteronomy 32:35 in Romans 12:19.

Rejoice, O Gentiles, with his people.

εὐφράνθητε, ἔθνη, μετὰ τοῦ λαοῦ αὐτοῦ (Rom 15:10/ Deut 32:43 LXX).

Deuteronomy 32:43 fits perfectly within the scriptural catena in Romans 15, for it invites the Gentiles to rejoice together with Israel in the salvation God has wrought for the entire world.[36] At the same time, Paul's citation of this text provides a deeply satisfying conclusion to his reading of Moses' Song in Romans 9–11. There, Paul appealed to Deuteronomy 32:21 in order to demonstrate that Israel's present resistance to the gospel is an integral part of God's plan to effect the salvation of the Gentiles and, in the end, to redeem Israel as well. God's purpose in embracing a "no-nation" is to provoke Israel to jealousy, to stir his people to forsake their idols and once again to seek deliverance in their God alone (32:19–21). As the Song of Moses unfolds, it ultimately is God himself who, for the sake of his glorious name,[37] takes the initiative to purify his people and res-

---

[36] Paul's interpretation depends on the form of this text found in the LXX, since in MT the first line of Deut 32:43 reads, "Praise his people, O nations," or possibly, "O nations, make his people sing out for joy" (הַרְנִינוּ גוֹיִם עַמּוֹ). In contrast, the LXX translator has apparently taken עם in a dual sense, rendering it twice, as both "with" and "people" (Wevers 1995:534). Evidence for a variant version of Deuteronomy 32:43 in Hebrew comes from a fragmentary manuscript of Deuteronomy from Qumran. In place of the wording found in 32:43a MT, 4QDeut[q] (4Q44) has two lines, הרנינו שמים עמו והשתחוו לו כל אלהים. The LXX translator apparently knew both the Hebrew tradition attested by 4Q44 (Deut 32:43ab) and a tradition similar in part to the text preserved in Deut 32:43a MT (LXX has a further line not found in MT or in 4Q44). Rather than choose between them, the translator decided simply to include them both, one right after the other (P. W. Skehan and E. Ulrich, DJD XIV, p. 141, note on lines 6–7):

εὐφράνθητε, οὐρανοί, ἅμα αὐτῷ	= 4Q44
καὶ προσκυνησάτωσαν αὐτῷ πάντες υἱοὶ θεοῦ·	= 4Q44
εὐφράνθητε, ἔθνη, μετὰ τοῦ λαοῦ αὐτοῦ,	= MT
καὶ ἐνισχυσάτωσαν αὐτῷ πάντες ἄγγελοι θεοῦ	≠ 4Q44 or MT

Contra Tigay 1996:516–17, this is not a "double translation" (as was the case with עם; cf. Deut 23:18 for another example), but a "double reading" (see Talshir 1987:22–23, 47–48). Interestingly, Targum Neofiti attests to an interpretation of Deuteronomy 32:43 similar to that of the LXX. It renders the words הרנינו גוים עמו as a call for both the nations and Israel to praise the Lord:

Shout before him, O you nations; praise him, O you his people, the house of Israel.

קלסו קדמוי אומייה שבחו יתיה עמיה בית ישראל

[37] The fierce polemic against other gods in the Song of Moses is phrased in terms reminiscent of similar tirades in Deutero-Isaiah (Deut 32:37–39 [cf. Isa 45:21; 43:13]; Deut 32:12 [cf. Isa 63:9]; Deut 32:17 [cf. Isa 65:3, 11]). Fishbane (1985:477–79)

cue them from their enemies (32:34–42). Israel's deliverance results in blessing not only for God's people, but also for the entire cosmos.[38] The Song closes with a rousing call to the heavenly beings as well as to all on earth—Israel and the nations together—to rejoice in what God has done (32:43). The use Paul makes of Deuteronomy 32:43 in Romans 15:10, then, provides a striking confirmation of my argument that Paul reads the Song as a whole as a narrative of God's faithfulness to redeem Israel and, through Israel, the entire world.[39]

"In Him Will the Gentiles Hope": Isaiah 11:10

The anchor for Paul's catena of scriptural witnesses is a quotation from Isaiah 11:10. Once more, Isaiah steps from the shadows to deliver his oracle *viva voce*. Once again the weighty presence of the prophet underscores Paul's foundational claim that his gospel has been revealed in the prophetic writings (1:1–3; cf. 16:25–26):

> And again, Isaiah says, "The shoot of Jesse will [come forth], even the one who rises to rule the Gentiles. In him the Gentiles will hope" (Rom 15:12).
>
> καὶ πάλιν Ἡσαΐας λέγει· ἔσται ἡ ῥίζα τοῦ Ἰεσσαὶ καὶ ὁ ἀνιστάμενος ἄρχειν ἐθνῶν, ἐπ' αὐτῷ ἔθνη ἐλπιοῦσιν.

Romans 15:12 forms a tight inclusio with the beginning of the section, for all the elements of Romans 15:8–9 are present here in one scriptural quotation. The promises God made to Israel long ago now find their realization in the coming of Jesus, "the shoot of Jesse." Moreover, this same Jesus, risen from the dead, has become the focal point for the hopes of the nations. In and through his ministry, he has brought Jew and Gentile together—to the glory of God.

Paul's quotation of Isaiah 11:10 is important for the present study not only because of its prominence as the final link in the lengthy

---

and Sommer (1998:134–36; 273–74 n. 8) discuss additional evidence for Deutero-Isaiah's use of the Song of Moses (e.g., Isa 48:20–21// Deut 32:1–5; Isa 58:11–14// Deut 32:9–13).

[38] It is perhaps not insignificant that, although Moses' Song depicts God's imminent vengeance on his enemies in chilling detail, it never identifies these enemies as "the Gentiles" *per se*. Instead of ἔθνη, the poet uses the terms οἱ ἐχθροί, οἱ ὑπεναντίοι and οἱ μισοῦντές με (Deut 32:27, 41–43). In Deuteronomy 32:28 LXX, the poet castigates Israel's enemies as ἔθνος ἀπολωλεκὸς βουλήν (cf. 32:21, 31), but this does not constitute a condemnation of τὰ ἔθνη as a whole.

[39] See especially pp. 190–201.

catena of citations that brings Paul's ἐπίλογος to a close, but also because, once again, Paul taps into the larger Isaianic story of Israel's restoration. The wider context in which Isaiah 11:10 is embedded (Isa 10–12) relates the story of God's merciful preservation of a remnant of Israel through judgment. It tells of God's faithfulness to rescue his people from their oppressors and—in a recapitulation of the exodus—to gather together their scattered exiles and lead them home to Zion. It envisions the restoration of Israel issuing in blessing for Gentiles and for the entire created order. Finally, the prophet's breathtaking vision culminates in a thundering chorus of praise, as Israel exalts God's glorious name in the presence of all nations.

Paul's citation follows LXX Isaiah closely (Fig. 5.2).[40] Its most significant departure from the LXX, the omission of the eschatological reference "in that day," probably reflects Paul's conviction that Isaiah's prophecy no longer refers to a future time, but is in the process of being realized in the present, in the lives of Paul and his hearers "on whom the ends of the ages have come together."[41]

Figure 5.2: Isaiah 11:10 LXX in Romans 15:12

Isaiah 11:10 LXX	Romans 15:12
καὶ ἔσται ἐν τῇ ἡμέρᾳ ἐκείνῃ <u>ἡ ῥίζα τοῦ Ιεσσαι</u> <u>καὶ ὁ ἀνιστάμενος ἄρχειν ἐθνῶν,</u> <u>ἐπ᾽ αὐτῷ ἔθνη ἐλπιοῦσι.</u>	καὶ πάλιν Ἡσαΐας λέγει· ἔσται <u>ἡ ῥίζα τοῦ Ἰεσσαὶ</u> <u>καὶ ὁ ἀνιστάμενος ἄρχειν ἐθνῶν,</u> <u>ἐπ᾽ αὐτῷ ἔθνη ἐλπιοῦσιν.</u>

Isa 11:10 MT: וְהָיָה בַּיּוֹם הַהוּא שֹׁרֶשׁ יִשַׁי אֲשֶׁר עֹמֵד לְנֵס עַמִּים אֵלָיו גּוֹיִם יִדְרֹשׁוּ

"Messianic Exegesis" of Isaiah 11

The quotation of Isaiah 11:10 in Romans 15:12 is notable because, of all the Isaianic texts quoted by Paul in Romans, it is the one that

---

[40] Paul has the distinctive reading of the LXX, καὶ ὁ ἀνιστάμενος ἄρχειν ἐθνῶν. In addition, his citation shares with LXX the verb ἐλπίζω, not an obvious Greek equivalent for דרשׁ (ἐλπίζω = דרשׁ only here in the entire LXX).

[41] The phrase in quotation marks is found only in 1 Corinthians 10:11 (εἰς οὓς τὰ τέλη τῶν αἰώνων κατήντηκεν), but it represents Paul's sense of his own location in history, and it functions as one of his foundational hermeneutical axioms.

most clearly reveals a "christological" hermeneutic at work.[42] It is not hard to see why Isaiah 11:10 LXX would have been especially attractive to Paul at this point in his argument in Romans. In addition to its clear reference to the messiah's Davidic ancestry—and Paul has taken pains to note that Jesus comes "from the seed of David according to the flesh" (1:3)[43]—the verb ἀνίστημι allows for a delicious double-entendre.[44] As in Romans 10:6–13, it is the resurrection and exaltation of Christ as Lord that makes him the focal point for God's salvation of Gentiles as well as Jews.[45] Moreover, Isaiah 11:10 portrays Gentiles *putting their hope in* this descendant of David.[46] As Romans 15:13 indicates, Paul understands this passage to prophesy that Gentiles—including his hearers at Rome—will give their allegiance to Israel's God ("the God of hope") and to his messiah and so will participate in the blessings of his saving reign:

> May the God of hope fill you with all joy and peace as you believe, so that you may abound in this hope[47] in the power of the Holy Spirit.

---

[42] Compare, however, what Paul does with the "stone" of Isaiah 8:14/28:16 in Romans 9:33–10:11, and see below (pp. 333–35) on the important christological reference he finds in the phrase περὶ αὐτοῦ in Isaiah 52:15 (Rom 15:21).

[43] Note the importance of the Davidic ancestry of Jesus in the opening salutation of Romans (Rom 1:3–4). See further Whitsett 2000.

[44] Paul usually employs ἐγείρω to speak about resurrection (24x; ἀνίστημι is found with this meaning in 1 Thess 4:14, 16; cf. ἀνάστασις, Rom 1:4; 6:5; 1 Cor 15:12, 13, 21, 42; Phil 3:10), but it would be ludicrous to suggest on this basis that Paul would not have recognized the paronomastic potential of ἀνίστημι in Isaiah 11:10.

[45] See above, pp. 161–65 for Paul's interpretation of Deuteronomy 30:12–14 in terms of Jesus' death, resurrection, and exaltation.

[46] Similar prophecies are found in Isaiah 42:4 and 51:5, and these may have influenced the translation of דרשׁ as ἐλπίζω in Isaiah 11:10 LXX (cf. Ziegler 1934:140–41).

καὶ ἐπὶ τῷ ὀνόματι αὐτοῦ ἔθνη ἐλπιοῦσιν (42:4).
And in his [the Servant's, 42:1] name the Gentiles will hope.

ἐγγίζει ταχὺ ἡ δικαιοσύνη μου, καὶ ἐξελεύσεται τὸ σωτήριόν μου, καὶ εἰς τὸν βραχίονά μου ἔθνη ἐλπιοῦσιν· ἐμὲ νῆσοι ὑπομενοῦσι καὶ εἰς τὸν βραχίονά μου ἐλπιοῦσιν (51:5).
My righteousness draws near speedily, and my salvation will come forth, and in my arm the Gentiles will hope. The islands will wait for me, and in my arm they will hope.

Although Ziegler (1939a) supposes ἐπὶ τῷ ὀνόματι in Isaiah 42:4 to be a scribal error for ἐν τῷ νόμῳ (= MT), there is not a scrap of manuscript evidence for this putative variant. Stendahl (1968:114–115 n. 6) and Gundry (1967:115 n. 115) rightly adopt ἐπὶ τῷ ὀνόματι as the original reading.

[47] Taking the article as anaphoric, referring not only to ἔλπις in 15:13a, but also to ἐλπιοῦσιν in the quotation in 15:12.

Ὁ δὲ θεὸς τῆς ἐλπίδος πληρώσαι ὑμᾶς πάσης χαρᾶς καὶ εἰρήνης ἐν τῷ πιστεύειν, εἰς τὸ περισσεύειν ὑμᾶς ἐν τῇ ἐλπίδι ἐν δυνάμει πνεύματος ἁγίου (Rom 15:13).[48]

Other Jewish groups of the Second Temple Period also found in Isaiah 11 fuel with which to stoke the fires of messianic and eschatological hopes.[49] The anonymous author of the Psalms of Solomon depicted the rule of the messiah,[50] whose coming he fervently awaited, in terms reminiscent of Isaiah 11 (*Pss. Sol.* 17:21–44).[51] The psalmist's expectation that the messiah will show mercy to the Gentiles who revere him,[52] an idea doubtless founded in part on Isaiah 11:10, is particularly interesting in light of the use Paul makes of Isaiah in Romans 15:12.

Both individual and corporate interpretations of Isaiah 11 are attested among the Dead Sea Scrolls. 4QpIsaᵃ (4Q161) includes a citation and interpretation of Isaiah 11:1–5,[53] finding in these verses a prophecy of a figure (further identified as "the Branch of David,"

---

[48] Paul elsewhere uses the language of "hope" to describe the response of believers to what God has done—and will yet do—for the world in Christ. "Hope" frequently occurs in his letters in close proximity to "faith" (Rom 4:18; 5:1–2; 15:13; 1 Cor 13:7, 13; Gal 5:5; 1 Thess 1:3; 5:8). Paul speaks of hoping in Christ (1 Cor 15:19; 1 Thess 1:3) as well as hoping in the future consummation of God's kingdom (Rom 5:2–5; 8:24–25; 2 Cor 3:12; 1 Thess 2:19; 4:13; 5:8). For Paul, the presence of the Spirit guarantees the certainty of this eschatological hope (Rom 15:13; Rom 8:26–27; Gal 5:5).

[49] M. Turner discusses Isaiah 11:1–4 in relation to Second Temple messianic expectations (1996:114–18, 132–33), arguing that Luke's portrayal of Jesus is heavily influenced by understandings of the messiah's character and role derived in large part from this passage. In addition to the texts discussed below, Turner notes the influence of Isaiah 11:1–4 on the portraits of the messiah in *1 En.* 49:2–3 and 62:1–2, in *T. Levi* 18:7 (he takes only the phrase "in the water" as a Christian gloss), and in *4 Ezra* 13:8–11 (132 and n. 41, 183). See also the discussions of Isaiah 11 in Collins 1995b:49–73 and in Chevallier 1958.

[50] *Pss. Sol.* 17:32; cf. 18:5, 7 and superscription.

[51] Note, for example, the allusions to Isaiah 11:2–3 in *Pss. Sol.* 17:37–40 and to Isaiah 11:4 in *Pss. Sol.* 17:24, 35–36. The psalmist evokes images from passages in Second Isaiah (e.g., Isa 42:4 in *Pss. Sol.* 17:37; Isa 49:20, 22–23; 66:18–20 in *Pss. Sol.* 17:31; Isa 60:3–4 in *Pss. Sol.* 17:31) and also draws on texts elsewhere in Israel's scriptures relating to the Davidic kingship, including Psalm 2 (*Pss. Sol.* 17:23–24), Psalm 89 (*Pss. Sol.* 17:4, 43), and 2 Samuel 7 (*Pss. Sol.* 17:4). See as well *Pss. Sol.* 18:7, whose description of the messiah's rule (ἐν φόβῳ θεοῦ αὐτοῦ, ἐν σοφίᾳ πνεύματος καὶ δικαιοσύνης καὶ ἰσχύος) incorporates a number of verbal recollections of Isaiah 11:1–4. On the use of scripture in these psalms, see further Holm-Nielsen 1977:97–109.

[52] "[The Lord's anointed] will show mercy to all the Gentiles [who come] before him with reverent fear" (καὶ ἐλεήσει πάντα τὰ ἔθνη ἐνώπιον αὐτοῦ ἐν φόβῳ, *Pss. Sol.* 17:34).

[53] 4Q161 frgs. 8–10 3.15–29.

צמח דויד) who will arise "at the end of days"[54] to defeat Israel's enemies and rule over the nations.[55] In 1QSb (1Q28b) 5.20–29, the blessing to be pronounced on the eschatological "Prince of the Congregation" (נשיא העדה) borrows a number of phrases from Isaiah 11:2–5.[56] A fragmentary text of the War Rule from Cave Four, 4QSM (4Q285), quotes Isaiah 11:1 (ויצא חוטר מגזע ישי), apparently in reference to the Prince of the Congregation, whom it then designates explicitly as "the Branch of David."[57] Though its exegesis may date from a later period, the Targum similarly finds in "the shoot" of Isaiah 11:1 a prophecy of the Messiah.[58]

---

[54] Reconstructing 3.22 to read, in part: [. . . צמח] דויד העומד באח[רית הימים. . .]. So J. M. Allegro (DJD V, p. 14 [his line 17]), followed by Horgan (1979:18, 85 and Charlesworth 2001:54 and n. 62). For the title, צמח דוד, see Jer 23:5; 33:15; cf. Isa 4:2; Zech 3:8; 6:12. It appears elsewhere among the Dead Sea Scrolls in 4QPBless (4Q252) 5.3–4; 4QFlor (4Q174) frgs. 1–2 1.11; 4QSM (4Q285) frg. 5, lines 3–4.

[55] 4Q161 frgs. 8–10 3.25–26 reads:
. . . And he shall rule all the na[tion]s and Magog . . . his sword will judge [al]l the peoples. . . .

²¹. . . ובכול הג[וא]ם ימשול ומגוג] . . . [²² כו]ל העמים תשפוט חרבו
A few lines earlier, Isaiah 10:34 is interpreted as a prophecy of the defeat of the Kittim (the Romans) by Israel (4Q161 frgs. 8–10 3.6–13).

[56] More distant echoes of Isaiah 11 may be discerned in the *Hodayot*. In 1QHᵃ 6[14].25–26, the anonymous poet may be thinking of Isaiah 11:2, 5 in claiming that God has given him "the spirit of knowledge" (ואני עבדך חנותני ברוח דעה; cf. 1QS 3.6, רוח עצת אמת אל). Likewise, in 1QHᵃ 10[2].13–14 the psalmist may allude to Isaiah 11:10–11 in calling himself "a banner for the chosen ones of righteousness" (ותשימני נס לבחירי צדק). Neither passage evinces any sustained dialogue with Isaiah 11, however.

[57] 4Q285 frg. 5, lines 2–4. On this text, which has been the focus of much publicity due to its alleged depiction of a "pierced messiah," see the balanced and sober discussion of VanderKam 1994:179–80. VanderKam rightly insists that the fragment be read first of all as an interpretation of Isaiah 11. Note also Vermes 1992; Lim 1992; R. P. Gordon 1992; Bockmuehl 1992; Abegg 1994. The alleged echo of Isaiah 11:2 in 4QBerᵇ [4Q287] frg. 10, line 13 (ונח]ה על משיחו רוח קוד[ש) ; see M. Turner 1996:116 n. 26; Eisenman and Wise 1993:228; Chilton and Evans 1994:555–556) must now be dismissed due to the publication of the *editio princeps*, which reads משיחי ("the *yod* is certain," B. Nitzan, DJD XI, p. 60). The editor notes further that an allusion to Isaiah 11:2 "has no basis in the context of 4QBerakhot" and suggests instead the reconstruction: לדבר סר]ה על משיחי רוח קוד[שו (p. 60; cf. 4QDᶜ [4Q270] frg. 2 2.13–14; 4QDᵇ [4Q267] frg. 2, lines 5–6 = CD-A 5.21–6.1).

[58] At Isaiah 11:1 the Targum reads, "And the king shall go out from the sons of Jesse, and the messiah shall grow up from his sons' sons" (ויפוק מלכא מבנוהי דיש(י) ומשיחא מבני בנוהי יתרבי). Note also the Targum's approach to the similar metaphor, צמח, in Isaiah 4:2. There, צמח יהוה is translated משיחא ייי (cf. the clear messianic connotations of צמח in Jer 23:5; 33:15; Zech 3:8; 6:12; see n. 54 above). On the messiah in the Isaiah Targum, see further Chilton (1982:86–96), who thinks that "the provenience of the messianic portrait in the Isaiah Targum is Tannaitic."

Isaiah 11:1 may also function as a point of reference for the community's understanding of its own role within the cosmic purposes of God. A series of psalms among the *Hodayot* depict the community as young tree planted and nurtured by God that will ultimately spread its branches over the whole earth. Common to all of these psalms is their use of the word נצר, "shoot," found in Isaiah 11:1 and 60:21 (cf. Dan 11:7).[59]

The LXX version of Isaiah 11:10 also betrays evidence of messianic exegesis. Where the Hebrew reads אשר עמד לנס עמים ("who will stand as a banner for the peoples"), the LXX has καὶ ὁ ἀνιστάμενος ἄρχειν ἐθνῶν ("even he who will rise to rule the nations"). The LXX reading is best explained, not by positing a different Hebrew *Vorlage*, but by recognizing this to be an interpretive translation, facilitated by the similarity of נס to נסיך and נשיא[60] and quite possibly influenced by the messianic vision in Ezekiel 37:25. This latter text promises that "David, my servant, [will be] their נשיא forever."[61]

Nevertheless, despite the fact that Paul interprets "the shoot of Jesse" explicitly in reference to Jesus,[62] his use of Isaiah 11:10 in

---

[59] 1QHᵃ 14[6].14–19; 1QHᵃ 15[7].19; 1QHᵃ 16[8].4–26. These psalms also draw on reflexes of the "tree" metaphor in scriptural texts such as Ezekiel 17:22–24; 19:10–14; 31:1–18; Daniel 4:7–24 (Eng., 4:10–27). Cf. Jesus' use of this image for the church in the parable of the Mustard Seed (Matt 13:31–32// Mark 4:30–32// Luke 13:18–21). The most elaborate version of the metaphor is found in 1QHᵃ 16[8].4–26. Though arguing that the psalm contains autobiographical references to the experiences of the Righteous Teacher, J. H. Charlesworth emphasizes that the author's intention is to shape the self-understanding of the *Yahad* as the elect, eschatological community in whom God is now secretly at work (1992:301). For arguments against reading the psalm as a record of the personal experiences of the Righteous Teacher, see Dombkowski Hopkins 1981:331–36.

[60] So also Ziegler 1934:82. Although these words do not appear in Isaiah, they are rendered elsewhere by Greek translators with forms of ἄρχω (for נסיך, Josh 13:21 A, B) or ἄρχων (for נסיך, Josh 13:21 [many minuscules], Ezek 32:30; often for נשיא in the Hexateuch and Ezekiel). Note that the subsequent occurrence of נס two verses later (Isa 11:12) is translated by a more appropriate Greek term, σημεῖον. As one would expect, α′ and σ′ follow the Hebrew of Isaiah 11:10 more closely than does LXX, translating: ἀνίσταται εἰς σύσσημον λαῶν.

[61] ודוד עבדי נשיא להם לעולם. I owe this suggestion to Goshen-Gottstein (1995:46, Apparatus IV, n. 2 on Isa 11:10). The נשיא העדה is, as we have seen, one of the eschatological figures who appears in some of the Dead Sea Scrolls (1QSb [1Q28b] 5.20–29; 1QM 5.14; CD–A 7.20; 4QpIsaᵃ [4Q161] frgs. 2–6 2.19; 4Q285 frg. 5, line 4).

[62] Cf. Revelation 5:5 and 22:16, which give to Jesus the title, ῥίζα Δαυίδ (cf. Isa 11:1, 10). Furthermore, the striking vision of Jesus with a sharp sword in his mouth (Rev 1:16; 2:12, 16; 19:11, 15, 21) may derive from a conflation of Isaiah 11:4 with Isaiah 49:2 (note the allusion to Isaiah 11:4 in the eschatological scene depicted in 2 Thess 2:8). On the use of Isaiah in the Apocalypse, see Fekkes 1994.

Romans 15:12 does not represent a fundamentally different hermeneutic from that operative in his reading of Isaiah elsewhere in Romans. Paul's christology is everywhere presupposed in Romans, and it is not far from the surface in many of his appeals to other portions of Isaiah in the letter.[63] At the same time, Paul's main concern in Romans 15:12 is not to "prove" something about Jesus, but to show that scripture prophesies the inclusion of Gentiles in the worshipping community as a result of what God has done in and through Jesus Christ. Moreover, although Isaiah 11:10 seems to have been chosen by Paul in large part because of the messianic reference it contains, its wider context is Isaiah's story of the eschatological restoration of Israel, a story that ties together nearly all of Paul's citations of and allusions to Isaiah examined thus far.

The Shoot of Jesse and the Restoration of Israel: Isaiah 11:10 in Context
As we have discovered previously, it is difficult to know exactly where to set the boundaries when seeking to illuminate the wider literary context of a particular passage in Isaiah. In the present case, there is a clear break after Isaiah 12:6, for the next verse, 13:1, bears the superscription of a new oracle, Isaiah's vision concerning Babylon. On the other hand, we should probably begin at least as far back as 10:5, where a transition is signalled by the final occurrence of the refrain, "For all this his anger has not turned away, but his hand is still upraised," in 10:4 (see 5:25; 9:12, 17, 21) and by the sudden shift to an oracle against Assyria in 10:5.[64] Even so, choosing to start here is little more than a concession to convenience. Isaiah 10:5ff. presupposes the situation depicted so vividly in the preceding chapters

---

[63] We saw in Chapter 3 the crucial role Romans 10:4 plays in setting the context for Paul's quotations of Isaiah 8:14/28:16 (Rom 9:33; 10:11), Isaiah 52:7 (Rom 10:15), and Isaiah 53:1 (10:16) as well as for his allusion to Isaiah 40:28 (Rom 10:18–19). See also the discussion of Isaiah 52:15 in Romans 15:21 below (pp. 333–35). Despite the fact that an obviously royal figure is prominent only in the account of Israel's restoration narrated in Isaiah 11, Paul, as an ancient reader, would not have hesitated to view the stories of Israel's redemption told in Isaiah 11 and those found in Second and Third Isaiah as essentially the same story, nor—given his christological presuppositions—would he have had difficulty finding messianic references in the latter half of Isaiah as well as in Isaiah 11 (cf. Seitz 1993:110). In the same way, *Pss. Sol.* 17 draws indiscriminately on Isaiah 11, 42, 49, 60, and 66 (n. 51 above), while the Isaiah Targum evinces a messianic reading not only of Isaiah 9 and 11, but also of several key passages in Second Isaiah (e.g., Isa 52:13–53:12; Isa 43:10, "my servant the messiah, in whom I delight," עבדי משיחא דאתרעיתי ביה).

[64] The Assyrians are mentioned here for the first time since chapters 7–8. Note that 11:11 refers to God's gathering Israel's exiles from Assyria.

of the book, where it is established that Israel's suffering is a direct consequence of their chronic rebellion against God.

In Isaiah 10:5–19, the Lord promises that when he finishes wielding his "Assyrian axe" to chastise Israel for their sins, he will turn and condemn his people's oppressors for their violent pride.[65] "In that day," when God's judgment of Israel is complete, his purified people will put their trust in him alone (10:20–21). The remnant *will* be saved, for God is bringing his work of judgment and deliverance to a swift and certain conclusion (10:22–23). Therefore, Israel's God calls his people to take courage (10:24). Soon he will strike down their oppressors and remove the Assyrian yoke from their shoulders, humbling the proud and bringing the lofty ones low (10:25–34).

The Lord's chosen agent for the restoration of Israel will be a scion of the house of David: "A staff will come from the shoot of Jesse, and from this shoot a flower will spring" (11:1). He will be empowered by God's Spirit to rule with wisdom, power, and godliness, securing justice for the humble and extirpating the wicked from the land (11:2–4). Righteousness and truth will characterize his rule (11:5).[66] All of creation will be freed from violence and will enter a state of Edenic peace and harmony, and the whole earth will be filled with the knowledge of the Lord (11:6–9). "In that day" when Israel is redeemed,[67] this "shoot of Jesse" will become the focal point for the hope not only of Israel, but of the Gentiles as well (11:10). "In that day," the Lord himself will be jealous for the remnant of his people scattered among the nations,[68] and he will gather Israel's exiles together from the four corners of the earth (11:11–12). Ephraim and Judah will be reunited, and together they will plunder and sub-

---

[65] See the detailed analysis of Isaiah 10 above, pp. 100–106.

[66] The portrait of the descendant of David who comes to deliver Israel in Isaiah 11 recalls the promise of a (Davidic) ruler in Isaiah 9. The LXX translator of Isaiah has recognized a number of verbal links between chapter 9 and chapters 10–11 and forged at least one of his own. Note Μαδιαμ (9:4; 10:26); compare ἀφαιρεθήσεται ὁ ζυγὸς ὁ ἐπ' αὐτῶν κείμενος (9:4) with ἀφαιρεθήσεται ... ὁ ζυγὸς αὐτοῦ ἀπὸ τοῦ ὤμου σου, καὶ καταφθαρήσεται ὁ ζυγὸς ἀπὸ τῶν ὤμων ὑμῶν (10:27) and καλεῖται τὸ ὄνομα αὐτοῦ· μεγάλης βουλῆς ἄγγελος (9:6) with ἀναπαύσεται ἐπ' αὐτὸν ... πνεῦνα βουλῆς (11:2). LXX alone has at 10:26 τῇ ὁδῷ τῇ κατὰ θάλασσαν, an echo of 9:1, ὁδὸν θαλάσσης (Isaiah 10:26 MT speaks of God lifting his rod over the sea, an allusion to the exodus).

[67] The temporal phrase, "in that day" (10:17, 20, 27; 11:10, 11; 12:1, 4), functions to bind together the larger section 10:5–12:6.

[68] Cf. Deuteronomy 32:19–21.

due the nations on their borders (11:13–14).[69] In words redolent both of the exodus from Egypt and of the myth of the Lord's cosmogonic defeat of chaos,[70] Israel's God vows that once again he will show his power and glory by delivering the people he has chosen for himself (11:15–16).

Israel responds to the Lord's saving deeds "in that day" by celebrating his mercy in rescuing them from exile, even as they acknowledge his justice in having visited them with wrath. The terrible refrain of the preceding oracles of judgment, "For all this, his anger has not turned away, but his hand is still upraised,"[71] has now modulated into a joyful song of thanksgiving:

> You will say in that day, "I bless you, Lord, because though you were angry with me you turned away your anger and dealt mercifully with me."

> καὶ ἐρεῖς ἐν τῇ ἡμέρᾳ ἐκείνῃ· εὐλογήσω σε, κύριε, διότι ὠργίσθης μοι καὶ ἀπέστρεψας τὸν θυμόν σου καὶ ἠλέησάς με (Isa 12:1).

The redeemed affirm their trust in God alone, just as Isaiah 10:20 prophesied,[72] and they vow to look to him only for deliverance:

> "Behold, the Lord is my God, my savior. I will trust in him, and I will be saved by him, and I will not be afraid, for the Lord is my glory and my praise, and he has become my salvation" (12:2).

---

[69] Needless to say, Paul can be quite selective in which details of the Isaianic vision he appropriates. It is a major burden of his ministry to see embodied in living communities his conviction that in Christ, Jew and Gentile stand before God on equal terms. Isaiah's depictions of the Gentiles coming to worship Israel's God provide Paul with plenty of material for advancing this view (e.g., 2:2–4; 19:19–25; 25:6–9; 42:4, 6, 10–12; 45:22–24; 49:6; 51:5; 56:3–8; 60:3, 5–9; 66:19–24). At the same time, however, Paul must ignore or subvert Isaianic (and other scriptural) traditions that work against him. It is no surprise that nowhere does he allude to the subjection of the Gentiles to Israel, even though this is an important theme in many Isaianic depictions of Israel's restoration (e.g., 14:1–2; 34:1–17; 45:14; 49:22–23; 54:3; 60:10–14; 61:5–6; 63:1–6; 66:12). The Targum moves in precisely the opposite direction from Paul, finding in Isaiah 11:10 a prophecy of Gentile *submission* to the Messiah. Whereas MT reads, "Gentiles shall seek him" (אליו גוים ידרשו), the Targum translates, "kingdoms shall submit to him" (ליה מלכון ישתמען). Chilton notes that the distinctive interpretation of the Targum at 10:27, "the Gentiles shall be shattered before the Messiah" (ויתברון עממיא מן קדם משיחא) "provides the governing context for the messianic teaching in chapter 11" (1987:29, note on 11:1–11:16).

[70] See Fishbane 1979b, 1985:350–57. On the exodus motif in Deutero-Isaiah, see further B. W. Anderson 1962, 1976; Blenkinsopp 1967; Fischer 1929; North 1950; Zimmerli 1963.

[71] Isa 5:25; 9:12, 17, 21; 10:4.

[72] ἔσονται πεποιθότες ἐπὶ τὸν θεὸν τὸν ἅγιον τοῦ Ισραηλ τῇ ἀληθείᾳ.

ἰδοὺ ὁ θεός μου σωτήρ μου κύριος, πεποιθὼς ἔσομαι ἐπ' αὐτῷ καὶ σωθήσομαι ἐν αὐτῷ[73] καὶ οὐ φοβηθήσομαι, διότι ἡ δόξα μου καὶ ἡ αἴνεσίς μου κύριος καὶ ἐγένετό μοι εἰς σωτηρίαν.

In keeping with the cosmic scope of Isaiah's vision, "in that day" the entire world will hear Israel's testimony to the glorious deeds of the God who has come to dwell in their midst:

> You will say in that day, ". . . Announce among the nations his glorious deeds . . . announce these things in all the earth. Be glad and rejoice, you who live in Zion, for the Holy One of Israel is exalted in your midst."
>
> καὶ ἐρεῖς ἐν τῇ ἡμέρᾳ ἐκείνῃ· . . . ἀναγγείλατε ἐν τοῖς ἔθνεσι τὰ ἔνδοξα αὐτοῦ . . . ἀναγγείλατε ταῦτα ἐν πάσῃ τῇ γῇ. ἀγαλλιᾶσθε καὶ εὐφραίνεσθε, οἱ κατοικοῦντες ἐν Σιων, ὅτι ὑψώθη ὁ ἅγιος τοῦ Ισραηλ ἐν μέσῳ σου (12:4–6).

For Paul, who has focused on Isaiah 11:10 as a promise of the inclusion of Gentiles in the worshipping community, it is natural to conclude that the praise of God's glorious name in Isaiah 12 pours forth not only from the lips of redeemed Israel, but also from the mouths of those among the Gentiles who have, through Christ, learned to hope in Israel's God.[74]

I have already alluded to the fact that there are important connections between the larger context of Isaiah 11:10 and the wider settings of many of Paul's previous citations of Isaiah. The oracles of salvation in Isaiah 10:5–12:6 presuppose the impassioned indictment of Israel's corruption and unfaithfulness that begins in Isaiah 1:2. A number of Paul's appeals to Isaiah to explain Israel's present state of unbelief and blindness either come from this opening sec-

---

[73] Ziegler (1939a) does not include καὶ σωθήσομαι ἐν αὐτῷ in his reconstruction of the LXX of Isaiah 12:2, even though it has good attestation, including the Alexandrian MSS Q–26–710, and even though its omission can be explained as due to harmonization with MT. The variations on this clause in a large number of MSS of different types further attest its presence in the Greek translation at a fairly early stage of textual transmission. The absence of the clause in the Alexandrian MSS A–106 may be due to haplography, as witnessed by the fact that these two MSS alone read ἐν αὐτῷ for ἐπ' αὐτῷ at the end of the previous clause. Seeligmann considers these words to be, "quite obviously, a Christian gloss" (1948:25), but it is difficult to see what about the clause commends it as particularly Christian.

[74] Isaiah 11–12, read through the lens provided by Romans 15:7–13, contains all of the principal themes of Paul's argument: Christ is the focal point for the hope of the Gentiles (Isa 11:10) and for the remnant of Israel (Isa 11:11–16), and he is the reason for their united praise of God (Isa 12:1–6).

tion of Isaiah or hark back to it in some way.[75] Furthermore, Paul has already quoted Isaiah 10:22–23 in Romans 9:27–28 to speak of God's promise to preserve a remnant of his people Israel.[76] This remnant will be characterized by trust in God alone (πεποιθὼς εἶναι, 10:20), an attitude Paul has commended, via Isaiah 8:14 and 28:16, as absolutely essential for salvation.[77] Now, in Romans 15:12, this believing remnant—which in Paul's version of the story will one day swell to encompass "all Israel"—is joined in its worship of YHWH by the Gentiles who have put their hope in "the shoot of Jesse."[78]

Similarly, there are significant points of correspondence between Isaiah 10–12 and the stories of Israel's restoration from which Paul draws his quotation in Romans 11:26–27 (Isa 59:20–21 and 27:9).[79] In particular, we should note the theme of the judgment and purification of God's people[80] and the promise that God will gather together Israel's exiles, who are scattered among the nations.[81] Moreover, both Isaiah 11 and Isaiah 25–26 emphasize the cosmic consequences of God's redemption of Israel, whether they are envisioned as a return of the natural world to Edenic bliss (11:6–9) or as the defeat of death and the resurrection of the dead (25:8; 26:19).

---

[75] Isa 29:16/45:9 in Rom 9:20; Isa 8:14/28:16 in Rom 9:33; Isa 53:1 in Rom 10:16; Isa 40:28 in Rom 10:18–19; Isa 65:2 in Rom 10:21; Isa 29:10/6:10 in Rom 11:8; Isa 59:20–21/27:9 in Rom 11:26–27.

[76] Cf. Isa 1:9 in Rom 9:29.

[77] Rom 9:33; 10:11. We saw above (pp. 101 and 140–41) the three-way connection established within LXX Isaiah itself between Isaiah 8:14–17, Isaiah 28:16, and Isaiah 10:22 via this language of faith/trust.

[78] Indeed, a number of the texts Paul cites (particularly as Paul interprets them!) resonate with the vision in Isaiah 11:10 of Gentiles sharing the blessings of redeemed Israel and joining in the worship of YHWH (Isa 52:7; 52:15; 65:1; cf. 25:6–9; 60:1–3, 6–7).

[79] According to Sommer (1998:86–87), Isaiah 11:1–10 has been worked into the fabric of the oracle in Isaiah 60:17–61:1. He notes the following parallels: נצר (11:1//60:21); רוח (11:2//61:1); √צדק (11:3–5//60:17); ארץ (11:4//60:21); the promise of peace within the city (11:6–9//60:18); the nations coming to Zion (11:11–12//60:5–10).

[80] Isa 11:1–5; 27:9–11; 59:20. There is an interesting verbal connection (only in the LXX) between 11:4 (καὶ ἐν πνεύματι διὰ χειλέων ἀνελεῖ ἀσεβῆ) and 59:20 (καὶ ἀποστρέψει ἀσεβείας ἀπὸ Ιακωβ).

[81] Isa 11:11–12; 27:12–13; 60:4, 8–9, 22. Compare Isaiah 27:13 (ἥξουσιν οἱ ἀπολόμενοι ἐν τῇ χώρᾳ τῶν Ἀσσυρίων καὶ οἱ ἀπολόμενοι ἐν Αἰγύπτῳ) and 11:12 (συνάξει τοὺς ἀπολομένους Ισραηλ καὶ τοὺς διεσπαρμένους τοῦ Ιουδα συνάξει ἐκ τῶν τεσσάρων πτερύγων τῆς γῆς. Cf. 11:11, which mentions Assyria and Egypt along with other regions). Note also the shared motif of travelling home in the "boats" of the Gentiles (11:14 and 60:9).

Isaiah and Moses in Concert: A Final Encore

A distinctive characteristic of Paul's interpretation of Isaiah in Romans 10 and 11 is the manner in which Paul links several Isaianic passages closely to quotations from Deuteronomy 29–32, with the result that the texts from Isaiah and Deuteronomy function together as mutually-interpreting witnesses to Paul's proclamation. The same phenomenon is evident in Paul's use of Deuteronomy 32:43 and Isaiah 11:10 in Romans 15:10–12.

The stories told in the Song of Moses and in the wider setting of Isaiah 10–12 are quite similar in outline. In both passages, God's fierce anger at Israel's idolatry leads God to punish his people at the hand of foreign nations. Both passages likewise emphasize the hubris with which the foreign oppressors carry out their divinely-appointed role,[82] and both proclaim God's determination to take vengeance on Israel's enemies when he has finished disciplining his people.[83] Finally, both the Song of Moses and Isaiah 10–12 depict the redemption of Israel as bringing blessing to the entire cosmos.[84] As Paul employs these two texts side by side, Deuteronomy 32:43 states explicitly what is implied in Isaiah's vision of the Gentiles hoping in the "shoot of Jesse": that Gentiles will worship YHWH in unity with Israel. In turn, Isaiah 11:10 clarifies that the redemption of Israel, which will result in the universal praise of God, takes place through the agency of the Christ, who unites Jew and Gentile in himself. As we have found previously in Romans, so also here the argument Paul makes by bringing together citations from Deuteronomy and Isaiah stands in continuity with both texts, even as it depends on features unique to one passage or the other.

In the climactic passage of the letter, Romans 15:7–13, Paul unveils an intricately-woven scriptural tapestry depicting the Church as a community of redeemed Jews and Gentiles who together praise God for his faithfulness and mercy. The passage closes with Paul's prayer (Rom 15:13) that the Roman Christians experience the reality of

---

[82] Isa 10:7–14, 33–34; Deut 32:27–33.

[83] Isa 10:15–19, 24–34; Deut 32:34–42. Note the common reference to the Lord's "hand" as the instrument of deliverance (Isa 11:11, 15; Deut 32:40, 41).

[84] Isa 11:6–10; Deut 32:43.

Isaiah's compelling vision of Jew and Gentile together putting their "hope" (Isa 11:10) in the Messiah, as he prays that the God of "hope" may enable them to abound in "hope" in the power of the Holy Spirit. Now, as he moves to bring the letter to a close, Paul appeals to the Romans Christians to join in actively supporting the crucial role his apostolic ministry plays in the realization of this vision.

PAUL'S MISSIONARY STRATEGY: ISAIAH 52:15 IN ROMANS 15:14–33[85]

Romans 15:14–33 offers an "apology" for Paul's letter and makes an appeal for assistance from the Roman churches for his planned missionary venture to the western Mediterranean. The passage revisits and extends many of the themes introduced by Paul in Romans 1:8–15 concerning the scope and purpose of his ministry and his desire to establish a partnership in ministry with the churches in Rome.[86] He takes pains to communicate that he hopes not only to minister to the Roman believers, but also to receive encouragement and support from their faith (15:24, 32; cf. 1:12). Paul seeks to secure their backing for this new evangelistic thrust to the west (15:24), and he asks them to begin partnering with him in prayer as he caps off his work in the eastern Mediterranean by accompanying the delegation from his Gentile churches to Jerusalem (15:30–32).

As part of his attempt to garner support for this new venture to Spain, Paul offers an account of the nature and purpose of his mission and a report of the fruit it has produced thus far. Although the churches in Rome show clear signs of God's working in their midst (15:14),[87] Paul has been bold enough to write to them in order to "remind" them (15:15) of the message and implications of the gospel (1:16–17). His rationale for doing this is the "grace given to [him]

---

[85] The remainder of this chapter incorportates (in a revised version) portions of Wagner 1998a:195–202.

[86] See Dunn's perceptive analysis of this section of the letter (1988b:856). See also Jewett 1995.

[87] In view of the many parallels between Romans 1 and 15, is it tempting to see in 15:14 a reversal of the language of 1:29 (μεστοὺς φθόνου, 1:29; μεστοί ἐστε ἀγαθωσύνης, 15:14; πεπληρωμένους πάσῃ ἀδικίᾳ, 1:29; πεπληρωμένοι πάσης [τῆς] γνώσεως, 15:14). These are the only two occurrences of μεστός and the only 2 occurrences of the perfect middle/passive participle of πληρόω in Romans. In these Christian communities composed of Jew and Gentile glorifying God together (15:10) the effects of human rebellion (1:21) are being overturned. For a similar suggestion, see Dunn 1988b:856.

by God" (15:15; cf. 12:3), that is, his calling as an apostle.[88] Paul understands the scope of his apostleship to encompass all the Gentiles (15:16; cf. 1:5), including the Roman Christians (1:6).

Paul figuratively places himself in the role of a priest, one whose ministry does not revolve around the altar but rather centers on the gospel (15:16; cf. 1:9). He describes his mandate as bringing about the obedience of faith (1:5; 16:26; cf. 15:18) or, employing a metaphor from the temple cult, as presenting the Gentiles to God as an acceptable and holy offering (15:16). Consequently, he is concerned not only with the initial proclamation of the gospel, but also with the formation of communities of believers who embody the truth of the gospel. In this light, it is possible to recognize that one of Paul's purposes in writing Romans is to discharge his ministry of bringing about the obedience of faith among the churches in Rome.[89] Longing to visit in order to strengthen them through the spiritual gifts he has been given (1:11), Paul writes this letter in part as a substitute for his presence—and perhaps in case he never reaches Rome (15:30–32).[90]

Despite his forebodings about this upcoming trip to Jerusalem, Paul continues to make plans for a visit to Rome on his way to proclaim the gospel in Spain. He tactfully hints that he hopes Rome will serve as a base of operations for his outreach to the western Mediterranean (15:24).[91]

Although Paul speaks of the success his mission has enjoyed to this point in eliciting the obedience of the Gentiles (15:18), he is swift to acknowledge that his "boast" is in Christ Jesus, who is work-

---

[88] Cf. Romans 1:5: ". . . through whom [Jesus Christ] we have received the grace of apostleship. . . ."

[89] So Kaye 1976:42; Jervis 1991:161; Smiga 1991; Klein 1991.

[90] Compare Paul's reference to "the disobedient in Judaea" (οἱ ἀπειθοῦντες ἐν τῇ Ἰουδαίᾳ) from whom he prays for deliverance (Rom 15:31) with his use of Isaiah 65:2 (Rom 10:21) to characterize his fellow Jews who reject the gospel as "a disobedient and contrary people" (λαὸς ἀπειθῶν καὶ ἀντιλέγων).

[91] In 2 Corinthians 10:15–16, Paul speaks of his strategy of using established churches as launching pads for further missions. Earlier in his missionary career, Antioch served as such a base. On the particular difficulties Paul faced in carrying out a mission to Spain, see Jewett 1988; Murphy-O'Connor 1996:329–31. Paul's use of προπέμπω suggests that he hopes the Romans will help outfit him for his journey. The word connotes the offering of some kind of material assistance to travelers: (1 Cor 16:6, 11; 2 Cor 1:16; Titus 3:13; Acts 15:3; 3 John 6; 1 Macc 12:4; 1 Esd 4:47; *Let. Aris.* 172). Cf. BDAG (873, s.v. προπέμπω, 2): "to assist someone in making a journey, *send on one's way* with food, money, by arranging for companions, means of travel, etc." Note the concern with when (and how much) to assist travelling teachers in *Didache* 11:6; 12:2. There may also be a double entendre in Paul's use of the idiom, ὑμῶν ἐμπλησθῶ, "have my fill of you"—both "enjoy your company" and "be supplied by you" (so also Jewett 1982:18).

ing through him, and not in anything he has done on his own (15:17–18).[92] His ministry is characterized by "the power of signs and wonders" and "the power of the Holy Spirit," markers that attest to the fact that Christ is working through him in his service of the gospel (15:19).[93] It is apparent now that Paul has told the story of Jesus in Romans 15:7–13 in such a way that Jesus' life prefigures the shape Paul's mission has taken.[94] By setting Christ forward as the archetypal missionary to Jew and Gentile—the one who not only became a servant to the circumcised but who also sings the praises of God in the midst of the Gentiles—Paul is able to claim that his apostolic ministry is nothing less than the continuation of Christ's own mission.

So powerful has been Christ's working through Paul's ministry that he is able to say that he has "fulfilled" (πεπληρωκέναι) the gospel of Christ from Jerusalem as far round in a circle as Illyricum (15:19), so that there is "no longer any room in these regions" for him to fulfill his apostolic calling (15:23). The precise meaning of Paul's claim has often been debated. John Knox is probably correct in suggesting that with the expression, "in a circle" (κύκλῳ), Paul is envisioning the spread of the gospel around the Mediterranean and speaking of the portion of the circle that he has been involved in completing.[95] Paul asserts that as a result of Christ's working through

---

[92] Note the echo here of Jer 9:23–24 LXX/1 Kgdms 2:10 (cf. 1 Cor 1:31; 2 Cor 10:17).

[93] See 2 Corinthians 12:12, "the signs of an apostle . . . signs and wonders and acts of power"; cf. Hebrews 2:4, "God testifying together with them through signs and wonders and various acts of power and distributions of the Holy Spirit. . . ."

[94] This is the corollary to the observation that Paul has a christomorphic vision of his life and ministry as an apostle. That is to say, Paul's understanding of his own mission has shaped the way he tells the story of Jesus, just as his knowledge of Jesus' ministry has influenced his conception of his own calling. For a similar analysis, see Grieb 1993. There appear to be important links between Paul's conception in Romans 15 of his mission as the outworking of Christ's ministry and his statements elsewhere about "sharing in" or "filling up what is lacking" in Christ's sufferings (Phil 3:10; 2 Cor 4:10–12; cf. Col 1:24–29). Paul's sense of participation in Christ lies at the root of his understanding of his own role as an apostle and missionary.

[95] Knox 1964:11. Cf. J. C. Beker's comment, following Knox: "Paul is a world apostle with a specific strategy. . . . He does not haphazardly missionize the Roman Empire but conceives of his mission in terms of a 'circle' (1980:71). The problem remains whether "Jerusalem" and "Illyricum" represent boundaries within which Paul has worked, exclusive of these areas (cf. μέχρι in Phil 2:30; Rom 5:14), or locations in which Paul has actually preached (cf. μέχρι in Phil 2:8; 2 Tim 2:9). Paul recounts two visits to Jerusalem in Gal 1:18 and 2:1–10, but he does not explicitly mention a preaching ministry as part of these visits. Acts places Paul in Jerusalem four times before his last trip (anticipated in Rom 15:25): Acts 9:26–30

him, he has "fulfilled" the gospel of Christ in these regions. In other words, he has faithfully discharged his vocation of bringing about the obedience of the Gentiles.[96] The surprising claim that his work is finished in the eastern Mediterranean is clarified by the explanation in 15:20: Paul has fulfilled his commission precisely by making it his goal "to boldly go where no one has gone before" with the gospel.[97] He has proclaimed the good news where Christ was not named[98] in order not to build on another missionary's foundation. Paul's ambition to go to unreached regions with the gospel does not simply reflect his own painful experience of outsiders thrusting themselves upon churches he had founded (as in Galatia and Corinth); rather, his policy derives from his understanding of the unique divine commission laid on him as an apostle.

Paul appeals to scripture in Romans 15:21 to justify his determination to preach the gospel to those who have not yet heard: "Those to whom it has not been announced concerning him will see, and those who have not heard will understand." Paul links the quotation to his argument in Romans 15:17–20 by means of the phrase, ἀλλὰ καθὼς γέγραπται. The strong adversative indicates that Paul's practice is quite the opposite of building on another's foundation. On the contrary, his strategy of pioneer church-planting is in accordance with what scripture prophesied would happen.[99]

(Paul preaches and is forced to leave); 11:29–30/12:25; 15:2; 18:22. It is probably futile to press Paul's language in Rom 15:19 too closely; the question of a Pauline ministry in Illyricum and in Jerusalem will not be decided from this text.

[96] Knox (1964:10) suggests that πληρόω has the sense, "fill in the gaps" left by other preachers. This interpretation seems strained in light of the common use of πληρόω to speak of the discharge of a commission (cf. Col 4:17; Col 1:25; Rom 8:4; koiné examples in BDAG, s.v. πληρόω, 4b; MM 520).

[97] The force of οὕτως δέ is "in this manner." It is important to recognize that φιλοτιμέομαι expresses an ambition or goal, not an inflexible rule. The contradiction some have found between Paul's statement of his purpose here and his desire expressed in Romans 1:13–15 to proclaim the gospel in Rome is a false problem created by an overly wooden reading of Paul's language.

[98] Paul refers to something more than name-recognition or "nominal Christianity." Romans 10:13 (Joel 2:32) speaks of "calling on the name of the Lord"; in 1 Corinthians 1:2 Paul characterizes Christians as "those who call on the name of our Lord Jesus Christ." Compare 2 Timothy 2:19 (quoting Isa 26:13), where "naming the name of the Lord" means giving exclusive allegiance to him. Paul's emphasis on the importance of the Christian community as the body of Christ would lead one to assume that, for Paul, Christ is not "named" in a region (however he defined it) where a church does not exist.

[99] In this instance, the καθώς of the quotation formula probably functions in a fully adverbial manner, modifying εὐαγγελίζομαι (v. 20).

Figure 5.3: Isaiah 52:15 LXX in Romans 15:21

Isaiah 52:15 LXX	Romans 15:21
	ἀλλὰ καθὼς γέγραπται·
οὕτως θαυμάσονται ἔθνη πολλὰ ἐπ᾽ αὐτῷ καὶ συνέξουσι βασιλεῖς τὸ στόμα αὐτῶν ὅτι οἷς οὐκ ἀνηγγέλη περὶ αὐτοῦ ὄψονται καὶ οἳ οὐκ ἀκηκόασι συνήσουσι	οἷς οὐκ ἀνηγγέλη περὶ αὐτοῦ ὄψονται, καὶ οἳ οὐκ ἀκηκόασιν συνήσουσιν

MT: כֵּן יַזֶּה גּוֹיִם רַבִּים עָלָיו יִקְפְּצוּ מְלָכִים פִּיהֶם כִּי אֲשֶׁר לֹא־סֻפַּר לָהֶם רָאוּ
וַאֲשֶׁר לֹא־שָׁמְעוּ הִתְבּוֹנָנוּ

As Figure 5.3 shows, Paul's quotation follows the LXX exactly; he omits only the initial ὅτι to effect a smoother transition from his sentence to the quotation.[100] The wording of the LXX, περὶ αὐτοῦ, is crucial to Paul's use of the quotation in Romans 15, for it speaks of an announcement centered on a particular person.[101] This prepositional phrase περὶ αὐτοῦ, then, provides a critical link between Romans 15 and Isaiah 52:15b. In Isaiah, the antecedent of αὐτοῦ is the "servant" (ὁ παῖς μου) introduced in 52:13. In Romans 15, the αὐτοῦ of the quotation clearly refers to Christ (15:20). Paul has been describing his activity as fulfilling τὸ εὐαγγέλιον τοῦ Χριστοῦ, the "gospel concerning Christ" (15:19).[102] Now in Isaiah 52:15b, Paul finds his own ministry "announced beforehand." He is one entrusted with the message about Christ, sent to those whom the message has not yet reached.

The immediately preceding half-verse of Isaiah 52:15 provides another important link between the quotation and Paul's exposition

---

[100] Stanley explains the reading of Vaticanus at Romans 15:21 as a reaction to the anacoluthon in the first line of Paul's quotation: the scribe responsible for the variant attempted to smooth out the grammar of the line by beginning with the verb (1992b:184 n. 344).

[101] MT's אֲשֶׁר (1QIsaᵃ, אֵת אֲשֶׁר) also clearly indicates that what they are seeing and hearing has to do with the "servant." The fact remains, however, that the wording περὶ αὐτοῦ found in LXX is much more conducive to Paul's interpretation than another translation of אֲשֶׁר, such as ὅ or ἅ, would have been.

[102] Compare Paul's expressions, "the gospel of his son" (1:9) and "the gospel of God, which was announced beforehand through the prophets in holy writings concerning his son," (1:1–3, εὐαγγέλιον θεοῦ ... περὶ τοῦ υἱοῦ αὐτοῦ).

of his calling to serve Christ among the Gentiles (Rom 15:16, 18). Isaiah 52:15a (LXX) reads, "thus many Gentiles will be amazed at him, and kings will shut their mouths" (οὕτως θαυμάσονται ἔθνη πολλὰ ἐπ᾽ αὐτῷ, καὶ συνέξουσι βασιλεῖς τὸ στόμα αὐτῶν). In Isaiah, the antecedent of the pronoun οἷς (52:15b) is none other than these "many Gentiles" and "kings."[103] Although Paul does not quote the first half of Isaiah 52:15, the wider context of 52:15b clearly resonates with his appropriation of the text as a prophecy of his own Gentile mission.[104] The impression that Paul has carried out a sustained reading of this section of Isaiah as a whole is strengthened as we recall that Paul has already cited the verse that immediately follows 52:15, Isaiah 53:1 (Rom 10:16)—also in reference to his ministry of proclamation.

The two verses quoted by Paul (52:15; 53:1) fall on either side of the seam joining the two parts of the so-called "servant song" of Isaiah 52:13–53:12: the prologue (52:13–15) and the song itself (53:1–12).[105] In addition, it appears that Paul's notion of Jesus being "handed over for us/for our transgressions" (Rom 4:25; 8:32) echoes Isaiah 53:6, 11–12.[106] Yet, surprisingly, nowhere in Romans does Paul quote explicitly from the heart of the passage. One possible explanation for this fact is basically an argument from silence: Paul did not read Isaiah 52:13–53:12 christologically, and so he found no particular relevance in the passage. It is true that, in Romans as a whole, Paul

---

[103] Cf. Isa 49:7: βασιλεῖς ὄψονται αὐτὸν [the Lord's servant] καὶ ἀναστήσονται ἄρχοντες καὶ προσκυνήσουσιν αὐτῷ ἕνεκεν κυρίου.

[104] Again, the pronoun αὐτῷ (Isa 52:15a) finds its antecedent in "my servant" (Isa 52:13).

[105] Although this poem is commonly analyzed as consisting of a central "we" section (53:1–11a) framed by the Lord's statements about the servant (52:13–15; 53:11b-12), the LXX recognizes no clear shift in speaker between 53:11a and 53:11b. Thus the two-part analysis suggested here seems appropriate.

[106] On the basis of shared language (παραδίδωμι; δικαίωσις) and thought (representation, "interchange in Christ"), M. D. Hooker now considers Rom 4:25 to be the "one clear echo of Isaiah 53 in Paul" (1998:101; contrast her earlier opinion in Hooker 1959:195). Although Hooker does not think Jesus interpreted Isaiah 53 as a prophecy of his own mission, she conjectures that the origin of a christological reading of Isaiah "may well have been with Paul" (1998:103). The case for an echo of Isaiah 53 in Romans 8:32 is somewhat weaker (παραδίδωμι), but it is strengthened considerably when Paul's earlier allusion to Isaiah 53 in Romans 4:25 is taken into account (note also the likelihood of an allusion to Isaiah 50:8 in Romans 8:33, where God is ὁ δικαιῶν). Romans 5:15–19 has also been suggested as a possible locus for echoes of Isaiah 53 (cf. NA²⁷ margin; Hays 1993b:88). See further Bellinger and Farmer 1998; Cerfaux 1951; Dinter 1983; Janowski and Stuhlmacher 1996; Kerrigan 1963; D. M. Stanley 1954.

gives surprisingly little attention to christology *per se*—although the "story" of Christ is never far from the surface of his argument. His primary concern in this letter is not with christology, but with the relationship of Jew and Gentile in God's redemptive purpose.

Another explanation commends itself, however, in view of Paul's use of Isaiah 52:7, 52:15, and 53:1 to speak of his own proclamation as a messenger of the gospel. In the context of Romans, the "him" of whom they have not heard or been told, but whom they shall see and understand (Isa 52:15), is Christ (Rom 15:20). The "good things" announced by the messengers of Isaiah 52:7 and the content of the rejected "message" of Isaiah 53:1, according to Paul, is the ῥῆμα Χριστοῦ (Rom 10:17). Paul completes two stages of the equation: (1) Heralds of Isaiah 52–53 = Paul and other preachers of the gospel; (2) Message concerning the return from exile and the servant of the Lord = gospel of Christ. Though the last step of the equation, (3) Servant = Christ, remains unarticulated, it lingers behind the text as a virtually unavoidable implication of Paul's larger reading of Isaiah.[107]

Paul's appeal to Isaiah 52:15 coheres with his use of other scriptural texts in Romans 9–11 to probe the mystery of God's inclusion of the Gentiles and God's concomitant hardening of Israel.[108] The negatively-phrased descriptions of the Gentiles in Isaiah 52:15—"those to whom it had not been announced . . . those who have not heard"— recall similar descriptions of the Gentiles earlier in the letter: "not my people . . . not loved";[109] "those who were not pursuing righteousness";[110] "those who are not a nation . . . a nation without understanding";[111] "those who were not seeking me . . . those who were not asking for me."[112] Isaiah 52:15 speaks of the inclusion of those formerly excluded, just as these previous designations of Gentile outsiders were themselves reversed by God's gracious intervention: "I

---

[107] Hays's judgment seems exactly right:

> [Paul] hints and whispers all around Isaiah 53 but never mentions the prophetic typology that would supremely integrate his interpretation of Christ and Israel. The result is a compelling example of metalepsis: Paul's transumptive silence cries out for the reader to complete the trope (Hays 1989:63).

[108] As a measure of the importance of the theme of Gentile inclusion in these chapters, note that 18 of 28 occurrences of the term ἔθνη in Romans are found in Romans 9–11 (9x) and Romans 15 (9x).

[109] Rom 9:25–26/Hos 2:23; 1:10 LXX.

[110] Rom 9:30.

[111] Rom 10:19/Deut 32:21.

[112] Rom 10:20/Isa 65:1.

will call them my people . . . beloved . . . children of the living God";[113]
"they attained righteousness, that is, the righteousness from faith";[114]
"I was found [by them] . . . I was revealed [to them]."[115]

The language of Isaiah 52:15 concerning "seeing" and "hearing"
further evokes the tragedy of Israel's spiritual insensibility, over which
Paul has agonized most poignantly in Romans 9–11. While the
Gentiles, through Paul's preaching, are now seeing, hearing, and
understanding, Israel has "heard," but has not believed the message.[116] God has given them "eyes that do not see and ears that do
not hear, to this very day."[117] The consonance of Isaiah 52:15 with
this larger theme of Romans suggests that Paul has found his own
ministry inextricably linked with the mysterious outworking of God's
redemptive purpose for Israel as well as for the Gentiles.

Excursus: Isaiah's Story and Paul's Ethics: Isaiah 45:23 in Romans 14:11
Paul turns in Romans 14:1–15:6 to address a point of tension in the life
of the Roman churches.[118] At its root, the problem involves two different
visions of what faithful discipleship entails. Paul's concern is not to elevate
one set of practices over the other, but to contextualize both within the
larger narrative of the community's life in Christ. Framing his exhortation
with the call to "accept one another" (14:1; 15:7), Paul commands each
group to refrain from judging the other (14:1, 3, 4, 10, 13). Significantly,
the basis for Paul's ethical paraenesis is the story of what God has done—
and will continue to do—for them in Christ. Paul invites his listeners to
fashion their common life in light of this story.[119] They must accept one

---

[113] Rom 9:25–26/Hos 2:23; 1:10 LXX.

[114] Rom 9:30.

[115] Rom 10:20/Isa 65:1.

[116] Rom 10:16–18.

[117] Rom 11:8 (Isa 29:10; Deut 29:4); cf. Rom 11:9–10. I suggested above (pp.
244–54) that in Romans 11:8, Paul's conflation of Isaiah 29:10 and Deuteronomy
29:4 was influenced by Isaiah 6:9–10, the first statement in the book of Isaiah of
the important motif of the Israel's obduracy. This motif is reprised again and again
throughout Isaiah's oracles. Isaiah 52:15, with its combination of "see," "hear," and
"understand," clearly echoes the language of Isaiah 6:9–10 (see Sommer 1998:93–95).

[118] Although a number of scholars believe Paul is addressing a topic that was
not actually a problem in the Roman churches (cf. Karris 1991; Sampley 1994),
there are good reasons to believe that Paul is aware of a real conflict in these communities. While both the "strong" and the "weak" may be primarily Gentile believers, the latter may be influenced by the practices of Jews or Jewish Christians. See
now the comprehensive study by M. Reasoner (1999; cf. Reasoner 1995).

[119] I am indebted to the insights of Richard Hays in his work on Paul's ethics
(1994, 1996a, 1996b). For the relationship between scripture, ethics, and eschatology in Paul (*contra* von Harnack 1928), see most recently Hays 1999; see also Rosner
1994. To the best of my knowledge, nowhere does Hays treat Romans 14:11 at
any length.

another because God, through Christ, has already accepted them (14:3; 15:7). Christ has died and returned to life in order exercise lordship over the living and the dead (14:9), and already Paul's hearers are participating in Christ's rule; moreover, Christ is able to preserve them until the eschatological consummation of God's rule over the entire cosmos (14:4). Because Christ is now Lord, they no longer belong to themselves, but to Christ, and they must seek in all they do to please their master (14:5–9). They stand in relation to one another as brothers and sisters (14:10, 13, 15, 21) for whom Christ died (14:15). And while they have an obligation to seek one another's welfare (14:19), they possess no authority to judge their fellow servants (14:4).

Paul appeals to scripture in Romans 14:11 to emphasize two closely-related points:

1) The Lord alone is the rightful judge;
2) Paul and his readers, who have already begun to experience the in-breaking of the new age, will soon stand before God's judgment seat:

As I live, says the Lord, to me every knee will bow,
and every tongue will confess to God.

Figure 5.4 shows that, apart from the introductory words, "As I live, says the Lord," the citation follows the wording of Isaiah 45:23b LXX[120] quite closely.[121] With this introductory phrase, Isaiah's lines fit smoothly into Paul's

---

[120] Paul's citation agrees with LXX in reading ἐξομολογήσεται against MT's תשבע (this latter reading also appears to lie behind the renderings of the Targum, Peshitta, and Vulgate). Barr 1994:600 asserts, *contra* Stanley 1992b:179, that there is no serious doubt that Paul is following the wording of his *Vorlage* here. Goshen-Gottstein 1963:156–58 notes that while ἐξομολογήσεται might be taken to reflect a *Vorlage* reading תשבה rather than תשבע, it is perhaps more likely that the translator has made an interpretive decision to read √שבע in the sense of הודה, "declare, confess, avow."

[121] Paul transposes the subject and verb in the second clause in Romans 14:11. One might argue that this is a deliberate modification of the text by Paul with the goal of creating a chiasm focused on "all." This hypothesis finds some support in noting the prominence of "all" and "each" in Paul's comments on either side of the citation (14:10, 12). Such a transposition could easily be chalked up to a slip of memory, however. It may be fruitless to look for a single source for Paul's introductory phrase, since this asseveration appears numerous times in Israel's scriptures (Num 14:21, 28; Deut 32:40; Zeph 2:9; Isa 49:18; Jer 22:24, 26:18; Ezek 5:11; 14:16, 18, 20; 16:48; 17:16, 19; 18:3; 20:3, 31, 33; 33:11, 27; 34:8; 35:6, 11). It is not clear that there is any reason to link Paul's wording with Isa 49:18 in particular (*contra* Koch 1986:184–85). Interestingly, there are a number of close verbal connections between Isaiah 45:21–23 and Deuteronomy 32:39–40:

Isa 45:21: ἐγὼ ὁ θεός, καὶ οὐκ ἔστιν ἄλλος πλὴν ἐμοῦ.
Isa 45:22: ἐγώ εἰμι ὁ θεός, καὶ οὐκ ἔστιν ἄλλος.
Deut 32:39: ἐγώ εἰμι, καὶ οὐκ ἔστιν θεὸς πλὴν ἐμοῦ.

Isa 45:23: κατ' ἐμαυτοῦ ὀμνύω ... ὅτι ἐμοὶ κάμψει πᾶν γόνυ....
Deut 32:40: ὀμοῦμαι τὴν δεξιάν μου καὶ ἐρῶ, Ζῶ ἐγω εἰς τὸν αἰῶνα.

present argument, for the citation now mentions both "the Lord" and "God,"[122] just as Paul has been speaking alternately of "the Lord" (Christ) and of "God" in Romans 14:1–10.[123]

Figure 5.4: Isaiah 45:23 LXX in Romans 14:11

Isaiah 45:23 LXX	Romans 14:11
κατ᾽ ἐμαυτοῦ ὀμνύω ἦ μὴν ἐξελεύσεται ἐκ τοῦ στόματός μου δικαιοσύνη οἱ λόγοι μου οὐκ ἀποστραφήσονται ὅτι ἐμοὶ κάμψει πᾶν γόνυ καὶ ἐξομολογήσεται πᾶσα γλῶσσα τῷ θεῷ.	γέγραπται γάρ· ζῶ ἐγώ, λέγει κύριος, ὅτι ἐμοὶ κάμψει πᾶν γόνυ καὶ πᾶσα γλῶσσα ἐξομολογήσεται τῷ θεῷ.

Isa 45:23 MT: בִּי נִשְׁבַּעְתִּי יָצָא מִפִּי צְדָקָה דָּבָר וְלֹא יָשׁוּב כִּי־לִי תִּכְרַע כָּל־בֶּרֶךְ תִּשָּׁבַע כָּל־לָשׁוֹן

While it is not necessary to make further reference to Isaiah in order to grasp the thrust of Paul's citation, the patterns uncovered in the preceding four chapters of this study suggest that it may be worth asking: "What would it mean to hear this citation as an allusion to Isaiah's larger story of Israel's restoration?" Isaiah 45:23, like so many of the Isaianic texts Paul cites in Romans, is part of a larger prophecy of Israel's restoration from exile (45:1–25).[124] Against all the false gods of the nations, "who do not save" (οἳ οὐ σῴζουσιν, 45:20), the Lord asserts that he alone is God. He alone is δίκαιος καὶ σωτήρ, and he calls to those dwelling at the ends of the earth to turn to him and "be saved" (σωθήσεσθε, 45:21). The Lord swears by his own name that "righteousness" (δικαιοσύνη) will go forth from his mouth and that his design for the redemption of Israel and of the comos will be accomplished. At that time, every knee will bow before him and every tongue confess that to God alone belong δικαιοσύνη and δόξα (45:24). All those who separate themselves from God "will be ashamed," (αἰσχυν-

---

In light of these verbal resemblances, and considering Paul's frequent linking of texts from Isaiah and from Deuteronomy 29–32, it is not impossible that in his quotation of Isaiah 45:23 Paul has borrowed the opening phrase from Deuteronomy 32:40.

[122] In Isaiah 45, of course, it is clear that the two terms share the *same* referent.

[123] Paul makes a similar interpretive move in his thoroughly christological rereading of Isaiah 45:23 in Philippians 2:10–11. In neither passage, however, does the christological reading displace God as the ultimate referent (cf. Rom 14:11b; Phil 2:11, εἰς δόξαν θεοῦ πατρός). In light of Paul's use of κύριος to refer to Christ, one wonders whether he might have understood ζῶ ἐγώ specifically as words of the *risen* Christ (I owe this suggestion to Richard Hays in private correspondence).

[124] I suggested in Chapter 2 that Paul draws on Isaiah 45:9 and its larger narrative context in Romans 9:20.

θήσονται, 45:24),[125] but "all the seed of the sons of Israel will be righteoused by the Lord (ἀπὸ κυρίου δικαιωθήσονται), and in God they will be glorified" (ἐν τῷ θεῷ ἐνδοξασθήσονται, 45:25).[126]

Tapping into this larger Isaianic narrative of the restoration of Israel and the salvation of the nations, Paul is able through his citation of Isaiah 45:23 to portray the Romans' present life in Christ as the proleptic realization of the eschatological deliverance promised in Isaiah.[127] Paul's citation invites those who hear the echoes of Isaiah's narrative to locate themselves imaginatively at the climactic moment of this story and to shape their communal life in light of what God has now accomplished for them in Christ. Paul does not merely warn of a future judgment to come, he insists that the time of judgment has already begun: that Christ, crucified and risen, has taken up his rule as Lord of the living and the dead.[128] This is the reality within which the Romans live; this is the story that must shape their

---

[125] Note the inversion of this idea in 45:17: Ισραηλ σῴζεται ὑπὸ κυρίου σωτηρίαν αἰώνιον· οὐκ αἰσχυνθήσονται οὐδὲ μὴ ἐντραπῶσιν ἕως τοῦ αἰῶνος. It is clear that for Isaiah, "being ashamed" (45:24) is the opposite of "being righteoused" (45:25). Cf. Paul's similar use of the idea of "not being ashamed" as he quotes Isaiah 28:16 in Romans 9:33 (ὁ πιστεύων ἐπ' αὐτῷ οὐ καταισχυνθήσεται) as a prophecy of God's determination in Christ to grant "righteousness" to all who "believe" (Rom 10:4) and as he affirms in Romans 1:16 his confidence in the gospel and mission entrusted to him (οὐ γὰρ ἐπαισχύνομαι τὸ εὐαγγέλιον).

[126] Once again the association of the δικ- root in Isaiah with the semantic field of "salvation" is evident. The term "glory" in Isaiah belongs to this semantic field as well (45:24, 25; see also Isa 5:16; 12:2; 40:5; 46:13; 58:8; 61:3; 62:2). Compare Isaiah 45:25 with Paul's statement about believers in Jesus in Romans 8:30: οὓς δὲ ἐδικαίωσεν, τούτους καὶ ἐδόξασεν. The apostle would presumably find in Isaiah's "seed" (45:25) a reference to both Jewish and Gentile believers.

[127] Paul's quotation of Deuteronomy 32:35 in Romans 12:19b functions in a similar manner (contra Hays 1996b:42). It is because they stand on the cusp of the new age that they are called to leave room for the Lord to deal justly with their oppressors (the import of ἡ ὀργή, Rom 12:19a). The very next verse of Moses' Song (32:36) associates the day of vengeance with the vindication of God's people: "the Lord will judge his people, and he will comfort his servants." For an eloquent argument that a firm commitment to Christian pacifism requires such an eschatological framework, see John Howard Yoder 1971.

[128] Note also the ethical warrant in Romans 13:11 (νῦν γὰρ ἐγγύτερον ἡμῶν ἡ σωτηρία ἢ ὅτε ἐπιστεύσαμεν), which Wilk (1998:329–30) argues is an echo of Isaiah 56:1 (ἤγγισεν γὰρ τὸ σωτήριόν μου παραγίνεσθαι). Though the echo is faint, it is certainly not inconceivable given Paul's thorough rereading of Isaiah's promises of restoration as words addressed to the believing community. Significantly, in Isaiah 56:1–2, the prophet uses the nearness of God's coming in salvation to exhort his hearers to act justly toward their neighbors (cf. Rom 13:8–10). If it is asked why Paul did not make greater use of passages from Isaiah 56, even though Gentiles figure prominently there, it might be pointed out that Isaiah 56 explicitly envisions Gentiles keeping the Law, an idea Paul might not have found particularly useful in his struggles with judaizers. At the same time, Paul's reference to "the offering of the Gentiles" (Rom 15:16, 27–28) may owe something to Isaiah's insistence on the full participation of Gentiles in the Temple cult (56:3, 6–8). On Gentile offerings during the Second Temple period, see Josephus, Ag. Ap. 2.48; J.W. 2.412–413;

life together, even with regard to such mundane activities as eating and drinking.[129] In such manner, Paul's reading of the larger story of Isaiah profoundly shapes the ethical vision he bequeaths to the Gentile communities he has founded.

Paul's reading of Isaiah in Romans 15 clearly stands in close continuity with his interpretation of Isaianic texts in Romans 9–11. In Romans 15, as in chapters 9–11, Isaiah steps forward as a witness to Paul's gospel that in Christ, God has now acted to redeem Jew and Gentile alike. As in Romans 9–11, the larger story Isaiah tells of Israel's restoration significantly shapes Paul's appropriation of the prophet's words in Romans 15. And once again, Isaiah prefigures the crucial role Paul himself will play in the proclamation of that message to those who have not yet heard.

And now, having traced the threads of Paul's appropriation of Isaianic texts through Romans, it remains to step back and consider this intricately-woven intertextual tapestry as a whole. Building on the detailed exegetical work that has preceded, I will offer in the concluding chapter a synthetic account of the complex interrelationships among scripture, theology, and mission that give Paul's argument in Romans its unique texture.

4.262; 5.562–63; *Ant.* 3.318–19; 20.49; cf. Mark 11:17 par. Rome subsidized a daily sacrifice at the Temple for the Emperor and the Roman people (Philo *Embassy* 157, 317; cf. 232, 291, 356–57; Josephus *Ag. Ap.* 2.77; *J.W.* 2.197, 409–410).

[129] It is intriguing to note the reappearance in Romans 14:13, 21 of the language of Isaiah 8:14 (cf. Rom 9:33): πρόσκομμα and σκάνδαλον (cf. 14:20–21). It is clear from the context of Romans 14 that the "stumbling" envisioned by Paul (like that in Isaiah 8) has serious consequences. To cause a brother to stumble is to "destroy one for whom Christ died" (14:15) and to "tear down the work of God" (14:20). As in Isaiah 8, it is πίστις that prevents one from stumbling (14:22–23). Wilk (1998:337–39) finds an allusion in Romans 14:21 (καλὸν τὸ μὴ φαγεῖν κρέα μηδὲ πιεῖν οἶνον μηδὲ ἐν ᾧ ὁ ἀδελφός σου προσκόπτει) to Isaiah 22:13 (αὐτοὶ δὲ ἐποιήσαντο εὐφροσύνην καὶ ἀγαλλίαμα σφάζοντες μόσχους καὶ θύοντες πρόβατα ὥστε φαγεῖν κρέα καὶ πιεῖν οἶνον λέγοντες· φάγωμεν καὶ πίωμεν, αὔριον γὰρ ἀποθνήσκομεν; note that Paul quotes Isaiah 22:13b in 1 Corinthians 15:32). However, this echo must be judged very faint indeed, for not only is there no marker in the text of Romans 14:21 that would lead one to expect an allusion, the language of the alleged echo does not appear distinctive enough to evoke the particular discussion of eating and drinking (quite mundane, every-day topics, after all) in this passage of Isaiah. Paul's phraseology arises naturally in the context of his argument (cf. βρῶσις καὶ πόσις, 14:17); compare Paul's language in a similar discussion (1 Cor 8:13: διόπερ εἰ βρῶμα σκανδαλίζει τὸν ἀδελφόν μου, οὐ μὴ φάγω κρέα εἰς τὸν αἰῶνα, ἵνα μὴ τὸν ἀδελφόν μου σκανδαλίσω; 1 Cor 10:31: εἴτε οὖν ἐσθίετε εἴτε πίνετε εἴτε τι ποιεῖτε, πάντα εἰς δόξαν θεοῦ ποιεῖτε).

CHAPTER SIX

HERALDS OF THE GOOD NEWS:
PAUL AND ISAIAH IN CONCERT

> How will they hear without a preacher?
> And how will they preach if they are
> not sent? Just as it is written, "How
> beautiful are the feet of those who pro-
> claim the good news."
>
> *Romans 10:14–15*

In Chapters Two through Five, I offered a close analysis of Paul's appropriation of Isaianic texts and traditions in the context of his unfolding argument in Romans. In this final chapter, I attempt to synthesize the numerous observations made along the way into a more comprehensive account of Paul's interpretation of Isaiah. Naturally, the validity of my synthesis depends on the soundness of the many interpretive decisions made in examining each individual citation of or allusion to Isaiah in Romans. Yet, at the same time, I trust that the "big picture" provided in this retrospect will enhance the plausibility of the interpretations I have advanced in the preceding chapters.

CITATIONS AND ALLUSIONS TO ISAIAH IN ROMANS

Figure 6.1 illustrates the distribution in Romans of the citations and allusions to Isaiah treated in this study. As already noted, these citations are concentrated in Romans 9–11 and, to a lesser extent, in chapter 15. Figure 6.2 displays the location and distribution within the book of Isaiah of the texts on which Paul draws in Romans.

As Figure 6.2 shows, Paul's citations of Isaiah in Romans range from Isaiah 1 to Isaiah 65. There are, however, three distinct clusters of citations, centered in Isaiah 1–11, Isaiah 28–29, and Isaiah 52–53. This latter cluster may be extended to encompass a number of citations and allusions to Isaiah 40–51 in Romans. Such a grouping is defensible on the basis of the numerous verbal and thematic connections between Isaiah 52 and Isaiah 40 within the book of Isaiah, connections that appear to have shaped Paul's use of these

Figure 6.1: Citations and Allusions to Isaiah in Romans (I)[1]

	Marked Citation	Allusion
Rom 2:24	Isa 52:5	
Rom 3:15–17	Isa 59:7–8 (+Eccl 7:20 etc.)	
Rom 4:25		Isa 53:6, 11–12
[Rom 8:32] Rom 8:33–34		[Isa 53:6, 11–12] Isa 50:8
[Rom 9:6] Rom 9:20 Rom 9:27–28 Rom 9:29 [Rom 9:30–31] Rom 9:33	**Isa 10:22–23/28:22** (+Hos 1:10a) **Isa 1:9** Isa 28:16/8:14	[Isa 40:7–8] Isa 29:26/45:9 [Isa 51:1]
Rom 10:11 Rom 10:15 Rom 10:16 Rom 10:18, 19 Rom 10:20 Rom 10:21	Isa 28:16 Isa 52:7 **Isa 53:1** **Isa 65:1** **Isa 65:2**	Isa 40:21/28
Rom 11:8 Rom 11:26–27 Rom 11:34	Isa 29:10 (+Deut 29:4; Ps 68:24) Isa 59:20–21/27:9	Isa 6:9–10 Isa 40:13
[Rom 13:11]		[Isa 56:1]
Rom 14:11	Isa 45:23 [+Deut 32:40?]	
Rom 15:12 Rom 15:21	**Isa 11:10** Isa 52:15	

---

[1] A "marked citation" is preceded by an introductory formula (Isa 28:16 in Rom 10:11 is, in context, an obvious re-citation of a portion of the text quoted in 9:33). Those in bold type are explicitly attributed to "Isaiah." "Allusions" are limited to those I have judged to be more probable cases of allusion. Allusions listed in square brackets are deemed to be less certain.

[2] See note to Figure 6.1. For comparative purposes, in Figure 6.2 I include in italic type quotations and strong allusions to Isaiah (those with a significant verbal correspondence) in Paul's other undisputed letters.

Figure 6.2: Citations and Allusions to Isaiah in Romans (II)[2]

	Marked Citation	Allusion
Isa 1:9	Rom 9:29	
Isa 6:9–10	(+Isa 29:10; Deut 29:4)	Rom 11:8
Isa 8:14	Rom 9:33 (+Isa 28:16)	
Isa 10:22a Isa 10:22b–23	Rom 9:27–28 (+Hos 1:10a) Rom 9:28 (+Isa 28:22)	
Isa 11:10	Rom 15:12	
Isa 22:13b		*1 Cor 15:32*
Isa 25:8	*1 Cor 15:54 (+Hos 13:14)*	
Isa 27:9	Rom 11:27 (+Isa 59:20–21)	
Isa 28:11–12 Isa 28:16 Isa 28:22	*1 Cor 14:21* Rom 9:33 (+Isa 8:14) Rom 9:28 (+Isa 10:22–23)	
Isa 29:10 *Isa 29:14* Isa 29:16	Rom 11:8 (+Deut 29:4; Ps 68:24) *1 Cor 1:19*	(+Isa 6:9–10) Rom 9:20 (+Isa 45:9)
[Isa 40:7–8] Isa 40:13 Isa 40:21/28		[Rom 9:6] Rom 11:34 Rom 10:18, 19
Isa 45:9 *Isa 45:14* Isa 45:23	 Rom 14:11 (+Deut 32:40?)	Rom 9:20 (+Isa 29:16) *1 Cor 14:25*
Isa 49:1 *Isa 49:4* *Isa 49:8*	 *2 Cor 6:2*	*1 Cor 15:10; Gal 1:15* *1 Cor 15:10; 2 Cor 6:1 etc.*
Isa 50:8		Rom 8:33–34
[Isa 51:1]		[Rom 9:30–31]
Isa 52:5 Isa 52:7 *Isa 52:11* Isa 52:15	Rom 2:24 Rom 10:15 *2 Cor 6:17 (+Ezek 20:34 etc.)* Rom 15:21	
Isa 53:1 Isa 53:6, 11–12	Rom 10:16 	 Rom 4:25; [8:32]
Isa 54:1	*Gal 4:27*	
Isa 55:10		*2 Cor 9:10 (+Hos 10:12)*
[Isa 56:1]		[Rom 13:11]
Isa 59:7–8 Isa 59:20 Isa 59:21	Rom 3:15–17 (+Eccl 7:20 etc.) Rom 11:26 Rom 11:27 (+Isa 27:9)	
Isa 65:1 Isa 65:2 *Isa 65:3, 11*	Rom 10:20 Rom 10:21 	 *1 Cor 10:20–21* *(+Deut 32:17, 21)*

texts in Romans 10.[3] Still, in light of the frequent claim that Isaiah
40–55 in particular has had a profound influence on Paul's thought,
it is important to note that, in Romans, his actual citations from
this section of the book are concentrated in Isaiah 52–53. With
regard to the rest of "Deutero-Isaiah," material from chapters 40,
45, 50, and 51 is quoted or evoked allusively by Paul in the course
of the letter.[4] But the fact that there are in Romans as many citations and allusions to Isaiah 28–29 as there are to Isaiah 52–53 and
that citations crucial to Paul's argument are drawn from Isaiah 1,
8, 10, 11, 27, 59, and 65 should caution us against asserting that
Paul shows a special interest in Isaiah 40–55 in distinction from the
rest of the book.[5]

Paul and His Vorlage

My own close examination of the wording of Paul's quotations and
allusions to Isaiah in Romans supports the consensus view that Paul
cites a Greek text (or texts) of this prophetic book. In most cases,
Paul's *Vorlage* seems to have been nearly identical with the Septuagint
version of Isaiah; at times, Paul's interpretation of a verse clearly
depends on the form of the text distinctive to LXX Isaiah.[6] In some
cases, however, it appears that Paul has drawn his citation from a
Greek text that reflects efforts to revise LXX Isaiah toward a Hebrew
exemplar.[7] Although I have given full consideration to the textual

---

[3] See pp. 183–84.

[4] Paul's other letters evince attention to chapters 49, 54, and 55 (See Figure 6.2).
On the importance of Isaiah 49 for Paul, see Bjerkelund 1977; Cerfaux 1951; Holtz
1966; Kerrigan 1963; Nickelsburg 1986; Radl 1986; Reinmuth 1991; cf. van der
Kooij 1997b; van de Sandt 1994.

[5] The only major blocks of material in Isaiah from which Paul does *not* draw
quotations or allusions in Romans are the pronouncements against the nations in
Isaiah 13–23, the various oracles in chapters 30–35, and the historical narrative in
chapters 36–39. The picture does not change significantly even when his other letters are taken into account (though note the allusion to Isa 22:13b in 1 Cor 15:32).
Wilk's findings are broadly similar to my own (1998:342–49), although he appears
to overreach in assigning a precisely-delineated "larger context" in Isaiah to each
of Paul's citations and allusions. Wilk ends up being much more specific about precisely which sections of Isaiah Paul found meaningful (e.g., 52:4–54:17; 59:1–61:3;
49:1–51:6; 43:18–45:25; 28:7–29:24; 24:23–27:13 [343]) than I think is warranted
by the evidence.

[6] E.g., ἐπ' αὐτῷ in Isaiah 28:16 (Rom 9:33/10:11); ὁ ἀνιστάμενος ἄρχειν ἐθνῶν
in Isaiah 11:10 (Rom 15:12); περὶ αὐτοῦ in Isaiah 52:15 (Rom 15:21). It will be
recalled that in this study the term "LXX" refers to the initial Greek translation
of a biblical book as critically reconstructed by scholars (see pp. 16–17 n. 60).

[7] See the general introduction to this phenomenon in Chapter 1 (pp. 16–17

evidence provided by MT, the Qumran finds (biblical MSS, *pesharim*, and quotations in other documents), the Targum, and the Peshitta, at no point has it been found necessary to suppose that Paul has relied on a Hebrew or Aramaic text of Isaiah.[8] This does not prove that Paul could not read these languages, nor does it show that he knew the book of Isaiah only in Greek. It does suggest, however, that Paul was intimately acquainted with a Greek version of Isaiah much like the LXX and that he apparently did not hunt down and exploit textual variants in other languages as he interpreted the book.[9]

It is also clear that, in a number of instances, Paul has altered the wording of his *Vorlage*, either in order to fit a citation smoothly into its context in Romans or to enable the text to express more clearly the point he wishes it to make.[10] Many of these adaptations are fairly inconsequential,[11] although a few prove crucial to Paul's

---

n. 60; cf. p. p. 130 n. 37), and note the detailed discussions of Isaiah 28:16/8:14 and Isaiah 52:7 above, pp. 126–36 and 170–74.

[8] *Contra* Lim 1997a. In addition to the instances in which Paul's citation agrees with the LXX against all other witnesses, there are several examples where Paul and the LXX agree in a distinctive translation of Hebrew into Greek (Rom 9:33/Isa 28:16: καταισχύνω; Rom 11:27/Isa 27:9: ἡ παρ' ἐμοῦ διαθήκη; Rom 10:20/Isa 65:1: ἐμφανὴς ἐγενόμην; Rom 15:12/Isa 11:10: ἐλπίζω). I have discovered no instance in which the hypothesis that Paul used a Greek text does not account for the data more simply and more satisfactorily than the supposition that Paul employed Hebrew and/or Aramaic texts.

[9] In the cases where Paul depends on a revised text of LXX Isaiah, however, it is conceivable that he deliberately chose from among two or more Greek versions the one that expressed his meaning most clearly (see, for example, the fairly dramatic differences between the LXX and the revised version of Isaiah 52:7).

[10] Lim is correct to point out that when one takes into account the great fluidity and plurality of scriptural texts in the first century, it becomes much more difficult to identify Pauline adaptations of the biblical text with certainty. Nevertheless, as we have seen, when a careful comparison of Paul's citations with all available textual evidence for the passage he quotes is carried out in conjunction with a close reading of the larger argument in which Paul appropriates the scriptural text, it is possible to identify—often with a fairly high degree of probability—cases in which Paul has adapted the wording of his *Vorlage*. Although I differ at points with one or more of them, I have found myself to be in general agreement with Koch, Stanley, and Wilk when it comes to identifying instances where Paul has altered his *Vorlage* (detailed discussion may be found in the notes to the preceding chapters). Although Stanley's conservative methodology is valuable for obtaining a set of fairly certain examples of Pauline adaptations from which to generalize about Paul's citation practices, his minimalist approach at times prevents him from taking contextual factors sufficiently into account. This fact may explain a number of places where I express more confidence in the identification of a Pauline adaptation than does Stanley.

[11] E.g., the omission of a conjunction such as καί or ὅτι (Rom 9:25/Hos 2:23; Rom 15:12/Isa 11:10; Rom 15:21/Isa 52:15); the substitution of ὑπόλειμμα for κατάλειμμα (Isa 10:22/Rom 9:27).

appropriation of the scriptural witness. For example, Paul's version
of Hosea 1:10 enables him to widen the scope of the prophetic oracle from its narrow focus on a particular time and place in Israel's
history. In Paul's hands, this word of comfort to exiled Israel becomes
an expansive promise that God will embrace even Gentiles as his
own people.[12] Similarly, Paul's omission of "on the mountains" in
his citation of Isaiah 52:7 and his subsitution of the plural εὐαγγελιζομένων for the singular participle in his *Vorlage* allows him to trans-
form Isaiah's depiction of a lone herald bringing news of YHWH's
victory to Jerusaelm into a prophecy of the numerous messengers
God has sent out all over the world to proclaim the good news of
Christ's lordship.[13]

Interpretive Strategies

Conflation of Texts
A notable characteristic of Paul's quotations of Isaiah in Romans is
the frequency with which Paul conflates a passage of Isaiah with
another text, whether from elsewhere in Isaiah or from another scriptural source. Interestingly, all but one of these conflated citations or
allusions occur in Romans 9–11 (see Figure 6.3).[14]

Figure 6.3: Isaiah in Romans: Conflated Citations/Allusions

Rom 9:20	Isa 29:16 and Isa 45:9
Rom 9:27	Isa 10:22 and Hos 1:10a
Rom 9:28	Isa 10:22–23 and Isa 28:22
Rom 9:33	Isa 28:16 and Isa 8:14
Rom 11:8	Deut 29:4, Isa 29:10, Isa 6:9–10 (allusion), and Ps 68:24
Rom 11:27	Isa 59:21 and Isa 27:9
Rom 14:11	Isa 45:23 (and Deut 32:40?)

---

[12] See pp. 84–85.
[13] See pp. 173–76. Perhaps the most thorough re-writing of a biblical text by Paul
in Romans, however, is his systematic replacement of the language of "doing" the
Law in Deuteronomy 30:12–14 with the idea of believing/confessing what God has
done in Christ's death, resurrection, and exaltation (Romans 10:4–13; see pp. 161–68).
[14] Discussions of individual passages may be found in Chapters 2–5 above. The
only conflated citation in Romans 9–11 that does not involve a text from Isaiah is
that in Romans 10:6, which brings together Deuteronomy 9:4 (8:17?) and Deuteronomy
30:12. (In addition, Romans 11:3 might be considered a conflation of 3 Kgdms
19:10, 14, and 18. On the problems involved in identifying the precise source of
Paul's citation, see pp. 233 n. 53.)

The striking number of these conflations and the variety of texts involved—Isaiah, Hosea, Deuteronomy, Psalms—suggests that they are the product of a mind steeped in Israel's scriptures.[15] Paul's frequent appeals to Isaiah, Psalms, and Deuteronomy bespeak his close familiarity with all of these texts. Moreover, the first six of these conflated citations fit so seamlessly into their respective contexts in Romans 9–11 that it appears Paul shaped them precisely for this particular argument. There are no compelling reasons to suppose that any of these conflations had a pre-Pauline origin.[16] On the contrary, in most instances important connections between Paul's argument in Romans and the wider contexts of each of the conflated passages suggest that Paul selected these texts for reasons beyond simple catchword associations.[17]

It is not always clear whether these conflated citations arise from a deliberate interpretive association or whether, in some instances, they might not reflect an unconscious fusion of similar texts and contexts in Paul's memory. In either case, the resulting citation is the product of a mind infused with the diction, cadences, and motifs of scripture. Even where one may suspect the blending of texts to be unintentional,[18] the conflation at the surface level betrays a deeper correspondence between the wider literary settings of the component texts that is of value for exploring Paul's understanding of scripture.

In many instances, however, we found good reasons to believe that Paul's fusion of discrete texts arises out of his own close reading of Israel's scriptures and his awareness of significant thematic as well as verbal connections between the texts. Here the Isaiah Targum and the LXX version of Isaiah prove to be important touchstones

---

[15] See p. 311 n. 16.

[16] See especially the series of arguments marshalled against Stanley's position that Romans 11:26–27 quotes a pre-Pauline conflation (pp. 281–86 above). Note also the evidence provided by 1 Peter 2:6, 8, which enables us with some confidence to trace the conflated citation in Romans 9:33 (Isa 28:16/8:14) to Paul (whether the particular form of text common to 1 Peter and Romans is thought to come from a revised text of the LXX or from a collection of testimonia).

[17] A much-needed corrective to the common assumption that by identifying a catchword connection one has thereby explained the *hermeneutical logic* behind the juxtaposition of texts is the observation of D. Jones concerning the process by which the book of Isaiah was formed (1955:238 n. 56):

As often in the collected oracles of Isaiah, connections of theme as understood by later disciples are betrayed by a catchword. But that is emphatically not to say that the sole reason for the association of the oracles is the catchword. The catchword reveals that aspect of the oracle which yields a connection.

[18] E.g., Isa 29:16/45:9 in Rom 9:20 or Isa 10:22–23/28:22 in Rom 9:28.

for evaluating Paul's reader-competence and interpretive strategies in their historical and cultural contexts. A number of Paul's conflations are anticipated in the interpretive activity of the LXX translator. Indeed, by pulling even more tightly the verbal and thematic threads linking discrete texts within the book of Isaiah in Hebrew, the Greek translator may actually have helped pave the way for Paul's intertextual connections.[19]

We also discovered a significant parallel to Paul's conflation of Isaiah 29:16/45:9 in the rendering of these two verses in the Isaiah Targum. The translators draw on features unique to each Hebrew text to create a composite phrase that they then employ in both passages.[20] In this case, the Targum's interpretive activity is of value to the present study, not because it establishes Paul's dependence on a particular tradition of interpretation, but because it demonstrates that other ancient interpreters could draw similar exegetical connections among widely-separated scriptural texts.[21] Similarly, attention to the manner in which the Dead Sea Scrolls and other Second Temple Jewish texts interpret the same passages from Isaiah cited by Paul reveals that the apostle has thoroughly imbibed the logic of scriptural interpretation prevalent in first century Jewish circles.[22]

---

[19] As we have seen, the LXX translator deliberately links together the following passages that are later conflated by Paul: Isa 29:16/45:9 (p. 60); Isa 10:23/28:22 (pp. 98–99); Isa 28:16/8:14/8:17 (pp. 145–46). See further pp. 145–51 on the numerous connections the translator draws between Isaiah 8 and 28–29.

[20] See pp. 60–62. We further saw that the Targum associates these two Isaianic texts with Jeremiah 18:6 by exactly the same technique of pastiche translation (pp. 70–71 n. 88).

[21] In the same way, the recognition in the targums and in rabbinic literature of affinities between Moses' Song (Deut 32) and the oracles of Isaiah reveals that Paul's association of Deuteronomy 29–32 with portions of Isaiah would have been quite at home in his cultural context (p. 189 nn. 205–206 above).

[22] I have argued that many of the similarities are *formal* rather than *material*. Given the crucial role Paul's gospel and mission play in his reading of scripture, we should not be surprised if Paul's particular interpretations, while based on methods widely in use in his cultural context, do not find close parallels in the writings of other Jewish groups. G. J. Brooke (1998) has discovered much the same thing to be true with regard to interpretation in the Dead Sea Scrolls and the New Testament:

> In those very passages in both the Scrolls and the New Testament where there are similar intertextual echoes, this study has observed that the interpretative differences are as numerous as the similarities. Attention to intertextuality shows the distinctiveness of each set of writings but also that much in the New Testament is the common stock of eschatologically oriented first century Palestinian Judaism (57).

Figure 6.4: Scriptural Clusters in Romans 9–11 and Romans 15

Rom 9:7 Rom 9:9 Rom 9:12 Rom 9:13	Gen 21:12 Gen 18:10, 14 Gen 25:23 Mal 1:2–3	"Not all from Israel are Israel" (Rom 9:6)
Rom 9:15 Rom 9:17 Rom 9:20	Exod 33:19 Exod 9:16 Isa 29:16/45:9	"There is not injustice with God, is there?" (Rom 9:14)
Rom 9:25–26 Rom 9:27–28 Rom 9:29	Hos 2:23/1:10 Isa 10:22–23/28:22 Isa 1:9	"He called us not only from among the Jews, but also from among Gentiles" (Rom 9:24)
Rom 9:33 Rom 10:5 Rom 10:6–8 Rom 10:11 Rom 10:13	Isa 28:16/8:14 Lev 18:5 Deut 30:12–14 Isa 28:16 Joel 2:32	"Christ is the goal of the Law, resulting in righteousness for everyone who believes" (Rom 10:4)
Rom 10:15 Rom 10:16 Rom 10:18 Rom 10:19 Rom 10:20 Rom 10:21	Isa 52:7 Isa 53:1 Ps 18:5 Deut 32:21 Isa 65:1 Isa 65:2	"Faith comes through hearing, and hearing through the word of Christ. . . . It is not that they have not heard . . . known, is it?" (Rom 10:17, 18, 19)
Rom 11:1–2 Rom 11:3 Rom 11:4	Ps 93:14/1 Kgdms 12:22 3 Kgdms 19:10, 14 3 Kgdms 19:18	"God has not rejected his inheritance, has he?" (Rom 11:1)
Rom 11:8 Rom 11:9–10	Deut 29:4/Isa 29:10 Ps 68:22–24	"The rest were rendered insensible" (Rom 11:7)
Rom 11:34 Rom 11:35	Isa 40:13 Job 41:3	"O the depth of the wealth of the wisdom and knowledge of God" (Rom 11:33)
Rom 15:9b Rom 15:10 Rom 15:11 Rom 15:12	Ps 17:50 Deut 32:43 Ps 116:1 Isa 11:10	"The Christ has become a servant of the circumcision . . . and [a servant] with respect to the Gentiles" (Rom 15:8–9a)

Juxtaposition of Texts

In addition to conflating originally discrete passages, Paul frequently associates quotations of Isaiah with other scriptural texts through the technique of juxtaposition. The lengthy catalogue of Israel's sins in Romans 3:10–18, which includes a portion of Isaiah 59:7–8 (Rom 3:15–17), takes the form of a series of scriptural texts cited one after the other under a single formula of introduction.[23] Similarly, in Romans 9:25–26, Paul quotes Hosea 2:23 and Hosea 1:10 in quick succession with only an initial citation formula, effectively treating the two texts as a single citation. In so doing, he allows the combination of texts to epitomize a much more extensive passage in the book of Hosea. Paul employs this technique in reverse in the case of his citation of Isaiah 65:1–2 in Romans 10:20–21. There, Paul's introduction of a second citation formula in Romans 10:21 allows him to drive a wedge between the two verses and to interpret 65:1 in reference to Gentiles while reading 65:2 in reference to Israel.

More commonly, juxtaposition takes the form of clusters of citations closely connected around a central theme. At times Paul offers a catena of texts separated only by introductory formulas and/or brief interpretive comments (Rom 9:24–29; 10:18–21; 11:7–10; 15:9–12). Other clusters of quotations (see Figure 6.4)[24] occur in the course of a more extensive argument and are tied together not so much by position as by their relation to the major point Paul is attempting to establish (Rom 9:6–13; 9:14–23; 9:30–10:13; 10:14–17; 11:1–6).[25] Nearly all of Paul's citations of Isaiah in Romans 9–11 are found in such a context.[26]

The striking exception to this rule is Paul's conflated quotation in Romans 11:26–27 (Isa 59:20–21/27:9), which stands as the lone explicit citation in the long stretch of text from Romans 11:11 down to the concluding doxology in Romans 11:33–36.[27] The isolated position of this citation reflects Paul's need to supply a more extensive

---

[23] As noted above (p. 288 n. 216) it is quite possible that Paul took over this catalogue as a pre-formed tradition. Whatever its origin, he identifies the words as scripture (3:10, καθὼς γέγραπται; 3:19, ὁ νόμος). In Romans 3:19 we find a clear instance in which Paul uses νόμος as a broad reference to Israel's scriptures (none of the texts in the catena is from the Pentateuch).

[24] Although a number of these texts do not bear introductory formulas (Rom 9:20 = Isa 29:16/45:9; Rom 11:2 = Ps 93:14/1 Kgdms 12:22; Rom 11:34 = Isa 40:13; Rom 11:35 = Job 41:3), I include them here in light of their high degree of verbal correspondence to their scriptural sources.

[25] See, for example, the extensive network of citations clustering around Romans 10:4 (Isa 28:16/8:14 [Rom 9:33]; Lev 18:5 [Rom 10:5]; Deut 9:4/30:12–14 [Rom 10:6–8]; Isa 28:16 [Rom 10:11]; Joel 2:32 [Rom 10:13]).

[26] Two interesting parallels to Paul's use of clustered citations interspersed with interpretive comments are *4QFlorilegium* (4Q174) and CD-A 5.13–17. See further Brooke 1985; J. G. Campbell 1995:116–131.

[27] There are, however, two prominent scriptural allusions in this section (Deut 32:21 in Rom 11:11–14 [cf. Rom 10:19]; Num 15:17–21 in Rom 11:16).

argument of his own at just this point in Romans 9–11 where he most radically reconfigures the anticipated sequence of events in Israel's eschatological story line. At the same time, its distance from other quotations enhances the rhetorical weight of the citation in Romans 11:26–27, allowing it to stand alone as the climactic moment of Paul's entire argument in chapters 9–11.

Isaiah among the Chorus of Witnesses

The frequency with which Paul either juxtaposes or conflates Isaianic material with other passages of scripture suggests that a deliberate interpretive strategy is at work here. Indeed, I have shown in some detail in the preceding chapters that the texts so joined are in some sense mutually interpreting for Paul. So, for example, Paul's positioning of the potter/clay metaphor (Rom 9:20 = Isa 29:16/45:9) at the end of two clusters of texts drawn from major episodes in Israel's covenant story—the election of the patriarchs, the exodus from Egypt, reaffirmation of election after the golden calf incident—highlights the theme of God's sovereignty in election already present in these foundational narratives.[28] At the same time, the location of the potter/clay text in Paul's argument indicates that he understands this metaphor not as a bare assertion of God's power over his creation, but as a particular claim about God's sovereign mercy shown in his dealings with Israel.

Similarly, Paul enlists Moses (Deut 32:21) and Isaiah (Isa 65:1–2) as fellow witnesses attesting to Israel's culpability for knowingly resisting God's plan to save Jews and Gentiles together in Christ (Rom 10:19–21). Here, the citation from Isaiah provides a specific interpretation of the scenario envisioned in Deuteronomy. God will make Israel jealous (Deut 32:21), not—as in the original context of Moses' Song—by allowing a foreign nation to oppress Israel, but rather by graciously making himself known to Gentiles. Conversely, Deuteronomy's story of the οὐκ ἔθνος that receives God's favor while Israel remains estranged from God facilitates Paul's radical bifurcation of Isaiah 65:1–2 into a prophecy of God's acceptance of Gentiles on

---

[28] The promise of seed for Abraham in Isaac: Gen 21:12 [Rom 9:7]; Gen 18:10, 14; the election of Jacob: Gen 25:23 [Rom 9:12]; Mal 1:2–3 [Rom 9:13]; forgiveness after the debacle of the golden calf: Exod 33:19 [Rom 9:15]; God's hardening of Pharaoh at the exodus: Exod 9:16 [Rom 9:17].

the one hand (65:1), and a lament over Israel's chronic rebelliousness toward their God on the other (65:2).

A further example of this phenomenon of mutually-interpreting
texts is found in the catena of citations that brings Paul's rhetorical
ἐπίλογος to its climax (Rom 15:9–12). Only when heard as a unity,
as the symphonic blending of harmonious scriptural voices, does the
catena support the point Paul is making in Romans 15:8–9. The
citations from Psalm 17:50 LXX, Deuteronomy 32:43, and Psalm
116:1 LXX state explicitly what is implied in Isaiah's prophecy that
Gentiles will "hope" in the root of Jesse (Isa 11:10): the nations will
join together with Israel in the worship and service of Israel's God.
In turn, Isaiah 11:10 specifies that the redemption of Israel and of
the nations, which calls forth the universal praise of God envisioned
in these texts, centers on the scion of David whom God has now
raised from the dead and exalted as Lord.

These examples, along with others discussed in the preceding chapters,[29] suggest that while Paul attends closely to the words of Isaiah,
he hears the prophet not simply as a solo voice, but also as a member of a larger scriptural chorus singing the epic story of God's
redemption of Jew and Gentile in Christ. To a great extent, Paul's
citation practice mirrors his interpretive practice. He gives a certain
prominence to Isaiah in Romans, mentioning him by name five times
(more than any other scriptural persona).[30] But because citations of
Isaiah nearly always occur in close connection with other quotations,
the prophet appears as one among a number of harmonious scriptural voices lending the weight of their cumulative authority to Paul's
argument. Isaiah does make significant and distinctive contributions
to Paul's particular retelling of the story of God, Israel, and the
Gentiles in Romans. Yet Isaiah's witness in this letter cannot adequately be treated in isolation from the testimony of other scriptural
voices, for they play a crucial role in shaping the meaning and force
of Isaiah's words in Paul's argument.

---

[29] See also the earlier discussions of Hos 1:10/Isa 10:22 (pp. 89–92); Deut 29:4/Isa
29:10 (pp. 240–57).

[30] Paul designates Isaiah as the speaker of a citation from scripture five times
(Rom 9:27; 9:29; 10:16; 10:20; 15:12). Moses appears twice as the source of a citation (Rom 10:5; 10:19); he is named two other times (Rom 5:14; 9:15). David is
mentioned three times, twice as speaker (Rom 1:3; 4:6; 11:9).

Plotting Isaiah's Story in the Letter to the Romans

Although Paul's citations and allusions to Isaiah are thoroughly entangled with his appeals to other scriptural texts, it is still possible to speak of the influence on Paul of characteristically Isaianic stories and motifs. In examining the Isaianic texts Paul appropriates in Romans and considering their wider literary settings in the book of Isaiah, we observed a number of recurrent themes. For example, Paul reads as prophecies of his own gospel and mission Isaianic texts that herald the deliverance of Israel from foreign oppression, particularly those that can be seen to intimate the inclusion of Gentiles in Israel's restoration.[31]

When addressing Israel's unresponsiveness to the gospel, however, Paul employs a quite different set of passages. The apostle repeatedly adduces texts from Isaiah that depict Israel as a nation deeply divided between those who have remained loyal to YHWH and the vast majority who have put their hope in other gods.[32] The small minority of the faithful appear as a remnant saved out of judgment, a seed that contains the germ of Israel's future restoration.[33] With reference to the majority of his kinspeople, Paul draws on passages from Isaiah whose wider contexts portray Israel as idolatrous and unfaithful, suffering under God's discipline in the form of foreign oppression or exile.[34] Rather than trusting in God's "righteousness"— God's power and faithfulness to deliver his covenant people—they

---

[31] Isa 28:16 (Rom 9:33/10:11); Isa 52:7 (Rom 10:15); Isa 65:1 (Rom 10:20); Isa 40:13 (Rom 11:34); Isa 11:10 (Rom 15:12); Isa 52:15 (Rom 15:21). Gentiles are actually in view in Isaiah 11:10 and in the context of Isaiah 52:15. Paul interprets Isaiah 28:16, 52:7, and 65:1 in such a way that they are made to speak of the extension of the message of salvation to the Gentiles. Cf. Paul's similar reinterpretations of Hos 2:23/1:10 (Rom 9:25–26); Deut 30:12–14 (Rom 10:6–8); Joel 2:32 (Rom 10:13); and Deut 32:43 (Rom 15:10).

[32] Isa 8:14 and Isa 28:16 (Rom 9:33); Isa 65:2 (Rom 10:21); Isa 29:10 (Rom 11:8). Cf. Paul's citations of Ps 93:14 (Rom 11:1–2); 3 Kgdms 19 (Rom 11:3–4); Ps 68:23–24 (Rom 11:9–10).

[33] Isa 10:22–23 (Rom 9:27–28) and Isa 1:9 (Rom 9:29).

[34] Isa 29:16/45:9 (Rom 9:20); Isa 10:22–23 (Rom 9:27–28); Isa 1:9 (Rom 9:29); Isa 8:14 and Isa 28:16 (Rom 9:33); Isa 65:2 (Rom 10:21); Isa 29:10 and Isa 6:9–10 (Rom 11:8); Isa 59:20–21 and Isa 27:9 (Rom 11:26–27). The charge of idolatry runs like a thread through many of Paul's citations and allusions to scripture in Romans 9–11, beginning with his evocation of the golden calf episode in Romans 9:3. Cf. the wider settings of Exod 33:19 (Rom 9:15); Hos 1–2 (Rom 9:25–26); Deut 32:21 (Rom 10:19); 1 Kgdms 8–12 (Rom 11:2); 3 Kgdms 19 (Rom 11:3–4); Deut 29:4 (Rom 11:8).

place their trust in the gods of the nations that threaten them.[35] The greater part of Israel has been afflicted by YHWH with spiritual blindness and insensibility.[36] God's people languish under their oppressors, unable to save themselves,[37] but they stubbornly refuse to believe the proclamation of the redemption that God has already accomplished.[38] Likewise in Romans, for "the rest" of Israel, the promise of deliverance—which Paul claims has now become reality in and through the gospel of Christ—remains as yet unrealized.

In terms of Isaiah's larger three-act "plot line" of rebellion, punishment, and restoration, Paul locates himself and his fellow believers (Jew and Gentile) in the final act of the story, where heralds go forth with the good news that God has redeemed his people. Surprisingly, however, most of Israel remains mired in acts one and two, still rebellious and estranged from God, still blinded to the reality of the redemption God has wrought for Israel and for the world in Christ. It is illuminating to lay Paul's analysis of Israel's plight in Romans 9–10 alongside Isaiah's frequent depiction of an Israel trusting in other gods for deliverance and refusing to believe the prophet's message of redemption. Paul charges that, rather than submitting to "God's righteousness," revealed now in Christ for all who believe (Rom 10:4), most of his kinspeople stubbornly prefer "their own righteousness," that is, the righteousness available only to Jews who observe the Law ὡς ἐξ ἔργων (Rom 9:32, 10:3). Ironically, their trust in their own manner of following the Law blinds them to the gospel that Paul—and Isaiah—proclaim (Isa 53:1/Rom 10:16), the gospel that is none other than the τέλος to which the Law itself would lead them if pursued ἐκ πίστεως (Rom 10:4).

Isaiah and Deuteronomy 29–32
Isaiah's narrative of sin, punishment, and redemption, onto which Paul plots his own story of contemporary Israel, has close counter-

---

[35] Israel's questioning of God's wisdom and of his ability to deliver them appears as a persistent motif in the wider context of many of these citations and allusions: Isa 29:16/45:9 (Rom 9:20); Isa 28:16/8:14 (Rom 9:33); Isa 53:1 (Rom 10:16); Isa 40:21/28 (Rom 10:18, 19); Isa 40:13 (Rom 11:34). Note this theme also in 1 Kgdms 8–12 (where God's "righteousness" is clearly defined in 12:7 as "the things the Lord did for you and your ancestors" [i.e., delivering you from Egypt]).

[36] See the conflated citation of Isa 29:10/Deut 29:4/Ps 68:24 and the probable allusion to Isa 6:9–10 in Rom 11:8.

[37] See the context of Isa 59:20–21 (Rom 11:26–27).

[38] Note especially Isa 53:1 (Rom 10:16); Isa 65:2 (Rom 10:21).

parts elsewhere among Israel's scriptures.[39] A quite similar version of Israel's story constitutes the narrative substructure of Deuteronomy 29–32. As we have seen, Paul quotes a number of key verses from these chapters in Romans 9–11 and Romans 15.[40] Of particular significance is the fact that three times Paul links a citation from the last chapters of Deuteronomy to a passage from Isaiah.[41] This interpretive strategy suggests that Paul understands Isaiah and Deuteronomy to be telling the same epic story of the triumph of God's faithfulness over Israel's unfaithfulness.[42]

Just as he does with the Isaianic texts, Paul plots his contemporary situation onto these latter chapters of Deuteronomy. Paul and his fellow Jewish and Gentile followers of Jesus live in the final act of the story narrated by Deuteronomy 29–32. These believers have had their hearts cleansed by God, as Deuteronomy 30:6 promised, and they have found that the word of salvation has indeed come near, into their hearts and into their mouths, as a result of God's mighty act of deliverance in Christ (Deut 30:12–14; Rom 10:6–10). Having been united together in one community by Christ's ministry, Jew and Gentile with one voice celebrate God's faithfulness and mercy (Deut 32:43; Rom 15:10).

In contrast, "the rest" of Israel remain stuck back in Deuteronomy 29:4, where "to this day" God has not given them "eyes to see or ears to hear or a heart to understand" (Rom 11:8). Paul goes so far as to identify his contemporaries with the profligate and rebellious Israel of Deuteronomy 32:21. Yet Paul does not make this connection

---

[39] Such a narrative stands behind the portions of Hosea quoted by Paul in Romans 9:25–26, for example. O. H. Steck has argued that the Sin-Exile-Restoration Pattern permeates Palestinian Jewish thought in the period 200 BCE–100 CE (1967, 1968). J. M. Scott has developed the implications of this insight for Paul's theology in a number of articles (1993a, 1993b, 1994). See also Gowan 1977; Knibb 1976, 1983; Scott 1997; Thielman 1989; Wright 1992:268–72.

[40] Deut 29:4 (Rom 11:8); Deut 30:12–14 (Rom 10:6–8); Deut 32:21 (Rom 10:19); Deut 32:35 (Rom 12:19); Deut 32:43 (Rom 15:10). Note allusions to Deuteronomy 32:21 (Rom 11:11–14) and Deuteronomy 32:4 (Rom 9:14).

[41] Deut 32:21 and Isa 65:1–2 (Rom 10:19–21); Deut 29:4 and Isa 29:10 (cf. Isa 6:9–10; Rom 11:8); Deut 32:43 and Isa 11:10 (Rom 15:10–12).

[42] My findings support the observation made by Hays that the Song of Moses "becomes in Paul's hands a hermeneutical key of equal importance with the prophecies of Deutero-Isaiah" (1989:164). Hays notes that both Isaiah and Deuteronomy "have already read the history of YHWH's dealing with Israel typologically, as a prefiguration of a larger eschatological design" (164). At the same time, the present study extends Hays's insight by showing that, in Romans, Paul consistently cites and interprets the two texts *in light of one another*.

in order to prove that God has rejected his people. On the contrary, Paul argues from Deuteronomy 32:21 and its wider context that "the rest" of Israel, far from being cast off, are now the objects of a lover's ploy designed to win them back. God has embraced Gentiles and lavished on them Israel's rightful inheritance with the express purpose of provoking his people to jealousy and to renewed zeal for their God (Deut 32:21; Rom 10:19). Thus, Paul finds in Deuteronomy, as in Isaiah, rock-solid assurances that God has not rejected his inheritance or abandoned his covenant people.

Conclusion: Scripture, Theology, and Mission

Paul's citations and allusions to Isaiah are not plunder from random raids on Israel's sacred texts. Rather, they are the product of sustained and careful attention to the rhythms and cadences of individual passages as well as to larger themes and motifs that run throughout the prophet's oracles. Paul finds in Isaiah a fellow preacher of the gospel, the message that reveals God's righteousness for all who believe, for the Jew first and also for the Greek. He uncovers in Isaiah's heralds a veiled prefiguration of his own mission to proclaim the good news to those among the Gentiles who have not yet heard news of the victory of Israel's God. Faced with the paradox of Israel's unbelief, Paul discovers that Isaiah's words give voice to his own agony of heart: "Lord, who has believed our message?" And finally, through adopting as his own the stories Isaiah and his fellow scriptural witnesses tell about God's unquenchable love for his people, Paul finds assurance that God will be faithful to redeem and restore his covenant people Israel, so that Jew and Gentile together can sing the glories of God's name.

The story of God, Israel, and the Gentiles that Paul tells in Romans reflects the dynamic interplay of his foundational convictions, his reading of Israel's scriptures, his labors in mission, and his cultural and historical contexts. By no stretch of the imagination can Paul be said to interpret Isaiah and other scriptural texts in Romans in a detached and disinterested manner. Rather, his scriptural interpretations serve the ends of the larger argument he is constructing in the letter, an argument that is called forth by a complex set of circumstances and concerns that have arisen in the context of his mission to the Gentiles. And yet, at the same time, the letter to the

Romans reveals, perhaps more clearly than any other of Paul's letters, the deep and pervasive influence that Israel's scriptures exert on the shape of his thought and on the contours of his apostolic ministry.[43]

This complex and dynamic interrelationship of scripture, theology, and mission within a particular cultural and historical context is nowhere more evident than in Paul's retelling of Israel's story in Romans 9–11. Believing that Israel's hopes for deliverance have been realized and God's promises to the patriarchs fulfilled *in Christ*, Paul appropriates Isaianic images in order to depict his ministry of the gospel as the proclamation of Israel's long-awaited release and restoration. At the same time, convinced that in redeeming Israel, God has also embraced Gentiles, and that God has determined to include Jew and Gentile in the one people of God on the same basis of faith, Paul revises the scriptural story to give Gentiles a prominent part in the drama of Israel's restoration. In so doing, he even goes so far as to cast Gentiles in a role originally written for Israel.[44]

Even more radical rewriting of the script is occasioned by the actual course the early Christian mission has taken. By the time Paul composes Romans, it has become clear that, in defiance of all expectations, the majority of Israel have not embraced the gospel, while at the same time Gentiles have been responding to the message in ever increasing numbers. Nevertheless, God's sovereignty, God's election of Israel, and God's fidelity to the covenant remain bedrock convictions for Paul. Consequently, he must believe that what has happened to Israel has been part of the divine playwright's script all along.

In a bold and sweepingly revisionary rereading of scripture, Paul argues in Romans 9–11 that God has designed the redemption of

---

[43] Though much separates Paul from the tradents of Israel's sacred texts who preceded him, Fishbane's characterization of the mindset of "the purveyors and creators of aggadic exegesis" provides an apt description of Paul as well (1985:435; emphasis original):

> [They] appear to live with 'texts-in-the-mind'—that is, with texts (or traditions) which provide the imaginative matrix for evaluating the present, for conceiving of the future, for organizing reality (the inchoate, the negative, the possible), and even for providing the shared symbols and language of communication. With aggadic *traditio* the world of Israelite culture is thus one which talks and thinks, which imagines and reflects, and which builds and rejects, *through* the traditions.

[44] Hos 2:23/1:10 (Rom 9:25–26); Isa 28:16 (Rom 10:11); Joel 2:32 (Rom 10:13); Isa 65:1 (Rom 10:20).

Israel to take place in *two stages* in order to allow room for the Gentiles to enter the community of God's people. And yet, it is telling that even where he most thoroughly transmutes the plot of the scriptural story, Paul continues to draw on the vocabulary, images, and themes of Israel's sacred texts. As Paul narrates it, through their acceptance of the gospel, *already* "a remnant" and "seed" of Israel have received the deliverance and restoration promised by God long ago; moreover, this is but the earnest of a fuller redemption yet to come.[45] In the present time, however, the rest of Israel remain suspended in the earlier acts of the drama, still suffering under the burden of foreign oppression, still estranged from God.[46] Intent on pursuing the Law "as if by works" and so establishing "their own righteousness," they have stumbled over the stumbling stone about which Isaiah had warned them.[47] They remain disobedient and rebellious,[48] questioning the divine plan for their deliverance announced in the gospel[49] and stubbornly refusing to believe the message of release and restoration that Paul—and Isaiah!—preach.[50]

So profound is Israel's blindness to the truth of the gospel that Paul can only conclude that *God himself* has rendered them insensible.[51] Yet this must be a temporary condition, for scripture insists that "God has not forsaken his people, whom he foreknew."[52] It is a text from the Song of Moses, Deuteronomy 32:21, that provides Paul the key to understanding the divine blinding of "the rest" of Israel.[53] Interpreting this text in terms of his contemporary situation, Paul finds that Israel's present stumbling does not signify God's rejection of Israel, but rather represents God's determination to use the temporary hardening of a portion of Israel to open a window of opportunity for his salvation to be extended to the Gentiles. This temporal scheme allows Paul in Romans 9–11 to integrate his "rem-

---

[45] Isa 10:22–23/1:9 (Rom 9:27–29); 3 Kgdms 19:10/14, 18 (Rom 11:3–4).

[46] My claim that Paul figuratively places his contemporaries "in exile" should be distinguished from the *historical* argument advanced by Scott, Wright, and others that many Second Temple Jews considered themselves in fact *to be* "in exile." See above, p. 30 n. 105.

[47] Isa 28:16/8:14 (Rom 9:33; cf. Rom 9:31–32; 10:3).

[48] Isa 65:2 (Rom 10:21).

[49] Isa 29:16/45:9 (Rom 9:20); Isa 40:21/28 (Rom 10:18, 19).

[50] Isa 53:1 (Rom 10:16).

[51] Deut 29:4/Isa 29:10/(Isa 6:9–10) and Ps 68:23–24 (Rom 11:8–10).

[52] Ps 93:14/1 Kgdms 12:22 (Rom 11:1–2).

[53] Rom 10:19; 11:11–14.

nant theology" with his ultimate insistence on the salvation of "all Israel." It is not that Paul suddenly abandons in mid-argument the remnant motif in favor of a more inclusive conception of Israel's election. Rather, for Paul, the future salvation of all Israel is implicit in—and, indeed, guaranteed by—the present survival of a remnant.

Significantly, in this revisionary retelling of the story of Israel's deliverance as a two-stage process it is Paul's mission to the Gentiles that will ultimately lead to the redemption of "the rest" of Israel. When the "fullness of the Gentiles" has come in, the Lord himself will go forth to redeem and purify his people and restore them to himself in righteousness.[54] In this way, "all Israel will be saved," just as in the original version of the stories told by Isaiah and Moses.[55] Until then, Paul finds himself playing a pivotal role in this drama of cosmic redemption: he is not only a herald bearing the message of redemption to the Gentiles,[56] but also a chosen instrument through whom God will provoke his own people to jealousy and so effect their salvation.[57]

And so, confident that as he faithfully discharges his commission to proclaim the gospel to the Gentiles, God will prove faithful to redeem Israel, Paul prepares to go to Jerusalem. From there he will begin a new journey leading to Rome, and thence, ultimately, to Spain, so that

> those to whom it has not been announced concerning him will see,
> and those who have not heard will understand.

For indeed,

> How will they hear without a preacher,
> and how will they preach if they have not been sent?
> Just as it is written:

> > How beautiful are the feet
> > of those who proclaim the good news. . . .

---

[54] Isa 59:20–21 and Isa 27:9 (Rom 11:26–27).
[55] Isa 59:20–21/27:9 (Rom 11:26–27); cf. Deut 32:34–43.
[56] Isa 52:7 (Rom 10:15); Isa 52:15 (Rom 15:21); cf. Hos 2:23/1:10 (Rom 9:25–26); Ps 18:5 (Rom 10:18); Isa 65:1 (Rom 10:20).
[57] Rom 11:11–14, alluding to Deut 32:21.

APPENDIX

ISAIAH AND ITS ANCIENT VERSIONS:
A SELECTED REFERENCE LIST

LXX Isaiah
In this study, "Isaiah LXX" refers to the critical text edited by Ziegler in the Göttingen Septuagint (1939a). In his introduction, Ziegler discusses in detail the character of the textual witnesses to Isaiah LXX and sets forth the principles on which he has assembled this eclectic text and its apparatuses. Important studies of LXX Isaiah include Ziegler 1934, 1939b; Seeligmann 1948; Ottley 1906–1909; Scholz 1880; Koenig 1982; Laberge 1978; Fischer 1930. Briefer but helpful treatments of the subject are provided by Tov 1997:17–29, 1988:173–78; Brockington 1954; van der Kooij 1989, 1997a, 1997c; Porter and Pearson 1997.

Later Greek Versions
Readings attributed to Aquila, Symmachus, and Theodotion in patristic writers or in the margins of LXX manuscripts are listed in Ziegler's second apparatus. Still an important resource for studying the later Greek versions is Field 1964. For Aquila, I have utilized the valuable index by J. Reider and N. Turner (Reider 1966; cf. Reider 1916, along with the methodological refinements proposed by Katz and Ziegler 1958). For Symmachus, I have consulted Liebreich 1944 and the lexicographical study by González Luis (1981). On the evidence of the Greek versions in Isaiah, see further Ziegler 1939b.

Hebrew Texts
For MT, I have examined both Codex Leningradensis and the Aleppo Codex, along with variants from other masoretic manuscripts and rabbinic writings. My source for much of this information is the Hebrew University Bible Project text of Isaiah edited by M. H. Goshen-Gottstein (1995). See also van der Kooij 1981.

The Qumran Isaiah scrolls have now all been published (cf. Ulrich 1995; Skehan 1979):

    1QIsaᵃ: Burrows 1950:xiii–xviii; Plates I–LIV.
    1QIsaᵇ: Sukenik 1955:30–34; Plates I–XV.
    1Q8 [fragments belonging to 1QIsaᵇ]: D. Barthélemy, DJD I:66–68; Plate XII.
    4Q55–69b: P. W. Skehan and E. Ulrich, DJD XV:7–143; Plates I–XXIII.
    5Q3: J. T. Milik, DJD III:173; Plate XXXVI.
    MurIsa: J. T. Milik, DJD II:79–80; Plate XXII.

The most thorough investigation of 1QIsaᵃ to date is the monumental study by E. Y. Kutscher (1974). In addition, see Morrow 1973; Skehan 1955, 1957. On the relationship of the Qumran Isaiah scrolls to LXX Isaiah, see Ziegler 1959; van der Kooij 1992; Orlinsky 1959; Tov 1992. Van der Kooij notes that while LXX Isaiah and 1QIsaᵃ do not share a particularly close textual affinity, "both texts, dating from the same period, the second half of the second century BCE, differ markedly from MT, and both reflect a free approach towards their *Vorlagen*" (201). On interpretation in 1QIsaᵃ, see the many perceptive observations offered by Kutscher (1974: *passim*). See further Brownlee 1964; Goshen-Gottstein 1954; van der Kooij 1986, 1988; Rosenbloom 1970; Talmon 1962, 1989.

In addition, there are six fragmentary *pesharim* on Isaiah:

3Q4: M. Baillet, DJD III:95–96; Plate XVIII.
4Q161–165: J. M. Allegro, DJD V:11–30; Plates IV–IX (see Strugnell 1969–71:183–99 for important corrections to Allegro's edition); Horgan 1979:15–37, 70–138. For the Isaiah *pesharim*, I have followed the carefully-revised text in Charlesworth 2001, which the editors graciously made available to me before publication of the volume.

Important quotations of or allusions to Isaiah in non-biblical scrolls are noted where possible. Identification of such quotations and allusions has been greatly facilitated by The Princeton Dead Sea Scrolls Project's *Graphic Concordance* (Charlesworth 1991). Also helpful have been Brownlee 1953, 1954; J. G. Campbell 1995; Carmignac 1956, 1960; Goshen-Gottstein 1953; Holm-Nielsen 1960; Rabin 1958; Starkova 1992; Wernberg-Møller 1955. Citations of the Dead Sea Scrolls follow the format: scroll name/number, fragment number(s), column number(s), and line number(s). So, for example, 4Q161 frgs. 8–10 3.6–13 refers to lines 6–13 of column three of the joined fragments 8 through 10 of 4Q161. I normally follow the numbering of the *editio princeps*; for the *pesharim*, however, I follow the revised text of Charlesworth 2001. For the *Hodayot*, I adopt the numbering of García Martínez and Tigchelaar 1997–98 (following the reconstruction of Stegemann/Puech) and provide Sukenik's numbers (1955) in brackets.

Isaiah Targum
I have relied on the editions by J. F. Stenning (1949) and A. Sperber (1962; cf. van Zijl 1965, 1968–69). J. B. van Zijl's concordance (1979) has been invaluable. On the targumists as exegetes, see J. F. Stenning's insightful introduction to his edition of the Isaiah Targum. See further Brockington 1954; Chilton 1982, 1987; Churgin 1927; R. P. Gordon 1978; Goshen-Gottstein 1991; Le Déaut 1974; E. Levine 1996; Rowlands 1959; Ribera 1994; Smolar and Aberbach 1983. Although we now have evidence for written targums as early as the first century BCE (11QtgJob [11Q10]; see S. A. Kaufman 1973; 4QtgLev [4Q156] and 4QtgJob [4Q157]), the dating of targumic traditions is notoriously difficult. Rather than searching for

specific *precursors* of Paul's interpretations, I have investigated the targum as a potential source for *analogous* strategies of reading Isaiah (cf. the methodological cautions of Chilton 1995).

Peshitta

For the Peshitta, I use the text edited by S. P. Brock (1987). On evidence for exegetical activity in the Peshitta, see M. P. Weitzman 1994, 1996, 1999; Goshen-Gottstein 1991; Rowlands 1959; Running 1965–66 (see also the critique of Running by van der Kooij 1981:261–70); Delekat 1957; Brock 1983, 1984.

Latin Versions

I also make occasional reference to the Vulgate, relying on the standard critical texts: *Biblia Sacra iuxta latinam Vulgatam versionem* (Rome: Typis polyglottis Vaticanis, 1926–) and Weber 1994.

SELECTED BIBLIOGRAPHY

Aageson, J. W. 1983. "Paul's Use of Scripture: a Comparative Study of Biblical Interpretation in Early Palestinian Judaism and the New Testament, with Special Reference to Romans 9–11." Ph.D. diss., Oxford.
———. 1986. "Scripture and Structure in the Development of the Argument in Romans 9–11." *CBQ* 48:265–89.
———. 1987. "Typology, Correspondence, and the Application of Scripture in Romans 9–11." *JSNT* 31:51–72.
Abegg Jr., M. G. 1994. "Messianic Hope and 4Q285: A Reassessment," *JBL* 113: 81–91.
Abel, E. L. 1968. "Were the Jews Banished from Rome in 19 AD?" *REJ* 127:383–86.
Achtemeier, Paul J. 1990. "*Omne Verbum Sonat*: The New Testament and the Oral Environment of Late Western Antiquity." *JBL* 109:3–27.
Ackroyd, P. R. 1978. "Isaiah I–XII: Presentation of a Prophet." *Congress Volume: Göttingen 1977*, 16–48. Leiden: Brill.
———. 1982. "Isaiah 36–39: Structure and Function." *Von Kanaan bis Kerala*. FS J. P. M. van der Ploeg. Ed. W. C. Delsman et al., 3–21. Neukirchen-Vluyn: Neukirchener Verlag.
Ackroyd, P. R. and C. F. Evans, eds. 1970. *Cambridge History of the Bible, Vol. I: From the Beginnings to Jerome*. Cambridge: Cambridge University Press.
Albl, Martin C. 1999. "*And Scripture Cannot Be Broken*": *The Form and Function of the Early Christian* Testimonia *Collections*. NovTSupp 96. Leiden: Brill.
Alexander, Philip S. 1983. "Rabbinic Judaism and the New Testament." *ZNW* 74:237–46.
———. 1990. "Quid Athenis et Hierosolymis? Rabbinic Midrash and Hermeneutics in the Graeco-Roman World." *A Tribute to Geza Vermes: Essays on Jewish and Christian Literature and History*. Ed. P. R. Davies and R. T. White, 101–24. JSOTSup 100. Sheffield: JSOT Press.
Allen, L. C. 1983. *Psalms 101–150*. WBC 21. Waco: Word.
Allison, D. C., Jr. 1980. "The Background of Romans 11:11–15 in Apocalyptic and Rabbinic Literature." *Studia Biblica et Theologica* 10:229–34.
———. 1985. "Romans 11:11–15: A Suggestion." *Perspectives in Religious Studies* 12:23–30.
———. 1993. *The New Moses: A Matthean Typology*. Minneapolis: Fortress.
———. 1999. "Jesus and the Victory of Apocalyptic." *Jesus and the Restoration of Israel*. Ed. C. C. Newman, 126–41. Downer's Grove, IL: IVP.
Anderson, Bernhard W. 1962. "Exodus Typology in Second Isaiah." *Israel's Prophetic Heritage*. Ed. B. W. Anderson and W. Harrelson, 177–95. New York: Harper.
———. 1976. "Exodus and Covenant in Second Isaiah and Prophetic Tradition." *Magnalia Dei: The Mighty Acts of God*. Ed. F. M. Cross et al., 339–60. Garden City, NY: Doubleday.
———. 1988a. "The Apocalyptic Rendering of the Isaiah Tradition." *The Social World of Formative Christianity and Judaism*. FS H. C. Kee. Ed. J. Neusner et al., 17–38. Philadelphia: Fortress.
———. 1988b. "'God With Us'—In Judgment and in Mercy: The Editorial Structure of Isaiah 5–10(11)." *Canon, Theology and Old Testament Interpretation*. Ed. G. M. Tucker et al., 230–45. Philadelphia: Fortress.
Anderson, F. I. and D. N. Freedman. 1980. *Hosea*. AB 24. Garden City, N.Y.: Doubleday.

Aune, David E. 1983. *Prophecy in Early Christianity and the Ancient Mediterranean World*. Grand Rapids: Eerdmans.

———. 1991. "Romans as a *Logos Protreptikos*." *The Romans Debate*. Ed. K. P. Donfried, 278–96. Rev. ed. Peabody, MA: Hendrickson.

Aus, R. D. 1979. "Paul's Travel Plans to Spain and the 'Full Number of the Gentiles' of Rom. XI 25." *NovT* 21:232–62.

Badenas, R. 1985. *Christ, the End of the Law: Romans 10.4 in Pauline Perspective*. JSNTSup 10. Sheffield: JSOT Press.

Bader-Saye, Scott. 1999. *Church and Israel after Christendom: The Politics of Election*. Boulder: Westview.

Bahr, Gordon J. 1966. "Paul and Letter Writing in the Fifth [*sic*, read "First"] Century." *CBQ* 28:465–477.

Barclay, J. M. G. 1996. *Jews in the Mediterranean Diaspora: From Alexander to Trajan (323 BCE–117 CE)*. Edinburgh: T & T Clark.

Barr, James. 1979. *The Typology of Literalism in Ancient Biblical Translations*. MSU 15. Göttingen: Vandenhoeck & Ruprecht.

———. 1994. "Paul and the LXX: A Note on Some Recent Work." *JTS* 45:593–601.

Barrett, C. K. 1957. *A Commentary on the Epistle to the Romans*. HNTC. New York: Harper & Row.

———. 1968. *A Commentary on the First Epistle to the Corinthians*. HNTC. New York: Harper & Row.

———. 1970. "The Interpretation of the Old Testament in the New." *Cambridge History of the Bible I: From the Beginnings to Jerome*. Ed. P. R. Ackroyd and C. F. Evans, 377–411. Cambridge: Cambridge University Press.

———. 1982. "Romans 9:30–10:21: Fall and Responsibility of Israel." *Essays on Paul*, 132–53. London: SPCK.

———. 1994. *Acts 1–14*. ICC. Edinburgh: T & T Clark.

———. 1995. "Paul: Missionary and Theologian." *Jesus and the Word and Other Essays*, 149–62. PTMS 41. Allison Park, PA: Pickwick.

Barthélemy, D. 1963. *Les devanciers d'Aquila*. VTSup 10. Leiden: Brill.

Bartlett, A. H. 1996. *The Book Around Immanuel: Style and Structure in Isaiah 2–12*. Biblical and Judaic Studies 4. Winona Lake, IN: Eisenbrauns.

Barton, John. 1986. *Oracles of God*. London: Darton, Longman and Todd.

Basser, H. W. 1984. *Midrashic Interpretations of the Song of Moses*. American University Studies, Series VII: Theology and Religion 2. New York: Peter Lang.

Bassler, J. M. 1993. "Paul's Theology: Whence and Whither?" *Pauline Theology III: 1 & 2 Corinthians*. Ed. D. M. Hay, 3–17. Minneapolis: Fortress.

Bauckham, R. A. 1988. "James, 1 and 2 Peter, Jude." *It is Written: Scripture Citing Scripture*. FS B. Lindars. Ed. D. A. Carson and H. G. M. Williamson, 303–17. Cambridge: Cambridge University Press.

Baumert, Norbert. 2000. "Diener Gottes für Wahrheit und Barmherzigkeit: Eine Rückmeldung zu J. R. Wagner's 'Fresh Approach to Romans 15:8–9'." *Biblische Notizen* 104:5–10.

Baumgarten, A. I. 1983. "The Name of the Pharisees." *JBL* 102:411–28.

Baumgarten, Joseph M. 1992. "A 'Scriptural' Citation in 4Q Fragments of the Damascus Document." *JJS* 43:95–98.

Beale, G. K. 1991. "Isaiah vi 9–13: A Retributive Taunt Against Idolatry." *VT* 41:257–78.

Beard, Mary. 1991. "Writing and Religion: Ancient Literacy and the Function of the Written Word in Roman Religion." *Literacy in the Roman World*. Ed. J. H. Humphrey, 35–58. Journal of Roman Archaeology Supplement 3. Ann Arbor.

Beckwith, R. 1985. *The Old Testament Canon of the New Testament Church*. Grand Rapids: Eerdmans.

Beentjes, Pancratius C. 1982. "Inverted Quotations in the Bible: A Neglected Stylistic Pattern," *Bib* 63:506–23.

———. 1997. "Wisdom of Solomon 3,1–4,19 and the Book of Isaiah." *Studies in the Book of Isaiah.* FS W. A. M. Beuken. Ed. J. van Ruiten and M. Vervenne, 413–420. BETL 132. Leuven: Leuven University Press.

Beker, J. C. 1980. *Paul the Apostle: The Triumph of God in Life and Thought.* Philadelphia: Fortress.

———. 1986. "The Faithfulness of God and the Priority of Israel in Paul's Letter to the Romans." *HTR* 79:10–16; reprinted in *The Romans Debate.* Ed. K. P. Donfried, 327–32. Rev. ed. Peabody, MA: Hendrickson, 1991.

Bekken, Per Jarle. 1995. "Paul's Use of Deut 30,12–14 in Jewish Context. Some Observations." *The New Testament and Hellenistic Judaism.* Ed. P. Borgen and S. Giversen, 183–203. Aarhus: Aarhus University Press.

Bell, Richard H. 1994. *Provoked to Jealousy: The Origin and Purpose of the Jealousy Motif in Romans 9–11.* WUNT 2.63. Tübingen: Mohr-Siebeck.

Bellinger, W. H. and W. R. Farmer, ed. 1998. *Jesus and the Suffering Servant: Isaiah 53 and Christian Origins.* Harrisburg, PA: Trinity Press International.

Ben-Porat, Ziva. 1976. "The Poetics of Literary Allusion." *PTL: A Journal for Descriptive Poetics and Theory of Literature* 1:105–28.

Berkley, Timothy W. 2000. *From a Broken Covenant to Circumcision of the Heart: Pauline Intertextual Exegesis in Romans 2:17–29.* SBLDS 175. Atlanta: Society of Biblical Literature.

Bernstein, Moshe J. 1994. "Introductory Formulas for Citation and Re-citation of Biblical Verses in the Qumran Pesharim: Observations on a Pesher Technique." *DSD* 1:30–70.

———. 1996. "The Employment and Interpretation of Scripture in 4QMMT: Preliminary Observations." *Reading 4QMMT: New Perspectives on Qumran Law and History.* Ed. John Kampen and M. J. Bernstein, 29–51. SBL Symposium Series 2. Atlanta: Scholars.

Bertrangs, A. 1954. "La vocation des gentils chez Saint Paul. Exégèse et heuristique Pauliniennes des citations Vétéro-Testamentaires." *ETL* 30:391–415.

Betz, O. 1957. "Felsenmann und Felsengemeinde (Eine Parallele zu Mt 16,17–19 in den Qumranpsalmen)." *ZNW* 48:49–77.

Birch, B. C. 1976. *The Rise of the Israelite Monarchy: The Growth and Development of 1 Samuel 7–15.* SBLDS 27. Missoula, MT: Scholars.

Bjerkelund, Carl J. 1977. "'Vergeblich' als Missionsergebnis bei Paulus." *God's Christ and His People.* FS N. A. Dahl. Ed. J. Jervell and W. A. Meeks, 175–91. Oslo: Universitetsforlaget.

Black, M. 1971–72. "The Christological Use of the Old Testament in the New Testament." *NTS* 18:1–14.

Blenkinsopp, Joseph. 1967. "Scope and Depth of Exodus Tradition in Deutero-Isaiah 40–55." *The Dynamism of Biblical Tradition.* Concilium 20. Ed. P. Benoit and R. E. Murphy, 41–71. New York: Paulist.

———. 1981. "Interpretation and the Tendency to Sectarianism: An Aspect of Second Temple History." *Jewish and Christian Self-Definition.* Vol. 2. Ed. E. P. Sanders, A. I. Baumgarten and Alan Mendelson, 1–26. Philadelphia: Fortress.

Bloch, Renée. 1955. "Note méthodologique pour l'étude de la littérature rabbinique." *RSR* 43:194–227; ET, "Methodological Note for the Study of Rabbinic Literature." *Approaches to Ancient Judaism: Theory and Practice.* Ed. W. S. Green, 51–75. BJS 1. Missoula: Scholars, 1978.

———. 1957. "Midrash." *DBSup* 5:1263–81; ET, in *Approaches to Ancient Judaism: Theory and Practice.* Ed. W. S. Green, 29–50. BJS 1. Missoula: Scholars, 1978.

Bockmuehl, Markus N. A. 1990. *Revelation and Mystery in Ancient Judaism and Pauline Christianity.* WUNT 2.36. Tübingen: Mohr-Siebeck.

———. "A 'Slain Messiah' in 4Q Serekh Milhamah (4Q285)?" *TynBul* 43:155–69.

Boers, H. 1981. "The Problem of Jews and Gentiles in the Macro-Structure of Romans." *Neot* 15:1–11.

——. 1993. "Polysemy in Paul's Use of Christological Expressions." *The Future of Christology*. Ed. A. J. Malherbe and W. A. Meeks, 91–108. Minneapolis: Fortress.

Böhl, E. 1878. *Die alttestamentlichen Citate im Neuen Testament*. Vienna: W. Braumüller.

Bonsirven, J. 1939. *Exégèse rabbinique et exégèse paulinienne*. Bibliothèque de théologie historique. Paris.

Booth, Wayne C. 1961. *The Rhetoric of Fiction*. Chicago: University of Chicago Press.

Borgen, Peder. 1996. "In Accordance with the Scriptures." *Early Christian Thought in Its Jewish Context*. Ed. J. Barclay and J. Sweet, 193–206. Cambridge: Cambridge University Press.

Bornhäuser, K. 1921. *Das Wirken des Christus durch Taten und Worte*. BFCT 2.2. Gütersloh: C. Bertelsmann.

Bornkamm, G. 1967. "μυστήριον." *TDNT* 4:802–28.

——. 1971. *Paul*. New York: Harper & Row.

——. 1991. "The Letter to the Romans as Paul's Last Will and Testament." *The Romans Debate*. Ed. K. P. Donfried, 16–28. Rev. ed. Peabody, MA: Hendrickson.

Botha, P. J. J. 1992a. "Greco-Roman Literacy as Setting for New Testament Writings." *Neot* 26:195–215.

——. 1992b. "Letter Writing and Oral Communication in Antiquity." *Scriptura* 42:17–34.

Bowman, A. K. and G. Woolf, eds. 1994. *Literacy and Power in the Ancient World*. Cambridge: Cambridge University Press.

Boyarin, Daniel. 1990. *Intertextuality and the Reading of Midrash*. Indiana Studies in Biblical Literature. Bloomington: Indiana University Press.

——. 1994. *A Radical Jew: Paul and the Politics of Identity*. Berkeley.

Braun, M. A. 1977. "James' Use of Amos at the Jerusalem Council: Steps Toward a Possible Solution of the Textual and Theological Problems (Acts 15)." *JETS* 20:113–21.

Bring, Ragnar. 1966. "Das Gesetz und die Gerechtigkeit Gottes: Eine Studie zur Frage nach der Bedeutung des Ausdruckes *telos nomou* in Röm. 10:4." *ST* 20:1–36.

Brock, Sebastian P. 1974. "The Phenomenon of Biblical Translation in Antiquity." *Studies in the Septuagint: Origins, Recensions, and Interpretations*. Ed. S. Jellicoe, 541–71. New York: KTAV.

——. 1983. "Towards a History of Syriac Translation Technique." *III Symposium Syriacum, 1980*. Ed. R. Lavenant, 1–14. Orientalia Christiana Analecta 221. Rome: Pontificium Institutum Studiorum Orientalium.

——. 1984. "Aspects of Translation Technique in Antiquity." *Syriac Perspectives on Late Antiquity*, 69–87. London: Variorum Reprints.

——, ed. 1987. *The Old Testament in Syriac According to the Peshiṭta Version 3.4: Isaiah*. Peshiṭta Institute. Leiden: Brill.

——. 1988. "Translating the Old Testament." *It is Written: Scripture Citing Scripture*. Ed. D. A. Carson and H. G. M. Williamson, 87–98. Cambridge: Cambridge University Press.

——. 1992. "To Revise or Not to Revise: Attitudes to Jewish Biblical Translation." *Septuagint, Scrolls and Cognate Writings*. Ed. G. J. Brooke and B. Lindars, 301–338. SBLSCS 33. Atlanta: Scholars.

Brockington, L. H. 1954. "Septuagint and Targum." *ZAW* 66:80–86.

Brooke, A. E., N. McLean, and H. St.-J. Thackeray, eds. 1906–40. The Old Testament in Greek. Cambridge University Press.

Brooke, George J. 1985. *Exegesis at Qumran: 4QFlorilegium in Its Jewish Context*. JSOTSup 29. Sheffield: JSOT.

——. 1991. "The Kittim in the Qumran Pesharim." *Images of Empire*. Ed. Loveday Alexander, 135–59. JSOTSup 122. Sheffield Academic Press.

——. 1994. "Isaiah 40:3 and the Wilderness Community." *New Qumran Texts and Studies*. Ed. George J. Brooke with Florentino García Martínez, 117–32. Leiden: Brill.

——. 1997a. " 'The Canon within the Canon' at Qumran and in the New Testament."

The Scrolls and the Scriptures: Qumran Fifty Years After. Ed. S. E. Porter and C. A. Evans, 242–66. JSPSup 26. Sheffield: JSOT.

——. 1997b. "The Explicit Presentation of Scripture in 4QMMT." *Legal Texts and Legal Issues: Proceedings of the Second Meeting of the International Organization for Qumran Studies: Cambridge, 1995.* Ed. Moshe Bernstein et al., 67–88. Leiden: Brill.

——. 1997c. "Review of J. G. Campbell, *The Use of Scripture in the Damascus Document 1–8, 19–20.*" *DSD* 4:112–16.

——. 1998. "Shared Intertextual Interpretations in the Dead Sea Scrolls and the New Testament." *Biblical Perspectives: Early Use and Interpretation of the Bible in Light of the Dead Sea Scrolls.* Ed. M. E. Stone and E. G. Chazon, 35–57. Leiden: Brill.

Brown, R. E. 1968. *The Semitic Background of the Term "Mystery" in the New Testament.* FBBS 21. Philadelphia: Fortress.

Brown, Stephen G. 1993. "The Intertextuality of Isaiah 66.17 and 2 Thessalonians 2.7: A Solution for the 'Restrainer' Problem." In *Paul and the Scriptures of Israel.* Ed. C. A. Evans and J. A. Sanders, 254–77. JSNTSup 83/SSEJC 1. Sheffield: JSOT.

Brownlee, W. H. 1953. "The Servant of the Lord in the Qumran Scrolls I." *BASOR* 132:8–15.

——. 1954. "The Servant of the Lord in the Qumran Scrolls II." *BASOR* 135:33–38.

——. 1964. *The Meaning of the Qumran Scrolls for the Bible: With Special Attention to Isaiah.* Oxford.

Broyles, C. G. and C. A. Evans, eds. 1997. *Writing and Reading the Scroll of Isaiah: Studies of an Interpretive Tradition.* 2 Vols. VTSup 70. Leiden: Brill.

Budd, P. J. 1984. *Numbers.* WBC 5. Waco: Word.

Bultmann, R. 1964. "γινώσκω κτλ." *TDNT* 1:689–719.

Burrows, M., ed. 1950. *The Dead Sea Scrolls of St. Mark's Monastery. Vol. I.* New Haven: ASOR.

Campbell, Jonathan G. 1995. *The Use of Scripture in the Damascus Document 1–8, 19–20.* BZAW 228. Berlin: de Gruyter.

——. 2000. "4QMMT^d and the Tripartite Canon," *JJS* 51:181–190.

Campbell, W. S. 1982. "The Place of Romans ix–xi within the Structure and Thought of the Letter." *SE* 7/*TU* 126:121–31.

Carmignac, Jean. 1956. "Les citations de l'Ancien Testament dans 'La guerre des fils de lumière contre les fils de ténèbres.'" *RB* 63:234–60, 375–90.

——. 1960. "Les citations de l'Ancien Testament et spécialement des poèmes du serviteur dans les Hymnes de Qumran." *RevQ* 2:357–94.

Carr, David M. 1992. "What Can We Say about the Tradition History of Isaiah? A Response to Christopher Seitz's *Zion's Final Destiny.*" *SBLSP*, 583–97.

——. 1993. "Reaching for Unity in Isaiah." *JSOT* 57:61–80.

Carroll, Robert P. 1978. "Second Isaiah and the Failure of Prophecy." *ST* 32:119–31.

——. 1980. "Prophecy and Dissonance: A Theoretical Approach to the Prophetic Tradition." *ZAW* 92:108–119.

——. 1997. "Blindsight and the Vision Thing: Blindness and Insight in the Book of Isaiah." *Writing and Reading the Scroll of Isaiah: Studies of an Interpretive Tradition.* 2 Vols. Ed. C. G. Broyles and C. A. Evans, 1:79–93. VTSup 70. Leiden: Brill.

Carson, D. A. 1981. *Divine Sovereignty and Human Responsibility: Biblical Perspectives in Tension.* Atlanta: John Knox.

Carson, D. A. and H. G. M. Williamson, eds. 1988. *It is Written: Scripture Citing Scripture.* FS B. Lindars. Cambridge: Cambridge University Press.

Cassuto, U. 1973a. "The Song of Moses (Deuteronomy Chapter xxxii 1–43)." *Biblical and Oriental Studies I: Bible.* Jerusalem: Magnes, 41–46.

——. 1973b. "The Prophet Hosea and the Books of the Pentateuch." *Biblical and Oriental Studies I: Bible.* Jerusalem: Magnes, 79–100.

Cerfaux, Lucien. 1951. "Saint Paul et le 'Serviteur de Dieu' d'Isaïe." *Studia Anselmiana* 27–28:351–65.

Chadwick, H. 1969. "Florilegium." *RAC* 7:1131–59.

Charlesworth, James H. 1987. "The Pseudepigrapha as Biblical Exegesis." *Early Jewish and Christian Exegesis*. Ed. C. A. Evans and W. F. Stinespring, 139–52. Atlanta: Scholars.

———, ed. 1991. *Graphic Concordance to the Dead Sea Scrolls*. PTSDSSP. Tübingen: Mohr-Siebeck; Lousiville: Westminster/John Knox.

———. 1992. "An Allegorical and Autobiographical Poem by the Moreh haṣ-Ṣedeq (1QH 8:4–11)." *"Sha'arei Talmon": Studies in the Bible, Qumran, and the Ancient Near East Presented to Shemaryahu Talmon*. Ed. M. Fishbane and E. Tov, 295–307. Winona Lake, IN: Eisenbrauns.

———, ed. 1993. *The Dead Sea Scrolls: Hebrew, Aramaic, and Greek Texts with English Translations. Vol. 1: Rule of the Community and Related Documents*. PTSDSSP. Tübingen: Mohr-Siebeck; Lousiville: Westminster/John Knox.

———, ed. 1995. *The Dead Sea Scrolls: Hebrew, Aramaic, and Greek Texts with English Translations. Vol. 2: Damascus Document, War Scroll, and Related Documents*. PTSDSSP. Tübingen: Mohr-Siebeck; Lousiville: Westminster/John Knox.

———, ed. 1997a. *The Dead Sea Scrolls: Hebrew, Aramaic, and Greek Texts with English Translations. Vol. 4A: Pseudepigraphic and Non-Masoretic Psalms and Prayers*. PTSDSSP. Tübingen: Mohr-Siebeck; Lousiville: Westminster/John Knox.

———. 1997b. "Intertextuality: Isaiah 40:3 and the Serek Ha-Yaḥad." *The Quest for Context and Meaning: Studies in Biblical Intertextuality in Honor of James A. Sanders*. Ed. C. A. Evans and S. Talmon, 197–24. Leiden: Brill.

———, ed. 2001. *The Dead Sea Scrolls: Hebrew, Aramaic, and Greek Texts with English Translations. Vol. 6B: Pesharim and Related Documents*. PTSDSSP. Tübingen: Mohr-Siebeck; Lousiville: Westminster/John Knox. Forthcoming.

Charlesworth, James H. and Craig A. Evans, eds. 1993. *The Pseudepigrapha and Early Biblical Interpretation*. JSPSup 14/SSEJC 2. Sheffield: JSOT Press.

Chazon, Esther G. 1992. "4QDibHam: Liturgy or Literature?" *RevQ* 15:447–55.

———. 1997. "*Dibre Hamme'orot*: Prayer for the Sixth Day (4Q504 1–2 v–vi)." *Prayer from Alexander to Constantine: A Critical Anthology*. Ed. M. Kiley et al., 23–27. London: Routledge.

———. Forthcoming. *"Words of the Luminaries" (4QDibHam): A Liturgical Document from Qumran and Its Implications*. STDJ. Leiden: Brill.

Chevallier, M.-A. 1958. *L'Esprit et le Messie dans le Bas-Judaïsme et le Nouveau Testament*. Études d'Histoire et de Philosophie Religieuses 49. Paris: Presses Universitaires de France.

Chilton, Bruce D. 1982. *The Glory of Israel: The Theology and Provenance of the Isaiah Targum*. JSOTSup 23. Sheffield: JSOT.

———. 1987. *The Isaiah Targum: Introduction, Translation, Apparatus and Notes*. The Aramaic Bible 11. Wilmington, DE: Michael Glazier.

———. 1995. "Reference to the Targumim in the Exegesis of the New Testament." *SBLSP*, 77–81.

Chilton, B. D. and C. A. Evans, eds. 1994. *Studying the Historical Jesus*. Leiden: Brill.

Churgin, Pinkhos. 1927. *Targum Jonathan to the Prophets*. New Haven: Yale University Press.

Clayton, Jay and Eric Rothstein. 1991. "Figures in the Corpus: Theories of Influence and Intertextuality." *Influence and Intertextuality in Literary History*. Ed. J. Clayton and E. Rothstein, 3–36. Madison: University of Wisconsin Press.

Clements, R. E. 1974. "The Deuteronomistic Interpretation of the Founding of the Monarchy in 1 Sam. VIII." *VT* 24:398–410.

———. 1980a. "The Prophecies of Isaiah and the Fall of Jerusalem in 587 BC" *VT* 30:421–36.

———. 1980b. "'A Remnant Chosen by Grace' (Romans 11:5): The Old Testament Background and Origin of the Remnant Concept." *Pauline Studies*. Ed. D. A. Hagner and M. J. Harris, 106–21. Grand Rapids: Eerdmans.

——. 1985. "Beyond Tradition-History: Deutero-Isaianic Development of First Isaiah's Themes." *JSOT* 31:95–113.

——. 1991. "The Immanuel Prophecy of Isa. 7:10–17 and Its Messianic Interpretation." *Die Hebräische Bibel und ihre zweifache Nachgeschichte.* FS R. Rendtorff. Ed. E. Blum et al., 225–40. Neukirchen-Vluyn: Neukirchener Verlag.

Cohn-Sherbok, Dan. 1982. "Paul and Rabbinic Exegesis." *SJT* 35:117–32.

Collins, John J. 1995a. "Before the Canon: Scriptures in Second Temple Judaism." *Old Testament Interpretation: Past, Present, and Future.* Ed. J. L. Mays et al., 225–41. Nashville: Abingdon.

——. 1995b. *The Scepter and the Star: The Messiahs of the Dead Sea Scrolls and Other Ancient Literature.* Anchor Bible Reference Library. New York: Doubleday.

——. 1997. "A Herald of Good Tidings: Isaiah 61:1–3 and Its Actualization in the Dead Sea Scrolls." *The Quest for Context and Meaning: Studies in Biblical Intertextuality in Honor of James A. Sanders.* Ed. C. A. Evans and S. Talmon, 225–40. Leiden: Brill.

Conzelmann, H. 1975. *1 Corinthians.* Hermeneia. Philadelphia: Fortress.

Coppens, J. 1968. " 'Mystery' in the Theology of Saint Paul and Its Parallels at Qumran." *Paul and Qumran.* Ed. J. Murphy-O'Connor, 132–58. Chicago: Priory Press.

Cosgrove, C. H. 1996. "Rhetorical Suspense in Romans 9–11: A Study in Polyvalence and Hermeneutical Election." *JBL* 115:271–87.

——. 1997. *Elusive Israel: The Puzzle of Election in Romans.* Louisville: Westminster/John Knox.

Cox, C. E. 1998. "The Reading of the Personal Letter as the Background for the Reading of the Scriptures in the Early Church." *The Early Church in Its Context.* Ed. A. J. Malherbe et al., 74–91. NovTSup 90. Leiden:Brill.

Cranfield, C. E. B. 1964. "St. Paul and the Law." *SJT* 17:43–68.

——. 1975a. "Some Notes on Romans 9:30–33." *Jesus und Paulus.* FS W. G. Kümmel. Ed. E. E. Ellis and E. Grässer, 35–43. Göttingen: Vandenhoeck & Ruprecht.

——. 1975b. *A Critical and Exegetical Commentary on the Epistle to the Romans. Vol I: Introduction and Commentary on Romans I–VIII.* ICC. Edinburgh: T & T Clark.

——. 1979. *A Critical and Exegetical Commentary on the Epistle to the Romans. Vol II: Commentary on Romans IX–XVI and Essays.* ICC. Edinburgh: T & T Clark.

——. 1987. "Some Comments on Professor J. D. G. Dunn's *Christology in the Making* with Special Reference to the Evidence of the Epistle to the Romans." *The Glory of Christ in the New Testament.* Ed. L. D. Hurst and N. T. Wright, 267–80. Oxford: Clarendon.

Cross, F. M. 1972. "The Evolution of a Theory of Local Texts." *1972 Proceedings: IOSCS and SBL Pseudepigrapha Seminar,* 108–26. SBLSCS 2. Missoula, MT: Scholars.

Dahl, Nils A. 1962. "The Particularity of the Pauline Epistles as a Problem in the Ancient Church," *Neotestamentica et Patristica,* 261–71. NovTSup 6. Leiden: Brill.

——. 1977a. "A Fragment and Its Context: 2 Cor. 6:14–7:1." *Studies in Paul,* 62–69. Minneapolis: Augsburg.

——. 1977b. "Missionary Theology in the Epistle to the Romans." *Studies in Paul,* 70–94. Minneapolis: Augsburg; orig. pub. 1956.

——. 1977c. "The Doctrine of Justification: Its Social Function and Implications," *Studies in Paul,* 95–120. Minneapolis: Augsburg.

——. 1977d. "The Future of Israel." *Studies in Paul,* 137–58. Minneapolis: Augsburg.

——. 1978. "Review of *Paul and Palestinian Judaism.*" *RSR* 4:153–58.

Dahood, M. 1965. *Psalms I (1–50).* AB 16. Garden City, N.Y.: Doubleday.

——. 1968. *Psalms II (51–100).* AB 17. Garden City, N.Y.: Doubleday.

——. 1970. *Psalms III (101–150).* AB 17A. Garden City, N.Y.: Doubleday.

Daube, D. 1949. "Rabbinic Methods of Interpretation and Hellenistic Rhetoric." *HUCA* 22:239–64.

——. 1956. *The New Testament and Rabbinic Judaism.* London.

——. 1977. "Alexandrian Methods of Interpretation and the Rabbis." *Essays in Greco-Roman and Related Talmudic Literature.* Ed. H. A. Fischel, 165–82. New York.

Davies, W. D. 1974. *The Gospel and the Land: Early Christianity and Jewish Territorial Doctrine*. Berkeley: University of California Press.

———. 1980. *Paul and Rabbinic Judaism*. 4th ed. Philadelphia: Fortress.

———. 1983. "Reflections about the Use of the Old Testament in the New in its Historical Context." *JQR* 74:105–36.

———. 1984a. "Paul and the People of Israel." *Jewish and Pauline Studies*, 123–52. Philadelphia: Fortress.

———. 1984b. "Paul and the Gentiles: A Suggestion Concerning Romans 11:13–24." *Jewish and Pauline Studies*, 153–63. Philadelphia: Fortress.

———. 1999. "Paul from the Jewish Point of View." *Cambridge History of Judaism III: The Early Roman Period*. Ed. W. Horbury, W. D. Davies, and J. Sturdy, 678–730. Cambridge: Cambridge University Press.

Deissmann, G. A. 1903. *Bible Studies*. 2d ed. Edinburgh: T & T Clark.

Delekat, Lienhard. 1957. "Die Peschitta zu Jesaja zwischen Targum und Septuaginta." *Bib* 38:185–335.

———. 1958. "Ein Septuagintatargum." *VT* 8:225–52.

Denniston, J. D. 1950. *The Greek Particles*. 2d ed. Rev. K. J. Dover. Oxford: Oxford University Press.

Díez Macho, A. 1968–79. *Neophyti 1*. 6 Vols. Madrid and Barcelona: Consejo Superior de Investigaciones Científicas.

Díez Merino, Luis. 1994. "Targum Manuscripts and Critical Editions." *The Aramaic Bible: Targums in their Historical Context*. Ed. D. R. G. Beattie and M. J. McNamara, 51–91. JSOTSup 166. Sheffield: JSOT Press.

Dinter, P. E. 1980. "The Remnant of Israel and the Stone of Stumbling in Zion According to Paul (Romans 9–11)." Ph.D. diss., Union Theological Seminary.

———. 1983. "Paul and the Prophet Isaiah." *BTB* 13:48–52.

Dittmar, W. 1903. *Vetus testamentum in novo: Die alttestamentliche Parallelen des Neuen Testaments im Wortlaut der Urtexte und der Septuaginta*. Göttingen: Vandenhoeck and Ruprecht.

DJD I. 1955. *Qumran Cave I*. Ed. D. Barthélemy and J. T. Milik. Oxford: Clarendon.

DJD II. 1961. *Les Grottes de Murabba'ât*. Ed. P. Benoit, J. T. Milik, and R. de Vaux. Oxford: Clarendon.

DJD III. 1962. *Les 'Petites Grottes' de Qumrân: Exploration de la falaise. Les Grottes 2Q, 3Q, 5Q, 6Q, 7Q à 10Q. Le rouleau de cuivre*. Ed. M. Baillet, J. T. Milik, and R. de Vaux. Oxford: Clarendon.

DJD IV. 1965. *The Psalms Scroll of Qumrân Cave 11 (11QPsᵃ)*. Ed. J. A. Sanders. Oxford: Clarendon.

DJD V. 1968. *Qumrân Cave 4. I (4Q158–4Q186)*. Ed. J. M. Allegro. Oxford: Clarendon.

DJD VI. 1977. *Qumrân Cave 4. II.1. Archéologie*. Ed. R. de Vaux. *II.2. Tefillin, Mezuzot et Targums (4Q128–4Q157)*. Ed. J. T. Milik. Oxford: Clarendon.

DJD X. 1994. *Qumran Cave 4. V. Miqṣat Ma'aśe Ha-Torah*. Ed. E. Qimron and J. Strugnell. Oxford: Clarendon.

DJD XI. 1998. *Qumran Cave 4. VI. Poetical and Liturgical Texts, Part I*. Ed. C. Newsom, E. Schuller et al. Oxford: Clarendon.

DJD XIII. 1994. *Qumran Cave 4. VIII. Parabiblical Texts Part I*. Ed. J. VanderKam, E. Tov et al. Oxford: Clarendon.

DJD XIV. 1995. *Qumran Cave 4. IX. Deuteronomy, Joshua, Judges, Kings*. Ed. E. Ulrich, F. M. Cross et al. Oxford: Clarendon.

DJD XV. 1997. *Qumran Cave 4. X. The Prophets*. Ed. E. Ulrich, F. M. Cross et al. Oxford: Clarendon.

DJD XXIII. 1998. *Qumran Cave 11. II. 11Q2–18, 11Q20–31*. Ed. F. García Martínez, E. J. C. Tigchelaar, and A. S. van der Woude. Oxford: Clarendon.

Dodd, C. H. 1932. *The Epistle of Paul to the Romans*. MNTC. London: Hodder and Stoughton.

———. 1935. *The Bible and the Greeks*. London: Hodder & Stoughton.

——. 1952a. *According to the Scriptures: The Substructure of New Testament Theology.* London: Nisbet.

——. 1952b. *The Old Testament in the New.* London: Athlone.

van Dodewaard, J. A. E. 1955. "La force évocatrice de la citation mise en lumière en prenant pour base l'Évangile de S. Matthieu." *Bib* 36:482–91.

Dogniez, C. and M. Harl. 1992. *La Bible d'Alexandrie 5: Le Deutéronome.* Paris: Cerf.

Dombkowski Hopkins, Denise. 1981. "The Qumran Community and 1QHodayot: A Reassessment." *RevQ* 10:323–64.

Donaldson, T. L. 1983. "Parallels: Use, Misuse and Limitations." *EvQ* 55:193–210.

——. 1986. "The 'Curse of the Law' and the Inclusion of the Gentiles: Galatians 3:13–14." *NTS* 32:94–112.

——. 1993. "'Riches for the Gentiles' (Rom 11:12): Israel's Rejection and Paul's Gentile Mission." *JBL* 112:81–98.

——. 1997. *Paul and the Gentiles: Remapping the Apostle's Convictional World.* Minneapolis: Fortress.

Doty, William G. 1973. *Letters in Primitive Christianity.* Philadelphia: Fortress.

Duncan, Julie A. 1997. "Excerpted Texts of Deuteronomy at Qumran." *RevQ* 18:43–62.

Dunn, J. D. G. 1987. "'Righteousness from the Law' and 'Righteousness from Faith': Paul's Interpretation of Scripture in Romans 10:1–10." *Tradition and Intepretation in the New Testament.* FS E. E. Ellis. Ed. G. F. Hawthorne and O. Betz, 216–28. Grand Rapids: Eerdmans.

——. 1988a. *Romans 1–8.* WBC 38A. Dallas: Word.

——. 1988b. *Romans 9–16.* WBC 38B. Dallas: Word.

——. 1989. *Christology in the Making: A New Testament Inquiry into the Origins of the Doctrine of the Incarnation.* 2d ed. London: SCM.

——. 1998. *The Theology of Paul the Apostle.* Grand Rapids: Eerdmans.

Du Toit, Andrie B. 2000. "A Tale of Two Cities: 'Tarsus or Jerusalem' Revisited." *NTS* 46:375–402.

Ehrman, Bart D. 1993. *The Orthodox Corruption of Scripture: The Effect of Early Christological Controversies on the Text of the New Testament.* New York: Oxford.

Eisenbaum, Pamela M. 1997. *The Jewish Heroes of Christian History: Hebrews 11 in Literary Context.* SBLDS 156. Atlanta: Scholars.

Eisenman, R. H. and M. Wise. 1993. *The Dead Sea Scrolls Uncovered.* New York: Penguin.

Eißfeldt, Otto. 1966. "Die Umrahmung des Moseliedes Dtn 32,1–43 und des Mosesgesetzes Dtn 1–30 in Dtn 31,9–32,47." *Kleine Schriften III*, 322–34. Tübingen: Mohr-Siebeck.

Elledge, C. D. 2001. "A Graphic Index of Citation and Commentary Formulae in the Dead Sea Scrolls." In J. H. Charlesworth, ed. *The Dead Sea Scrolls: Hebrew, Aramaic, and Greek Texts with English Translations. Vol. 6B: Pesharim and Related Documents.* PTSDSSP. Tübingen: Mohr-Siebeck; Lousiville: Westminster/John Knox. Forthcoming.

Ellingworth, P. 1978. "Translation and Exegesis: A Case Study (Rom 9,22ff.)." *Bib* 59:396–402.

Elliott, J. K. 1981. "The Language and Style of the Concluding Doxology to the Epistle to the Romans." *ZNW* 72:124–30.

——. 1995. "Thoroughgoing Eclecticism in New Testament Textual Criticism." *The Text of the New Testament in Contemporary Research: Essays on the Status Quaestionis.* Ed. B. D. Ehrman and M. W. Holmes, 321–33. SD 46. Grand Rapids: Eerdmans.

Elliott, Mark Adam. 2000. *The Survivors of Israel: A Reconsideration of the Theology of Pre-Christian Judaism.* Grand Rapids: Eerdmans.

Elliott, Neil. 1990. *The Rhetoric of Romans: Argumentative Constraint and Strategy and Paul's Dialogue with Judaism.* JSNTSup 45. Sheffield: JSOT Press.

Ellis, E. Earle. 1957. *Paul's Use of the Old Testament.* Edinburgh: Oliver and Boyd; reprinted, Grand Rapids: Baker, 1981.

———. 1978. *Prophecy and Hermeneutic in Early Christianity*. WUNT 18. Tübingen: Mohr-Siebeck.

———. 1988. "Biblical Interpretation in the New Testament Church." *Mikra*. Ed. M. J. Mulder, 691–725. CRINT II/1. Assen: Van Gorcum/Philadelphia: Fortress.

Elwolde, John. 1997. "Distinguishing the Linguistic and the Exegetical: The Case of Numbers in the Bible and 11QTᵃ." *The Scrolls and the Scriptures: Qumran Fifty Years After*. Ed. S. E. Porter and C. A. Evans, 129–41. JSPSup 26. Sheffield: JSOT.

Emerton, J. A. 1982. "The Translation and Interpretation of Isaiah vi. 13." *Interpreting the Hebrew Bible*. Ed. J. A. Emerton and S. C. Reif, 85–118. Cambridge: Cambridge University Press.

Epp, E. J. 1991. "New Testament Papyrus Manuscripts and Letter Carrying in Greco-Roman Times." *The Future of Early Christianity*. FS H. Koester. Ed. Birger A. Pearson, 35–56. Minneapolis: Fortress.

Evans, Craig A. 1984a. "Paul and the Hermeneutics of 'True Prophecy': A Study of Romans 9–11." *Bib* 65:560–70.

———. 1984b. "1QIsaiahᵃ and the Absence of Prophetic Critique at Qumran." *RevQ* 11: 537–42.

———. 1985. "An Interpretation of Isa 8,11–15 Unemended." *ZAW* 97:112–13.

———. 1989. *To See and Not Perceive: Isaiah 6.9–10 in Early Jewish and Christian Interpretation*. JSOTSup 64. Sheffield: JSOT Press.

———. 1993. "Listening for Echoes of Interpreted Scripture." *Paul and the Scriptures of Israel*. Ed. C. A. Evans and J. A. Sanders, 47–51. JSNTSup 83/SSEJC 1. Sheffield: JSOT.

———. 1995. "Early Rabbinic Sources and Jesus Research." *SBLSP*, 53–76.

———. 1997. "David in the Dead Sea Scrolls." *The Scrolls and the Scriptures: Qumran Fifty Years After*. Ed. S. E. Porter and C. A. Evans, 183–97. JSPSup 26. Sheffield: JSOT.

———, ed. 2000. *The Interpretation of Scripture in Early Judaism and Christianity: Studies in Language and Tradition*. JSPSup 33/SSEJC 7. Sheffield: Sheffield Academic Press.

Evans, Craig A. and James A. Sanders, eds. 1993. *Paul and the Scriptures of Israel*. JSNTSup 83/SSEJC 1. Sheffield: JSOT.

———, eds. 1997. *Early Christian Interpretation of the Scriptures of Israel: Investigations and Proposals*. JSNTSup 148/SSEJC 5. Sheffield: Sheffield Academic Press.

———, eds. 1998. *The Function of Scripture in Early Jewish and Christian Tradition*. JSNTSup 154/SSEJC 6. Sheffield: Sheffield Academic Press.

Evans, Craig A. and W. Richard Stegner, eds. 1994. *The Gospels and the Scriptures of Israel*. JSNTSup 104/SSEJC 3. Sheffield: Sheffield Academic Press.

Falk, D. K. 1997. *Daily, Sabbath and Festival Prayer in the Dead Sea Scrolls*. STDJ 27. Leiden: Brill.

Feeney, Denis. 1995. "Criticism Ancient and Modern." *Ethics and Rhetoric*. Ed. D. Innes et al., 301–12. Oxford: Clarendon.

Fekkes, Jan, III. 1994. *Isaiah and Prophetic Traditions in the Book of Revelation: Visionary Antecedents and their Development*. JSNTSup 93. Sheffield: JSOT.

Feldman, L. H. 1993. *Jew and Gentile in the Ancient World: Attitudes and Interactions from Alexander to Justinian*. Princeton: Princeton University Press.

Fiedler, Martin J. 1970. "Δικαιοσύνη in der diaspora-jüdischen und intertestamentarischen Literatur." *JSJ* 1:120–43.

Field, Fridericus. 1964. *Origenis hexaplorum quae supersunt sive veterum interpretum graecorum in totum vetus testamentum fragmenta*. 2 vols. Hildesheim: Georg Olms.

Fischer, Johann. 1929. "Das Problem des Neuen Exodus in Isaias c. 40–55." *Theologische Quartalschrift* 110:111–30.

———. 1930. *In welcher Schrift lag das Buch Isaias den LXX vor? Eine textkritische Studie*. BZAW 56. Giessen: Töpelmann.

Fishbane, Michael. 1977a. "The Qumran Pesher and Traits of Ancient Hermeneutics." *Proceedings of the Sixth World Congress of Jewish Studies*. Vol. I, 97–114. Jerusalem: World Union of Jewish Studies.

———. 1977b. "Torah and Tradition." *Tradition and Theology in the Old Testament*. Ed. D. A. Knight, 275–300. Philadelphia: Fortress.

———. 1979a. "The 'Eden' Motif/The Landscape of Spatial Renewal." *Text and Texture: Close Readings of Selected Biblical Texts*, 111–120. New York: Shocken.

———. 1979b. "The 'Exodus' Motif/The Paradigm of Historical Renewal." *Text and Texture: Close Readings of Selected Biblical Texts*, 121–140. New York: Shocken.

———. 1980. "Revelation and Tradition: Aspects of Inner-biblical Exegesis." *JBL* 99:343–61.

———. 1982. "Jewish Biblical Exegesis: Presuppositions and Principles." *Scripture in the Jewish and Christian Traditions: Authority, Interpretation, Relevance*. Ed. F. E. Greenspahn, 92–110. Nashville: Abingdon.

———. 1985. *Biblical Interpretation in Ancient Israel*. Oxford: Oxford University Press.

———. 1989. *The Garments of Torah: Essays in Biblical Hermeneutics*. Indiana Studies in Biblical Literature. Bloomington: Indiana University Press.

———. 1998. *The Exegetical Imagination: On Jewish Thought and Theology*. Cambridge: Harvard University Press.

Fisk, Bruce N. 1997. "Retelling Israel's Story: Scripture, Exegesis and Transformation in Pseudo-Philo's *Liber Antiquitatum Biblicarum* 12–24." Ph.D. diss., Duke University.

Fitzmyer, Joseph A. 1957. "'4QTestimonia' and the New Testament." *TS* 18:513–37; reprinted in *Essays in the Semitic Background of the New Testament*, 59–89. London: Geoffrey Chapman, 1971.

———. 1960–61. "The Use of Explicit Old Testament Quotations in Qumran Literature and in the New Testament." *NTS* 7:297–333; reprinted in *Essays in the Semitic Background of the New Testament*, 3–58. London: Geoffrey Chapman, 1971.

———. 1967. "Further Light on Melchizedek from Qumran Cave 11." JBL 86:25–41; reprinted in *Essays in the Semitic Background of the New Testament*, 245–67. London: Geoffrey Chapman, 1971.

———. 1993. *Romans*. AB 33. New York: Doubleday.

Flamming, J. 1968. "The New Testament Use of Isaiah." *SWJT* 11:89–103.

Flint, Peter W. 1997. *The Dead Sea Psalms Scrolls and the Book of Psalms*, 228–36. STDJ 17. Leiden: Brill.

———. 1998. "The Contribution of the Cave 4 Psalms Scrolls to the Psalms Debate." *DSD* 5:320–33.

Fowl, S. E. 1990. *The Story of Christ in the Ethics of Paul: An Analysis of the Function of the Hymnic Material in the Pauline Corpus*. JSNTSup 36. Sheffield: JSOT.

Fowl, S. E. and L. G. Jones. 1991. *Reading in Communion*. Grand Rapids: Eerdmans.

Fox, Michael. 1980. "The Identification of Quotations in Biblical Literature." *ZAW* 92:416–31.

Fraade, S. 1991. *From Tradition to Commentary: Torah and Its Interpretation in the Midrash Sifre to Deuteronomy*. SUNY Series in Judaica. Albany: SUNY Press.

Fredriksen, Paula. 1988. *From Jesus to Christ: The Origins of the New Testament Images of Jesus*. New Haven: Yale University Press.

———. 1991. "Judaism, the Circumcision of Gentiles, and Apocalyptic Hope: Another Look at Galatians 1 and 2." *JTS* 42:532–64.

Frid, Bo. 1983. "Jesaja und Paulus in Röm 15,12." *BZ* 27:237–41.

Frymer-Kensky, Tikva, et al. ed. 2000. *Christianity in Jewish Terms*. Boulder, CO: Westview Press.

Gager, John G. 2000. *Reinventing Paul*. Oxford: Oxford University Press.

Gamble, Harry Y. 1977. *The Textual History of the Letter to the Romans*. SD 42. Grand Rapids: Eerdmans.

———. 1990. "The Pauline Corpus and the Early Christian Book." *Paul and the Legacies of Paul.* Ed. W. Babcock, 265–80. Dallas: Southern Methodist University Press.

———. 1995. *Books and Readers in the Early Church.* New Haven: Yale University Press.

García Martínez, F. and E. J. C. Tigchelaar. 1997–98. *The Dead Sea Scrolls Study Edition.* 2 Vols. Leiden: Brill.

Gelston, A., ed. 1980. "Dodekapropheton." *The Old Testament in Syriac According to the Peshiṭta Version 3.4: Dodekapropheton—Daniel-Bel-Draco.* Peshiṭta Institute. Leiden: Brill.

Gerhardsson, B. 1961. *Memory and Manuscript: Oral Tradition and Written Transmission in Rabbinic Judaism and Early Christianity.* ASNU 22. Lund: Gleerup.

———. 1964. *Tradition and Transmission in Early Christianity.* ConNT 20. Lund: Gleerup.

Gertner, M. 1962. "Midrashim in the NT." *JSS* 7:267–92.

Gignac, Alain. 1999. "La Bonne Nouvelle d'Ésaïe au service de l'Évangile de Paul. Rm 10,14–17 comme relecture de Es 52,6–53,1." *SR* 28:345–61.

Gill, D. H. 1974. "ΤΡΑΠΕΖΟΜΕΤΑ: A Neglected Aspect of Greek Sacrifice." *HTR* 67:117–37.

Gillespie, T. W. 1994. *The First Theologians: A Study in Early Christian Prophecy.* Grand Rapids: Eerdmans.

Given, Mark D. 1999. "Restoring the Inheritance in Romans 11:1." *JBL* 118:89–96.

González Luis, J. 1981. "La versión de Símaco a los Profetas Mayores." Ph.D. diss., Universidad Complutense de Madrid.

Goodman, M. D. 1994a. *Mission and Conversion: Proselytizing in the Religious History of the Roman Empire.* New York: Oxford University Press.

———. 1994b. "Texts, Scribes and Power in Roman Judaea." *Literacy and Power in the Ancient World.* Ed. A. K. Bowman and G. Woolf, 99–108. Cambridge: Cambridge University Press.

Goodwin, W. W. 1892. *Syntax of the Moods and Tenses of the Greek Verb.* 5th ed. London: Macmillan.

Gordis, R. 1949. "Quotations as Literary Usage in Biblical, Oriental, and Rabbinic Literature." *HUCA* 22:157–219.

Gordon, R. P. 1978. "The Targumists as Eschatologists." *Congress Volume: Göttingen 1977,* 113–30. VTSup 29. Leiden: Brill.

———. 1992. "The Interpretation of 'Lebanon' and 4Q285." *JJS* 43:92–94.

Gordon, T. David. 1992. "Why Israel Did Not Obtain Torah-Righteousness: A Translation Note on Rom 9:32." *WTJ* 54:163–66.

Goshen-Gottstein, M. H. 1953. "Bible Quotations in the Sectarian Dead Sea Scrolls." *VT* 3:79–82.

———. 1954. "Die Jesaia-Rolle im Lichte von Peschitta und Targum." *Bib* 35:51–71.

———. 1963. "Theory and Practice of Textual Criticism: The Text-critical Use of the Septuagint." *Textus* 3:130–58.

———. 1991. "Exercises in Targum and Peshitta I." *Textus* 16:117–25.

———, ed. 1995. *The Book of Isaiah.* The Hebrew University Bible. Jerusalem: Magnes Press.

Gosse, B. 1991. "Isaïe 52,13–53,12 et Isaïe 6." *RB* 98:537–43.

Gowan, D. E. 1977. "The Exile in Jewish Apocalyptic." *Scripture in History and Theology.* Ed. A. L. Merrill and T. W. Overholt, 205–23. PTMS 17. Pittsburgh: Pickwick.

Graham, William. 1987. *Beyond the Written Word: Oral Aspects of Scripture in the History of Religion.* Cambridge: Cambridge University Press.

Green, R. P. H. ed. and trans. 1995. *Augustine: De Doctrina Christiana.* Oxford: Clarendon.

Greenspoon, L. 1998. "The Dead Sea Scrolls and the Greek Bible." *The Dead Sea Scrolls after Fifty Years, Volume I.* Ed. P. W. Flint and J. C. VanderKam, 101–27. Leiden: Brill.

Grieb, A. K. 1993. "The Root of Jesse Who Rises to Rule the Gentiles: Paul's Use of the Story of Jesus in Romans 15:7–13." *Proceedings: Eastern Great Lakes and Midwest Biblical Societies* 13:71–88.

Guelich, R. A. 1989. *Mark 1–8:26.* WBC 34A. Dallas: Word.

Guerra, A. J. 1995. *Romans and the Apologetic Tradition: The Purpose, Genre and Audience of Paul's Letter*. SNTSMS 81. Cambridge: Cambridge University Press.

Gundry, Robert H. 1967. *The Use of the Old Testament in St. Matthew's Gospel*. NovTSup 18. Leiden: Brill.

Gundry-Volf, J. M. 1990. *Paul and Perseverence*. WUNT 2.37. Tübingen: Mohr-Siebeck.

Hafemann, S. J. 1990. *Suffering and Ministry in the Spirit: Paul's Defense of His Ministry in II Corinthians 2:14–3:3*. Grand Rapids: Eerdmans.

Hahn, Ferdinand. 1965. *Mission in the New Testament*. SBT 47. London: SCM.

———. 1982. "Zum Verständnis von Römer 11.26a: '. . . und so wird ganz Israel gerettet werden.'" *Paul and Paulinism: Essays in Honour of C. K. Barrett*. Ed. M. D. Hooker and S. G. Wilson, 221–36. London: SPCK.

Hanhart, R. 1983. "Die Septuaginta als Interpretation und Aktualisierung: Jesaja 9:1(8:23)–7(6)." *Isac Leo Seeligmann Volume, Vol III: Non-Hebrew Section*, 331–46. Jerusalem: Rubinstein's Publishing House.

———. 1984. "Die Bedeutung der Septuaginta in neutestamentlicher Zeit," *ZTK* 81:395–416.

———. 1992. "The Translation of the Septuagint in Light of Earlier Tradition and Subsequent Influences." *Septuagint, Scrolls and Cognate Writings*. Ed. George J. Brooke and Barnabas Lindars, 339–79. Atlanta: Scholars.

Hanson, A.T. 1963. *Paul's Understanding of Jesus*. Hull: University of Hull.

———. 1973. "The Oracle in Romans 11:4." *NTS* 19:300–302.

———. 1974. *Studies in Paul's Technique and Theology*. London: SPCK.

———. 1980. *The New Testament Interpretation of Scripture*. London: SPCK.

———. 1981. "Vessels of Wrath or Instruments of Wrath? Romans IX.22–3." *JTS* 32:433–43.

Harding, Mark. 1998. "The Salvation of Israel and the Logic of Romans 11:11–36." *AusBR* 46:55–69.

Harl, Marguerite. 1993. "Le grand cantique de Moïse en Deutéronome 32: Quelques traits originaux de la version grecque des Septante." *Rashi 1040–1990: Hommage à Ephraïm E. Urbach*. Ed. G. Sed-Rajna, 183–201. Paris: Cerf.

von Harnack, Adolf. 1928. "Das Alte Testament in das paulinischen Briefen und in den paulinischen Gemeinden." *Sitzungsberichte der Preussischen Akademie der Wissenschaften 1928. Philosophisch-Historische Klasse*. Berlin: Verlag der Akademie der Wissenschaften, 124–41; ET, "The Old Testament in the Pauline Letters and in the Pauline Churches." *Understanding Paul's Ethics: Twentieth Century Approaches*. Ed. Brian S. Rosner, 27–49. Grand Rapids: Eerdmans, 1995.

Harner, P. B. 1967. "Creation Faith in Deutero-Isaiah." *VT* 17:298–306.

Harper, W. R. 1905. *Amos and Hosea*. ICC. Edinburgh: T & T Clark.

Harrington, D. J. 1992. *Paul on the Mystery of Israel (Rom 11:25–32)*. Collegeville, MN: Liturgical Press.

Harris, J. Rendel. 1916–20. *Testimonies*. 2 Vols. Cambridge: Cambridge University Press.

Harris, William V. 1989. *Ancient Literacy*. Cambridge: Harvard University Press.

Hartung, Matthias. 1999. "Die kultische bzw. agrartechnisch-biologische Logik der Gleichnisse von der Teighebe und vom Ölbaum in Röm 11.16–24 und die sich daraus ergebenden theologischen Konsequenzen." *NTS* 45:127–40.

Harvey, Graham. 1996. *The True Israel: Uses of the Names Jew, Hebrew, and Israel in Ancient Jewish and Early Christian Literature*. AGJU 35. Leiden: Brill.

Hasel, G. F. 1962. "Remnant," *IDBSup*, 735–36.

———. 1974. *The Remnant: The History and Theology of the Remnant Idea from Genesis to Isaiah*. AUSS 5. 2d ed. Berrien Springs, MI: Andrews University Press.

Hatch, Edwin. 1889a. "On Early Quotations from the Septuagint." *Essays in Biblical Greek*, 131–202. Oxford: Clarendon.

———. 1889b. "On Composite Quotations from the Septuagint." *Essays in Biblical Greek*, 203–14. Oxford: Clarendon.

Hay, David M. 1993. *Pauline Theology II: 1 & 2 Corinthians*. Minneapolis: Fortress.

Hay, David M. and E. Elizabeth Johnson, eds. 1995. *Pauline Theology III: Romans.* Minneapolis: Fortress.

Hays, Richard B. 1983. *The Faith of Jesus Christ: An Investigation of the Narrative Substructure of Galatians 3:1–4:11.* SBLDS 56. Chico, CA: Scholars.

——. 1985. "'Have We Found Abraham to be Our Forefather According to the Flesh?' A Reconsideration of Rom 4:1." *NovT* 27:76–98.

——. 1989. *Echoes of Scripture in the Letters of Paul.* New Haven: Yale University Press.

——. 1991. "Crucified with Christ: A Synthesis of the Theology of 1 and 2 Thessalonians, Philemon, Philippians, and Galatians." *Pauline Theology, Vol. I: Thessalonians, Philippians, Galatians, Philemon.* Ed. J. M. Bassler, 227–46. Minneapolis: Fortress.

——. 1992. "Justification." *ABD* 3:1129–33.

——. 1993a. "Christ Prays the Psalms: Paul's Use of an Early Christian Exegetical Convention." *The Future of Christology.* FS L. E. Keck. Ed. A. J. Malherbe and W. A. Meeks, 122–36. Minneapolis: Fortress.

——. 1993b. "On the Rebound: A Response to Critiques of *Echoes of Scripture in the Letters of Paul.*" *Paul and the Scriptures of Israel.* Ed. C. A. Evans and J. A. Sanders, 72–96. JSNTSup 83/SSEJC 1. Sheffield: JSOT.

——. 1994. "Eschatology and Ethics in 1 Corinthians." *Ex Auditu* 10:31–43.

——. 1995. "Adam, Israel, Christ: The Question of Covenant in the Theology of Romans," *Pauline Theology III: Romans.* Ed. D. M. Hay and E. E. Johnson, 68–86. Minneapolis: Fortress.

——. 1996a. *The Moral Vision of the New Testament: Community, Cross, New Creation.* San Francisco: HarperSanFrancisco.

——. 1996b. "The Role of Scripture in Paul's Ethics." *Theology and Ethics in Paul and His Interpreters.* FS V. P. Furnish. Ed. E. H. Lovering, Jr. and Jerry L. Sumney, 30–47. Nashville: Abingdon.

——. 1997. *First Corinthians.* IBC. Louisville: Westminster/John Knox.

——. 1998. "'Who Has Believed Our Message?' Paul's Reading of Isaiah." *SBLSP*, 205–25.

——. 1999. "The Conversion of the Imagination: Scripture and Eschatology in 1 Corinthians." *NTS* 45:391–412.

Hengel, M. 1991. *The Pre-Christian Paul.* Philadelphia: TPI.

Hickling, C. J. A. 1980. "Paul's Reading of Isaiah." *Studia Biblica 1978. III. Papers on Paul and Other New Testament Authors.* Ed. E. A. Livingstone, 215–23. JSNTSup 3. Sheffield: JSOT Press.

Hiebert, Robert. 1989. *The "Syrohexaplaric" Psalter.* SBLSCS 27. Atlanta: Scholars.

Hodgson, Robert. 1979. "The Testimony Hypothesis." *JBL* 98:361–78.

Hollander, John. 1981. *The Figure of Echo: A Mode of Allusion in Milton and After.* Berkeley: University of California Press.

Holm-Nielsen, Svend. 1960. *Hodayot: Psalms from Qumran.* ATDan 2. Aarhus: Universitetsforlaget.

——. 1977. "Die Psalmen Salomos." *Poetische Schriften.* Ed. W. G. Kümmel, 49–112. Jüdische Schriften aus hellenistisch-römischer Zeit 4.2. Gütersloh: Gütersloher Verlagshaus Gerd Mohn.

Holmes, A. R. and J. Parsons. 1798–1827. *Vetus Testamentum Graecum cum Variis Lectionibus.* 5 Vols. Oxford: Clarendon.

Holmes, Michael W. 1995. "Reasoned Eclecticism in New Testament Textual Criticism." *The Text of the New Testament in Contemporary Research.* Ed. B. D. Ehrman and M. W. Holmes, 336–60. SD 46. Grand Rapids: Eerdmans.

Holtz, T. 1966. "Zum Selbstverständnis des Apostels Paulus." *TLZ* 91:321–30.

——. 1990. "The Judgment on the Jews and the Salvation of All Israel: 1 Thes 2,15–16 and Rom 11,25–26." *The Thessalonian Correspondence.* Ed. R. F. Collins, 284–94. BETL 87. Leuven: Leuven University Press.

Hooker, Morna D. 1959. *Jesus and the Servant: The Influence of the Servant Concept of Deutero-Isaiah in the New Testament.* London: SPCK.

———. 1971. "Interchange in Christ." *JTS* 22:349–61.

———. 1982. "Paul and Covenantal Nomism." *Paul and Paulinism*. Ed. M. D. Hooker and S. G. Wilson, 47–56. London: SPCK.

———. 1990. *From Adam to Christ: Essays on Paul*. Cambridge: Cambridge University Press.

———. 1991. *A Commentary on the Gospel According to Saint Mark*. BNTC. Peabody, MA: Hendrickson.

———. 1998. "Did the Use of Isaiah 53 to Interpret His Mission Begin with Jesus?" *Jesus and the Suffering Servant: Isaiah 53 and Christian Origins*. Ed. W. H. Bellinger, Jr. and W. R. Farmer, 88–103. Harrisburg, PA: Trinity Press International.

Horgan, M. P. 1979. *Pesharim: Qumran Interpretations of Biblical Books*. CBQMS 8. Washington, DC: Catholic Biblical Association of America.

Horton, Fred L. 1971. "Formulas of Introduction in the Qumran Literature." *RevQ* 7:505–14.

Howard, G. E. 1969. "Christ the End of the Law: The Meaning of Romans 10:4ff." *JBL* 88:331–37.

Hübner, Hans. 1984. *Gottes Ich und Israel: zum Schriftgebrauch des Paulus in Römer 9–11*. FRLANT 136. Göttingen: Vandenhoeck and Ruprecht.

———. 1991. "Intertextualität—die hermeneutische Strategie des Paulus." *TLZ* 116: 881–98.

———. 1993. *Biblische Theologie des Neuen Testaments: Band 2: Die Theologie des Paulus*. Göttingen: Vandenhoeck & Ruprecht.

———. 1997. *Vetus Testamentum in Novo. Band 2: Corpus Paulinum*. Göttingen: Vandenhoeck & Ruprecht.

Huebsch, R. W. 1981. "The Understanding and Significance of the 'Remnant' Motif in Qumran Literature: Including a Discussion of the Use of this Concept in the Hebrew Bible, the Apocrypha and the Pseudepigrapha." Ph.D. diss., McMaster University.

Hultgren, Arland J. 1985. *Paul's Gospel and Mission: The Outlook from His Letter to the Romans*. Philadelphia: Fortress.

Hulton, A. O. 1957. "ʾAN with the Future: A Note." *ClQ* NS 7:139–42.

Hurst, L. D. 1990. *The Epistle to the Hebrews: Its Background of Thought*. SNTSMS 65. Cambridge: Cambridge University Press.

Hurtado, Larry W. 1981. "The Doxology at the End of Romans." *New Testament Textual Criticism: Its Significance for Exegesis*. FS B. M. Metzger. Ed. E. J. Epp and G. D. Fee, 185–99. New York: Oxford.

Hvalvik, R. 1990. "A 'Sonderweg' for Israel: A Critical Examination of a Current Interpretation of Romans 11.25–27." *JSNT* 38:87–107.

———. 1996. *The Struggle for Scripture and Covenant: The Purpose of the Epistle of Barnabas and Jewish-Christian Competition in the Second Century*. WUNT 2.82. Tübingen: Mohr-Siebeck.

Instone Brewer, D. 1992. *Techniques and Assumptions in Jewish Exegesis Before 70 CE*. Texte und Studien zum antiken Judentum 30. Tübingen: Mohr-Siebeck.

Irwin, William H. 1977. *Isaiah 28–33: Translation with Philological Notes*. BibOr 30. Rome: Pontifical Biblical Institute Press.

Iser, Wolfgang. 1974. *The Implied Reader: Patterns of Communication in Prose Fiction from Bunyan to Beckett*. Baltimore: Johns Hopkins University Press.

Jacobson, Howard. 1996. *A Commentary on Pseudo-Philo's* Liber Antiquitatem Biblicarum, *with Latin Text and English Translation*. 2 Vols. AGJU 31. Leiden: Brill.

Jaffee, Martin S. 1992. "How Much 'Orality' in Oral Torah? New Perspectives on the Composition and Transmission of Early Rabbinic Tradition." *Shofar* 10:53–72.

———. 1994. "Writing and Rabbinic Oral Tradition: On Mishnaic Narrative, Lists and Mnemonics." *Journal of Jewish Thought and Philosophy* 4:123–46.

———. 1995. "Figuring Early Rabbinic Literary Culture: Thoughts Occasioned by Boomershine and J. Dewey." *Orality and Textuality in Early Christian Literature*, 67–73. Semeia 65. Atlanta: Scholars.

Janowski, Bernd and Peter Stuhlmacher, eds. 1996. *Der leidende Gottesknecht: Jesaja 53 und seine Wirkungsgechichte*. Forschungen zum Alten Testament 14. Tübingen: Mohr-Siebeck.

Jay, Nancy B. 1992. *Throughout Your Generations Forever: Sacrifice, Religion, and Paternity*. Chicago: University of Chicago Press.

Jellicoe, Sidney. 1993. *The Septuagint and Modern Study*. Winona Lake, IN: Eisenbrauns; orig. pub. Oxford: Clarendon, 1968.

Jenson, Robert. 1999. "Toward a Christian Theology of Israel." *Reflections* 3:2–21. Princeton: Center of Theological Inquiry.

Jeremias, J. 1958. *Jesus' Promise to the Nations*. London: SCM.

Jervell, J. 1991. "The Letter to Jerusalem." *The Romans Debate*. Ed. K. P. Donfried, 53–64. Rev. ed. Peabody, Mass: Hendrickson.

Jervis, L. A. 1991. *The Purpose of Romans: A Comparative Letter Structure Investigation*. JSNTSup 55. Sheffield: JSOT.

Jewett, Robert. 1982. "Romans as an Ambassadorial Letter." *Int* 36:5–20.

———. 1988. "Paul, Phoebe, and the Spanish Mission." *The Social World of Formative Christianity and Judaism*. FS H. C. Kee. Ed. J. Neusner et al., 142–61. Philadelphia: Fortress.

———. 1995. "Ecumenical Theology for the Sake of Mission: Romans 1:1–17+ 15:14–16:24." *Pauline Theology, Volume III: Romans*. Ed. D. M. Hay and E. E. Johnson, 89–108. Minneapolis: Fortress.

Johnson, E. Elizabeth. 1989. *The Function of Apocalyptic and Wisdom Traditions in Romans 9–11*. SBLDS 109. Atlanta: Scholars.

Johnson, E. Elizabeth and D. M. Hay, eds. 1997. *Pauline Theology IV: Looking Back, Pressing On*. SBL Symposium Series 4. Atlanta: Scholars.

Johnson, F. 1896. *The Quotations of the New Testament from the Old Considered in the Light of General Literature*. Philadelphia: American Baptist Publication Society.

Johnson, Luke Timothy. 1997. *Reading Romans*. New York: Crossroad.

Jones, D. 1955. "The Traditio of the Oracles of Isaiah of Jerusalem." *ZAW* 67:226–46.

de Jonge, M. and A. S. van der Woude. 1965–66. "11Q Melchizedek and the New Testament." *NTS* 12:301–26.

Joüon, P. and T. Muraoka. 1993. *A Grammar of Biblical Hebrew*. 2 Vols. Subsidia Biblica 14. Rome: Pontifical Biblical Institute Press.

Jowett, B. 1859. "On the Quotations from the Old Testament in the Writings of St. Paul." *The Epistles of St. Paul to the Thessalonians, Galatians, Romans. With Critical Notes and Dissertations*. Vol. I, 401–16. London: John Murray.

Juel, Donald. 1988. *Messianic Exegesis: Christological Interpretation of the Old Testament in Early Christianity*. Philadelphia: Fortress.

———. 1994. *A Master of Surprise: Mark Interpreted*. Minneapolis: Fortress.

Kaiser, O. 1974. *Isaiah 13–39*. OTL. Philadelphia: Westminster.

Karris, R. J. 1991. "Romans 14:1–15:13 and the Occasion of Romans." *The Romans Debate*. Ed. K. P. Donfried, 65–85. Rev. ed. Peabody, MA: Hendrickson.

Käsemann, Ernst. 1969. "The Righteousness of God in Paul." *New Testament Questions of Today*, 168–82. Philadelphia: Fortress.

———. 1971. "Justification and Salvation History in the Epistle to the Romans." *Perspectives on Paul*, 60–78. Philadelphia: Fortress.

———. 1980. *Commentary on Romans*. Grand Rapids: Eerdmans.

Katz, P. and J. Ziegler. 1958. "Ein Aquila-Index in Vorbereitung." *VT* 8:264–85.

Kaufman, S. A. 1973. "The Job Targum from Qumran." *JAOS* 93:317–217.

Kautzsch, E. F. 1869. *De Veteris Testamenti Locis a Paulo Apostolo Allegatis*. Leipzig: Metzger and Wittig.

Kaye, B. N. 1976. " 'To the Romans and Others' Revisited." *NovT* 18:37–77.

Keck, L. E. 1977. "The Function of Romans 3:10–18—Observations and Suggestions." *God's Christ and His People*. FS N. A. Dahl. Ed. J. Jervell and W. A. Meeks, 141–57. Oslo: Universitetsforlaget.

——. 1990. "Christology, Soteriology, and the Praise of God (Romans 15:7–13)." *The Conversation Continues*. FS J. L. Martyn. Ed. R. T. Fortna and B. R. Gaventa, 85–97. Nashville: Abingdon.

Keesmaat, Sylvia C. 1994a. "Exodus and the Intertextual Transformation of Tradition in Romans 8:14–30." *JSNT* 54:29–56.

——. 1994b. "Paul's Use of the Exodus Tradition in Romans and Galatians." D. Phil. diss., Oxford University.

Keller, Winfrid. 1998. *Gottes Treue, Israels Heil: Röm 11, 25–27: die These vom "Sonderweg" in der Diskussion*. SBB 40. Stuttgart: Katholisches Biblewerk.

Kenyon, F. G. 1951. *Books and Readers in Ancient Greece and Rome*. 2d ed. Oxford: Clarendon.

Kerrigan, Alexander. 1963. "Echoes of Themes from the Servant Songs in Pauline Theology." *Studiorum Paulinorum Congressus Internationalis Catholicus 1961*, 2:217–28. AnBib 18. Rome: Pontifical Biblical Institute Press.

Kertelge, K. 1971. *"Rechtfertigung" bei Paulus*. 2d ed. Münster: Aschendorff.

Kilpatrick, G. D. 1980. "The Text of the Epistles: The Contribution of the Western Witnesses." *Text-Wort-Glaube*. FS K. Aland. Ed. M. Brecht, 47–68. Arbeiten zur Kirchengeschichte 50. Berlin: de Gruyter.

Kim, Johann D. 2000. *God, Israel, and the Gentiles: Rhetoric and Situation in Romans 9–11*. SBLDS 176. Atlanta: Society of Biblical Literature.

Kim, S. 1984. *The Origin of Paul's Gospel*. WUNT 2.4. Tübingen, 1981; 2d ed.

——. 1997. "The 'Mystery' of Rom 11.25–6 Once More." *NTS* 43:412–29.

Klein, G. 1991. "Paul's Purpose in Writing the Epistle to the Romans." *The Romans Debate*. Ed. K. P. Donfried, 29–43. Rev. ed. Peabody, MA: Hendrickson.

Knibb, M. A. 1976. "The Exile in the Literature of the Intertestamental Period." *HeyJ* 17:253–72.

——. 1983. "Exile in the Damascus Document." *JSOT* 25:99–117.

——. 1996. "Isaianic Traditions in the Book of Enoch." *After the Exile: Essays in Honour of Rex Mason*. Ed. J. Barton and D. J. Reimer, 217–29. Macon: Mercer University Press.

Knox, John. 1964. "Romans 15.14–33 and Paul's Conception of His Apostolic Mission." *JBL* 83:1–11.

Kobelski, P. J. 1981. *Melchizedek and Melchireša'*. CBQMS 10. Washington, DC: Catholic Biblical Association of America.

Koch, Dietrich-Alex. 1986. *Die Schrift als Zeuge des Evangeliums: Untersuchungen zur Verwendung und zum Verständnis der Schrift bei Paulus*. BHT 69. Tübingen: Mohr-Siebeck.

Koenig, Jean. 1982. *L'herméneutique analogique du judaïsme antique d'après les témoins textuels d'Isaïe*. VTSup 33. Leiden: Brill.

van der Kooij, Arie. 1981. *Die alten Textzeugen des Jesajabuches. Ein Beitrag zur Textgeschichte des Alten Testaments*. OBO 35. Göttingen: Vandenhoeck and Ruprecht.

——. 1986. "Accident or Method? On 'Analogical' Interpretation in the Old Greek of Isaiah and in 1QIsᵃ." *BibOr* 43:366–76.

——. 1988. "*1QIsᵃ* Col. VIII, 4–11 (Isa 8, 11–18): A Contextual Approach of Its Variants." *RevQ* 13:569–81.

——. 1989. "The Septuagint of Isaiah: Translation and Interpretation." *The Book of Isaiah*. Ed. J. Vermeylen, 127–33. BETL 81. Leuven: Leuven University Press.

——. 1992. "The Old Greek of Isaiah in Relation to the Qumran Texts of Isaiah: Some General Comments." *Septuagint, Scrolls and Cognate Writings*. Ed. George J. Brooke and Barnabas Lindars, 195–213. Atlanta: Scholars.

——. 1997a. "Isaiah in the Septuagint." *Writing and Reading the Scroll of Isaiah: Studies of an Interpretive Tradition*. 2 Vols. Ed. C. G. Broyles and C. A. Evans, 2:513–29. VTSup 70. Leiden: Brill.

——. 1997b. "'The Servant of the Lord': A Particular Group of Jews in Egypt According to the Old Greek of Isaiah. Some Comments on LXX Isa 49,1–6 and

Related Passages." *Studies in the Book of Isaiah*. FS W. A. M. Beuken. Ed. J. van Ruiten and M. Vervenne, 383–96. BETL 132. Leuven: Leuven University Press.
———. 1997c. "Zur Theologie des Jesajabuches in der Septuaginta." *Theologische Probleme der Septuaginta und der hellenistischen Hermeneutik*. Ed. H. G. Reventlow, 9–25. Gütersloh: Chr Kaiser/Gütersloher.
Kraabel, A. T. 1987. "Unity and Diversity among Diaspora Synagogues." *The Synagogue in Late Antiquity*. Ed. Lee I. Levine, 49–60. Philadelphia: ASOR.
Kraft, Robert A. 1960. "Barnabas' Isaiah Text and the 'Testimony Book' Hypothesis." *JBL* 79:336–50.
———. 1961. "Barnabas' Isaiah Text and Melito's Paschal Homily." *JBL* 80:371–73.
Kraftchick, S. J. 1993. "Seeking a More Fluid Model." *Pauline Theology III: 1 & 2 Corinthians*. Ed. D. M. Hay, 18–34. Minneapolis: Fortress.
Kraus, H.-J. 1993. *Psalms 60–150*. Continental Commentary. Minneapolis: Fortress.
Kugel, James L. 1990. *In Potiphar's House: The Interpretive Life of Biblical Texts*. Cambridge: Harvard University Press.
———. 1998. *Traditions of the Bible: A Guide to the Bible as It Was at the Start of the Common Era*. Cambridge: Harvard University Press.
Kugel, James L. and Rowan A. Greer. 1986. *Early Biblical Interpretation*. Library of Early Christianity 3. Philadelphia: Westminster.
Kutscher, E. Y. 1974. *The Language and Linguistic Background of the Isaiah Scroll (1QIsaᵃ)*. STDJ 6. Leiden: Brill.
Kuyper, L. J. 1977. "Righteousness and Salvation." *SJT* 30:233–52.
Laberge, Léo. 1968. "Isaïe 28–33. Étude de tradition textuelle, d'après la Pešiṭto, le texte de Qumrân, la Septante et le texte massorétique." Ph.D. diss., Université Saint-Paul, Ottawa.
———. 1978. *La Septante d'Isaïe 28–33. Étude de tradition textuelle*. Ottawa: By the author.
Labuschagne, C. J. 1971. "The Song of Moses: Its Framework and Structure." *De Fructu Oris Sui*. Ed. I. H. Eybers et al., 85–98. Pretoria Oriental Series 9; Leiden: Brill.
———. 1997. "The Setting of the Song of Moses in Deuteronomy." *Deuteronomy and Deuteronomic Literature*. Ed. M. Vervenne and J. Lust, 111–29. BETL 133. Leuven: Leuven University Press.
de Lagarde, P. 1967. *Prophetae Chaldaice, e fide codicis reuchliniani*. Osnabrück: O. Zeller; orig. pub. 1872.
Lagrange, M.-J. 1916. *Saint Paul Épitre aux Romains*. EBib. Paris: Gabalda.
Lambrecht, Jan. 1999. "The Caesura Between Romans 9.30–3 and 10.1–4." *NTS* 45:141–47.
Lampe, P. 1985. "Zur Textgeschichte des Römerbriefes." *NovT* 27:273–77.
Lamsa, G. M. 1957. *The Holy Bible from Ancient Eastern Manuscripts*. Nashville: Holman.
Lane Fox, Robin. 1994. "Literacy and Power in Early Christianity." *Literacy and Power in the Ancient World*. Ed. A. K. Bowman and G. Woolf, 126–48. Cambridge: Cambridge University Press.
Lanier, David E. 1991. "With Stammering Lips and Another Tongue: 1 Cor 14:20–22 and Isa 28:11–12." *Criswell Theological Review* 5:259–86.
Lauterbach, J. Z. 1933–35. *Mekilta de-Rabbi Ishmael*. 3 Vols. Philadelphia: Jewish Publication Society.
Le Déaut, R. 1974. "Targumic Literature and New Testament Interpretation." *BTB* 4:243–89.
Leenhardt, F. J. 1995. *L'Épitre de Saint Paul aux Romains*. 3d ed. Geneva: Labor et Fides.
Leiman, S. 1976. *The Canonization of Hebrew Scripture: The Talmudic and Midrashic Evidence*. Hamden, CT: Archon Books.
Leon, H. J. 1960. *The Jews of Ancient Rome*. Philadelphia: Jewish Publication Society.

Levine, Étan. 1996. "The Targums: Their Interpretative Character and Their Place in Jewish Text Tradition." *Hebrew Bible/Old Testament: The History of Its Interpretation* 1:1. Ed. M. Sæbø, 323–331. Göttingen: Vandenhoeck & Ruprecht.

Levine, M. H., trans. and ed. 1976. *Falaquera's Book of the Seeker* [*Sefer Ha-Mebaqqesh*]. Studies in Judaica 7. New York: Yeshiva University Press.

Lichtenberger, Hermann. 1996. "Das Rombild in den Texten von Qumran." *Qumranstudien.* Ed. H.-J. Fabry et al., 221–31. Schriften des Institutum Judaicum Delitzschianum 4. Göttingen: Vandenhoeck & Ruprecht.

Lieberman, S. 1950. "Rabbinic Interpretation of Scripture." *Hellenism in Jewish Palestine*, 47–82. New York: Jewish Theological Seminary.

Liebreich, L. 1944. "Notes on the Greek Version of Symmachus." *JBL* 63:397–403.

Lim, Timothy H. 1991. "Attitudes to Holy Scripture in the Qumran Pesharim and Pauline Letters." D. Phil. diss., University of Oxford.

———. 1992. "11QMelch, Luke 4 and the Dying Messiah." *JJS* 43:90–92.

———. 1997a. *Holy Scripture in the Qumran Commentaries and Pauline Letters.* Oxford: Clarendon.

———. 1997b. "Midrash Pesher in the Pauline Letters." *The Scrolls and the Scriptures: Qumran Fifty Years After.* Ed. S. E. Porter and C. A. Evans, 280–92. JSPSup 26. Sheffield: JSOT.

Lincoln, A. T. 1990. *Ephesians.* WBC 42. Dallas: Word.

Lindars, Barnabas. 1961. *New Testament Apologetic: The Doctrinal Significance of the New Testament Quotations.* Philadelphia: Westminster.

———. 1985. "The Sound of the Trumpet: Paul and Eschatology." *BJRL* 67:766–82.

Lindbeck, George. 1988. "Scripture, Consensus, and Community." *This World* 23:5–24.

Literacy in the Roman World. 1991. Journal of Roman Archaeology Supplement Series 3; Ann Arbor, MI.

Litwak, K. D. 1998. "Echoes of Scripture? A Critical Survey of Recent Works on Paul's Use of the Old Testament." *Currents in Research: Biblical Studies* 6:260–88.

Loewe, Raphael. 1990. "Jewish Exegesis." *Dictionary of Biblical Interpretation.* Ed. R. J. Coggins and J. L. Houlden, 346–54. London: SCM.

Lohfink, N. 1962. "Der Bundesschluß im Land Moab. Redaktionsgeschichtliches zu Dt 28,69–32,47." *BZ* 6:32–56.

Longenecker, Bruce W. 1989. "Different Answers to Different Issues: Israel, the Gentiles and Salvation History in Romans 9–11." *JSNT* 36:95–123.

Longenecker, Richard N. 1975. *Biblical Exegesis in the Apostolic Period.* Grand Rapids: Eerdmans.

De Lorenzi, Lorenzo, ed. 1977. *Die Israelfrage nach Röm. 9–11.* Rome: St. Paul's Abbey.

Ludwig, T. M. 1973. "The Traditions of the Establishing of the Earth in Deutero-Isaiah." *JBL* 92:345–57.

Lust, J., E. Eynikel, and K. Hauspie. 1992–96. *A Greek-English Lexicon of the Septuagint.* 2 Vols. Stuttgart: Deutsche Bibelgesellschaft.

Macintosh, A. A. 1997. *A Critical and Exegetical Commentary on Hosea.* ICC. Edinburgh: T & T Clark.

Macleod, M. D. 1956. "'AN with the Future in Lucian and the *Solecist*." *ClQ* NS 6:102–11.

Maillot, A. 1982. "Essai sur les citations veterotestamentaires contenues dans Romains 9 à 11." *ETR* 5:55–73.

Manley, Johanna, ed. 1995. *Isaiah Through the Ages.* Menlo Park, CA: Monastery Books.

Marcovich, Miroslav. 1997. *Iustini Martyris Dialogus cum Tryphone.* PTS 47. Berlin: De Gruyter.

Marcus, Joel. 1992. *The Way of the Lord: Christological Exegesis of the Old Testament in the Gospel of Mark.* Louisville: Westminster/John Knox.

———. 1995. "Mark and Isaiah." *Fortunate the Eyes that See.* FS David Noel Freedman. Ed. A. B. Beck et al., 449–66. Grand Rapids: Eerdmans.

Marrou, H. I. 1956. *History of Education in Antiquity*. 3d ed. New York: Sheed and Ward.

Marshall, Bruce D. 1997. "Christ and the cultures: The Jewish people and Christian theology." *The Cambridge Companion to Christian Doctrine*. Ed. C. E. Gunton, 81–100. Cambridge: Cambridge University Press.

Marshall, I. H. 1996. "Salvation, Grace and Works in the Later Writings in the Pauline Corpus." *NTS* 42:339–58.

Martin, W. J. 1954. *The Dead Sea Scroll of Isaiah*. London: Westminster Chapel.

Martyn, J. Louis. 1997a. *Galatians*. AB 33A. New York: Doubleday.

———. 1997b. "Romans as One of the Earliest Interpretations of Galatians." *Theological Issues in the Letters of Paul*, 37–45. Nashville: Abingdon.

Mason, Steve. 1991. *Flavius Josephus on the Pharisees: A Composition-Critical Study*. SPB 39. Leiden: Brill.

———. 1994. "'For I am not Ashamed of the Gospel' (Rom 1.16): The Gospel and the First Readers of Romans." *Gospel in Paul*. Ed. L. A. Jervis and P. Richardson, 254–87. JSNTSup 108. Sheffield: JSOT.

Matlock, R. B. 1996. *Unveiling the Apocalyptic Paul: Paul's Interpreters and the Rhetoric of Criticism*. JSNTSup 127. Sheffield: Sheffield Academic Press.

Mayes, A. D. H. 1978. "The Rise of the Israelite Monarchy." *ZAW* 90:1–19.

Mayser, E. 1906. *Grammatik des Griechischen Papyri aus der Ptolemäerzeit. I: Laut- und Wortlehere*. Leipzig: Teubner.

———. 1926. *Grammatik des griechischen Papyri aus der Ptolemäerzeit. II.1*. Berlin: de Gruyter.

McCarter, P. Kyle, Jr. 1980. *I Samuel*. AB 8. Garden City, N.Y.: Doubleday.

McCarthy, D. 1973. "The Inauguration of Monarchy in Israel: A Form-Critical Study of 1 Samuel 8–12." *Int* 27:401–12.

McCasland, S. V. 1958. "The Way." *JBL* 77:222–30.

McCormick, Michael. 1985. "The Birth of the Codex and the Apostolic Life-Style." *Scriptorium* 39:150–58.

McKnight, Scot. 1991. *A Light among the Gentiles: Jewish Missionary Activity in the Second Temple Period*. Minneapolis: Fortress.

McLaughlin, J. L. 1994. "Their Hearts *Were* Hardened: The Use of Isaiah 6,9–10 in the Book of Isaiah." *Bib* 75:1–25.

McNamara, M. 1966. *The New Testament and the Palestinian Targum to the Pentateuch*. AnBib 27. Rome: Pontifical Biblical Institute Press.

Meeks, Wayne A. 1990. "On Trusting an Unpredictable God: A Hermeneutical Meditation on Romans 9–11." *Faith and History*. Ed. J. T. Carroll et al., 105–24. Atlanta: Scholars.

Melugin, R. F. 1996. "Reading the Book of Isaiah as Christian Scripture." *SBLSP*, 188–203.

———. 1998. "On Reading Isaiah 53 as Christian Scripture." *Jesus and the Suffering Servant: Isaiah 53 and Christian Origins*. Ed. W. H. Bellinger, Jr. and W. R. Farmer, 55–69. Harrisburg, PA: Trinity Press International.

Mendenhall, G. F. 1993. "Samuel's 'Broken Rîb': Deuteronomy 32." *A Song of Power and the Power of Song: Essays on the Book of Deuteronomy*. Ed. D. L. Christensen, 169–80. Winona Lake, IN: Eisenbrauns; orig. pub. in *No Famine in the Land*. Ed. J. W. Flanagan and A. W. Robinson, 63–74. Missoula, MT: Scholars Press, 1975.

Menken, M. J. J. 1988. "Die Form des Zitates aus Jes 6,10 in Joh 12,40. Ein Beitrag zum Schriftgebrauch des vierten Evangelisten." *BZ* 32:189–209; ET, "'He Has Blinded Their Eyes . . .' (John 12:40)." *Old Testament Quotations in the Fourth Gospel: Studies in Textual Form*, 99–122. Contributions to Biblical Exegesis and Theology 15. Kampen: Kok Pharos, 1996.

Metzger, B. M. 1951. "Formulas Introducing Quotations of Scripture in the NT and the Mishnah." *JBL* 70:297–307.

——. 1983. "The Fourth Book of Ezra." *OTP* 1:516–59.

——. 1992. *The Text of the New Testament: Its Transmission, Corruption, and Restoration.* 3d ed. New York: Oxford University Press.

——. 1994. *A Textual Commentary on the Greek New Testament.* 2d ed. Stuttgart: Deutsche Bibelgesellschaft.

Meyer, L. V. 1992. "Remnant." *ABD* 5:669–671.

Meyer, P. W. 1980. "Romans 10:4 and the'End' of the Law." *The Divine Helmsman.* FS L. H. Silberman. Ed. J. L. Crenshaw and S. Sandmel, 59–78. New York: KTAV.

Meyers, C. L. and E. M. Meyers. 1987. *Haggai; Zechariah 1–8.* AB 25B. Garden City, N.Y.: Doubleday.

Michaels, J. R. 1988. *1 Peter.* WBC 49. Waco: Word.

Michel, O. 1929. *Paulus und seine Bibel.* Gütersloh: C. Bertelsmann; reprinted, Darmstadt: Wissenschaftliche Buchgesellschaft, 1972.

——. 1966. *Der Brief an die Römer.* 4th ed. Meyer K. Göttingen: Vandenhoeck & Ruprecht.

Mielziner, M. 1968. *Introduction to the Talmud.* New York: Bloch.

Milgrom, J. 1990. *Numbers.* The JPS Torah Commentary. Philadelphia: Jewish Publication Society.

Milik, J. T. 1972. "Milkî-Sedeq et Milkî-Reša'." *JJS* 23:95–144.

Millard, Alan. 2000. *Reading and Writing in the Time of Jesus.* New York: New York University Press.

Miller, M. P. 1969. "The Function of Isa 61:1–2 in 11QMelchizedek." *JBL* 88:467–69.

——. 1971. "Targum, Midrash and the Use of the Old Testament in the New Testament." *JSJ* 2:29–82.

Miller, P. D. 1990. *Deuteronomy.* IBC. Louisville: John Knox Press.

Mitchell, Margaret M. 1992. "New Testament Envoys in the Context of Greco-Roman Diplomatic and Epistolary Conventions: The Example of Timothy and Titus." *JBL* 111:641–62.

——. 2000. *The Heavenly Trumpet: John Chrysostom and the Art of Pauline Interpretation.* HUT 40. Tübingen: Mohr Siebeck.

Mitton, C. L. 1955. *The Formation of the Pauline Corpus of Letters.* London: Epworth.

Moessner, David P. 1989. *Lord of the Banquet: The Literary and Theological Significance of the Lukan Travel Narrative.* Minneapolis: Fortress.

——, ed. 1999. *Jesus and the Heritage of Israel: Luke's Narrative Claim Upon Israel's Legacy.* Harrisburg: TPI.

Moo, Douglas J. 1983a. "'Law,' 'Works of the Law,' and Legalism in Paul." *WTJ* 45:73–100.

——. 1983b. *The Old Testament in the Gospel Passion Narratives.* Sheffield: Almond.

——. 1996. *The Epistle to the Romans.* NICNT. Grand Rapids: Eerdmans.

Moorhouse, A. C. 1946. "AN with the Future." *ClQ* 40:1–10.

——. 1959. "A Reply on ἄν with the Future." *ClQ* NS 9:78–79.

Morawski, S. 1970. "The Basic Functions of Quotations." *Sign, Language, Culture.* Ed. A. J. Greimas, 690–705. The Hauge: Mouton.

Morrow, F. J., Jr. 1973. "The Text of Isaiah at Qumran." Ph.D. diss., Catholic University of America.

Motyer, J. A. 1993. *The Prophecy of Isaiah.* Downer's Grove, IL: InterVarsity Press.

Mulder, Martin Jan, ed. 1988. *Mikra: Text, Translation, Reading and Interpretation of the Hebrew Bible in Ancient Judaism and Early Christianity.* CRINT II/1. Assen: Van Gorcum/Philadelphia: Fortress.

Munck, J. 1959. *Paul and the Salvation of Mankind.* Richmond: John Knox.

——. 1967. *Christ and Israel: An Interpretation of Romans 9–11.* Philadelphia: Fortress.

Muraoka, Takamitsu. 1973. "Literary Device in the Septuagint." *Textus* 8:20–30.

——. 1984. "On Septuagint Lexicography and Patristics." *JTS* 35:441–48.

———. 1993. *A Greek-English Lexicon of the Septuagint (Twelve Prophets)*. Louvain: Peters.
———. 1994. "Bible Translation, Ancient Versions." *Encyclopedia of Language and Linguistics*. Ed. R. Asher and J. M. Y. Simpson, 1:349–51. Oxford: Pergamon.
———. 1998. *Hebrew/Aramaic Index to the Septuagint: Keyed to the Hatch-Redpath Concordance*. Grand Rapids: Baker.
Murphy-O'Connor, J. *Paul: A Critical Life*. Oxford: Oxford University Press.
Murray, J. 1959–65. The Epistle to the Romans. 2 Vols. NICNT. Grand Rapids: Eerdmans.
Mußner, F. 1976. "Ganz Israel wird gerettet werden (Röm. 11,26)." *Kairos* 18:241–55.
Nanos, Mark D. 1996. *The Mystery of Romans: The Jewish Context of Paul's Letter*. Minneapolis: Fortress.
Nehamas, Alexander. 1981. "The Postulated Author: Critical Monism as a Regulative Ideal." *Critical Inquiry* 8:133–49.
———. 1986. "What an Author Is." *Journal of Philosophy* 83:685–91.
———. 1987. "Writer, Text, Work, Author." *Literature and the Question of Philosophy*. Ed. A. J. Cascardi, 265–91. Baltimore: Johns Hopkins University Press.
Nickelsburg, G. W. E. 1972. *Resurrection, Immortality and Eternal Life in Intertestamental Judaism*. HTS 26. Cambridge: Harvard University Press.
———. 1981. *Jewish Literature Between the Bible and the Mishnah*. Philadephia: Fortress.
———. 1984. "The Bible Rewritten and Expanded." Jewish Writings of the Second Temple Period. Ed. M. E. Stone, 89–156. CRINT II/2. Assen: Van Gorcum/Philadelphia: Fortress.
———. 1986. "An ΈΚΤΡΩΜΑ, though Appointed from the Womb: Paul's Apostolic Self-Description in 1 Corinthians 15 and Galatians 1." *Christians Among Jews and Gentiles*. Ed. G. W. E. Nickelsburg and G. W. MacRae, 198–205. Philadelphia: Fortress.
———. 1991. "The Incarnation: Paul's Solution to the Universal Human Predicament." *The Future of Early Christianity*. FS H. Koester. Ed. B. A. Pearson, 348–57. Minneapolis: Fortress.
Noack, B. 1965. "Current and Backwater in the Epistle to the Romans." *ST* 19:155–66.
Norris, F. W. 1994. "Black Marks on the Communities' Manuscripts." *JECS* 2:443–66.
North, C. R. 1950. "The 'Former Things' and the 'New Things' in Deutero-Isaiah." *Studies in Old Testament Prophecy*. Ed. H. H. Rowley, 111–26. Edinburgh: T & T Clark.
Nygren, A. 1949. *Commentary on Romans*. Philadelphia: Fortress.
Oates, John F. et al. 1992. *Checklist of Editions of Greek and Latin Papyri, Ostraca and Tablets*. 4th ed. Bulletin of the American Society of Papyrologists Supplements 7. Atlanta: Scholars Press, 1992. Updated version available on-line at http://odyssey.lib.duke.edu/papyrus/texts/clist.html.
O'Brien, P. T. 1995. *Gospel and Mission in the Writings of Paul*. Grand Rapids: Baker.
O'Day, Gail R. 1990. "Jeremiah 9:22–23 and 1 Corinthians 1:26–31: A Study in Intertextuality." *JBL* 109:259–67.
Olley, John W. 1979. *"Righteousness" in the Septuagint of Isaiah: A Contextual Study*. SBLSCS 8. Missioula: Scholars.
———. 1998. "A Precursor of the NRSV? 'Sons and Daughters' in 2 Cor 6.18." *NTS* 44:204–12.
Olofsson, S. 1990. *God is My Rock: A Study of Translation Technique and Theological Exegesis in the Septuagint*. ConBOT 31. Stockholm: Almqvist & Wiksell.
Olson, Dennis T. 1994. *Deuteronomy and the Death of Moses: A Theological Reading*. OBT. Minneapolis: Fortress.
Orlinsky, H. M. 1959. "Qumran and the Present State of Old Testament Text Studies: The Septuagint Text." *JBL* 78:26–33.
———. 1975. "The Septuagint as Holy Writ and the Philosophy of the Translators." *HUCA* 46:89–114.

Ottley, Richard R., trans. and ed. 1906–1909. *The Book of Isaiah According to the Septuagint (Codex Alexandrinus). Vol. I: Introduction and Translation with a Parallel Version From the Hebrew; Vol. II: Text and Notes.* 2d ed. Cambridge: Cambridge University Press.

Paget, J. C. 1994. *The Epistle of Barnabas: Outlook and Background.* WUNT 2.64. Tübingen: Mohr-Siebeck.

Pao, David W. 2000. *Acts and the Isaianic New Exodus.* WUNT 2.130. Tübingen: Mohr-Siebeck.

Patte, D. 1975. *Early Jewish Hermeneutic in Palestine.* SBLDS 22. Missoula: Scholars.

———. 1999. *The Challenge of Discipleship.* Harrisburg, Pa: Trinity Press International.

Pawlikowski, J. T. 1979. "The Historicizing of the Eschatological: The Spiritualizing of the Eschatological: Some Reflections." *AntiSemitism and the Foundations of Christianity.* Ed. A. T. Davies, 151–66. New York: Paulist.

Penna, A. 1957. "Testi d'Isaia in S. Paolo." *RivB* 5:25–30, 163–79.

Penna, R. 1989. "Narrative Aspects of the Epistle of St. Paul to the Romans." *Parable and Story in Judaism and Christianity.* Ed. C. Thoma and M. Wyschogrod, 191–204. New York: Paulist.

Peters, Melvin K. H. 1992. "Septuagint." *ABD* 5:1093–1104.

Petersen, Norman R. 1985. *Rediscovering Paul: Philemon and the Sociology of Paul's Narrative World.* Philadelphia: Fortress.

———. 1991. "On the Ending(s) to Paul's Letter to Rome." *The Future of Early Christianity: Essays in Honor of Helmut Koester.* Ed. Birger A. Pearson, 337–47. Minneapolis: Fortress.

Pfitzner, V. C. 1967. *Paul and the Agon Motif: Traditional Athletic Imagery in the Pauline Literature.* NovTSup 16. Leiden: Brill.

Piper, J. 1993. *The Justification of God: An Exegetical and Theological Study of Romans 9:1–23.* 2d ed. Grand Rapids: Baker.

Ponsot, Hervé. 1982. "Et ainsi tout Israel sera sauvé: Rom XI,26a." *RB* 89:406–17.

Porter, Stanley E. 1989. *Verbal Aspect in the Greek of the New Testament.* SBG 1. New York: Peter Lang.

———. 1997. "The Use of the Old Testament in the New Testament: A Brief Comment on Method and Terminology." *Early Christian Interpretation of the Scriptures of Israel: Investigations and Proposals.* Ed. C. A. Evans and J. A. Sanders, 79–96. JSNTSup 148/ SSEJC 5. Sheffield: Sheffield Academic Press.

Porter, Stanley E. and Brook W. R. Pearson. 1997. "Isaiah through Greek Eyes: The Septuagint of Isaiah." *Writing and Reading the Scroll of Isaiah: Studies of an Interpretive Tradition.* 2 Vols. Ed. C. G. Broyles and C. A. Evans, 2:531–46. VTSup 70. Leiden: Brill.

Porton, Gary G. 1979. "Midrash: Palestinian Jews and the Hebrew Bible in the Greco-Roman Period." *ANRW* 2.19.2:103–38.

Prigent, Pierre. 1961. *Les Testimonia dans le Christianisme primitif. L'épître de Barnabé (I–XVI) et ses sources.* EBib. Paris: Gabalda.

———. 1964. *Justin et l'Ancien Testament.* EBib. Paris: Gabalda.

Przybylski, B. 1980. *Righteousness in Matthew and His World of Thought.* SNTSMS 41. Cambridge: Cambridge University Press.

Puech, Emile. 1987. "Notes sur le manuscrit de XIQMelkîsédeq." *RevQ* 12:483–513.

———. 1988. "Quelques aspects de la restauration du Rouleau des Hymnes (1QH)." *JJS* 39:38–55.

———. 1992. "Une Apocalypse messianique (4Q521)." *RevQ* 15:475–519.

Rabin, Chaim. 1958. *The Zadokite Documents.* 2d ed. Oxford: Clarendon.

———. 1968. "The Translation Process and the Character of the Septuagint," *Textus* 6:1–26.

von Rad, G. 1965. "Deutero-Isaiah." *Old Testament Theology. Volume II: The Theology of Israel's Prophetic Traditions*, 238–62. San Francisco: Harper & Row.

———. 1966. "The Theological Problem of the Old Testament Doctrine of Creation." *The Problem of the Hexateuch and Other Essays*, 131–43. New York: McGraw-Hill.

Radermacher, L. 1925. *Neutestamentliche Grammatik.* HNT 1. Tübingen: Mohr-Siebeck.
Radl, W. 1986. "Alle Mühe umsonst? Paulus und der Gottesknecht." *L'Apôtre Paul: personalité, style, et conception du ministère.* Ed. A. Vanhoye, 144–49. BETL 73. Leuven: Leuven University Press.
Rahlfs, A., ed. 1935. *Septuaginta. Id est vetus testamentum graece iuxta LXX interpretes.* 2 vols. Stuttgart: Privilegierte Württembergische Bibelanstalt, 1935; reprinted in 1 Vol., Stuttgart: Deutsche Bibelgesellschaft, 1979.
——, ed. 1979. *Psalmi cum Odis.* 3d ed. Vetus Testamentum Graecum Auctoritate Academiae Scientiarum Gottingensis editum 10. Göttingen: Vandenhoeck & Ruprecht.
Räisänen, Heikki. 1987. "Römer 9–11: Analyse eines geistigen Ringens." *ANRW* 2.25.4:2891–2939.
——. 1988. "Paul, God, and Israel: Romans 9–11 in Recent Research." *The Social World of Formative Christianity and Judaism.* FS H. C. Kee. Ed. J. Neusner et al., 178–206. Philadelphia: Fortress.
——. 1995. "Romans 9–11 and the 'History of Early Christian Religion.'" *Texts and Contexts: Biblical Texts in Their Textual and Situational Contexts: Essays in Honor of Lars Hartman.* Ed. Torn Fornberg and David Hellholm, 743–65. Oslo: Scandinavian University Press.
Reasoner, M. 1995. "The Theology of Romans 12:1–15:13." *Pauline Theology III: Romans.* Ed. D. M. Hay and E. E. Johnson, 287–99. Minneapolis: Fortress.
——. 1999. *The Strong and the Weak: Romans 14.1–15.13 in Context.* SNTSMS 103. Cambridge: Cambridge University Press.
Refoulé, F. 1984. ". . . *Et ainsi tout Israël sera sauvé": Romains 11.25–32.* LD 117. Paris: Cerf.
Reider, Jospeh. 1916. *Prolegomena to a Greek-Hebrew and Hebrew-Greek Index to Aquila.* Philadelphia: Dropsie College.
——. 1966. *An Index to Aquila.* Completed and revised by N. Turner. VTSup 12. Leiden: Brill.
Reinmuth, E. 1991. "'Nicht Vergeblich' bei Paulus und Pseudo-Philo, *Liber Antiquitatem Biblicarum.*" *NovT* 33:97–123.
Rendtorff, Rolf. 1954. "Die theologische Stellung des Schöpfungsglaubens bei Deuterojesaja." *ZTK* 51:3–13.
——. 1989. "Jesaja 6 im Rahmen der Komposition des Jesajabuches." *The Book of Isaiah.* Ed. J. Vermeylen, 73–82. BETL 81. Leuven: Leuven University Press; ET, "Isaiah 6 in the Framework of the Composition of the Book." *Canon and Theology,* 170–80. OBT. Minneapolis: Fortress, 1993.
——. 1993a. "Rabbinic Exegesis and the Modern Christian Scholar." *Canon and Theology,* 17–24. OBT. Minneapolis: Fortress.
——. 1993b. "Where Were You When I Laid the Foundation of the Earth? Creation and Salvation History." *Canon and Theology,* 92–113. OBT. Minneapolis: Fortress.
——. 1993c. "The Composition of the Book of Isaiah." *Canon and Theology,* 146–69. OBT. Minneapolis: Fortress.
Rengstorff, K. H. 1978. "Das Ölbaum-Gleichnis in Röm 11, 16ff.: Versuch einer weiterführenden Deutung." *Donum Gentilicium.* FS D. Daube. Ed. E. Bammel et al., 127–64. Oxford: Clarendon.
Reuther, R. R. 1974. *Faith and Fratricide: The Theological Roots of Anti-Semitism.* New York: Seabury.
Rhyne, C. T. 1981. *Faith Establishes the Law.* SBLDS 55. Chico, CA: Scholars.
——. 1985. "*Nomos Dikaiosynews* and the Meaning of Romans 10:4." *CBQ* 47:486–99.
Ribera, J. 1994. "The Targum: From Translation to Interpretation." *The Aramaic Bible: Targums in their Historical Context.* Ed. D. R. G. Beattie and M. J. McNamara, 51–91. JSOTSup 166. Sheffield: JSOT Press.
Riesenfeld, H. 1972. "ὑπέρ." *TDNT* 8:507–16.

Riesner, R. 1998. *Paul's Early Period: Chronology, Mission Strategy, Theology*. Grand Rapids: Eerdmans.

Roberts, C. H. 1970. "Books in the Graeco-Roman World and in the New Testament." *Cambridge History of the Bible, Vol. I*. Ed. P. R. Ackroyd and C. F. Evans, 48–66. Cambridge: Cambridge University Press.

Robertson, A. T. 1934. *A Grammar of the Greek New Testament in the Light of Historical Research*. Nashville: Broadman.

Robinson, J. A. 1902. "ΠΩΡΩΣΙΣ AND ΠΗΡΩΣΙΣ." *JTS* 3:81–93.

Rosenbloom, J. R. 1970. *The Dead Sea Isaiah Scroll: A Literary Analysis*. Grand Rapids: Eerdmans.

Rosenthal, J. M. 1969–70. "Biblical Exegesis of 4QpIs [*sic*]." *JQR* 60:27–36.

Rosner, Brian S. 1994. *Paul, Scripture and Ethics: A Study of 1 Corinthians 5–7*. AGJU 22. Leiden: Brill.

Rowlands, E. R. 1959. "The Targum and the Peshiṭta Version of the Book of Isaiah." *VT* 9:178–91.

Royse, J. R. 1981. "Scribal Habits in Early Greek New Testament Papyri." Th.D. diss., Graduate Theological Union.

Running, L. G. 1965–66. "An Investigation of the Syriac Version of Isaiah." *AUSS* 3:138–57; 4:37–64, 135–48.

Ryle, H. E. 1895. *Philo and Holy Scripture or the Quotations of Philo from the Books of the Old Testament*. New York: Macmillan.

Sæbø, Magne, ed. 1996. *Hebrew Bible/Old Testament: The History of Its Interpretation* 1:1. Göttingen: Vandenhoeck & Ruprecht.

Safrai, S. 1976. "Education and the Study of Torah." *The Jewish People in the First Century, Vol II*. Ed. S. Safrai and M. Stern, 945–70. CRINT I/2; Assen: Van Gorcum.

Sailhamer, J. H. 1992. *The Pentateuch as Narrative: A Biblical-Theological Commentary*. Grand Rapids: Zondervan.

Sampley, J. P. 1994. "The Weak and the Strong: Paul's Careful and Crafty Rhetorical Strategy in Romans 14:1–15:13." *The Social World of the First Christians*. FS W. A. Meeks. Ed. L. M. White and O. L. Yarbrough, 40–52. Minneapolis: Fortress.

Sanday, W. and A. C. Headlam. 1902. *A Critical and Exegetical Commentary on the Epistle to the Romans*. ICC. Edinburgh: T & T Clark.

Sanders, E. P. 1977. *Paul and Palestinian Judaism*. Philadelphia: Fortress.

——. 1978. "Paul's Attitude Toward the Jewish People." *USQR* 33:175–87.

——. 1983. *Paul, the Law and the Jewish People*. Minneapolis: Fortress.

——. 1985. *Jesus and Judaism*. Philadelphia: Fortress.

——. 1987. "Jesus and the Kingdom: The Restoration of Israel and the New People of God." *Jesus, the Gospels, and the Church*. Ed. E. P. Sanders, 225–39. Macon: Mercer University Press.

——. 1990. *Jewish Law from Jesus to the Mishnah: Five Studies*. Philadelphia: Trinity Press International.

——. 1991. *Paul*. Past Masters. Oxford: Oxford University Press.

——. 1992. *Judaism: Practice and Belief, 63 BCE–66 CE*. Philadelphia: Trinity Press International.

Sanders, James A. 1973. "The Old Testament in 11Q Melchizedek." *JANESCU* 5:373–82.

——. 1975a. "From Isaiah 61 to Luke 4." *Christianity, Judaism and Other Greco-Roman Cults*. Ed. J. Neusner, 75–106. Leiden: Brill; reprinted in Craig A. Evans and James A. Sanders. *Luke and Scripture*, 46–69. Minneapolis: Fortress, 1993.

——. 1975b. "Torah and Christ." *Int* 29:372–90.

——. 1977a. "Hermeneutics in True and False Prophecy." *Canon and Authority*. Ed. G. W. Coats and B. O. Long, 21–41. Philadelphia: Fortress.

——. 1977b. "Torah and Paul." *God's Christ and His People*. FS N. A. Dahl. Ed. J. Jervell and W. A. Meeks, 132–40. Oslo: Universitetsforlaget.

Sandmel, Samuel. 1962. "Parallelomania." *JBL* 81:1–13.
van de Sandt, Huub. 1994. "The Quotations in Acts 13,32–52 as a Reflection of Luke's LXX Interpretation." *Bib* 75:26–58.
Saß, G. 1993. "Röm 15,7–13 als Summe des Römerbriefs gelesen." *EvT* 53:510–27.
Savran, G. 1988. *Telling and Retelling: Quotation in Biblical Narrative.* Bloomington, IN: Indiana University Press.
Sawyer, John F. A. 1996. *The Fifth Gospel: Isaiah in the History of Christianity.* Cambridge: Cambridge University Press.
Schaller, Berndt. 1980. "Zum Textcharakter der Hiobzitate im paulinischen Schrifttum." *ZNW* 71:21–26.
———. 1984. "ΗΞΕΙ ΕΚ ΣΙΩΝ Ο ΡΥΟΜΕΝΟΣ: Zur Textgestalt von Jes. 59.20–21 in Rom. 11.26–27." *De Septuaginta.* FS J. W. Wevers. Ed. A. Pietersma and C. Cox, 201–206. Mississauga, Ont.: Benben.
Schaper, J. 1995. *Eschatology in the Greek Psalter.* WUNT 2.76. Tübingen: Mohr-Siebeck.
Schildenberger, Johannes. 1959. "Parallelstellen als Ursache von Textveränderungen." *Bib* 40:188–98.
Schleusner, J. F. 1822. *Novus Thesaurus Philologico-Criticus sive Lexicon in LXX et Reliquos Interpretes Graecos ac Scriptores Apocryphos Veteris Testamenti.* 3 Vols. Glasgow: A. & J. Duncan.
Schmidt, K. L. and M. A. Schmidt. 1967. "παχύνω κτλ." *TDNT* 5:1022–31.
Schmitt, J. 1979. "Qumran et l'exégèse apostolique." *DBSup* 9:1011–14.
Scholz, Anton. 1880. *Die alexandrinische Uebersetzung des Buches Jesaias.* Würzburg: Leo Woerl.
Schuller, E. M. 1986. *Non-Canonical Psalms from Qumran: A Pseudepigraphic Collection.* HSS 28. Atlanta: Scholars.
———. 1992. "4Q380 and 4Q381: Non-Canonical Psalms from Qumran." *The Dead Sea Scrolls: Forty Years of Research.* Ed. D. Dimant and U. Rappaport, 90–100. STDJ 10. Leiden: Brill.
———. 1997. "Qumran Pseudepigraphic Psalms." *The Dead Sea Scrolls: Hebrew, Aramaic, and Greek Texts with English Translations. Vol. 4A: Pseudepigraphic and Non-Masoretic Psalms and Prayers.* Ed. J. A. Charlesworth, 1–39. PTSDSSP. Tübingen: Mohr-Siebeck/Louisville: Westminster/John Knox.
Scott, James M. 1992. *Adoption as Sons of God: An Exegetical Investigation into the Background of ΥΙΟΘΕΣΙΑ in the Pauline Corpus.* WUNT 2.48. Tübingen: Mohr-Siebeck.
———. 1993a. " 'For as Many as are of Works of the Law are under a Curse' (Galatians 3.10)." *Paul and the Scriptures of Israel.* Ed. C. A. Evans and J. A. Sanders, 187–221. JSNTSup 83/SSEJC 1. Sheffield: JSOT.
———. 1993b. "Paul's Use of Deuteronomistic Tradition." *JBL* 112:645–65.
———. 1994. "The Use of Scripture in 2 Corinthians 6.16c–18 and Paul's Restoration Theology." *JSNT* 56:73–99.
———, ed. 1997. *Exile: Old Testament, Jewish and Christian Conceptions.* JSJSup 56. Leiden: Brill.
Seeligmann, I. L. 1948. *The Septuagint Version of Isaiah: A Discussion of Its Problems.* Mededelingen en Verhandelingen van het vooraziatisch-egyptisch Genootschap "ex oriente lux" 9. Leiden: Brill.
———. 1953. "Voraussetzungen der Midraschexegese." VTSup 1, 150–81. Leiden: Brill.
———. 1961. "Indications of Editorial Alteration and Adaptation in the MT and LXX." *VT* 11:201–21.
Seitz, Christopher R. 1991. *Zion's Final Destiny: The Development of the Book of Isaiah.* Minneapolis: Fortress.
———. 1993. *Isaiah 1–39.* IBC. Louisville: Westminster/John Knox.
———. 1999. "The Call of Moses and the 'Revelation' of the Divine Name: Source-Critical Logic and Its Legacy." *Theological Exegesis.* FS B. S. Childs. Ed. C. R. Seitz and K. Greene-McCreight, 145–61. Grand Rapids: Eerdmans.

Selwyn, E. G. 1947. *The First Epistle of St. Peter.* London: Macmillan.

Sheppard, Gerald T. 1992. "The Book of Isaiah: Competing Structures according to a Late Modern Description of Its Shape and Scope." *SBLSP*, 549–84.

———. 1996. "Isaiah as a Scroll or Codex Within Jewish and Christian Scripture." *SBLSP*, 204–24.

Siegert, F. 1985. *Argumentation bei Paulus gezeigt an Röm 9–11.* WUNT 34. Tübingen: Mohr-Siebeck.

Sievers, Joseph. 1997. " 'God's Gifts and Call are Irrevocable': The Interpretation of Rom 11:29 and its Uses." *SBLSP*, 337–57.

Skarsaune, Oskar. 1987. *The Proof from Prophecy: A Study in Justin Martyr's Proof-Text Tradition: Text-Type, Provenance, Theological Profile.* NovTSup 56. Leiden: Brill.

Skehan, Patrick W. 1940. "Isaiah and the Teaching of the Book of Wisdom." *CBQ* 2:289–99.

———. 1955. "The Text of Isaias at Qumran." *CBQ* 17:38–43.

———. 1957. "The Qumran Manuscripts and Textual Criticism." *Volume de Congrès: Strasbourg 1956*, 148–69. VTSup 4. Leiden: Brill.

———. 1969. "The Scrolls and the Old Testament Text." *New Directions in Biblical Archaeology.* Ed. D. N. Freedman and J. C. Greenfield, 89–100. Garden City, N.Y.: Doubleday.

———. 1979. "Littérature de Qumran. A. Textes bibliques." *DBSup* 9:805–22.

Skehan, Patrick W. and Alexander A. Di Lella. 1987. *The Wisdom of Ben Sira.* AB 39. New York: Doubleday.

Smallwood, E. M. 1981. *The Jews Under Roman Rule: From Pompey to Diocletian.* SJLA 20. Leiden: Brill.

Smiga, G. 1991. "Romans 12:1–2 and 15:30–32 and the Occasion of the Letter to the Romans." *CBQ* 53:257–73.

Smith, D. Moody. 1972. "The Use of the Old Testament in the New." *The Use of the Old Testament in the New and Other Essays.* Ed. J. M. Efird, 3–65. Durham, N.C.: Duke University Press.

———. 1984. "The Setting and Shape of a Johannine Narrative Source." *Johannine Christianity: Essays on Its Setting, Sources, and Theology*, 80–93. Columbia: University of South Carolina Press; orig. pub. *JBL* 95 (1976):231–241.

———. 1988. "The Pauline Literature." *It is Written: Scripture Citing Scripture.* Ed. Carson, D. A. and H. G. M. Williamson, 265–91. Cambridge: Cambridge University Press.

———. 1996. "The Love Command: John and Paul?" *Theology and Ethics in Paul and His Interpreters.* FS V. P. Furnish. Ed. E. H. Lovering, Jr. and Jerry L. Sumney, 207–17. Nashville: Abingdon.

Smolar, L. and M. Aberbach. 1983. *Studies in Targum Jonathan to the Prophets, and Targum Jonathan to the Prophets by Pinkhos Churgin.* New York: KTAV.

Smyth, H. W. 1956. *Greek Grammar.* Rev. G. M. Messing. Cambridge: Harvard University Press.

Snodgrass, Klyne R. 1977–78. "I Peter ii.1–10: Its Formation and Literary Affinities." *NTS* 24:97–106.

Sommer, Benjamin D. 1994. *"Leshon Limmudim*: The Poetics of Allusion in Isaiah 40–66." Ph.D. diss., University of Chicago.

———. 1996a. "Allusions and Illusions: The Unity of the Book of Isaiah in Light of Deutero-Isaiah's Use of Prophetic Tradition." *New Visions of Isaiah.* Ed. R. F. Melugin and M. A. Sweeney, 156–86. JSOTSup 214. Sheffield: JSOT.

———. 1996b. "The Scroll of Isaiah as Jewish Scripture, Or, Why Jews Don't Read Books." *SBLSP*, 225–42.

———. 1998. *A Prophet Reads Scripture: Allusion in Isaiah 40–66.* Stanford: Stanford University Press.

Songer, Y. H. 1968. "Isaiah and the New Testament." *RevExp* 65:459–70.

Sonnet, Jean-Pierre. 1997. *The Book Within the Book: Writing in Deuteronomy.* Leiden: Brill.

Soulen, R. K. 1996. *The God of Israel and Christian Theology*. Minneapolis: Fortress.
Sperber, A., ed. 1962. *The Bible in Aramaic. Based on Old Manuscripts and Printed Texts. III. The Latter Prophets According to Targum Jonathan*. Leiden: Brill.
Stanley, Christopher D. 1992a. "The Importance of *4QTanhumim* (4Q176)." *RevQ* 15:569–82.
———. 1992b. *Paul and the Language of Scripture: Citation Technique in the Pauline Epistles and Contemporary Literature*. SNTSMS 74. Cambridge: Cambridge University Press.
———. 1993a. "'The Redeemer Will Come ἐκ Σιων': Romans 11.26–27 Revisited." *Paul and the Scriptures of Israel*. Ed. C. A. Evans and J. A. Sanders, 118–42. JSNTSup 83/SSEJC 1. Sheffield: JSOT.
———. 1993b. "The Significance of Romans 11:3–4 for the Text History of the LXX Book of Kingdoms." *JBL* 112:43–54.
———. 1997. "The Rhetoric of Quotations: An Essay on Method." *Early Christian Interpretation of the Scriptures of Israel: Investigation and Proposals*. Ed. Craig A. Evans and James A. Sanders, 44–58. JSNTSup/SSEJC 4. Sheffield: JSOT.
———. 1998. "Review of *Holy Scripture in the Qumran Commentaries and Pauline Letters* by Timothy H. Lim." *JTS* 49:781–84.
———. 1999. "'Pearls Before Swine': Did Paul's Audiences Understand His Biblical Quotations?" *NovT* 41:124–44.
Stanley, D. M. 1954. "The Theme of the Servant of Yahweh in Primitive Christian Soteriology, and Its Transposition by St. Paul." *CBQ* 16:385–425.
Stansell, Gary. 1996. "Isaiah 28–33: Blest Be the Tie that Binds (Isaiah Together)." *New Visions of Isaiah*. Ed. R. F. Melugin and M. A. Sweeney, 68–103. JSOTSup 214. Sheffield: JSOT Press.
Stark, Rodney. 1996. *The Rise of Christianity*. Princeton, NJ: Princeton University Press.
Starkova, K. B. 1992. "The Ideas of Second and Third Isaiah as Reflected in the Qumran Literature." *Qumran Chronicle* 2:51–62.
Steck, O. H. 1967. *Israel und das gewaltsame Geschick der Propheten: Untersuchungen zur Überlieferung des deuteronomistischen Geschichtsbildes im Alten Testament, Spätjudentum und Urchristentum*. WMANT 23. Neukirchen-Vluyn: Neukirchener Verlag.
———. 1968. "Das Problem theologischer Strömungen in nachexilischer Zeit." *EvT* 28:445–58.
Stegner, W. Richard. 1984. "Romans 9.6–29—A Midrash." *JSNT* 22:37–52.
Stemberger, G. 1996. *Introduction to the Talmud and Midrash*. Trans. and ed. M. Bockmuehl. 2d ed. Edinburgh: T & T Clark.
Stendahl, K. 1954. *The School of St. Matthew*. ASNU 20. Lund: Gleerup.
———, ed. 1958. *The Scrolls and the New Testament*. London.
———. 1976. *Paul Among Jews and Gentiles*. Philadelphia: Fortress.
———. 1995. *Final Account: Paul's Letter to the Romans*. Minneapolis: Fortress.
Stenning, J. F., ed. and trans. 1949. *The Targum of Isaiah*. Oxford: Clarendon.
Stockhausen, Carol K. 1989. *Moses' Veil and the Glory of the New Covenant: The Exegetical Substructure of II Cor 3,1–4,6*. AnBib 116. Rome: Pontifical Biblical Institute Press.
———. 1993. "2 Corinthians 3 and the Principles of Pauline Exegesis." *Paul and the Scriptures of Israel*. Ed. C. A. Evans and J. A. Sanders, 143–64. JSNTSup 83/SSEJC 1. Sheffield: JSOT.
Stowers, S. K. 1994. *A Rereading of Romans: Justice, Jews, and Gentiles*. New Haven: Yale University Press.
Strugnell, J. 1970. "Notes en marge du volume V des 'Discoveries in the Judaean Desert of Jordan.'" *RevQ* 7:163–276.
Stuhlmacher, Peter. 1965. *Gerechtigkeit Gottes bei Paulus*. FRLANT 87; Göttingen: Vandenhoeck & Ruprecht.
———. 1971. "Zur Interpretation von Römer 11:25–32." *Probleme biblischer Theologie*. Ed. H. W. Wolff, 555–70. Munich: Chr. Kaiser.
———. 1987. "The Hermeneutical Significance of 1 Cor 2:6–16." *Tradition and Inter-*

pretation in the New Testament. FS E. E. Ellis. Ed. G. F. Hawthorne and O. Betz, 328–47. Grand Rapids: Eerdmans.

Stuhlmueller, C. 1959. "The Theology of Creation in Second Isaiah." *CBQ* 21:429–67.

———. 1967. "'First and Last' and 'Yahweh-Creator' in Deutero-Isaiah." *CBQ* 29:295–311.

———. 1970. *Creative Redemption in Deutero-Isaiah.* AnBib 43. Rome: Pontifical Biblical Institute Press.

Suggs, M. J. 1957. "Wisdom of Solomon 2.10–5.1: A Homily Based on the Fourth Servant Song." *JBL* 76:26–33.

———. 1967. "'The Word is Near You': Romans 10:6–10 Within the Purpose of the Letter." *Christian History and Interpretation.* FS J. Knox. Ed. W. R. Farmer et al., 289–312. Cambridge.

Sukenik, E. L. 1955. *The Dead Sea Scrolls of the Hebrew University.* Jerusalem: Magnes.

Suleiman, Susan and Inge Crosman, eds. 1980. *The Reader in the Text.* Princeton, NJ: Princeton University Press.

Sullivan, K. 1963. "EPIGNOSIS in the Epistles of St. Paul." *Studiorum Paulinorum Congressus Internationalis Catholicus, Rome, 1961,* 2:405–16. AnBib 18. Rome: Pontifical Biblical Institute Press.

Sundberg, A. 1964. *The Old Testament of the Early Church.* HTS 20. Cambridge: Harvard University Press.

Swartley, W. M. 1994. *Israel's Scripture Traditions and the Synoptic Gospels: Story Shaping Story.* Peabody, MA: Hendrickson.

Sweeney, Marvin A. 1988. *Isaiah 1–4 and the Post-exilic Understanding of the Isaianic Tradition.* BZAW 171. Berlin: de Gruyter.

Swete, H. B. 1914. *An Introduction to the Old Testament in Greek.* Rev. R. R. Ottley. Cambridge: Cambridge University Press.

Talmon, Shemaryahu. 1962. "DSI[a] as a Witness to Ancient Exegesis of the Book of Isaiah." *ASTI* 1:62–72; reprinted in *The World of Qumran from Within: Collected Studies,* 131–41. Jerusalem: Magnes Press/Leiden: Brill, 1989.

———. 1989. "Observations on Variant Readings in the Isaiah Scroll (1QIsa[a])." *The World of Qumran from Within: Collected Studies,* 117–30. Jerusalem: Magnes Press/Leiden: Brill.

———. 1993. "The Desert Motif in the Bible and in Qumran Literature." *Literary Studies in the Hebrew Bible: Form and Content. Collected Studies,* 216–54. Jerusalem: Magnes Press/Leiden: Brill.

Talshir, Z. 1987. "Double Translations in the Septuagint." *VI Congress of the International Organization for Septuagint and Cognate Studies.* Ed. C. E. Cox, 21–63. SBLSCS 23. Atlanta: Scholars.

Tasker, R. V. G. 1946. *The Old Testament in the New Testament.* London: SCM.

Tate, M. 1990. *Psalms 51–100.* WBC 20. Dallas, Word.

Tatum, G. T. 1997. "Putting Galatians in Its Place: The Sequence of Paul's Undisputed Letters." Ph.D. diss., Duke University.

Thackeray, H. St. J. 1909. *A Grammar of the Old Testament in Greek According to the Septuagint. Vol. I: Introduction, Orthography and Accidence.* Cambridge: Cambridge University Press.

———. 1929. *Josephus, the Man and the Historian.* New York: Jewish Institute of Religion Press.

Thielman, F. 1989. *From Plight to Solution: A Jewish Framework for Understanding Paul's View of the Law in Galatians and Romans.* NovTSup 61. Leiden.

Thompson, M. 1991. *Clothed with Christ: The Example and Teaching of Jesus in Romans 12.1–15.13.* JSNTSup 59. Sheffield: JSOT.

Thrall, M. 1962. *Greek Particles in the New Testament.* NTTS 3. Leiden: Brill.

Tigay, J. H. 1996. *Deuteronomy.* The JPS Torah Commentary. Philadelphia: Jewish Publication Society.

Tov, Emanuel. 1976. "Three Dimensions of LXX Words." *RB* 83:529–44.
———. 1982. "A Modern Textual Outlook Based on the Qumran Scrolls." *HUCA* 52:11–27.
———. 1984. "Did the Septuagint Translators Always Understand Their Hebrew Text?" *De Septuaginta.* FS J. W. Wevers. Ed. A. Pietersma and C. Cox, 53–70. Mississauga, Ont.: Benben.
———. 1988. "The Septuagint." *Mikra: Text, Translation, Reading and Interpretation of the Hebrew Bible in Ancient Judaism and Early Christianity.* Ed. M. J. Mulder, 161–88. CRINT II/1. Assen: Van Gorcum/ Philadelphia: Fortress.
———. 1992. "The Contribution of the Qumran Scrolls to the Understanding of the LXX." *Septuagint, Scrolls and Cognate Writings.* Ed. G. J. Brooke and B. Lindars, 11–47. Atlanta: Scholars.
———. 1995. "Excerpted and Abbreviated Biblical Texts from Qumran." *RevQ* 16:581–600.
———. 1997. *The Text-Critical Use of the Septuagint in Biblical Research.* 2d ed. Jerusalem: Simor.
———. 1999. "Theologically Motivated Exegesis Embedded in the Septuagint." Chap. in *The Greek and Hebrew Bible: Collected Essays on the Septuagint,* 257–69. VTSup 72. Leiden: Brill.
Toy, C. H. 1884. *Quotations in the New Testament.* New York: Charles Scribner's Sons.
Trever, J. C. 1950. "The Isaiah Scroll." *The Dead Sea Scrolls of St. Mark's Monastery, Vol. I: The Isaiah Manuscript and the Habakkuk Commentary.* Ed. M. Burrows, xiii–xviii. New Haven: ASOR.
Trobisch, David. 1994. *Paul's Letter Collection: Tracing the Origins.* Minneapolis: Fortress.
Tuckett, Christopher M. 2000. "Paul, Scripture and Ethics. Some Reflections." *NTS* 46:403–24.
Turner, M. 1996. *Power from on High: The Spirit in Israel's Restoration and Witness in Luke-Acts.* Journal of Pentecostal Theology Supplement Series 9. Sheffield: Sheffield Academic Press.
Turner, N. 1959. "The Preposition *en* in the New Testament." *BT* 10:113–20.
Turpie, D. M. 1868. *The Old Testament in the New: A Contribution to Biblical Criticism and Interpretation.* London: Williams and Norgate.
———. 1872. *The New Testament View of the Old: A Contribution to Biblical Introduction and Exegesis.* London: Hodder and Stoughton.
Ulrich, Eugene C. 1994. "An Index of the Passages in the Biblical Manuscripts from the Judean Desert (Genesis—Kings)." *DSD* 1:113–29.
———. 1995. "An Index of the Passages in the Biblical Manuscripts from the Judean Desert (Part 2: Isaiah—Chronicles)." *DSD* 2:86–107.
———. 1998. "The Dead Sea Scrolls and the Biblical Text." *The Dead Sea Scrolls after Fifty Years, Volume I.* Ed. P. W. Flint and J. C. VanderKam, 79–100. Leiden: Brill.
———. 1999. *The Dead Sea Scrolls and the Origins of the Bible.* Grand Rapids: Eerdmans.
VanderKam, James C. 1994. *The Dead Sea Scrolls Today.* Grand Rapids: Eerdmans.
———. 1998. "Authoritative Literature in the Dead Sea Scrolls." *DSD* 5:382–402.
Vermes, G. 1970. "Bible and Midrash: Early Old Testament Exegesis." *Cambridge History of the Bible: Vol. I. From the Beginnings to Jerome.* Ed. P. R. Ackroyd and C. F. Evans, 199–231. Cambridge: Cambridge University Press.
———. 1973. *Scripture and Tradition in Judaism: Haggadic Studies.* Rev. ed. SPB 4. Leiden: Brill.
———. 1975. *Post-biblical Jewish Studies.* SJLA 8. Leiden: Brill.
———. 1980. "Jewish Studies and New Testament Interpretation." *JJS* 31:1–17.
———. 1992. "The Oxford Forum for Qumran Research Seminar on the Rule of War from Cave 4 (4Q285)." *JJS* 43:85–90.
Via, D. O. 1974. "A Structuralist Approach to Paul's Old Testament Hermeneutic." *Int* 28:201–20.

Vielhauer, P. 1969. "Paulus und das Alte Testament." *Studien zur Geschichte und Theologie der Reformation.* FS E. Bizer. Ed. L. Abramowski and J. F. G. Goeters, 33–62. Neukirchen-Vluyn; reprinted in *Oikodome: Aufsätze zum Neuen Testament* 2:196–228. TBü 65. Munich: C. Kaiser, 1979.

Vis, A. 1936. *The Messianic Psalm Quotations in the New Testament: A Critical Study on the Christian "Testimonies" in the Old Testament.* Amsterdam: Menno Hertzberger.

Vollmer, H. 1895. *Die alttestamentlichen Citate bei Paulus textkritisch und biblisch-theologisch gewürdigt.* Freiburg: Mohr-Siebeck.

de Waard, Jan. 1965. *A Comparative Study of the Old Testament Text in the Dead Sea Scrolls and the New Testament.* STDJ 4. Leiden: Brill.

———. 1997. *A Handbook on Isaiah.* Textual Criticism and the Translator, Vol. 1. Winona Lake, IN: Eisenbrauns.

Wagner, J. Ross. 1997a. "The Christ, Servant of Jew and Gentile: A Fresh Approach to Romans 15:8–9." *JBL* 116:473–85.

———. 1997b. "Psalm 118 in Luke-Acts: Tracing a Narrative Thread." *Early Christian Interpretation of the Scriptures of Israel: Investigation and Proposals.* Ed. Craig A. Evans and James A. Sanders, 154–78. JSNTSup 148/SSEJC 5; Sheffield: Sheffield Academic Press.

———. 1998a. "The Heralds of Isaiah and the Mission of Paul: An Investigation of Paul's Use of Isaiah 51–55 in Romans." *Jesus and the Suffering Servant: Isaiah 53 and Christian Origins.* Ed. W. H. Bellinger, Jr. and W. R. Farmer, 193–222. Harrisburg, PA: Trinity Press International.

———. 1998b. " 'Not Beyond the Things Which are Written': A Call to Boast Only in the Lord (1 Cor 4:6)." *NTS* 44:279–87.

———. 1999a. "From the Heavens to the Heart: The Dynamics of Psalm 19 as Prayer." *CBQ* 61:245–61.

———. 1999b. " 'Who Has Believed Our Message?': Paul and Isaiah 'In Concert' in the Letter to the Romans." Ph.D. diss., Duke University.

———. 2001. "Review of *Holy Scripture in the Qumran Commentaries and Pauline Letters* by Timothy H. Lim." *JBL* 120:175–78.

Ward, Richard F. 1995. "Pauline Voice and Presence as Strategic Communication." *Orality and Textuality in Early Christian Literature*, 95–107. Semeia 65. Atlanta: Scholars.

Wasserburg, Günter. 2000. "Romans 9–11 and Jewish-Christian Dialogue: Prospects and Provisos." *Reading Israel in Romans.* Ed. C. Grenholm and D. Patte, 174–86. Harrisburg, PA: TPI.

Watson, F. 1986. *Paul, Judaism and the Gentiles: A Sociological Approach.* SNTSMS 56. Cambridge: Cambridge University Press.

Watts, J. D. W. 1985. *Isaiah 1–33.* WBC 24. Waco: Word.

———. 1987. *Isaiah 34–66.* WBC 25. Waco: Word.

Watts, J. W. 1988. "The Remnant Theme: A Survey of New Testament Research, 1921–1987." *Perspectives in Religious Studies* 15:109–29.

Watts, Rikki. 1990. "Consolation or Confrontation? Isaiah 40–55 and the Delay of the New Exodus." *TynBul* 41:31–59.

———. 1997. *Isaiah's New Exodus and Mark.* WUNT 2.88. Tübingen: Mohr-Siebeck.

Weber, R. et al. eds. 1994. *Biblia Sacra iuxta Vulgatam Versionem: Editio Minor.* Stuttgart: Deutsche Bibelgesellschaft.

Wedderburn, A. J. M. 1989. "Paul and the Story of Jesus." *Paul and Jesus: Collected Essays.* Ed. A. J. M. Wedderburn, 161–89. JSNTSup 37. Sheffield: Sheffield Academic Press.

———. 1991. *The Reasons for Romans.* Minneapolis: Fortress.

Weitzman, M. P. 1994. "Peshitta, Septuagint and Targum." *VI Symposium Syriacum, 1992.* Ed. R. Lavenant, 51–84. Orientalia Christiana Analecta 247. Rome: Pontificio Instituto Orientale.

———. 1996. "The Interpretative Character of the Syriac Old Testament." *Hebrew*

Bible/Old Testament:The History of Its Interpretation 1:1. Ed. M. Sæbø, 587–611. Göttingen: Vandenhoeck & Ruprecht.
———. 1999. *The Syriac Version of the Old Testament: An Introduction.* University of Cambridge Oriental Publications 56. Cambridge: Cambridge University Press.
Weitzman, S. 1996. "Allusion, Artifice and Exile in the Hymn of Tobit." *JBL* 115:49–61.
———. 1997. *Song and Story in Biblical Narrative.* Bloomington, IN: Indiana University Press.
Wellhausen, J. 1899. "Zur apokalyptischen Literatur." *Skizzen und Vorarbeiten* 6:225–34.
Wernberg-Møller, P. 1955. "Some Reflections on the Biblical Material in the Manual of Discipline." *ST* 9:40–66.
Westerholm, Stephen. 1988. *Israel's Law and the Church's Faith: Paul and His Recent Interpreters.* Grand Rapids: Eerdmans.
———. 1996. "Paul and the Law in Romans 9–11." *Paul and the Mosaic Law.* Ed. J. D. G. Dunn, 215–37. WUNT 89. Tübingen: Mohr-Siebeck.
Wevers, John William. 1968. "Septuaginta: Forschungen seit 1954." *TRu* 33:18–76.
———, ed. 1977. *Deuteronomium.* Vetus Testamentum Graecum Auctoritate Academiae Scientiarum Gottingensis editum 3.2. Göttingen: Vandenhoeck & Ruprecht.
———. 1982. "An Early Revision of the Septuagint of Numbers." *ErIsr* 16:235–39.
———. 1995. *Notes on the Greek Text of Deuteronomy.* SBLSCS 39. Atlanta: Scholars.
———. 1998. *Notes on the Greek Text of Numbers.* SBLSCS 46. Atlanta: Scholars.
White, Sidnie Ann. 1990. "4QDtⁿ: Biblical Manuscript or Excerpted Text?" *Of Scribes and Scrolls.* FS J. Strugnell. Ed. H. W. Attridge et al., 13–20. College Theology Society Resources in Religion 5. Lanham: University Press of America.
Whitsett, Christopher G. 2000. "Son of God, Seed of David: Paul's Messianic Exegesis in Romans 2:3–4 [*sic*; read 1:3–4]." *JBL* 119:661–81.
Wiefel, W. 1991. "The Jewish Community in Ancient Rome and the Origins of Roman Christianity." *The Romans Debate.* Ed. K. P. Donfried, 85–101. Rev. ed. Peabody, MA: Hendrickson.
Wilckens, U. 1978–82. *Der Brief an die Römer.* 3 Vols. EKKNT 6. Zurich: Benzinger/Neukirchen-Vluyn: Neukirchener.
———. 1982. "Statements on the Development of Paul's View of the Law." *Paul and Paulinism.* FS C. K. Barrett. Ed. M. D. Hooker and S. G. Wilson, 17–26. London: SPCK.
Wilcox, Max. 1979. "On Investigating the Use of the Old Testament in the New Testament." *Text and Interpretation.* Ed. E. Best and R. McL. Wilson, 231–43. Cambridge: Cambridge University Press.
———. 1988. "Text Form." *It is Written: Scripture Citing Scripture.* Ed. D. A. Carson and H. G. M. Williamson, 193–204. Cambridge: Cambridge University Press.
Wilk, Florian. 1998. *Die Bedeutung des Jesajabuches für Paulus.* FRLANT 179. Göttingen: Vandenhoeck & Ruprecht.
———. 1999. "Paulus als Interpret der prophetischen Schriften." *KD* 45:284–306.
Wilken, Robert L. 1989. "Who Will Speak *For* the Religious Traditions?" *JAAR* 57:699–717.
Willey, Patricia Tull. 1997. *Remember the Former Things: The Recollection of Previous Text in Second Isaiah.* SBLDS 161. Atlanta: Scholars.
Williams, Sam K. 1980. "The 'Righteousness of God' in Romans." *JBL* 99:241–90.
Williamson, H. G. M. 1994. *The Book Called Isaiah: Deutero-Isaiah's Role in Composition and Redaction.* Oxford: Clarendon.
———. 1997. "Isaiah 6,13 and 1,29–31." *Studies in the Book of Isaiah.* FS W. A. M. Beuken. Ed. J. van Ruiten and M. Vervenne, 119–28. BETL 132. Leuven: Leuven University Press.
Winston, David. 1979. *The Wisdom of Solomon.* AB 43. Garden City, N.Y.: Doubleday.
Witherington, Ben, III. 1994. *Paul's Narrative Thought World.* Louisville: Westminster/John Knox.

Wolff, H. W. 1974. *Hosea*. Hermeneia. Philadelphia: Fortress.

———. 1986. *Obadiah and Jonah*. Minneapolis: Augsburg.

van der Woude, A. S. 1965. "Melchisedek als himmlische Erlösergestalt in den neuge-fundenen eschatologischen Midraschim aus Qumran Höhle XI." *OtSt* 14:354–73.

Wright, G. E. 1962. "The Lawsuit of God: A Form-Critical Study of Deuteronomy 32." *Israel's Prophetic Heritage*. Ed. B. W. Anderson and W. Harrelson, 26–67. New York: Harper.

Wright, N. T. 1991. *The Climax of the Covenant: Christ and the Law in Pauline Theology*. Edinburgh: T & T Clark.

———. 1992. *The New Testament and the People of God*. Minneapolis: Fortress.

———. 1995. "Romans and the Theology of Paul." *Pauline Theology III: Romans*. Ed. David M. Hay and E. Elizabeth Johnson, 30–67. Minneapolis: Fortress.

———. 1996. "Paul, Arabia, and Elijah (Galatians 1:17)." *JBL* 115:683–92.

———. 1998. "Justification in Paul and Qumran: Some Exegetical and Theological Reflections." Paper presented at the Center of Theological Inquiry, Princeton, N.J., November 19, 1998.

Yoder, J. H. 1971. "Peace Without Eschatology?" Reprinted as, "If Christ is Truly Lord." *The Original Revolution: Essays on Christian Pacifism*, 55–90. Scottdale, PA: Herald Press.

Zeller, Dieter. 1973. *Juden und Heiden in der Mission des Paulus: Studien zum Römerbrief*. FB 8. Stuttgart: Verlag Katholisches Bibelwerk.

———. 1984. *Der Brief an die Römer*. Regensburg: Pustet.

Zerwick, M. 1963. *Biblical Greek*. Rome: Pontifical Biblical Institute Press.

Ziegler, Joseph. 1934. *Untersuchungen zur Septuaginta des Buches Isaias*. ATAbh 12.3. Münster: Aschendorffschen Verlagsbuchhandlung.

———, ed. 1939. *Isaias*. Vetus Testamentum Graecum Auctoritate Academiae Scientiarum Gottingensis editum 14. Göttingen: Vandenhoeck & Ruprecht; 3d ed., 1983.

———. 1939. "Textkritische Notizen zu den jüngeren griechischen Übersetzungen des Buches Isaias." *Nachrichten der Akademie der Wissenschaften zu Göttingen, Philologische-Historische Klasse*, 75–102 (= Septuaginta Arbeiten 1); reprinted, *Sylloge: Gesammelte Aufsätze zur Septuaginta*, 43–71. MSU 10. Göttingen: Vandenhoeck & Ruprecht, 1971.

———, ed. 1943. *Duodecim Prophetae*. Vetus Testamentum Graecum Auctoritate Academiae Scientiarum Gottingensis editum 13. Göttingen: Vandenhoeck & Ruprecht; 2d ed., 1967.

———. 1959. "Die Vorlage der Isaias-LXX und die erste Isaias-Rolle von Qumran (1 Q Is^a)." *JBL* 78:34–59; Reprinted in *Sylloge: Gesammelte Aufsätze zur Septuaginta*, 34–59. MSU 10. Göttingen: Vandenhoeck & Ruprecht, 1971.

Ziesler, John. 1972. *The Meaning of Righteousness in Paul*. SNTSMS 20. Cambridge: Cambridge University Press.

van Zijl, J. B. 1965. "Errata in Sperber's Edition of Targum Isaiah." *ASTI* 4:189–91.

———. 1968–69. "A Second List of Errata in Sperber's Edition of Targum Isaiah." *ASTI* 7:132–34.

———. 1979. *A Concordance to the Targum of Isaiah: Based on the Brit. Mus. Or. MS. 2211*. SBLAS 3. Missoula, MT: Scholars Press.

Zillesin, A. 1902. "Bemerkungen zur alexandrinischen Übersetzung des Jesaia (c. 40–66)." *ZAW* 22:238–63.

Zimmerli, W. 1963. "Der 'neue Exodus' in der Verkündigung der beiden grossen Exilspropheten." *Gottes Offenbarung*, 192–204. Munich: Kaiser.

Zink, James K. 1963. "The Use of the Old Testament in the Apocrypha." Ph.D. diss., Duke University.

Zuntz, Günther. 1953. *The Text of the Epistles: A Disquisition upon the Corpus Paulinum*. The Schweich Lectures of the British Academy, 1946. London: Oxford University Press.

INDEX OF MODERN AUTHORS

INDEX OF ANCIENT SOURCES

OLD TESTAMENT*

---

* For the numbering of chapters and verses in this section, I follow the LXX [Göttingen edition where available; Rahlfs 1935 elsewhere]. Numbers in brackets refer to the MT.

31:29	166, 191, 192, 193, 195, 200
31:30	199
31:30–32:43	193
32	23, 52, 72, 191–205, 238, 254, 256, 266–67, 348
32:1	189, 200, 203
32:1–5	203, 317
32:4	52, 192, 198, 315, 355
32:5	23, 192, 194
32:5–6	195
32:6	194, 195
32:7–9	196
32:8	196
32:8–9	225, 315
32:9	197, 225
32:9–13	203, 317
32:10	225
32:12	316
32:13	203
32:15	195, 249
32:15–17	195
32:16	195, 198, 202
32:16–17	202
32:16–23	205
32:17	23, 192, 202, 203, 317
32:18–19	195
32:19	192, 195, 198, 199–200, 202
32:19–21	316, 324
32:20	193, 194, 200, 275
32:21	23, 83, 184, 187–204, 206, 210, 212, 216–17, 225, 254, 266–71, 275, 292–93, 299, 315, 316, 317, 335, 350, 351, 353, 355, 356, 358, 359
32:21–26	195
32:24	195
32:25	195
32:26	195
32:27	317
32:27–33	270, 328
32:28	317
32:31	317
32:34–42	267, 270, 317, 328
32:34–43	359
32:35	23, 192, 254, 315, 339

32:35–36	23
32:36	198, 339
32:37–39	316
32:39	203, 337
32:40	328, 337, 338
32:41	198, 328
32:41–43	317
32:43	23, 192, 198, 254, 270, 271, 310, 315–17, 328, 352, 353, 355
32:44	193, 199, 200
32:44–47	192
33	162
33:13	164
33:26–29	203
34:4	112

Joshua

2:22	210
8:22	110
10:20	110
10:28	110, 111
10:30	110, 111
10:33	110, 111
10:37	110
10:39	110
10:40	110
11:8	111
13:21	322
22:3	243
22:7	243
23–24	229
23:13	263
24:3	112
24:4	51

Judges

2:12	195
2:17	195
2:19	140
5:13	110
5:31	280
6:13	227
8:34	289

1 Kingdoms/1 Samuel

2:10	223, 331
2:31	113
4–6	72
6:6	54
8–12	223, 228–31, 238, 254, 353, 354
8:5	229, 230
8:6–18	229

NEW TESTAMENT

	189, 205, 221, 327, 352, 353	10:6–8	54, 162–65, 192, 254, 350, 353, 355
9:30	49, 83, 119, 120, 122, 125, 152, 159, 168, 188, 207, 209, 212, 213, 266, 272, 335, 336	10:6–10	355
		10:6–13	256, 319
		10:7	49, 167–68
		10:8	49, 164, 165, 174, 179, 180, 185
9:30–31	122, 125, 238–39	10:8–10	165, 186, 294
9:30–32	40, 188	10:8–13	170
9:30–33	125	10:9	167, 168, 175, 176
9:30–10:4	120–57, 159	10:9–10	179
9:30–10:13	350	10:9–11	170
9:30–10:21	40, 119, 151, 186	10:10	168, 169, 175
9:31	49, 122, 123, 152, 161, 168, 266	10:11	62–63, 99, 129, 130, 143, 156, 159, 168–70, 179, 205, 215, 254, 323, 327, 344, 350, 353, 357
9:31–32	358		
9:31–33	125		
9:32	50, 124, 156, 158, 188, 236, 238, 354	10:11–13	168–70, 178
9:32–33	124, 126, 155–57	10:12	156, 169, 170
9:33	17, 24, 62–63, 99, 100, 120, 125, 126–36, 145, 150, 151, 156, 161, 169, 215, 254, 263, 275, 305, 323, 327, 339, 340, 344, 345, 347, 350, 353, 354, 358	10:12–13	170
		10:13	156, 169, 174, 175, 179, 209, 332, 350, 353, 357
		10:14	164
		10:14–15	170, 174, 179, 341
		10:14–17	170–80, 350
		10:15	17, 24, 126, 164, 170–74, 178, 183, 185, 286, 292, 323, 353, 359
9:33–10:11	319		
10:1	93, 106, 125, 161, 175, 220, 265		
10:1–3	125, 214	10:15–16	254, 305
10:1–4	125, 238	10:16	54, 78, 92, 119, 170, 174, 178–80, 181, 185, 188, 189, 205, 209, 214, 251, 323, 327, 352, 354, 358
10:2	187		
10:2–3	153		
10:2–4	154, 210		
10:3	68, 153, 161, 168, 187, 188, 354, 358		
10:3–4	229	10:16–17	173, 187, 313
10:4	120, 122, 125, 152, 156, 157, 160, 161, 168, 169, 178, 179, 186, 188, 199, 238, 266, 323, 339, 350, 354	10:16–18	178, 181, 336
		10:17	164, 165, 174, 180, 181, 184, 335
		10:18	7, 23, 57, 98, 165, 181, 184–86, 190, 305, 359
10:4–13	157–70, 346	10:18–19	119, 180–86, 187, 323, 327, 354, 358
10:5	92, 160, 168, 189, 205, 350, 352		
10:5–6	123, 159–62	10:18–21	110, 155, 257, 350
10:5–10	153, 159–68	10:19	23, 83, 92, 178, 181, 188–91, 192, 194, 196, 198, 205, 212, 225, 254, 266, 315, 335, 350, 352, 353, 355, 356, 358
10:5–13	124, 161, 305		
10:6	49, 160, 161, 165, 167–68, 205, 346		
10:6–7	163, 167–68		

DEUTEROCANONICAL BOOKS

OLD TESTAMENT PSEUDEPIGRAPHA

JOSEPHUS

TARGUMS

PESHITTA

OTHER ANCIENT CHRISTIAN WRITINGS

Augustine, *De Doctrina Christiana*
Preface, 1   27
2:30   26–27
2:31   27

Clement of Alexandria, *Stromateis*
2.9.42.4–5   210
2.9.43.1   210
2.9.43.2   210
2.9.43.4   210

Dialogue of Athanasius and Zacchaeus
111   133

Justin, *Dialogue with Trypho*
20   192

119   192
119:2–4   205
119.4   219
119.6   219
123   192

Origen, *Contra Celsum*
II.78   210

Tertullian, *Adversus Marcionem*
5.5   133

Tertullian, *Adversus Judaeos*
14   133

SUPPLEMENTS TO NOVUM TESTAMENTUM

ISSN 0167-9732

2. Strobel, A. *Untersuchungen zum eschatologischen Verzögerungsproblem auf Grund der spätjüdische-urchristlichen Geschichte von Habakuk 2,2 ff.* 1961. ISBN 90 04 01582 5
16. Pfitzner, V.C. *Paul and the Agon Motif.* 1967. ISBN 90 04 01596 5
27. Mussies, G. *The Morphology of Koine Greek As Used in the Apocalypse of St. John.* A Study in Bilingualism. 1971. ISBN 90 04 02656 8
28. Aune, D.E. *The Cultic Setting of Realized Eschatology in Early Christianity.* 1972. ISBN 90 04 03341 6
29. Unnik, W.C. van. *Sparsa Collecta.* The Collected Essays of W.C. van Unnik Part 1. Evangelia, Paulina, Acta. 1973. ISBN 90 04 03660 1
31. Unnik, W.C. van. *Sparsa Collecta.* The Collected Essays of W.C. van Unnik Part 3. Patristica, Gnostica, Liturgica. 1983. ISBN 90 04 06262 9
34. Hagner, D.A. *The Use of the Old and New Testaments in Clement of Rome.* 1973. ISBN 90 04 03636 9
37. Reiling, J. *Hermas and Christian Prophecy.* A Study of The Eleventh Mandate. 1973. ISBN 90 04 03771 3
43. Clavier, H. *Les variétés de la pensée biblique et le problème de son unité.* Esquisse d'une théologie de la Bible sur les textes originaux et dans leur contexte historique. 1976. ISBN 90 04 04465 5
47. Baarda, T., A.F.J. Klijn & W.C. van Unnik (eds.) *Miscellanea Neotestamentica.* I. Studia ad Novum Testamentum Praesertim Pertinentia a Sociis Sodalicii Batavi c.n. Studiosorum Novi Testamenti Conventus Anno MCMLXXVI Quintum Lustrum Feliciter Complentis Suscepta. 1978. ISBN 90 04 05685 8
48. Baarda, T., A.F.J. Klijn & W.C. van Unnik (eds.) *Miscellanea Neotestamentica.* II. 1978. ISBN 90 04 05686 6
50. Bousset, D.W. *Religionsgeschichtliche Studien.* Aufsätze zur Religionsgeschichte des hellenistischen Zeitalters. Hrsg. von A.F. Verheule. 1979. ISBN 90 04 05845 1
52. Garland, D.E. *The Intention of Matthew 23.* 1979. ISBN 90 04 05912 1
53. Moxnes, H. *Theology in Conflict.* Studies in Paul's Understanding of God in Romans. 1980. ISBN 90 04 06140 1
56. Skarsaune, O. *The Proof From Prophecy.* A Study in Justin Martyr's Proof-Text Tradition: Text-type, Provenance, Theological Profile. 1987. ISBN 90 04 07468 6
59. Wilkins, M.J. *The Concept of Disciple in Matthew's Gospel, as Reflected in the Use of the Term 'Mathetes'.* 1988. ISBN 90 04 08689 7
64. Sterling, G.E. *Historiography and Self-Definition.* Josephos, Luke-Acts and Apologetic Historiography. 1992. ISBN 90 04 09501 2
65. Botha, J.E. *Jesus and the Samaritan Woman.* A Speech Act Reading of John 4:1-42. 1991. ISBN 90 04 09505 5
66. Kuck, D.W. *Judgment and Community Conflict.* Paul's Use of Apologetic Judgment Language in 1 Corinthians 3:5-4:5. 1992. ISBN 90 04 09510 1
67. Schneider, G. *Jesusüberlieferung und Christologie.* Neutestamentliche Aufsätze 1970-1990. 1992. ISBN 90 04 09555 1
68. Seifrid, M.A. *Justification by Faith.* The Origin and Development of a Central Pauline Theme. 1992. ISBN 90 04 09521 7

69. Newman, C.C. *Paul's Glory-Christology*. Tradition and Rhetoric. 1992. ISBN 90 04 09463 6

70. Ireland, D.J. *Stewardship and the Kingdom of God*. An Historical, Exegetical, and Contextual Study of the Parable of the Unjust Steward in Luke 16: 1-13. 1992. ISBN 90 04 09600 0

71. Elliott, J.K. *The Language and Style of the Gospel of Mark*. An Edition of C.H. Turner's "Notes on Marcan Usage" together with other comparable studies. 1993. ISBN 90 04 09767 8

72. Chilton, B. *A Feast of Meanings*. Eucharistic Theologies from Jesus through Johannine Circles. 1994. ISBN 90 04 09949 2

73. Guthrie, G.H. *The Structure of Hebrews*. A Text-Linguistic Analysis. 1994. ISBN 90 04 09866 6

74. Bormann, L., K. Del Tredici & A. Standhartinger (eds.) *Religious Propaganda and Missionary Competition in the New Testament World*. Essays Honoring Dieter Georgi.1994. ISBN 90 04 10049 0

75. Piper, R.A. (ed.) *The Gospel Behind the Gospels*. Current Studies on Q. 1995. ISBN 90 04 09737 6

76. Pedersen, S. (ed.) *New Directions in Biblical Theology*. Papers of the Aarhus Conference, 16-19 September 1992. 1994. ISBN 90 04 10120 9

77. Jefford, C.N. (ed.) *The* Didache *in Context*. Essays on Its Text, History and Transmission. 1995. ISBN 90 04 10045 8

78. Bormann, L. *Philippi – Stadt und Christengemeinde zur Zeit des Paulus*. 1995. ISBN 90 04 10232 9

79. Peterlin, D. *Paul's Letter to the Philippians in the Light of Disunity in the Church*. 1995. ISBN 90 04 10305 8

80. Jones, I.H. *The Matthean Parables*. A Literary and Historical Commentary. 1995. ISBN 90 04 10181 0

81. Glad, C.E. *Paul and Philodemus*. Adaptability in Epicurean and Early Christian Psychagogy. 1995 ISBN 90 04 10067 9

82. Fitzgerald, J.T. (ed.) *Friendship, Flattery, and Frankness of Speech*. Studies on Friendship in the New Testament World. 1996. ISBN 90 04 10454 2

83. Tilborg, S. van. *Reading John in Ephesus*. 1996. 90 04 10530 1

84. Holleman, J. *Resurrection and Parousia*. A Traditio-Historical Study of Paul's Eschatology in 1 Corinthians 15. 1996. ISBN 90 04 10597 2

85. Moritz, T. *A Profound Mystery*. The Use of the Old Testament in Ephesians. 1996. ISBN 90 04 10556 5

86. Borgen, P. *Philo of Alexandria - An Exegete for His Time.* 1997. ISBN 90 04 10388 0

87. Zwiep, A.W. *The Ascension of the Messiah in Lukan Christology*. 1997. ISBN 90 04 10897 1

88. Wilson, W.T. *The Hope of Glory*. Education and Exhortation in the Epistle to the Colossians. 1997. ISBN 90 04 10937 4

89. Peterson, W.L., J.S. Vos & H.J. de Jonge (eds.). *Sayings of Jesus: Canonical and Non-Canonical*. Essays in Honour of Tjitze Baarda. 1997. ISBN 90 04 10380 5

90. Malherbe, A.J., F.W. Norris & J.W. Thompson (eds.). *The Early Church in Its Context*. Essays in Honor of Everett Ferguson. 1998. ISBN 90 04 10832 7

91. Kirk, A. *The Composition of the Sayings Source*. Genre, Synchrony, and Wisdom Redaction in Q. 1998. ISBN 90 04 11085 2

92. Vorster, W.S. *Speaking of Jesus*. Essays on Biblical Language, Gospel Narrative and the Historical Jesus. Edited by J. E. Botha. 1999. ISBN 90 04 10779 7

93. Bauckham, R. *The Fate of Dead*. Studies on the Jewish and Christian Apocalypses. 1998. ISBN 90 04 11203 0

94. Standhartinger, A. *Studien zur Entstehungsgeschichte und Intention des Kolosserbriefs.* ISBN 90 04 11286 3 *(In preparation)*
95. Oegema, G.S. *Für Israel und die Völker.* Studien zum alttestamentlich-jüdischen Hintergrund der paulinischen Theologie. 1999. ISBN 90 04 11297 9
96. Albl, M.C. *"And Scripture Cannot Be Broken".* The Form and Function of the Early Christian *Testimonia* Collections. 1999. ISBN 90 04 11417 3
97. Ellis, E.E. *Christ and the Future in New Testament History.* 1999. ISBN 90 04 11533 1
98. Chilton, B. & C.A. Evans, (eds.) *James the Just and Christian Origins.* 1999. ISBN 90 04 11550 1
99. Horrell, D.G. & C.M. Tuckett (eds.) *Christology, Controversy and Community.* New Testament Essays in Honour of David R. Catchpole. 2000. ISBN 90 04 11679 6
100. Jackson-McCabe, M.A. *Logos and Law in the Letter of James.* The Law of Nature, the Law of Moses and the Law of Freedom. 2001. ISBN 90 04 11994 9
101. Wagner, J.R. *Heralds of the Good News.* Isaiah and Paul "In Concert" in the Letter to the Romans 2002. ISBN 90 04 11691 5
102. Cousland, J.R.C. *The Crowds in the Gospel of Matthew.* 2002. ISBN 90 04 12177 3
103. Dunderberg, I., C. Tuckett and K. Syreeni. *Fair Play: Diversity and Conflicts.* Essays in Honour of Heikki Räisänen. 2002. ISBN 90 04 12359 8
104. Mount, C. *Pauline Christianity.* Luke-Acts and the Legacy of Paul. 2002. ISBN 90 04 12472 1